Postmetropolis

POSTMETROPOLIS

Critical Studies of Cities and Regions

Edward W. Soja

BLACKWELL
Publishers

First published 2000

2 4 6 8 10 9 7 5 3 1

Blackwell Publishers Ltd
108 Cowley Road
Oxford OX4 1JF
UK

Blackwell Publishers Inc.
350 Main Street
Malden, Massachusetts 02148
USA

British Library Cataloguing in Publication Data

A CIP catalogue record for this book is available from the British Library.

Library of Congress Cataloging-in-Publication Data

Soja, Edward W.
    Postmetropolis : critical studies of cities and regions / Edward W. Soja.
      p. cm.
    Includes bibliographical references and index.
    ISBN 1–57718–000–3 (alk. paper) — ISBN 1–57718–001–1 (pbk. : alk. paper)
      1. Cities and towns.   2. Metropolitan areas.   3. Urbanization.   4. Spatial behavior.   5.
    Postmodernism.   6. Los Angeles (Calif.)   I. Title.
    HT119.S65 2000
    307 — dc21   99-047607

Typeset in 10½ on 12 pt Palatino
by Best-set Typesetter Ltd, Hong Kong
Printed in Great Britain by MPG Books Ltd, Bodmin, Cornwall

This book is printed on acid-free paper.

Contents

Illustrations

Preface

As we enter the new millennium, the field of urban studies has never been so robust, so expansive in the number of subject areas and scholarly disciplines involved with the study of cities, so permeated by new ideas and approaches, so attuned to the major political and economic events of our times, and so theoretically and methodologically unsettled. It may indeed be both the best of times and the worst of times to be studying cities, for while there is so much that is new and challenging to respond to, there is much less agreement than ever before as to how best to make sense, practically and theoretically, of the new urban worlds being created.

Ever since the emphatically urban crises of the 1960s, nearly all the world's major (and minor) metropolitan regions have been experiencing dramatic changes, in some cases so intense that what existed thirty years ago is almost unrecognizable today. These changes have been described by urban scholars, following broader developments in the world economy, as the product of a process of *urban restructuring*. Almost every urbanist agrees that this restructuring process has been particularly widespread and intense over the past three decades, but here agreement ends. At one extreme, there are some who claim that the urban transformations have been so profound as to make virtually useless all traditional frameworks of urban analysis and interpretation. They contend that wholly new constructs need to be developed to understand the radically transformed urban scene. At the other extreme, many historically-minded scholars proclaim, over and over again, the pre-eminence of continuities with the past, that *plus ça change, plus c'est la même chose*. In their view, the way we do urban studies is not fundamentally flawed, so it does not need to be radically changed, merely updated. To add to the confusion, both these views are probably correct in more ways than either extreme is willing to admit.

It is almost surely too soon to conclude with any confidence that what happened to cities in the late twentieth century was the onset of a revolutionary change or just another minor twist on a old tale of urban life. Yet, by the very title of this book, I have taken a position closer to the former possibility than to the latter. In my view, there has been a significant transition if not transformation taking place in what we familiarly describe as the modern metropolis, as well as in the ways we understand, experience, and study cities. To distinguish what has changed the most from what remains most constant and continuous, I have chosen the term "postmetropolis" as a working title for what might otherwise be called the new urbanism, had not this term been taken up by architects and designers for other and narrower purposes. As a result, this book is first and foremost an attempt to explore what is new and different in the contemporary city and in the scholarly field I describe as critical studies of cities and regions.

One way of reading this book, then, is as an introductory text in contemporary critical studies applied to cities and regions. Even when I delve into the distant past, it is from a perspective that derives from the present and is infused with more recently developed ways of understanding the urbanization process and interpreting urbanism as a way of life. More conventional ways of studying cities and our accumulated knowledge about cities and urban life are not neglected, but these continuities will not be highlighted or summarized at length. There are other texts that do this better. Brought to the foreground instead are a wide variety of new approaches to studying cities and regions, many of which, like the book's title, are prefixed with *post-*, to indicate not a complete break but a significant departure from established practices and disciplinary traditions. While I would prefer not to hinge the title of this book solely around the most controversial and misunderstood of these *post*-prefixed terms, postmodernism, I adopt throughout *Postmetropolis* what I consider to be an insightful and critical postmodern approach to urban studies, focusing on what is new and different today rather than what is the same. The title term can thus be used interchangeably with *postmodern metropolis* and interpreted as an expression of what some now call *postmodern urbanism.*

Layered into this interpretive text on cities and regions are other *post*-prefixed methods of critical thinking and analysis that are often gathered under the broad field of cultural studies: poststructuralism, postmodern feminism, postcolonial critiques, postmarxist analysis. At the same time, I remain informed, but more critically than I once was, by non-*post*-prefixed forms of these approaches, especially the innovative structuralist and Marxist epistemologies that shaped the development of Radical Geography and the hybrid fields of urban, regional, and international political economy that I have joined together to call *geopolitical economy.* Indeed, one of my objectives here is to encourage a more productive synergy between critical cultural studies and geopolitical economy, two zones of intellectual inquiry and identity that were teasingly coming together in the 1990s only to break apart again in seemingly irresolvable incompatibilities. If any reader feels that this attempt at bringing culture and political economy more closely together is compromised by my espousal of postmodernism, I suggest they skip over the sections where my postmodernism is most explicit. I hope there will be enough left to be of interest to even the most cynical of the growing legion of anti-postmodernists.

Taking such an eclectic approach has its costs. It will no doubt disturb those committed to narrower and more focused ways of studying cities and urban life as well as those committed to purer forms of postmodernist interpretation, freed of any vestiges of modernist thinking. My eclecticism is bounded, however, by two guiding emphases which give greater focus and I hope clarity to the text. The first I share with all critical scholars: a commitment to producing knowledge not only for its own sake but more so for its practical usefulness in changing the world for the better. This intentionally progressive and emancipatory project has often been ascribed exclusively to modernist thought and practice, and therefore considered incompatible with a postmodern perspective. I reject such simplistic logic and its implied categorical opposition between modernism and postmodernism, and find it challenging and revealing to draw selectively upon both. Modernist critical theory and modes of interpretation continue to inform my explorations of the postmetropolis, especially in understanding what remains the same today as it was in the past. As for understanding the practical and theoretical significance of what is new and different in the contemporary world, I find postmodernism does it better, as I will try to demonstrate in every chapter.

What makes this book different from most other forms of critical scholarship is that I am also committed to an explicitly spatial or, if you wish, geographical perspective on the production of practical knowledge and the promotion of a political practice that seeks to reduce the oppressions and inequities associated with class, race, gender, and other sources of differential social power. In this sense, I focus my critical studies of cities and regions on such achievable goals as *spatial justice* and *regional democracy*, terms which have rarely appeared in such explicit juxtaposition elsewhere in the literature. Without neglecting other critical social and/or historical approaches, I literally and figuratively "put space first," foregrounding the power and insight of an assertively spatial or geographical imagination. The language throughout the text is drenched with an intentional spatialization that aims to bring to the interpretive surface the fundamental and all-embracing, but frequently buried or backgrounded, spatiality of human life.

A similar foregrounding of the critical spatial imagination has shaped my selection of particular references from the vast literature on cities and regions to emphasize here. I glean the literature for sources of specifically spatial insight, whether the subject is the earliest appearance of cities or the most recent responses to the postmetropolitan transition. Left out, then, are many scholarly writings, some of great insight, that do not in my view evince a significant critical spatial consciousness or do not help in advancing the interpretive project of spatializing critical thinking and practice. For many readers, this may seem to be an excessive narrowing of scope, but my intent is just the opposite. My objective is to expand the scope of critical thinking about cities and regions across all disciplines by opening up new ways to understand how specifically urban spatiality is empirically perceived, theoretically conceptualized, and experientially lived.

This brings me to a second way of reading this book. *Postmetropolis* began as part of a large manuscript I submitted to Blackwell over six years ago with the title *Thirdspace: Journeys to Los Angeles and Other Real-and-Imagined Places.* Then Senior Editor John Davey, in his warmly demanding way, suggested that the proposed book be split in two, with the first half published under the given title and what was then Part III, three long chapters on "Exploring the Post-metropolis," to come out in the following year in what he thought would be a much smaller volume. I agreed, rather uncomfortably, to the split and went about trying to make *Thirdspace* stand on its own, without what was its most empirical punchline, the more practical application of what I theoretically defined as a thirdspace perspective and epistemology. *Thirdspace* was published in 1996 and, soon after, Blackwell optimistically announced the imminent appearance of *Postmetropolis* as its companion volume. But *Postmetropolis* took on a life of its own, expanding into a much more ambitious and comprehensive project. Tracing what happened to the three original chapters provides a brief synopsis of what is contained in the present volume.

The first of the three original chapters, in revised form, is now chapter 5. It concludes Part I: *Remapping the Geohistory of Cityspace* with a detailed look at the historical development of the representative conurbation of Los Angeles, drawing from a version of the same material published as chapter 14 in Scott and Soja (eds.), *The City* (1996). The preceding four chapters of Part I are filled with new material written over the past three years. They contain a broad-brush tracing of what I purposefully call the *geohistory* of cities and urbanism from 11,000 years ago to the present. I begin by introducing several key concepts, such as the *spatial specificity of urbanism* and, as one of its most intrinsic developmental forces, what I describe as *synekism*, the stimulus of urban agglomeration. Also emphasized here and elsewhere in the text is the inherently *regional* nature of urbanization and urbanism. These concepts guide the discussion of the geohistory of *cityspace* – another purposefully spatialized term – through three epochal transformations or Urban Revolutions.

The first of these Urban Revolutions took place in the upland regions of Southwest Asia more than ten millennia ago and led, I will argue, to the initial urban-based invention of full-scale agriculture. The second, contextualized originally in the alluvial lowlands of the Fertile Crescent roughly 5,000 years later, spurred a political revolution which led to the formation of the city-state and city-based empires, kingship, organized social classes, and patriarchal social power. After another 5–6 millennia, urbanism entered a new phase with the beginnings of the Industrial Revolution in western Europe, forming the foundations of specifically urban-industrial capitalism. This sequence is traced in the first three chapters. Chapter 4 carries forward the development of the industrial capitalist city and the intellectual field of urban studies through a series of alternative modernizations, culminating in the urban crises of the 1960s and the new approaches to geopolitical economy that arose to make sense of this important turning point. The concluding chapter on Los Angeles thus serves to raise the question of whether what we are witnessing today, after thirty years of intense urban restructuring, may be the start of a fourth Urban Revolution, a question that, like many others, I leave open to alternative viewpoints.

What was formerly the middle chapter of the original manuscript has become the six chapters that now constitute Part II: *Six Discourses on the Post-metropolis*. Here I expand upon the different but interrelated schools of thought that have consolidated over the past few decades to make sense of the *new urbanization processes* affecting the world in the late twentieth century. These scholarly representations alternatively describe the postmetropolis as: (1) a flexibly specialized Postfordist Industrial Metropolis; (2) a globalized city-region or Cosmopolis; (3) a postsuburban Exopolis or megacity; (4) a Fractal City of intensified inequalities and social polarization; (5) a Carceral Archipelago of fortressed cities; and (6) a collection of hyperreal Simcities, where daily life is increasingly played out as if it were a computer game. The aim of Part II is to argue that the postmetropolis is best understood by combining all six of these interpretive discourses, without privileging any one over the others, while keeping open the possibility of developing additional interpretive frameworks of equal significance in the future. Featured prominently in these chapters is the work of scholars based in or writing about Los Angeles. If indeed there is a distinctive Los Angeles "school" of critical urban and regional studies, as some have claimed, then these six discourses represent its major overlapping subdepartments.

The old final chapter has been expanded into the three found in Part III, *Lived Space: Rethinking 1992 in Los Angeles*. Here I concentrate attention on a singular event, the Justice Riots that took place after the first trial of the police officers involved in the beating of Rodney King, using this particular moment to trigger more general interpretations of what has been happening in the postmetropolis since 1992. In a somewhat experimental vein that will surely not please all readers, I compose chapters 12 and 13 entirely around quotations from the rich literature that has emerged to make specifically spatial sense of what happened in 1992, relegating my commentary to the footnotes. Featuring most prominently here is material taken, with her cautious and admonishing permission, from an unpublished paper by Barbara Hooper, "Bodies, Cities, Texts: The Case of Citizen Rodney King"; and from a stylistically very different treatment of the 1992 events, the performative text *Twilight – Los Angeles, 1992*, written and enacted by the documentary theater artist Anna Deveare Smith. I conclude *Postmetropolis* not with an exhaustive summing up of what has gone before but with an open-ended and cautiously speculative discussion – entirely in my own words I might add – of two new twists to the postmetropolitan transition taking place in the 1990s: the emergence after thirty years of urban restructuring of what I describe as a series of restructuring-generated crises; and the beginnings at least of significant collective struggles to take greater control over the new urbanization processes and steer the postmetropolis toward greater spatial justice and regional democracy.

While *Postmetropolis* and *Thirdspace* can be read as separate and distinct books, they remain closely interconnected. *Postmetropolis* continues to be a direct sequel to its earlier companion volume, applying its broad theoretical arguments and "trialectical" approach to studying what has been happening to cities over the past thirty years from simultaneously spatial, social, and historical perspectives. In both, there is an affirmative attempt to "put space first," not in the sense of a perspective that excludes historical and social-theoretical modes of understanding but rather in one that transcends their long-established privileging in critical thought and practice by reasserting an equivalent power to the critical spatial imagination, an argument that I first developed in *Postmodern Geographies: The Reassertion of Space in Critical Social Theory* (1989). I carry forward the theoretical arguments of *Thirdspace* in all the chapters that follow and often refer back to particular passages and chapters to reinforce these connections. But I have tried to make it possible for readers who are not familiar with the earlier book to understand its most relevant ideas and arguments, especially in the Introduction to Part I. Although it would certainly help, it is not necessary to read *Thirdspace* first, before venturing into *Postmetropolis*.

In addition to being an introduction to contemporary critical studies of cities and regions and an applied sequel to *Thirdspace*, there is a third book rolled into *Postmetropolis*. It is a book on Los Angeles and to some degree a direct expression of the remarkable expansion of scholarly writing focused on this exemplary urban region that has been accumulating over the past thirty years. In much the same way that I foreground a critical spatial perspective, I put Los Angeles first, that is, I explore the postmetropolis and exemplify the critical study of cities and regions primarily, but not exclusively, through Los Angeles and the literature that has grown around what can be called its "generalizable particularities." There is so much about Los Angeles (and indeed every city) that is unique and incomparable. But even these exceptional qualities can be used to contribute to a more general and global understanding of contemporary urban life and the impact of the still ongoing postmetropolitan transition.

I thus treat Los Angeles as a symptomatic lived space, a representative window through which one can observe in all their uniquely expressed generality the new urbanization processes that have been reshaping cities and urban life everywhere in the world over the past thirty years. The effects of these restructuring processes may be more intensely developed and perhaps also easier to see in their complex interconnections in Los Angeles than in most other places, but this does not mean that the same windows of interpretation cannot be opened for other cities. Stated differently, what has been happening in Los Angeles can also be seen taking place in Peoria, Scunthorpe, Belo Horizonte, and Kaohsiung, with varying intensities to be sure and *never* in exactly the same way. The new urbanization processes are evident everywhere if one knows what to look for, but they take on a rich diversity of forms and expressions as they become localized and situated in particular geographical contexts.

Like every social process, the postmetropolitan transition has developed unevenly over space and time, faster and thicker in some places than in others. This process of geohistorically uneven development is an integrative theme and leitmotif in all studies of the human condition. What it suggests here is that wherever one's critical attention is focused, there will be something to learn about postmodern urbanism. Every reference to Los Angeles contained in this book thus serves a double purpose. It is at once both an illustration of the specific contextual effects of the postmetropolitan transition in one urban region and an *invitation to comparative analysis* in all other lived spaces wherever they may be located.

I alone am responsible for trying to combine three books in one and for whatever problems this may cause the reader. I too am wholly responsible for the many lengthy quotations I have taken from the works of others to advance my own arguments. If in any way I have misused these references, I apologize in advance. On a more positive note, I would like to thank all those who have contributed in some way to the writing of this book, beginning with the present and former students of the Urban Planning Department at UCLA: Barbara Hooper, Mark Garrett, Larry Barth, Marco Cenzatti, Clyde Woods, Alfonso Hernandez-Marquez, Olivier Kramsch, Mustafa Dikec, and so many others whom I have taught and who have taught me.

Thanks also to Jill Landeryou at Blackwell for asking the archeologist Ian Hodder to read and comment on the final manuscript. Hodder's supportive but cautionary and corrective comments helped greatly in toning down my overenthusiastic treatment of the events and places I associate with the first Urban Revolution that I contend, against the grain of most archeological texts, occurred more than 10,000 years ago. But I must add that whatever mistakes and exaggerations still exist are entirely my own. In an oddly related way, I would like to extend my appreciation to the Getty Foundation, which some years ago supported a collaborative research project with Janet Abu-Lughod on "The Arts of Citybuilding." Although the project was never completed as promised, my research on urban art led me to discover the remarkable city mural of Çatal Hüyük painted more than 8,000 years ago. This was the primary spark that led me to the concept of synekism, to a rethinking of the debates on the origins of cities, to a rereading of Jane Jacobs and Lewis Mumford, and to much of the new material that appears in Part I.

One of the major differences between *Thirdspace* and *Postmetropolis* has to do with the visual and creative contributions of my friend Antonis Ricos. Financial considerations prevented me from utilizing his great skills to create original visual material for this book as he did so brilliantly for its earlier companion volume. The more traditional illustrative material for *Postmetropolis* thus requires more conventional acknowledgment.

Acknowledgments

The author and publisher would like to thank the following for permission to reproduce copyright material:

Berry, Brian J. L., and Kasarda, John D., "Integrated spatial model of the metropolis," from *Contemporary Urban Ecology* (London and New York: Macmillan, 1977).

Bhabha, Homi K., "Twilight #1," from Anna Deveare Smith, *Twilight – Los Angeles 1992* (copyright © 1994 by Anna Deveare Smith; used by permission of Doubleday, a division of Random House, Inc.).

Davis, Mike, extracts from *City of Quartz: Excavating the Future in Los Angeles* (London and New York: Verso, 1990).

Gates, Daryl, "It's Awful Hard to Break Away," from Anna Deveare Smith, *Twilight – Los Angeles 1992* (copyright © 1994 by Anna Deveare Smith; used by permission of Doubleday, a division of Random House, Inc.).

Hockney, David, *Pearblossom Highway, 11–18 April 1986*, photographic collage; © David Hockney (The J. Paul Getty Museum, Los Angeles).

Kenyon, Kathleen, "Air view of the mound at ancient Jericho," "Head portrait of plaster on a human skull from Jericho," and "Plan of Jericho," from *Archeology in the Holy Land* (London: Ernest Benn, 1960; Jericho Excavation Fund).

Kim, Richard, "Don't Shoot," from Anna Deveare Smith, *Twilight – Los Angeles 1992* (copyright © 1994 by Anna Deveare Smith; used by permission of Doubleday, a division of Random House, Inc.).

Lugones, Maria, "Purity, Impurity and Separation," *Signs*, 19 (Winter 1994) (copyright © University of Chicago Press, Chicago, 1994).

Maisels, Charles Keith, "Relations of Production, Subordination and Stratification in Mesopotamia," from *The Emergence of Civilization* (London and New York: Routledge, 1993).

Mellaart, James, "Pictorial View of Çatal Hüyük" by Grace Huxtable, from *Çatal Hüyük* (London: Thames and Hudson, 1967).

Morris, A. E. J., "City Map of Ur" and "Present-day Erbil," from *History of Urban Form: Before the Industrial Revolution* (New York: John Wiley and Sons, 1974).

Okantah, Mwatabou S., "America's Poem, or 81 Seconds and 56 Blows," from Haki R. Madhubuti, ed., *Why L.A. Happened: Implications of the '92 Los Angeles Rebellion* (Chicago: Third World Press, 1993).

Scott, Allen J., and Soja, Edward W., eds., "Technopoles of the San Fernando Valley," from *The City* (Berkeley and Los Angeles: University of California Press, 1996).

Scott, Allen J., and Soja, Edward W., eds., "Industrial Geography of Los Angeles," from *The City* (Berkeley and Los Angeles: University of California Press, 1996).

Soja, Edward W., "Evolution of Urban Form in the US," from *Postmodern Geographies* (London: Verso, 1989).

Waters, Maxine, "The Unheard," from Anna Deveare Smith, *Twilight – Los Angeles 1992* (copyright © 1994 by Anna Deveare Smith; used by permission of Doubleday, a division of Random House, Inc.).

Part I
Remapping the Geohistory
of Cityspace

Introduction

This book opens with a city that was, symbolically, a world: it closes with a world that has become, in many practical aspects, a city.

Lewis Mumford, *The City in History* (1961)

What I am saying is that every city has a direct economic ancestry, a literal economic parentage, in a still older city or cities. New cities do not arise by spontaneous generation. The spark of city economic life is passed on from older cities to younger. It lives on today in cities whose ancestors have long since gone to dust . . . These links of life may extend – perilously tenuous at times but unbroken – backward through the cities of Crete, Phoenicia, Egypt, the Indus, Babylonia, Sumeria, Mesopotamia, back to Çatal Hüyük itself and beyond, to the unknown ancestors of Çatal Hüyük.

Jane Jacobs, *The Economy of Cities* (1969): 176

To investigate the city is therefore a way of examining the enigmas of the world and our existence.

Lea Virgine, in Mazzoleni, *La città e l'immaginario* (1985)[1]

As with Lewis Mumford's *The City in History*, *Postmetropolis* opens with a city that was symbolically a world – the very first such "city-world" in human history – and closes with a world that, in so many ways, has become very much like a city, where urban ways of life extend to every corner of the globe.[2] What happens in between this opening and closure is presented as a selective journey through more than 10,000 years of what I will describe as the *geohistory of cityspace*. Part I outlines and reinterprets the broad sweep of this geohistory, tracing back to its generative sources the ancestry of what Jane Jacobs identified as the defining "spark of city economic life" and what I will call *synekism*, the stimulus of urban agglomeration.

My intent here is not simply to track down the ancient roots of urbanism for their own sake or to engage in another of those often desperate and nostalgic searches for origins, authenticity, and comforting continuities between the past

1 Quoted in Ian Chambers, "Some Metropolitan Tales," chapter 3 in *Border Dialogues: Journeys in Postmodernity*, London and New York: Routledge, 1990: 51. Chambers's journeys into postmodernity will guide us in many other chapters of *Postmetropolis*.
2 By the time this book is published, the majority of the world's population, for the first time in history, will be living in cities.

and present. I aim instead to initiate through this excursion back in space and time a more intrusive rethinking of the ways scholars have written about cities and the role of the urban condition in the historical development of human societies. In this sense, what follows is not just about how cities develop and change but also an explicitly spatialized narrative of the broad field of inquiry that is concerned with *critical studies of cities and regions* as vital components of our world and our existence. We look to the past, then, with decidedly contemporary eyes, and with the primary goal of enhancing our practical and theoretical understanding of the most recent episode in the social production of cityspace, the still ongoing transition from the modern metropolis to the expansive postmetropolis. This currently unfolding *postmetropolitan transition*, in one way or another, will be the focus of all subsequent chapters.

Outlining the Geohistory of Cityspace

The sequence of chapters in Part I compresses the geohistory of cityspace around three epochal moments. The first and perhaps most controversial, because it challenges many long-established assumptions about the early historical development of human societies, pushes back the beginnings of urbanization and urbanism as a way of life, and hence of what we have traditionally called "civilization," to at least ten millennia ago. This *first Urban Revolution* is most clearly evident at two representative and generative sites, Jericho in the Jordan Valley and Çatal Hüyük in southern Anatolia, although recent archeological evidence is multiplying the number of such "founder" cities, at least in Southwest Asia. Both Jericho and Çatal Hüyük began as pre-agricultural urban settlements of hunters, gatherers, and traders. Through the impact of *synekism* (the developmental impetus that derives from densely settled habitats and the stimulus of urban agglomeration) these first cities, I will argue, incubated the development of full-scale agriculture and organized animal husbandry, inverting what has conventionally been seen as a historical sequence in which the so-called Agricultural Revolution preceded the development of the first true cities.

Chapter 1 is provocatively titled "Putting Cities First" and exemplifies in a particularly striking way the distinctive interpretive emphasis that threads through every chapter of this book and helps to link *Postmetropolis: Critical Studies of Cities and Regions* to its companion volume, *Thirdspace: Journeys to Los Angeles and Other Real-and-Imagined Places* (1996). This interpretive emphasis builds on the increasingly far-reaching "spatial turn" that has been developing across many different disciplines in the 1990s and the closely related contemporary resurgence of interest in cities and urbanism as both objects of study and modes of understanding and explaining what in the last of the three quotations above is so encompassingly described as "the enigmas of the world and our existence." Simply stated, I foreground in every chapter – put first in an interpretive sense – the potential explanatory power of a critical spatial perspective on cities and regions. My intent in doing so is not to project a deterministic spatial explanation for everything being discussed but to open up alternative viewpoints that have been relatively unexplored because of a long-established tendency in the scholarly literature to downplay the importance of critical spatial inquiry and analysis. Proposing the possibility of an urban origin for agriculture and rooting the development of cities in what can be described as the *spatial specificity of urbanism*, and in particular those interdependencies that arise from dense proximity in urban agglomerations, is but the first step in a more comprehensive and critical spatialization of urban and regional studies that I began in *Postmodern Geographies* (1989), continued to develop in *Thirdspace*, and now flesh out in *Postmetropolis*.

Chapter 2 revolves around a *second Urban Revolution* that built upon the first but shifted its primary geographical locus from the highland regions of Southwest Asia to the alluvial plains of the Tigris and Euphrates rivers beginning about 7,000 years ago. This is what the archeological texts usually proclaim as the first and only Urban Revolution and associate directly with two intertwined events, the invention of writing (and hence of "recorded" history) and the development of a distinctive form of urban governmentality called the *city-state*, or in its later Greek elaboration, the *polis*. Represented through the epitomizing Sumerian city of Ur, this second Urban Revolution expands the complex of social production and the scale of social organization centered in the city beyond simple agrarian society to new territorially-defined forms of social and spatial control and regulation based on kingship, military power, bureaucracy, class, property, slavery, patriarchy, and empire.[3]

After a long period of development and diffusion that lasted well into the Second Millennium A.D., a third Urban Revolution explodes (and implodes) with the development of the industrial capitalist city, epitomized in its purest form in Manchester and Chicago. For the first time in history, social production becomes primarily concentrated inside the core of cities, setting off not just a radical transformation in the size and internal organization of cityspace but a more general process of societal urbanization. Here, in chapter 3, a new story enters the picture, focused on the formation of a distinctive field of pragmatic and reflective scholarship that has come to be known specifically as urban studies. The third Urban Revolution is discussed via the discourse on modernity and the rise of the modern industrial metropolis, and moves through the first century of modern urban studies (ca. 1850–1950) via the "schools" that arose to make practical as well as theoretical sense of urbanism as a way of life in the rich social and spatial laboratories represented by Manchester and Chicago.

---

3 I apologize in advance to those readers whose familiarity with the history of cities centers on developments in classical Athens, ancient Rome, the medieval and Renaissance cities of Mediterranean Europe, and the Hanseatic seaports of the North Sea and the Baltic; as well as those particularly interested in the urbanization of Asia, Africa, Mesoamerica, and the Andes. Many excellent sources exist to cover these geohistories, including Mumford (1961) and Morris (1972 [1994]). They are skipped over here not because I consider them unimportant or uninteresting, but rather as a way of focusing particular attention on the three most revolutionary turning points in the geohistory of cityspace.

In chapter 4, new developments in our understanding of the industrial capitalist metropolis in the aftermath of the urban crises of the 1960s are critically assessed, focusing not on representative and epitomizing cities but rather on two representative and epitomizing texts, Manuel Castells's *The Urban Question* (1977; in French 1972) and David Harvey's *Social Justice and the City* (1973), each indicative of significantly new directions being taken in the field of critical urban studies, especially with respect to an emerging "school" of radical geopolitical economy. This chapter concludes with a summarizing overview of the cyclical rhythms of capitalist urban development through four major periods of restructuring, the latest of which stretches from around 1970 to the present and takes us to the formation of the contemporary post-metropolis. To exemplify the geohistory of the postmetropolis and to illustrate the development of still another round of new approaches to critical urban studies, a detailed look at the "Conurbation of Los Angeles" presented in chapter 5 concludes Part I, leaving open the question of whether or not the postmetropolis signifies the beginnings of yet another Urban Revolution.

Defining the Conceptual Framework[4]

Every chapter in *Postmetropolis* reflects the recently reinvigorated and trans-disciplinary interest and emphasis on all aspects of what can be described as the *spatiality of human life*. Perhaps more than ever before, we are becoming consciously aware of ourselves as intrinsically spatial beings, continuously engaged in the collective activity of producing spaces and places, territories and regions, environments and habitats. This process of producing spatiality or "making geographies" begins with the body, with the construction and performance of the self, the human subject, as a distinctively spatial entity involved in a complex relation with our surroundings. On the one hand, our actions and thoughts shape the spaces around us, but at the same time the larger collectively or socially produced spaces and places within which we live also shape our actions and thoughts in ways that we are only beginning to understand. Using familiar terms from social theory, human spatiality is the product of both human agency and environmental or contextual structuring.

Moreover, our "performance" as spatial beings takes place at many different scales, from the body, or what the poet Adrienne Rich once called "the geography closest in," to a whole series of more distant geographies ranging from rooms and buildings, homes and neighborhoods, to cities and regions, states and nations, and ultimately the whole earth – the human geography furthest out. Although there is some "distance decay" out from the body in

---

4 Much of what follows condenses (as well as builds upon) the arguments I developed in *Thirdspace* (1996). For a shorter and more accessible synthesis of these arguments, see Edward W. Soja, "Third-space: Expanding the Scope of the Geographical Imagination," in D. Massey, J. Allen, and P. Sarre, eds., *Human Geography Today*, Cambridge, UK: Polity Press, 1999: 260–78.

the degree to which we individually influence and are influenced by these larger spaces, every one of them must be recognized as products of collective human action and intention, and therefore susceptible to being modified or changed. This infuses all (socially constructed) scales of human spatiality, from the local to the global, not just with activity and intentionality, but also with built-in tensions and potential conflicts, with openness and freedom as well as enclosure and oppression, with the perpetual presence of geohistorically uneven development, and hence with politics, ideology, and what, borrowing from Michel Foucault, can be called the intersections of space, knowledge, and power.

This enhanced definition of human spatiality may seem obvious to many of us, but until relatively recently it has remained significantly understudied by most scholars. There is an abundant literature on cities and urban life, for example, and some key moments when the social production of urban spatiality became the center of attention for rigorous scholarship. But for the most part even the field of urban studies has been underspatialized until recently, with the spatiality of urban life predominantly seen as the mere adjunct or outcome of historical and social processes that are not in themselves intrinsically spatial, that is, with spatiality in itself having little or no causal or explanatory power. Much the same can be said for all other scales of spatial analysis, from our understanding of the body and individual psychology, to the formation of community and cultural identities, to the analysis of the nation-state and its politics, to the dynamics of the world economy.

During the late 1990s, however, this situation began to change, initiating what some have described as a transdisciplinary spatial turn. For perhaps the first time in the past two centuries, critical scholars in particular have begun to interpret the *spatiality* of human life in much the same way they have traditionally interpreted history and society, or the *historicality* and *sociality* of human life. Without reducing the significance of life's inherent historicality and sociality, or dimming the creative and critical imaginations that have developed around their practical and theoretical understanding, a reinvigorated critical perspective associated with an explicitly spatial imagination has begun to infuse the study of history and society with new modes of thinking and interpretation. At the turn of the twenty-first century, there is a renewed awareness of the simultaneity and interwoven complexity of the social, historical, and spatial dimensions of our lives, their inseparability and often problematic interdependence. It is with this rebalanced perspective that we begin our remapping of the geohistory of cityspace.

The spatial specificity of urbanism

The very use of the terms "geohistory" and "cityspace" immediately reflects the preferential foregrounding of a critical spatial perspective. Geohistory, for example, emphasizes the unprioritized inseparability of geography and history, their necessary and often problematic interwovenness. But, at least for present purposes, it is the *geo* that comes first, for too often history, used without its spatial qualifier, squanders the critical insights of the geographical or spatial imagination, merely adding geographical facts and a few maps in their place. Another intentional foregrounding relates to the interweaving of spatiality and sociality, or what I once called the socio-spatial dialectic. While it may be easy to grasp the idea that everything spatial is simultaneously, even problematically, social, it is much more difficult to comprehend the reverse relation, that what is described as social is always at the same time intrinsically spatial. This inherent, contingent, and complexly constituted spatiality of social life (and of history) must be persistently and explicitly stressed, lest it be forgotten or submerged. That the social, the historical, and the spatial dimensions can stand alone as analytical objects is obvious, but I ask readers always to keep the other two in mind whenever one of these terms is used without qualification – for keeping the three co-equally linked together is a vital part of the spatial turn and the spatialization of urban studies.

As it has been the spatial dimension that is most often left out or underemphasized, the spatial and the geographical will be "put first" in many of the terms and concepts used in this book, starting here with the geohistory of cityspace. Cityspace refers to the city as a historical-social-spatial phenomenon, but *with its intrinsic spatiality highlighted* for interpretive and explanatory purposes. Also coming to the foreground in this definition of cityspace and adding more concreteness to its meaning is what can be described as the *spatial specificity of urbanism*, a concept that will be used repeatedly in subsequent chapters. Urban spatial specificity refers to the particular configurations of social relations, built forms, and human activity in a city and its geographical sphere of influence. It actively arises from the *social production of cityspace* as a distinctive material and symbolic context or habitat for human life. It thus has both formal or morphological as well as processual or dynamic aspects.

As urban form, spatial specificity can be described in terms of the relatively fixed qualities of a *built environment*, expressed in physical structures (buildings, monuments, streets, parks, etc.) and also in the mappable patternings of land use, economic wealth, cultural identity, class differences, and the whole range of individual and collective attributes, relations, thoughts, and practices of urban inhabitants. As urban process, it takes on more dynamic qualities that derive from its role in the formation of cityspace and the social construction of urbanism, a constantly evolving, intentionally planned, and politically charged *contextualization* and *spatialization* of social life in its broadest sense. As both form and process, the spatial specificity of urbanism is synonymous with what can be called the historically evolving *specific geography* of cityspace.

The specific geography of cityspace has frequently been relegated to an unproblematic background in the intellectual practices of critical historiography and insistently social and/or socialist science. Social processes, such as stratification by status and class or the formation of urban communities, are seen as shaping cities but very rarely are these social and historical processes and events recognized as being significantly shaped by the intrinsic nature of city-ness itself. Even when cityspace becomes the focus of inquiry, as in the field of urban studies, it has tended to be viewed primarily as an architecturally built environment, a physical container for human activities, shaped and reshaped over time by professional or vernacular citybuilders and a host of non-spatial but distinctly social and historical processes of urban development. This has concentrated attention on the distilled material forms of urban spatiality, too often leaving aside its more dynamic, generative, developmental, and explanatory qualities.

Rephrasing Foucault's often-quoted observation comparing how scholars have traditionally viewed space as opposed to time, cityspace in nearly all these approaches is typically seen as fixed, dead, socially and politically ineffectual, little more than a constructed stage-set for dynamic social and historical processes that are not themselves inherently urban. In contrast, urban history and the historical development of urban society (the historical and social specificity of urbanism) are typically privileged and prioritized as vitally involved in the ongoing dynamics of human and societal development and change, vibrantly alive, complexly dialectical, the primary field and focus of human action, collective consciousness, social will, and critical interpretation. Shaping every chapter in *Postmetropolis* is a delicate (re)balancing act that attempts to break down this long-established privileging of time over space in urban studies, without, however, simply reversing the order of privilege, that is, subordinating time and history to an overriding spatial determination or spatialism.

Opening up the investigation of cityspace to this more comprehensive perspective of spatio-temporal "structuration," to use a term closely associated with the work of the social theorist Anthony Giddens, makes it possible to link the dynamic production and reproduction of cityspace more directly to other familiar and well-studied configurations of social life such as the family, the cultural community, the structure of social classes, the market economy, and the governmental state or polity. Not only does this linkage suggest that these other institutionalized structures have their own specific geographies that need to be more rigorously studied and understood, but also that the production of cityspace generates additional local, urban, and regional forms of social organization and identity that are worthy of study in themselves.

In my view, the most insightful and affirmative conceptualization of this complex but distinctively urban process of social configuration can be found in the work of Henri Lefebvre, one of the twentieth century's leading urbanists. Lefebvre grounded his embracing conceptualization of the relations between spatiality, society, and history in a fundamentally *urban problematic*, a tension-filled and often highly contested spatial dynamic and framework for political action that he projected into the more social and historical specificities of urban life. Following Lefebvre's most assertive argument, all social relations, whether they are linked to class, family, community, market, or state power, remain abstract and ungrounded until they are specifically *spatialized*, that is, made into material and symbolic spatial relations. Moreover, this process of real and imagined materialization and contextualization is not a simple matter of being coincidentally mapped into specific and fixed geographies, but is filled with movement and change, tensions and conflict, politics and ideology, passions and desires, and, to quote Virgine again, "the enigmas of the world and our existence." That this problematic process is intrinsically urban is powerfully evoked in the quotation from Lefebvre that begins chapter 1, where he states that "the development of society is conceivable only in urban life, through the realization of urban society."

Lefebvre argued that this specifically urban problematic derives from the complex interaction between macro- and micro-geographical configurations of cityspace. When viewed "from above," these developmental geographies describe the overall condition and conditioning of urban reality in general or global terms. Viewed "from below," they are more grounded in localized spatial practices and the particular experiences of everyday life. The tensions and contradictions that arise from these different *scales* of spatial specificity, as well as from the contrasting perspectives used to interpret them, are resolved – or at least unfold – in a third process, which Lefebvre described most comprehensively as the (social) production of (social) space.[5] This alternative and intensely politicized way of looking at cityspace, combining both macro and micro perspectives without privileging one over the other, has been much less frequently explored in the literature on cities, for too often the views from above and below have been defined as separate and competitive empirical and interpretive domains rather than interactive and complementary moments in our understanding of urbanism and its spatial specificities.[6] Here again, I will try to put into practice this alternative Lefebvrean conceptualization of cityspace in all the chapters that will follow.

The trialectics of cityspace

Building further on Lefebvre and my extensions of his work in *Thirdspace* (1996), the production of cityspace in its combined expression as contextualizing form-and-process can be studied in at least three different but interrelated ways. From what I described as a Firstspace perspective (Lefebvre called its object of analysis *perceived* space), cityspace can be studied as a set of materialized "spatial practices" that work together to produce and reproduce the concrete forms and specific patternings of urbanism as a way of life. Here cityspace is physically and empirically perceived as form and process, as measurable and mappable configurations and practices of urban life. This

---

5   This parenthetical inclusion of the social should not be interpreted, as some more sociological readers of Lefebvre have done, as somehow privileging the social over the spatial. As I read his intent, it is to keep the two simultaneously entwined, lest we forget the social as Lefebvre forcefully asserts the critical power of specifically urban spatiality and spatial thinking.

6   For further discussion of this more comprehensive approach, see "Postscript I: On the Views from Above and Below," *Thirdspace*, 1996: 310–14.

fundamentally materialist approach has been by far the dominant perspective in looking at and interpreting urban spatiality.

From a Secondspace perspective, cityspace becomes more of a mental or ideational field, conceptualized in imagery, reflexive thought, and symbolic representation, a *conceived* space of the imagination, or what I will henceforth describe as the urban imaginary. One example of these representations of cityspace is the "mental map" we all carry with us as an active part of how we experience a city. Another is the envisioning of an urban utopia, an imagined reality which also can affect our urban experience and behavior. A third and even more complex example is the construction of an urban epistemology, a formal framework and method for obtaining knowledge about cityspace and explaining its specific geography. While Firstspace perspectives are more objectively focused and emphasize "things in space," Secondspace perspectives tend to be more subjective and concerned with "thoughts about space."

Various combinations of these two modes of understanding cityspace have traditionally filled the entire scope of the urban geographical imagination and have helped to rivet attention in urban studies on what might be described as the measurable surface appearances of urban spatiality, even when conceived as a field of utopian dreams and subjective imaginings. Extending an argument I developed in some detail in *Thirdspace*, such a pronounced concentration on real and/or imagined surface appearances places certain constraints on our ability to recognize cityspace – as well as other forms of human spatiality – as an active arena of development and change, conflict and resistance, an impelling force affecting all aspects of our lives. Viewed exclusively within these two modes of spatial thinking and epistemology, the spatial specificity of urbanism tends to be reduced to fixed forms, whether micro or macro in scale, that are described and interpreted as the materialized products of what tend to be seen as non-spatial processes: historical, social, political, economic, behavioral, ideological, ecological, and so on. The intrinsic, dynamic, and problematic spatiality of human life is thus significantly muted in its scope and explanatory power. Cityspace is seen as something to be explained, reduced to an outcome or product of essentially social action and intention. Only rarely is it recognized as a dynamic process of (social) spatial construction, as *a source of explanation in itself*.

The central argument of *Thirdspace* was that there is another way of thinking about the social production of human spatiality that incorporates both Firstspace and Secondspace perspectives while at the same time opening up the scope and complexity of the geographical or spatial imagination. In this alternative or "third" perspective, the spatial specificity of urbanism is investigated as fully *lived space*, a simultaneously real-and-imagined, actual-and-virtual, locus of structured individual and collective experience and agency. Understanding lived space can be compared to writing a biography, an interpretation of the lived time of an individual; or more generally to historiography, the attempt to describe and understand the lived time of human collectivities or societies. In all these "life stories," perfect or complete knowledge is impossible. There is too much that lies beneath the surface, unknown and perhaps unknowable, for a complete story to be told. The best we can do is selectively explore, in the most insightful ways we can find, the infinite complexity of life through its intrinsic spatial, social, and historical dimensions, its interrelated spatiality, sociality, and historicality.

In this sense, studying cityspace presents a potentially endless variety of exemplifications and interpretations. Faced with such complexity, we explore and explain as much as we can, choosing those specific examples and instances which most closely reflect our particular objectives and projects for obtaining useful, practical knowledge, knowledge that we can use not just to understand the world but to change it for the better. Although there is a degree to which Part I highlights a Firstspace perspective, Part II a Secondspace perspective, and Part III a Thirdspace perspective, every chapter is informed by all three modes of investigating the city and by the challenges arising from the interconnectedness of perceived, conceived, and lived spaces.

Synekism: the stimulus of urban agglomeration

To guide our remapping of the geohistory of cityspace, another term needs to be introduced to capture in a clearer way one of the most important human dynamics that arises from the very nature of urban life, from what can be broadly called cityness. For this purpose, I have chosen to adapt an ancient Greek word that appears from time to time in the archeological and historical literature on cities and urbanism in its English form, "synoecism" (pronounced "sin-ee-sism"). For several reasons, I have chosen to spell and pronounce the word as *synekism*, although whenever synoecism appears in the literature I will retain the original spelling.

Synekism is directly derived from *synoikismos*, literally the condition arising from dwelling together in one house, or *oikos*, and used by Aristotle in his *Politics* to describe the formation of the Athenian *polis* or city-state. Many other terms have been spun off from the root term *oikos* and its intrinsic sense of organizing and managing a shared space or common habitat: *economics* (originally "home economics" or "household management," expanded to encompass much larger territories from the local to the global), *ecology* (the study of how various living organisms "dwell together" in shared spaces or environments), *ecumene* (the "inhabited world" and/or its core regions of occupation), and most recently *ekistics* (a term developed by the Greek architect and planning theorist Constantinos Doxiades to refer to the comprehensive study of all human settlements from the household to the global scales). All these extensions of *oikos* have retained the hard k-sound of the Greek root. They are also imbricated in the extended meaning of *synoikismos*. Synekism thus connotes, in particular, the economic and ecological interdependencies and the creative – as well as occasionally destructive – synergisms that arise from the purposeful clustering and collective cohabitation of people in space, in a "home" habitat.

In ancient Greece, synekism referred specifically to the union of several smaller urban settlements under a "capital" city, thus implying a form of urban-based governmentality (what we have called, for example, the city-state) as well as the idea of an *urban system*, an interconnected network of settlements of varying sizes interacting within defined and defining *regional* boundaries (the term *region* being derived from the Latin *regere*, to rule). Thus, from the beginning, synekism connoted a regional concept of cityspace, a form and process of political governance, economic development, social order, and cultural identity that involved not just one urban settlement or node but many articulated together in a multi-layered meshwork of nodal settlements or city-centered regions. In this sense, synekism carries with it a similar socio-spatial dynamic to what is implied in the equally ancient Greek word *metropolis*, literally "mother-city," the capital or dominating center of a "colonized" constellation of cities, towns, and villages, along with their less densely settled hinterlands, that defines the territorial (and often imperial) *homeland*, another regional variation of *oikos*. In modern Greek, synekism retains its connotation of a particular spatial dynamic in the urbanization or city-formation process, often referring to the accretion of new settlement spaces (villages, towns, neighborhoods, suburbs) around a dominant and centripetal urban core.[7]

As with our definitions of cityspace, both synekism and metropolis can be seen as static descriptions of spatial form, but also as the spatially specific context for active and affective processes of social formation, innovation, development, growth, and change. Without neglecting the importance of urban form, it is the latter, more processual and impelling aspect that warrants our particular attention here. As an active and motive force in geohistory, synekism involves the formation of a nucleated and hierarchically nested regional network of settlements capable of generating innovation, growth, and societal (as well as individual) development from within its defined territorial domain. In this sense, it resembles what economic geographers have called *agglomeration economies*, the economic advantages (and at times disadvantages) that derive from the dense clustering of people and the sites of production, consumption, administration, culture, and related activities in nodal concentrations that form the focal points of a regional system of settlements, a nested network of "central places" and their dependent hinterlands.

Synekistic agglomeration is a behavioral and transactional as well as political and economic concept that activates, makes into a social and historical force, the spatial specificity of urbanism. It is not the only such force arising from the specific geography of cities, but it is crucial in explaining why cityspace and the spatialized culture and political economy of *city-regions* play a powerful and enduring role in human historical and societal development, albeit a role that has been infrequently recognized and rarely theorized explicitly. The stimulus of urban agglomeration becomes especially relevant in

---

7 Another contemporary usage of *synoikismos* is to refer to recent areas of immigrant settlement in cities such as Athens.

attempting to explain one of the most enigmatic and challenging questions in geohistory: why do some regions of the world develop faster than others? This is the leading question for all studies of *geohistorically uneven development*, perhaps the most integrative thematic subject in all the human sciences.

Much of the contemporary work of economic geographers and others on the stimulus of urban agglomeration, a subject which will be returned to in later chapters, was provocatively foreshadowed in a small book published in 1969 by the iconoclastic urban critic Jane Jacobs. In her speculative introduction to *The Economy of Cities*, Jacobs reached back to the origins of cities to develop an argument that roots urban growth in what she called "the spark of city economic life," a spark that closely resembles synekism and the reflexive, generative, and innovative forces associated with spatial agglomeration and nodality. She defines the city as a settlement that consistently generates its economic growth from its own localized economy and resources. This endogenous or intra-urban synergy (boosted by interurban connections) extends itself in the creation of a local city-region of dependent towns, villages, and countrysides (which by her definition are incapable of producing self-generated growth); more extensive metropolitan areas where cities, towns, and villages coalesce into a regional network of settlements; and a "national economy," defined as "the sum of a nation's city economies and the past and current secondary effects of city economies upon the economies of towns, villages, countrysides and wildernesses" (1969: 258–9). Some cities may cease to grow (she calls them stagnant cities), but her key argument is that all propulsive forces for economic growth and development (and she emphatically adds: throughout history) emerge from the particular sociospatial milieux of cities, from that extraordinary but too often overlooked condition of human life that can be described as the spatial specificity of urbanism.

In a brief interview in the *Los Angeles Times*, conducted in conjunction with a five-day symposium honoring Jacobs in Toronto in October 1997, she repeats her argument in her characteristically straightforward and challenging style.

> Cities are the mothers of economic development, not because people are smarter in cities, but because of the conditions of density. There is a concentration of need in cities, and a greater incentive to address problems in ways that haven't been addressed before. This is the essence of economic development. Without it, we'd all be poor.

> It's only with development and trade that poverty is overcome. The most rural places, without cities to act as their economic motors, are the poorest . . . All through organized human history, if you wanted prosperity, you've had to have cities. Places that attract new people, with new ideas . . . [Newcomers] bring new ways of looking at things, and maybe new ways of solving old problems.[8]

8   Steve Proffitt, "Jane Jacobs: Still Challenging the Way We Think About Cities," *Los Angeles Times* (Opinion), October 12, 1997: M3.

More recently, the economic geographer and planner Michael Storper has vigorously reasserted the importance of this creative stimulus of urban agglomeration. Here are a few of his observations taken from "The World of the City: Local Relations in a Global Economy," chapter 9 in *The Regional World: Territorial Development in a Global Economy* (1997):

> [T]he nature of the contemporary city is as a local or regional "socio-economy" ... an ensemble of specific, differentiated and localized social relations ... concrete relations between persons and organizations which are necessary to the economic functioning of those entities. Cities are sites where such relations are conventional, and they are different from one city to another. Economic activities that cluster together in cities ... are frequently characterized by interdependencies that are indirect or untraded and take the form of these conventions and relations. (1997a: 222)

Storper links these socially and spatially constructed conventions and interdependencies to what he calls *economic reflexivity*, the ability to "shape the course of economic evolution through reflexive human action," and to what he describes as "competitive learning." He then adds (emphasis deleted):

> Important and distinctive dimensions of this reflexivity, in both production and consumption, in manufacturing as well as in services, take place in cities; they are dependent on the concrete relations between persons and organizations that are formed in cities; and they are coordinated by conventions that have specifically urban dimensions. (ibid.)

> [I]t is not just the geometry of these [urban worlds of reflexive action] which is of interest, but the constructed mentalities and frameworks by which the actors involved evaluate and interpret their contexts in an ongoing way, and on that basis adjust their participation in the context. (1997a: 246)

Although Storper does not see this generative reflexivity as exclusively urban, he nonetheless emphasizes the vital role of spatial proximity and the stimulus of dense urban agglomeration.

> [R]eflexivity involves complex and uncertain relationships between organizations, between the parts of complex organizations, between individuals, and between individuals and organizations, in which proximity is important because of the substantive complexity and uncertainty of these relationships ... In other words, the transactional tissue of these urban activities is of a conventional/relational nature, and it is urban because certain conventions and relations only work in the context of proximity. (1997a: 245)

Significantly, Storper, even more so than Jacobs, couches his analysis of urban economic reflexivity in a regional perspective, in what he describes as "regional worlds of production." It is useful to elaborate further on this "regionality" of synekistic cityspace.

The regionality of cityspace

As already noted, the concept of synekism is implicitly regional in scope. It applies not just to a singular, peak density, city center but more emphatically to a larger polycentric regional system of interacting nodal settlements, a city-region. This regionality enlarges the *scale* of cityspace right from the start, and points to the need to see even the earliest cities as regional agglomerations. Keeping in mind the regionality of cityspace is not easy, for we tend to see the city as a formally bounded area distinct from its surrounding "non-city" or "sub-urban" or "rural" hinterland and countryside. It is only in this inner area that we conventionally attribute the distinctive qualities of urban-ness or the experiences of urbanism as a way of life. Cityspace, however, involves a much larger and more complex configuration, a specific geography that, by its very definition, tends to be dynamic and expansive in its territorial domain. It will always contain inhabited or, for that matter, uninhabited or wilderness areas that do not look urban in any conventional way, but nonetheless are *urbanized*, part of a regional cityspace and thereby deeply affected by urbanism as a way of life and by the synekism that inheres to dwelling together in a shared space.

As a regional network of settlements, cityspace is hierarchically structured, in that it consists of settlements of different sizes, some relatively freestanding, others once so but subsequently coalesced into a continuous urban tissue. There probably has never existed any regional cityspace in which all settlements were of equal size. This has been the fundamental premise of what geographers have called "central place theory," an attempt to describe the characteristic geometry of hierarchical settlement systems in terms of size, relative location, and the distribution of service functions. Furthermore, these size hierarchies tend to be pyramidal, with many more smaller than larger settlements. Again, there are no known city-regions in which the largest cities outnumber the smallest. Indeed, there has always been a tendency for regional cityspace to revolve around a single dominant urban core, the "capital" or mother-city of the metropolitan region, where synekism in all its positive and negative manifestations can be presumed to be most intensely, but not exclusively, concentrated.

Other descriptive generalizations can be made about the material form of cityspace. For example, even in smaller settlements there is likely to be a distance-decay function in population densities, peaking in or near a definable center and declining outward more or less regularly, depending on the size of the agglomeration, the location of other nodal centers, and other factors such as the rate of population expansion. The resultant tentlike structure of cityspace densities is often associated, in contemporary urban economic analysis, with land values and other measures of attraction and comparative locational advantage based on accessibility, density of activity, and potential for stimulating further urban development. Not surprisingly, when you think about it, these dense nodal centers also tend to generate various types of concentric and axial zonation around them, shaping at least some patterns of urban land use and related behavior and activity. Concentric zonation into rings of specialized activity is not always visible in the built environment, especially in pre-industrial cityspaces, but is nearly always there to find if one looks hard enough. Also likely to be there patterning land use, modifying concentricity and the tentlike density distribution, are "preferred" axes, usually major transit arteries that typically cross in the city center, another reflection of the centripetal power of nodality. If proximity breeds advantage, then the spatial specificity of urbanism generates a field of real and imagined competition for advantageous access that makes cityspace far from randomly or uniformly organized.

Rephrasing one of the maxims of mathematical geography, cityspace can be seen internally as a spatial system in itself, and also as externally nested within a larger spatial system of similar cityspaces. Agglomeration and synekism thus operate at several different levels and also extend their effects in at least three different directions: from the center to its immediate hinterland (an intra-urban effect), from each center to other centers of relatively similar size (inter-urban linkages), and between the many different-sized settlements in the regional network (a hierarchical effect that most often but not always filters from the larger centers to the smaller). Furthermore, agglomeration is not exclusively a process of attraction, a movement inward to a center. It also works the other way, as a force of decentralization and diffusion. There thus exists in every regional cityspace a complex and dynamic relation between the forces of agglomeration and centralization (centripetal forces) and dis-agglomeration and decentralization (centrifugal forces), again operating at several different scales, differing in resultant effects from place to place, and changing over time.

Seeking, finding, and perhaps also explaining the origins of these morphological patternings of cityspace has preoccupied generations of geographical urbanists over the past century. Although some of the findings of these studies will be referred to in our remapping of the geohistory of cityspace as interesting continuities from the oldest to the newest cities, they will not play a major role in the attempt to make practical and theoretical sense of the spatial specificity of urbanism and the emergence of the postmetropolis. This is not because they are irrelevant or uninteresting, but rather because they too often tend to distract attention from an explicit exploration of the dynamics of synekism and the larger project of demonstrating how the spatiality of social life acts as a motive force in geohistory.

Synekism is much more than a pattern variable that can be directly measured by population statistics, activity patterns, income distribution, or other "outcome" densities and accessibilities. Its less tangible effects are not so easily perceived, for they lie beneath these surface appearances and often out of conscious awareness, shaping and helping to explain the formation of cityspace as well as many of its empirically defined morphological "regularities" in more subtle ways. To use a perhaps overly presumptuous biological comparison, synekism can be seen as a vital part of the DNA of urbanism, a kind of presuppositional code for the generation, growth, and development of city-space and its metropolitan regionality. By this I mean that it can be used to help decipher and therefore aid in understanding not just the origins of city-space and the evolution of urban form, but the entire geohistorical trajectory of urbanism and urban development in all human societies from the past to the present. Recognizing its potential explanatory power significantly broadens the scope of urban studies, enabling it to deal more effectively and insightfully with much larger and more diverse issues than have hitherto been included within its traditional purview, including those "enigmas of the world and our existence" mentioned in the lead quote by Lea Virgine.

Through such redefined concepts as the spatial specificity of urbanism, synekism as the stimulus of urban agglomeration, and the multinodal regionality of cityspace, we are made much more aware that the social-spatial-historical processes that shape our lives do not simply operate *in* and *on* cities, but to a significant degree also emanate *from* cities, from those complex specificities and stimulations of urban life. Mainstream social science perspectives and the orthodoxies of scientific socialism have tended to lose sight of the potential explanatory power of these spatial specificities in their interpretations of human history and society. It is time to bring this "hidden dimension" back into the picture.

Chapter 1
Putting Cities First

The development of society is conceivable only in urban life, through the realization of urban society.

Henri Lefebvre, *Le droit à la ville/Espace et Politique"* (1968)

Until recently, theoretical thinking conceived the city as an entity, as an organism and a whole among others, and this in the best of cases when it was not being reduced to a partial phenomenon, to a secondary, elementary or accidental aspect, of evolution and history. One would thus see in it a simple result, a local effect reflecting purely and simply general history . . . [This view] did not contain theoretical knowledge of the city and did not lead to this knowledge; moreover, [it] blocked at a quite basic level the enquiry . . . Only now are we beginning to grasp the *specificity* of the city.

Kofman and Lebas, *Henri Lefebvre: Writings on Cities* (1996): 100

This city is the outcome of a *synoecism*.

Ibid.: 87

Re-excavating the Origins of Urbanism

The search for origins, like all forms of historical inquiry, is often shaped by a predetermination of results, a kind of reverse teleology that leads the searcher to find roots and starting points that reflect his or her personal views of the present. We are comfortable looking back to the past for we believe that understanding history helps us grapple better with the problems affecting the present day. But even the most objective historian tends to be less aware of the degree to which an understanding of the past is powerfully shaped by prevailing contemporary modes of thought, whether they are personal political beliefs, entrenched disciplinary paradigms, or currently fashionable methods of inquiry. That is why history is intrinsically destined to be rewritten over and over again.

I begin my rewriting of the geohistory of cities, the urbanization process, and urbanism as a way of life fully aware that I too have a particular project that shapes my search for origins and destinations. What I will find is therefore likely, indeed it is intended, to differ significantly from the established ways of describing and explaining the origins of what has been called the Urban Revolution. My approach is grounded in and guided by the belief that there has been a tendency in even the most geographically-conscious writings on the origins of cities, from V. Gordon Childe's original and still paradigmatic conceptualization of the Urban Revolution to Lewis Mumford's brilliant foray into the "crystallization" of the city in history, to some of the best contemporary writings of critical archeologists and anthropologists, to downplay the importance of the dynamic processes associated with the spatiality of social life and the social construction of specific human geographies. What I plan to do in this chapter, and indeed in all the chapters that will follow, is to take a different look at the literature that deals with cities, starting with the debates on urban origins, with the intention of demonstrating the potential interpretive power that can come from the application of a more comprehensive and assertive critical spatial perspective. The objective is not only to show that thinking spatially makes a difference, but also to illustrate how putting critical spatial thinking first, foregrounding the spatial with respect to the social and the historical dimensions of our lives, can result in significant new insights that challenge much that has been taken for granted in history, geography, and social thought more generally.

The conventional sequence: hunting and gathering – agriculture – villages – cities – states

The prevailing contemporary discourse on the origins of cities and the ensuing Urban Revolution, upgraded by some recent discoveries and critical reinterpretations, usually moves through an evolutionary sequence that begins with small-scale human societies organized as relatively egalitarian bands of hunters and gatherers. For most of the first three million years of humankind, we lived in groups that probably averaged around 25–30 people and were marked by strong gendered roles. Although many now question just how narrowly specialized this gender division of labor actually was, men tended to be the primary hunters. They worked to maintain and defend hunting and gathering territories, fished, and did some minor collecting of wild food. Women were the primary food gatherers, helped to maintain gathering territories, and tended to the demands of everyday life in the temporary home compounds.

Beginning at least 40,000 years ago, hunters and gatherers in scattered parts of the world became increasingly sedentary. Compounds became specifically and more substantially constructed, usually consisting of clusters of circular huts organized in a kraal-like settlement. This was a significant advance on the protected cave-dwelling or rock shelter because it allowed for much greater mobility in the search for food. The settlement was easily dismountable or could be abandoned and rebuilt when necessary. Although few if any permanent settlements were constructed by these semi-nomadic hunters and gatherers, recent evidence suggests that in Southwest Asia at least, the compounds had become quite complex and multinodal. In addition to the base camps, which tended to remain for increasingly longer periods of time, there were also scattered locations of smaller temporary camps, hunting stations, rock shelters, and quarry workshops for making stone tools, the defining technology of the Paleolithic or Old Stone Age.[1] Most bands remained relatively isolated, but there is increasing evidence of some trade in such items as salt, and stone for tools as well as ornamentation.

Between about fifteen and ten thousand years ago, with the retreat of Pleistocene glaciation and the beginnings of the transition from the Paleolithic to the Neolithic (New Stone Age), something quite dramatic, if gradual – some archeologists call it a "broad spectrum revolution" – began to happen in Southwest Asia and perhaps also the Nile Valley and surrounding Saharan oases. Hunters and gatherers intensified their exploitation of wild cereal grains and wild animals, possibly in response to changing climatic conditions. The ecological milieu of Southwest Asia and Egypt, especially in the arc of highlands surrounding the Tigris-Euphrates valleys running from present-day Iran through the Anatolian Plateau and Iraq and then south through Syria and Palestine to the Lower Nile, was particularly propitious for these developments. Wild varieties of wheat, barley, lentils, and nuts were especially abundant in the well-watered highlands, and similarly there were large numbers of the wild ancestors of sheep, goats, cattle, and pigs. In these advantageous circumstances, hunting and gathering bands became more rooted in place, creating the world's first known permanent settlements and accelerating the processes that would lead to the domestication of plants and animals, bringing human society to the brink of full-scale and intentional farming and animal husbandry, the hallmark of what has been called the Neolithic or Agricultural Revolution.

The transition from hunting to farming and the formation of the first fully agrarian societies is typically seen as developing in association with the rise and multiplication of small villages linked in larger trading networks facilitating the exchange of ideas, food, stone ornaments and tools, and other valued resources. This probably first occurred in the highland regions of Southwest Asia at least 10,000 years ago, with later and probably related developments in the Nile, Indus, and Tigris-Euphrates valleys, and southeastern Europe.[2] It was here that the process of domestication accelerated into

---

1   See, for example, Anthony E. Marks, "The Middle Paleolithic of the Negev, Israel," in J. Cauvin and P. Sanlavalle, eds., *Préhistoire du Levant: chronologie et organisation de l'espace depuis les origines jusqu'au VIe millénaire*, Paris: Éditions du Centre National de la Recherche Scientifique, 1981: 288–302. Also useful here and in the subsequent discussion is Ofer Bar-Yosef, "On the Nature of Transitions: the Middle to Upper Paleolithic and the Neolithic Revolution," *Cambridge Archeological Journal* 8, 1998: 141–63. Bar-Yosef is a leading specialist on the "prehistory" of Southwest Asia and in particular on the eventful developments taking place in the Levantine Corridor.

2   Similar processes of transition from hunting-gathering to farming-animal husbandry occurred, it is presumed independently, in many other parts of the world several thousands of years later than in Southwest Asia. The best known of these independent hearths of agricultural development are the

intentional cultivation, beyond the mere side job it may have been for hunters and gatherers. Over the past few years, new archeological research has confirmed the primary location of early plant and animal domestication in a roughly T-shaped region (from Iran to western Anatolia and south through the Levantine Corridor to the Nile) and uncovered a remarkable concentration of these developments in the relatively short period between 10,000 and 9,500 years ago. Where the two bars of the T cross, in south-central Anatolia, DNA testing has revealed three major "founder crops," the earliest known cultivated species of chickpeas, bitter vetch, and, most important, einkorn wheat.[3] In surrounding extensions of the T during roughly the same period are found the first domesticated sheep, pigs, goats, and cattle, and a whole array of plant crops, including grapes, olives, barley, emmer as well as bread wheat (*Triticum aestivum*), peas, lentils, broad beans, and flax.[4]

Sedentarization was essential for agrarian society and villages grew to substantial size throughout Southwest Asia in the early Neolithic after about 10,000 B.P. This new settlement form and socio-economic organization arising from the development of full-scale agriculture consisted of denser clusters of rectangular mud and daub houses (as opposed to the beehive huts of the hunter-gatherer compound) and a social order that was increasingly based on wider kinship or ethnic ties in the form of nucleated and extended families,

Hwang Ho-Yangtze river basins in China, Mesoamerica (Aztec and Maya), and highland Peru (Inca). The list of other major centers of plant and animal domestication has been growing over the years and now includes at least the large river basins of Southeast Asia (from the lower Ganges to Tonkin), Ethiopia and West Africa, the upper Amazon basin, northern Europe and eastern North America, and Papua-New Guinea, where there is some evidence of pig and taro domestication almost as early as in Southwest Asia. For an excellent recent overview of the debates on agricultural origins see T. Douglas Price and Anne Birgitte Gebauer, eds., *Last Hunters – First Farmers: New Perspectives on the Prehistoric Transition to Agriculture*, Santa Fe, NM: School of American Research Press, 1995.

3   The research referred to here was conducted by scientists from the Agricultural University of Norway in Ås and the Max Planck Institute in Cologne. For a report on their findings see M. Heun et al., *Science* 278, November 14, 1997: 1312. Also in this issue is a commentary by the UCLA physiologist and biogeographer Jared Diamond entitled "Location, Location, Location: The First Farmers" (1997: 1243–4). Diamond uses these discoveries to reinforce the arguments he develops in *Guns, Germs, and Steel: The Fates of Human Societies* (New York: Norton, 1997) that "a long straight line runs through world history" triggered by the origins of food production and followed by the emergences of kings, bureaucrats, scribes, professional soldiers, metal workers, writing, stratified society, empires, advanced weapons, as well as smallpox and other epidemic diseases. In this process, he notes, "location is almost everything." In all these writings, including newspaper reports (see Robert Lee Holtz, "Scientists Follow a Grain to the Origins of Agriculture," *New York Times*, November 14, 1997), the core region is defined as the "Fertile Crescent," the whole area is called "Eurasia," and the spread of agriculture to Europe (as opposed, say, to the Indus or Nile Valleys) is given major emphasis. For several reasons, I have chosen not to use the term Fertile Crescent, which normally emphasizes lowland Mesopotamia, and instead describe the region as T-shaped, to include more of western Anatolia, the huge peninsula of Turkey that was originally called "Asia" by the Greeks and Romans. To describe the whole region as "Eurasia" is as Eurocentric as calling it the "Near East."

4   The rapidity of domestication of einkorn wheat in this region is compared with the "drastic biological reorganization" required for the domestication of maize in Mexico and Mesoamerica from its wild ancestor, teosinte. Diamond in *Science* (278, 1997) claims that this "helps explain why densely populated agrarian societies arose so much earlier and developed so much more rapidly in the crescent [*sic*] than in the New World."

clans, and lineages. These "tribal" societies developed more complex religious or cultic associations, production technologies, and new social arrangements based not only on gender but increasingly on age, experience, descent, and military skill. Although reciprocity, a form of mutual exchange and symbolic bartering, continued to be important, the primary exchange relationship in kinship societies increasingly focused on methods of redistribution, giving rise to a new political form, alternatively called the "chiefdom" or the "village-state." These new agrarian societies, multiplying on a regional scale, not only increased regional population densities and created a substantial social surplus of food, but also embarked on important technological innovations, including the earliest development of irrigation. But city-state institutions, large-scale irrigation works, a distinctively urban division of labor, and the "recorded history" that comes from the written word – the accouterments of what we call "civilization" – are still considered to have been in their infancy. Another "big bang" was necessary to create the more substantive Urban Revolution and the first "true" cities.

The "proto-urbanization" process begun in such sites as Jericho, Abu Hureyra, Mureybat, and Aşikli Hüyük more than 10,000 years ago is most often described, when it is recognized at all, as not having crystallized into true cities until at least 4,000 years later; and not in the highlands but on the alluvial plains of the Tigris and Euphrates, and particularly in the area known as Sumeria, where there were relatively few agricultural settlements before that time. Although some continue to focus on singular explanations of this great shift in the geographical locus of societal innovation in Southwest Asia, the origin of cities is usually viewed as arising from an integrated package of causal influences: the administrative demands of large-scale irrigation and flood control technology; the new economic opportunities arising from long-distance trade and commerce; the closely related creation of a more reliable and sustained food surplus; the increasing institutional development of kingship and its administrative bureaucracy; the expansion of religious and ceremonial activities and their capability to maintain and reproduce larger-scale communities than ever before; the growing need for defense against the vagaries of nature and the invasion of "outsiders"; and the demographic pressures brought about by both increasing numbers and environmental degradation. To this list, some might add the impact of synekism, at least in the sense of an amalgamation of existing villages and towns into one large and consolidated urban entity. But whatever the causes, the result was the virtually simultaneous creation of two new forms of human social spatiality: the city and the state, conveniently coupled by a dash in the city-state or combined in a new way in the long-lasting notion of *civilization*, from the Latin root *civitas*, or city.

Thus begins the recorded history of cities, materially and symbolically initiated by the invention of writing and the associated formation of the city-state. The onset of recorded history also begins another trend in more contemporary interpretations of the past, an inclination towards giving primary attention to the development of the monarchial state and its imperial extensions rather than to the city and the specificities of cityspace. From its earliest origins in

Mesopotamian sites such as Eridu, Uruk, and Ur, the city-state is seen as multiplying and mutating into that remarkable sequence that underpins the intentionally recorded history of civilization, highlighted in Western historiography by developments in "classical" Athens and Rome, where the city-state and city-empire are alleged by Western scholars to have reached their most advanced and distinctively European form. Parallel (and occasionally intersecting) city-state histories rise and fall in Egypt, the Indus Valley (Harappa and Mohenjo-daro), in China and Southeast Asia, in upland Mexico and Mesoamerica, in the Andes and coastal Peru, in the African Sahel and Ethiopia, and, it is now becoming clear, even in the colder reaches of North America and northern Eurasia. As these histories unfold, at least from the viewpoint of the West, the empowerment of city-ness, the spatial specificity and synekism of urban life, tends to be portrayed, if it is seen at all, as declining in overall importance, reduced largely to the production of clustered architectural monuments and creatively designed built environments. Increasingly, the state and its extended definition in the form of empire and, much later, the "imagined community" of the nation-state, subsumes the city as a motive force in history. Symbolic of this subsumption, the definition of citizenship shifts from inhabitant of the city to inhabitant of the (no longer city-prefixed) state.

A provocative inversion: putting cities first

The narrative discourse outlined above is recaptured succinctly in the title of an excellent text written by Charles Keith Maisels: *The Emergence of Civilization: From Hunting and Gathering to Agriculture, Cities, and the State in the Near East.*[5] Maisels carries on the traditions of V. Gordon Childe and other critical prehistorians in blending a materialist interpretation of history (at least partly inspired by Marx) with an explicitly anthropological and geographical perspective, enervated by contemporary developments in critical social science.[6] In comparison with most other current texts, it is infused with a rich geographical imagination and a particular interest in what I will later describe as geopolitical economy. In addition to emphasizing, as many scholars do, the physical environment and its influential explanatory power in history, Maisels roots his analysis of the origins of cities in Southwest Asia and the emergence of civilization directly in that vital endogenous component of the city's spatial specificity, the dynamic and propulsive force of synekism.

---

5   Published by Routledge in 1990 (paperback edition 1993). See also Maisels, *The Near East: Archeology in the "Cradle of Civilization,"* London and New York: Routledge, 1993.

6   V. Gordon Childe, "The Urban Revolution," *Town Planning Review* 21, 1950: 3–17. Childe's new synthesis of prehistory, in which he recasts the old sequence of Neolithic, Bronze, and Iron Ages around two epochal revolutions, the Agricultural and the Urban, can be traced through a series of texts: *Man Makes Himself*, Glasgow: Collins (1936), *What Happened in History?* (1942), and *Social Evolution* (1951). Also relevant here is the work of C. Daryll Forde, beginning with *Habitat, Economy, and Society: A Geographical Introduction to Ethnology*, London: Methuen (1934).

Maisels places synekism at the heart of his analysis of the origins of cities, civilization, and urbanism. He does so, however, by concentrating his consideration of its impact almost exclusively at one moment in history: the initial formation of the city-state and hence of civilization as it has come to be formally defined.

> By *urban*, I mean a population sufficiently numerous and nucleated that the social relations of production mutate to express the principle of synoecism itself (which is interdependence arising from dense proximity), the emergent expression of which is the crystallization of government. In turn, government manifests itself as the state through administration based on writing, plus monumental building representing the professionalization of ideological, economic, and armed force. It is not coincidental, then, that the first form of the city, or for that matter the state, takes the form of the city-state.   (1993: 155)

Using a phrase that resonates well with Henri Lefebvre's description of the perceived space of Spatial Practice (what I called Firstspace), Maisels notes that urbanism as synekism operates by *"secreting relations of production appropriate to a dense interdependent population"* (1993: 302, emphasis added); and goes further to suggest that the city-state may be a better way of defining and naming, at least in the particular form it takes in Mesopotamia, a key offshoot from what Marx described as the Asiatic mode of production. Maisels distinguishes a Mesopotamian city-state mode of production, which is described as being integrated by an "ideology of order, hegemony, and dependence," from the chiefdom, with its "ideology of ranked matri-lineages" as well as from all other examples of the Asiatic or, as he calls it, the "village-state" mode of production, which are united around an "ideology of (divine) descent patri-lineages." In these distinctions, the role of the city versus the village (as well as the relative roles and power of men and women) features prominently. Following Marx, Maisels argues that, in the Asiatic or village-state mode, cities are "exceptional" and "quite unproductive," royal "islands in a sea of peasant villages." Only in the city-states of Sumeria does full-fledged urban society and increasingly stratified class-like relations of production take hold.

Looking back to what might be behind the highly specific nucleation-mutation-crystallization dynamic that gave rise to the city-state in Mesopotamia, he conventionally sites the origins of the city in agriculture, and especially in the formation of agricultural villages, village-states, and presuppositionally rural development. In other words, Maisels (and almost every other scholar writing on the origins of cities) unquestioningly puts agriculture first and presumes a consequential path in which small farming villages grow ever larger until some threshold of synekism is surpassed and true cities and city-states "crystallize" in very particular locations.

> [O]nly agriculture can sustain a relatively high population density over a wide area and thus, at a regional level, produce high population numbers. Under those

circumstances it does not take much to crystallize population around a central place, administrative, cultic, military, or commercial in the first instance, and tending over time to incorporate all those functions in a new synthesis, so developing a further dynamic. A city presupposes, then, both a durable nucleation and a fairly stable relationship to a hinterland, which, depending on circumstances, need not be very large.   (1993: 302)

Maisels thus attaches to the spatial specificity of urbanism a powerful developmental impulse capable of generating and sustaining innovative changes in human society and in its modes of production, a simultaneously social, historical, and spatial dynamic that is rooted specifically in the synergistic stimulus of urban agglomeration and the related production and reproduction of localized cityspace. Cities from the very start are seen as centers of innovation, places where dense propinquity and interdependent co-presence are important shaping features of daily life, human development, and social continuity. They represent a very special form of human habitat and habitation in which social life is both structured by and materially manifested in the ongoing process of producing urban spatiality. These observations alone are enough to begin a deep critical inquiry into Western social theory, philosophy, historiography, and empirical analysis, where the meanings of these fundamentally spatial arguments are too often either taken for granted (and thus left unstudied), or else are subsumed into other processes that cover up or deflect from a critical understanding of the synekistic spatiality of urban life.

How then might we build upon this recognition of "developmental" or generative synekism and the dynamic spatial specificity of urbanism? More specifically, how can we use it to rethink the early geohistory of cityspace that is embedded in *The Emergence of Civilization*, and even more rigidly in the conventional texts of prehistory and archeology? First, it is necessary to free synekism from Maisels's narrow confinement of it to the moment of city-state formation, and to see it as a fundamental and continuous force in the entire sequence of human societal development outlined earlier and continuing to the present. Such an expansion in the spatial and temporal scope of this key concept opens up the possibility of rethinking the specific sequence evoked in Maisels's subtitle – from hunting and gathering to agriculture and farming villages, and then to cities and states – and considering the possibility of putting cities first, that is, pushing back the origins of cities to a time *before* the Agricultural Revolution. This enables us to conceive of a process in which the first cities and distinctive cityspaces were produced by hunters, gatherers, and traders at the same time as the domestication of plants and animals was accelerating. It also becomes possible to see these early cities and the stimulus of urban agglomeration playing a key role first in speeding up domestication and then in the rise of organized and intentional cultivation and the development of "true" agrarian society, indeed what might more accurately be called urban-agrarian society.

Such a re-energizing of the *geo* in geohistory allows for a conceptualization of the stimulus of urban agglomeration as a primary motor force not just for the development of agriculture itself, inverting the usual chain of causality, but also for the appearance of agricultural villages, rural life, pastoralists and peasants, and later, writing, class formation, and the state. In opening up this potential revisioning, I am not suggesting that the conventional sequence is wrong and needs to be scrapped, but rather that we recognize that another course of originating events may have occurred, in Southwest Asia at least, leading to a very different interpretation of the historical importance of the spatial specificity of urbanism. To illustrate further this provocative amplification on the conventional sequence, let us turn to two startling places, Jericho in the rift valley of the Jordan River and Çatal Hüyük in south-central Anatolia.

Learning from Jericho

Once man is settled in one spot, the rest follows.
              Kathleen M. Kenyon, *Archeology in the Holy Land* (1960): 20[7]

Excavations at Jericho, located in a spring-fed oasis well below sea level on a low plateau above the Jordan River in Palestine, present some significant challenges to the conventional wisdom on the origins of cities. The original settlement – possibly the first in history capable of self-generated growth and development – dates back at least to 8350 B.C., that is, more than 10,000 years ago in a period some archeologists call the Epipaleolithic. During the earliest phases of this important but relatively little-known transitional period between the last hunters and the first farmers, Jericho was the largest center of the innovative Natufian culture that stretched along the Mediterranean coast in the region now known as the Levant. The Natufians practiced what was then a highly advanced form of hunting, gathering, and fishing that centered around increasingly permanent settlements, now widely considered the first known example of a sedentary human society. They came to Ain es Sultan, ancient Jericho's life-giving spring, around 9000 B.C. and began constructing what would become a dense and innovative urban agglomeration that may have reached a population of at least 3,000 at its peak. And it is here, in this urban settlement of hunters and foragers, that archeologists would find some of the earliest evidence for that revolutionary event in human history, the invention of settled agriculture as the systematic and intentional cultivation of domesticated food crops.[8]

7 Kathleen Kenyon was a leading figure in mid-twentieth-century British archeology, and her reputation was built primarily on her work at Jericho. In addition to *Archeology in the Holy Land* (London: Ernest Benn, 1960), see her *Digging Up Jericho*, from the same publisher, first published in 1957; and "Some Observations on the Beginnings of Settlement in the Near East," *Journal of the Royal Anthropological Institute* 89(1), 1959: 35–43.
8 Full-scale agriculture can be seen as developing through three phases. Simple domestication comes first and is discoverable through seed remains displaying signs of selective mutation or other biolog-

Figure 1.1 *Air view of the mound at ancient Jericho*   (Source: Kathleen Kenyon, *Digging Up Jericho*, London: Ernest Benn, 1957: 104)

With only one major interruption, the mound or *tell* of Jericho (located a few miles north of the present-day city) was continuously occupied for almost 4,000 years. During these four millennia, a number of other urban centers developed in the broad T-shaped region and became linked together in an expansive trading network of cities: Abu Hureyra (even larger in size than Jericho), Bouqras, and Mureyra along the upper reaches of the Euphrates and

ical changes. The oldest evidence of domesticated food-plants yet found is at Wadi Kubbaniya, a tributary of the Nile, dated to 18,000 years ago. The second phase is intentional planting and harvesting, usually but perhaps not always associated with some degree of sedentarism, in essence an advanced form of gathering. Here there seems little doubt that the most advanced area for this second phase was the T-shaped region of highland Southwest Asia starting around 10,000 years ago, at about the time Jericho was first established. True agriculture and the beginnings of what can be called agrarian society come with more systematic food production, as indicated by more elaborate storage facilities, food-processing tools, and organized production processes such as irrigation. At present, Jericho remains the richest site for this third phase, but what is becoming clear from more recent discoveries is that all three phases were highly compressed in time in the T-region, leaving open some interesting possibilities for rethinking the whole process of agricultural development.

Ras Shamra on the coast in present-day Syria; Ain Ghazal, Abu Gosh, and Beidha in the southern Levant; Zawi Chemi, Jarmo, and Ali Kosh in the borderlands of Iraq and Iran drained by the Tigris; and, from east to west in Anatolia, Çayönü, Aşikli Hüyük, Çatal Hüyük (probably the largest and most intensely studied of the first cities), and Haçilar. In many of these sites, and especially in Çatal Hüyük, one can trace in rich detail the developmental transition from intensified hunting and gathering to organized cultivation and animal husbandry.[9] Of this group, Jericho continues to stand out for its combination of size, continuity, built environment, and dating of the earliest known evidence of settled agriculture.

Maisels, like many contemporary archeologists, tends to downplay the significance of Jericho in the history of urbanization. He almost grudgingly acknowledges that "true full-scale agriculture" may have developed first in Jericho by at least 7000 B.C., but he doubts the estimated size of the agglomeration, considering it to be no more than an enlarged village, and hence ignores the possibility of a creative synekism operating. Another leading specialist, Glyn Daniel, is even more skeptical, arguing that "neither Jericho nor Çatal Hüyük were civilisations: they were large settlements that could be called towns or proto-towns. They did not have the other requirements of the Kluckhohn formula [for defining civilization]. They may have been unsuccessful experiments towards civilisation, a synoecism that did not succeed; or we might label them just as overgrown peasant villages."[10] Setting aside the question of population size, was not the extraordinary innovation of the "full-

9 Some of the best recent information I have found on the period between 9000–6000 B.C. in Southwest Asia is in Ofer Bar-Yosef and Richard H. Meadow, "The Origins of Agriculture in the Near East," in Price and Gebauer eds., *Last Hunters – First Farmers*, 1995: 39–94. This chapter includes a map showing the main late Epipaleolithic and Neolithic sites (73 of them); a series of maps depicting the evolving zones of sedentary hunter-gatherers, early farmers, and early herders over this period; and a listing by hectare of the largest sites. Topping this last list at around 12 hectares are Çatal Hüyük, Aşikli Hüyük, Abu Hureyra, Ain Ghazal, and Basta (to the south, near the Gulf of Aqaba). While not mentioning synekism, the authors write that "sedentarism was a prerequisite for cereal cultivation and both were essential for animal husbandry," indicating that herding did not develop independently but out of established permanent settlements. They also argue that agriculture "both depended upon and intensified a concern for real as well as productive and alienable property – a concern that was the essential foundation for the development of complex urban societies in the region during subsequent millennia" (1995: 41).

10 See Glyn Daniel, *The First Civilisations: The Archeology of their Origins*, London: Thames and Hudson, 1968. Writing in the early 1960s, Lewis Mumford in *The City in History* also reflected the dominant view that cities and synekism arose from the coalescence of farming villages and what he calls the "crystallization" of cities around 5,000 years ago, primarily in Sumeria. In other words, agriculture and village formation were the necessary precursors of urbanization. But he does recognize that the "earliest foundations" for these developments were found in the Valley of the Jordan and, noting the new discoveries at Jericho taking place at that time, very parenthetically opens up some possibilities for significant rethinking. In his annotated bibliography, for example, he notes that Kathleen Kenyon's *Digging Up Jericho* (1957), if correct in its dating of the "earliest urban settlement in the Near East," provides "a discovery that may revolutionize the archeology and chronology of this area and urban development generally" (1961: 606).

scale" Agricultural Revolution enough to affirm the successful synekism of such "overgrown villages" as Jericho? Not, it would seem, if the observer cannot see the generative "precession" of the urban in this innovative process, or so exclusively links synekism with the invention of writing and the development of the city-state as to make other expressions of its effects invisible.

Let us look deeper into the cityspace of Jericho, for in it can be found further indications of inventive synekism. The oldest excavated layers at Jericho, known as PPNA (Pre-Pottery Neolithic-A), indicate that the first known settlement consisted of rectangular mud-brick houses with rounded edges, like a bread loaf, built on strong stone foundations. The PPNA period, lasting to about 6250 B.C., is distinguished from the PPNB, which ended around 5000 B.C., by the use of hog-back-shaped bricks dimpled by the thumbs of the makers to improve adhesion. In addition to other improvements, the PPNB, still aceramic or without pottery, is associated with the plastering of floors as well as other surfaces, a technique that is found elsewhere such as in Çatal Hüyük and was, as Kenyon (1957) suggests, probably introduced into Jericho from other towns in the region, indicating in another way the existence of an extensive and interactive trading network of settlements. But even from the oldest PPNA layers of Jericho's settlement mound (*tell* in Arabic, *höyük* or *hüyük* in Turkish) there is evidence of impressive architectural achievement and the beginnings of planned public building. Rooms were large, some at least 20 × 12 feet in area, with wide openings and often with a complex of smaller rooms attached, probably used for storage. The houses were grouped around large courtyards used for cooking and other collective activities. At least one building has been discovered that was ceremonial in function and probably served as a focus for the cult of skulls that was well developed throughout the Pre-Pottery Neolithic period. Human skulls were plastered and carefully preserved as "portraits" that can stand as one of the world's first major artistic achievements. As Kenyon notes wryly, the inhabitants of Jericho could have made pottery, but probably did not need to.

Clear evidence of domesticated wheat and barley, as well as lentil and chickpea cultivation, have also been found at these lower PPNA levels. The original settlers, however, were almost surely primarily hunters and gatherers rather than farmers, suggesting that agriculture, the conventional keystone of the Neolithic Revolution, may have grown to its earliest advanced stage in and from the urban settlement of Jericho. It is also often overlooked that as early as 12,000 years ago there is evidence of a geographically extensive trading system that connected the Jericho area northward along the eastern Mediterranean coast (including Cyprus) and into Anatolia and possibly as far east as Iran, where, among other resources, there were important sites of volcanic obsidian, a vital commodity with multiple uses for hunting, gathering, and fishing societies. Even before plant domestication, obsidian, flint, and other Stone Age resources were traded for wild seeds (gathered and possibly also milled or processed in some other way inside the settlement), as well as live animals and animal products. This ancient trading system, like

Figure 1.2 *Head portrait of plaster on a human skull from Jericho* (Source: Kathleen Kenyon, *Archeology in the Holy Land,* London: Ernest Benn, 1960: plate 13 (after page 96), Neolithic portrait head of plaster on a human skull from Jericho)

agriculture itself, was developed by hunters, gatherers, foragers, and fishermen well before the formation of anything that can be called an agrarian village.

By 7000 B.C., simple irrigation methods had developed in Jericho to expand the scale and scope of agricultural cultivation, at least in the Jordan River valley, and Jericho's cityspace came to be materially defined, confined, and symbolized by the construction of those famous walls. Here the technology, artistic skills, environmental knowledge, and social organization that would much later produce the Egyptian pyramids, Stonehenge, and many other free-standing megalithic structures in Eurasia, were applied specifically to a public works project designed to enhance, organize, and consciously *plan* a permanent human habitat, initiating a major transformation in the scale and scope of sedentarism and the social production of a built environment.

Figure 1.3 *Early town wall at Jericho* (Source: Kathleen Kenyon, *Digging Up Jericho*, 1957: 128, early town wall, underlying later one)

Visibly marking this extraordinary achievement were the massive stone fortifications that surrounded Jericho in a series of arcs that were open perhaps only on the west, at the site of the life-sustaining permanent spring of fresh water that probably attracted the earliest settlers. First, there was an impressive rock-cut ditch, nearly thirty feet wide and ten feet deep (9 × 3 m), that at one time may have stretched for a distance of 2,000 feet. Even the most ancient of the series of walls built around Jericho were five feet thick and rose as high as twelve feet, and were much more formidable than the walls felled by the

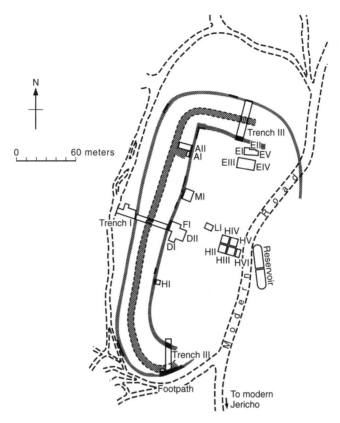

Figure 1.4 *Plan of Jericho* (Source: Kathleen Kenyon, *Archeology in the Holy Land*, 1960: 40, plan of Jericho, showing Bronze Age walls and excavated areas)

biblically trumpeted Joshua many millennia later. They were buttressed, perhaps at several points, with even more astonishing constructions, huge circular stone towers thirty feet in height and girth, containing stone-built staircases and small rooms, and like the walls themselves associated with the cult of skulls. The walls concretely defined a city and the city, almost certainly, began to define an urban and regional culture as a discrete geographical, economic, political, social, and territorial unit, a unit in which the generative imprint of collective propinquity and synekism was added to kinship and lineage ties, and possibly also a proto-state, as foundations for social order and continuity. For a rough plan of Jericho, see figure 1.4.

From somewhat later evidence, we know that the floors and walls of the houses and shrines contained within the sturdy perimeter of Jericho were plastered and painted, and that arts and crafts were flourishing. Many small carvings of a mother goddess and of animals, probably associated with a fertility cult, have been found, along with the aforementioned human skulls remodeled into plaster portraits with inlaid seashell eyes and painted hair (with one specimen clearly mustached). We do not know what guided the overall spatial design of Jericho, what cosmological and religious symbolism was attached to the walled-in urban form, but it is clear that the interior spaces of the shrines and households were elaborately decorated to express and signify a collective belief system, and that the built environment was not simply a random construction. From the very start, then, urban space was designed and produced as a self-conscious expression of local and territorial culture, a materialized "symbolic zone," to use Iain Chambers's term, in which the real and the imagined commingled to comprehend, define, and ceremonialize a much-enlarged scale of social relations and community, the beginnings of *urbanism as a way of life*, to use that famous phrase of the Chicago School of urban studies founded 10,000 years later.

Kathleen Kenyon summarizes her work in digging up Jericho in this way:

> We may therefore envisage pre-pottery Neolithic Jericho as a culture with all the attributes of civilisation, except that of a written language. The town must have been almost modern, or at least medieval in appearance, and it must have been surrounded by fertile fields. In the neighbourhood we can assume that there were other similar towns, and since materials such as obsidian, turquoise matrix and cowrie shells must have been obtained from a considerable distance away, we can assume trade with and relations between neighbouring districts. This is the revolutionary picture that Jericho has given us of a period nine or ten thousand years ago.   (1957: 76)

The original Jericho was destroyed before 5000 B.C., but by this time it had already influenced the development of other settlements in the Levantine Corridor. One of the best known and studied of these concurrent urban settlements is Beidha, located near Petra in present-day Jordan. Beidha is described by Maisels as an "early Neolithic village dating from about 7000 to 6500 B.C." (1993: 79), but there is sufficient archeological evidence at this site to suggest a more advanced process of urbanization, carrying forward the synekism of Jericho. There was craft specialization and what are clearly workshops filled with bone, wood, stone, and ochre, as well as chipped and polished flint axes. A series of large well-built houses appear to have been constructed around an open plaza, with lesser houses relegated to more peripheral locations, suggesting the beginnings of simple class privileges expressed in the spatial specificity of the urban settlement. A large building, over 600 square feet in area, inside the city-village is clearly a religious or cultic center and there is an impressive complex of buildings with an obvious religious function about 50 yards away from the center, built by highly skilled (and organized) laborers mainly of huge sandstone blocks from the nearby mountains. What seems somewhat clearer in Beidha than in Jericho is the emergence of a distinctly urban social *and spatial* division of labor manifested in cityspace in the formation not only of a proto-"civic" center but also of new center–periphery relations of unequal power.

In Jericho, as well as in Beidha, Çatal Hüyük, and other sites in Southwest Asia, there is sufficient evidence to demonstrate that hunters and gatherers, along with smaller numbers of traders, animal herders, farmers, cultic specialists, craftspersons, and artists clustered together in dense settlements that were far larger than the size usually attributed to agricultural villages, even after 5000 B.C. These large urban settlements certainly did not originate as agricultural villages nor can they be seen as consolidations of pre-existing agricultural settlements. No specialized agricultural villages have yet been discovered anywhere in the world that significantly predate the founding of Jericho. So how can it continue to be thought that there had to be a simple linear progression of human settlement or sedentarism, from tiny encampments of hunters and gatherers to small hamlets to the first small farming villages, to a few overgrown villages and proto-towns, and only then to true cities? Yet it is this view of city formation that dominates the contemporary literature not only for Southwest Asia but even more presumptively for the independent invention of agriculture and urban settlement in all other areas of the world.[11]

If one sidesteps the traditional insistence of prehistorians that the origins of urbanism require the development of writing, then there is a strong argument to label Jericho as a "founder" city (analogous to founder crops in agriculture) of what can be called the first Urban Revolution, dating back to more than 10,000 years ago. If this is accepted, then the Neolithic or Agricultural Revolution, as well as the subsequent development of writing, monumental architecture, the state, and indeed all the prerequisites of civilization itself, may be best viewed as primarily *arising from*, rather than giving rise to, the origins of cities. What this means cuts even deeper against the grain of many established interpretations of prehistory, especially those that emphasize evolving social relations of production, for it suggests that, rather than an agricultural surplus being necessary for the creation of cities, *it was cities that were necessary for the creation of an agricultural surplus*. As an adjunct to this very real possibility comes another challenge to more conservative contemporary visions of the past, a recognition that major innovations and substantial societal development can come from relatively egalitarian communalist cultures, another example of the reinterpretive power that arises from putting cities first. To dig deeper into the spatial specificities of this generative process of urbanization, let us look next at Çatal Hüyük.

---

11 I want to make clear that I am not arguing that the process I have described for Southwest Asia was necessarily repeated in Mesoamerica, upland Peru, China, Southeast Asia, and other regions of early plant and animal domestication and agricultural development. But I do want to raise the possibility that even in these areas, the transition between the "last hunters" and the "first farmers" hinged more on the creation of permanent settlements (sedentarism) than is usually acknowledged; that these settlements were first established by hunters and gatherers, with some reaching a substantial size (<2,000 inhabitants); and that these larger urban settlements played a much more critical role in generating new developments and innovations than most scholars recognize. In a broader sense, I am also arguing that too much attention is given to exogenous forces (climatic change, environmental degradation, generalized population to resource ratios) and not enough to social and spatial dynamics internal to the settlement, or as described in Price and Gebauer (1995), "the complex social organizations already in place," a significant part of which derives from the stimulus of agglomeration itself.

Learning from Çatal Hüyük

The wealth of material produced by Çatal Hüyük is unrivalled by any other Neolithic site. Moreover, not being a village but a town or city, its products have a definitely metropolitan air: Çatal Hüyük could afford luxuries such as obsidian mirrors, ceremonial daggers, and trinkets of metal beyond the reach of most of its known contemporaries. Copper and lead were smelted and worked into beads, tubes and possibly small tools, thus taking the beginnings of metallurgy back into the seventh millennium [B.C.]. Its stone industry in local obsidian and imported flint is the most elegant in the period; its wooden vessels are varied and sophisticated, its woollen textile industry fully developed . . . Funeral gifts, though not rich by later standards, are less sparing than among other contemporary cultures . . . Trade is well established . . . [and] there is evidence for Neolithic religion in the form of numerous shrines, artistically decorated with reliefs in plaster . . . or with wall-paintings in one or more colours. (James Mellaart, *Çatal Hüyük: A Neolithic Town in Anatolia*, 1967: 22–3)[12]

Çatal Hüyük (pronounced cha-TAHL-hu-yook) is, in many ways, even more compellingly revealing of the earliest development of cityspace than Jericho. This is not because it predated that ancient settlement or can claim to have older indications of advanced agriculture, but rather because its excavations present an extraordinary glimpse into everyday life and into a startling array of technological and artistic innovations. Moreover, the site from its discovery in the late 1950s has become the focal point of a much larger interpretive literature not just on the origin of cities but on more general aspects of the human condition.[13] I will trace these larger debates in three steps, first through the work of James Mellaart, the leading archeologist and popularizer of this remarkable Neolithic city, then in the extensions made by the urbanist Jane Jacobs, and finally in the very recent and ongoing digs of the Çatalhöyük Research Project, directed by Ian Hodder, a former student of Mellaart and perhaps today's best-known theoretical and critically postmodern archeologist.

James Mellaart and the urban Neolithic

As Mellaart states, between 7000 and 5000 B.C. the central Anatolian Plateau may have surpassed the Natufian Levant as the most culturally advanced

---

12   James Mellaart, *Çatal Hüyük*, London: Thames and Hudson, 1967. An earlier report of his findings, "A Neolithic City in Turkey," appeared in a widely cited article in *Scientific American* 210–14, 1964: 94–104. See also Mellaart, *Earliest Civilisations of the Near East*, London: Thames and Hudson, 1965, *The Neolithic of the Near East*, London: Thames and Hudson, 1975, and numerous reports in the journal *Anatolian Studies*. Mellaart's discoveries and interpretations of the site have stimulated several iconoclastic reinterpretations of the origins of cities, including Jane Jacobs, *The Economy of Cities* (1969); and more recently, Murray Bookchin, *From Urbanization to Cities: Towards a New Politics of Citizenship*, New York: Cassell (1995).

13   As far as I know, no such larger literature has developed around Jericho, which continues to be remembered beyond its archeological significance primarily for its biblical connotations and extensions. For an interesting comparison, check the Internet hits for the two places. My last connection via Yahoo! listed 3,186 web pages for Çatal Hüyük, only 34 for Jericho (mainly concerning several US cities with that name, a wrestler, and a rock band from Los Angeles).

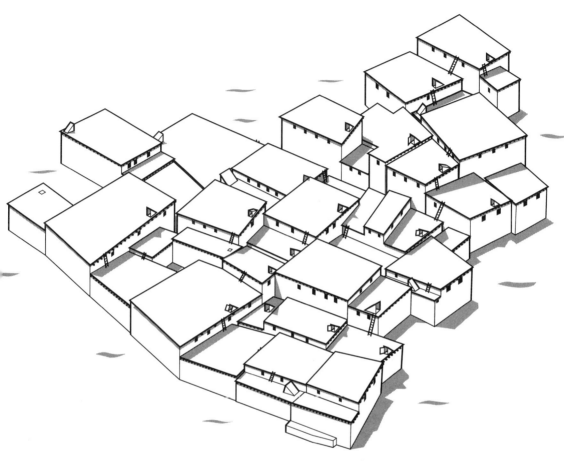

Figure 1.5 *Pictorial view of Çatal Hüyük by Grace Huxtable* (Source: James Mellaart, *Çatal Hüyük*, London: Thames and Hudson, 1967: 62, schematic reconstruction of a section of Level VI with houses and shrines rising in terraces above each other)

region of the Neolithic world, with a developing system of urban settlements spread over thousands of square miles and a local urban society with "a definitely metropolitan air."[14] He and his team excavated twelve successive building levels in about one acre of the 32-acre site of Çatal Hüyük, and provided an unusually vivid picture of the early evolution of urbanism as a way of life. Unlike Jericho, Çatal Hüyük was never surrounded by massive stone fortifications. As shown in the schematic reconstruction of figure 1.5, the cityspace consisted of a dense pueblo-like agglomeration of attached houses without any streets or paths between them, at least at ground level. Access and move-

14 Archeological research in Anatolia after Mellaart's work has identified a whole string of large settlements, many such as Aşikli and Çayönü that significantly predate Çatal Hüyük. See, for example, Ufuk Esin, "Salvage Excavations at the Pre-Pottery Site of Aşikli Höyük in Central Anatolia," *Anatolica* 17, 1991: 123–74.

ment within the settlement occurred on the laddered roofs, with defense against human and natural intrusions provided simply by the continuous perimeter of timber-reinforced and doorless house walls. There was at least one public square, which may have served as a marketplace, and many small open courts probably used mostly as refuse pits. There was also an abundance of shrines, about one to every four houses, but no indication of a dominant religious center or temple. The shrines and many homes were elaborately decorated with wall paintings, plaster reliefs, cult statuettes, animal heads, and bull horns.

Female deities and cult statuettes, depicting all stages of the life cycle (youth, marriage, pregnancy, birth, motherhood, respected elder), increasingly dominate over male figures; and wall paintings depicting hunting scenes decline significantly in number in favor of realistic and abstract representations of fertility symbols, agricultural production, and urban life. These changes suggest not only the Neolithic transition from hunting and gathering to agriculture but also the consolidation of a new gender-based, and possibly matricentric, division of labor associated with the early stages of urbanization. Permanent and stable urban settlement may have made what we presume to be women's work (grain milling, baking, weaving, tending animals, household caretaking, childcare) and even more so their religious and secular power (as Mother Goddess, ruler over wild animals, and metaphorical symbol of fertility, nurture, and social reproduction) more central to the production and reproduction of urban spatiality and sociality, the material and symbolic foundations of culture. The relative openness of the town plan, the absence of monumental fortifications such as those at Jericho, the fact that few signs of violent death have been found among the abundant skeletal remains excavated, and other indications that urban society in Çatal Hüyük was remarkably peaceful and productive for nearly a millennium, probably continued to enhance, and also to be enhanced by, the social power of women, at least until the rise of the first more formally institutionalized Mesopotamian city-states around 4000 B.C.

Mellaart's observations on the role of women and especially his discussion of the Mother Goddess as the city's supreme deity has sparked widespread debate that continues today, especially in academic feminist critiques of established patriarchal religions and in the recent expansion of interest in Goddess theories and cults.[15] Mellaart writes in his popular article in *Scientific American*:

---

15 The debates on the Great Goddess are closely associated with the work of Marija Gimbutas, an archeologist from Eastern Europe who authored such books as *The Goddesses and Gods of Old Europe, 6500–3500 B.C.: Myths and Cult Images*, Berkeley: University of California Press, 1974; and *The Language of the Goddesses: Unearthing the Hidden Symbols of Western Civilization*, San Francisco: Harper and Row, 1989. Inspired in part by Mellaart's findings, she argues that the earliest Neolithic symbols and images revolved around a "self-generating Goddess" who was a Giver-of-Life, Wielder-of-Death and Regeneratrix. Although probably matrilineal and "matristic," these early religions were not strictly matriarchal, she argues, but rather they emphasized ways of nurturing and nourishing people's lives, in contrast to the "androcentric focus on domination" that would replace them in the later development of city-states.

> I would maintain, perhaps wrongly, that the Neolithic religion of Çatal Hüyük
> . . . was created by women. In contrast to nearly all other earlier and later "fer-
> tility cults" of the Near East, it significantly lacks the element of sexual vulgar-
> ity and eroticism that is almost automatically associated with fertility and
> probably is the male's contribution. If the Çatal Hüyük religion is a creation of
> women, one has the rare opportunity of exploring Neolithic woman's mind by
> studying the symbolism she used in her effort to comprehend and influence the
> mysteries of life and death.   (1964: 101)

At the very least, what is represented here is an aspect of primitive gender egal-
itarianism, a time when there appeared to be no major difference in social power
between men and women, that remains relatively understudied and poorly
understood. At most, it provides useful symbolic and political information relevant to contemporary debates on gender and power and, in particular, the
effort to uncover a persistent masculinist bias in the writings of many archeologists, prehistorians, and others. I will return to these issues later in the chapter.

Other reconstructions of the lived spaces of Çatal Hüyük provide additional
glimpses of the specifically urban social and spatial division of labor that was
developing in the new habitat that, at its height, may have contained more
than 6,000 people, some now say as many as 10,000, packed together in what
must have been by far the densest settlement of the known Neolithic world,
as far from an agricultural village of the time as can be imagined. At least until
later stages, the primary occupation in the settlement was hunting and gathering, but the dense agglomeration also included some of the earliest known
sedentary farmers and herders, pioneers in the Neolithic domestication of
plants and animals. In contrast with the contemporary and still aceramic
Haçilar to the west, a great variety of food-plants was cultivated in and around
Çatal Hüyük, including emmer, einkorn, and bread wheat, barley, peas, lentils,
various vetches, and oil-bearing plants. The diet was supplemented by other
intentionally planted seeds, including acorns, almonds, pistachio, apple,
juniper, and hackberry, the latter used for making wine.

Equally significant, Çatal Hüyük's population also consisted of an extraordinary collection of highly skilled artists, craftsworkers, manufacturers, and
merchants. Mellaart's list of probable occupations include:

> . . . the weavers and basketmakers, the matmakers; the carpenters and joiners;
> the men who made the polished stone tools (axes and adzes, polishers and
> grinders, chisels, maceheads and palettes); the bead makers who drilled in stone
> beads holes that no modern steel needle can penetrate and who carved pendants
> and used stone inlays; the makers of shell beads from dentalium, cowrie and
> fossil oyster; the flint and obsidian knappers who produced the pressure-flaked
> daggers, spearheads, lance heads, arrowheads, knives, sickle blades, scrapers
> and borers; the merchants of skin, leather and fur; the workers in bone, who
> made the awls, punches, knives, scrapers, ladles, spoons, bows, scoops, spatu-
> las, bodkins, belt hooks, antler toggles, pins and cosmetic sticks; the carvers of
> wooden bowls and boxes; the mirror-makers, the bowmakers; the men who
> hammered native copper into sheets and worked it into beads, pendants, rings
> and other trinkets; the builders; the merchants and traders who obtained all the

raw materials; and finally the artists – carvers of statuettes, the modelers and the painters. (Mellaart, 1964: 99)

The list begins with the weavers, probably mainly women, who produced the oldest textiles and woven rugs yet discovered at any archeological site. Another first is represented by the workers in native copper and lead, stamping out the beginnings of metallurgy. Here too is perhaps the first sizeable weapons industry, and, more certainly, the producers of that ultimate symbol of human self-reflection and identity, the mirror. Constructed of polished obsidian in the form of a plaster-backed half-globe, the first intentionally made mirrors marked another kind of new beginning emanating from the remarkably industrious population of Çatal Hüyük. Notably absent from the list, in part because Mellaart downplays the heavy emphasis given to it by most archeologists, is pottery-making. But even here there were some pathbreaking achievements. Although it was rather simply made, easily breakable, and mostly undecorated, the world's earliest pottery can also be traced to Çatal Hüyük and the nearby region of northern Syria.

The list ends with the artists – carvers, modelers, and painters – and here also one finds truly extraordinary creativity and innovation, including the world's first carved wooden bowls (much better than the ceramic vessels) and remarkable religious statues, some of the finest found anywhere at the time. Of particular significance for the geohistory of cityspace, however, is one very special – and spatial – fresco. Found in one of the oldest shrines, it is a wall painting or mural that may be not only the first true landscape ever painted, as recognized in most art history textbooks, but also an original example of a distinctively and self-consciously panoramic *urban* art form that brilliantly expresses a popular awareness of the spatial specificity of urbanism.[16] As shown in figure 1.6, the wall painting, dating back to ca. 6150 B.C., depicts in the foreground a creatively cartographic representation of cityspace, stunningly detailed yet abstractly perceived. One can count about 75 separate buildings in this detailed portion of the painting, all similar in form but each one uniquely portrayed, hinting at an egalitarian yet individualized built environment.[17] What is even more remarkable is that until the *veduta* paintings of Venice, Florence, and other Renaissance cities starting about 1300 and perhaps a few Chinese landscapes with some urban features drawn at about the same time, the Çatal Hüyük panoramic cityscape remained the only painting of its kind to be found anywhere in the world for the next 7,000+ years.[18]

16   The Çatal Hüyük fresco is also listed in the Guinness Book of Records as the world's first "nature painting."

17   In looking at this townscape, I am reminded of the canal houses of contemporary Amsterdam that I discussed in chapter 9 of *Thirdspace*, each one both similar and unique; and of the Dutch genius in painting panoramic cityscapes dating back to the fifteenth century.

18   I have been searching for exceptions to this statement ever since coming across its innocent mention in such texts in art history as H. de la Croix, R. G. Tansey, and D. Kirkpatrick, *Art through the Ages*, New York: Harcourt Brace Jovanovich (1991 edn.). There are some paintings of port scenes in the Greek islands that depict pre-Christian urban landscapes and many maps of ancient Rome and murals showing major buildings and street scenes. But I have not yet found any paintings showing the kind of bird's-eye overview of a city depicted in Çatal Hüyük produced before around 1200.

Figure 1.6 *Reconstruction and original of cityscape painting at Çatal Hüyük* (Source: (*top*) James Mellaart, *Çatal Hüyük*, 1967: Plate 60; (*bottom*) de la Croix, Tansey, and Kirkpatrick, *Art through the Ages*, 9th edn, New York: Harcourt Brace Jovanovich, 1991: 46, figure 2-8, landscape with volcanic eruption (?), detail of a copy of a wall painting from Level VII, Çatal Hüyük, ca. 6150 B.C.)

The represented cityspace sprawls against a backdrop highlighted by a twin-peaked and gently erupting volcano, depicted in vivid vermilion. The cinnabar mountain, almost surely the 10,600-foot high Hasan Dag, floats above the plotted town, yet there appear to be purposeful lines connecting the two worlds of nature and culture, the "raw" and the "cooked," the sacred and the profane. An important part of the urban economy was built on the trade in obsidian, a gift of the volcano that would need to be socially reciprocated and ecologically respected.[19] Nature is to be both feared and propitiated, for it can provide that "embarrassment of riches" that every civilized urban culture depends on. Nature does not just exist outside the city at Çatal Hüyük, it is also incorporated within its territorial culture and symbolic zone as a vital part of the local economy and society, signaling the beginning of the social production of a "second nature" intricately involved with the urbanization process.

Although he never uses the term, Mellaart's findings at Çatal Hüyük (backed by developments at Jericho) support, even encourage, the possibility of conceiving of an "Urban Neolithic," hitherto an impossible juxtaposition of terms. It is not surprising that no reputable archeologist or prehistorian has made this leap in the more than thirty years since Mellaart's major excavations, given the tight hold of the canonical sequence that makes agriculture an absolute prerequisite to urbanism. But one of the leading urbanists of the 1960s was quick to see the possibilities of putting the urban before the agricultural revolution, or at least combining them as a simultaneous and intertwined dynamic. Let us turn next to Jane Jacobs.

Learning from New Obsidian

In *The Economy of Cities* (1969), Jacobs reflects on Mellaart's work and launches into her own richly imaginative revisioning of the Urban Revolution and the evolution of cities, using Çatal Hüyük as a kind of Proustian madeleine to recall the primordial (and contemporary) origins of urbanization. While all of her claims probably cannot withstand the most rigorous evidential criteria of the ancient historians and archeologists, the core argument is sufficiently powerful and insightful to deserve serious attention here, especially for its demonstration of the geohistorical as well as contemporary significance of putting cities first.

The date of publication for *The Economy of Cities* is significant. Not only did the book appear soon after the peak of the 1960s urban uprisings, when the world's attention was focused on cities, it also marked the emergence of Jacobs as a powerful competitor with Lewis Mumford as the country's leading public intellectual and critic of contemporary urban life. Mumford's *The City in*

---

19 Here again I am reminded of Amsterdam and those urban panoramas that take in the formidable incursions of the North Sea and the polderlands that have been created from the watery mud of nature.

History had appeared in 1961 and was widely considered his *magnum opus*, a definitive interpretive history of the city from its ancestral forms to its present-day retrogressions and problems. Like all good histories, Mumford's book plumbed the past with a very contemporary project in mind, one that reflected the soft and anti-big-city anarchism and regionalism that shaped all of his writings. Of particular relevance to the debates on the origins of cities and to Jane Jacobs's reconstruction of these events was Mumford's romancing of the pre-urban agricultural village. Synekism and hence the city are simply defined as "a union of villages," by his implication a destructive, violent, and male-dominated process transforming traditional village cultures. Separating the two strands of development, Mumford states that "the village multiplied and spread over the entire earth more rapidly and more effectively than the city; and though it is now on the verge of being overwhelmed by urbanization, it maintained the ancient folkways for thousands of years and survived the continued rise and destruction of its bigger, richer, more alluring rivals" (1961: 28). He follows this with a quaint verse on the capacity of the village to survive the urban onslaught, suggested to him by his most inspirational mentor, Patrick Geddes, the Scottish polymath whose work shaped the new field of regional planning.

> Musselburgh was a burgh
> When Edinburgh was nane
> And Musselburgh will be a burgh
> When Edinburgh is gane

Sharing some of Mumford's anarchism and disdain for megalopolitan sprawl but little of his utopian regionalism and environmentalism, Jacobs re-entered the debate on the origin of cities and its adjunct, the search for the essential qualities of urbanness, with a very different viewpoint. Inspired by the work of Mellaart on Çatal Hüyük, which appeared after *The City in History* was published, and taking a more pragmatic approach focused on economic development, Jacobs assertively put cities first, attached the formation of agricultural and herding villages to the first cities, and reconstituted her own version of the city in history.

Jacobs starts her revisionist prehistory by imagining the world's first putative city, which she names New Obsidian and locates at or near the site of Çatal Hüyük, into which she projects it would eventfully evolve. She describes New Obsidian as a "pre-agricultural city of hunters" established more than 11,000 years ago and centered around the crucial obsidian trade, as well as growing skills in animal husbandry and the exchange of gathered foodstuffs, including the hard seeds of wild varieties of wheat and barley. New Obsidian was not simply a home base for hunting and gathering but also a performatively urban agglomeration that was capable of generating economic growth from its own internal resources, from the construction of a cityspace that both stimulated and reflected economic innovation, new forms of productive work, and an expanding division of labor, the hallmarks of her definition of the urbanization process and very close to my definition of synekism.

A key group in this real-and-imagined New Obsidian were the traders and associated artisans, who were part of a network of bartered exchange that stretched for nearly 2,000 miles from east to west and may have extended as far south as the Nile Delta and north at least to the shores of the Black Sea.[20] The traders obtained obsidian (in exchange for craft items produced in the city, such as hide bags, knives, spearheads, mirrors, religious talismans, ornaments, as well as extra supplies of food grains and seed) from non-urban Paleolithic hunters who controlled defined territories around such volcanic mountains as Hasan Dag to the north, visible on a clear day to the city-dwellers. Hunters were also used as middlemen to trade for other raw materials such as copper, shells, and pigments, as well as supplies of wild cereal grass and seeds, beans, lentils, and nuts that were increasingly being collected in subsidiary settlements throughout the region. Jacobs suggests that barter points and non-local trader camps were located on the periphery of the city where trade routes converged on the settlement, such as is hinted in figure 1.6 for the space between the settlement and the fertile, erupting Hasan Dag, source of apparently endless supplies of that valuable volcanic glass. This "barter square" – a budding "edge city" or perhaps more accurately a "suburb" – was probably the only public open space in New Obsidian, a bustling business center where the worlds of the local inhabitants and the "outsiders" met.

Part of the food supply for local inhabitants came from the old hunting and gathering territories surrounding New Obsidian, but a large proportion was imported, at first mainly in the form of live animals and hard seeds. Appealing to a process that we would call today a strategy of import substitution, Jacobs begins to unravel the propulsive inner workings of the first self-generating urban economy. What Jacobs calls "stewards," budding wholesale and retail traders drawn from the local population, control the flow of food into the city households, where over time some seeds are sown in family patches or simply spill and sprout in mixed batches that encourage crosses, hybrids, and mutations. Seed trading, probably organized by women, also develops, selectively improving seed quality, just as similar processes operate for the meat and hides of sheep, goats, cattle, and pigs (domesticated first in northern Anatolia). Eventually, a small but growing proportion of food is locally produced in what can be called, in much more than a biological sense, the *domestication* (making domestic, part of the *domus* or household) of food plants. For Jacobs, the product of this synekistic social and spatial process is the *urban* origin of the Agricultural Revolution.

Grain growing in particular intensified in and around Jacobs's New Obsidian and provided an increasingly reliable source of food and, in particularly good years, a small surplus that could be traded for other goods and services. At this time and well into the peak growth period of Çatal Hüyük, there was no such thing as rural agriculture nor any specialized agricultural villages. To

20 This is only a slight enlargement of what is known today to have been the Natufian trading network more than 11,000 years ago.

be sure, in the city, agriculture was at first only a small part of the local economy, which, in addition to hunting and gathering, had already become specialized in commerce and craft-based industry. The rural world still revolved around small and simple hunting and gathering settlements, but even here the population was becoming increasingly attached to the growing cityspace and its imagined community. Rather than grain cultivation, it was probably animal husbandry, transplanted from the city, that first began to change the rural economy of hunting and gathering. Herding large numbers of domesticated sheep, goats, and cattle required too much space to be effectively maintained in the immediate city region. As Jacobs argues, herds and the work of tending them were spun off to grazing areas more than a day's animal journey from the city, spawning small villages consisting of households with the knowledge of grain cultivation and urban ways of life but specialized in producing meat, hides, and wool for the city population. She likens these offshoot villages to company towns and suggests that they gradually grew in part by absorbing into the small settlements increasing segments of the rural hunting and gathering population, not always in a peaceful manner. Only much later did urban farmers, or what today is called the rural peasantry, decentralize in significant numbers.

Jacobs's theorization hinges upon this process of specifically urban innovation, endogenous growth, and both centrifugal and centripetal regional development and diffusion. It contains within it not only the seeds of such contemporary ideas about economic expansion as import substitution strategies and export base models, but also, by putting cities first, she has constructed a comprehensive, powerful, and pervasively spatial theory of agglomeration economies that would influence a more contemporary generation of geopolitical economists such as Allen Scott and Michael Storper, who will feature prominently in Part II of *Postmetropolis*. Building on these ideas, she turns the conventional sequential model of prehistorical societal development upside down. In the first chapter of *The Economy of Cities*, indicatively titled "Cities First – Rural Development Later," Jacobs creatively formulates her "theory of city origins of the first agriculture." Here are some of her conclusions:

> If my reasoning is correct, it was not agriculture then, for all its importance, that was the salient invention, or occurrence if you will, of the Neolithic Age. Rather it was the fact of sustained, interdependent, creative city economies that made possible many new kinds of work, agriculture among them.   (1969: 34)

> Both in the past and today, then, the separation commonly made, dividing city commerce and industry from rural agriculture, is artificial and imaginary. The two do not come down two different lines of descent. Rural work – whether that work is manufacturing brassieres or growing food – is city work transplanted. (1969: 16; note the implied critique of Mumford)

> I have asked anthropologists how they know agriculture came before cities. After recovering from surprise that this verity should be questioned, they tell me the

economists have settled it. I have asked economists the same thing. They tell me archeologists and anthropologists have settled it. It seems that everyone has been relying on somebody else's say-so. At bottom, I think, they are all relying on a pre-Darwinian source, Adam Smith.   (1969: 42)

Whatever we make of this "origins" controversy, it can be concluded that Jericho and Çatal Hüyük represent a revolutionary leap in the social and spatial scale of human societies and culture, with scale being measured not just in numbers of people but in the intensity and geographical extent of human interaction. The stimulating interdependencies and cultural conventions created by socio-spatial agglomeration – moving closer together – were the key organizing features or motor forces driving virtually everything that followed. Such propinquity and interdependent co-presence made social cooperation more efficient and effective, not only for defense and for the collective production (and consumption) of food and "social" services, but also for the production of social and spatial order, long-distance trade, an increasingly specialized division of labor, and locational continuity, all part and product of the intrinsically spatial "spark" that would play an important role at every transformative moment in the geohistory of human development up to the present.[21] By reducing the friction of distance in everyday life while increasing population densities, human interaction and sociality were creatively intensified. More time and opportunity were opened for leisure, for arts and crafts, for religious ceremonies, for expanding the exchange of goods and services well beyond the family unit, clan, or band, for adding new kinds of productive work, and for the new challenges of urban planning and the application of what the Greeks would later call *phronesis*, the practical and political reason involved in creating, managing, and sustaining a territorially defined community, a synekistic metropolis.

Learning more from Çatal Hüyük

Çatal Hüyük and I, we bring each other into existence.
                               Ian Hodder, *The Domestication of Europe* (1990): 20

This rather apt encapsulation of the controversial contemporary debates over the relative power of human agency versus the shaping force of social structure was written by the English-speaking world's leading critical and theoretical archeologist. Ian Hodder was an undergraduate student of James Mellaart at the Institute of Archeology in London and became familiar early

---

21   This is a central theme running through every subsequent chapter of this book, from the second Urban Revolution which comes next, to the third Urban Revolution that arises from the development of what is also an essentially *urban* industrial capitalism, continuing through the series of significant restructurings of urban industrial capitalism that is today in its fourth phase, a period defined by the emergence of still another variation of urbanism as a way of life, what I call the postmetropolis.

on with the excavations at Çatal Hüyük and with Mellaart's evocative and enthusiastic, if at times overdrawn, style of "interpretive" archeology. Without losing the creative insight of such an approach, Hodder has for the past thirty years been building a "new archeology" that is both more analytically rigorous and theoretically sophisticated.

During the 1970s, Hodder was among the first to incorporate new social science methodologies into archeology, and, in particular, the methods and models emanating from the so-called "quantitative revolution" in the field of geography.[22] These positivist approaches, using models from systems analysis and spatial science (for example, the "central place theory" of human settlements) fixed attention on the material evidence of culture and spatial organization, or what I call Firstspace geographies. But Hodder was also deeply concerned with the "meaning of things," with the interpretation of "symbolic evidence" that was not so obviously manifested in material, empirical forms; and with the relations between material culture and symbolic expression, the real and the imagined. In a series of books and edited collections, he opened what was called "processual" archeology (a mixture of positivist science and naturalist anthropology) to new theoretical perspectives derived from critical theory, structuralism, neo-Marxism, hermeneutics, constructivist philosophies of science, and, more recently, poststructuralism, the new ethnography, feminism, postcolonial critiques, and critical postmodernism.[23] Hodder describes this eclectic interpretive approach simply as "postprocessual archeology" and roots it in what he calls *contextual reading*, first as an interpretation of the environmental, technological, and behavioral context of action, but also as discourse or narrative, linking the contextual meanings of material cultural traits with the meaning of words in a text or in written language. Through these contextual readings, the objects studied by archeologists are seen as both materially and conceptually constructed, simultaneously real-and-imagined, to refer back to the phrase I have used to describe the critical study of lived spaces.

22 See Ian Hodder and Clive Orton eds., *Spatial Analysis in Archeology*, Cambridge and New York: Cambridge University Press, 1976; Ian Hodder ed., *The Spatial Organisation of Culture*, London: Duckworth, 1978; and *Simulation Studies in Archeology*, Cambridge and New York: Cambridge University Press, 1978.

23 Ian Hodder ed., *Symbolic and Structural Archeology* (1982), *Symbols in Action: Ethnoarcheological Studies of Material Culture* (1982), *The Archeology of Contextual Meanings* (1987), and (sole author) *Reading the Past: Current Approaches to Interpretation in Archeology* (1991), all published by Cambridge University Press; Hodder ed., *The Meaning of Things: Material Culture and Symbolic Expression*, London and Boston: Unwin Hyman, 1989; Hodder, *Theory and Practice in Archeology*, London and New York: Routledge, 1992; Hodder, *The Domestication of Europe: Structure and Contingency in Neolithic Societies*, Oxford, UK, and Cambridge, MA: Basil Blackwell, 1990; Hodder et al. eds., *Interpreting Archeology: Finding Meaning in the Past*, London and New York: Routledge, 1995; and Robert Preucel, Ian Hodder eds., *Contemporary Archeology in Theory*, Oxford, UK, and Cambridge MA: Basil Blackwell, 1996. Through his position as Professor of Archeology at Cambridge University, Hodder clearly had some contact with Anthony Giddens, until recently Professor of Sociology at Cambridge and now Director of the London School of Economics, for Giddens's work features prominently in Hodder's retheorizations of archeology.

While being recognized as a leading theoretician and philosopher of archeology and a specialist on Neolithic cultural symbolism and the spread of agriculture to Europe, Hodder has until recently never led a major archeological dig, as much a symbolic mark of a renowned archeologist's identity as the construction of a major building project is for the architect. Putting his armchair reflections on postprocessual archeology to the test of the "trowel's edge," however, Hodder has become the lead archeologist for a major new excavation taking place in, of all possible sites, Çatal Hüyük.[24] The Çatalhöyük Research Project was conceived and is directed by Hodder, building in part on a grant given in 1993 to the Çatal Hüyük Research Trust for a 25-year program to conserve, display, and learn more from this 9,000-year-old city. He leads a global team of more than 100 specialists from Great Britain, the United States, Canada, South Africa, Spain, Greece, Germany, and Pakistan, along with dozens of Turkish scholars and students. The team is working not only at the main site but also in other areas, such as Pinarbisi, about 25 km to the east, where there is evidence of settled encampments by a permanent lake that may predate the occupation of Çatalhöyük by several thousand years. The entire project takes advantage of multimedia technology to keep its work open to the world and to multiple forms of interpretation, reflecting one of the principles of postprocessual archeology.

Hodder's digging began in 1995 with excavations into three of the twelve layers of settlement found in the eastern wing of the ancient site. Each of these layers contains more than 3,000 houses, suggesting that the population for most of the city's existence may have consisted of at least 10,000 permanent residents, bringing it much closer in size to the first Sumerian city-states. Early findings confirm most of Mellaart's picture of urban life, with a few key exceptions. Mellaart assumed the existence of a priestly group concentrated in a special area and organizing religious functions on a citywide basis, while new excavations show no evidence of such an elite group. Each household has organized spaces devoted to both ritual and domestic uses, suggesting a highly decentralized, simpler, and more egalitarian form of religious practice. In an even more controversial break with Mellaart, Hodder and his team downplay the importance of the Mother Goddess cult, arguing that the iconic goddess figurines Mellaart discusses were not venerated, for none have yet been found in burial or other religiously significant contexts. In both cases, Mellaart, who is alive and kicking, has been vigorously defending his views against his former student and others on the team.

The project has attracted widespread attention from feminist scholars as well as the "Goddess community," who arrive on organized tours to celebrate their own interpretations of the site.[25] Hodder has been especially open to both

24 I first discovered this reading Edward DeMarco, "New Dig at a 9,000-Year-Old City is Changing Our Views of Ancient Life," *New York Times* (Science), November 11, 1997. My subsequent knowledge has come primarily from the outstanding web pages available at http: //catal.arch.cam.ac.uk/catal.
25 See, for example, "Discussions with the Goddess Community," an e-mail exchange between Hodder and Anita Louise accessible through the catalhoyuk web page.

the more rigorous feminist and softer cult interest in Çatalhöyük, promoting what he has called "feminist archeologies." In *Reading the Past* (1991), he recognized not only the need to address the imbalance in the representation of women in the archeological profession and the use of sexist language in archeological publications, but also other more subtle "androcentric strands" being recognized by feminists in the field.

> ... archeologists have tended to view the past sexual division of labour as similar to that of the present. For example, hunting and trade are often seen as male pursuits, while gathering and weaving are female. Projectile points and well-made tools are linked to men, while non-wheel-made pots are linked to women. This sex-linking of past activities makes present sexual relations seem inevitable and legitimate ... Second, greater interest is shown in the "dominant" male activities. Males are generally portrayed as stronger, more aggressive, more dominant, more active and more important than women, who often appear as weak, passive and dependent. The past is written in terms of leadership, power, warfare, the exchange of women, man the hunter, rights of inheritance, control over resources, and so on ... If we want to show how gender relations are experienced and given meaning, how they are used to define personhood and how they are involved in subtle ways in multi-dimensional relations of power, a critical hermeneutic or contextual approach may be necessary. (1991: 169–71)

Thus far, relatively little that is new and surprising has been found at Çatalhöyük and nothing significant has been added specifically to the debate on putting cities first.[26] What is most significant, however, is not the preliminary findings but rather that this site is being excavated and interpreted by archeologists and other scholars who are unusually well-informed in critical theory; acutely aware of the relevance of the past to contemporary issues of democracy, citizenship, gender, race, and class; assertively spatial in their outlook and methods; and equipped with a "postmodern attitude," which Hodder has described as an openness to difference, alterity, multivocality, and experimentation aimed at "the empowerment of marginal political and cultural constituencies."[27] This may be another entry on the lengthening list of firsts for Çatal Hüyük/Çatalhöyük.

26 The first major publication of the project's early findings is Ian Hodder ed., *On the Surface: Çatalhöyük, 1993–1995*, Cambridge: McDonald Institute for Archeological Research and British Institute of Archeology at Ankara, 1996. See also the papers presented on "Postprocessual Methodology at Çatal" at a conference in Liverpool in 1996, available through the Newsletter web page. Hodder's introductory talk, presented in note form, is particularly interesting with regard to his engagement with new ideas about globalism and contemporary globalization processes, as well as related postmodern approaches to postprocessual interpretation. His title is "Glocalising Çatal," using a term I will return to in chapter 7.
27 See the Glossary entry for *postmodernity and postmodernism* in Hodder et al. eds., *Interpreting Archeology*, 1995: 241–2.

Chapter 2
The Second Urban Revolution

The first cities [as city-states] appeared with the simultaneous concentration of commanding symbolic forms, *civic centers* designed to announce, ceremonialize, administer, acculturate, discipline, and control. In and around the institutionalized locale of the *citadel* (literally, a "little city") adhered people and their spatially focused social relations, creating a *civil society* and an accordingly built environment . . . The city continues to be organized through two interactive processes, surveillance and adherence, looking out from and in towards the citadel and the panoptic eye of *power*. To be urbanized means to adhere, to be made an adherent, a believer in a collective ideology and culture rooted in the extensions of *polis* (politics, policy, polity, police) and *civitas* (civil, civic, civilian, citizen, civilization) . . . For Foucault, *space* is where the discourses about *power* and *knowledge* are transformed into actual relations of power. Here, the knowledge in the forefront is that of aesthetics, of an architectural profession, of a science of planning. But these "disciplines" never constitute an isolated field. They are of interest only when one looks to see how they mesh with economics, politics, or institutions. Then both architecture and urban planning offer privileged instances for understanding how power operates.

Extracts from *Thirdspace* (1996): 205, 234

[T]he origin of the emergence of a thing and its ultimate usefulness, its practical application and incorporation into a system of ends, are worlds apart . . . Anything in existence, having somehow come about, is continually interpreted anew, transformed and redirected to a new purpose by a power superior to it [via a process through which its] former "meaning" and "purpose" must necessarily be obscured or completely obliterated.

Nietzsche, *On the Genealogy of Morality* (1994, orig. 1887): 55

The city came into being to preserve life, it exists for the good life.

Inscription on the external wall of Los Angeles City Hall[1]

Between 5000 and 2500 B.C., the technologies of irrigated agriculture were significantly expanded, the wheel was invented, more formally institutionalized

1 This particular inscription, like the first use of the term synekism, is attributable to Aristotle's observations on cityspace in his writings on politics. Los Angeles City Hall was built in 1926–8 and until the 1950s it was the only structure allowed to exceed a 150-foot height limit designed to protect against earthquakes. Its 28 storeys, capped by an ersatz version of the Mausoleum at Halicarnassus, reach a height just about equal to the ziggurat at Babylon, the biblical Tower of Babel, built around 2000 B.C.

religions, markets, and states took shape, and with the decidedly urban invention of cuneiform writing in the "new cities" of Sumeria, near the confluence of the Tigris and Euphrates, there dawned what subsequent scholarship would consecrate as "recorded history." Deeply involved in all these developments, condensing them in specific socio-spatial contexts, was a far-reaching transformation in the organization of cityspace and in urbanism as a way of life. The standard texts conventionally refer to this transformation as the one and only Urban Revolution, the singular crystallization of "the city" as a distinctive form of human habitat. While it may indeed have produced the first cities in *recorded* history, such overemphasis on the invention of writing as a key criterion of city formation has obscured the equally revolutionary developments that occurred in the highland collar surrounding the Fertile Crescent several millennia earlier. It thus becomes more appropriate and revealing to represent what happened in Sumeria beginning around 7,000 years ago as the onset of a second Urban Revolution.

The New Urbanization

The second Urban Revolution, when seen as a singular event, is traditionally explained as both the cause and the consequence of the shift of agricultural production and dense human settlement into the fertile river valleys, first in Mesopotamia beginning in the sixth millennium B.C., and then in Egypt, Persia, the Indian subcontinent, China, and elsewhere in Eurasia and Africa, and later in the New World. This rise of what some have described as "hydraulic civilizations" was intimately associated with the development of independent *city-states* and the attendant creation of an interconnected network of urban settlements that functioned as metropolitan nodal points for a far-reaching diffusion of trade, technology, culture, knowledge, and governmental-military power. The rise of the city-state *per se* did not represent a complete break from what was happening throughout highland Southwest Asia starting as early as 11,000 years ago. Small but actively metropolitan city-based states and extensive urban trading systems had emerged throughout the T-shaped highland region soon after the early expansion of agriculture, and their continuing synekism probably helped significantly to spawn innovative changes in all spheres of life, including the invention of writing and its effective use in building and administering the urban geopolitical economy.

What, then, distinguishes the second from the first Urban Revolution? And why is its origin so clearly associated with the region of Sumer, at the mouth of the Tigris-Euphrates, rather than, say, the Nile Delta or elsewhere in the lowland Fertile Crescent? The answer to the first question will become clearer when we look at the most representative Sumerian cityspaces in more detail. As for the second, the most commonly accepted explanation for specifically Sumerian origins links city-state development to the special needs for larger-scale irrigation works to cultivate the fertile alluvium in the arid lowlands, where there is little evidence of city-formation or even significant permanent settlement until after 6000 B.C. Without such technology and the social organization necessary for its sustainable use, urbanization in the arid lowlands was difficult to achieve. Similarly, the demands of large-scale irrigated agriculture were such that cities with less than 10,000 inhabitants, probably the maximum size of the first round of city development, were inadequate, as were their simpler and relatively egalitarian lineage-based polities. A leap in the scale, scope, and authoritarian power of both the city and the state was required to "crystallize" – the term so often used to describe what happened in Sumeria – the second Urban Revolution. It is this leap in scale, scope, and political authority that makes the invention of writing appear to be a vital prerequisite, for it allowed for greater surveillance and control over labor power, improved organization of agricultural production and the storage and distribution of the social product, and the enlarged local urban culture that was necessary for everything to work together to construct not just a city-state but one capable of significant political and economic expansion.

There is no reason to challenge the broad outlines of this general explanation. But there remains the question of why first in Sumeria. Here we can continue to learn from Jericho and Çatal Hüyük, both with regard to the particular importance of trade in city formation and in appreciating the innovative power of advanced forms of hunting, gathering, and fishing societies. Sumeria's location at the head of the Persian Gulf thus becomes just as important as its position along the lower reaches of the Tigris-Euphrates. By the time the first full-blown Mesopotamian city-states were established, Sumerian merchants had developed an extensive trading network that stretched through the Persian Gulf to the Indian Ocean and beyond, with particularly close contacts established with the early Indus Valley civilizations. The earliest major city-states ('Ubaid, Eridu, Ur, and Uruk) were located closest to the Gulf and to the marshlands that, while not well suited to cereal agriculture, were rich in fish and birdlife as well as other useful resources capable of sustaining small permanent settlements. Their strategic location as seaports and trading centers may have been essential to their leading role in launching the second Urban Revolution.

Although I have not read anything in the literature to confirm this, it may very well be that the first permanent settlements in Sumeria, like those much earlier in the Natufian Levant, were established by people who hunted, fished, gathered wild food and other resources, and also engaged in regional trade. Unlike the earlier Natufian settlements, the Sumerians knew about agriculture and simple methods of irrigation from the Neolithic urban centers of the highland arc, and had begun to grow some crops, with the date palm providing particularly useful sources of food and building materials. What is clearer in the literature is that these southern Sumerian settlements were probably the main sites for the invention of cuneiform writing which, much more so than Egyptian hieroglyphics and early Chinese writing, developed largely as a practical accounting device for storage, ownership, distribution, and exchange of various goods produced and collected from local and distant places.[2] Mainly written with a stylus on clay tablets, cuneiform became the most widely used writing system of the many created in Southwest Asia, producing a significant body of literary and mathematical texts while also being used as the basis for other writing systems that would develop in the region.[3]

Recognizing some of the continuities between the first and second Urban Revolutions thus helps us to understand better the particular geohistorical conditions that gave southern Sumeria a head start in the formation of city-states that were larger in size, more potent in controlling the natural environment, and more capable of expanding their political and economic reach than any others that preceded them. This grounded the urbanization process more permanently in place, allowing not only for larger agglomerations to form but also sustaining their greater locational continuity and social reproduction. Before moving on to explore these developments, however, a perplexing set of questions remains concerning Egypt and the Nile Valley. Although there are many reasons to assume that city-states of the Sumerian form should have also taken shape in Egypt, there is very little evidence of large cities much before 1500 B.C., 4,000 years after the earliest developments of pre-dynastic Egypt. Although there is evidence of several small walled cities existing early on along the Nile, nothing like the mosaic of centralized and expansive city-states that filled Mesopotamia ever covered the "unified kingdom of Egypt," leading many prominent archeologists of the past to claim that "the city was really non-existent."[4] Yet there can be no doubt that Egypt was a city-centered, urban civilization from the start. How can this seeming anomaly be explained?

First of all, the most prominent and permanent city in ancient Egypt was the necropolis, the city of the dead, where tombs and temples, pyramids and sphinxes, monopolized the attention and labor of the city-builders. Cities of the dead tended to occupy the west bank of the Nile, where the sun sets, while the city of the living was located to the east, the site of the rising sun. The living city was considered much more temporary and would frequently be abandoned after a generation or two, as each successive pharaoh moved his sacred city to another site different from that of his predecessor. Thus there were few if any of the multi-layered city mounds or *tells* of Southwest Asia to provide tangible evidence of urban continuity. The city of everyday life, of institutional administration, trade, commerce, and political culture was rarely

---

2 Egyptian and Chinese writing systems were devised more specifically to keep track of kinship and lineage ties and major historical events, thereby maintaining symbolic connections between the living and the dead.

3 This "pragmatic" writing system was also closely associated with the development of numerical systems and mathematics. Sumeria is usually seen as the original source of such familiar concepts as the 60-minute hour and the 360-degree circle. Reflecting these developments, historians also attribute to Sumeria the invention of the wheel for both transport and pottery making and the first use of the true arch, the corbel vault, and the dome in public building and architecture.

4 See Jacquetta Hawkes and Leonard Woolley, *Prehistory and the Beginnings of Civilisation*, London: Allen and Unwin, 1963.

walled, for the desert provided protection against outside invasion, and internal conflict was relatively limited due to an overarching cultural unity. Furthermore, the enormous investment in time and labor involved in building and maintaining city walls would be lost when the city was abandoned. Similarly, the inhabited city also had no great monuments or ziggurats, for all these more permanent buildings were displaced to its necropolitan neighbor. Housing was simply built and easily left to crumble back into the soil from which it came, leaving few remains in comparison with the sturdier stone houses of Southwest Asian cities. The same was true for the even more temporary housing for the sizeable population that needed to be close by the growing necropolis. It is no surprise that the city appeared to be absent in Egypt, for all that remains are the monumental fragments of cityspace seemingly scattered randomly in the open desert.

Egyptian urbanization thus seems to be exceptional. But even granting its unique qualities, it can also be argued that it is the extreme case of a more general urbanization process that may be much more widespread than archeologists and historians have imagined. From the onset of urbanization more than 10,000 years ago, the formation of cityspace may have taken two different paths, one more densely agglomerated, designed with permanence and continuity in mind, and invested with monumental forms that help to centralize the urban polity, economy, and culture; the other more dispersed, agglomerated around multiple nodes, and open enough to permit residential resettlement in new areas rather than continuous rebuilding at the same sites.[5] Lewis Mumford noticed this bifurcation in *The City in History* (1961) and tried to associate it with totalitarian (the enclosed or fortressed city) versus more democratic forms (the Open City model he called it, more regional and village-like). Whether or not these two paths carry with them additional political or ideological connotations, it is important to recognize that the first and, even more notably, the second Urban Revolution involved an urbanization process that spanned a fairly wide range of agglomeration and dispersal. New World civilizations (Maya, Aztec, Inca) and several others outside Mesopotamia may have been closer to the Egyptian than the Sumerian model, at least in their early stages of development. Excavations of their remains may suggest that there were no cities or city-states of significance until much later, but there is now some reason to believe that they too may have been fundamentally urbanized cultures right from the start.

This raises some new questions about synekism. For example, is the innovative stimulus of dense proximity inherently greater in more concentrated rather than dispersed agglomerations? Given that we still know so little about

---

5 The second path brings to mind what contemporary scholars in Italy call the *città diffusa*, the diffused city, consisting of multiple centers linked closely together but without a dominant large metropolis, a characteristic feature of Emilia Romagna and other parts of what is today called the Third Italy. One might also ask whether this "modal split" in the urbanization process also relates to the contrasts between the sprawling polycentricities of Los Angeles as opposed to the amazing densities of New York City or Hong Kong.

how synekism works, it may not be possible to answer this question with any confidence. It should be noted, however, that even the extreme case of dispersed urbanism in Egypt was nonetheless urban and that the great achievements of Egyptian civilization arose primarily from people living in cities, from the stimulus of urban agglomeration, and not from its scattered rural villages. At the same time, size surely mattered in Sumeria, for it signified a culturally conscious investment and commitment to a permanent, if not cosmologically eternal, cityspace. With many such committed, permanent sites, both cooperation and competition may have stimulated greater inventiveness, especially with regard to technologies and conventions of territorial control and administration. It must be remembered, after all, that it was the Sumerian, not the almost concurrently developed Egyptian, model that would initiate a major urban revolution that would affect societal development in Eurasia and Africa for at least the next 4,000–5,000 years. What happened in Sumeria triggered a new phase in the geohistory of cities that would significantly redefine, on a *much larger scale*, the modes of production and the methods of social regulation that hitherto had organized human societies. And it would attach new societal institutions, expanded economic production, and specifically *political* development even more directly to the material, symbolic, and governmental powers of a radically expanded and restructured cityspace.

Space, Knowledge, and Power in Sumeria

The most distinctive *new urbanization processes* (a phrase that will be used repeatedly in this book) associated with the second Urban Revolution revolved primarily around a far-reaching reconstitution of power relations inside and outside the city, and hence of what can be called *societal governmentality*. The older, simpler class-like divisions of lineage-based societies were both broadened and deepened as the social and spatial relations of production and governance expanded in scale and scope to produce larger surpluses, more extensive mercantile trade, and more expansive political cultures than were possible before. The fundamental production complex of agriculture and animal husbandry, backed by substantial development of trade, crafts, art, and services having to do with the collection and distribution of food and other necessities, developed in the earliest round of urban development. The social surplus obtainable from this urban-based production complex was significantly increased in the new city-states, but the greatest innovations of the second Urban Revolution revolved not so much around social production as societal *reproduction*, the creation of institutional structures that could maintain in place political, economic, and cultural continuity.

Imbricated in these changes was the apparent rise of a more definitively *patriarchal* social order, reshaping the older sexual division of labor and initiating what would become a long-lasting cultural subordination of women in practically all subsequent urban societies. We know very little about this rise of urban patriarchy and the significant social struggles that must have accompanied it, but it stands as one of the most profound differences between the first and second Urban Revolutions. What we do know is that by 4000 B.C., the power to control and shape everyday life in and around the city and the associated spatial practices of phronesis and citybuilding became much more highly concentrated, centralized, and male-dominated.[6]

Building on trends that were becoming well established in the cities of the first Urban Revolution, the new cities of Sumeria consolidated political power in a genealogically defined *ruling class* that combined and connected two major spheres of legitimate authority. On the one hand were the citizen-patriarchs, now ensconced as recognized leaders of the traditional communal sector of the urban economy, as well as the new subclass of private land and property owners. On the other hand was the citizen-nobility of the rapidly expanding "public" or state sector. The two came together under the ultimate authority of a royal palace and temple community centered around a theocratic monarchy, with the divine king seen as the creator of the city-state and as its cosmological personification. For a social (rather than spatial) mapping of the structures of power in the Mesopotamian city-state, see figure 2.1, a diagram of the relations of production, subordination, and stratification from Maisels (1990: 272).

Urban politics in the Sumerian city-state became much more competitive and complex than it had ever been before, often straining the new institutions of power and authority. Over the centuries, divine rule came to be increasingly challenged, especially as the elite citizenry of the communal/private and state/public sectors jostled for greater autonomy and strategic privilege. Maisels argues that what was beginning in Sumeria was a slow process of dissolving the "ideology of divine descent patrilineages" that had defined all the most advanced human societies and modes of production up to that time and would persist relatively unchanged in Egypt, India, China, and Mesoamerica. What was also beginning was the rise of a distinctive and semi-autonomous "civil society" in between the state and private sectors, a process that probably did not reach its most advanced stage in Mesopotamia but rather, at least as seen through the eyes of Western scholarship, in the Athenian *polis* during the fifth century B.C.[7] But let us not be diverted by this European trajectory,

6   Lewis Mumford speculates frequently on this patriarchal shift in *The City in History* (1961), linking it to the development of the plow and ox-drawn power (versus the digging stick and hoe), the greater difficulty in cultivating the heavier soils of the alluvial river valleys, and, with his persistent preference for the former, the contrasts between village and city life. He argues that woman's power derived from symbolizing fertility and specializing in the intimate "arts of life," while the growing empowerment of urbanized man "lay in feats of aggression and force, in showing his ability to kill and his own contempt for death; in conquering obstacles and forcing his will on other men, destroying them if they resisted" (1961: 27). For Mumford, the new city-states of Mesopotamia were essentially totalitarian and oppressive, especially when compared to less city-centric and more peaceful Egypt, reminding us again that one of the best-known books ever published about the city was written by an anti-city regionalist and environmentalist.

7   There is evidence to suggest that, in many Sumerian cities, there arose "assemblies of citizens" with the power to ratify or reject the ruler's decisions, especially with regard to warfare and defense.

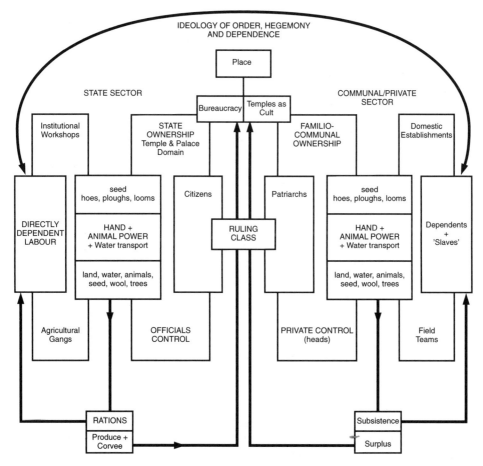

Figure 2.1 *Relations of production, subordination, and stratification in Mesopotamia* (Source: Charles Keith Maisels, *The Emergence of Civilization*, London and New York: Routledge, 1990: 272, figure 9.7, same title)

for there is much more to be learned from the developments in Sumeria, especially with regard to the conjunctions of space, knowledge, and power in the city-state.

Reinforcing the processes of city-state formation was the opening up of city-space to four new specialized populations: (1) entrepreneurial merchant-financiers, (2) an organized military armed force doubling as an urban police, (3) the first institutionalized civic bureaucracy, and (4) an impoverished urban "underclass." Much more than they ever were in the earlier cities, merchants involved in local, regional, and "foreign" trade became city-dwellers as well as civil servants, private landowners, and speculative developers within the urban space economy. Sumerian merchants not only financed long-distance trading expeditions, enhancing the wealth of the palace and state, they offered loans to farmers and fishermen, helped the state authorities to collect taxes and tribute, invested in the urban built environment, and organized a proto-market economy based in large part on the exchange value of silver.[8] This resolutely "private" sector was not particularly influential before about 3000 B.C., but after this date its power and freedom in the urban space economy grew along with its increasing autonomy from palace control.[9]

Drawing upon those who were in the past either defenders of hunting and gathering territories or, even more likely, age-graded male "warrior" communities, new and more specialized military cadres emerged with the capability of defending the entire city-region against outside invaders, expanding the territorial control of the state into city-based empire, and, probably of at least equal importance, maintaining internal peace and order. As an urban "police" (another term deriving from the Greek *polis*), the military functioned in part to assure (and enforce) the adherence of all citizens and others to the unsettling new social and spatial order emerging in the expanding regional cityspace. Military forts and their watchful service populations thus became an integral part of the built environment and everyday life of the city. And as with the merchant citybuilders and patriarchs, the new military class would establish a territorial power base in the city-state and, after about 3000 B.C., play a growing role in checking the absolutist power of the royal class and in shaping the very definition of *citizenship*.[10]

Armed with more subtle means of surveillance, regulation, and control was an expanding urban-based public bureaucracy of government officials and their assistants, charged with meeting the expanded demands of phronesis, maintaining and managing the territorial community and cultural identity of the city-state. These first "civil servants" were primarily the land-owning nobility (with close ties to the resident merchants and warriors) directly attached to the temple and/or palace. Over time, a more specialized and increasingly autonomous governing bureaucracy would emerge and find its

8 Interestingly, the major deposits of silver in Southwest Asia at this time were found in Anatolia, also the site of the most important sources of obsidian and flint. For a description of this proto-market formation and an argument against Polanyi and others who state that there was nothing resembling true markets in the ancient Near East, see Marc van de Mieroop, *Society and Enterprise in Old Babylonian Ur*, Berlin: Dietrich Reimer Verlag, 1992.

9 Keep this group in mind, for it will emerge later in the "leagues" of cities along the North Sea–Baltic and Mediterranean shores of Western Europe as perhaps the most important driving force leading to the third Urban Revolution.

10 The Weberian view of the origins of citizenship (Max Weber, *The City*, New York: Free Press, 1958, orig. 1921) fixes its first emergence in the Greek *polis*. Arguing that citizenship presupposes the breakdown of hegemonic kinship ties and the associated dominance of a monarchical royal class, this classical view excludes the residents of Sumerian city-states (as well as those in the Indus and Nile valleys, China, and Mesoamerica) from being described as "citizens" (as opposed to "subjects"). Even without connecting such views with Eurocentrism, I believe it can be argued that the origins of citizenship can usefully be pushed back to an earlier date and, in particular, to the dynamic development of the city-states of Mesopotamia. For an interesting contemporary overview of the debates on the "genealogy of citizenship," albeit one that accepts the Weberian argument that Greece was the place where "the first practice of citizenship becomes visible," see Engin F. Isin, "Who is the New Citizen? Towards a Genealogy," *Citizenship Studies* 1, 1997: 115–32.

turf in the spatial specificity of the city-state, further differentiating the internal residential and institutional geography as well as expanding the external territorial scope and efficiency of city-state power and city-centered governmentality.

Over time, a new underclass would also emerge. It comprised domestic slaves, corvée laborers, and gangs of "contingent" workers used not only to facilitate agricultural production and help in the households, but also to meet the growing demands of citybuilding, which now expanded well beyond what must have been necessary to build the famous walls of Jericho. Male and female slaves, clearly treated as private property, became an important part of the urban economy. They were traded as a commodity in commercial exchanges, given away in marriage dowries, used as a guarantee for loans, and proffered as gifts to the temple. There is even evidence of debt slavery, affecting those unable to repay their outstanding loans. Very little is known about the processes of enslavement, but the number of slaves residing in the city seems to have been quite large, with some households having more than twenty.

These developments worked to redefine the differences between city and countryside, the urban and the rural, the citizen and the peasant, the center and the periphery. The restructured power relations revolved fundamentally around the political differences between *polites* (Greek for those who adhered to collective urban life and society) and *idiotes* ("independent" rural dwellers, relatively isolated and "idiosyncratic" peasants, or worse, barbarians). All together, these new urbanization processes crystallized in the formation of the city-state as a territorial and *presuppositionally urban* institutional structure. This was not the first territorial state in history, nor was it the first example of an urban-generated polity. What was most different about the city-state was its new class composition, its restructured social and spatial relations of production, and the expansion of a civic or (city) state sector positioned in between the rulers and the ruled and capable of developing its autonomous bases of power through localized resources and control over space and knowledge (now existing in written form).

In the first Urban Revolution, synekism – the stimulus of urban agglomeration – worked primarily in the realm of revolutionizing social production through the invention of agriculture (farming and animal husbandry), the creation of specialized forms of craft production, and the development of associated trading and exchange networks. In the second Urban Revolution, synekism continued to be involved with technological innovation in agriculture (the creation of much larger-scale irrigation systems, for example), but became most potently focused on the realm of societal reproduction, generating an essentially political revolution that revolved around extraordinary innovations in geographical governmentality, making possible the maintenance and administration of cohesive societies and cultures of unprecedented population size and territorial scope. The crystallizing moment of this synekism was the *urban invention of the imperial state* and all its ancillary apparatuses, including those that would permit the exceptional expansion in societal scale and scope associated with the formation of city-centered empires. To elaborate further on these observations, let us look at just one of the first independent city-states, a real-and-imagined place whose name has become a popular trope for all discourses on origins and roots, the invitingly metonymic Ur.

Ur and the New Urbanism

The sanctuary Ur, the dais of kingship, the pure city, may bring barley, sesame-oil, precious and exquisite clothes on big ships to you.
> From a literary text of the early second millennium B.C.[11]

The city of Ur, the point of departure . . . The State was not formed in progressive stages; it appears fully armed, a master stroke executed all at once; the primordial *Urstaat*, the eternal model of everything the State wants to be and desires . . . the basic formation, on the horizon throughout history . . . Every form that is more "evolved" is like a palimpsest: it covers a despotic inscription . . .
> Deleuze and Guattari, *Anti-Oedipus* (1983): 217–18

The Sumerian city-state of Ur was one of the earliest centers of what would become a sprawling, more or less loosely connected mosaic of city-states in the Fertile Crescent, with outliers stretching from Egypt to India, from Memphis and Thebes to Mohenjo-daro and Harappa, and later into Europe. This proto-world wide web, the first expansive "global" network of metropolitan cities, greatly expanded the spatial scale and scope of local urban life by articulating a vast transactional system for interregional trade, cultural and technological diffusion, population movements, and military conquest. But rather than expanding on these external relations, as most historians do, let us look first at the major internal transformations in the social and spatial structure of cityspace.

Evidence from Ur suggests that it was one of the earliest focal points for the elaboration of a distinctively urban social and spatial division of labor, based on the development of new relations of production rooted in private property, land ownership, patriarchy, and the formation of hierarchically organized social classes. Class formation, and its associated process of city-state development and change, was based initially on a stratification of prestige and empowerment that arose largely from real or putative kinship ties to key ancestral figures. This patrilineage-based social order developed to its fullest extent in the last stages of the first Urban Revolution, centering around divine rulers with absolute patrimonial prerogatives. Over time and space, these dif-

---

11   Cited in Marc van de Mieroop, *Society and Enterprise*, 1992: 196. As the major port for Mesopotamia, Ur's trade extended through the Persian Gulf to the Indian subcontinent and northeast Africa, and was already established by 5000B.C. This may be the first recorded example of urban commercial boosterism.

ferentiated kinship ties took on more formalized religious and cosmological significance and symbolism that tightly integrated the polity, the economy, and the material and symbolic culture.

As suggested earlier, a key difference in governmentality that would arise in the Sumerian city-state was the development of a distinctive and increasingly autonomous *civic* sphere. Urban governance, the development of the urban economy, and the social production of cityspace, even with the continuation of divine kingship, became more secular and specialized, and increasingly *self-generating* and autonomous. As Maisels notes, and roots in the intensified synekism of city-states such as Ur:

> . . . city-state urbanism is an organic polity, self-centered on its immediate hinterland and largely self-sustaining, therefore usually self-governing through its own specifically "civic" institutions . . . [W]hile the city-state may be headed by a king it does not owe its existence to kingship and to the spending of royal revenues drawn from the dispersed villages of the territorial state. Rather the *urbs* of the city-state regime owes its existence to its own economic activities, which are largely autonomous from the political, in times of peace at least.   (1993: xvi)

At first, the top of the new urban social hierarchy at Ur and other Mesopotamian city-states consisted of a divine sovereign, king and/or queen, and an associated cadre of priest and priestess counselors and scribes serving as a ruling elite over a population consisting primarily of farmers and a small but growing group of artisans, merchants, soldiers, and civil servants. By the end of the period between 2500 and 1500 B.C., however, Ur had developed a more specialized and expanded administrative, religious, and economic bureaucracy; and the royal leadership became both more secular and, it would seem, more dominantly male-centered in its symbolic and material power, reflecting the intensifying patriarchy that grew in close association with class formation. Maintaining this emergent social hierarchy of dominant and subordinate classes created new demands for urban governance. In this revolutionary transformation of social and spatial relations, the city became the center not only for simple household reproduction based on agriculture, now greatly expanded through large-scale irrigation methods, but also for the more complex phronetic process of societal reproduction and social regulation on a much larger territorial scale than ever before.

The deepened and broadened societal division of labor – another indication of the increasing spatial scale of human sociality that clearly distinguishes the first from the second Urban Revolution – was concretely expressed in and dialectically related to the material and symbolic geography of the Mesopotamian city-state. We do not know very much about the details of everyday life in Ur, but we can learn a great deal about local socio-spatial practices by looking at Ur's exemplary and widely repeated urban morphology.

Ur was built on a raised mound (*tell*) almost adjacent to the Euphrates and not far from what was then the marshy coast of the Persian Gulf. Ur was not the first city in Sumer. That title is usually given to Eridu, located 12 miles south of Ur and dated back to around 5500 B.C., the start of what is called the

'Ubaid period. Nor is it to Ur but rather to Uruk, 35 miles to the north, that archeologists and ancient historians attribute the origins of writing and wheel-made pottery. Uruk was most likely the first true city-state, while Babylon under Hammurabi (1792–1750 B.C.) and the vast Babylonian empire conventionally marks the peak of city-state development in Mesopotamia. Ur's popular recognition and its symbolic use to denote the origins of practically everything come largely from its unusually detailed cuneiform documentation, the remarkably well preserved quality of its monumental structures, and the immense popularity of the biblically inspired book, *Ur of the Chaldees*, written by Leonard Woolley, the most famous excavator of its cityspace.[12]

Ur's location was significant for its access to the rich marshlands known today as the Shatt al Arab, one of the earliest areas in the desert basin of Mesopotamia to be settled by hunters, fishermen, and farmers; and for its proximity to the trading networks that extended from the Gulf to the Indian Ocean. Throughout its history, from its origins around 4500 B.C. to its abandonment four millennia later, Ur would be an important trade entrepot for the entire region, exchanging the surplus wealth of its urban-based agriculture and craft industries for copper, lapis-lazuli and other semi-precious stones, shells, ivory, spices, and condiments. The Arabic name for the site is Tell el-Mukuyyar, the Mound of Pitch, almost surely an indication of the rich "black gold" deposits that underlie and infuse the thick blanket of alluvium that defined the fecundity of ancient Mesopotamia. The raised location of the settlement mound not only afforded a view of the nearby cities of Eridu and 'Ubaid as well as protection against flood and foreign invasion, it also brought the population of Ur closer to heaven and the sphere of the gods. This vertical reach pinned down and pivoted the organization of Ur's cityspace in both symbolic and material terms.

Like most of the great cities of the ancient world, Ur was walled and roughly circular, although the greater pull of the North–South axis, sanctified in Sumerian cosmology, made it more oval or egg-shaped. Perpendicular to the dominant N–S axis (some experts claim it was actually tilted either to the northeast or northwest) was the secondary E–W axis, marked on one side by a military fort and on the other by what Sir Leonard Woolley called the "West harbour." Although this distinctive geometry is clearer in other Mesopotamian cityspaces, the two axes in Ur must have crossed at a central place, dividing the internal space into roughly four quadrants and punctuating the peripheral city walls with gates located approximately at the four cardinal points. This immanent spatial structure of the quartered circle pivoting on the crossroads of at least four directional axes would be repeated, with many local variations, in almost every other city-state in the world over the next 4,000 years. The earliest pictorial sign for "city" in Egyptian writing systems was simply a circle with a cross (a circle with a dot in the middle stood for the sun), while

---

12 See Sir Leonard Woolley, *Ur "of the Chaldees," The Final Account*: *Excavations at Ur*, revised and updated by P. R. S. Moorey, London: Herbert Press, 1982.

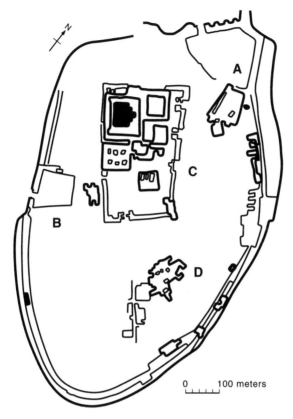

Figure 2.2   *City map of Ur* (A: North Harbour; B: West Harbour; C: *temenos*; D: housing area)   (Source: A. E. J. Morris, *History of Urban Form: Before the Industrial Revolution*, New York: John Wiley and Sons, 1974: 7, adapted from Sir Leonard Woolley, *Ur of the Chaldees*, London: Herbert Press, 1982)

the early Chinese form was a square with thick pointed arrows extending from it in the four cardinal directions.[13]

   This characteristic urban morphology was jointly attuned to astronomical knowledge, cosmological symbolism, secular power, and the practicalities of everyday urban life. For perhaps the first time in geohistory, the spatial specificity of urbanism came to revolve around a simultaneously sacred and secular centralization. The profoundly centered cityspace, so different from anything produced during the first Urban Revolution, created a new focus for the entire resident population of the city-state, one that would shape everyday life and determine access to the symbolic power bases of the local territorial culture.

---

13   Oddly enough, in Sumerian cuneiform the simple circle with a cross stood for sheep. The city was symbolized instead by a thick L-shape, probably linked to the form of houses. See Maisels, 1990: 193.

Figure 2.3 *The Ziggurat at Ur* (Source: de la Croix, Tansey, and Kirkpatrick, *Art Through the Ages*, 1991: 49, figure 2-13, ziggurat (northeastern façade with restored stairs), Ur, ca. 2100 B.C.)

In the metropolis of Ur, as in nearby Eridu and Uruk, this new centrality was celebrated monumentally in the construction of the *ziggurat*, an enormous temple built on a solid mass of mud brick at least fifty feet in height, and raised even closer to the heavens in two additional storeys, the topmost a shrine reachable only by three ramp-like stairways. The sacred ziggurat visibly asserted a break in the homogeneity of the surrounding flat environment and symbolized the creation of a transcendent axis of communication between heaven and earth. It projected itself as the center of the world, the locus of creation, the fixed point of the cosmos, the sacred space that repeated "the paradigmatic work of the gods."[14] That it also had phallic connotations is very likely. See figure 2.3.

The relatively well-preserved ziggurat at Ur, constructed around 2100 B.C., was part of a skyscraper-building boom that would culminate in Babylon further to the north, in what the Hebrews would later call the Tower of Babel, a ziggurat that reached 270 feet in height, rivaling the free-standing necropolitan pyramid-tombs of Egypt. Unlike the latter, the ziggurat was an integral part of the living city, a symbol of cultural permanence, investment, and commitment. As was typical, it was not located in the exact geographical center of the city, but in Ur's case slightly to the north and west as the focal

14 Mircea Eliade, *The Sacred and the Profane: The Nature of Religion*, New York: Harcourt, Brace and World, 1959: 32. For further discussion of these urban symbols of transcendence, see Yi-Fu Tuan, *Topophilia: A Study of Environmental Perception, Attitudes, and Values*, Englewood Cliffs, NJ: 1974.

point of the *temenos*, the clearly marked-off sacred space of the city, conse-
crated to the gods and excluded from profane use. Also typical, the temenos
at Ur was rectangular in shape, suggesting to some observers such as
Mumford the assertion of male power as opposed to the more "female" semiotics of the circle.

Like a microcosm of the city itself, the temenos was also aligned to the major
N–S and E–W axes, although actually positioned, as noted, toward the northwest. This "temple city" was the center of an elite religious community that
controlled access to the highest shrine and thereby controlled many other
dimensions of urban life and culture. There were many shrines in the temenos,
along with open courtyards and buildings serving as administrative centers
and storehouses. Within it was also the royal palace, another accentuation of
a sacred and secular centrality that would over time make the king virtually
synonymous (and metonymous) with the city-center. In this composite spatial
condensation of administrative, military, religious, and economic power was
formed the world's first real-and-imagined *citadel*, a city within the city, a monumentally commanding "civic center" of government buildings designed to
protect and control urban life and civil society.

For the residents of Ur, the combined ziggurat-palace-citadel-king became
the iconically materialized manifestation of the local territorial culture and
identity. Many names came to be attached to this powerful node. It was called
the "summit of Sumer," the "center of the universe," an edenic bridge between
heaven and earth. In a particularly vivid phrase that can be applied to the
citadels of almost all the ancient world's great city-states, from Teotihuacan to
Beijing, it was also described as the *pivot of the four quarters*.[15] The monumental citadel almost surely dominated the urban imaginary, the mental maps and
urban representations carried by the inhabitants of the city-state. It is perhaps
here that we can find some explanation for the prolonged absence of the
panoramic cityscape painting found in Çatal Hüyük. The artistic representation of cityspace now involved a dominant cosmological and sacred symbolism that was metonymically concentrated in the divine kingship and its
concrete expressions in monumental architecture. The secular and mundane
residential city, and perhaps also the natural landscape, may have simply disappeared from the representational urban imaginary as a relevant – or per-
mitted – subject of pictorial expression.[16]

It is possible to speculate from available evidence and an appreciation for
the powerful frictions of distance that there was probably at least the beginnings of both a concentric and radial zonation of residential land use and

---

15 For an expansion on this latter description of the city center, see Paul Wheatley, *The Pivot of the
Four Quarters: A Preliminary Enquiry into the Origins and Character of the Ancient Chinese City*, Chicago:
University of Chicago Press, 1971. Wheatley has been the pre-eminent scholar arguing for an empha-
sis on the ceremonial origins of cities.
16 One major exception to this absence of pictorial representation of the city is the famous map of
Nippur, constructed around 1500B.C. and considered by many to be the oldest known map in history.
The cartography demonstrates a remarkable ability to picture complex urban forms, including several
prominent buildings, without resort to abstract symbols.

lifestyle in Ur, which at its peak may have contained around thirty-five thousand inhabitants in the slightly more than two square miles inside its walls, with perhaps a quarter of a million in the regional mosaic of city-states and subordinate areas under its imperial control. Proximity to the sacred center, where the main grain storehouses and at least one major marketplace were located, offered significant political and economic advantages that were related to class formation and the increasingly uneven distribution of power.[17] The ring that surrounded the centralized temple community-citadel-market, the most favored site of the "inner city," was in turn most likely to be occupied by better-established and longer-settled urban dwellers; whereas locations closer to the wall, especially furthest from the entry gates and especially to the semiotically less preferred south side of the city, probably suffered somewhat from the everyday frictions of distance from the centers of power. Such emerging concentricities were probably stretched out along the four major radial avenues connecting the center to the gates, especially to the north where the temenos was sited.

Pictorial art forms found in other Mesopotamian city-states suggest that the four quarters that pivoted around the city center may have also begun to specialize in different kinds of urban activities. There is evidence in Ur of a well-established financial and mercantile district and an area of specialized craft production. A bas-relief found in the palace at Nimrud, along the northern reaches of the Tigris, shows a quartered circular city, with each quadrant filled with specific activities: pottery making, hairdressing, iron forging, laundry. For a contemporary picture of what Ur may have looked like, figure 2.4 portrays the city of Erbil (ancient Arbela) in northeast Iraq at the foot of the Kurdistan mountains, a cityspace that has more or less been continuously lived in for the past 6,000–8,000 years.

Woolley's work also suggests that "Greater Ur" was surrounded by the first suburbs, both in the form of the villa, with its spacious gardens and perhaps residences for domestic help, and the scattering of clustered buildings that extended beyond the built-up area of the city along the four-mile route to the temple at 'Ubaid. As Mumford writes (1961: 483), "the suburb becomes visible almost as early as the city itself, and perhaps explains the ability of the ancient town to survive the insanitary conditions that prevailed within its walls." But one should not exaggerate the orderliness of these patterning of secular urban space and spatial practices. After all, one of the Sumerian terms most widely used during this period to describe the urban built environment translates as "labyrinth." But there can be no doubt that the production and reproduction of social life in Ur were becoming increasingly ordered and regulated by the *spatial* institutionalization of the city-state, or, recalling Foucault, through the development of "disciplinary technologies" that seek to control the localized nexus of space, knowledge, and power.[18]

---

17   The two major types of market space of contemporary Southwest Asia were probably already well established at Ur, the open plaza or covered bazaar and the booth- or stall-lined street. Mumford even goes so far as to describe the largest site in the temple precinct as a "supermarket."
18   This Foucauldian reference brings to mind a tour of the citadel of Los Angeles that I described in chapter 7 of *Thirdspace*, the source of the lead quotes to this chapter.

Figure 2.4 *Present-day Erbil (ancient Arbela) in northeast Iraq* (Source: A. E. J. Morris, *History of Urban Form: Before the Industrial Revolution*, New York: John Wiley and Sons, 1974: 9, figure 1.11)

Fast Forward > > to the Third Urban Revolution

The intervening time span, between the decline of Ur in 1500 B.C. and the onset of what I will describe as the third Urban Revolution more than 3,000 years later, can be seen as a period in which the city-state form of territorial governmentality, culture, and mode of production was elaborated, diffused, and reinvented all over the world with relatively little change in its fundamental spatial specificities. For the most part, this globalization of the city-state continued to build, with creative local variations, on the innovative developments that were initiated in Mesopotamian cityspaces. Vast city-based empires, which we continue to call civilizations, rose and fell for many different reasons, perhaps the most common having to do with the uneven development of those disciplinary technologies and their material and ideological command over space, knowledge, and power. Like Ur at the height of its power, these imperial civilizations were "mosaic states" clearly centered in the dominant metropolis (although "patropolis" or father city may more accurately define the prevailing patriarchal order).

Surrounding the core "pantile" of the imperial mosaic was a fluid tesselation of subordinate and tributary city-states, each the culminating focus of its own local territorial culture and its own regional hierarchy of cities, towns, and villages. Adherence and territorial authority in the dependent periphery was maintained primarily through military force and bureaucratic promises of economic advantage, especially with respect to defense against alien hordes bent on conquest and/or plunder, the barbarians and *idiotes* (the uncivilized), as well as other expansive city-states. A few imperial core cities such as Rome and Teotihuacan grew to great size, with perhaps more than a million inhabitants and a concentric accretion of walls defining the inner boundaries of the city-state empire. A shifting and less concretized set of territorial boundaries and borders defined the outer reaches of authoritative and allocative power.

Inside the city, the monolithic powers of the citadel became increasingly differentiated into separate spheres – each symbolically and materially represented at specific sites. The adjoined palace-ziggurat was split into a series of clustered headquarters for the ruling political, military, religious, commercial, judiciary, and bureaucratic elites: castle, palace, fortress, cathedral, marketplace, public square, city hall, courthouse – each located atop a growing hierarchy of such sites organizing cityspace into a multi-tiered and nested system of nodal regions that stretched from the privileged core of the mosaic state to the "outer cities" of its subordinate and dependent peripheries.

Urban growth continued almost everywhere to pivot around the visually prominent and politically hegemonic city-center, intensifying concentricities both inside and outside the city walls. What urban historians call unplanned or "organic" expansion tended to be more haphazard and irregular, but cityspace became increasingly planned and regulated as new geometries were added to the simple model of the (head)quartered circle. Rectangular grids conveniently plotted new areas of expansion while the older settled areas continued to be structured in radial sectors defined in large part by the major transportation axes emanating from the citadel. The spatial practices and mental maps of city-dwellers almost surely continued to reflect the symbolic geometry and cosmology that have always been attached to cityspace, but more secular sites took on new meaning in everyday urban life and in the social production (and reproduction) of cityspace. Although the specific shape and internal geography of cities took on many different forms and patternings, especially with regard to the particularities of site and situation, there was also a remarkable regularity in the urban morphologies created all over the world in the 3,000 years following the decline of Ur, so much so that little more needs to be said for this period in our remapping of the geohistory of cityspace.[19]

It must be remembered, however, that the vast majority of the population almost everywhere in the world until the nineteenth century lived outside the major cities, although mainly within their sphere of territorial control. The necessary production of a social surplus was based, in almost every city-state and empire, on agriculture and other "primary sector" activities (animal husbandry, mining, fishing, hunting) that benefited much less from nodality and agglomeration than did the work of administration and social control as well as commerce and craft industry. With social production taking place primarily in what appear to be non-urban areas, most materialist histories of human societies and modes of production have tended to overlook the spatial specificities of urbanism and synekism, and to take a functional or technological rather than a territorial or spatial approach. A more explicitly geohistorical reading, however, suggests that these societies and modes of production were fundamentally urban from the very start and that much of their dynamism was generated from the dense nucleations of cityspace and the persistent stimulus of urban nodality.

Not only agriculture and the peasantry, but also animal husbandry and pastoralism, commerce and industry, wholesale and retail trade, centralized political authority and planning, class formation and class struggle, began in and from cities and have always been integrally related to evolving and *specifically urban* social divisions of labor. Social relations of production and reproduction, and associated relations of class exploitation, patriarchal authority, and cultural domination, were not only concretized – made real, Lefebvre would argue – in material spatial practices and their symbolic representations in cities and city-regions, but these material and symbolic urban spatialities were in themselves powerful forces in shaping the very nature of social production and reproduction. In other words, there was a vital and often problematic *socio-spatial dialectic* to the historical development of human societies and modes of production that has been frequently overlooked or de-emphasized in Western scholarship and even the most critical forms of historiography. For these reasons, a strong argument can be made to insist that every mode of production beyond the most primitive forms of hunting and gathering deserves to be described as intrinsically *urban and city-centric* in its origins and development.

With that bold conclusion, we can pass quickly through (and leave to others the challenge of spatially rethinking) the long and fascinating geohistory of

19 For an excellent overview of the development of the urban built environment over this long period, see A. E. J. Morris, *History of Urban Form: Before the Industrial Revolutions*, New York: John Wiley and Sons, originally published in 1972. There is, of course, an extraordinary wealth of references to the development of Greek, Roman, Chinese, and other civilizations that are relevant here, but these classic histories pay very little attention to the generative stimulus of urban agglomeration and the influential role played by the spatial specificity of urbanism. See, for example, the otherwise groundbreaking work of Max Weber, *The Agrarian Sociology of Ancient Civilizations*, written in 1908 and reissued by Verso in 1998 as a Verso Classic.

the city-state and its globally uneven development, to enter another time and place, a new point of origin for a third convulsive transformation in the social production and reproduction of cityspace that brings us much closer to the present. From Mesopotamia and its immediately surrounding regions we shift to Western Europe in the aftermath of the Renaissance and the Enlightenment, to the early stages of the Industrial Revolution, to engage more directly with that poignant spatial narrative that, in Iain Chambers's words, can "help some of us to locate our home in modernity."

Chapter 3
The Third Urban Revolution: Modernity and Urban-industrial Capitalism

The metropolis has invariably functioned as the privileged figure of modernity . . . [It] represents the highest form assumed by both economic and aesthetic forces. The metropolis becomes both a model of economic and social development, and a metaphor of modernity, a metaphysical reality . . .

The metropolis is, above all, a myth, a tale, a telling that helps some of us to locate our home in modernity, there to find the new gods, the new myths, called for by Nietzsche. The metropolis is an allegory; in particular it represents the allegory of the crisis of modernity that we have learnt to recognize in the voices of Baudelaire, Benjamin, and Kafka. To go beyond these bleak stories of exile and that grey, rainy country of the anguished soul, is to establish a sense of being at home in the city, and to make of tradition *a space of transformation* rather than the scene of a cheerless destiny. For this metropolis is not simply the final stage of a poignant narrative, of apocalypse and nostalgia, it is also the site of the ruins of previous orders in which diverse histories, languages, memories and traces continually entwine and recombine in the construction of new horizons.

Iain Chambers, *Border Dialogues: Journeys in Postmodernity* (1990): 55, 112; emphasis added

Understanding the third Urban Revolution and its role in the geohistory of cityspace takes us away from the Southwest Asian heartland of urbanization and into postfeudal Europe and its globalizing network of colonial metropolises and mercantile capitalist cities. Here the evolving spatial specificities of urbanism and the developmental dynamics that emanate from them become attached to a new narrative framework that contemporary Western scholarship has retrospectively associated with a European Age of Enlightenment and the rise of a collective consciousness of *modernity*. Another timeline is also added, explicitly linking the social production of cityspace to the development of capitalism since the sixteenth century. A brief scene-setting in this broader discourse on capitalist modernity and modernization begins a discussion that takes us into the exemplary cityspaces of Manchester and Chicago, where both the modern industrial capitalist metropolis and the field of urban studies were most paradigmatically developed.

Cityspace and the Succession of Modernities

Modernity as a motive force in societal development arises most generally from ways of thinking and acting that are specifically based on a practical consciousness of the contemporary, an explicit and purposeful awareness of what Marshall Berman (1982) called the "perils and possibilities" inherent in being alive in a particular time, place, and social milieu.[1] Stephen Kern (1983) associated the concept of modernity with an evolving "culture of time and space," or what might be referred to as a combined *zeitgeist* and *raumgeist*, a temporal and spatial spirit of the contemporary moment.[2] Being modern, in whatever field of endeavor one chooses, is thus contingent upon a critical awareness of contemporaneity, the "just now" (from the Latin *modo*), as a source of practical knowledge that can be used to change the world for the better rather than to continue to reinforce and faithfully reproduce the status quo.

As such a critical awareness, what can be defined as modernity-in-general is driven by two key questions. What difference does today, what is going on just now, in this world and this period of time, make with respect to yesterday? Assuming that some significant differences exist, how might we use this knowledge of what is new and different to change our thinking and our practices to make for a better world? In other words, what is significantly new and what is to be done about it, right here and now? From the answers to these questions derive all modernizing movements, all assertive modern*isms*. Following Berman (1982) again, the practical consciousness of modernity is produced and reproduced by individuals and social movements through the specific interaction between modernization (the more concrete and objective processes of societal change and development) and modernism (the diverse cultural, ideological, and reflexive responses to the contemporary condition, to ongoing modernization processes, and especially to the generative and intrinsically spatio-temporal question of what *now/here* is to be done).[3]

Modernism as an intentional framework for "progressive" thought and action is thus radically open to the accumulation of new understanding and knowledges. It is also, reflecting this openness, susceptible to being spatio-temporally restructured, recomposed, taken in new and different directions

---

1   Marshall Berman, *All that is Solid Melts into Air*, New York: Simon and Schuster, 1982.
2   Stephen Kern, *The Culture of Time and Space, 1880–1918*, Cambridge, MA: Harvard University Press, 1983.
3   One irony of the conjunction of now and here is that it produces the word "nowhere." Another is that "nowhere" is a rough translation of the Greek root for "utopia." All this wordplay gives additional meaning to Iain Chambers's commentary on modernity.

from those already established. Modernity is not something that is created once and for all, but changes over time and is spatially unevenly developed. Its practices are especially prone to change during periods of societal turmoil and crisis, when, quoting Marx via Berman, all that was once solid seems to melt into air. It is with these broad and dynamic definitions of modernity, modernization, and modernism that we begin to address what Iain Chambers describes as the "poignant narrative" of the modern metropolis, "the site of the ruins of previous orders in which diverse histories, memories and traces continually entwine and recombine in the construction of new horizons."

What has been described earlier as the first two Urban Revolutions can be recast as epochal modernizations of human society, rooted in the creative dynamics of urban spatiality that are associated with such terms as agglomeration economies, synekism, and phronesis. These major transformations in the social and spatial relations of production and reproduction, however, were most likely not accompanied by a socially and spatially comprehensive (and critical) consciousness of "being modern" as a strategy for societal betterment and development. Although the question of where and when such a systematic contextualization of a collective and critical consciousness of modernity first appeared must be kept open, the contemporary Western discourse conventionally locates its origins in the European Enlightenment and the earliest appearance of an explicit social differentiation of spatial practices and practitioners around the opposition between what were explicitly called the "Ancients" and the "Moderns."

The European Renaissance answered the question of what is to be done to improve society by an appeal to what was perceived and conceived to have been the primary achievements of specifically European civilizations and city-states of the past, most pointedly classical Athens and Rome. It was rooted in a reinforced urban-based theologism that looked to faithful belief in scriptured Christian history as the foundation for action in the present and the future. By defining itself in affirmatively European terms, the Renaissance was the first assertive expression of what contemporary scholars describe as Eurocentrism in the arts, sciences, and philosophy. Given its definition of the "Other," against which a European identity was forged after the crusades and the expulsion of the "Moors" from the continental mainland, it can also be seen as the beginning of what Edward Said (1979) described as "Orientalism," the active construction of the non-European world as backward, un-Christian, and semi-barbarian. These worldviews and their associated ideologies and action frameworks would be instilled in the emerging new consciousness of European modernity and would subsequently profoundly affect the social production of cityspace, as well as much of the rest of Western scholarship, for the next 500 years.

In part, the European Enlightenment was a direct reaction to Renaissance classicism, a search for alternatives to theocratic faith and classical learning. The first modern movements, distinguishing themselves from the Ancients, increasingly turned to a new secular science and scientific understanding as a basis for *praxis*, another Greek word referring to the transformation of knowledge into presumably beneficial, progressive, socio-spatial action. Ever since, the discourse on modernity has been deeply implanted in what we still call the epistemology and philosophy of *science*, a form of potentially emancipatory critical thinking that Jean Baudrillard described as revolving around the benign episteme of the mirror, the scientific gathering of good and useful reflections from the empirical world.[4] Obtaining their primary footholds in the major capital cities and trading centers of western Europe, these modern movements began playing a minor but growing role in urban development, putting science to public use in the management and social improvement of urban communities and their territorial hinterlands.

This new modernity-as-Enlightenment, however, did not remain constant. It evolved in a complex multiplicity of unevenly developed regional forms in Europe and became increasingly exported through colonization and the expansion of mercantile trade, creating the outlines of the first consciously modern, modernist, and modernizing world system. After several centuries of elaboration and consolidation, modernity-as-Enlightenment met with a formidable new challenge. In what we now call the Age of Revolution (1776–1848), the course of modernity became radically restructured. In this (first?) major internal crisis of European modernity, generated almost entirely in and from the major metropolises of the time, conflicts arose between those who wished to maintain the best of Enlightenment modernization practices and an avant-garde of what today might be called postmodernists who promoted an alternative view of modernism, of what is to be done here and now, that departed significantly from existing strategies and practices.

The first truly *modern* social revolutions, in the American colonies in 1776 and then in France (or more specifically in Paris) in 1789, marked the development of a new modern age of liberal democracy emblazoned in the calls for liberty, equality, fraternity, and the universal rights of "man."[5] Significantly, these were also explicit calls for greater rights to the city, to cityspace, to citizenship, inspired above all perhaps by the words and ideas of Jean-Jacques Rousseau, the "Citizen of Geneva." They aimed at obtaining urban-based territorial control from monarchical city-state mosaics and colonial empires either from a position in the periphery (the mercantile cities of the American colonies) or more directly in the core (the citadel of Paris). In many ways, the Age of Revolution can be seen as marking the final chapter of the second Urban Revolution's evolving experimentation with increasing urban

---

4   Jean Baudrillard, *Simulations*, New York: Semiotext(e), 1983; see also pp. 326–30.

5   That these masculinisms must be taken literally and not sublimated in language conventions opens up an alternative critical history of modernity – and of modernization and modernism – as the material and conceptual products of Eurocentric patriarchy. Although rife with exceptions, the prevailing discourse on modernity-in-general has always been dominated by white male envisionings of what's new and what is to be done, disguised under the assumed universality of "man." One of the most distinctive and disruptive features of the contemporary critical discourse on postmodernity has been its concerted unraveling of this discursive hegemony and the assertion of postmodern feminist and postcolonial alternatives. See *Thirdspace* (1996), chapter 4.

democracy and the beginning of a radically new phase in the geohistory of cityspace.

Modernity-as-Enlightenment and modernity-as-Liberal Democracy struggled for urban and state power, the two still tightly enmeshed, over a long unsettled period that lasted to about 1850. By this time, the third Urban Revolution was already well advanced in a few European regions, shaped in part by this ideological crisis of modernity but even more by the conjunction of the economic and cultural rhythms of modernization with concurrent developments of the Industrial Revolution that had begun outside the city centers of power more than a century earlier. By 1850, the narrative of modernity had adopted a different plot and narrative form, becoming absorbed in the storyline of the development of urban-industrial capitalism and its profound innovation of territorial governmentality, the capitalist nation-state. When Kant asked *"Was ist Aufklärung?"* (What is Enlightenment?) in 1784, he could answer with no mention of capitalism or the nation-state. After 1789, this became inconceivable as the discourses and consciousnesses of modernity were significantly transformed.

The comprehensive deconstruction and reconstitution of modernity arising from its spatio-temporal convergence with urban-industrial capitalism and the rising power of the nationalist state changed the critical discourse in nearly every field of knowledge and action. In particular, it radically redefined and refocused political theory, philosophy, and socio-spatial praxis. In 1848, both Marx and Comte would paper the revolutionary moment in Paris, described by some as the capital of the nineteenth century, with their very different emancipatory "positivist" manifestos. Marx's ideas gave impetus to a revolutionary scientific socialism, Comte's to a liberal social scientism. Each in their own way provided a totalizing vision of a new modernity that differed significantly from Rousseau's universalizing and humanistic liberal democracy, while maintaining many continuing links to it.

Major attention in both of these new modernisms was given to the worsening problems of urban immiseration that were associated with the early phases of urban-industrial capitalism. Attempts to explain the root causes of such extensive immiseration and to seek "progressive" social and spatial strategies to significantly improve these terrible conditions, especially in the major industrializing cities, widened the split between the two new modern movements. An establishmentarian and state-centered liberal reformism, now led by scientists and professionals in medicine, engineering, and law, theorized a praxis based on improved public health, moral betterment, and technological innovation. This praxis was rationalized and projected through a fundamentally capitalist metanarrative of *development* that wrapped world history in the necessity for continuous progress and modernization. In stark contrast was a fundamentally Marxist or scientific socialist metanarrative of *social justice* that saw reforms as temporary palliatives and argued for the necessity of a more radical if not revolutionary transformation in order for social justice – and development – to be achieved. This fundamental split would shape the specifically political and urban discourse and deeply polarize modernist social movements for the next 150 years.

In the expansive Age of Capital, as E. J. Hobsbawm called the period after the revolutions of 1848–9, these two opposed but nonetheless modernist movements would consolidate increasing power in their separate spheres and extend their influence – and their particular programs for what is to be done "just now" – around the globe in tune with the dynamic rhythm of boom and bust cycles that defined capitalist urban and industrial development. In other words, what had been a postmodernist avant-garde growing out of the Age of Revolution became the dominant new modernisms of the second half of the nineteenth century, superseding its competition until it would itself contend with another crisis and a rising new postmodernism in the *fin de siècle*. It is within the spatial and temporal setting of this "long" nineteenth century, stretching through Hobsbawm's Ages of Revolution, Capital, and Empire to the First World War, that we can refocus the story of the third Urban Revolution.[6]

The Rise of the Modern Industrial Metropolis

The first sites of factory production were located outside the major pre-industrial cities, although, following Jane Jacobs, they are probably best viewed as transplants of urban crafts such as weaving to places where energy sources and cheaper, less well-organized workers were more plentiful. It was the insertion into cityspace of large-scale manufacturing industry, however, that was the primary trigger of the third Urban Revolution.[7] From this moment on, there developed a fully symbiotic and expansive relation between the urbanization and industrialization processes on a scale and scope never before achieved, very much like the propulsive effects of the first cities on the development of agriculture. It was a relation so formidable that it would define industrial capitalism as a fundamentally *urban* mode of production (and also imbue much of oppositional socialist thought with an associated, if at times somewhat quixotic, anti-urban bias).

---

6 Eric Hobsbawm's magnificent series of books on what I am calling the succession of modernities include *The Age of Revolution, 1789–1848*, New York: New American Library, 1962; *The Age of Capital, 1848–1878*, New York: Charles Scribner's, 1975; *The Age of Empire, 1875–1914*, New York: Pantheon, 1987; and *The Age of Extremes: A History of the World, 1914–1991*, New York: Pantheon, 1994.
7 Why manufacturing industry returned to cityspace is a fascinating question, for more than any other event it defines the third Urban Revolution and the new course taken by capitalist development. Many historians of capitalism and the Industrial Revolution rivet attention to originary moments such as the appearance of the first factories, and conclude from their characteristically rural location that cities were not the initiating sparkplug of the revolution. From all that we have seen in remapping the geohistory of cityspace, it would seem that this "origins" argument is seriously misleading. Something inherent in the social and spatial conditions of urbanism was primarily responsible for the massive expansion of manufacturing inside the city, and this "something" is almost surely connected to the reflexive qualities of agglomeration, synekism, and phronesis that have always been a part of the social production of cityspace.

Prior to this epochal urban transformation, there were three kinds of cities, each the center of coordination, control, and administration of territorial cultures and modes of production based primarily in agriculture, mining, and other primary sector activities, as well as of the systems of trade and commerce built upon these primary production complexes. Most large cities were elaborations of the old city-state model described in chapter 2, although by the late eighteenth century in Western Europe they were increasingly being incorporated into an inter-regional hierarchy of cities defined by the territorial borders of the emerging nation-state and national market. Within these new national systems of cities – perhaps better described as state-cities rather than city-states – there were at least two more specialized nodes where the reach of the citadel's political, economic, and cultural power expanded well beyond the national territory: imperial state-cities and mercantile state-cities. In such major conurbations as London and Paris, all three types of city were combined in a more complex regional metropolis, or "world city," that for the first time in over a thousand years began to approach ancient Rome and Teotihuacan in population size.

The third Urban Revolution involved not so much an increase in the size of cities as an expansive recomposition of the urban population and the associated urbanization of entire national societies. In Britain, for example, the population shifted from being more than 80 percent rural in 1750 to being over 80 percent urban in 1900. This unprecedented societal urbanization-cum-modernization was brought about primarily by the entry into cityspace of millions of representatives of the two new classes that defined urban-industrial capitalism, the proletariat and the bourgeoisie, each as definitively and pre-suppositionally urban as industrial capitalism itself. This extraordinary mass migration radically restructured earlier distinctions between city and countryside, urban and rural, *polites* and *idiotes*, the sacred and the profane, to inscribe a new urban order in which the production of a social surplus was not only coordinated and controlled by the city but, for the first time in history, also took place predominantly inside the city proper, in and around the dense core of cityspace. On a very basic level, this revolutionary reorganization of cityspace required not only making room for the millions of new migrants and for the infrastructure of industrial production but also for the development of new ways to keep this emerging industrialized space economy of urbanism together, to administer and reproduce the social and spatial relations of capitalism at its now tightly nested global, national, regional, and local state scales.

In addition to the micro-technologies of labor discipline so brilliantly observed by Marx and Engels, there developed new macro-technologies of social and spatial control. Most potent perhaps was the material and symbolic construction of "imagined" territorial cultures on the scale of the nation-state. Although this "nationalism" broke away from many of the established foundations of the city-state and its elaborations, at least in its ideological appearance, there continued to be a fundamentally spatial and urban-based strategy for social cohesion and adherence. The nation-state was both a material expansion of the territorial culture of the city-state and also an abstraction and con-solidation of its more tangible control over the nexus of space, knowledge, and power. What was formerly the fluid accretion of city-states and their tributary regions into an imperial mosaic became the more formal establishment of the nationally bounded territorial state, bent on erasing the regional borders and cultural identities of the city-states contained within it through its homoge-nizing powers and those of the expanding market.[8] The long nineteenth century can be read not just through the interplay of urbanization and indus-trialization but also through the extraordinary ascendancy and empowerment of a new scale in the multi-layered hierarchy of nodal regions that shapes the spatiality of social life, a scale of socially constructed individual and collective identity and "citizenship" located between the city-state and the mosaic empire.

The nation-state may have originated centuries earlier with the shift from the Merovingian King of the Franks to the Carolingian King of France, but it took the Industrial Revolution and the liberal social revolutions of 1776 and 1789 to institutionalize, restructure, and culturally homogenize the real-and-imagined territorial community to meet the now more voracious and compelling modernization demands of urban-industrial capitalism. The nation-state can therefore also be seen as a product of the cities, of a new kind of urbanism that could be sustained and regulated only through a massive, hierarchical, and centrally managed expansion of its political and economic control well beyond the immediate city region. But we must rush again through this urban revisioning of the complex geohistory of the nation-state to look more specifically at what was happening to cityspace during the long nineteenth century.

Made in Manchester

There is no town in the world where the distance between the rich and the poor is so great, or the barrier between them so difficult to be crossed.

    Friedrich Engels writing on Manchester in 1844

The Ur-metropolis of the third Urban Revolution was Manchester, the first major city and cityspace to be socially produced almost entirely by the socio-spatial practices of industrial capitalism. In 1750, Manchester was a small compact market town in southern Lancashire, then the most densely popu-

---

8   This national homogenization or nation-building process triggered vigorous regionalisms through-out the nineteenth century, often in association with anarchist or libertarian socialist political move-ments. These anarchist-inspired regionalisms sought to preserve "subnational" cultures and identities against the increasingly centralized powers of the state and market. Ironically, anarchist thought and practice, from Proudhon to Bakunin, Reclus, and Kropotkin, was seen as a growing threat not only to liberal social scientism and nation building, but also to radical scientific socialism, explaining in part why Marx reserved some of his most vitriolic critiques for his libertarian socialist brethren.

lated area of England outside the immediate environs of London. It grew as a collection point for a system of towns, villages, and farmsteads engaged in handweaving primarily cotton textiles to supplement decreasing incomes from agricultural production. The product of this distinctly rural-yet-urban industry was sold locally and throughout England, but also began to be exported through the growing port of Liverpool, already established as a major center of the global slave trade and the source of raw cotton imported from the plantations of North America. This link was consolidated in the 1760s by the construction between Manchester and Liverpool of the first major long-distance canal in Britain, and reinforced in the 1830s by the first major interurban railway line. Until the beginning of the nineteenth century, however, Manchester remained little more than an overgrown trading center. It had no walls surrounding it, was not incorporated as a city, had few if any strong guilds organizing local artisans and craftsmen, and contained a relatively small non-agriculturally rooted urban population or civic bureaucracy.

Between 1770 and 1850, Manchester (along with nearby Salford) was transformed into the first fully industrial capitalist metropolis and manufactory, the "chimney of the world," a regional conurbation of 400,000, second in size only to London, by then on the verge of becoming the largest city in history. The story of this remarkable transformation is a complex one, but it can be focused around a cluster of new urbanization processes that help to define the third Urban Revolution. First there was the implantation of the factory system into the city. By 1830, there were nearly 100 steam-powered textile factories in Manchester, located mainly along the Irwell and Irk rivers, near whose confluence lay the city center. Although most of the factories employed about 100 workers, employment at a few grew to more than 1,000. This intrusion of industrial production into the urban fabric dramatically reorganized cityspace. Large cotton warehouses were constructed in the city center, many in the converted dwellings of established merchants who were abandoning their once-prestigious central location for bus-linked. suburbs away from the growing industrial grime. What was happening here was not just the origins of "middle-class" suburbanization – what Fishman (1987) would later call the creation of "bourgeois utopias" – but the beginnings of a great inversion of locational prestige in the concentric zonation of cityspace.[9]

Still without substantial civic institutions (self-governing borough status was given in 1838), a powerful clergy, or well-organized guilds, Manchester

---

9 The following quote from Robert Fishman, *Bourgeois Utopias: The Rise and Fall of Suburbia*, New York: Basic Books, 1987, both highlights the importance of Manchester in the history of suburbanization and warns of too easy extensions from the Anglo-Saxon urban experience.

By the 1840s Manchester had established a model for middle-class suburbanization that was to endure fundamentally unchanged for a century. In the 1850s and 1860s this suburban model established itself outside the rapidly growing cities of the United States but was decisively rejected in France. There . . . the bourgeoisie maintained their hold on the urban core. This dichotomomy creates an important problem for any history of suburbia: why did this bourgeois utopia take hold only among the "Anglo-Saxon" bourgeoisie, when the equally bourgeois French followed a very different vision.

had a weakly developed citadel. The Tory aristocracy and landed gentry lived primarily outside the city on sprawling rural estates. Only a small military garrison represented the national state, a descendant of the old Roman fort of Mancunium that was built in the first century A.D. and after which, as "Mancunians," the residents of Manchester are still named. It was therefore relatively easy for the new industrial bourgeoisie to establish its control over the "inner city," even with its dense population of shopkeepers, merchants, traders, and independent weavers and spinners. With the new factories nearby, although not particularly clustered around the defined city center, the dense inner city became the home of the working class and still another vital component of industrial capitalism, what Marx and Engels would call the "reserve army" of unemployed and casual laborers. There developed around what would subsequently be defined as the Central Business District (a substantial elaboration of the main marketplace or agora of the city-state), a broad band of crowded working-class housing quarters stretching out for several miles from the city center. And within this ring, two additional new urbanization processes would be spatially concentrated and expressed: "pauperization" and the formation of what can be called "intentional" urban slums.

These two processes, often overlooked in more conventional studies of the industrial capitalist city, were closely interrelated. Both are linked to one of the most powerful disciplinary strategies of urban-industrial capitalism, the creation of a real-and-imagined "underclass" of extreme poverty and destitution that could be used materially and symbolically to threaten individual "free" workers as a likely destiny or destination should their work falter or they challenge the established social relations of production, or what we call today the prerogatives of management. Pauperization was the creation of a population that was virtually divorced from any means of constructing their own livelihood, including factory work. In rural areas, pauperization was primarily a matter of finding ways to eliminate peasant landownership, farmwork, and domestic industry, such as handloom weaving in the Manchester region, which began to disappear with the development of mechanized textile factories. The intent here was not only to create a pool of potential workers but also a reservoir of non-workers, the unemployed, the landless, the destitute, all of whom would have little choice but to enter the city, and especially the inner city, to survive. In no previous urban society, including those based on slavery, was such a population so necessary and so numerous.

Pauperization was inscribed within the city by what I have described as the formation of intentional urban slums, areas of the most abject poverty that are actively created by the very nature of capitalist urban-industrial development. The cumulative demographic result of these new urbanization processes was a mass migration to the cities. Within Manchester and other large British cities, this mass urbanization movement created what were probably the most densely populated inner urban cores in history and, in Manchester in particular (Dickensian London notwithstanding), some of the worst conditions of urban life ever experienced anywhere until then. In the 1840s, half the children born in Manchester's poorest areas died before the age of six, and the average age of death was seventeen. Constantly faced with labor shortages, the booming space economy of Manchester extended its devastating reach beyond its immediate hinterland to other regions within England and to such "internal colonies" as Ireland, where pauperization (enhanced by socially stimulated "natural" events such as the potato famine) pumped thousands of poor migrants into the industrial city cores, in such enclaves as "Little Ireland," where Manchester's worst housing conditions could be found.

From the beginning, then, the new classes of urban-industrial capitalism entered the city in spatially segregated concentric zones: workers and the reserve army in the densest and most haphazardly jumbled inner zone, the new "middle-class" bourgeoisie settled in the more regularly gridded second ring, and the upper bourgeoisie in a suburban commuting zone of gardened villas and countryside estates. While concentric zonation has, at least since Ur, been an integral part of the city's spatial fabric, it was never so clearly defined, homogeneously composed, and attuned to the dominant class interests. And, as noted, the prestige gradient of residential sites with respect to distance from the city center was virtually inverted, creating not only a new centrifugal force pushing outward the boundaries of the city region but also a new dynamic of internal circulation that came increasingly to revolve around the now more extended daily journey to work. For the first time ever, the vast majority of the urban population had to travel between their places of residence and their places of work *inside* the city. This created major new demands for urban planning and provided yet another disciplinary technology for maintaining the social and spatial divisions between classes, for the journey to work was a cost to both capital and labor that could be manipulated through civic institutions and public works to the maximum benefit of the dominant class.

This set up a decision-making matrix that would become a pervasive organizing feature of industrial capitalist cityspace everywhere in the world. All sites in the city were commodified by the establishment of locational rents that combined the ownership and rental costs of land, the costs of transit (especially the journey to work but also to other civic services), and the costs of density, now clearly defined in a gradient extending steeply outward from the city center to the new "suburbs." Decision-making with regard to land use and housing choice was increasingly shaped by monetary trade-offs between these locational costs and, of course, the ability to pay them. The economic logic contained within this spatial decision-making matrix can be seen as both producing the class-based concentric zonation of the city and being produced and reproduced by it, giving a new economic calculus to the socio-spatial dialectic played out in cityspace and its built environment. Increasingly over time, this economic calculus would attract the attention of urban scholars as the primary theoretical and explanatory framework for understanding the social and spatial formation of the industrial capitalist metropolis, from its earliest stages to the present.

At least until the end of the nineteenth century, when the Age of Capital entered a period of crisis and restructuring sparked by such events as the fleeting creation of the Paris Commune and the financial panics of the early 1870s, the new urbanization processes affecting Manchester and many other expanding industrial cityspaces created a relatively simple urban spatial structure, although it should be noted that the situation in older mercantile and imperial state-cities experiencing industrialization was much more complex due to their sizeable pre-industrial built environments. There was an intense centralization of population, employment, and production; and a well-defined concentric zonation of classes and residential quality, broken only by a few "protected" transit routes. This characteristic patterning of cityspace was acutely observed by a resident Mancunian of the time in what would be the first paradigmatic reading of the newly formed cityspace of the third Urban Revolution. Here are the prescient words of Friedrich Engels, who migrated to Manchester in 1842 to work for his father's textile-manufacturing firm.

> The separation between the different classes and the consequent ignorance of each other's habits and condition, are far more complete in this place than in any other country . . . There is far less communication between the master cotton spinner and his workmen . . . than there is between the Duke of Wellington and the humblest labourer on his estate.   (p. 114)[10]

> The working-people's quarters are sharply separated from the sections of the city reserved for the middle-class . . . Manchester contains, at its heart, a rather extended commercial district, perhaps half a mile long and about as broad, and consisting almost wholly of offices and warehouses. Nearly the whole district is abandoned by dwellers, and is lonely and deserted at night . . . [Surrounding it are] unmixed working-people's quarters, stretching like a girdle, averaging a mile and a half in breadth . . . Outside, beyond the girdle, lives the upper and middle bourgeoisie, the middle bourgeoisie in regularly laid out streets in the vicinity of the working quarters . . . the upper bourgeoisie in remoter villages and gardens . . . in free, wholesome country air, in fine comfortable homes, passed once every half or quarter hour by omnibuses going to the city. And the finest part of the arrangement is this, that the members of this money aristocracy can take the shortest road through the middle of all the labouring districts . . . without ever seeing that they are in the midst of grimy misery . . . For the thorough fares are lined, on both sides, with an almost unbroken series of shops [that] suffice to conceal from the eyes of the wealthy . . . the misery and grime which form the complement of their wealth.   (pp. 79, 80)

He would add to these comments that Manchester in the 1840s was "less built according to plan . . . than any other city." Indeed, Engels and others would argue that the absence of strong civic institutions responsible for guiding and

10   See Friedrich Engels, *The Condition of the Working Class in England*, originally published in 1844. These passages are from the Panther (1969) edition, as quoted in James Anderson, "Engel's Manchester: Industrialization, Worker's Housing, and Urban Ideologies," a working paper published by the Planning School of the Architectural Association in London around 1974 (no date is given on the original publication). See also Steven Marcus, *Engels, Manchester and the Working Class*, New York: Vintage, 1974.

regulating the social production of urban space was a major factor in the rapid early growth of Manchester as an industrial capitalist city as well as for at least some of the abominable conditions of the working class.[11] By the end of the Age of Revolution, it had also become clear to many others, including the industrial bourgeoisie, that the immiseration of the working class was not only morally unjustifiable but had an economically dysfunctional side to it as well. It is not surprising, then, that there developed in Manchester the first identifiable "school" of urban studies, and that it was immediately concerned with seeking explanations and progressive "policy" solutions for the all too evident problems of the city. And it is also not surprising, given the earlier discussion of the split between liberal reformist and radical socialist modern movements, that the broadly defined Manchester School of political economy would reflect this bifurcation.

The dominant approach to the "applied" political economy of urbanization in Manchester explained the city's problems as a result of "foreign and accidental causes" and, given the powerful laissez-faire ideology of the time, on national government policy and other restrictions on the free play of market competition. The "foreign" causes frequently focused on the fluctuating influx of immigrants, especially the Irish, unaccustomed to life in the big city; while the "accidental" tended to blame corrupt and greedy land speculators, moneylenders, and shopkeepers, a two-sided scapegoating strategy that continues to influence urban public policy and planning to this day. As for possible solutions to the problems, two major arguments were presented. The first, implicitly absolving the factory system from blame, sought answers through laissez-faire policies with regard to labor-management relations and the market in goods, services, and labor power. The general assumption, so persuasively promulgated in the classic works of Adam Smith, was that the free market and its "magic" would elevate every member of the social body, bringing about the greatest good for the greatest number. The second argument assumed that, under continuing constraints on the market economy, certain problems would persist and that they could be best handled through the development of a reform-minded local government assisted by specialist-professionals in alliance with the industrial bourgeoisie – in other words, through active urban planning and astute surveillance, especially with regard to public health and safety.

Engels represented best the radical socialist wing – or perhaps better, the opposing pole – of the Manchester School. He too would apportion some

---

11   It is tempting to view Engels's observation in a more contemporary light. What he was seeing was a disjunction between an already established and expansive "regime of accumulation" (the earliest and purest form of urban-industrial capitalism) and the still emerging and weak "mode of regulation," the administrative and managerial structures and local institutions that could effectively hold the new economy together, assuring its continuity over time and space. A similar situation can be said to exist today with the emergence of another new regime of "flexible" and "global" capitalist accumulation and the formation of the postmetropolis under conditions where there is not yet well established an accompanying system of societal regulation. In this sense at least, Manchester in 1850 is not unlike Los Angeles in 1990.

blame to the Irish, but in almost all other ways he would present a very different interpretation of the urban problems and their resolution in Manchester. While he paid major attention to the restructured cityspace and to the inherently urban housing question, he would abstract himself from the spatial specificities of the urban scene to seek deeper structural explanations and more radical calls for social action. What was happening in the industrial capitalist city, Engels argued, was what was happening everywhere: the imposition and empowerment of industrial capitalist relations of production played out through the factory system and its urban contextualization. Even the best of liberal reformist planning would only touch the surface, and even there only temporarily and with the likelihood that a problem resolved in one place would reappear in another. But with an ironical eye to the powers of spatiality, he also saw the segregation and compaction of the working class as a potential source of strength, a synekistic breeding ground for the class consciousness that would necessarily lead the way to resolving the problems of industrial capitalism through organized resistance and, ultimately, revolutionary transformation.[12]

The liberal reformism of the Manchester School of urban studies would win out over the more radical solutions of scientific socialism and shape cityspace through urban planning for the next century. But a new Babylon would rise far away from the Mancunian Ur and stimulate the development, soon after the end of the "long" nineteenth century, of the most clearly identifiable and self-conscious school of urban studies ever established. A brief look at this Chicago School of urban studies will conclude the discussion of the origins of the third Urban Revolution and move us closer to the present.

Remade in Chicago

The city is not an artifact or a residual arrangement. On the contrary, the city embodies the real nature of human nature. It is an expression of mankind in general and specifically of the social relations generated by territoriality.

Morris Janowitz, Introduction to a new edition of Robert E. Park,
Ernest W. Burgess, and Roderick D. Mackenzie, *The City: Suggestions
for Investigation of Human Behavior in the Urban Environment* (1967)[13]

---

12 Missed by both sides was the emphatic "break with nature" induced by the third Urban Revolution. Pre-industrial urbanization was dependent on maintaining appropriate adaptations to the physical environment to assure continued agricultural and other primary forms of production. The shift to the "secondary" sector of manufacturing industry made these adaptive ties appear much less important, creating a more blindly exploitative relation between the city and its natural environment. The anarchists and regionalists of the nineteenth century saw this more clearly as a major "urban" problem, but, as noted earlier, they were attacked and dismissed by both liberal reformers and scientific socialists.

13 *The City* was the classic text of the Chicago School. Originally published in 1925 by the University of Chicago Press, its title was taken from an essay written by Robert E. Park in 1916 (*American Journal of Sociology* 20: 577–612). The quote from Morris Janowitz is taken from his introduction to the new edition, published in 1967. For a not totally unrelated book with the same main title, see Allen Scott and Edward Soja eds., *The City: Los Angeles and Urban Theory at the End of the Twentieth Century*, Berkeley and Los Angeles: University of California Press, 1996.

Chicago was to the second half of the nineteenth century what Manchester was to the first: a relatively uncluttered urban laboratory for examining the formation of the industrial capitalist city and its reflexive cityspace. Like Manchester, Chicago started as a military fort (Fort Dearborn, built in 1803), was incorporated as a city in the 1830s, and began booming soon after the construction of a long-distance canal (opened in 1848, connecting its site on the Great Lakes with the Ohio-Mississippi river basin) and the arrival of the railroad (in 1852–3, linking it to the eastern seaboard). Unlike New York, Philadelphia, Baltimore, and other major eastern cities, Chicago did not have an extensive mercantile cityspace to complicate the urban-industrialization process, although today it too has an identifiable "old town," as these mercantile vestiges came to be called. Buoyed by the rapid westward expansion of the American urban-industrial frontier in the last half of the century, Chicago grew even faster than Manchester and reached a million inhabitants before the turn of the century. Moreover, Chicago was built on a flatter surface and with a much more regular grid of streets and residences, allowing for an even clearer reading of the superficial spatial organization, the "trend surfaces," of the new urban-industrial order.

Such a superficial reading of the cityspace of Chicago did not take place until the 1920s and 1930s, well after the "classic" industrial cityscape had become blurred somewhat through a selective decentralization of industry and labor to satellite cities such as Gary, Indiana; and the beginnings of residential suburbanization by an expanding middle class that overlapped (and blurred) the boundary between the lower bourgeoisie and the better-established working class. The nineteenth-century spatial order remained empirically visible, however, and became the focus of attention for a group of social scientists and planners at the University of Chicago, imbued with the achievements of European natural sciences and the creative spatial imagination of such European social theorists as Georg Simmel. These cross-Atlantic influences, however, soon became wrapped in a distinctly American blend of liberal reformism, professional managerialism, and pragmatic idealism.

By this time, Chicago and its premier university had become a major seedbed for this prototypically American approach to understanding the city, and for uplifting attempts to resolve its inherent problems through a uniquely American brand of planned modernization. Some of the earliest urban reform and social welfare movements developed in Chicago, stimulating the growth of the so-called "helping professions." The University of Chicago was also the workplace of Thorstein Veblen, a key figure in the development of professional-managerialist thought (he would call for a "Soviet of Technicians" to run the country); and John Dewey, the leading voice in American pragmatism, described as the most important, if not only, major philosophical doctrine originating in the USA. Also influential in the local development of this Chicago School of urban studies was the World's Columbian Exhibition of 1893. Its resplendent "White City" model crystallized the utopian possibilities of industrial capitalist modernization as a progressive force and positioned the pragmatic and idealist "city planner" as a heroic figure in American modernism. The "White City," with all its attached symbolism, intended or otherwise, became an originary moment in the history of urban planning in the USA. By its celebration of the new possibilities for urban reform through planning and design, it, too, significantly shaped the urban consciousness of the emerging Chicago School.

Although they were similarly concerned with the problems and challenges of persistent urban immiseration and poverty, what the Chicago School pragmatists and planners saw in the spatial specificity of their home city was far removed from the class analysis and political economy that characterized the Manchester School. As disciplined sociologists and geographers, they instrumentally abstracted cityspace out from the geohistory (and critique) of industrial capitalism, reconceptualized it as a pseudo-biological organism, and liberally universalized its morphology as part of a natural-cum-social, or social Darwinian, process of "organic" evolution. The concentric class geography seen by Engels, for example, was remodeled as the product of a socially mediated but intrinsically "natural" process of invasion and succession, competition and cooperation, evolution and retrogression (leaving some room for accident and mutation), producing an essentially organic or social physics interpretation of "the city" (the title of the School's most representative text) and "urbanism as a way of life" (the evocative phrase coined by one of the intellectual leaders of the Chicago School, Louis Wirth).

Hence the description of the School's focus as *urban ecology*. The use of the term ecology was itself an abstraction, an almost metaphorical adoption of a natural science point of view and epistemology rather than a scientific analysis of the relation between the city and its natural environment. Indeed, the organism of the city, with "urban culture" as its contextual expression, was essentially isolated from its larger physical environment and studied sociobiotically, in terms of its internal anatomy and circulatory systems, its symptoms of sickness and health, and its life cycles of youth, maturity, and old age. In this urban ecology, still powerful in the contemporary urban imaginary, visible appearances were what mattered most, and it was on these measurable appearances of regular ecological patterning (in what Lefebvre would call perceived space) that the School focused its theoretical attention. As would be the case in all social sciences of urbanism throughout the twentieth century, urban theory came to be rooted in the measurement and mapping of empirically-defined social and spatial covariations of "human behavior in the urban environment," the correlations between one set of surface patternings (often deemed to be independent or causal variables) and another (so-called dependent variables, the direct objects of explanation).

The Chicago School's modeling of the social and spatial morphology of the city is by now familiar to all students of urban sociology and geography. Burgess's concentric zone model provided the foundation, with its neat depiction of annular rings emanating from nodal concentrations in the Central Business District, the new *temenos* of the industrial capitalist city. Immediately surrounding this dominant agglomeration, with its skyscraping ziggurats, was the Zone in Transition (filled with new immigrants to the city, boarding houses, ethnic enclaves, slums, vice, and various underworlds); then the Zone of Workingmen's Homes (more stable and independent, often with second-generation immigrant families); followed by the Zone of Better Residences (the main middle-class area, with apartment complexes, bright-light areas, and a few single-family dwellings) and finally the Commuter's Zone, where the "higher class" lived (the term "bourgeoisie" had virtually filtered out of American usage). Within this idealized spatial specificity of urbanism emerged "natural areas," territorial units whose distinctive physical, economic, and cultural characteristics Burgess described as arising from the "unplanned operation of ecological and social forces" formed in the "ecological crucible of the city."

Influenced by the rise of neoclassical economics and its break from an integrated political economy, Homer Hoyt, a land economist, represented the residential class geography somewhat differently. His sector model saw cityspace being shaped through a set of widening wedges extending outward from the city center through the operations of the urban land and housing markets and the linear axes of the transit system. What was in Engels's Manchester only a narrow corridor connecting the suburban villas to the city center was now fleshed out as a continuous and homogeneous sectoral zone of the wealthy cutting across all the concentric rings to establish the presence of the rich in every zone, from the core to the periphery. Similar but foreshortened wedges formed by lower-income groups also edged out from the center, but never quite reached the "bourgeois utopias" of the suburbs.

The integration of these two models of an orderly and monocentric cityspace was reinforced by dozens of rich empirical studies of the "natural areas" and characteristic "human behavior" emerging within the "ecological crucible" of Chicago. Here, in alphabetical order, is a sampling of Chicago School books, all published by the University of Chicago Press: N. Anderson (1923), *The Hobo: The Sociology of the Homeless Man*; P. G. Cressey (1932), *The Taxi-Dance Hall: A Sociological Study in Commercialized Recreation and City Life*; H. Hoyt (1933), *One Hundred Years of Land Values in Chicago*; R. E. Park and E. W. Burgess (1921), *Introduction to the Science of Sociology*; W. Reckless, *Vice in Chicago* (1933); E. H. Shideler (1927 doctoral dissertation), *The Chain Store: A Study of the Ecological Organization of a Modern City*; F. M. Thrasher (1927), *The Gang: A Study of 1313 Gangs in Chicago*; L. Wirth (1928), *The Ghetto*; L. Wirth and E. W. Burnert eds. (1940), *Local Community Fact Book of Chicago*; H. Zorbaugh (1929), *The Gold Coast and the Slum*. These natural areas and their associated behaviors came to be defined as urban "subcultures," more localized expressions of the ecological processes that shaped urban society and sociology.

There was a greater emphasis on race and ethnicity in Chicago than in more culturally homogeneous Manchester (the Irish notwithstanding). Given the mass migrations from the USA and especially from Europe in the period between 1880 and 1920, "immigrant status" played an increasingly central role in shaping the hypothesized surface appearances and natural areas of cityspace. Indeed, new migrants to the city, clustering in the inner Zone of Transition, were seen as the motive force behind the spatial dynamics of residential land use and household decision-making, pushing the boundaries of the city ever-outward in a process of "filtering." There was also less overt scapegoating of "problem minorities," for they too were seen to have their appropriate if not natural place within the city. Particular attention was given to the largest of these special places, the so-called Black Belt or black ghetto, which appeared in every American city through what was seen as an ambiguous mixture of voluntary and involuntary residential choice. There was racism and sexism embedded in the Chicago School, but it was relatively benign and liberal, especially in comparison with academia elsewhere in the USA.

The Chicago School models and theories were confidently built on the presumption of a dominating urban nucleus, an extraordinary composite pivot of every quarter that contained virtually all factories, jobs, government offices, corporate headquarters, etc. The population of this hypothesized metropolis, with minor exceptions, consisted of individuals of no particular class, race, or gender shaping their lives and lived spaces primarily through a tradeoff between locational rent (what would be paid to locate one's residence or a business firm at a particular place) and the costs of the daily "journey to work," both varying significantly with distance to the Central Business District. What was most amazing about these modelings was that they succeeded in describing, with some accuracy, many characteristic features of the macrospatial organization of cityspace. There was (and probably still is) some degree to which almost every cityspace is organized around a dominant center in a series of concentric zones, radial sectors, and specialized enclaves. What is specifically contained in these zones, wedges, and enclaves, how many there might be, and how clearly they can be defined, differs significantly over time and place, but the overall surface patterning has been a remarkably regular feature of the spatiality of urban life, from ancient Ur to contemporary Los Angeles.

Cityspace was therefore much more complex, multi-layered, and multiethnic in the Chicago than in the Manchester model. But it was also much more opaque and superficial, in the sense of being focused on visible and measurable appearances and behavior. The deeper processes presumed to be structuring cityspace were confined to the realm of ecology, filtered through a social matrix of individualistic agents (including households and business firms) and their decision-making behavior.[14] The most glaring absence in this modeling of cityspace was the industrialization process and its formative impact on urban geography. By not directly addressing the factory system and the capital–labor relation as underlying forces in the organization of cityspace, the dynamic interplay between urbanization and industrialization that defined the industrial capitalist city was essentially ignored. The deep structural dualism of capital versus labor, the (urban) bourgeoisie versus the

---

14 Although rarely couched in an ecological or spatial framework, this "methodological individualism" had become the core epistemology in Western social science. In the postwar development of urban economics and later, regional science, it would completely recast the Chicago School models in its powerful purview.

(urban) proletariat, that energized the urban observations of Engels and others seemed to melt away in the new American metropolis.

The Chicago School at its peak defined urban sociology in America. Despite its weaknesses, it represented the most serious attempt to make the spatial specificity of urbanism both a focus for theory-building and a rich domain for empirical and practically applicable research in the social sciences. In the 1940s, however, the Chicago School began to come under serious attack, from sociologists in particular, for its simplistic "ecologism," its overemphasis on what were perceived as "natural" or "organic" processes that hid from view the more significant social and cultural dimensions of urban life. In sociology outside the University of Chicago, the onslaught of critiques produced a redirected urban sociology almost devoid of explicitly spatial explanations. Stripped of its dynamic spatiality, the city came to be seen merely as an incidental backdrop to powerful social, psychological, cultural, and economic processes that just happened to take place in cityspace but were no longer considered to be intrinsically urban. An untheorized and unproblematic cityspace was pushed into the background of an increasingly empirically-minded and much less city-centric discipline. Through what was called Social Area Analysis, some sociologists continued to describe in great detail the surface geographies of the city, but with rather timid attempts to understand the spatial dynamics of what they were describing.[15]

In 1945, the Chicago urban geographer Chauncey Harris and his colleague Edward Ullman attempted to reinvigorate the human ecological or geographical perspective in their essay, "The Nature of Cities."[16] They broke somewhat from the monocentric model of cityspace to recognize multiple nuclei and more complex processes of urban development, although each center continued to be seen as shaping regularly ordered cityspaces around them, miniature if somewhat truncated versions of the original model. Viewed in retrospect, their work marked a shift in impetus of the Chicago School, opening a new phase in its development that brought the discipline of geography to the forefront more than ever before. In the 1950s, beginning with Amos Hawley's *Human Ecology* and soon after the closely related work of Beverly and Otis Dudley Duncan, there was also a minor revival outside of Chicago of the ecological approach to studying cities.[17] It bolstered the "new"

15 Pertinent here is Eshref Shevky and Marianne Williams, *The Social Areas of Los Angeles: Analysis and Typology*, Berkeley: University of California Press, 1949. Also denoting a California shift in this new approach is Wendell Bell, "The Social Areas of the San Francisco Bay Region," *American Sociological Review* 18, 1953: 29–47; and Shevky and Bell's *Social Area Analysis: Theory, Illustrative Application and Computational Procedures*, Stanford: Stanford University Press, 1955.

16 C. Harris and E. Ullman, "The Nature of Cities," *Annals of the American Academy of Political and Social Sciences* 242, 1945: 7–17.

17 Amos Hawley, *Human Ecology: A Theory of Urban Structure*, New York: Ronald Press (1950) and *The Changing Face of Metropolitan America*, Glencoe, IL: The Free Press (1956); Otis Dudley Duncan and Beverly Duncan, *The Negro Population of Chicago: A Study of Residential Succession*, Chicago: University of Chicago Press (1957); Otis Dudley Duncan and Leo F. Schnore, "Cultural, Behavioral, and Ecological Perspectives in the Study of Social Organization," *American Journal of Sociology* 65: 132–46.

Chicago School and helped it persist up to the present day, albeit on the periphery rather than at the center of mainstream social science.

One major strand of the Chicago School revival, led primarily by urban geographers, turned to the rich multivariate statistical analyses of a new field of factorial ecology.[18] In this rejuvenated ecological synthesis, pioneered by the then Chicago geographer Brian Berry, a place was found for everything and everything seemed to settle in its appropriate place. What social area analysts called Ethnic Status was confined to enclaves, both voluntary and "induced," worlds unto themselves in the larger urban order. Family Status, or stage in the life cycle, followed a regular concentric zonation that cut across all income groups, with older childless apartment households in the densely populated center and younger families in detached suburban homes. Hoyt-like sectoral wedges of social class, defined as Economic Status, broke through the concentricity to radiate in many different directions from the real-and-imagined Central Business District. The composite model, as seen in figure 3.1, incorporated all the elements of the Chicago School into a statistically defined "spatial system" that redefined urban ecology as the spatial organization of the city. In Berry's phrase, the city was a system within a system of cities, part of a nested hierarchy of central places ranging from the hamlet to the largest metropolis, definable and explainable through the powerful tools of a new spatial science.

Factorial ecology, building on the growth of new hybrid fields such as urban economics and regional science, presented itself as a rigorous new approach to studying what I have been calling the spatial specificity of urbanism. This spatial specificity became increasingly encoded in statistically defined mappings of the transportation networks, income differences, rent geographies, commercial establishments, housing markets, and land-use patterns of cityspace, all presumed to be produced by the locational strategies of "independent" households and business establishments in the industrial capitalist urban environment, with Chicago again serving as the primary laboratory. In *Contemporary Urban Ecology* (1977), Brian Berry and John Kasarda summarized the new perspective bluntly.

> An orderly social ecology results through like individuals making like choices, through regularities in the operation of the land and housing markets, and through the collaboration of similar individuals in excluding those of dissimilar characteristics from their neighborhood or in restricting certain minority groups to particular areas.[19]

18 Factorial ecology was an adaptation to spatial analysis of what was more generally called factor analysis, a method of reducing a massive amount of statistical data to a set of common factors or components based on their intercorrelations. Factor analysis developed out of attempts to measure human intelligence and skills among military recruits. Its uses expanded rapidly with advances in computational capability, to the point that, in the 1960s, it was hailed by some as the new "calculus" for the social sciences.

19 Brian J. L. Berry and John D. Kasarda, *Contemporary Urban Ecology*, New York and London: Macmillan, 1977: 130.

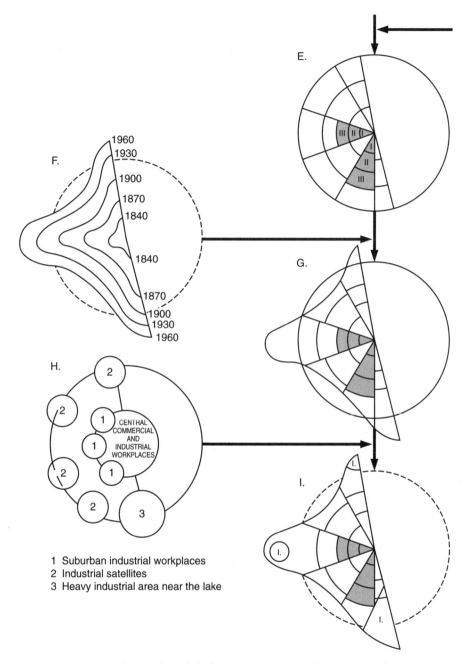

Figure 3.1 *Integrated spatial model of the metropolis – Chicago School* (Source: Brian J. L. Berry and John D. Kasarda, *Contemporary Urban Ecology*, New York: Macmillan, and London: Collier Macmillan, 1977: 125, figure 7.13, integrated spatial model of the metropolis)

On a larger scale, this logic of the urban land market took on a more comprehensive and ideological role in shaping how the specific geography of cityspace was studied. Each urban activity, from finding a home to starting a business, was seen as having the ability to derive "utility" from every site in the urban area, with this utility measured primarily by the rent the individual decision-maker was willing to pay for the use of the site. Extrapolating this process in the long run, it was assumed that the forces of competition in the urban land market would lead, if not interfered with or ignored, to the occupation of each site by what has been faithfully described as the "highest and best" use, that is, the activity or land use which is able to derive the greatest utility from the site and, therefore, willing and able to pay most to occupy it. Growing out of this presumed tendency for sites to be occupied by the "highest and best" uses was the expectation of an orderly "ideal" pattern of land utilization that simultaneously maximized rents throughout the urban system and "optimally" located all urban activities in their economically proper and rational place. Some version or another of this idealized methodologically individualist economic logic was hypothesized as the primary cause for all the regular patternings discoverable in cityspace.

The close association between this reconceptualization of urban studies and the field of economics provided many new opportunities to intervene in the social construction of cityspace that were not available to the original Chicago School urbanists. Economists, building on their important role in the New Deal and the recovery from depression and war, had become increasingly powerful in the federal government and in the formulation of national policies regarding economic development and related issues during the long postwar boom in the American economy. With the urban crises of the 1960s, the "new urbanists" piggy-backed on the economists to expand their "applied" role in the national policy arena, and to redefine and reinvigorate the field of urban planning. Through its innovative interdisciplinary program in Planning, Economics, and Geography, led by Rexford Tugwell and Harvey Perloff and extended by such students in the 1950s as John Friedmann, the University of Chicago took the lead in inculcating urban planners with a national policy perspective and training them in the most advanced theories and methods of the social sciences, especially economics. With the move of Perloff and Friedmann to UCLA in the late 1960s, the new Chicago School established a significant, if often quite revisionist, outpost on the West Coast, from which a lot more will be heard in later chapters of *Postmetropolis*.[20]

Meanwhile, the Department of Sociology at the University of Chicago persisted in its traditional approaches, building especially on the work of Morris Janowitz and Gerald Suttles. Janowitz expanded his research realm into polit-

---

20 To add a personal note: When the new School of Architecture and Urban Planning was established at UCLA in 1969, with Perloff as founding dean and Friedmann as chair, a search was begun to attract one of the new urban geographers/regional scientists to the Urban Planning Program. Brian Berry was an obvious first choice, but he refused to leave Chicago. Suboptimizing, the School hired a young geographer teaching at Northwestern University named Soja.

ical and military sociology, publishing books on the rising power of the New Military, the changing role of the professional soldier, and the redefinition of national patriotism, but he maintained an intellectual and often policy-oriented foothold in Chicago and in urban studies. One specific example of this is contained in the statement in his introduction to a new edition of the School's classic text, *The City*, quoted above as a lead-in to this section.

It was Suttles, however, who added most to the ecological and spatial traditions of the Chicago School, especially to our understanding of its putative core focus: "the social relations generated by territoriality." In *The Social Order of the Slum* (1968) and *The Social Construction of Community* (1972), Suttles investigated the importance of territorial behavior – for gangs as well as middle-class suburban homeowners – as an integral part of the spatial specificity of urbanism. Still imbued with that search for "moral order" that is a hallmark of the Chicago School tradition, he grounded his work in one of the most important roots of synekism. "Copresence alone," he writes, "makes people captive judges of each other's conduct and requires them to develop some communicative devices for anticipating and interpreting each other's judgements." He also gently chides mainstream sociology for its rampant despatialization and abandonment of urban ecology.

> [S]ociologists seem uncomfortable with such a principle or organization as territoriality, [but] their skepticism is scarcely warranted by what seems an implicit judgement of the arbitrariness of territorial selection. In retrospect such selective principles as age, sex, kinship, race, or ethnicity are similarly arbitrary in the sense that they involve human choice rather than a subsocial (e.g., innate, determined) pattern. More positively, however, such a forthright inclusion of territoriality needs to be initiated because we are surrounded by examples of it that will go unstudied unless they are frankly approached as social facts. (1972: 17)

Looking back, the Chicago School and its followers must be duly recognized as the first successful attempt to develop and sustain an explicitly spatial theorization of the city, no small achievement given the despatializing theories of scientific socialism and the equally despatializing tendencies that accompanied the late nineteenth-century formation of the social sciences. But at the same time, it was also a confusing diversion away from a more critical understanding of spatiality and the revealing spatial specificities of urban life. The Chicago School and its followers locked into a myopic view of the geohistory of cities and created a depoliticizing illusion of urban specificity that concentrated interpretation solely on surface appearances and behaviors.[21] Under this "realist illusion," as Henri Lefebvre called it, the perceived space of the city and the most directly evident expressions of material spatial practices – the focus for what I have described as a Firstspace perspective – are

---

21   As an example of this depoliticization of space and spatiality, see Dennis Smith, *The Chicago School: A Liberal Critique of Capitalism*, New York: St. Martin's Press, 1988. Despite a valiant effort to picture the Chicago School as a social movement deeply critical of capitalism, the book is an exercise in sociologism, almost devoid of any spatial imagination.

made into the only real geography to be studied, explained, and attended to in public policy, urban planning, and social as well as spatial science. What lies beneath the surface of social spatiality is either naturalized as naively given and "ecologically" determined, and hence subject to the action-numbing adage "That's the way it is and there is nothing much we can do about it"; or else it remains invisible and thus irrelevant to both theory and practice.

This, by the way, does not mean that the views of Marx and Engels on city-space are intrinsically much better. They lead too easily to what Lefebvre described as the "illusion of transparency," in which the concrete spatialities of urbanism become luminous, completely knowable through the application of an epistemologically rigid but all-seeing mode of explanation, what contemporary critical scholars call a totalizing metanarrative. In such a hyper-metropic (excessively farsighted) as opposed to myopic view, perceived space and spatial practices are seen merely as empirical projections of a deeper rational or logical imperative (no matter how complex these appearances might be); or they are virtually dispensed with entirely, as meaningless complications of the metanarrativized blueprint of empirical social reality. Either way, what I have been describing as the spatial specificity of urbanism tends to disappear as a subject worthy of serious analysis. Geohistory becomes just history, the socio-spatial dialectic is subsumed by the determinative power of sociality, class analysis loses touch with its specifically urban origins, and urban theory becomes sidetracked into studying social processes that may take place incidentally *in* cities but are not intrinsically shaped, in any significant way, *by* cities. To get the discussion back on track, and to explore a very different view of the spatial specificity of urbanism, we must leave Chicago and go elsewhere.

Chapter 4
Metropolis in Crisis

Space is not a "reflection of society," it *is* society . . . Therefore, spatial forms, at least on our planet, will be produced, as all other objects are, by human action. They will express and perform the interests of the dominant class according to a given mode of production and to a specific mode of development. They will express and implement the power relationships of the state in an historically defined society. They will be realised and shaped by the process of gender domination and by state-enforced family life. At the same time, spatial forms will be earmarked by the resistance from exploited classes, from oppressed subjects, and from dominated women. And the work of such a contradictory historical process on the space will be accomplished on an already inherited spatial form, the product of former history and the support of new interests, projects, protests, and dreams. Finally, from time to time, social movements will arise to challenge the meaning of spatial structure and therefore attempt new functions and new forms.

Manuel Castells, *The City and the Grass Roots* (1983): 4

Capital represents itself in the form of a physical landscape created in its own image, created as use values to enhance the progressive accumulation of capital. The geographical landscape which results is the crowning glory of past capitalist development. But at the same time it expresses the power of dead labour over living labour and as such it imprisons and inhibits the accumulation process within a set of physical constraints . . . Capitalist development has therefore to negotiate a knife-edge path between preserving the exchange values of past capitalist investments in the built environment and destroying the value of these investments in order to open up fresh room for accumulation. Under capitalism, there is then a perpetual struggle in which capital builds a physical landscape appropriate to its own condition at a particular moment in time, only to have to destroy it, usually in the course of crises, at a subsequent point in time. The temporal and geographical ebb and flow of investment in the built environment can be understood only in terms of such a process.

David Harvey, "The Urban Process Under Capitalism" (1978): 124

Rehearsing the Break: the Urban Crisis of the 1960s

The urban crisis that exploded all over the world in the 1960s was one of several signals that the long postwar economic boom in the advanced industrial countries was coming to an end. Just as the Vietnam War, the rise of OPEC, and other reassertions of the power of the less industrialized world began to challenge the long-established global order that helped to sustain the boom, the specifically urban order of the large capitalist metropoles that were the national and regional control centers for the global economy began to disintegrate in uprisings of those who had profited least from the postwar economic expansion. This was no passing phase of rebelliousness that could be responded to with piecemeal reforms. By 1973–4, the world economy had entered its steepest decline since the Great Depression and many leading economic and political figures had become convinced that "business as usual" could no longer be as confidently depended upon to assure continued economic expansion, especially in the face of such explosive social resistance. While most clung stubbornly to the old ways, a few began exploring alternative economic and organizational strategies that might hopefully lead the way to economic recovery and deal effectively with the spreading unrest.

With hindsight, what was being initiated during this period can be described as a *crisis-generated restructuring* process that would be felt at every scale of human life, from the global to the local, marking another critical turning point in the geohistory of urban-industrial capitalism. It was also a period that, with similar hindsight, can be looked at as a transformative moment in the geohistory of modernity, a time of accelerated change when seemingly all that was solid and dependable in the recent past melted into the intensely unsettling "air" of the present. Paralleling the crisis-generated restructuring of capitalism, the emerging crisis of modernity generated calls for alternative modernisms and new forms of modernization to redirect the effort to make practical and theoretical sense of the then contemporary world.

As had occurred in previous periods of accelerated and crisis-driven restructuring (from the Great Depression to the Second World War, during the last decades of the nineteenth century, and in the Age of Revolution), the future course of modernity and capitalism became embroiled in an ideological and strategic competition between establishmentarian, reformist, and radical restructuring camps, each operating across the political spectrum, from far Left to far Right. The conservative establishmentarians or unreconstructed Modernists demanded continued adherence to the tried and true. The reformists or neo-Modernists opened their orthodoxies to new ideas and strategies, but placed significant limits on the extent and depth of restructuring that would be allowed. For the third group, those most comfortable with the label Postmodernist, the changes taking place were of such magnitude that old ways of thinking and acting had to be radically deconstructed and reconstituted, if not abandoned entirely, to meet the new demands and challenges of the contemporary moment.

Such brief characterizations of the major political alignments that arose in response to the 1960s urban crisis and its aftermath of intensified and highly competitive material and ideological restructuring oversimplify what has been a much more complex and nuanced set of developments over the past thirty years. They provide a useful starting point, however, for re-entering the discourse on urban studies and extending the discussion of the geohistory of cityspace closer to the present. It has now become increasingly clear that the urban crisis of the 1960s exposed deep weaknesses and serious gaps in the urban theories and practices that had evolved over the previous century. Nearly all explicitly urban theory and the empirical investigations of the city and its spatial specificity up to that time were in one way or another involved in a search for regularity and *order*, a moral order in the case of the early Chicago School sociologists, a geo-statistical order for the new urban geographers and new urban economists following in their footsteps. Throughout the social sciences, various forms of systems analysis, backed by increasingly sophisticated and "cybernetic" computer technology, invigorated this emphasis on order, equilibrium, and continuous evolution, often in the form of stagelike models of modernization and progressive development. When the modern urban order began to break down on the streets of Los Angeles, New York, Paris, Mexico City, and almost every other major modern metropolis, there was thus little available in established social science approaches to help us understand what was happening in cities, why this was happening, and what could be done in response.

Into this theoretical and empirical breach, new approaches to understanding the dynamics of industrial capitalist cityspace began to develop. Most of these new approaches drew heavily on the writings of Marx and Engels, an intellectual tradition that, although not specifically focused on cities, was more attuned than mainstream urban studies to conditions of disorder, discontinuity, social upheaval, and economic crisis. Influenced mainly by sociologists in France and Italy and geographers in Britain and North America, a neo-Marxist variant of urban studies emerged and took the lead in making practical and theoretical sense not just of the urban crisis but of the very nature of the urbanization process and the social production of cityspace. This neo-Marxist School of Urban Political Economy created a new paradigm for studying the city and its complex geohistory that would deeply influence and radically politicize urban scholarship up to the present.[1]

The focus for this new school of urban studies was the modern Fordist-Keynesian metropolis, the agglomerations of mass production, mass consumption, social welfare practices, and governmental power that were the most propulsive centers leading the postwar economic boom. Although Paris probably came closest, no single city became the dominant social laboratory for the new urban political economists. Their efforts hinged instead on constructing a more general theory of the industrial capitalist city in which explanations for the spatial specificity of urbanism (and for urban crisis) became rerooted in the social relations of class and power underlying capitalism as the dominant mode of production. In some ways, this marked a return to Engels and his writings on Manchester, a revived radical political economy of urbanization that revolved around the inbuilt social necessity within capitalism to produce and reproduce poverty and inequality. Almost everything that

---

1 For a comprehensive collection and overview of the major writings in this new field, see Michael Dear and Allen J. Scott eds., *Urbanization and Urban Planning in Capitalist Society*, London and New York: Methuen, 1981.

was happening in the postwar metropolis was attached to this neo-Marxist interpretive framework: mass suburbanization, the rise of an automobile-based culture of consumerism, metropolitan political fragmentation, the decline of the inner city, increasing segregation and ghettoization, changing labor – management relations, the disciplinary technologies of "philan-thropic" Fordism and the Keynesian welfare state, and the rise of new social movements aimed at achieving greater social justice in the city.

A particularly favored focus of the new School of Urban Political Economy was the practice of urban planning. Even in its most progressive forms, urban planning was seen as functioning primarily, if often unintentionally, to serve the basic needs of capital and the capitalist state. Indeed, it was this focus on urban planning and its role in shaping the built environment via the provision of housing, transportation, social services, and "urban renewal" that kept the urban political economists most in touch with the spatial specificity of urbanism. One side effect of this emphasis on urban planning and the associated realm of urban politics was a fixation on what would be called *collective consumption* rather than on the foundational industrial production processes of the capitalist city. The vital links between industrialization and urbanization were not ignored, but they were assumed to be already understood within Marxism itself. What was less well understood was mass consumption and consumerism, the consolidation of the centralized welfare state, mass suburbanization and the rapid growth of the middle class, and the growing political force of new social movements organized around gender, race, and ethnicity, as well as geographical location within the sprawling urban fabric, such as homeowners' movements and related efforts to control urban growth. For the most part, issues relating to the natural environment remained in the background.

As cityspace was increasingly conceived as the specialized context for collective consumption, urban politics came to be defined primarily around a struggle for these collective goods and services that pitted the local and national state (with the assistance of urban planners) against the empowerment strategies of the new urban social movements. That the ultimate struggle was centered in the industrial workplace and the labor process was taken for granted by the urban political economists, but its immediate political expression in the urban context was located primarily in the place of residence and in neighboring communities of resistance. The fields of contention were thus explicitly spatialized, emplaced within the specific geography of urbanism, and centered not so much on industrial production as on the social and spatial reproduction of cityspace and the urban order. Although the term was never explicitly used, a new dimension was being added to synekism, the stimulus of urban agglomeration, in these reformulations. Engels had already hinted at the potency of spatial propinquity and agglomeration in stimulating proletarian class consciousness. In the Fordist–Keynesian metropolis, the potential power of smaller-scale urban social movements organized around a consciousness of specifically urban spatiality was brought to the forefront of radical urban studies and politics.

The two quotes that head this chapter provide perhaps the most insightful and explicitly spatial encapsulations of the neo-Marxist approach to urban political economy and, more specifically, to understanding the causes and consequences of the urban crises of the 1960s. In the language of the Marxist sociologist, Manuel Castells links space and society in a historical process of social production that expresses and performs the interests of the dominant class and implements the power of the state, which specifically includes gender domination and the shaping of family life. At the same time, the spatial forms that arise from these social processes become focal points for resistance from exploited classes, oppressed subjects, dominated women. Finally, from time to time, these communities of resistance crystallize into powerful social movements that challenge the meaning of spatial structure and attempt to reorganize cityspace to support new functions, forms, interests, projects, protests, and dreams. There is thus a constant tension embedded in cityspace that revolves around the power differentials between social classes, between men and women, between the state and civil society, that is manifested and performed in and around the evolving spatial specificity of urbanism.

The Marxist geographer David Harvey, whose work was closely intertwined with Castells's at least until the early 1980s, paints a similar picture, albeit one that is centered much more specifically on the power and logic of capital. Whereas he gives less attention than Castells to social movements organized around collective consumption and radical urban subjectivity, Harvey uncovers another urban dynamic (and source of urban crisis and restructuring) that is deeply embedded in the spatial specificity of the capitalist city. Like Castells, he argues that a particular landscape, a specific urban geography, is created by capitalism in its own image, designed above all to facilitate the accumulation process. But the very fixity of the urban built environment, he notes, creates problems for continued capitalist accumulation, for it locks into particular spatial locations investments that, over time and especially during periods of crisis, may no longer be as effective (profitable) as they were in the past. The impossibility of moving built forms (think, for example, of the Empire State Building) freely around the physical landscape when they no longer meet immediate needs, creates a perpetual dilemma for capital and for the social construction of capitalist cityspace. Capitalist development must therefore always negotiate a precarious balance between the creation and the destruction of its specific geography, a knife-edge path that becomes most problematic during times of crisis and restructuring.

Harvey (1982) would later add to this formulation the notion of a *spatial fix* to describe how capital seeks to reorganize its specific urban and regional geography in the attempt to respond to crisis and open up "fresh room for accumulation." Although Harvey would insist that this search for a "magical" spatial solution to the problems of capitalism can never be completely successful, his conceptualization of the spatial fix, added to his observations on the built environment, opened up a new and assertively geographical dynamic to the study of urban crisis and restructuring, and even more broadly to our understanding of the materialist geohistory and uneven development of capitalism. Harvey's ideas were not adopted by all radical political economists, in part because they often appeared too spatially assertive and deterministic. But it was precisely this creative spatialization of Marx's analysis of the logic and "inner workings" of capitalism, its inbuilt "anarchy of production" and tendencies toward crisis, and especially the restructuring process itself as a search for a spatial fix, that may, in retrospect, prove to be Harvey's greatest achievement.

Combining these brief condensations from the work of Castells and Harvey provides a fitting introduction to the new school of urban studies that developed out of the 1960s urban crisis; and also offers one of the best ways of understanding the origins not just of the general crisis itself but of the subsequent three decades of crisis-generated urban restructuring. During these three decades, through a remarkable series of books, both Castells and Harvey would maintain their intellectual and political leadership in what can be broadly defined as the "marxification" of urban scholarship. They would not be without their critics, but each has proven capable of responding to the most cogent criticisms with creative and flexible restructuring of their own theoretical and political perspectives and projects, so much so that their most recent work contributes significantly to the reconceptualization of the new "postmetropolitan" cityspaces that are emerging today and form the focus of all subsequent chapters.

To continue our critical remapping of the geohistory of cityspace through the eyes of Manuel Castells and David Harvey, it is useful to look back to the books each produced almost simultaneously in the early 1970s, in the immediate aftermath of the 1960s urban upheavals: Manuel Castells, *La Question urbaine*, published in 1972 and translated as *The Urban Question* in 1977; and David Harvey, *Social Justice and the City*, published in 1973. These two books were the primary launching pads for the radical school of Urban Political Economy that would influence critical studies of cities and regions for the next twenty years.

Manuel Castells and the Urban Question

The student uprising and related social unrest in May 1968 in Paris was the trigger for a radical rethinking of "the city" and "urbanism as a way of life," to refer back to the terms used by the Chicago School. The leading intellectual figure inspiring the uprising, with his calls for politicizing the spatial specificity of urbanism and taking control over the social production of cityspace, was Henri Lefebvre.[2] As I argued in the first two chapters of *Thirdspace* (1996),

2   For an interesting discussion of Lefebvre's inspirational role for the student uprising in May 1968, see Rob Shields, *Henri Lefebvre: Love and Struggle*, London and New York: Routledge, 1998. For Lefebvre's own interpretation of these events, see *L'Irruption de Nanterre au sommet*, Paris: Anthropos, 1968 (translated as *The Explosion: From Nanterre to the Summit*, New York: Monthly Review Press, 1969). In May 1968, Lefebvre was the head of the Institute of Sociology at the University of Nanterre, in suburban Paris. Also there at around the same time were Alain Touraine, Jean Baudrillard, and Manuel Castells.

Lefebvre's work on "the rights to the city," "everyday life in the modern world," the social struggles over "the production of space," and the need for a specifically "urban revolution," introduced a trenchant new perspective on the politics and ideology of cityspace as well as the geohistory of modernity and capitalism. More than anyone else, Lefebvre creatively initiated if not an actual urban revolution then a conceptual revolution in urban studies that would culminate, albeit after two decades of relative neglect and misunderstanding, in a pronounced "spatial turn" that would be felt not just in urban studies but throughout all the human sciences.

La Production de l'espace, published in 1974, was the key work in this radical transformation of urban studies.[3] It established, more clearly than his earlier work, the philosophical foundations for a dramatic recovery of the spatial specificity of urbanism as a theoretical object as well as a problematic and consciousness-raising context for progressive political action. But the impact of Lefebvre's expansive geographical imagination was immediately deflected in the intellectual ferment that followed the failure of the May 1968 uprisings in Paris to stimulate significant change. This put a shroud of suspicion over Lefebvre's ideas that would weaken his impact on the new radical political economy and sociology developing not just in Paris but in Britain and North America. Leading the way in this deflection was Manuel Castells and his provocative work, *La Question urbaine*, published two years before *La Production de l'espace*.

A Spaniard from Catalonia, Castells was a sociology student in Paris in the early 1960s, where he came under the influence of three of the most prominent French scholars of the time: Henri Lefebvre, Alain Touraine, and Louis Althusser. In the original French version of *The Urban Question*, Castells creatively synthesized Lefebvre's writings on cities and space, Touraine's sociology of social movements, and Althusser's structuralist Marxism in one of the most influential books written about cities in the second half of the twentieth century. From the very first chapters, it became clear that a primary target for his hard-lined structuralist critique of urban studies was the explanatory power given to the spatial specificity of urbanism and to cityspace in general within the broad field of urban sociology and in particular in the work of both the Chicago School and Henri Lefebvre.

Castells begins his critical attack by reformulating the geohistory of the third Urban Revolution. "The development of industrial capitalism," he writes, "contrary to an all too widespread naive view, did not bring about a strengthening of the city, but its virtual disappearance as an institutional and relatively autonomous social system, organized around specific objectives" (1977: 14). He describes this as a "loss of the city's ecological and cultural particularism" and uses this loss as a springboard to deprivilege "the city" and its "spatial forms" as a theoretical object for (Marxist) sociological analysis. In

---

3   Its very late translation into English in 1991, the year of Lefebvre's death, stimulated both a revival of interest in his work throughout the English-speaking world and a significant rethinking of existing geographical and spatial theory and practice. See *The Production of Space*, tr. Donald Nicholson-Smith, Oxford, UK, and Cambridge, MA: Blackwell, 1991.

his view, industrial capitalism (shorn of its intrinsic urbanness) and the industrial bourgeoisie (no longer rooted in *bourg*) take control over the social production of urban space and diffuse their citybuilding prowess to a global scale, leaving the city behind as merely the container or canvas for capitalism's inscriptions.

These appeared to many to be reasonable observations on the transition from the second to the third Urban Revolution. The rise of the modern capitalist nation-state was in part defined by its usurpation of authoritative territorial power from the old city-states. But at the same time, the new territorial power did not float in the air. It was grounded in a national system of state-cities charged with maintaining not just the political geography of the nationalist state but also its integrity as a cultural and economic space, both real and imagined. The state was no longer coterminous with the city, nor was the city as autonomous and hegemonic as it was in the era of city-states. But too much is lost, in my view, by claiming the "virtual disappearance" of the city as a "relatively autonomous social system, organized around specific objectives." Destroyed in the wake of such a formulation are the self-generating capacity of synekism and virtually all other dynamic effects arising from the spatial specificity of urbanism. Indeed, it might be argued that the capitalist nation-state was created in and from cityspace, following a pattern of generative synekism that has characterized the innovative "crucible" of cities for the past 10,000 years.

Nevertheless, this was a particularly appealing interpretation of what Castells called "the historical process of urbanization," especially for Marxists whose insistently historical materialism left little room for spatial or any other form of ostensibly extra-social or "external" causality. What was happening then was perhaps not so much an actual weakening of the importance of cityspace in the rise of urban-industrial capitalism, as a virtual expunging of urbanism and its specific geography from Marxist and socialist theory and critique, a process I have argued had its roots in a space-blinkered historicism arising in both scientific socialism and the new social sciences in the late nineteenth century. But why did Castells, with his rich geographical imagination and focus on the urban question, take such a dismissive stance? Whose voices was he combating? What was behind this subordination of the spatial?

At the time *La Question urbaine* was published, most of liberal and radical urban sociology was no longer under the ecological sway of the Chicago School, but it was the Chicago School that Castells turned on most fiercely. Behind this attack, which many considered the most formidable of all the critiques of the Chicago urbanists, was a more personal and political target: Henri Lefebvre's "urbanistic" views that so inspired the failed uprising of 1968. To explain historically how what he considered to be such an errant and politically "naive" view persisted in urban studies, Castells castigated both the liberal Chicago School and the radical urbanism of Lefebvre for their promotion of what he called an "urban ideology" and a "myth of urban culture."

The urban ideology . . . sees the modes and forms of social organization as characteristic of a phase of the evolution of society, closely linked to the technico-natural conditions of human existence and, ultimately, to its environment. It is this ideology that, in the final analysis, has very largely made possible a "science of the urban", understood as theoretical space defined by the specificity of its object. (1977: 73–4)

To this he would add, concluding his chapter on "The Myth of Urban Culture":

The social efficacity of this ideology derives from the fact that it describes the everyday problems experienced by people, while offering an interpretation of them in terms of natural evolution, from which the division into antagonistic classes is absent. This has a certain concrete force and gives the reassuring impression of an integrated society, united in facing up to its "common problems". (1977: 85)

Castells describes Chicago School sociology and its extensions as a "science of the new forms of social life appearing in the great metropolises" (1977: 76). This new science of the urban, he argues, was built primarily on the "confusion-fusion" that arose from causally linking a "certain ecological form" to a "specific cultural content." The Chicago urbanists were thus captured on both sides of this relation by either a narrow "ecologism" or an equally reductionist "culturalism," with each narrowing further exacerbated by an overarching evolutionary and organic historicism. In a pithy phrase, Castells captures all that he saw as wrong with the Chicago School and the many different branches of urban studies derived from it: *The "city" takes the place of explanation* (1977: 73). In other words, all aspects of social life in the city are presumed to be explainable as a product of cityness itself, a form of simplistic and circular reasoning that he contended was filled with unprogressive political consequences. It is easy to see how the power of this critique can lead to the throwing away of the vital dynamic of synekism with the dirtied bathwater of ecologism and culturalism.

At one level, Castells was doing little more here than elaborating on the internal critiques that had already developed within mainstream urban sociology to despatialize urban theory and empirical analysis and to shift attention to presumably non-spatial *social* processes in the construction of urbanism as a way of life. At another level, however, Castells was also redirecting modern sociology and the sociological imagination to a new set of (also presumably non-spatial) social processes that were related to capitalist industrialization, the social relations that lay behind "the division into antagonistic classes," and the neo-Marxist precepts of the emerging field of radical urban political economy. In a fundamental, if not fundamentalist, way, Castells was centering urban sociology in the structured and structuring effects of the social relations of production, consumption, exchange, and administration. Everything one might want to understand and explain in contemporary urban life was a product of this dynamic nexus of social relations, including the spatial specificity of urbanism.

Reflecting Lefebvre's influence or perhaps just carrying forward the greater comfort with space and spatial concepts that has marked francophone as against anglophone philosophy and social theory for more than a century, Castells consistently spatialized the definitions of these fundamental social processes and relations, often creating great confusion among those adopting his ideas, especially anglophone sociologists. Production is equated to the "spatial expression of the means of production" (exemplified in industry and offices); consumption is the "spatial expression of labour power" (housing, public amenities); exchange derives "from the spatialization of the transferences between production and consumption" (traffic, commerce); and administration is the "articulation of the politico-institutional system with space" (municipal administration, urban planning). He adds to this the ideological system, which "organizes space by marking it with a network of signs, whose signifiers are made up of spatial forms and whose signifieds are ideological contents" (1977: 126–7). But at the same time, he remains cautious of falling into the urbanistic spatialism of Lefebvre, his early mentor. Drawing a clear line of separation, he argues that "although spatial forms may accentuate or deflect certain systems of behavior, *they have no independent effect*, and, consequently, there is no systematic link between different urban contexts and ways of life" (1977: 108, emphasis added). The spatial specificity of urbanism must remain in view, but only as a product or outcome of social processes, never as an explanatory variable in itself.[4]

Castells politically taunted Lefebvre for producing a "left-wing version" of the Chicago School urban ideology, tossing out such labels as libertarian, spontaneist, millenarist, utopian, and humanist (a term of derision in Althusserian structuralism). In Castells's eyes, at least at that time, Lefebvre's primary misadventure was in moving away from a "Marxist analysis of the urban phenomenon" to an "urbanistic theorization of the Marxist problematic." As I have been arguing now for nearly twenty years, it is exactly this "provocative inversion" of Marxist analysis, from the marxification of spatial analysis to the spatialization of Marxism, that was Lefebvre's most momentous contribution to urban studies and more broadly to all the human sciences.[5] Lefebvre would

4 Most British and American radical sociologists, historians, and even some geographers would ignore these persistent but to them perplexing spatializations. A few would even use Castells to justify a further purging of any hint of spatial causality in studying cities and practically every other subject as well. A peak point in this backlash against the spatialization of sociology was reached in the second edition of *Social Theory and the Urban Question*, an influential text written by Peter Saunders and published by Hutchinson in 1986. Saunders sought literally to strip urban sociology from its "traditional preoccupation with spatial units such as cities or regions" and deemed the study of social-spatial interrelationships to be "both futile and diversionary" to what should be the true theoretical object: the non-spatial sociology of consumption.

5 Edward W. Soja, "The Socio-Spatial Dialectic," *Annals of the Association of American Geographers* 70, 1980: 207–25. See also *Postmodern Geographies: The Reassertion of Space in Critical Social Theory*, London: Verso, 1989.

never abandon the Marxist analysis of urban phenomena. Instead, he would add to its pre-eminent emphasis on historical materialism and social relations and processes an equally forceful and problematic spatial dimension. This expansion and reinvigoration of Marxism was rooted in both a dialectically entwined historical *and geographical* materialism (or more broadly, a geohistorical perspective), and what I described as a "socio-spatial dialectic" in which social processes/relations shape, for example, the spatial specificities of urbanism but are at the same time also significantly shaped by these spatial specificities.

Castells would never completely subscribe to this radical spatial re-theorization of Marxism, although his view of Lefebvre and the spatial problematic would soften significantly after *The Urban Question*. But even in *The City and the Grass Roots* (1983), from which the quote that heads this chapter is taken and in which Castells most forcefully breaks from the Althusserian structuralism that shaped the earlier volume, a boundary remains in effect, limiting how far his spatial sociology would be allowed to go. While space and spatial forms are activated prominently in the history of society, they still remain only as social products, performative and expressive outcomes of inherently historical and social, but not spatial, processes and forces.

Castells's writings have taken many different trajectories since *The Urban Question*, the most recent of which will be returned to in later chapters, for they continue to make important contributions to our understanding of city-space and urban development. In the 1970s and 1980s, his work focused on making practical and theoretical sense of the postwar Fordist-Keynesian metropolis and the social movements that arose, primarily around issues of collective consumption, to "challenge the meaning of spatial structure" and sustain "new interests, projects, protests, and dreams." During this period, Castells was particularly influential in North American (as well as South American) sociology, although in the USA his persistent and rich spatial imagination had relatively little effect on sociologists. The impact of his spatial thinking (much more so than Lefebvre's, at least until recently) was felt more directly in the fields of urban planning and geography. In 1979, he was appointed as a professor of Urban Planning at the University of California, Berkeley. By this time, he was already widely recognized by geographers as a leading Marxist urban theorist and had significantly influenced the work of David Harvey and other Marxist geographers. It is to Harvey, and specifically to his *Social Justice and the City*, that our story of the postwar development of urban studies now turns.

David Harvey's *Social Justice and the City*

Looking back over the second half of the twentieth century, it is difficult to find a book which has had a more definitive agenda-setting influence on so many different disciplines than David Harvey's *Social Justice and the City*

(1973).[6] Its impact on the field of modern geography was especially profound, for by the date of its publication, Harvey had already published *Explanation in Geography* (1969), a philosophical and methodological treatise that had catapulted him into being one of the leading geographers in the world. When in *Social Justice and the City* Harvey dramatically switched from mainstream liberal approaches to geography (Part I) to an avowedly Marxist perspective (Part II), virtually all of geography felt its effects. Geography being a relatively small field, Harvey's political and intellectual turn had a much wider and deeper impact than, say, if the economist Milton Friedman had announced his own conversion to Marxism. Here is Harvey's own description of this shift and his careful attempt to show that it was not a complete rejection or abandonment, but rather a creative expansion.

> The evolution which occurs in these essays naturally gives rise to contradictions and inconsistencies between them. The general approach contained in Part 2 is substantially different (and, I believe, substantially more enlightening) than that in Part 1. Yet the later chapters take on more meaning if it is understood how the general viewpoint they espouse was arrived at – hence the importance of recording the search process as it threads its way through the various essays here assembled. It is also important to note that the material content of Part 1 is not rejected but is incorporated and given new meaning by the evolving framework of Part 2.   (1973: 10)

Enough has been said for the moment about Harvey's Marxist formulations. What I wish to do here is recapture the arguments presented in the earlier chapters (Part I) of *Social Justice and the City* where Harvey presents his "liberal formulations" and brilliantly explores their most powerful interpretive possibilities, and ultimately their most severe limitations. In the Introduction, Harvey organizes this exploration around four intertwining themes: the "nature," as he called it, of Theory, Urbanism, Justice, and Space. In the first of two chapters on "Social Processes and Spatial Form," subtitled "the conceptual problems of urban planning," Harvey begins with the first extensive discussion of the differences between what he called the geographical and (following C. Wright Mills) the sociological imaginations. He concludes the discussion this way:

> The general point should be clear: the only adequate conceptual framework for understanding the city is one which encompasses and builds upon both the sociological and the geographical imaginations. We must relate social behavior to the way in which the city assumes a certain geography, a certain spatial form. We must recognize that once a particular spatial form is created it tends to institutionalize and, in some respects, to determine the future development of social process. We need, above all, to formulate concepts which will allow us to harmonize and integrate strategies to deal with the intricacies of social

6 David Harvey, *Social Justice and the City*, Edward Arnold, London, and Johns Hopkins University Press, Baltimore, 1973.

process and the elements of spatial form. And it is to this task that I now want to turn. (1973: 27)

In the second chapter, subtitled "the redistribution of real income in an urban system," Harvey applies his simultaneously geographical and sociological imagination to an analysis of the dynamics of cityspace in the modern metropolis in the aftermath of the 1960s urban crisis. Here he develops one of his most memorable and lasting insights: that the "normal workings" of the urban system, the day-to-day practices and particularities of urbanism as a way of life, tend all on their own to produce and reproduce a regressive redistribution of real income that persistently benefits the rich at the expense of the poor. Harvey described the capitalist city as an inequalities-generating machine *by its very nature*, thereby creating in the context of urban geographies and the interrelations of social processes and spatial form a fertile terrain for the cumulative aggravation of injustices. He specified this redistributive dynamic in three realms. One was the normal operations of the free market in land, labor, retailing, and finance, from the changing value of private property rights (especially when amplified or depleted by public investments) to the risk-avoiding redlining of banks and the location and pricing systems of supermarkets to make the "poor pay more." These free-market-generated inequalities arose, Harvey argued, not through conspiracy or corruption so much as from standard market conventions and competition, from how the unfettered urban space economy worked toward achieving maximum organizational efficiency for capitalist development. If there was a magic to the market, it was a dark and bleak sort of magic for many.

To this he added the everyday operations and practices of urban planning and public sector decision-making, providing a new and different explanation for the familiar problem of why the "good intentions" of liberal (and even some radical) planners so often result in those "unexpected consequences" and "great planning disasters" that urban critics like to write about, like the transformation of "urban renewal" into "poor people removal." The urban public realm never acts as a free agent, Harvey argued, but always within the powerful economic and political fields shaped by market competition and profit-maximizing behavior. Without public control over these market forces, even the most innovative and progressive planning programs are susceptible to co-optation by the invisible hands that generate, by their very nature, increasing inequality.

Finally, Harvey broadened his focus to what he would later call the "urbanization process under capitalism," especially as it is manifested in the evolution of urban form, the production of the built environment, and the territorial problems of metropolitan government. For these formulations alone, *Social Justice and the City* became required reading in virtually every major urban planning and geography department in the USA. It also infused the largely descriptive field of urban geography with a new theoretical framework and a more practical and applied orientation, bringing it into closer contact than ever before with the education and practice of urban planners.

Harvey capped his liberal formulations on the interplay of social process and spatial form with an explicitly spatial conceptualization of social justice based on these endemic redistributive effects of urbanization. Pushing the liberal discourse and its universalized principles of social justice to its limits, he creatively extended the concept of "territorial redistributive justice" and grounded it in a set of achievable goals based on need, contribution to the common good, and "merit," which he defined primarily in terms of maximizing the prospects of the "least advantaged territory" and its poorest residents. In this search for the means to achieve a just distribution of real income and resources justly arrived at, Harvey reached the end of his universalizing liberal formulations with a growing frustration that these laudable goals might never be achievable given the persistent power of the "normal workings" of the capitalist city.

In a philosophical transformation that would resonate throughout the field of urban studies and beyond, Harvey at this point vaulted into a Marxist critique that radically shifted the terrain defined by his four themes of Theory, Urbanism, Justice, and Space. Rather than in liberal formulations, he rooted the origins of redistributive injustice in the matrix of the social relations of production and, more generally, in what came to be called the class-structured "specific geography" of capitalism, a concept and a focus that bring us closer to a critical understanding of the spatial specificities of the capitalist city than at any earlier time in the twentieth century. For the next twenty years, the effort to make practical and theoretical sense of the specific geography of the capitalist city, where Harvey's work has always been concentrated, attracted the attention of progressive urban scholars from many different disciplines. A new critical discourse on urban political economy emerged, tying together what were formerly separate debates on social justice, urbanism, the social production of space, and the nature of social theory.

Social Justice and the City also contained another twist that would have a long-lasting effect. Without being overly explicit, Harvey opened up his neo-Marxist critique to what might be called radical modernist cultural politics. More than just an appreciation for the superstructural elements that impinge upon the urban economic base, this attention to culture and community, to race and ethnicity, to struggles over issues of collective consumption, social reproduction, and the built environment of urbanism arose most emphatically in his liberal formulations, but were also given some room in the construction of radical socialist subjectivity and in the struggles to overcome the exploitative class dynamics of urbanization.[7] Influenced by Lefebvre's spatial critique of everyday life in the modern world and Manuel Castells's theorization of

---

7 Significantly, perhaps, especially given the developments that would occur over the years after 1973, there is almost no mention of gender issues or feminism in *Social Justice and the City*, and very little attention is given to the writings of women on the themes of social theory, justice, urbanism, and space. Of the 144 authors cited in the Author Index, for example, only four are women; and while "Man–Nature Relationship" appears in the Subject Index, there is little in the listings or the text to suggest that women are involved too.

urban social movements, Harvey, from the very beginning, recognized the need to give more substantive attention to cultural issues in the new urban political economy and the Marxist geography that was developing around it. In subsequent years, this challenge would be raised again and again by almost everyone involved in studying the capitalist city and the political economy of urbanization. And it would provide the context and conjuncture for another transformative rethinking of social justice and the city as significant as that expressed in Harvey's shift from liberal to socialist formulations.

For a more detailed discussion of the development of a postmodern reconceptualization of cultural politics and of the intertwining strands of theory, urbanism, justice, and space, I refer you to chapters 3 and 4 of *Thirdspace* and to my essay written to commemorate the twentieth anniversary of the publication of *Social Justice and the City*.[8] In that essay, I rephrased Harvey's description, quoted above, of his transition from liberal to socialist formulations as a means of describing the move from modernist to postmodernist cultural politics. Repeating this rephrasing with slight revisions provides an apt conclusion to discussing Harvey's earlier take on theory-justice-urbanism-space as well as a fitting indicative introduction to the remaining chapters of *Postmetropolis*.

> The evolution which occurs between our approaches to the old (modernist) and the new (postmodernist) cultural politics naturally gives rise to contradictions and inconsistencies. The general approach to the new cultural politics is substantially different (and, I believe, substantially more enlightening). Yet the new approach takes on more meaning if it is understood how the viewpoints it espouses were arrived at – hence the importance of recording the search process as it threads its way through the various essays here assembled. It is also important to note that the material content and action strategies of the old cultural politics are not being rejected but incorporated and given additional meaning by the evolving framework of the new.

Summarizing the Geohistory of Capitalist Cityspace

From the mid-eighteenth century to the present, the geohistory of the third Urban Revolution can be told through the increasingly globalized economic and cultural rhythms of capitalist development and the associated interplay of modernization and modernism. Crucial to these globalizing rhythms has been a remarkably regular periodicity that has both fascinated and perplexed scholars and other observers throughout the twentieth century. Theorizing this periodicity and explaining its primary causal mechanisms continue to be controversial, but its broad outline seems increasingly to conform to past geohistorical events and retrospective interpretations of global development pat-

8   Edward W. Soja, "Margin/Alia: Social Justice and the New Cultural Politics," in Andy Merrifield and Erik Swyngedouw eds., *The Urbanization of Injustice*, London: Lawrence and Wishart, 1996. Parts of the discussion of *Social Justice and the City* presented here have been taken from this essay.

terns over at least the past 150 years. Moreover, what has been happening to cities, nation-states, and the world economy during the past 30 years has revived interest in these macroeconomic rhythms and increased their usefulness as a framework for making practical and theoretical sense of the contemporary moment.

Roughly 50-year cycles define this "long-wave" periodization of urban-industrial capitalism. The first clearly defined cycle begins in the middle of the nineteenth century, although some project back an earlier cycle to cover the preceding Age of Revolution (1789–1848). Each cycle or wave begins with several decades of accelerated economic growth and expansion in the most advanced industrial countries, such as characterized what Hobsbawm called the Age of Capital (1848–1878), the period of extraordinary economic expansion that followed the consolidation of the Industrial Revolution in northwestern European cities. These boom periods eventually peak in disruptive crises usually related in some way to growing constraints on continued capitalist accumulation and profits, and are followed by equally long periods of decelerated economic growth, increasingly frequent social crises, and what present-day scholars have termed *restructuring processes*, described most simply as attempts to restore the conditions for accelerated economic expansion. These periods of restructuring usually conclude in another round of crisis and upheaval, somewhat different from the better-understood "overaccumulation" crises that ended the boom years and generated the restructuring processes. Successful recovery from this second round of crises initiates the next long wave.

Three distinct periods of crisis-generated restructuring can be clearly identified. Each represents unusually turbulent times of experimentation, redirection, and change when, to use more contemporary terms, long-established economic, political, and cultural practices are selectively deconstructed and reconstituted in new and different forms. The first of these periods of restructuring and turbulent change followed the Age of Capital and lasted to the end of the nineteenth century, a period called the Long Depression in Europe and looked back on today as the *fin de siècle*. The second stretched from the 1920s through the Great Depression and the end of the Second World War. The third began in the late 1960s and early 1970s, and is still with us today as we enter the twenty-first century.

A recurrent feature of these macroeconomic cycles has been a tendency for distinctive new modes of capitalist development to emerge during the restructuring phase. The most successful lead the new growth period of the next cycle, consolidate as its dominant developmental paradigm, and then peak in their own distinctive period of crisis. Thus the initial phase of highly competitive free-market and strictly laissez-faire industrial capitalism was rooted in the stormy years between the revolutions of 1830 and 1848–9, consolidated in the Age of Capital, and peaked in the early 1870s, after which there were several decades of restructuring and transition during which another mode of capitalist development emerged. Lenin interpreted this late nineteenth-century restructuring as the onset of an age of imperialism (Hobsbawm's Age of Empire) and over-optimistically described it as capitalism's "last stage." Others emphasized the rise of large corporations and other new organizational forms that reshaped competition and control over domestic or national economies and reduced free-market competition through limited state intervention and the emerging power of corporate monopolies and oligopolies. Taking its initial shape in the last three decades of the nineteenth century, this new corporate-monopoly-imperialist mode of capitalist development would boom in the early twentieth century, only to fall into deep crisis again in the Great Depression.

A third phase, which in retrospect has been closely associated with the names of Henry Ford and John Maynard Keynes, emerged between 1920 and 1940 and defined the postwar boom years as Fordist and Keynesian, metonyms for a different mode of capitalist development built on mass production, mass consumption, mass suburbanization, and a widely established "social contract" drawing together big capital (symbolized by the automobile industry), large national labor unions, and big government intervention in the economy to stimulate growth and provide for expanded social welfare (hence the Keynesian label). It is this Fordist-Keynesian phase of capitalist development that entered into a crisis period in the late 1960s and is currently being significantly restructured, leading many scholars to describe the present era as post-Fordist (now often simplified to postfordist), post-Keynesian, postindustrial, postmodern, etc.

Ever since Lenin, there have been many attempts to define, explain, and learn from this increasingly apparent long-wave rhythm in the geohistory of the past two hundred years. The Russian economist Kondratieff provided abundant statistics to describe these cyclical rhythms, which to this day are typically called Kondratieff waves. Schumpeter and Keynes made similar observations during the interwar years, recognizing both shorter cycles and longer waves of crisis and restructuring (which Schumpeter famously described as periods of "creative destruction"). Beginning in the early 1960s, the Marxist economist Ernest Mandel gave an important geographical twist to these rhythms and composed perhaps the most elaborated and convincing long-wave analysis, capping his work with the prediction of an emerging new crisis period that he, also optimistically perhaps, defined as "Late Capitalism."[9] Without ever subscribing explicitly to long-wave models, Eric Hobsbawm chronicled in wonderful detail the concatenated progression of the "Ages" of capitalist development in ways that conform very closely to the long-wave periodization. More recently, W. W. Rostow recast his well-known "stages of growth" model into the rhythms of Kondratieff's waves, and, more relevant for present purposes, a cluster of geographer-planners, including Peter Hall, Brian Berry, and Ron Johnston, have used variations of

---

9 Ernest Mandel, *Late Capitalism*, London: Verso, 1975; and *Long Waves and Capitalist Development: The Marxist Interpretation*, Cambridge: Cambridge University Press, 1980.

the Kondratieff model to reinterpret urban development over the past two centuries.[10]

These later contributions have helped to connect the literature on the periodicity of capitalist development and modernization to our understanding of the geohistory of the industrial capitalist city. In *Postmodern Geographies* (1989), I attempted to build on these connections by presenting a series of prototype mappings, drawn mainly from North American cities, depicting the evolution of urban form in the period from 1820 to 1970. As reproduced with some changes in figure 4.1, the maps provide a useful way to move the geohistory of cityspace forward to the contemporary emergence of the postmetropolis as, in large part, a product of the most recent wave of crisis-generated restructuring.

The simplified maps begin with the small and compact Mercantile city of the USA, with its dense mixture of residences of many different income levels and social classes clustered around the key site of trade and commerce, the port or central railway station. Industry is still located outside the city in a mill town, typically where energy to power the machines is readily available. Also usually outside the city, but closer by, were the poorest residential areas, little more than clusters of ramshackle shelters. As noted by David Gordon (1978), this mercantile cityspace was filled with its own distinctive tensions and contradictions in early nineteenth-century America.[11]

> Commercial accumulation tended to generate uneven development among buyers and sellers . . . Because different socioeconomic groups were living and working closely together . . . these spreading inequalities became more and more physically evident . . . As inequalities reached their peak during the 1820s and 1830s, popular protests also seemed to intensify . . . Because the Commercial City retained the precapitalist transparencies of immediate, intimate, and integrated social relationships, commercial capitalist profits could not be masked. The quest for such a disguise . . . played a central role in prompting a turn to a new and ultimately more opaque mode of capital accumulation.   (1978: 36)

Gordon provides a more contextual and crisis-driven explanation for the transformation of the Mercantile city, one that is rooted in local responses to the "transparencies" of mercantile capitalism. In his view, the Mercantile or Commercial city contained the seeds of its own spatial restructuring even

---

10   Peter Hall and Paschal Preston, *The Carrier Wave: New Information Technology and the Geography of Innovation, 1846–2003*, London and Boston: Unwin Hyman, 1988; Brian J. L. Berry, *Long-Wave Rhythms in Economic Development and Political Behavior*, Baltimore: Johns Hopkins University Press, 1991; R. J. Johnston, *The American Urban System: A Geographical Perspective*, New York: St. Martin's Press, 1982.
11   David Gordon, "Capitalist Development and the History of American Cities," in W. Tabb and L. Sawers eds., *Marxism and the Metropolis*, New York: Oxford University Press, 1978. On a larger scale and with much greater variation and complexity, a similar situation existed in the more numerous and older commercial port cities of Europe, from London and Liverpool to Amsterdam, Hamburg, Venice, Genoa, and many others.

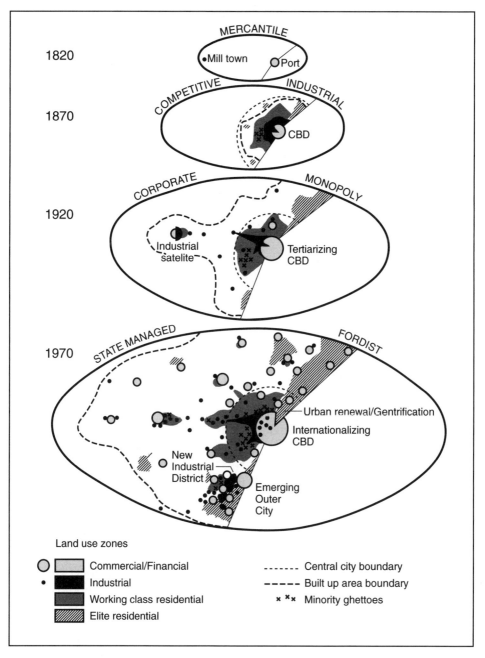

Figure 4.1 *Evolution of urban form in the USA* (Source: Soja, *Postmodern Geographies*, Verso, 1989: 174)

before its expansive industrialization. What emerged so paradigmatically in places such as Manchester and Chicago can thus be seen as a far-reaching "spatial fix," to use David Harvey's insightful term, the creation of a new specific geography designed to mask the most obvious transparencies of capitalist accumulation as a means of enhancing not just industrial production per se but also the ability to control and discipline the burgeoning urban population.

This "more opaque" model of the centralized and zoned Competitive Industrial capitalist city emerged erratically through the Age of Revolution and would help propel the expansive boom that lasted from the late 1840s to the 1870s, Hobsbawm's "Age of Capital." But as in the Mercantile City, this classic form of industrial capitalist cityspace would eventually breed its own forms of internal tensions and political unrest, necessitating another fix, another round of crisis-generated restructuring. As Engels acutely observed, the deep immiseration of workers and their extraordinary residential concentration in the inner ring of the city spawned an increasing class consciousness and mobilization, despite the opaqueness, the near invisibility, of the opulent bourgeoisie, now living in their distant gardened suburbs. Over the last three decades of the nineteenth century, which in the USA marked the end of the expansionary western frontier, the classic Competitive Industrial cityspace was significantly recomposed in an effort to provide a new spatial fix to the problems facing urban-industrial capitalism. This created not a fourth urban revolution but the first of a series of major restructurings of industrial capitalist cityspace, characteristically cloaked in the guise of modernization and redevelopment.

With the consolidation of what I earlier called the Corporate-Monopoly city in the early twentieth century, the discussion of the evolution of capitalist urban form becomes much more complex, for this restructuring process would generate a much greater diversity of specific geographies in the cities of the industrialized world. The classic cityspace observed by Engels and described by the Chicago School did not disappear, but its formerly well-defined and highly centralized structure began to disintegrate in many different ways. Much of what occurs can be described as a sequential and selective decentralization, of factories, residences, offices, warehouses, retail stores, public services and other urban activities. This not only stretched the concentric zones outward in a sprawling and increasingly haphazard process of suburbanization, it also made each of the existing zones much less homogeneous than they once were. Cityspace and urban life became increasingly fragmented, not just in terms of residential land use but also in patterns of local governance, social class, and race and ethnicity. Between 1870 and 1920, cities such as New York and Chicago also experienced a significant recentralization, especially with the concentration of financial and banking activities, corporate headquarters, and skyscraper office buildings in the Central Business District and civic center. These new occupants of the citadel took on increasing responsibility for planning and regulating the expansion and restructuring of cityspace in tandem with local government officials, an accommodating arrangement that was accompanied by a significant return of the "higher classes" to residences in the city center.

During the Great Depression and the Second World War, a second round of crisis-generated urban restructuring reshaped cityspace again. For the most part, this restructuring process would extend and elaborate many of the same tendencies that were evident in the last three decades of the nineteenth century, but the cumulative effect would produce some significant changes in the specific geography of the industrial capitalist city. Backed by the powerful alliance of big government, capital, and labor, the growth of mass production and its space-consuming assembly lines, along with the even more space-demanding rise of consumerism and mass suburbanization, led to an increasing dispersal of the once highly centralized location of factories and blue-collar workers in and around the downtown area of the central city. What was emerging was the Fordist regional metropolis, with its increasingly split personality and mentality, simultaneously yet separately urban and suburban. The enlarged "suburbia" that grew around most USA cities was deeply fragmented into scores of autonomous municipalities, each offering different kinds of escape from the growing problems of urbanism. Los Angeles and Detroit represented these developments particularly well, especially the dramatic rise of *suburbanism* as a distinctive way of life for a significant portion of the metropolitan population. The primary citadel of political and economic power, however, remained in the old city center, along with a residual infrastructure of hotels, restaurants, boutiques, and other specialized services for a small resident elite as well as for tourists and other occasional visitors.

The central core of the State-Managed Fordist city was constantly faced with decay and potential unrest, creating an open field for competing economic and governmental forces seeking entirely different "futures" for downtown "renewal." The battles over downtown, pitting those who wished to destroy and rebuild anew against those who sought a less destructive form of renaissance, were as much a defining feature of the Fordist-Keynesian regional metropolis as the rise of peripheral suburbia. After the urban explosions of the 1960s, Castells used the term *la ville sauvage*, the wild city, to describe the new urban forms that consolidated in the postwar period in North America and Europe. Trying to understand and explain this highly unstable and volatile cityspace, split into two worlds by suburbanization, metropolitanization, and political fragmentation, became the center of attention for the new school of neo-Marxist sociologists, geographers, political economists, and planners that would reshape urban studies for the next several decades. But by the time a more rigorous understanding of its inner workings was achieved, the wild city had begun to be significantly restructured into something else that could no longer be explained with the same success that was achieved for the postwar regional metropolis. Because we do not yet have a better or more specific term to describe this currently emerging metropolitan cityspace, I have chosen to call it the *postmetropolis* and will devote the remaining chapters to investigating how contemporary scholars have approached the task of trying to make practical and theoretical sense of its development. As Los Angeles has played a particularly representative and exemplary role in these investigations as well as in all three periods of restructuring of the industrial capitalist city, it will provide the primary empirical and theoretical focus for all that follows, starting in the next chapter with an extensive description of its geohistory of urbanization.

Chapter 5
An Introduction to the Conurbation of Greater Los Angeles

The contemporary city has many layers. It forms what we might call a *palimpsest*, a composite landscape made of different built forms superimposed one upon the other with the passing of time. In some cases the earliest layers are of truly ancient origin, rooted in the oldest civilizations whose imprint can still be discerned beneath today's urban fabric. But even cities of relatively recent date comprise distinctive layers accumulated at different phases in the hurly-burly of chaotic urban growth engendered by industrialization, colonial conquest, neocolonial domination, wave after wave of speculative change and modernization. In the last two hundred years or so the layers seem to have accumulated even thicker and faster in response to burgeoning population growth, strong economic development and powerful technological change.

David Harvey, "Urban Places in the 'Global Village': Reflections on the Urban Condition in Late Twentieth Century Capitalism" (1988)

De Certeau has suggested that the technology of perspective vision is complicitous with the conceptual construction of the mortifying screen. Lyotard, also, has described the flattening of visibility in textual space by analogy with the geometry of perspectival representation. Certainly, this technology of visual representation is one of many which intercede between reference to the city and our conceptualization of it, and we might include the map, the plan, or even the aerial photograph as additional examples of visual representation of the city whose technologies produce the two-dimensionality of the perspective view . . . [T]hese technologies of representation do not so much flatten the space of visibility as introduce its different spatiality of the visible into the very activity of reading . . . The reading of the image of the city involves a perpetual alternation between vision and its forgetting, an alternation which disrupts any neat reduction of either the image or its referent to a two-dimensional textual space.

Lawrence Barth, "Immemorial Visibilities: Seeing the City's Difference" (1996): 482

Here, alone of all the cities of America, there was no plausible answer to the question, "Why did a town spring up here and why has it grown so big?"

Morris Markey, seeing Los Angeles in 1938

Los Angeles – from Space: A View from My Window

On the wall in front of my desk at home in Los Angeles is a photographic image of Los Angeles taken from 450 miles above the ground. Its origins and provenance are printed below the picture: Scale 1" = 2.3 miles, Image Supplied by Earth Observation Satellite Company, Image Produced and Marketed by Spaceshots Inc. (with a street address and a local as well as 800 telephone number), copyright 1987 Spaceshots Inc. In an odd way, it reminds me again of that remarkable panorama of ancient Çatal Hüyük. It also provokes me to think again about the puzzling question raised in one of the headquotes: why did a town spring up here and why has it grown so big?

Stretching before me is one of the largest industrial metropolises the world has ever seen, an expressive peak point of the third Urban Revolution. Since the beginning of the twentieth century, more people have moved over greater distances to settle in the area shown in the satellite photo than in almost any other equivalent area on earth. In an ever-widening orbit of attraction, a swelling series of migratory waves has poured into the area south of the Tehachapi Mountains, inducing a net population growth in the larger region of Southern California that has averaged close to two million per decade, or over 500 new inhabitants appearing every day for almost one hundred years. And close to 80% of this growth has packed into the remotely sensed picture of "Los Angeles – From Space."

Los Angeles seen from outer space is one of the most visible human creations on the planet, the Cannibal City, Mike Davis called it, sprawling voraciously over the earthly landscape.[1] There are some natural breaks in the color-enhanced picture before me. Along most of the northern edge are the browned national forest preserves of the San Gabriel Mountains, peaking at over 10,000 feet, and extending still further east in the even higher San Bernardinos, partially powdered with snow. The thinner line of the Santa Monica Mountains comes in from the left along the vibrantly blue Pacific and almost connects to the San Gabriels; while jutting in at an angle from the southeast corner are the Santa Ana Mountains, gradually being eaten away by human settlement, like the Santa Monicas, as they approach the thick webs of occupation around downtown Los Angeles. Almost everywhere else are the gray and beige tones of the menacing metropolitan sea, lapping upslope like a rising tide.

An almost continuous ribbon of humanity stretches nearly a hundred miles from east to west across the entire picture, just below the transverse ranges. Running roughly from the city of San Bernardino to LAX (Los Angeles International Airport) on the Pacific rim, it is the continental approach path to Los Angeles from the east, lit nightly by the most dazzling urban kilowattage in the world, the air traveler's starry introduction to the vast metropolitan uni-

---

1 Mike Davis, "Cannibal City: Los Angeles and the Destruction of Nature," in *Urban Revisions: Current Projects for the Public Realm*, R. Ferguson, ed., Los Angeles: Museum of Contemporary Art, and Cambridge, MA: MIT Press, 1994: 39–57.

verse, the most breathtaking sight of the region. Overviewing this stretch in 1958, William Whyte used it to epitomize his vision of urban sprawl. He describes flying between Los Angeles and San Bernardino as providing "an unnerving lesson in man's infinite capacity to mess up his environment," an experience where "the traveler can see a legion of bulldozers gnawing into the last remaining tract of green between the two cities, and from San Bernardino another legion of bulldozers gnawing westward."[2]

Almost as long but much wider is the broad gray carpet unfolding southeastward from the Santa Monica Mountains into Orange County, defining what is locally called the LA Basin, the core of Greater Los Angeles, matted with freeways and so continuously built upon that it is virtually impossible to discern any residual green spaces whatsoever from 450 miles above or, for that matter, on the ground. There are probably fewer parks and open spaces in this vast swathe of Greater Los Angeles than in any other comparable urbanized region in the US. Squeezed into the upper left-hand corner of the picture, on the other side of the Santa Monicas, is the almost equally parkless expanse of the filled-up San Fernando Valley, America's prototype of televisual suburbia.

The satellite view provides a crude map of the occupied territory of Greater Los Angeles: the broad Basin in the center, nosing into the Pacific in the Palos Verdes Pensinsula, petering out in the southern flanks of Orange County, and containing a present-day population of over 8 million; the burgeoning Greater San Fernando Valley tucked away north of the Santa Monica Mountains and growing well beyond the picture to the High Desert and into Ventura County to the west, with a resident population of around 3 million; and the string of other Valleys (San Gabriel, Pomona, Santa Ana) wedged in between the San Gabriel and Santa Ana Mountains and opening eastward through what is locally called the Inland Empire, past San Bernardino and Riverside, and into the Low Desert toward Palm Springs, with another 3 million inhabitants. Nearly 15 million people come together here in five counties: Los Angeles, Orange, San Bernardino, Riverside, Ventura. And embedded in it all is a galaxy of more than 170 separate municipalities, an agglomeration of agglomerations, each one with its own geohistory, its own spatial specificity of urbanism. It is difficult to know where to start.

A Perpetual Alternation Between Vision and its Forgetting

The geohistory of the twentieth-century *conurbation* of Greater Los Angeles begins most effectively in 1870, after two decades of ethnic cleansing had erased much of the Latino heritage built up from the original founding

---

2   William H. Whyte, "Urban Sprawl," *Fortune* 57, 1958: 102–9; quoted in Mike Davis, "Cannibal City," footnote 1.

of El Pueblo de Nuestra Señora la Reina de Los Angeles in 1791.[3] It is at this point that the development of Los Angeles becomes attuned to the rhythms of crisis and restructuring that have shaped (and reshaped) industrial capitalist cityspace. Roughly using the periodization discussed in the previous chapter, the conurbation of Los Angeles can be seen as giving its own localized stamp to the general sequence of long waves: 1870–1900 (restructuring), 1900–1920 (boom), 1920–1940 (restructuring), 1940–1970 (boom), 1970–present (restructuring). What becomes most striking when this sequence is applied to Los Angeles is its remarkably continuous expansion, even during the periods of most intense crisis, depression, and restructuring. As Carey McWilliams, probably the finest critical historian of Southern California, has stated, "every city has had its boom, but the history of Los Angeles is the history of booms. Actually, the growth of Southern California since 1870 should be regarded as one continuous boom punctuated at intervals with major explosions.[4]

Taking a cue from McWilliams, a panoramic picture of the conurbation of Los Angeles – the social production of the gray matter that appears in the view from space – can be described in the rhythm of a virtually continuous expansion, occasionally slowed down somewhat but never reversed by national and global recessions, but nonetheless punctuated by some of the most violent urban social upheavals in American history. Some population growth statistics help to chart this rhythm of conurbation decade by decade (table 1).

Five waves of urban growth can be identified from these population figures, the first peaking in the 1880s, the next in the Progressive Era of the 1900s, and then in the "roaring" 1920s, in the two decades following the Second World War, and finally – and perhaps most anomalously – in the contemporary period of crisis-generated restructuring. Decennial figures for percentage growth rates at the crest of these waves decline over time, but the absolute numbers added consistently increase. Each wave drenched the landscape with a constellation of new municipalities, while from the center the City of Los Angeles grew like an octopus, desperately seeking its routes to the Pacific while reaching out for freshwater lifelines even further, to the Sierra Nevadas and the Colorado River. Here, then, are some snapshots of these population waves filling in the map of Greater Los Angeles, paying particular attention to the multiplication of municipalities as nodal points of agglomeration and to the equally punctuating moments of urban social explosion.

---

3 I revive the old term conurbation, first used by the Scottish planner-urbanist Patrick Geddes, in both its formal and processual meanings, that is, as a description of a particular spatial organization of urbanism and as a dynamic process of socio-spatial construction. Conurbation, as the coming together of a polycentric agglomeration of cities, towns, and villages, thus carries with it much the same meaning as synekism.

4 I have taken this quote and many other bits of information from Gordon DeMarco, *A Short History of Los Angeles*, San Francisco: Lexikos, 1988. Carey McWilliams's classic work on Los Angeles is *Southern California: An Island on the Land*, Salt Lake City: Peregrine Smith, 1979.

Table 1 Population growth in the five-county region of Los Angeles (000s)

Census year	LA County (percent)	Orange	SanBern	Riverside	Ventura	Region
1870	15 (79)	—	4	—	—	19
1880	33 (72)	—	8	—	5	46
1890	101 (67)	14	25	—	10	151
1900	170 (68)	20	28	18	14	250
1910	504 (78)	34	57	35	18	648
1920	936 (81)	61	73	50	28	1,150
1930	2,209 (85)	119	134	81	55	2,597
1940	2,786 (86)	131	161	106	70	3,253
1950	4,152 (84)	216	282	170	115	4,934
1960	6,011 (78)	709	501	303	199	7,724
1970	7,042 (71)	1,421	682	457	378	9,981
1980	7,478 (65)	1,932	893	664	530	11,490
1990	8,863 (61)	2,411	1,418	1,170	669	14,531

1870–1900: the WASPing of Los Angeles

The first surge of urban growth, peaking in the 1880s, added over 230,000 new residents to the tiny regional population of about 20,000 in 1870. The long-resident Californio population, a major target for Protestant racial purification ever since the American conquest of the Mexican southwest, dwindled in relative size and importance as their ranchos were transformed into prime real estate to feed the flood of White Anglo-Saxon Protestant American migrants. Rail connections were made to San Francisco in 1871, but it was the transcontinental links (the Southern Pacific in 1876 and the Santa Fe in 1885) that opened the floodgates, initially to the northeastern states and then, rolling westward like the American frontier itself, to Ohio, Indiana, Illinois, Michigan, Wisconsin, Nebraska, Kansas, and Iowa. By 1900, some were calling Los Angeles "Double Dubuque" and Long Beach "Iowa's seaport," as the region was filled with middle-class, middle-aged, middle-brow, and conventionally middle-western Americans intent on building not a centralized city but a far-flung network of middle-sized towns. What was being produced was indeed a new kind of urbanism, quite unlike Manchester or London, or even New York and Chicago, perhaps the first purely American cityspace.

This growth surge coincided with the first major restructuring of the competitive industrial capitalist city, but there was no such city to be found in the extreme southwest corner of the US. The urban crises arising in the larger industrial cities, the most densely centralized urban forms that ever existed, were not directly felt in Southern California. The old Pueblo and its downtown extensions continued to anchor the regional urbanization process, as it would up to the present, but around this center a much freer and more flexible urbanization process took place, reflecting the particularities of the local setting as well as some of the new urbanization processes that were reshaping cities "back East." In many ways, the cityspace of Los Angeles was created almost entirely by these new trends (suburbanization, the growth of satellite cities, the decentralization of manufacturing activities) unencumbered by the pre-existence of an established urban-industrial fabric. During this early period in its growth, Los Angeles felt the positive effects of urban restructuring without directly experiencing the crises from which they were being generated.

Twenty new municipalities were created in this period, adding to the three established cities of Los Angeles (incorporated in 1850), San Buenaventura about sixty miles to the west (1866) and San Bernardino sixty miles or so due east (1869). For those who would like to track the spatio-temporal punctuation of cities on the emerging map (see figure 5.2 for a composite picture), I will list for each period the new municipalities and their date of incorporation in a sidebar.

1870–1900

1878: Anaheim
1883: Riverside
1886: Santa Monica
        Santa Ana
1887: Colton
        Monrovia
1888: Compton
        Orange
        Redlands
        San Jacinto
        Lake Elsinore
        South Pasadena
        Pomona
1891: Ontario
1892: Redondo
Beach
1896: Corona
        Pasadena
1897: Long Beach
1898: Whittier
        Azusa

One can see very clearly that the polycentric sprawl of Greater Los Angeles was established right from the start. The nearly 100-mile-long East–West ribbon visible from 450 miles in space was already strung with its primary nodal centers, mainly along the new railway lines: San Bernardino, Riverside, Redlands, Colton, and Corona on the eastern flank; followed westward by Ontario, Pomona, Azusa, Monrovia, South Pasadena, Pasadena, and, a little to the south, to Whittier, where Richard Nixon would grow up; and then, west of downtown, a skip to the Pacific shores in Santa Monica and Redondo Beach. The great sprawl to the south (through Compton to the port city of Long Beach) and southeast into Orange County (Anaheim, Santa Ana, Orange) had also already begun.

How is this first burst of growth explained? Agricultural production plays a prominent role. The region's vineyards, citrus groves, beef ranches, and vegetable gardens would make it the richest agricultural area in the country by the turn of the century. Also significant were the sunny climate and the wondrous combination of beaches, mountains, and deserts that would attract health-seekers, retirees, vacationers, and "tourists" (a word some claim originated in its present usage in Southern California) from the great midwestern flatlands. And by 1900, the first gush from what would prove to be one of the richest petroleum pools in the world began to flow at a site located just west of the downtown core of the City of Los Angeles. But the one force that has been given the most emphasis and attention in the historical literature has been "boosterism," a term which, even if it was not first used in Southern California, was certainly developed here to its most skillful promotional effect.

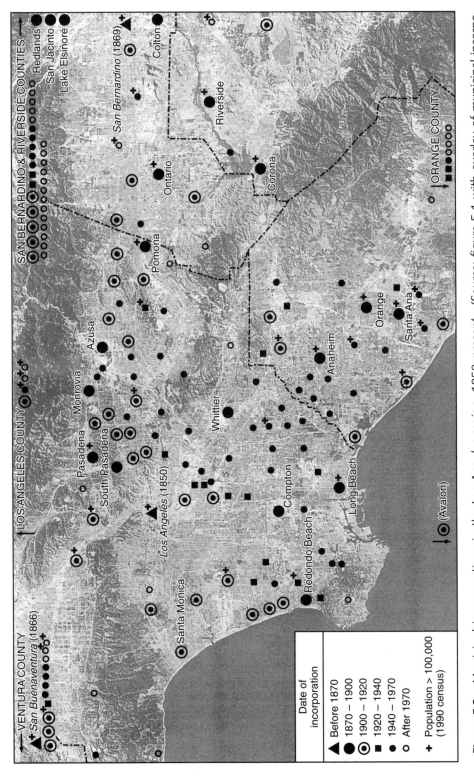

Figure 5.2 *Municipal incorporations in the Los Angeles region, 1850–present* (Source: figure 5.1 with overlay of municipal incorporations over time)

As early as 1886, it was claimed that Los Angeles had more real estate agents per capita than any other city in the world. Land speculators and developers were everywhere, and they worked closely with municipal officials (mainly real estate agents and land developers themselves) and the local media (the *Los Angeles Times* was established in 1881) to advertise and sell the regional attractions all over the country. Such "civic moonshine" became rampant in the aftermath of the Chinese Massacre in 1871 and reached full blast in the 1880s, boosted itself by the extraordinary national popularity of Helen Hunt Jackson's romantic idyll, *Ramona*, published in 1884; and the successful promotional efforts of Charles Fletcher Lummis, who aimed to make Los Angeles the new Eden for middle-class, white and Protestant American homeseekers. Even as boom turned to bust by 1890, an urban mythology of the grandest proportions had been created. It so successfully entered the national cultural imaginary that Los Angeles would continue to define the American Dream more than any other real or imagined place for the next hundred years.

My references to the Chinese Massacre and *Ramona* are meant to suggest that underneath this booming boosterism is another story that is less frequently told. In October 1871, a band of Yankee vigilantes, assisted by a few police officers, killed at least 20 of the 200 Chinese residents concentrated in and around the city center. Chinese stores and homes were looted in revenge for the accidental death of a white man who attempted to make a citizen's arrest of someone he thought was involved in a tong feud. Following the raucous downtown trial that convicted only seven of the twenty rioters arrested (with none serving more than a year in jail) and the payment to China of reparations by the federal government for the murder of its nationals, some eastern churches were ready to send special missionaries to the "Hell Town" out west.[5] But a new set of missionaries was already in place, prepared to rebuild Los Angeles's tarnished image along new lines that turned the city's back on its past, using creative local simulations of geohistory to redirect the local and national urban imaginary.

Over the next thirty years, a more subtle form of Chinese massacre would occur as "anti-oriental" hysteria continued to be felt along the entire Pacific coast. Despite the intensity of discrimination, the Chinese played a significant role in the 1880s surge of urban expansion as merchants, laborers, fishermen, and vegetable farmers. Thriving Chinatowns grew in almost every urban center in Southern California. The severe recession which hit the entire country in the early 1890s, however, hit hardest on the Chinese. Legislative and less official forms of racial discrimination, including some of the earliest zoning regulations designed to control the location of Chinese businesses and shops, added to the growing influx of Mexican labor and Japanese farmers, effectively squeezed out the Chinese presence in the urban economy, emptied

---

5   Hell Town was the name given to Los Angeles during the period following the American conquest of California in 1858, when on average there was a murder every day. See my discussion of Hell Town and the Chinese Massacre in *Thirdspace*, 1996: 221–2.

most of the Chinatowns, and confined the remaining Chinese to a small enclave adjoining the old Pueblo, near its present location.

A pattern was set by such disciplining of a "troublesome" minority. It exposed a teeming undercurrent of violent and institutionalized racism and xenophobia that would periodically burst to the surface in this "most American" city, briefly interrupting but also redirecting the urbanization process. In the aftermath of such outbursts, powerful private interests would gather in force to plan and promote their visions of an idealized urban future, often in the absence of effective public leadership and at the expense of a perceived "problem minority."

The "Ramona Myth" represented more subtle dimensions of this institutionalized racism. Jackson's *Ramona*, written as a social protest against the treatment of the American Indian, became a promotional and mythmaking spectacular that would last for at least fifty years. A full-blown tourist industry was built around the novel, with special tours to the "real" fictional sites and every imaginable replica of the story (baskets, pincushions, postcards) made available to the trainloads of curious visitors. The mythmaking, however, fed more than curiosity. By romanticizing the life of the Mission Indians, a more benevolent European era was recreated to contrast with the implied evils of the Mexican Californios. In more ways than one, it contributed significantly to the WASPing of Los Angeles.

1900–1920: the Regressive–Progressive Era

The first surge of urban growth sold an idyllic Los Angeles to Protestant America and rooted the regional economy in agriculture, land speculation, real-estate boosterism, tourism, and the provisioning of specialized health and leisure services to such groups as wealthy white retirees. The depression of the 1890s, however, demonstrated the weaknesses of this economic base for larger-scale urbanization. The regional population growth rate plummeted from 226% in the 1880s to 66% in the following decade. As it would all over the country, however, the new century opened with a boom in Los Angeles, one which shifted the focus of LA boosterism increasingly to industrial development and successfully plugged the region, as an auxiliary western outlier, into the dynamo of the American Manufacturing Belt in the northeast. In 1920, Greater Los Angeles was still behind most other major metropolitan areas in manufacturing employment, but it had just experienced a decade of employment growth that surpassed all other urban regions except Detroit, the powerhouse for the budding new Fordist economy that would consolidate triumphantly through the Great Depression and lead the long post-Second World War boom. A trajectory had clearly begun that would make the Los Angeles conurbation the country's leading industrial metropolis by 1990, after seven consecutive decades in which Los Angeles led all other city-regions in new manufacturing jobs added to the existing base.

Rapid economic development between 1902 and 1914 helped to quadruple the regional population to well over one million in the 1920 census. By 1920, Los Angeles had become one of the major petroleum-producing regions in the world and its leadership in motion picture production was firmly established.[6] A budding aircraft industry, producing the design for the first passenger plane, was born from the talents of local entrepreneurs named Douglas, Loughead (later Lockheed), and Northrup. An expanded port complex in San Pedro (annexed to the City of Los Angeles in 1906) and in Long Beach (now well established as the region's second largest city) had already passed nearly all its Pacific coast competitors, and the completion of the California Aqueduct in 1913 assured a sufficient water supply for large-scale urban expansion, speeding up the annexation process.

Significant migration streams from southern and central Europe, Japan, and especially Mexico (in 1920 Mexicans had become the largest immigrant group in Los Angeles and were for the first time since the late nineteenth century more numerous than African Americans) added to the growing influx of black and white American workers to create a substantial industrial labor force in what had already become the most racially diverse – and racially segregated – of Pacific coast cities.[7] Finally, the booming regional complex was effectively tied together by the automobile (Los Angeles in 1920 was ahead of all other major American cities in automobile registration and traffic was already gridlocking downtown), and by what was reputed to be the most extensive network of metropolitan mass transit in the world, dominated by the "red cars" of the Pacific Electric Railway Company.

Forty widely scattered new cities were incorporated during this period, reinforcing the sprawling, polycentric character of the urban built environment. Many of these municipalities were "black gold suburbs" built on the scattered pools of petroleum. Others grew at new industrial and warehousing sites, resorts, and studio locations. A very different looking American metropolis was taking shape, one where the oil derrick, the automobile, the airfield, the movie studio, the beach and mountain community, the immigrant labor camp and factory town, and the all-

1900–1920

1901: Covina
1902: Santa Paula
1903: Alhambra
    Arcadia
    Oxnard
1904: Fullerton
1905: Vernon
1906: Newport
    Beach
    Huntington
    Park
1907: Hermosa
    Beach
    Claremont
    Sierra Madre
1908: Inglewood
1909: Huntington
    Beach
1910: Chino
    Hemet
1911: Burbank
    Glendora
    Rialto
    Perris
    San Fernando
    San Gabriel
    San Marino
    Banning
    Needles
1912: Manhattan
    Beach
    El Monte
    Beaumont
1913: Avalon
    La Verne
    Glendale
    Upland
1914: Fillmore
    Beverly Hills
1915: Seal Beach
1916: Blythe
    Monterey Park
1917: Culver City
    El Segundo
    Brea

6 In addition to the attractions of sunshine and "open shop" labor practices, the motion picture industry moved away from its earlier center in and around New York to avoid the "patent thugs" of Thomas Edison's Kinetoscope Company, which then controlled the production of filmmaking equipment. The first local footage was shot in 1907, the first feature film (*The Heart of a Racing Tout*) in 1909.

7 For a more detailed picture of multi-ethnic Los Angeles in the 1920s, see Robert M. Fogelson, *Fragmented Metropolis: Los Angeles, 1850–1930*, Cambridge, MA: Harvard University Press, 1967 (reissued Berkeley and Los Angeles: University of California Press, 1993).

purpose tourist resort both stretched the urban fabric and pinned it down in a swirling multiplicity of localized cityspaces.

At the same time, the City of Los Angeles was assuming its peculiar contours, spreading into the San Fernando Valley to the north, extending an annexed "shoestring" salient south to the port at San Pedro, and gobbling up most of the communities along its western march to the Pacific (leaving a few holes in such places as Beverly Hills and Culver City, where local movie moguls and real estate developers were powerful enough to resist annexation and incorporate on their own). A bustling downtown grew just south of the old Pueblo, choked with traffic jams and surrounded by picturesque Victorian "inner suburbs" and growing ethnic enclaves to house the new migrations.

The downtown core of the region was also alive with extraordinary fervor for radical political change and new utopias designed for communities other than those dominated by the white Protestant elite. The Progressive Era brought major government reforms and encouraged the growth of a strong labor movement and an expanding Socialist Party. A significant part of the Mexican and Chinese revolutions were planned and trained for in and around downtown LA. Non-whites made up 14% of the City's population, compared with 6% in San Francisco and 8% in Detroit. Only Baltimore, among the largest US cities, exceeded this figure. Moreover, the "minority" population was already unusually diverse, with more than 11,000 from Asia (including 8,500 Japanese), 22,000 from Mexico, and nearly 16,000 African Americans.

The turbulent second decade of this first wave of industrial urbanization began with an explosion in the downtown offices of the powerful *Los Angeles Times*, the 1911 trial of its alleged "anarchist unionist" perpetrators, and what national labor leaders described as the working class-led "Battle for Los Angeles." By the time the decade ended, the population growth rate had been cut in half, the labor movement was roundly defeated in its fight against the open shop, the once confident Socialist Party was reduced to tatters, and the reins controlling the regional economy moved even more firmly into the hands of the new boosters of industry. The First World War reinforced this control and prepared the regional economy to boom again.

1920–1940: roaring from war to war

The 1920s may have roared more loudly in Los Angeles than anywhere else in America. The regional population more than doubled over the decade to 2.6 million, the last time it would ever increase at so rapid a rate. Although population growth and economic expansion would slow down dramatically following the stock market crash in 1929, the persistence of the "continuous boom" softened the impact of the Great Depression relative to most of the rest of the country. The most powerful engines of the regional economy recovered rapidly in the 1930s and, as had occurred before after periods of crisis and unrest, Los Angeles moved to the edge of another growth surge as the era ended in the global explosions of the Second World War.

Like the first wave from 1870 to 1900, this was a period marked by severe economic crises and rapidly accelerated urban restructuring in all the world's major industrial cities. The new industrial base established in Los Angeles in the early 1900s, however, was not so much restructured as it was intensified and kept open to accommodate the expansion of the new mass production and mass consumption industries that would come to define Fordism in America. In comparison to the cities of the American Manufacturing Belt, Los Angeles would never become dominated by Fordist assembly-line industries, but by 1940 it had become the largest concentration of such industries (automobile manufacturing, steel, glass, tires, consumer durables) west of the Mississippi.

Petroleum production and refining spurted again after huge new finds, especially in southern Los Angeles and nearby Orange County. Along with the expanding Fordist industries, this stimulated the growth of the twinned ports of Los Angeles-Long Beach and, between the ports and the downtown core, the formation of a vast urban industrial zone, reputed to be one of the largest in the world. The motion picture industry soundly transcended the silent era to grow more rapidly than ever. It was the leading industrial sector throughout this period, employing 30,000 to 40,000 workers. Still centered in Hollywood, "The Industry," as it came to be called, expanded in a broad arc north and west of downtown from North Hollywood (in the San Fernando Valley) to Culver City in the Westside. The aircraft industry also boomed in the interwar years, establishing itself as the conduit through which the high-technology industrialization stimulated by Defense Department contracts would flood the region in later years.

1920–1940

1920:	Montebello*
1921:	Torrance*
	Lynwood*
	Ojai
1922:	Hawthorne*
1923:	West Covina*
	South Gate*
1924:	Maywood*
	Signal Hill*
1925:	La Habra
1926:	Placentia
1927:	Tustin
	Laguna Beach
	Bell*
1928:	San Clemente
1930:	Gardena*
	Indio
1938:	Palm Springs
1939:	Palos Verdes
	Estates

The 1920s and 1930s marked the peak period of growth of Los Angeles County. A map of the built-up area in 1940 would show an almost complete filling in of the county's southwest quadrant, mainly by the City of Los Angeles, now with close to its present, oddly shaped boundaries that include almost all of the suburban San Fernando Valley; and the array of working-class suburbs attached to the industrial zone between downtown and Long Beach. The population of Los Angeles County in 1940 was 86% of the total for the five-county region, the highest percentage it would ever reach. Municipal incorporations between 1920 and 1940 slowed down significantly to only nineteen, but the majority (marked with an asterisk in the sidebar) were in Los Angeles County in and around the major industrial zone.

By 1935, Los Angeles was the fifth largest industrial county in the US and had established an unusually broad and diverse industrial base. It led the country in motion picture production, oil refining, airplane manufacturing, and secondary automobile assembly; was second in tires and fourth in furniture and women's apparel. The image of the industrial might of America was so centered on the Fordist

Manufacturing Belt of the northeast, however, that the extraordinary industrialization of Los Angeles passed almost unnoticed in academic urban studies and in the popular media, both of which tended to see only the region's exceptionalism, its Hollywood aura as a bizarre Babylon by the sea, a unique and inimitable kind of city.

The American working class, however, was not so blinkered. The enormous job machine that began rolling in the 1920s attracted not only a growing stream of Mexican peasants but also what would turn out to be the largest urban-focused domestic migration in US history. The Dust Bowl migration of the 1930s poured in a new population of poor whites from the southern states, as "Okies" and "Arkies" filled in the industrial suburbs of southern LA County. An even larger black migration would begin in the same period, from many of the same states, and with similar but residentially separated local destinations. These flows created in the south central core of Los Angeles County a compacted racial geography that replicated many of the conditions of rural life in the Lower Mississippi Delta, then and now one of the poorest, most racially-divided regions in the USA.[8]

The Depression and the volatile concentration of a domestic white and black working class rekindled the undercurrent of anti-Mexican feelings that had burst violently to the surface many times before in post-conquest Los Angeles. These feelings were aggravated by the peculiarly ambiguous qualities of the Mexican population in California, where they were both "foreign" immigrants and "domestic" residents in what was once Mexican territory. Growing out of these local conditions was the leading edge of a national movement, significantly supported by the federal government, that led to mass deportations of Mexicans (especially as "indigent aliens") from the USA. It is estimated that the Mexican population of Los Angeles County dropped by as much as a third during this period, through both deportations and voluntary emigration.[9]

1940–1970: the Big Orange explodes

Following the twentieth-century pattern, the long postwar economic boom in the USA was nowhere more intense than in the Los Angeles conurbation. Between 1940 and 1970, the regional population would triple in size to nearly

---

8 For an excellent critical regional and historical analysis of the Lower Mississippi Delta, see Clyde Adrian Woods, *Development Arrested: The Delta Blues, the Delta Council and the Lower Mississippi Delta Commission*, doctoral dissertation, Urban Planning, UCLA, 1993. A shortened and revised form of this work, entitled *Development Arrested: Race, Power, and the Blues in the Mississippi Delta* was published by Verso in 1998. Woods is currently extending his "blues epistemology" to an understanding of the role of African Americans in the construction of Fordism in the USA and in the development of Los Angeles.
9 See Abraham Hoffman, *Unwanted Mexican Americans in the Great Depression: Repatriation Pressures, 1929–1939*, Tucson, AR: University of Arizona Press (1974); and Carey McWilliams, "Getting Rid of the Mexicans," *American Mercury* 28 (1933). I thank Janet Abu-Lughod for making me aware of these references.

10 million, a net addition of almost 7 million new residents, one of the fastest growth spurts in the history of First World urbanization. Although Los Angeles County grew from a population of 2.8 million to over 7 million, the rate of population growth in the peripheral counties was even greater. With less than half a million residents at the beginning of the period, the four outer counties grew to nearly 3 million in thirty years. The largest surge of growth took place in Orange County, which increased more than tenfold to 1.4 million, about equal to the other three peripheral counties combined. What was occurring in the regional metropolis of Los Angeles was mass suburbanization on a scale never before encountered.

An unprecedented housing boom platted the urban landscape with suburban tracts that quickly grew into independent municipalities. Nearly 60 cities were incorporated between 1940 and 1970, bringing the total number to about 140, as the already fragmented metropolis was shattered into even tinier pieces.[10] Lakewood (incorporated in 1954) was the exemplary model of the new, primarily white "upper" working-class suburban municipality, Los Angeles's version of eastern Levittowns. A "city by contract," Lakewood purchased its basic services from the county in a scheme that would stimulate a frenzied incorporation game that in retrospect looks like a cross between chess and *SimCity*, the popular computer game of simulated city-building that I will refer again to in chapter 11. Residential developments of different types, with different ethnic and occupational mixes and differing degrees of backing from real estate agencies, competed for turf with powerful commercial and industrial interests seeking municipal tax havens. Eastern Los Angeles County was a particularly lively war zone, containing almost half of the 57 new incorporations spawned by the success of the Lakewood model.

Cities of sorts sprouted to serve highly specialized local constituencies. A City of Industry (1957) and a City of Commerce (1960) bluntly announced their roots, while such places as Irwindale (1957) hid their evasiveness along the lines of Vernon, incorporated in 1905 with the tiniest of residential populations (still today with less than 100) as an industrial and commercial warehousing tract. Tiny Bradbury (1957) was designed and zoned for the horsey set with large lots, no sidewalks, and privileged bridle paths. Out on the Palos Verdes Peninsula, Rolling Hills and Rolling Hills Estates (1957) joined the older Palos Verdes Estates (1939) as archetypes of the gated and walled community protected by visibly armed guards. Mainly white, relatively poor southerners concentrated near the industrial zone in Bellflower,

1940–1970

1946: Coachella
1947: Barstow
1948: Port Hueneme
1952: Fontana
1953: Costa Mesa
    Buena Park
1954: Lakewood
1955: La Palma
    Cabazon
    Duarte
    Industry
    Irwindale
    Norwalk
    Paramount
    Santa Fe
    Springs
    San Juan
    Capistrano
    Hidden Hills
1956: Baldwin Park
    Cerritos
    Cypress
    Downey
1957: Rolling Hills
    Rolling Hills
    Estates
    Westminster
    Fountain
    Valley
    Bellflower
    Bradbury
1958: La Puente
    Pico Rivera
    South El
    Monte
1959: Artesia
    Lawndale
    Rosemead
    Walnut

10   See Gary Miller, *Cities by Contract: The Politics of Municipal Incorporation*, Cambridge, MA: MIT Press, 1981.

Bell Gardens, Cudahy, and Downey, separated by a "Cotton Curtain" along Alameda Avenue from the burgeoning black ghetto to the west (located primarily within the City of Los Angeles). Better-off white working-class families began moving to the fringes of Los Angeles County and beyond, into Ventura County (Camarillo, Thousand Oaks, Simi Valley), Orange County (a dozen new incorporations, including Garden Grove, Costa Mesa, and Nixon's home base of Yorba Linda), and into the High and Low Deserts.

There was an incorporated place for everyone, it seemed, somewhere to escape the various burdens perceived to exist within the central City of Los Angeles. Left behind, however, were two areas which, if they had become incorporated as cities of their own in the 1960s, would probably have become the region's second and third largest in population. About half a million African Americans were concentrated in the area that has come to be known as South Central (including a few incorporated and many unincorporated areas nearby); and a similar number of Mexican Americans were clustered in and around the barrio of East Los Angeles, mainly on still unincorporated county land. Without either a substantial tax base or any significant degree of local control, these areas imploded with poverty and a housing and employment crisis of such extraordinary proportions that any prospects for local solutions were made to seem beyond the realm of possibility. Under these conditions, only the federal government had the powers to make a difference.

1960:	San Dimas
	Commerce
	Cudahy
	La Mirada
	Los Alamitos
	Temple City
1961:	Bell Gardens
	Garden Grove
	Montclair
	Stanton
1962:	Villa Park
	Palmdale
	Victorville
1963:	Desert Hot Springs
1964:	Norco
	Hawaiian Gardens
	Lomita
	Camarillo
	Thousand Oaks
1967:	Yorba Linda
	Indian Wells
1968:	Carson
1969:	Simi Valley

The primary attention of the federal government in Greater Los Angeles was, however, focused elsewhere. Sustaining this surge of economic growth was the series of Pacific wars, from the Japanese invasion of Pearl Harbor to the Korean War and Vietnam, that propelled the region into undisputed leadership of what President Eisenhower called the American "military-industrial complex." While all the other engines of the regional economy continued to expand through this period, the aerospace industry (now including missiles and other paraphernalia of war as well as civilian aircraft manufacture) literally soared, enveloping itself in an expansive regional network of components manufacturers, service providers, research centers, and a growing electronics industry, all sharing in the lift-off provided by huge contracts from the Department of Defense. Broken only by the Santa Monica Mountains, the combined aerospace-defense-electronics industry became centered in an almost continuous band running from the San Fernando Valley in the north, through the "Aerospace Alley" along the coastal fringe of Los Angeles County from Santa Monica to Long Beach, and then into the northern half of Orange County. Taken together, these areas formed a high-technology industrial complex far larger than any of its competitors, including Silicon Valley.

Given the long history of white American xenophobia in Los Angeles, it should not be surprising that this long boom period was also marked by intensified racial, gender, and class tension. Now, however, these localized tensions took on a more global significance, for here in Southern California was both America's Arsenal and its most strategic ideological fortress for the world-wide diffusion of the Pax Americana. During the war years of the 1940s, the longstanding anti-Mexican tradition exploded again after the "Zoot Suit" riots of 1943, instigated in part by the presence in and around the barrio of strategic military personnel at work and play. The equally longstanding anti-Asian tradition reached another low point in the confinement of more than thirty thousand Japanese Americans from Los Angeles in concentration camps following Executive Order 9066 of 1942. During the nascent Cold War years of the 1950s, socialism and militant unionism became prime targets. After many decades of relative quiescence, "Red Scare" tactics again entered the local political agenda in an explosive way, especially in two important areas of the booming regional economy: housing and Hollywood.

Just after the end of the Second World War, the City of Los Angeles was en route to becoming a national leader in the provision of racially integrated public housing. More than 10,000 units of public housing were being planned for, with a major site proposed for Chavez Ravine just north of downtown. In a counter-offensive reminiscent of the events of 1910–11, the *Los Angeles Times* and a cohort of pro-business organizations crushed these initiatives under the guise of American resistance to a socialist plot. Urban renewal (and minority removal) was the preferred plan for downtown. Chavez Ravine was cleared away to provide the site for Dodger Stadium and the public housing that was built was concentrated almost entirely in Watts and East Los Angeles, the racially segregated ghetto and barrio.[11] No significant public housing for the poor has been built since the intensive Red-baiting of the early 1950s and the housing that was built was essentially neglected for the next forty years.

Hollywood provided another target for misguided patriotism. In the pre- and postwar years, unions and guilds associated with the motion picture industry had become among the most militant in the region. Large numbers of European intellectuals and others fleeing fascism had moved to Los Angeles and their growing influence fanned fears of a socialist/communist takeover of the industry that, more than any other, controlled the image and imagineering of America, both internally and for the rest of the world. Aside from federal government officials and members of Congress, the McCarthy-led House Un-American Activities Committee (HUAC) inquisitions focused most insistently on Los Angeles in a fierce and locally supported attempt to purge the entertainment industry of any real or imagined radical tendencies. These and other national offensives and supportive local maneuvers shattered the promising multiracial labor, community, and housing alliances and social movements that had been growing after the end of the war. Many would say

---

11   On this "headline-happy housing war," as he called it, see Don Parson, *Urban Politics during the Cold War: Public Housing, Urban Renewal and Suburbanization in Los Angeles*, doctoral dissertation, Urban Planning, UCLA (1985); and "The Development of Redevelopment: Public Housing and Urban Renewal in Los Angeles," *International Journal of Urban and Regional Research* 6 (1982), 393–413.

that these well-organized progressive forces would never again gain such power and prominence on the local urban scene.

By the mid-1960s, Greater Los Angeles had become a federally produced metropolis to a degree surpassed only by the much more territorially confined District of Columbia. The gargantuan suburban sprawl was significantly fostered by federal mortgage and home-loan programs, the most rapid industrial growth in US history was stimulated and sustained by billions of dollars from the Department of Defense and other federal agencies, and federal funds for the development of an interstate system of superhighways (also designed with national defense in mind) played a key role in the construction of the dense urban freeway network. Federal legislation had other lasting effects. After 1942, when Executive Order 8802 forced war contractors to stop their racist hiring practices, the region became the country's major target for African American migration, attracting nearly 600,000 new residents over the following thirty years and providing the booming regional economy with a vital source of relatively cheap and non-unionized labor.

Taken together, these unplanned federal inducements were instrumental in making Greater Los Angeles the country's, and arguably the entire First World's, most successful economic "growth pole" during the postwar boom. No other metropolis so effectively and efficiently exemplified the propulsive synergy of demand-driven mass production-mass consumption that defined the principles of the Fordist welfare state. Further federal interventions, from the HUAC purges to the intimate linkages developing between the FBI and the LAPD to the presumed safety net provided by growing welfare provisions, strengthened the powers of local elites and helped to intensify the control of the private sector over regional economic expansion.

This renewed version of the realizable American Dream, now made visible everywhere through the expansive mass media and boosted by the spectacular success of Disneyland and the TV situation comedies of suburban life, exploded in 1965 in the Watts Rebellion, the most violent urban social unrest the country had experienced in the twentieth century. The continuous boom was interrupted again by racial and economic tensions, but this time the interruption was much less localized in its causes and consequences.

Looking back to the future: Los Angeles in 1965

To outsiders and many of its own inhabitants, the Los Angeles that erupted in the Watts Rebellion was a virtually unknown city hidden behind the thick sheathing of a hyperactivated American imaginary. The academic world of urban studies, still being swayed by the appealing orderliness of Chicago and the incomparable density of power and culture in New York, steered clear of Southern California, leaving all hope of accurate understanding to other observers more in tune with the region's seemingly bizarre exceptionalism. What was more generally known about Los Angeles in both the academic and popular literatures was characteristically vicarious and impressionistic, built on a collection of heavily mediated images passing, almost by default, for the real thing.

Every city generates such imagery, internally and externally, but Los Angeles was in 1965 (and remains) more specialized in image production and more prone to be understood through its created imagery than any other urban region. On location here since the 1920s is the multitude of "dream factories" that comprise what is still called "the Industry," mass-producing moving pictures of Los Angeles that insistently substitute reel stories for real histories and geographies. Camera crews "shooting" scenes depicting practically every place on earth (and often off-earth) are a familiar sight on the streets of the city, and a constant local reminder of the confusing interplay between fantasy and reality that pervades everyday urban life in the City of Angels.

By 1965, ten years after its opening, Disneyland had added new layers to this landscape of vicarious unreality. Its imaginative proto-geography of America reconfigured the mental maps of the national subconscious to fit the familiar artifice deposited in a tiny corner of Orange County. A cleverly concocted Main Street centered the map and led the all-consuming visitor to separate worlds of fantasy, the future, the frontier, the "happiest places" on earth. With the addition of mass-audience television, the blanket of consciousness-shaping imagery was not only thicker than anywhere else, it was more creatively heterogeneous and diverting in Los Angeles, the place where urban imagineering was invented, commodified, mass-produced, and projected to a worldwide scale and scope.

Behind these broadcast scenes, however, was another Los Angeles that is only now, in retrospect, coming into focus. Amidst the iconic runes of this extendable past, a clearer picture of the "actually existing" Los Angeles of 1965 is beginning to take shape. What it depicts can be seen as both the darkest side of the American Dream and a crowning moment of twentieth-century urban modernity, a particularly vivid exaggeration of the simultaneously utopian and dystopian urbanization that has been etched into Los Angeles since its origins.

More than a century of obsessive Anglo-fication (posing as patriotic Americanization) had "purified" the population to the point that, in 1960, more than 80 percent of the inhabitants were non-Hispanic whites or "Anglos" (a term deeply and defiantly rooted in the recolonization of formerly Spanish America). Although the statisticians might quibble, this Anglo population was almost entirely suburban in lifestyle, not unlike the situation comedies of television, constructing places where city and countryside blended together in a new experiential synthesis. This situational synthesis was decidedly WASPish, for Los Angeles had for decades contained the highest percentage of native-born Protestants of all the largest US cities. With a substantial dose of irony, Los Angeles in 1965 could still be described as the first truly American metropolis. Not surprisingly, an almost crusade-like mentality pervaded this white, often anti-papist, and racially proud Christian majority, supremely confident in its successful inhabitation and preservation of an earthly and preternaturally American paradise.

Few areas of Los Angeles contained the conventional densities of urban life, even among the poor and working-class communities of every color, for the city's ghettoes and barrios were more suburban than anywhere else in America. "Sixty Suburbs in Search of a City" became the catchall description of life in Los Angeles in the 1960s and many of those suburbs wore blue collars. Built into this homogeneously un-urban sprawl of American Dream-like communities was what two of the best academic treatments of Los Angeles at the time called a "fragmented metropolis" and a "non-place urban realm," the former reflecting the mass production of suburban municipalities or "cities by contract," the latter tapping the rootlessness and artificiality of place-named identities and "proximate" community.[12] Having escaped the claustrophobic tightness of small-town America and the imperfect urbanity of the big cities, well-off Angelenos atomistically constructed far-flung networks of contacts and activities centered around increasingly protected homespaces rather than in well-defined neighborhood communities. The unlisted telephone number and the gated and walled-in residence symbolized this most privatized of urban landscapes. Truly public spaces were few and far between, as what the social theorists call "civil society" seemed to melt into the airwaves and freeways and other circuitries of the sprawling urban scene.

Mass suburbanization and other centrifugal forces had emptied the gridlocked downtown of the 1920s, leaving only a decaying financial and retail center, a few hotels, and the still imposing civic center, which had been recently philanthropically revived by the opening in December, 1964, of the Music Center, a product of a fantastically successful effort by the Anglo elite to put their acropolitan culture high up on the real and imagined map of the city. Towering still more morosely over downtown, however, was City Hall, which by 1965 had become a global symbol of the American justice system after being portrayed each week on *Dragnet* and other no-nonsense TV crime shows. *Dragnet's* sober Sergeant Joe Friday curtly epitomized modernist justice for white America by always insisting on "just the facts, ma'am" in scripts that were checked for verisimilitude by then police chief William H. Parker of the Los Angeles Police Department (LAPD). No fluffy imagery here, for there was a threatening dark side to life in the brightness of the simulated City of Angels, a tough counterpoint landscape that teemed with stygian dangers, never very far from the glittering surface.

Downtown Los Angeles has been the dystopian Main Street of the world's most visible Noir City at least since the 1920s, a lineage that traces easily from the gritty Bunker Hill of Raymond Chandler to the acid-rain-swept streets of Ridley Scott's only slightly futuristic *Blade Runner*. And by 1965, the contrapuntal dark side of the Southern California dreamscape seemed to be partic-

---

12   Robert M. Fogelson, *The Fragmented Metropolis*. Fogelson would also become a leading critic of the McCone Commission and other official interpretations of the Watts Riots. See his edited compilation, *Mass Violence in America: The Los Angeles Riots*, New York: Arno Press and New York Times Press, 1969; and *Violence as Protest: A Study of Riots and Ghettoes*, Garden City, NJ: Doubleday, 1971. The vision of Los Angeles as a "non-place urban realm" is from Melvin Webber, "Culture, Territoriality, and the Elastic Mile," *Papers of the Regional Science Association* 11 (1964), 59–69.

ularly rife with what many upholders of the peace were convinced was their greatest threat ever, nothing short of a global alliance of evil forces bent on planetary domination, echoing the many villainous scripts shot on Los Angeles's meaner streets.

When Watts exploded in the summer of 1965, the unfolding events immediately appeared to many as the product of some Disney-maniac staging an evil TV spectacular in Negroland, the darkest and most secretive zone of Noir City. Police Chief Parker, whose name now enshrines the riot-damaged downtown headquarters of LAPD that was a primary target in the 1992 uprising, not unexpectedly saw everything in black and white, with a little red thrown in for good measure. The revolutionary "monkeys" in the "zoo" of Negroland were running amok, he said, stirred by the "communists" and their hordes of Hollywood sympathizers. With little accurate knowledge and understanding to distinguish the difference between the two, the real Los Angeles once again seemed to collapse into its vivid simulations. How else could one understand the latest event staged in this dystopic utopia, this place where the unique and the paradoxical are somehow universalized for all to see?

Only well after the rioting, burning, and looting spread to other cities, did a different picture begin to develop of late modern Los Angeles and the deeper – and wider – meaning of the Watts Rebellion. Spurred by its increasing role as America's military arsenal for three successive Pacific wars, the Los Angeles region had experienced the most rapid industrial growth of any region in the country after the Great Depression. Federally subsidized suburbanization combined with federally fostered industrial growth to create an exceedingly efficient urban machine for simultaneously stimulating both mass production and mass consumption, making Los Angeles one of the crown jewels of the Fordist-Keynesian "social contract" in the USA.

More than half a million African Americans migrated into Los Angeles County alone between 1942 and 1965, after the passage of Executive Order 8802.[13] They carried with them the cutting edge of national black politics, enhanced by the growing power of the civil rights movement, the War on Poverty, the dreams of Martin Luther King, and the raised fist of black nationalism. A second large migration stream, similarly attracted to the hyperactive Los Angeles job machine ever since the Great Depression, added almost equal numbers of relatively poor white southerners to the cultural mix of the fragmented metropolis.

Not surprisingly perhaps, both groups concentrated around the large industrial zone stretching from downtown to the ports of Los Angeles and

---

13 The year 1942 was especially interesting for Los Angeles. The first concentration camps were created to remove Japanese Americans from their property and businesses in the city, a Japanese submarine shelled an oilfield near Santa Barbara, and a purely imaginary air raid led to a crazed scenario in which a faux "hostile aircraft" was reported to have been shot down on Vermont Avenue. Five citizens died in this imaginary invasion, three from car crashes and two from heart attacks. In the same year, Camp Pendleton Marine Corps base was founded and the "Sleepy Lagoon" murder triggered another hispanophobic frenzy in which as many as 150 Mexican American "boy gang" members (as they were then called) were arrested for the death of one youth at a party in East Los Angeles.

Long Beach, a zone bounded on its western edge by Alameda Avenue, which in 1965 had become one of the most pronounced racial divides in any American city. On one side of this so-called Cotton Curtain were the factories and jobs and such exemplary white working-class suburbs as South Gate; immediately on the other was a string of equally exemplary African American suburban communities, many on unincorporated county land and all strikingly bereft of major industrial establishments as well as of basic social services: Florence, Watts, Willowbrook, Compton. Despite a tantalizing physical proximity to one of the largest pools of high-wage, unionized, blue-collar jobs in the country, nearly one-third of the African American workforce was unemployed and almost 60 percent lived on welfare. This southside racial geography provided the immediate backdrop to the urban "civil war" that was an integral part of the events of 1965, once again illustrating how race divides America in ways that often cut across powerful class divisions.

Although concentrated in the Watts district of the City of Los Angeles, the rebellion peaked along the entire corridor just west of Alameda, an area that had become one of the major local, national, and global centers of radical black consciousness in the 1960s. Perhaps nowhere else were conditions more ripe for rebellion. Los Angeles, after a long and violent history of racist public administration, housing codes, zoning practices, and police work, had become one of the most segregated cities in the country; its mayor, police chief, and dominant newspaper had given sufficient indications that this tradition of recalcitrant racism was still flourishing in the centers of political power; and another obsessive tradition, of McCarthyesque anti-communism, fed by the vicious trials of Hollywood "sympathizers" and the defeat of the vigorous "socialist" public housing movement in the 1950s, had excitedly centered its attention on uppity blacks as the great revolutionary threat to the white American dream. The mood of the time was captured one month before the August insurrection. In an attempt to stem what seemed to be a rising tide of police brutality, then LAPD lieutenant and later mayor Tom Bradley formally protested against the widespread posting of John Birch Society literature on LAPD bulletin boards, literature that labeled Martin Luther King and other black leaders as dangerous communists and implicitly promoted white and thin-blue-line terrorism against the enemy within.

At the national level, urban blacks had assumed, both by default and by active choice, the leadership of American social movement politics and were thus the most powerful voice of resistance against the status quo and racially uneven development of the Fordist-Keynesian economic boom. Although African Americans in Los Angeles had probably benefited from the boom more than those of any other major urban region, the segregated social geography of the larger metropolis all too visibly presented itself as an extraordinarily polarized mosaic of extreme and conspicuous wealth and poverty, a consciousness-raising tableau of racially-intensified relative deprivation. That the worst civil disturbance of the century would occur where and when it did was therefore as predictable as the immediate reaction to it. Thirty-four people were killed (31 by police gunfire), 1,032 were injured, and 3,952 were arrested (the vast majority African American). Property damage topped $40 million and 6,000 buildings were damaged, most heavily along 103rd Street, which came to be called Charcoal Alley.

Looked at myopically, the riots, burning, and looting appeared to be a self-inflicted local wound instigated by the particular frustrations and impatience of a long-impoverished and racially isolated population. In retrospect, however, the events were of considerably more global significance. They can be seen today as one of the earliest violent announcements that "business as usual" in urban and industrial America could no longer continue without explosive resistance, even in the most successful boomtown of the twentieth century. The Watts Rebellion and the series of urban uprisings which followed it in the late 1960s all over the world (and again in Los Angeles in August, 1970, with the anti-Vietnam war Chicano Moratorium, the largest mass protest of Mexican Americans in US history) marked one of the symptomatic beginnings of the end of the postwar economic boom and the Fordist-Keynesian state planning that underpinned its propulsiveness. As occurred a century earlier, the peculiar articulations of race and class in the USA ruptured the booming space economy at about the time it was reaching its peak performance. The worldwide recession of the early 1970s, the worst since the Great Depression, helped to confirm the turning-pointedness of the preceding decade, but even more convincing confirmation can be derived from the dramatic restructuring processes that have been radically transforming the urban landscape and the very nature of urban modernity over the past three decades. As seen from the present, the urban worlds of 1965 have not only been deconstructed, they have also become comprehensively reconstituted in many different ways.

1970 and beyond: the New Urbanization

In Los Angeles, the next surge of growth would have much lower rates of industrial and population increase than ever before. But the "continuous boom" would keep on rolling toward the twenty-first century. As it did so successfully during the two earlier periods of deepening economic crisis and accelerated urban restructuring (1870–1900 and 1920–40), the Los Angeles conurbation would adjust rapidly to changing local, national, and global conditions to lead the (American) way to economic recovery, at least until another explosive moment would punctuate the continuous boom. Before moving on to Part II, an expanded and generalized interpretation of what has been happening to Los Angeles and other major city-regions over the past thirty years, and Part III, a more explicitly political interpretation of the events of 1992 and their aftermath, let us briefly conclude the big-picture overview of the booming conurbation, sketching out again its most obvious social and spatial punctuation points.

Although rates of population growth since 1970 have been lower than in any previous surge, recent estimates indicated that by the turn of the century the total regional population would have increased by more than seven million, a net addition that surpasses the figures for the preceding three decades. If present trends continue, Greater Los Angeles will pass Greater New York as the country's largest (post)metropolis in the first decade of the new millennium. Los Angeles County has continued its population growth, adding three million over the past 30 years, but the outer four counties have grown even faster, with a combined population growth of almost four million during the same period. At least 39 new municipalities have been established since 1970, bringing the total for the five-county region to well over 170.

Several of these municipalities top the 1990 census list of the fastest-growing small cities (from 50,000 to 150,000) in the country: Irvine, Mission Viejo, Lancaster, Moreno Valley. They are indicative of the new "postsuburban" cityscape filling in the "exopolitan" Outer Cities (see chapter 8) and marking the transition from mass suburbanization to what might be called mass regional urbanization, a process that may be more advanced in Southern California than anywhere else in the United States. The only example of inner-city incorporation is West Hollywood, the product of a gay-elderly-renter coalition that created the first gay and lesbian majority city council in the region, if not in the US, on a leftover enclave of county land just east of Beverly Hills. Many of the other new municipalities were located well off the picture of Los Angeles – From Space, in the Low Desert around and beyond plush Palm Springs (e.g., Palm Desert, Rancho Mirage, La Quinta, Twentynine Palms, Cathedral City).

The most dramatic change in the regional population since 1970, however, has come from another round of mass migration. For more than a hundred years, hard times in the national and global economies seem to magnify the attractions of Southern California. As in previous surges, the new pool of migrants opportunely provided an abundant supply of cheap labor to fuel continued economic expansion and help control labor costs (and militancy), typically at the expense of established working-class communities. After that portentous year of 1965, when federal legislation on immigration quotas was passed and the Bracero program was officially terminated, these migration waves reached unprecedented heights, transforming Los Angeles into the country's major port of entry for immigrants and making it one of the world's most ethnically and racially diverse metropolises. In Los Angeles County, the population shifted from 70 percent Anglo to 60 percent non-Anglo between 1970 and 1990, as what was once the most white and Protestant of American cities changed into what some observers are now calling America's leading Third World metropolis as well as the reputed site of the world's largest Catholic archdiocese.

1970–present

1970: Loma Linda
        Adelanto
1971: Irvine
1973: Rancho Palos
        Verdes
        Palm Desert
        Rancho Mirage
1976: La Canada-
        Flintridge
1977: Rancho
        Cucamonga
        Lancaster
1978: La Habra
        Heights
        Grand Terrace
1980: Big Bear Lake
1981: Westlake
        Village
1982: La Quinta
        Agoura Hills
1983: Moorpark
1984: West Hollywood
        Moreno Valley
1987: Santa Clarita
        Highland
        Twentynine
        Palms
1988: Mission Viejo
        Apple Valley
        Hesperia
1989: Laguna Niguel
        Dana Point
        Yucaipa
        Diamond Bar
        Temecula
1990: Calimesa
        Canyon Lake
1991: Cathedral City
        Calabasas
        Laguna Hills
        Malibu
        Lake Forest
        Murietta
        Chino Hills
        Yucca Valley

African Americans numbered close to 1 million in 1990, an increase of about 230,000 over the two decades, but their rate of growth and their proportion of the total county population have been declining and there are some signs of an absolute decrease in population in the 1990s, as many leave Los Angeles County for the outer cities of the region or to return to the southern states. The old geographical core of African American Los Angeles has dropped significantly in density and has shifted westward, with its once-rigid eastern black–white boundary now completely dissolved not by the elimination of racial barriers but by the massive in-migration of Latinos, the preferred local term for all persons, Spanish-speaking or not, whose original homeland lies south of the USA–Mexico border.

The census category of Asian and Pacific Islander has experienced the highest rate of growth, as large numbers of Koreans, Chinese, Vietnamese, Thai, Pilipino (from the Philippines), Cambodians, South Asians, Samoans, and Tonga Islanders moved into the metropolitan region and raised their proportion of Los Angeles County's population to more than 10 percent, almost equal to the percentage of African Americans. The first three groups named have probably clustered together most visibly. A large and expanding Koreatown is now located west of downtown, a new "suburban Chinatown" centered on Monterey Park has taken shape to the east, and a band of Vietnamese and Cambodian communities has grown to the south, stretching from the older Japanese community in Gardena to Long Beach and into Orange County, where the city of Westminster is now known as "Little Saigon," the largest concentration of Vietnamese in the US and a vital source of relatively cheap but highly skilled labor for the Orange County "technopoles," a term that will be discussed in more detail in chapter 6.

The largest surge of population growth has led to the re-Latinization of Los Angeles and more specifically to its re-Mexicanization. More than two million new migrants from Mexico account for the majority of the increase in the Hispanic census category, with at least another half million coming from El Salvador, Guatemala, and other Central American countries. Given some undercounting in the 1990 census, Latinos (including migrants from all countries south of the US border as well as resident Chicanas and Chicanos) are almost certainly now the largest population group in Los Angeles County, for the first time in more than a century. The most dramatic Latino population growth has taken place in the southeast quadrant of the county, where many municipalities have changed from more than 75 percent Anglo to almost 95 percent Latino in a little over a decade. A more detailed discussion of ethnic Los Angeles will be presented in chapter 9.

The regional economy has also experienced a profound change since 1970. Reflecting the deindustrialization happening almost everywhere else in the USA, most of the Fordist manufacturing sectors in Los Angeles (automobile assembly, tires, glass, steel, consumer durables) have almost disappeared, decimating many of the working-class neighborhoods and suburbs that had grown around them. With a more diverse economy than, say, Detroit or Cleveland, however, Los Angeles was able to reindustrialize more flexibly around either its well-established and labor-intensive craft-based industries (including motion picture production, clothing, furniture, jewelry, leather working, printing) or the new high-technology production systems (led by the electronics-defense-aerospace complex). See chapter 6 for further discussion of this economic restructuring.

At least until the late 1980s, while metropolitan areas in the northeastern "Rustbelt" states were losing manufacturing industries and employment at a rapid pace, Los Angeles continued to grow, maintaining its record of leading all other urban regions in the net increase of manufacturing workers for every decade since 1920. Most other sectors of the economy, especially services and the FIRE sector (finance, insurance, real estate), also expanded as the region churned out far more jobs than there were jobseekers. In the 1970s, more than 1.3 million additional jobs were generated, a little more than the total regional population increase during the decade.

The massive wave of global migration was absorbed primarily into low-wage, low-skill service jobs in hotels, hospitals, restaurants, domestic service, and retail stores, as well as in the undergrowth of sweatshops that is now such a vital part of the entire manufacturing system of Los Angeles, from the garment industry to high-technology electronics assembly. Labor markets for the millions of "working poor" have become increasingly segmented along ethnic lines. Latinos, for example, dominate in the furniture and clothing industries while Asians are more specialized in electronics assembly and in retailing. At the same time, many of the new immigrants have moved out from these initial bases to become entrepreneurs in their own right – ethnic restaurant owners, Korean clothing industry contractors, Mexican jewelry manufacturers – adding significantly to the continued growth of the regional economy.

The reindustrialization of Los Angeles has also added significant new jobs in the upper end of the labor market, reflecting the concentration in the region of what is reputed to be the world's largest collection of engineers, scientists, mathematicians, industrial designers, and computer specialists. This has increasingly bifurcated economic expansion around the twin poles of the new technocracy (enhanced by entertainment industry moguls and FIRE sector millionaires) and the working poor (the most successful segment of a much larger urban underclass), squeezing the once bulging middle-class segments more tightly than at any time since the Great Depression. The end result has been a widening income gap between the rich and the poor, and a growing social and spatial polarization as great as if not greater than in any other major urban region, despite the "continuous boom."

In the mid-to-late 1980s, manufacturing employment hit its peak in the region and by 1990 it had begun to decline in all five counties during what some claim to be the worst regional recession of the century. The end of the Cold War and major cuts in prime Defense Department contracts threw the regional economy into a pronounced but brief tailspin. Employment in Los Angeles County aerospace–defense–electronics industries fell from 312,500 in 1987 to 259,600 in 1990 and to 234,800 in 1991. Some forecasters predicted that not many more than 100,000 workers would be left by the end of the decade. Waves of decline also hit the FIRE sector, the construction industry, and most of the region's craft industries, which began to feel the pinch of cheap foreign competition more than ever before. The major exception to this decline has been the entertainment industry and its ancillary economy, which today has again become the region's largest industrial employer, as it was during the interwar years.

Increasing income inequalities and social polarization, massive legal and illegal immigration, the magnification of cultural diversity and inter-cultural tensions, the squeeze on middle-class households, increasing homelessness, and the rising urban densities in both Inner and Outer Cities created a much more volatile "new" Los Angeles. During times of economic boom, this volatility was rather effectively controlled, but with the crises of the 1990s, arising to a significant degree directly from the "successful" restructuring processes of the past thirty years, the new Los Angeles erupted again, in late April–early May 1992, surpassing the Watts Riots as the century's most violent and destructive urban uprising. Why the "Justice Riots" occurred, what we can learn from their aftermath, and how the events of 1992 can be seen as a more general shift from crisis-generated restructuring to what I will call a restructuring-generated crisis are the leading questions that will underlie the discussions in all the following chapters.

Part II
Six Discourses on the Postmetropolis

Introduction

The City is an ideogram: the Text continues.

Roland Barthes, *Empire of Signs* (1982): 31

Border Dialogues: Previewing the Postmetropolitan Discourses

In the headquotes to chapter 3, I drew upon Iain Chambers to allegorize the modern metropolis as a moving metaphor of modernity. In his *Border Dialogues: Journeys in Postmodernity* (1990), Chambers represents the modern metropolis as "a myth, a tale, a telling," a "poignant narrative" that builds on the past to continually produce "new horizons." In Part II, I will take this construction of new horizons literally and figuratively, and use Chambers's evocative travels in the cultural and philosophical borderlands between modernity and postmodernity as a preliminary envisioning of the latest stage in the geohistory of cityspace: the formation of the postmetropolis. Previewing the postmetropolis through the eyes of a critical cultural theorist widens the scope of the attempt to make practical and theoretical sense of the new urbanization processes that have been restructuring the modern metropolis over the past thirty years. It does so by representing the postmetropolis not only as an epitomizing model of contemporary social and economic development, but also as a "metaphysical reality," a place where the real and the imagined are persistently commingled in ways we have only begun to understand.

Chambers never uses the term *postmetropolis* in his border dialogues, but its substance and meaning are clearly present in the rich imagery he attaches to contemporary cityspace in his transgressive journeys into the postmodern world. There are many different *posts* packed into the postmetropolis, but the first among them is "postmodern," at least in the way I have defined this effusive and often elusive adjective. Chambers represents the emergent postmodern metropolis as both a new mode of contemporary life and one that is marked by deep and immutable continuities with the past. This is an important starting point for exploring the postmetropolis, for at least at present there are no signs that the metropolitan allegory of modernity arising from the third Urban Revolution has been completely transcended. Of all the *posts* that can be applied to the contemporary metropolis, the *least* applicable are post-urban, post-industrial, and post-capitalist.

Even the new urbanization processes are not entirely new. In many ways, the postmetropolis can be seen as a distinctive variation on the themes of crisis-generated restructuring and geohistorically uneven development that have been shaping (and reshaping) cityspaces since the origins of urban-industrial capitalism. More immediately, there are powerful continuities today with the geohistories of Manchester and Chicago, and still more so with the modern Fordist-Keynesian metropolis that consolidated so formidably in the postwar decades and whose inner workings were captured so well by the neo-Marxist school of urban and regional political economists. The postmetropolis thus represents, in large part, an outgrowth or, better, an extension of that modern and modernist urbanism, a still partial and incomplete metamorphosis that will always bear traces of earlier cityspaces.

But at the same time, the postmodern, postfordist, postkeynesian metropolis does represent something significantly new and different, the product of an era of intense and extensive restructuring as profound in its impact on every facet of our lives as any other period in at least the past two centuries – that is, since the origins of the industrial capitalist city. As such, it demands to be studied in its own right and not just as a geohistorical extension, especially in those areas of the world where the postmetropolitan transition has advanced furthest. To use the terms that have become so closely associated with postmodern and poststructuralist critical theory and the allied field of critical cultural studies, what has been happening over the past thirty years can be described and interpreted as a selective deconstruction and still evolving reconstitution of the modern metropolis. Each chapter in Part II will chart out different but interconnected channels of discourse that have arisen specifically to make practical and theoretical sense of this ongoing transformation of the modern metropolis.

Using Chambers to preview the postmetropolis serves several other purposes. Right from the start, his provocative observations expand the frame of reference for the study of contemporary urban development well beyond the confines of conventional urban studies. As a revealing window on to the intertwining historicality, sociality, and spatiality of human life, they give new meaning and depth to the epigraph from Lea Virgine that heads both the Introduction to Part I and Chambers's chapter 3, "Some Metropolitan Tales": "to investigate the city is . . . a way of examining the enigmas of the world and our existence." More specifically, Chambers introduces a far-reaching and critical cultural dimension to the powerful political economy perspectives that dominated urban studies in the late twentieth century. The stimulating synergies as well as interpretive frictions generated from this encounter between critical cultural and radical political economic studies of the city form an intentional backdrop to the discussion of all six discourses on the postmetropolis.

Conceptualizing the New Urbanization Processes

In the late twentieth century, cities in North America and Europe are coming less and less to represent the culmination of local and territorial cultures. Many of these cities themselves threaten to become residual; abandoned and obsolete monuments to an earlier epoch. Or else, as twilight regions of once confident and rational projects, they are transformed into aestheticized cityscapes (in architecture and art galleries, cultural and heritage centres, loft living and designer homes), while their previous populations, if they have no role to play in this act, are inserted into other discourses: ethnic communities, urban poverty, inner-city decay, industrial decline, drugs, organized crime. This particular metro-network does not simply represent an extension of the previous urban culture of the mercantile and industrial city and its form of nation state; for it no longer necessarily represents a fixed point or unique referent. While the earlier city was a discrete geographical, economic, political and social unit, easily identified in its clearcut separation from rural space, the contemporary western metropolis tends toward drawing that "elsewhere" into its own symbolic zone. The countryside and suburbia, linked up via the telephone, the TV, the video, the computer terminal, and other branches of the mass media, are increasingly the dispersed loci of a commonly shared and shaped world. Towns and cities are themselves increasingly transformed into points of intersection, stations, junctions, in an intensive metropolitan network whose economic and cultural rhythms, together with their flexible sense of centre, are no longer even necessarily derived from Europe or North America.   (Chambers, 1990: 53)

Chambers and his "metropolitan tales" are charged by a recognition that something extraordinary happened to cities in the late twentieth century, a kind of sea change that makes our old ways of understanding the city and cityspace appear increasingly anachronistic. This double-sided recognition of the substantial material changes taking place in our contemporary urban worlds and the challenge these changes represent for those who study cities is the necessary first step in understanding the postmetropolis. Chambers is not the first to note these extraordinary changes. A few present-day observers have gone so far as to proclaim that this current urban transformation may be the most dramatic in the more than 10,000-year history of urbanization. I am also tempted to raise the speculative possibility that the still ongoing transition from the modern to the postmodern metropolis may eventually lead to a fourth Urban Revolution. While such speculations are not needed to appreciate the unusual intensity of the new urbanization processes and the different urban forms and spatial practices they are producing, they have the effect of keeping open the implicative and interpretive scope and scale of what has been happening to cities as we have approached the new millennium. Such openness is useful, if only to protect against the premature closure of debate by those who stubbornly see the new as only a minor perturbation in the continuous flow of geohistory.

Chambers focuses his exploration of the new urbanization processes on *a profound change in what the city represents*, a deep restructuring of the meanings, cultural symbolism, and prevailing discourses attached to what I have been calling the spatial specificity of urbanism and its more abstract conceptual and experiential expression in the *urban imaginary*, the ways we think about cities and urban life. In particular, he argues that cities, in Europe and North America at least, are coming less and less to represent the "culmination of local and territorial cultures," an intrinsic quality of urbanness that can be traced back to the origins of cities. Building on a tendency that may have been initiated in the earliest development of urban-industrial capitalism, the contemporary city seems to be increasingly unmoored from its spatial specificity, from the city as a fixed point of collective reference, memory, and identity. Chambers expands upon this dislocation and decentering in the paragraph following the one quoted above.

> With this semiotic extension in details, and a simultaneous loss in focus, references to an "outside" increasingly fall away. At the most there is the sweeping urban fringe of endless suburbs, satellite towns and ribbon development, or else inner-city housing projects, unofficial, subterranean economies and those pockets of hard, local, realities – whether Brixton, south London, the back streets of Naples or the *barrios* of east Los Angeles – that are invariably distinguished by poverty, often ethnicity, and local languages of identity. But the earlier separation between an obvious "natural" exterior and an "artificial" urban interior weakens and tends toward collapse. The referents that once firmly separated the city from the countryside, the artificial from the "natural", are now indiscriminately reproduced as potential signs and horizons within a common topography. It is this habitat, the metropolis, as much an imaginary reality as a real place, that has become the myth of our times.   (1990: 53–4)

He adds immediately that we can no longer hope to map the modern metropolis, because we can no longer assume that we know "its extremes, its borders, confines, limits." It is more difficult than ever before to represent the city as a discrete geographical, economic, political, and social unit rooted in its immediate environs and hinterlands. The boundaries of the city are becoming more porous, confusing our ability to draw neat lines separating what is inside as opposed to outside the city; between the city and the countryside, suburbia, the non-city; between one metropolitan city-region and another; between the natural and the artificial. What was once clearly "elsewhere" to the city is now being drawn into its expanded symbolic zone. An increasing blurriness intercedes between the real and imagined city, making "the city" as much an imaginary or simulated reality as a real place. Chambers also notes that we can no longer represent the postmodern metropolis as merely an extension of the industrial capitalist city, with its decidedly fixed referents and established urban epistemologies. New ways of making practical and theoretical sense of the empirically perceived, conceptually represented, and actually lived spaces of the city need to be developed.

Several other contemporary scholars have noticed a similar territorial unmooring of cityspace. In her own insightful journeys into postmodernity, Celeste Olalquiaga microscopically roots this urban malaise in a transformation of the body, the geography closest in, as the poet Adrienne Rich once called it. She characterizes this malaise as a specifically urban and contemporary form of psychasthenia, the Modern Greek word used to refer generally to mental disorder.

Defined as a disturbance in the relation between self and surrounding territory, psychasthenia is a state in which the space defined by the coordinates of the organism's own body is confused with *represented space*. Incapable of demarcating the limits of its own body, lost in the immense sea that circumscribes it, the psychasthenic organism proceeds to abandon its own identity to embrace the space beyond. It does so by camouflaging itself into the milieu. This simulation effects a double usurpation: while the organism successfully reproduces those elements it could not otherwise apprehend, in the process it is swallowed up by them, vanishing as a differentiated entity. (Olalquiaga, 1992: 1–2; emphasis added)

Psychasthenia is one of the psychological syndromes associated with life in the postmetropolis, where the boundaries of identity are rapidly changing and many of the old spatial specificities of urbanism seem to melt into air. As Olalquiaga writes: "Bodies are becoming like cities," with the self-perception and identity of both tied increasingly to "the topography of computer screens and video monitors," giving us the "languages and images that we require to reach others and see ourselves" (1992: 17). This reference to an invasive new electronic "topography" picks up on a similar connection made by Chambers and by many others studying the contemporary city. In our new Information Age, with its inveigling webs of virtual reality, artificial intelligence, netscapes, cyberspatial communications, and "digital communities," the hard materialities of cityspace seem to evaporate as the whole world (and more) is drawn into every city's symbolic zone. In this "semiotic extension of details," there is a simultaneous "loss in focus" for there is no longer a definable "outside" to cities.

Chambers follows this ensnaring web into the simultaneously decentered and recentered cartography of postmetropolitan cityspace. A "sweeping urban fringe" of "endless suburbs" blurs the outer reaches of the postmetropolis, while a more "flexible sense of centre" redefines the inner city as "unofficial" and "subterranean." Some of the sites in this expansive "metro-network" are abandoned as obsolete monuments to an earlier era of modernity, forming new ruins to explore in "twilight regions" of the city. Other sites are reconstituted as simulated and aestheticized cityscapes, boutiqued and gentrified to feed new kinds of virtual communities occupying privileged places in an increasingly niched cityspace. Still others become little more than "points of intersection, stations, junctions" in a worldwide web, what Manuel Castells in his most recent work calls the Network Society. Those who have no role to play in the new metropolis are made virtually invisible by being "inserted into other discourses," or else they become demonized as the enemy within, floating populations of urban nomads filling "pockets of hard, local realities," carriers of poverty, decay, disease, drugs, crime, and violence.

All these observations reflect the simultaneous interplay of *deterritorialization* and *reterritorialization*, another of the many paradoxical pairings of *de-re* words that have come to describe the effects of the new urbanization processes. Deterritorialization refers to the weakening attachments to place, to territorially defined communities and cultures ranging from the household, the urban neighborhood, and the town or city, to the metropolis, the region, and that most powerful of contemporary territorial communities of identity, the modern nation-state. Although such deterritorialization is not unique to the contemporary era, there probably has never been a period in which its effects have been so intense and far-reaching, leading some to proclaim the creation of a "borderless world" and the "end of geography." At the same time, however, there has also been a reterritorialization process, creating new forms and combinations of social spatiality and territorial identity that, if not actually replacing the old, are producing human geographies that are significantly different and more complex, from those we have recognized in the past. It is this turbulent restructuring of territorial identity and rootedness amidst a sea of shifting relations between space, knowledge, and power that has given rise to a *new cultural politics* in the postmetropolis, significantly different from the politics of the economy that dominated modernist urbanism. And far from marking the end of geography, this new politics is increasingly attaching itself to the spatial specificities of urbanism and to a strategic consciousness of how space acts as a means of subordination and social control.

Still another way of describing the postmetropolitan transition is as a simultaneous implosion and explosion in the *scale* of cities, an extraordinarily far-reaching turning of cityspace both inside-out and outside-in at the same time. At one level today, the entire world is rapidly becoming urbanized, from Antarctica to the Amazon, as the spatial reach of city-based cultures, societies, and economies expands into every region on the planet. At another level, every individual urban center, from the largest to the smallest, seems increasingly to contain the entire world within it, creating the most culturally heterogeneous cityspaces the world has ever seen. Again, the origins of this transformation in urban scale can be traced back to much earlier urban eras, but never before has it approached such an embracing scope and depth. It has made the discourse on *globalization* one of the most revealing entry points in making sense of the new urbanization processes.

The postmetropolis can be represented as a product of intensified globalization processes through which the global is becoming localized and the local is becoming globalized at the same time. Chambers sees this simultaneity as leading to a kind of "worlding" of the city via its emplacement in a vast global metro-network of hitherto dispersed loci that increasingly absorbs everyone, everywhere, into commonly shared economic and cultural rhythms. What was once central is becoming peripheral and what was the periphery is becoming increasingly central, an observation that pertains to cityspace, with the intensive urbanization of the suburbs into Outer Cities or Edge Cities while the Central Cities or Inner Cities become edgily filled with diasporic migrants from the world's poorest regions. A similar combination of decentralization and recentralization is happening on a global scale within what is being called a New International Division of Labor, where a few formerly poor regions of the Third World become NICs, Newly Industrializing Countries, the Second World disintegrates into a new kind of periphery, and many regions in the First World suffer widespread deindustrialization and decay.

While bodies are becoming like cities, cityspace is coming more and more to resemble global geographies, incorporating within its encompassing reach a cosmopolitan condensation of all the world's cultures and zones of international tension. The postmetropolis thus becomes a replicative hub of fusion and diffusion, implosive and explosive growth, a First-Second-Third World city wrapped into one. In Europe and North America, as Chambers notes, postmetropolitan culture is no longer necessarily derived from local or even national territories. This is bringing about another radical change in the cultural politics of cityspace, highlighting in new ways the practical and theoretical meaning of difference, identity, subjectivity, multiplicity, integration; as well as race, class, gender, sexual orientation, age, and so on. Old binary categories such as black-white, man-woman, capital-labor, colonizer-colonized are breaking down and becoming reconstituted in different ways that we are only beginning to understand. And our understanding can no longer depend exclusively on indigenous sources. Lagos, São Paulo, Bombay, or Singapore provide as revealing a window from which to comprehend the postmetropolis as Los Angeles, Paris, Chicago, or Manchester.

To conclude this quick preview of the postmetropolis and provide a motivating political challenge to move forward, I turn once more to Iain Chambers.

The present world does not automatically augur an info-tech paradise . . . It does, however, usher in a new horizon of possibilities. It produces a space (in both the physical, temporal and symbolic sense) in which previous social relations, economic organization and established knowledge and expertise are thrown into question, crisis and movement; in which work may become discontinuous; in which ecology will not be a peripheral concern to the economy but part of the same social budget; in which the gender of power and politics can no longer be assumed or ignored; in which the exhaustion of the post-war consensus and the hardening of certain ideological discourses may, paradoxically, encourage the creation of transversal connections over previous political divisions, as, for example, in the case of sexual rights and freedoms; in which native perspectives may be frequently interrupted and forced to accommodate transnational tendencies and realities; and in which consumerism is not a by-product of industrial production but a self-generating economy and way of life no longer limited to the "family unit" but now characterized by highly fluid and heterogeneous channels of consumption that, in turn, are symptoms of important changes in the very conception of "production" and "markets". In this *uprooting* and *rerouting* of earlier histories, structures and traditions, in their mutation and contamination in a contingent world, we can begin to discern a wider sense. . . .

[A] new sense of both "politics" and "democracy", if they are not to disappear forever behind policed poverty, structural unemployment, the legal surveillance and public ostracism of minorities, authoritarian government and into dust-free data banks . . . has to be discovered and contested in the space of what is potentially and socially possible, and not in abstract solicitations to an abstract "emancipation" or nostalgic appeals to an imaginary past. For ultimately it is only by testing our imagination on the possibilities of this present – "the only times we've got," as the painter David Hockney recently put it – that we can hope to reconstruct both in the realization of a "socialized individuality" (Henri Lefebvre), and attempt to enter another history.   (1990: 47–8)

Grounding the Discourses

The empirical conurbation of Los Angeles discussed in chapter 5 sets the geo-historical scene for the six chapters that comprise Part II. Each of these chapters, in different but interconnected ways, *represents* Los Angeles as a synekistic milieu for the development and expression of the new urbanization processes as well as for the generation of interpretive discourses aimed at making theoretical and practical sense of the postmetropolitan transition. In these representations of the *conceived space* of the postmetropolis, the Los Angeles region is thus both a primary empirical object of analysis and a generative site and source for the analysis itself.

This grounding of the postmetropolitan transition in Los Angeles is not meant to constrict interpretation of the postmetropolis just to this singular and often highly exceptional city-region. Rather, it is guided by an attempt to emphasize what might be called its *generalizable particularities*, the degree to which one can use the specific case of Los Angeles to learn more about the new urbanization processes that are affecting, with varying degrees of intensity, all other cityspaces in the world. In this sense, what will be represented here is an *invitation to comparative analysis*, to using what can be learned from Los Angeles to make practical and theoretical sense of what is happening wherever the reader may be living.

What follows then interweaves the general and the particular, or what the philosophers call nomothetic and idiographic approaches, into six distinct discourses, each representing a different way of analyzing and interpreting the restructuring of the modern metropolis. The first two discourses focus on what have become the most influential interpretive frameworks or windows through which scholars have attempted to explain the primary causes of the new urbanization processes. Chapter 6 represents the postmetropolis through the discourse on the restructuring of the geopolitical economy of urbanization and the emergence of the flexibly specialized *Postfordist Industrial Metropolis*. In chapter 7, the primary explanatory emphasis shifts to the globalization and localization of capital, labor, and culture, and the concurrent formation of a new hierarchy of global or world cities. Here the postmetropolis is seen as a new *Cosmopolis*, generating the most economically, politically, and culturally heterogeneous cityspaces that may have ever existed.

The second pair of discourses focuses primarily on the *outcomes* or urban consequences of globalization and postfordist economic restructuring. Chapter 8 looks specifically at the restructuring of urban *spatial* form, the decentering and recentering of cityspace that is turning the modern metropolis inside-out and outside-in at the same time, challenging conventional definitions of urban, suburban, exurban, non-urban, and rural. The postmetropolis is represented and regionally restructured as an *Exopolis*, a new urban form that challenges the very foundations of contemporary urban studies. Chapter 9 turns our attention to the restructured *social* mosaic of the postmetropolis and the emergence of new forms of metropolarity, inequality, and ethnic and racial marginalization in the midst of extraordinary wealth. The postmetropolis here becomes a *Fractal City*, fragmented and polarized, but also the scene of creative new "hybridities" and a cultural politics aimed not just at reducing inequalities but also at preserving difference and fostering flexible "transversal" identities.

The last two discourses are concerned with how the postmetropolis, especially as it has taken shape in and around Los Angeles, has managed to survive its turbulent and socially fractious globalization and economic restructuring. Chapter 10 describes the archipelago of *Carceral Cities*, fortressed spaces with sophisticated surveillance and adherence technologies that respond to an "ecology of fear" by increasingly substituting *police* for *polis*. Another, more subtle, form of social regulation is explored in chapter 11. The postmetropolis is seen as an agglomeration of *Simcities*, where the urban imaginary is being restructured in electronic as well as more materially manifested cyberspace, increasing what can be called the hyperreality of everyday life. In this implosion of simulation, urban life is increasingly being played out as if it were a computer game, further blurring the boundaries between real and imagined worlds. As with all six of the discourses, this chapter begins with a list of representative texts. These relevant book titles provide key phrases and metaphors that guide the discussion and also serve as supplementary as well as alternative readings.

These six discourses are not intrinsically better or more important than other ways of approaching and understanding the contemporary city. They have been selected because each has become the focus for the development of a significant international cluster of research and researchers explicitly concerned with making practical and theoretical sense of the new urbanization processes and their effects on the spatial specificities of contemporary urbanism. Furthermore, each of these discourses has emerged and consolidated with significant roots in the intellectual environment and synekistic milieu of one of the most precursory if not paradigmatic postmetropolises, the conurbation of Los Angeles. If there exists a distinctive "LA School" of critical urban and regional studies, these six discourses define its areas of greatest scholarly concentration.

Chapter 6
The Postfordist Industrial Metropolis: Restructuring the Geopolitical Economy of Urbanism

Representative Texts

- *Metropolis: From Division of Labor to Urban Form* (Scott, 1988)
- *Technopolis: High Technology Industry and Regional Development in Southern California* (Scott, 1993)
- *Pathways to Industrialization and Regional Development* (Storper and Scott eds., 1993)
- *New Industrial Spaces: Flexible Production, Organization and Regional Development in North America and Western Europe* (Scott, 1988)
- *Production, Work, Territory: The Geographical Anatomy of Industrial Capitalism* (Scott and Storper eds., 1986)
- *The Capitalist Imperative: Territory, Technology, and Industrial Growth* (Storper and Walker eds., 1989)
- *Worlds of Production: The Action Frameworks of the Economy* (Storper and Salais, 1997)
- *The Regional World: Territorial Development in a Global Economy* (Storper, 1997)
- *The New Social Economy: Reworking the Division of Labour* (Sayer and Walker, 1992)
- *Technopoles of the World: The Making of Twenty-first Century Industrial Complexes* (Castells and Hall, 1994)
- *Manufacturing Matters: The Myth of the Post-Industrial Economy* (Cohen and Zysman, 1987)
- *The Deindustrialization of America* (Bluestone and Harrison, 1982)
- *The Great U-Turn: Corporate Restructuring and the Polarizing of America* (Harrison, 1988)
- *Lean and Mean: The Changing Landscape of Corporate Power in the Age of Flexibility* (Harrison, 1994)
- *The Second Industrial Divide: Possibilities for Prosperity* (Piore and Sabel, 1984)

- *The Urbanization of Capital* and *Consciousness and the Urban Experience* (Harvey, 1985)
- *Spatial Divisions of Labor* (Massey, 1984)
- *Post-Fordism: A Reader* (Amin ed., 1994)

Book titles often contain the most concentrated distillations of a discourse. For each of the six discourses on the postmetropolis, I will use key phrases from a list of representative book titles as thematic entry points into the discursive space under consideration. Within this space, the conurbation of Los Angeles will continue to supply a heuristic grounding, both as the primary source of empirical illustrations of the new urbanization processes shaping the postmetropolis and as a stimulating milieu from which a significant portion of the discourse itself originates.

Pathways into Urban Worlds of Production

The first discourse on the postmetropolis is woven of many strands, but motivating each is an interpretive emphasis on the role of *industrial production* and the impact of *industrial restructuring* on contemporary urban life. The evolving postmetropolis is thus viewed primarily as a space, a territory, a region, a "world" of production, with chains or *filières* of penetrating influence that extend into every aspect of urban and regional development. Crystallized within this enmeshing network of dense transactional linkages is a cityspace that is represented discursively as a *postfordist industrial metropolis.* This particular way of looking at cityspace and its postmetropolitan restructuring has developed over the past fifteen years as one of the most powerful and rigorously formulated theoretical and empirical perspectives in contemporary critical urban studies. In what follows, the development of this still-evolving discourse on *industrial urbanism* is presented in a series of conceptual layers, each of which captures different facets of postfordist industrial cityspace.

The geographical anatomy of industrial urbanism

How do cities develop and grow within the production system of modern capitalism? What forces govern the internal and external organization of their economies? How is the intraurban geography of production arranged, and how does it change through time? How is the labor of the citizenry mobilized over the urban system and deployed in productive work? What impacts does the economy have on the structure of urban life? Conversely, what influence does urban life have on the structure of local economic activity? These questions ... represent preliminary windows onto a theoretical problematic of industrialization and urbanization ... and they have important consequences for the ways in which we set about the tasks of understanding the modern metropolis ... how an urban process emerges – via complex patterns

and dynamics of the division of labor – from the basic production apparatus of capitalist society.
            Allen J. Scott, *Metropolis: From the Division of Labor to Urban Form* (1988): 1, 234

These excerpts from the first and last pages of *Metropolis*, perhaps the most academically iconic work on the postmetropolitan geopolitical economy in Southern California, outline the underlying conceptual framework and pre-vailing analytical approach – as well as the ambitious scope – of the first dis-course on the postmetropolitan transition. Framing and focusing the discourse is a perspective on cities and the "urban process" that is centered on the specif-ically geographical impact of industrial production on the changing "land-scape of capitalist society." The "basic production apparatus," manifested in the production space of the city-region, provides the chosen "window" on to the central "theoretical problematic" that arises from the geohistorical inter-play of urbanization and industrialization. This dynamic link between indus-trial and urban development is seen as the fundamental or foundational force shaping what is described in the subtitle of a representative text co-edited by Allen Scott and Michael Storper (1986) as "the geographical anatomy of indus-trial capitalism" or, in other words, capitalism's specific geography. It is from this theoretical framework of industrial urbanism that interpretations are drawn of the new urban and regional restructuring processes that have been reconstituting the spatial specificity of urbanism in the modern metropolis over the past thirty years.

    The general discourse on industrial urbanism has emerged from a wider search to understand the geographical logic and resultant "anatomy" of urban-industrial capitalism and its persistent tendency to produce and repro-duce *geographically uneven development*. It approaches the postmetropolis with a mode of analysis consciously built on the selective recovery, reorientation, and assertive spatialization of old and new ways of studying the city that revolve specifically around the *dynamics of social production* and the intricate web of relations that compose and comprise social as well as spatial *divisions of labor*. As indicated in the subtitle of Scott's *Metropolis*, the main analytical channel runs from the division of labor and other forceful socio-economic processes to urban form and structure, although some attention is also given to the reverse relation: how the spatial specificity of urbanism rebounds to shape economic forces and the very nature of urban-industrial capitalism itself.[1]

----

1 I do not want to derail the discourse on industrial urbanism before it is appropriately introduced, but this issue of the balance between the way industry shapes urbanism and the way urbanism shapes industry is vital to one of the central arguments I have been developing in this book and therefore deserves some comment. Although Scott and a few other exponents of the discourse try hard to rec-ognize the dialectical relation between process and form, there remains a deeply embedded tendency to focus primarily on the economic processes/forces shaping the structural anatomy of urban form/geography rather than the other way around. That is, the analytical journey "from the division of labor to urban form" often leaves too little time to move in the reverse direction. It thus becomes

The leading exponents of the discourse on industrial urbanism, both in Los Angeles and elsewhere, have been economic geographers or geopolitical economists, especially those, like Scott, who played an important role in the neo-Marxist school of urban and regional political economy that developed out of the urban crises of the 1960s. Although the research cluster of industrial urbanists has expanded in recent years to include a wider variety of social scientists interested in industry–labor relations and institutions, the discourse continues to be forcefully shaped by an explicitly spatial version and vision of the political economy of urbanization. The object of study is decidedly focused on the spatial specificities of urbanism and the generative and occasionally degenerative economic stimulus of urban agglomeration, or what I have termed synekism. In this sense, the discourse is a direct extension of the insightful theorizations of the specific (and I would add primarily Firstspace or spatial practice-oriented) geography of capitalist urbanization developed by David Harvey, Manuel Castells, and others in the neo-Marxist school.

But the current discourse also represents a significant departure from this rich tradition. It is, for example, much more eclectic than its primary precursor, especially as it has taken shape in the cluster of researchers using postmetropolitan Los Angeles as its primary urban laboratory. The new discourse weaves together many different approaches to studying cityspace and the urban process, ranging from Engels's commentaries on Manchester, as well as Chicago School ecology and its extensions in neoclassical urban economics and regional science, to new developments in international political economy, evolutionary and institutional economics, poststructuralist critical theory, and postmodern cultural studies. There are borrowings from the classical industrial location theories of Alfred Weber, adding a certain "post-Weberian" flavor to the discourse;[2] from the economist Schumpeter on economic cycles and the "creative destruction" associated with crisis-generated restructuring processes; from the theories of regional development and planning concerned with growth centers and polarized development; and from such iconoclastic urban-

---

worthwhile recalling the most forceful assertion of how the spatial specificity of urbanism rebounds to shape the industrialization process, an observation by Henri Lefebvre that I used as the epigraph to my discussion of the socio-spatial dialectic in *Postmodern Geographies* (1989: 76):

> Space and the political organization of space express social relationships but also react back upon them . . . *Industrialization, once the producer of urbanism, is now being produced by it* . . . When we use the words "urban revolution" we designate the total ensemble of transformations which run throughout contemporary society and which bring about a change from a period in which questions of economic growth and industrialization predominate to the period in which the urban problematic becomes decisive. (emphasis added)

Keep this reblancing directive in mind as we move through the first discourse.

2   The Weber referred to here is not Max but his lesser known and much more spatially minded brother, whose writings on industrial location and agglomeration economies became one of the pillars of the new quantitative and theoretical geography that developed in the 1970s. Alfred Weber's *Uber den Standort der Industrien* was published in 1909; an English translation (*Theory of the Location of Industries*) was first published in 1929, by the University of Chicago Press.

ists as Jane Jacobs and her notions of the self-generating economic culture of cities.

Although most scholars playing a central role in generating the new discourse on industrial urbanism remain tacitly grounded in Marxist conceptions of the fundamental nature of capitalism, there is also a degree to which the discursive framework and language has moved closer to a post-Marxist position, at least in the sense of appearing to reject the "automatic" deep structuralist explanations of all urban phenomena as the product of a single overriding logic of capitalist accumulation. That deep structure and logic remains in play, not as a deterministic blueprint for explaining everything that is happening today, but as an assumed (and most often unstated) backdrop or stage-setting for making theoretical and practical sense of an unpredictable and increasingly complex contemporary world. There remains then a frequently puzzling ambiguity regarding just how much Marxism remains in the discourse, but it is clear that the totalizing metanarrative that dominated the radical school of urban and regional political economy is no longer as all-encompassing and inflexible as it once was.

There are many other ways to distinguish the new discourse on industrial urbanism and geopolitical economy from its predecessor. To elaborate further on these distinguishing features, I present a series of indicative themes that have been shaping the discourse over the past fifteen years, starting with how the "production apparatus of capitalist society" is conceived and treated.

Production-work-territory: reworking the divisions of labor

[T]he urban discourses of the 1960s and 1970s seemed to create a curiously truncated view of the city, i.e., a view in which the basic everyday world of production and work was subsumed as mere stage scenery to a series of consumptionist phenomena . . . In contrast to these theorists, I claim here that industrialization as a generalized process of economic organization and social integration is *the* basis of modern urban development. Above all, the intricate ramifications of the social division of labor, the transactional structure of production, and the dynamics of local labor market formation create a field of forces that pervasively underpins the whole spatial pattern of the metropolis.   (Scott, 1986: 35)[3]

Of the major epistemological premises that have shaped the first discourse and stylized its presentations and representations, the most prominent has been an insistent return to the generative problematic defined by the dynamics of social production, expanded to include not only goods and services but also information, entertainment, and the "production of culture" in what are

3   This quote is taken from the conclusion to A. J. Scott, "Industrialization and Urbanization: A Geographical Agenda," *Annals of the Association of American Geographers* 76, 1986: 25–37. This benchmark essay, building on the work of Scott and his students on industrial development and restructuring in Los Angeles and Orange counties, did indeed effectively set a "geographical agenda" that would shape research on industrial urbanism over the following decade.

called the "culture industries" or, in Scott's most recent work, the "cultural economy of cities".[4] This foundational accent on the contradictory forces and conflictful relations associated with the production process and the divisions of labor built around it is rooted primarily in the work of Marx and Engels. As Scott and others have argued, however, this classical tradition, with its emphasis on the dynamics of production, became sidetracked in the neo-Marxist discourse of the 1960s and 1970s, even in its most spatially explicit formulations.

The deeply embedded problematic of production was seen by most Marxist geographers and sociologists as having been so effectively conceptualized in *Capital* that little more needed to be done other than to use Marx's inspiring insights to stimulate radical political consciousness and action. The inherently exploitative social relations of capitalist production and their imprint on the space of the city and region were thus tacitly relegated to the most abstract and "universal" levels of analyzing capitalist society, becoming an all-encompassing presence that was taken for granted in the very definition of the inner workings of capitalism itself. Keeping the production problematic alive meant little more than maintaining vigilant support for the labor movement and its workplace struggles. But even here the support was diluted by the growing importance of the *consumption space* of the city and the struggles within it over social *reproduction* in households, neighborhood communities, and the overall built environment of urbanism. These struggles revolved around specifically urban social movements that connected progressive politics not so much with capital and the capital–labor relation in the workplace as with the local and national state and its functionaries.[5] In other words, collective consumption and social reproduction defined the most immediate and problematic sites of political contention, with the "production apparatus" of the city shunted into an ever-present but uninterrogated backdrop.

Particularly influential in these earlier neo-Marxist debates was a statement made by Manuel Castells in *The Urban Question* (1977) in which he relegated production to the regional scale, while condensing the spatial specificity of the urban almost exclusively around collective consumption and decidedly social, but only incidentally spatial, movements and politics. This not only narrowed the scope of critical urban studies, it reinforced the interpretive separation of the urban from the regional, and added further barriers to the development of an appropriately socio-spatial dialectic. Breaking down these persistent modernist dualisms (production–consumption, urban–regional, social–spatial) would become a central issue in the evolving discourse on industrial urbanism and an assertively geopolitical economy.

---

4   Allen J. Scott, "The Cultural Economy of Cities," *International Journal of Urban and Regional Research* 21, 1997: 323–39.

5   For the most part, these so-called urban social movements did not include workplace struggles directly relating to industrial production and the labor process. Production struggles continued to be of central importance, but they tended not to be seen as specifically *urban*.

Within the broader and less explicitly neo-Marxist realms of urban planning, urban sociology, and urban geography, a similar concentration on the "consumption apparatus" of the city prevailed, even when dealing with issues of employment, work, and income. Relatively little attention in urban theory, empirical analysis, and planning practice was given to industrial production *per se*, except as a source of gainful blue-collar employment and income, the economic base for labor unions as actors in the city, or a minor form of non-residential land use. As Scott noted, "there was fairly common agreement that the central agenda for urban research was defined by a conception of the city as a locus of consumption activities, housing processes, and neighborhood dynamics" (1986: 25).

The rapidly developing discourse on industrial urbanism thus took urban studies by surprise and was met with significant resistance from radical and liberal, as well as conservative urban scholars. There continues to this day a strong counterposition claiming that the industrial urbanist discourse remains narrowly "productionist," pushing too far into the unstudied margins such issues as the service-based economy, collective consumption, social welfare concerns, the importance of leisure-time activities, and even more importantly, culture and aesthetics, race and ethnicity, gender and sexuality, and many other vital dimensions of urban life not conventionally associated with industrial production and class analysis.

Although this persistent critique of industrial urbanism has helped to open up geopolitical economy to more nuanced interpretations, an argument can be made that the best work on the geopolitical economy of urbanism has always been attentive to issues of consumption, reproduction, and culture. Most industrial urbanists take care to avoid rejecting the inherent importance of such traditional subject matters as housing, the provision of social services, public welfare policies and anti-poverty programs, mass transit, land-use regulation, environmental degradation, and the urban social movements that arise around these collective consumption issues. After an initial period of neglect, new movements revolving around race, gender, sexual preference, and other forms of cultural identity have also been given increasing attention, although not without significant controversy and often rancorous debate.

In response to the critique, it was argued not only that these cultural and consumption issues and problems are important, but also that they can be better understood and acted upon through a rigorous rethinking of the dynamics of social production and divisions of labor, especially in relation to the dramatic industrial restructuring that occurred in the last third of the twentieth century. By the end of the 1980s, this industrial restructuring had advanced far enough to make it clear to most urbanists that many of the most serious problems of urban decay and uneven regional development, from the social disasters of urban renewal to the increasingly evident Frostbelt–Sunbelt "power shift," were implicated in the profound changes taking place in the corporate organization and technology of industrial production and in associated social and spatial divisions of labor.

In particular, it was argued that the industrial restructuring process was having the effect of hollowing out and polarizing *urban labor markets*, one of the primary expressions of the social division of labor in cityspace. The once-bulging middle sector of the labor market and the middle class more generally were being squeezed, with a lucky few rising above into technical and managerial occupations while much larger numbers, mostly unionized blue-collar workers, were experiencing severe reductions of household income and edging toward what has recently come to be called the welfare-dependent urban underclass. Charting the social and spatial impact of industrial restructuring on urban labor markets and their segmentation by gender, race, and ethnicity, as well as occupation and location has been a major research focus for the industrial urbanists.

Much of this research has been accomplished through *industrial or sectoral case studies*, detailed and specifically geographical analyses of the changing technology, corporate organization, labor process, employment structure, and locational patterns in particular industries and industrial sectors, ranging from automobiles to animated cartoons. In addition to mapping occupational patterns, firm locations, input–output relations, and the distribution of employment, these case studies went further and deeper into the division of labor to explore the "transactional web" of inter-firm and inter-personal linkages that surround the production process. Scott's work, dutifully recognizing its rich historical precursors, set the tone for many subsequent industrial case studies by focusing attention on the dynamics of *vertical disintegration*, defined as "the general process of the fragmentation of different elements of the labor process into specialized but functionally interlinked units of production" (1986: 27).

Increasing vertical disintegration became, for Scott and many other industrial urbanists, the interpretive focus for understanding and theorizing industrial restructuring and the new patterns of urban-industrial development arising from the economic crises of the 1960s and 1970s. Scott traced back the conceptualization of the dynamics of vertical disintegration to Adam Smith's parable of the division of labor in pin manufacturing, but added to Smith's pinpointing an acute spatialization, linking growing vertical disintegration and its inherent explosion of transaction costs to the cost-saving strategy of "horizontal" re-agglomeration, the formation of distinct *industrial complexes* or districts. These emerging clusters of industrial production, many established at sites some distance removed from the older urban-industrial cores, became the most symbolic representation of what was developing (again) in the geographical anatomy of contemporary industrial urbanism, especially with regard to organizational and technological innovation and what I have been calling an endogenously generated spatial synekism.

The economic and spatial logic here was simple and straightforward. Faced with increasing vertical and horizontal disintegration (due to such practices as subcontracting, outsourcing, establishing multiple production sites, and other transformations of the thoroughly integrated Fordist assembly line), "producers (whether engaged in manufacturing or office and service activities) will tend to locate near to one another so as to cut the costs of external transactional activity" (1986: 28). Pushing his spatialization still further, Scott argued that because "geographical association," with its amelioration of the frictions of distance, effectively reduces the costs of transactions, it induces still more vertical disintegration *and re-agglomeration.* "In these ways," says Scott, "intensely developed clusters of producers develop on the landscape, and with the growth of markets the clusters themselves grow in size and become increasingly internally differentiated" (1986: 29).

The three main sectors of the economy where this re-agglomeration appeared to be most propulsively intense were (1) high-technology-based production, especially in electronics, aerospace, and biomedicine, giving rise to a host of new terms such as technopoles, technopolis, and silicon landscapes; (2) craft-based and often highly labor- and design-intensive industries, ranging from the production of garments, furniture, and jewelry to guided missiles and movies; and (3) the so-called FIRE sector, consisting of finance-insurance-real estate firms as well as related activities in advertising, promotion, and legal services. Most of the empirical research as well as the major attempts at theory building have concentrated on these three "cutting-edge" or propulsive sectors of the new urban-industrial space economy, in the USA as well as in many other areas of the world.

Such industrial case studies, tracing the formation of specialized industrial agglomerations, have become methodologically emblematic of the first discourse. They have provided the most important empirical raw material for both theory-building and practical application, and have became the characteristic pathway for younger research scholars to enter the discourse. As a methodological hallmark, they have also helped to define the academic boundaries of the discourse, generating heated debates over inclusion and exclusion, especially with regard to gender and race. These debates have involved both the degree to which women and people of color are given conceptual and empirical attention in the industrial, sectoral, and labor market studies, and the degree to which women and people of color are academically recognized and respected as scholars within the division of labor inside the discourse itself.[6]

Manufacturing matters: against postindustrial sociology

Another thematic banner around which the industrial urbanists have rallied is the assertion that "manufacturing matters," a rhetorical celebration of the

6 See, for example, Susan Christopherson, "On Being Outside 'The Project,'" *Antipode* 21, 1989: 83–9; and Linda McDowell, "Multiple Voices: Speaking from Inside and Outside 'The Project,'" *Antipode* 24, 1992: 56–72. Christopherson and McDowell extended their critiques well beyond the industrial urbanism discourse, helping to generate a far-reaching critical feminist reinterpretation of all modes of geographical inquiry. For this larger and bolder critique, see Doreen Massey, *Space, Place and Gender*, Cambridge, UK: Polity Press, 1994; and Gillian Rose, *Feminism and Geography: The Limits of Geographical Knowledge*, Cambridge, UK: Polity Press, 1993.

centrality of industrial production. This double-barreled trope is first an assertive affirmation that manufacturing industry, despite dramatic statistical decline in employment in almost every advanced industrial country and the accompanying reductions in the power of industrial unions, remains the vital core of all national economies, the *sine qua non* of capitalist development. The battle to (re)establish this positioning has been fought on several fronts. It is noted, for example, that while industrial employment has dropped sharply in the USA and most other advanced industrial countries, the contribution of manufacturing to the Gross National Product has suffered relatively little decline. But aside from the statistical arguments, there are larger ideological and theoretical targets, perhaps the most prominent of which is the competing discourse on postindustrialism.

By now, almost everyone is aware of at least the concept of postindustrial society, the notion that in most of the developed countries there has been a pronounced shift into service-based economies, white-collar occupations, and information-generating technologies that are the vital cogs of what some allege is a new form of affluent capitalist society based primarily on consumption and consumerism rather than manufacturing industry. Some version of this postindustrial hypothesis and its more recent extensions in the notions of an Information Society have entered urban studies, especially among sociologists working in declining manufacturing regions in the USA and the UK. In this alternative discourse on urban restructuring, the industrial capitalist city has become the Postindustrial or Information Age city, signaling a fundamental shift away from the structure and logic of urban-industrial capitalism. In some extreme cases, this shift, with its declining emphasis on workplace struggles, industrial unions, and socialist politics, has provoked imaginative pronouncements of the "end of ideology," the "triumph of capitalism," and most recently "the end of history." Even in its more moderate forms, postindustrialism is associated with a deprivileging of industrialization processes as a foundation for studying contemporary urban phenomena.

It is not surprising to find that Allen Scott has taken the lead in attacking postindustrialism and its followers. At a most basic level, working in and on the Los Angeles region during a time when it rose to become the largest industrial metropolis in North America made the postindustrial hypothesis seem unusually off-base to Scott. In a frontal response, he concluded his discussion of "Urban Theories and Realities," the first chapter of *Metropolis* (1988), with "a brief exercise in deconstruction and reorientation." In his characteristically terse and unplayful writing style, he states: "The postindustrial hypothesis strikes me as being seriously misleading in several of its major implications, and utterly wrong insofar as it points to the latent transcendence of capitalism by a sort of new information-processing mode of economic organization" (1988: 7). He supports his position by arguing (1) that information and business services are to a significant degree also manufactured commodities and are "produced" in much the same way as steel, cars, and computers; (2) that even the provision of personal services (household finance, education, health) and of public and semipublic goods (collective consumption) can be seen as "important components of and/or adjuncts to the basic structures of production and work in modern capitalism" (1988: 8); and (3) that such specialized sectors as corporate administration, banking, insurance, accounting, advertising, and the like continue, as they always have, to manage, direct, and control the worldwide system of industrial commodity production, the "inner motor of the entire capitalist economy" (1988: 8).

There is another side to the commanding argument that manufacturing matters and to Scott's attack on postindustrialism. It has to do with a central issue in all the chapters of *Postmetropolis*, the importance of the spatial specificity of urbanism. The very words "manufacturing matters" can be seen as resonating with a discursive connection to an argument that has been at the forefront of what I once described, in a larger context, as "the reassertion of space in critical social theory," a claim that *geography matters* in every attempt to understand human behavior, history, and society.[7] Given the specifically spatial emphasis in the discourse on industrial urbanism, to recognize that manufacturing matters can be seen as, at the same time, a reavowal of the critical importance of the geographical imagination, at least in the study of cities. As the postindustrial and new information age perspectives have been particularly attractive to sociologists, indeed have been generated primarily by sociologists, and as these perspectives and discourses have often developed in ways that reduce the significance of spatial specificities and the geographical as against the historical and sociological imaginations, the resistance to them is also again in part a purposeful reassertion of the importance of space and geography in understanding the contemporary world.

To reduce industrial urbanism to a simple productionism or a structural obsession with the manufacturing sector is therefore to miss a vital point. Within this first discourse is one of the richest reassertions of the importance of a critical spatial perspective and what I have called a socio-spatial dialectic in all of contemporary urban studies. Although there remains a tendency to give more attention to the space-shaping power of industrialization than the industry-shaping power of spatiality, even this imbalance is being partially attended to in the more recent works of Scott, Storper, and many other geopolitical economists. What does remain in force, however, is a growing division between geographical and sociological approaches to urban studies over this reassertion of spatiality, a subject I will return to in later chapters.

Crossing industrial divides

Patterns of industrialization and urbanization have always been closely intertwined with one another, just as they have also always been jointly subject to periodic restructuring, right from the very historical initiation of capitalism. One distinctive expression of these phenomena can be observed in Britain in the early nineteenth century

---

7   See D. Massey and J. Allen eds., *Geography Matters! A Reader*, Cambridge, UK: Polity, 1984.

where dense urban concentrations of workshops, mills, and manual workers developed in response to the factory system in places like Birmingham, Bradford, Leeds, Manchester and Sheffield. Another expression of the same phenomena can be found in the Northeast of the United States in the decades following World War II, with Chicago and Detroit as its typical cases, where a hugely successful fordist mass production system was creating the bases of the American Dream. Yet another is discernible in the USA Sunbelt today where cities such as Dallas-Fort Worth, Denver, Houston, Phoenix, and the great megalopolis of Southern California have grown apace on the basis of a very different kind of capitalist industrialization from that which shaped the urban centers of the Northeast at an earlier period of time. All of the cases mentioned represent peculiar conjunctures in the historical geography of capitalism; they can be seen as particularly intense distillations of economic order and ways of life that have prevailed at different times in different places over the past couple of centuries.

> Allen Scott, "Industrial Urbanism in Southern California: Post-Fordist Civic Dilemmas and Opportunities," *Contention* (1995): 39

Here Scott leads us again into another discursive trope that threads through the literature on industrial urbanism. It involves a strategic emplacement of the discourse within the geohistory of capitalism and its episodic moments of intensive and extensive restructuring. Three of these "peculiar conjunctures" are identified by Scott, each giving rise to "distinctive expressions" or epitomizing representations of different modes of industrial urbanism: Manchester and other Industrial Revolution cities in Britain for what might be described as the classic or foundational model, the workshops and mills of the factory system; Chicago and Detroit for the "hugely successful fordist mass production system"; and, with deliberate emphasis, "the great megalopolis of Southern California" for the contemporary development of a distinctively postfordist industrial cityspace. This sequence of three modes of industrial urbanism, although defined, exemplified, and dated in different ways, is etched deeply into the geohistorical narrative that frames the discourse.[8]

In doing so, the discourse becomes intrinsically attached to some version or other of the long-wave models discussed earlier in conjunction with the macro-geohistory of modernity, urbanization, and capitalist development. Although the major theoreticians and empirical analysts of industrial urbanism tend to distance themselves from a full-blown long-wave model, a discursive consensus has developed around the most recent downturn in the national and global economies, variously dated from the late 1960s to the early 1970s. The empirical evidence of crisis formation during this period and sub-

---

8   While Southern California will remain the primary focus of discussion, it is important to note other significant exemplars of the new industrial urbanism, including Silicon Valley and the greater San Francisco Bay Area, the region around Boston strung primarily along Route 128, and the so-called Third Italy, consisting of such intermediate regions between the North and the South as Emilia-Romagna, Tuscany, and Venice. To this list might also be added the *cité scientifique* of Paris, the Baden-Württemberg and Bavaria regions of Germany, and various "technopoles" in Japan.

sequent indications of a profound economic shift arising from crisis-generated restructuring processes operating at all scales of the capitalist economy, from the local to the global, has become an interpretive fulcrum for the new discourse and its urban representations.

Bennett Harrison described this shift in the US economy and society as a *Great U-Turn* (1988) and attributed its causes to a breakdown of the "social contract" between giant corporations, big labor unions, and an interventionist state that sustained the Fordist-Keynesian postwar economic boom. At the root of this breakdown was a calculated restructuring of corporate power and decision-making that was associated with increasing subcontracting strategies, factory closures especially in the industrial heartland of the American Manufacturing Belt, union-busting campaigns, the flight of capital overseas in the search for cheaper labor supplies, and the reorganization of the corporate "landscape" around new labor-saving technologies. A parallel restructuring of big government was also leading to a reversal of priorities, as the earlier New Deal and later Great Society welfare programs lost their attraction because of worsening economic conditions. What was initially described as a process of *deindustrialization* developed into a "polarizing of America" that was intensifying poverty, decimating the blue-collar workforce, ruining once-thriving communities, and significantly pinching middle-class households as corporations sought new pathways to profitability.

On a wider international scale and with a more optimistic viewpoint, Michael Piore and Charles Sabel (1984) theorized this crisis-generated restructuring as the start of a "second industrial revolution" based in large part on a move away from what they termed the "necessity of bigness" that for two centuries had propelled capitalist development toward ever larger increases in the scale of industrial production. Fordist mass production, with its giant corporations and integrated assembly lines, was seen as having reached the limits of bigness and economies of scale. This crisis of Fordism made room for the fluorescence of a new economy built on what they called *flexible specialization*, derigidified hierarchies of labor-management relations and reorganized production processes and technologies that allowed clusters of small and middle-sized firms, no longer bound to old Fordist urban agglomerations, to take the lead in economic innovation and the generation of new "possibilities for prosperity," often in what Scott described as *new industrial spaces*. For Piore and Sabel, the paradigmatic example of these new industrial spaces was the Third Italy and its pattern of widely scattered and mainly craft-based industries.

Studying the Third Italy introduced several additional themes to the industrial urbanism discourse, based largely on the work of Italian scholars trying to make sense of this regional resurgence. The term *fabbrica diffusa* or diffused production described the wide scattering of production sites outside the largest urban centers. Rather than concentrating in big cities, production was clustered in what the Italian economist Giacamo Beccatini, drawing on the early work of the English economist Alfred Marshall, called *industrial districts*. Studying the dynamics behind the formation of these "Marshallian" industrial districts and what might be described as the synekistic innovation that arises in even small urban agglomerations, has become a central empirical and theoretical focus for industrial urbanists throughout the world, and has entered deeply into the work on the Los Angeles region, one of the most diffuse and polycentric of all major industrial metropolises.

In addition to conceiving of the current period of urban economic restructuring as reflecting a Great U-turn in the relations between capital, labor, and the state, and the passage across a Second Industrial Divide to an Age of Flexibility, there was another semantic layer used to conceptualize what was happening to cities in the late twentieth century. It drew upon the French Regulation School that was built initially on the work of Michael Aglietta and developed with a more explicitly spatial emphasis by Alain Lipietz.[9] From the regulationist viewpoint, a new *regime of accumulation* was developing in the world capitalist economy in response to the crisis of Fordism and the disintegration of the Fordist *mode of regulation*, a concept somewhat akin to the social contract between capital, labor, and the state. The terms usually associated with this emerging regime were neo-Fordist and neo-Taylorist, although there has been a tendency among many outside the Regulation School to lump all the new forms under the general label *postfordist*.

In their summative depiction of the geographical dynamics of "late capitalist industrialization," Allen Scott and David Harvey added a new label to the contemporary era of urban-industrial capitalism, describing it as a period of transition from Fordism to a regime of *flexible accumulation*.[10] But despite the widespread usage of this term, especially among those most interested in maintaining strong ties to Marxism, the dominant trope in the industrial urban discourse has continued to be postfordism.

Post-ford-ism

The emergence of postfordism as the prevailing metaphor for the contemporary world economy has sparked widespread critical discussion both within the field of geopolitical economy and among its outside observers. Let us look at the word *post-ford-ism*, breaking it down to its component parts. The middle syllable (with or without the capital letter) is perhaps least controversial. It emphatically expresses the centrality of industrial production and captures as well as any other trope the hegemonic economic system and social contract that most powerfully propelled the postwar boom in the USA. Its Gramscian

9   Michael Aglietta, *A Theory of Capitalist Regulation: The USA Experience*, London: Verso, 1979; Alain Lipietz, "New Tendencies in the International Division of Labor: Regimes of Accumulation and Modes of Regulation," in Scott and Storper eds., *Production, Work, Territory: The Geographical Anatomy of Industrial Capitalism*, Boston: Allen and Unwin, 1986: 16–40. For Lipietz, see also *Le Capital et son espace*, Paris: Maspero, 1977.
10   David Harvey and Allen Scott, "The Practice of Human Geography: Theory and Empirical Specificity in the Transition from Fordism to Flexible Accumulation," in Bill Macmillan ed., *Remodeling Geography*, Oxford: Blackwell, 1989: 217–29.

roots are appealing to the radical political economist and also appropriately place the origins of the (capitalized) Fordist regime back to the 1920s, when the Italian Marxist first used the term Fordism. Its specific reference to the automobile industry has equally attractive iconic power with respect both to mass-production assembly lines and to the mass-consumption productivity deals that generated the most well-off and socially mobile blue-collar working class in history. Some critical flurries have arisen over whether the dominance of Fordist mass production has been exaggerated in the immediate pre- and postwar decades (primarily outside the USA) and some analysts have urged that more attention must be given to Keynes, and hence to the role of the welfare state and state-stimulated mass consumption, in symbolizing the postwar economic system. These critiques, however, have probably had more to do with overenthusiastic assertions of the hegemony of postfordist spatial practices than with challenging the metonymical root term. Fordism has now entered into common usage to describe the era of capitalist development stretching from the 1920s to at least the early 1970s.

The prefixing of *post-* has been most controversial. As with the debates on postmodernity and postmodernism, certain categorical literalists insist that the prefix connotes "the end of," a clean break between two entirely different eras. Given abundant empirical evidence that Fordism has not disappeared, they claim that postfordism is therefore inherently misleading if not useless as a concept. Another version of such literalism, also prevalent in the postmodern debates, creates a dichotomy or binarism from the *post*-prefixing, thereby making postfordism a pure and polar opposite to Fordism, with no mixing allowed. When characteristically Fordist industries are seen engaging in typically postfordist practices, or vice versa, this becomes an unacceptable contradiction challenging the very meaning of the postfordist "ascendancy." It is no doubt true that one can rummage through the writings on postfordism and discover phrases and paragraphs that appear to intimate both a "clean break" and a "polar opposite" model of the relations between fordism and postfordism. But the wider context of these writings is sufficiently clear. Like other *posts*, postfordism represents neither a complete break with nor a binary opposite to its central referent, but rather a movement beyond its established regime of accumulation and mode of regulation to a significantly different economic order. In other words: a deconstruction (not destruction or erasure) and reconstitution (still only partial, ongoing, and incorporating selective components of the older order) of Fordist and Keynesian political economies.

Finally the *-ism*, a suffix most innocently denoting some form of intentional adherence to a particular way of doing things, but often used also to denote extremes of exclusion and/or passionate advocacy. For Fordism, the innocent meaning is probably most appropriate. It defines a specific composite of economic practices that are ideally typified in the production processes and labor–management relations initiated by Henry Ford; and which also characterized a cluster of industrial sectors that were primarily (but not exclusively) responsible for economic recovery from the Great Depression and sustaining the postwar boom in the USA and in other advanced industrial countries. Fordism thus refers to economic actors and their characteristic actions. Post-ford*ism*, then, similarly implies the development of an alternative "emergent" configuration of propulsive economic practices, significantly different yet not completely disconnected from Fordism. To push the-*ism* to its most advocative, promotional, and exclusionary extremes is therefore to over-extend its meaning.

For its analysts, postfordism is a useful portmanteau word to define and describe the emerging new forms and characteristic tendencies of contemporary urban-industrial capitalism. To be sure, it is often reified into a preferred course of action, the only way to go, so to speak, especially when the "success stories" described in the discursive texts are simplistically translated into planning and public policy debates and decision-making. Without its own metonymical referent, however, postfordism becomes a vaguer and more open-ended concept than Fordism. It is designed to capture all apparent departures from Fordism while simultaneously suggesting that something significantly new and different has already consolidated in Fordism's wake. Postfordism is thus best seen as a "holding" concept, tentatively open to multiple specifications, a temporary catch-all that can disappear when its distinctive qualities are unequivocally established, identified, and named. What crystallizes the discourse is the asserted ascension of a particular ensemble of economic practices over the past three decades to a position of increasing economic prominence. Identifying and naming the generative "inner workings" of this ascendancy and specifying its most important causes and consequences has been another important theoretical and practical project of the discursive exponents.

The empowerment of flexibility

Flexibility pervades the discourse on industrial urbanism. The contemporary literature abounds with references to flexible specialization (sometimes shortened to flexspec), flexible production systems, a capitalist regime of flexible accumulation, an Age of Flexibility, flexible labor–management relations, flexible technologies, even Flex-city or Flexopolis as a synonym for postfordist industrial cityspace. Increasing flexibility is seen as the key ingredient in the propulsive expansion and multiplication of the new technopoles, craft-based industrial districts, and FIRE stations, and indeed of the entire transition from Fordism to postfordism. The attractions of flexibility are manifold. It resounds with contrasts to the rigidities of Fordist mass production: committed assembly lines pouring out highly standardized products, huge hierarchically organized corporations, vertically integrated production systems that encompass everything from raw material inputs to marketing and advertising of the finished product, equally tightly structured and hierarchical labor agreements and management relations, and formally legislated government regulation and welfare provision.

Under the postwar social contract in the USA, Fordist industries were able to achieve historically unprecedented economies of scale and agglomeration. By the early 1970s, however, profits became increasingly squeezed, productivity was no longer increasing fast enough to cover promised wages and benefits to labor, intensified international competition created growing trade imbalances, key raw material imports were cut off, and stagflation significantly curtailed the mass consumption (and related welfare provisions) necessary for Fordism to work. However one might explain the emerging crisis in the US and world economies, it became clear to the leading economic actors that business as usual could no longer be depended upon to sustain continued economic expansion and that the built-in rigidities of Fordism were at least part of the problem. In Japan, Western Europe, and other advanced industrial countries, even where Fordist industries were not as prominent as in the USA, there was a similar realization that piecemeal reforms of the economy might not be enough to assure continued economic growth and social peace. More drastic measures needed to be taken.

The industrial restructuring processes generated by the economic crises that ended the postwar boom initially moved in many different directions. But soon, certain distinctive patterns of innovation seemed to emerge and consolidate as stable and successful economic practices. The earliest sociological descriptions of this new economic order benignly noted the birth of a "postindustrial" society in the USA, as manufacturing employment severely declined and service occupations exploded. Later, the discourse shifted to descriptions of the deindustrialization of America, focusing upon the vast American Manufacturing Belt, and the new regionalizations arising from the decline of the Frostbelt or Rustbelt, and the rise of the Sunbelt states and "sunrise industries."

In the discussions of deindustrialization, it became increasingly clear that manufacturing (and the working class) still mattered (a striking contrast to the postindustrial thesis) and that what was happening was describable not just as deindustrialization (largely emanating from the decline or deconstruction of Fordism) but also as *reindustrialization* (the rise of new industrial forms that reconstituted Fordism along significantly different lines). By the end of the 1980s, the discussions of industrial restructuring had become refocused on this postfordist reindustrialization process and, in particular, on the greater flexibility that seemed to characterize its most profitable spatio-economic practices. The discourse was also significantly internationalized to explore the many global variations on the theme of flexible production and specialization, with particular emphasis given to the Japanese and Italian models. Also emphasized as pathways to greater flexibility were the new information-based technologies (modern electronics, computers, robotics), corporate organizational innovations, emerging transactional economies of "scope" rather than scale, the growth of local and regional networks of enterprises and entrepreneurs, and a host of other causes and consequences of industrial restructuring too numerous to make note of here. What emanated from all these new developments was an enhanced ability to combine the variety of production that characterized nineteenth century craft industries with the enormous returns to scale that were associated with Fordist mass production.

Flexible production, indeed what might be called the flexible version of industrial urbanism, has been studied in three broad and interacting realms: technological, organizational, and territorial or spatial. New technologies are seen as promoting flexibility through computer-processed changes in product lines, just-in-time delivery systems, reduced inventory costs, and many other labor- and fixed cost-saving devices and strategies. Corporate organizational structures have become more flexible in various ways. Corporate mergers have formed huge conglomerates with many diverse specializations that, when successful, can be flexibly expanded or closed down depending on performance, without having negative effects on other units. Much more attention, however, has been given to the vertical disintegration of the production process and the externalization of risk through subcontracting, outsourcing, more effective control of labor–management relations, and many other forms of flexible specialization. The accumulating impact of these technological and organizational changes is viewed as generating new patterns of territorial development, driving the restructuring of the geopolitical economy of cityspace, and shaping the formation of the postfordist industrial metropolis.

Getting lean and mean: the surge in inequality

Much of the literature on industrial restructuring and flexible specialization has concentrated on the success stories and the growth and development of the leading sectors of the contemporary global economy. There is another side to the discourse on industrial urbanism, however, that centers around the negative impacts of postfordist industrial restructuring and flexible accumulation, especially on labor in general and women and ethnic-racial minorities and the poor in particular. These negative effects can be seen as arising from the very nature of economic restructuring itself: its origins in crisis and its double-edged driving force of seeking new ways of achieving sustainable and profitable economic expansion while also finding new ways to maintain social peace and stability, especially with respect to controlling and disciplining the vital workforce.

As it has in earlier periods of accelerated economic restructuring, the search for tighter social control over disruptive or potentially disruptive forces in the economy has characteristically involved an intensified disciplining process that has been ideologically rationalized and cloaked in such catch-phrases as the necessity for "creative destruction" or an emergency-generated "politics of austerity." The disciplining that has been occurring in conjunction with the current phase of economic restructuring has been formidable indeed, and deserves some specific attention, if only to counterbalance the tendency to dwell primarily on the success stories of postfordism.

The deconstruction and reconstitution of Fordism in America has had a significant disciplining effect on all three components of the Fordist social contract. Big Business, Big Government, and Big Labor have all been drastically "downsized" to become, in Bennett Harrison's pungent phrase, increasingly "lean and mean." As Harrison (1994, rev. edn. 1997) argues, this has allowed the Fordist trio to survive in the Age of Flexibility but at an enormous economic, political, and social cost to the general population. It is also becoming clear that the new postfordist economies and geographies, rather than relieving these costs, are compounding them in what increasingly appears to be a vicious cycle of social polarization and widening economic inequalities.

To illustrate: according to a recent Department of Commerce report, inflation-adjusted real wages for non-supervisory employees in private industry have been falling since 1973 (the most widely used starting date of the Great U-turn) at a compound rate of 0.7 percent a year, with declines occurring even during some boom years. As other studies have shown, full-time employees are working longer hours and receiving fewer benefits, paid time off has decreased, and part-time work has exploded to the point that Manpower, Inc. (a headhunting and temporary employment firm) is today the largest corporate employer in the country, having replaced General Motors, that even larger corporate icon of Fordism. The income gap between rich and poor has widened significantly to levels last seen in the Great Depression and the poor are made up, more than ever before, of women and children of color. There are some signs of a turnaround in recent years, but the cumulative negative impact of restructuring on the industrial workers of America has been of such magnitude as to make many observers view the postfordist industrial metropolis as inherently a magnifier of social and spatial inequalities.

Harrison describes "the dark side of flexible production" and its advancing "surge of inequality" in this way:

> From the vantage point of the 1990s, it is hard to find any serious observer who does *not* agree that inequality is on the rise. The polarization of the jobs that employers are making available to people searching for work is cleaving the whole population, white and black, Anglo and Latino, into highly paid haves and more poorly paid, increasingly insecure have-nots . . . [W]hat the M.I.T. economist Lester Thurow has called "the surge in inequality" may, at least in part be connected with the very industrial restructuring and business reorganization discussed thus far in this book. Lean production, downsizing, outsourcing, and the growing importance of spatially extensive production networks governed by powerful core firms and their strategic allies, here and abroad, are all part of business's search for "flexibility," in order to better cope with heightened global competition. But this very search for flexibility is also aggravating an old American problem – economic and social *dualism*.   (1994 [1997]: 190)

The primary discursive focus for explaining this negative side of postfordism and flexible production has been the apparent obsession, especially in Corporate America, with the tactics of cutting labor costs: the definitive program for getting lean and mean through drastic *downsizing*, now the most popular synonym for restructuring (and for what Schumpeter called "creative destruction") inside and outside the corporate landscape. So much of the contemporary economic condition in the USA emerges from the perceived necessity to reduce the costs of labor and its widespread implementation: the explosion in the numbers of part-time and "contingent" workers, the rising frequency of multi-job families and households, the massive entry of women (especially with children) into the labor market, the widening income gap and the growing polarization of wages, plant closures and relocations, corporate flight and overseas investment in cheap labor areas, rising homelessness and the health care crisis, government deregulation and union-busting, the growth of less labor-intensive high-technology industries, the rise of underground informal economies and industrial sweatshops, and a host of additional outcomes that are represented as contributing to the dark side of the new geopolitical economy.[11]

These more critical responses to the complex transition from Fordism to postfordism raise some challenging questions for the evolving discourse on industrial urbanism. As more evidence accumulates about the negative social and economic consequences of the new regime of flexible accumulation, it is becoming increasingly clear that we know much more about the success stories and positive indicators of contemporary urban and regional development than we do about the failures and deleterious effects of the new urbanization processes. What, then, does this mean with respect to our practical and theoretical understanding of the postmetropolitan transition? Looking back at the tumultuous events since 1989, starting with the symbolic fall of the Berlin Wall and the uprising in Tienanmen Square and moving through the Justice Riots of 1992 in Los Angeles to the 1997 economic breakdown in eastern Asia, a new question can be raised: Is what we are facing today, as we enter a new millennium, not just a successful recovery from the crisis of Fordism but also the beginning of a new crisis emanating from the expansion and diffusion of postfordist spatial practices, the Age of Flexibility, and the other new urbanization processes that have shaped the postmetropolis? In other words, have we moved from a crisis-generated restructuring to a *restructuring-generated crisis*? Keep this question in mind as you read further into the discourses on the postmetropolitan transition.

Into the regional world: the rediscovery of synekism

One last step is needed in outlining the development of the first discourse on the postmetropolis, a new twist on an old theme in the geohistory of cityspace that is reconceptualizing the discourse on industrial urbanism around an

---

11 For another view of the dark side of postfordism and flexible production, focused on questions of environmental degradation, environmental justice, and tightening labor discipline, see David Harvey, *Justice, Nature and the Geography of Difference*, Cambridge, MA, and Oxford, UK: Blackwell, 1996.

explicitly *regional* framing. There has always been a significant regional focus to the geopolitical economy of urbanism, but today, with renewed intensity, there is emerging an explicit attempt to reformulate and absorb the discourse on industrial urbanism into a more encompassing discourse on *industrial regionalism*. Taking the lead in this current effort is Michael Storper, another of the cluster of spatial scholars based in Los Angeles. Here is how Storper introduces this reformulation in the first chapter of *The Regional World: Territorial Development in a Global Economy* (1997), entitled "The Resurgence of Regional Economies":

> Something funny happened in the early 1980s. The region, long considered an interesting topic to historians and geographers, but not considered to have any interest for mainstream western social science, was rediscovered by a group of political economists, sociologists, political scientists, and geographers. Not that no attention had been paid to regions by social scientists before that: in regional economics, development economics, and economic geography, such topics as regional growth and decline, patterns of location of economic activity, and regional economic structure were well-developed domains of inquiry. But such work treated the region as an *outcome* of deeper political-economic processes, not as *a fundamental unit of social life* in contemporary capitalism equivalent to, say, markets, states or families, nor a *fundamental motor process in social life*, on the same level as technology, stratification, or interest-seeking behavior . . .
>
> In the early 1980s, in contrast, it was asserted that the region might be a fundamental basis of economic and social life "after mass production." That is, since new successful forms of production – different from the canonical mass production systems of the postwar period – were emerging in some regions and not others, and since they seemed to involve both *localization* and *regional differences and specificities* (institutional, technological), it followed then that there might be something fundamental that linked late 20th-century capitalism to regionalism and regionalization.   (1997: 3, emphasis added)

A key part of what was happening in the early 1980s was centered in the development of a new hybrid field of regional political economy.[12] The first products of the growing spatialization of Marxism that began in the early 1970s were concentrated at the *urban* and *international* scales, creating the radical urban political economy, sociology, and geography discussed in chapter 4 as well as the neo-Marxist theories of underdevelopment, dependency, and world systems analysis that significantly changed prevailing views of how the global economy operates. For the most part, these two fields, themselves hybrids, shared a similar underlying analytical framework but remained relatively distinct and separate from one another, with little cross-fertilization or synergy. As a latecomer, regional political economy was able to build on

---

12   Edward W. Soja, "Regions in Context: Spatiality, Periodicity, and the Historical Geography of the Regional Question," *Environment and Planning D: Society and Space* 3, 1985, 175–90.

and synthesize the best of both the more microspatial and internalist perspectives on urbanism and the "urban process" under capitalism; and the
more macrospatial and externalist perspectives of a broadly defined world
systems theory of global capitalism. It did so by adopting what Storper and
others would call a "meso-level" of analysis, an integrative third perspective
assertively positioned between the micro and the macro.[13]

In *The Regional World*, Storper looks back not just to the early 1980s but to
the entire development up to the present moment of the discourse on industrial urbanism and all the issues and approaches that have just been discussed
in this chapter. At the heart of his regionalist retheorizing, as well as of the
more empirically defined "resurgence of regional economies" he describes, is
one of the classical questions of all human geographical inquiry: what makes
things (people, activities, the built environment) cluster together in distinct
nodes or agglomerations and what are the consequences of this clustering?
Storper does not ask the question in so general a form, but instead concentrates on specifically economic activities, above all industrial production as the
generative force for what he calls "territorial development." In doing so, he
hones in on the distinctive territorial development processes currently observ-
able in the restructured global economy.

Drawing our attention to the self-generating developmental capacity of
agglomeration economies (also called externalization, urbanization, or localization economies in the literature), Storper identifies three prevailing
approaches to explaining the formation and expansion of dynamic industrial
agglomerations or, as they are alternatively called, industrial complexes,
industrial districts, and innovative milieux. He defines these approaches as
distinct "schools" focusing on (1) institutions, (2) industrial organization and
transactions, and (3) technological change and learning. Passing each through
the screen of what he calls the "holy trinity" of regional economic analysis,
Organizations-Technologies-Territories, he composes his own eclectic theory
of "regional economies as relational assets" and roots these regional assets and
specificities in what he calls *reflexivity*, described as "the central characteristic
of contemporary capitalism" (1997: 28). Reflexivity is seen as operating at two
levels, the first and "more limited" being the traditional sphere of market
relations, in which "localized input–output relations" constitute "webs of
user–producer" linkages through which flow information, knowledge, innovation, and learning. The second and "more general case" is keyed to "localized conventions" and "untraded interdependencies," those "softer" and
more subtle non-market-screened behaviors and "atmospheres" that "attach
to the process of economic and organizational learning and coordination" and
make regional development stick in place over long periods of time (1997: 21).
While the first level has been widely recognized and studied, the second opens

---

13 Although the terms were never used by the regional political economists, I am tempted to describe
the meso-level insertion, following my arguments in *Thirdspace*, as a critical thirding, deconstructing
and reconstituting in a new form and focus one of the most powerful binarisms (micro–macro) in all
of social science.

up significant new research directions in urban-regional development theory
and practice.

The concept of *purposeful economic reflexivity*, with its associated emphasis
on localized conventions and untraded interdependencies, is the keystone of
Storper's regional worlds of production. It is ontologically empowered as the
"becoming" of territorial development, and represented as the foundation for
learning and *innovation*, for our ability to develop, communicate, and interpret
knowledge as well as to stimulate people to do this in new and better ways.
In the present era of "reflexive capitalism," as Storper calls it, the "social organization of economic reflexivity" has become "a characteristic of contemporary modernity in which organizations – both private and public – and
individuals devote themselves to the deliberate and strategic shaping of their
environments, in part by taking a critical perspective on them" (1997: 245). He
identifies a "reflexivity class" shaping learning and innovation from the global
to the local scales, and "reflexive urban consumers and citizens" engaged in
"reflexive consumption."

The "enormous leap" in economic reflexivity that Storper argues defines
the present era makes it more possible than ever before for "groups of actors
in the various institutional spheres of modern capitalism – firms, markets,
government, households, and other collectivities – to shape the course of economic evolution" (1997: 29). Reflexivity thus becomes much more than a
network of transactions negotiated through market rules or the flows of information in what Castells calls in his recent work the rise of a Network Society.
Extending his interpretation of this enormous leap to still wider spheres,
Storper also offers some comments, with an economic emphasis to be sure, on
the commingling of the "real" and the "imagined" in the contemporary world,
a subject explored in *Thirdspace* and in more self-consciously postmodern critical cultural theory.

> Interpretations and constructed images of reality are now just as important as
> any "real" material reality, because these interpretations and images are diffused
> and accepted and become the bases on which people act: they become real. Such
> interpretations and images are central to the organization and evolution of
> markets, prices, and other key economic variables. They are, in this sense, as real
> and material as machines, people, and buildings.   (1997: 29)

But what is most relevant to the present discussion is Storper's explicit rooting
of purposive reflexive action in the spatial specificity of urbanism. Here I
repeat and extend the quoted statement from Storper used in the Introduction
to Part I.

> The organization of reflexivity is importantly, though not exclusively, urban. This
> is because reflexivity involves complex and uncertain relationships between
> organizations, between the parts of complex organizations, between individu-
> als, and between individuals and organizations, in which proximity is important
> because of the substantive complexity and uncertainty of these relationships . . .
> [T]he transactional tissue of . . . urban activities is of a conventional/relational

nature, and it is urban because certain conventions and relations only work in the context of proximity . . . *The economies of big cities, in other words, should be analyzed as sets of partially overlapping spheres of reflexive economic action*, and the structures of those activities, in addition to traditional economic descriptors, must include *their conventional and relational structures of coordination and coherence*. (1997: 245, emphasis in original)

Wrapped in the stiff prose of Storper's expansive theory of reflexivity are two important breakthroughs in the discourse on industrial urbanism, both of which take us back to the prescient if crudely formulated observations of Jane Jacobs on the origins of cities and the self-generating dynamics of urban economic development. The first involves the breakdown or deconstruction of the longstanding conceptual division between city and region, and its reconstitution as a new combinatorial form, some variant on city-region, urban-region, or more broadly regional urbanism. Storper's regional worlds of production are also specifically urban worlds as well. The resurgence of regional economies thus does not translate to the relative decline of urban economies but rather to the resurgence of urbanized regions. These city-regions are a "fundamental unit of social life," *comparable to the market, the state, and the family*. They are also a "fundamental motor process in social life," *as consequential and filled with causal power as technology, social stratification, and rational economic behavior*. They do not always revolve around just one large metropolitan core but should be seen rather as a network of urban nodes nested together in a regionally defined system comprising cities, suburbs, towns, villages, open space, wilderness areas, and other urbanized (and regionalized) landscapes.[14]

There is no widely accepted term to capture this distinctively regional character of urbanism, or more particularly, the regional character of industrial urbanism as it has been discussed here. Up to the present, the urban has tended to take precedence, as in the use of the term "urban region." Perhaps the time has come to shift the emphasis to the region, to absorb the urban into the regional, to see the urbanization process and the development of urbanism as a way of life as simultaneously a process of regionalization and the production of regionality. In doing so, however, the shift must not be seen as reducing the significance of the urban or of urban studies, but rather as the reframing of the urban condition and critical urban studies in a more explicitly regionalist perspective.[15]

The second breakthrough in Storper's work can be described as the rediscovery of synekism, the stimulus of (regional) urban agglomeration. Storper never defines reflexivity as exclusively urban, but does attach it intrinsically to regions and territories. In part, I think, this reflects the difficulties that still

---

14 A similar emphasis on urbanized regions is evident in Jane Jacobs's *The Economy of Cities*, New York: Random House, 1969; and even more emphatically in *Cities and the Wealth of Nations: Principles of Economic Life*, New York: Random House, 1984.

15 More will be said on this subject in the next chapter, when we turn to the discourse on globalization.

remain in what has been discussed in the previous paragraphs, especially with respect to a continued association of the urban with big cities. But in his discussion of proximity, propinquity, localization, interdependence, and agglomeration as key to the generation of purposeful reflexive action, innovation, and learning, he brings to the foreground a process which very closely resembles what I have defined earlier as synekism and the self-generating developmental capacity of cities and city-regions. And just as Jane Jacobs tied her conceptualization of these features embedded in the spatial specificity of urbanism to the export base of cities, so too does Storper.

> The distinction between export-oriented and locally serving activities is still relevant to the understanding of urban economies, in the sense that this is the fundamental source of their economic specialization, differentiation, and much of interurban growth transmission. *What is principally common to the export-oriented economic specialization activities of cities is that they are concerned with the social organization of economic reflexivity* . . . Reflexivity is given shape and order through the development of proximity-dependent relations and conventions, ensembles of which define cognitive and pragmatic contexts common to a group of actors and permit them to carry out a particular kind of purposeful collective economic action.   (1997: 245–6)

Storper may be perfectly correct in identifying an enormous leap in reflexivity as a hallmark of contemporary urban-industrial capitalism and in assigning to the relational assets of regions its fundamental driving force. But hidden in the intensity of his arguments is a still bolder assertion, that the innovative reflexivity that arises from the spatial specificity of urbanized regions – what I have defined as synekism – may be one of the most important driving forces behind every major innovative surge in human history, from the discovery of agriculture and the creation of the state to the Industrial Revolution and various technological, organizational, and spatial "fixes" that have marked the crisis-prone geohistory of urban-industrial capitalism up to the present.

Localizing Industrial Urbanism

As much as any of the six discourses, the discourse on industrial urbanism and the representation of the postmetropolis as a postfordist, flexible, and reflexive urban-regional world of production has been rooted in the empirical and intellectual context of Southern California. In this sense, a significant part of what has been discussed up to this point can be described as a process of learning from Los Angeles. What I propose to do here is to selectively synthesize from the specifically local discourse a few representative portrayals of the postfordist industrial metropolis as seen by its resident discursants.

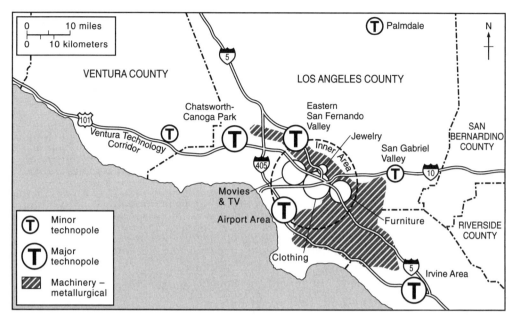

Figure 6.1 *Industrial geography of Los Angeles* (Source: Scott and Soja eds, *The City*, Berkeley and Los Angeles: University of California Press, 1996: 13, figure 1.1)

Postfordist industrial cartographies

Figure 6.1 is a composite sketch of the industrial geography of Los Angeles. As an indicative cartography, it not only captures the main features of the post-fordist industrial metropolis as it is particularly expressed in the Los Angeles urban region but is also suggestive of how one might cartographically portray other major urban regions from the industrial urbanist perspective.[16]

The map is clearly *centered* on the downtown core of the City of Los Angeles, and this centering is accentuated by a dashed circle defining the "Inner Area." Note the apparent neutrality of this designation. The actual boundaries of the City of Los Angeles are not shown (its notorious irregularity would only confuse the picture), and nowhere is there an explicit symbol to show where the exact center is located. There is no indication of an "inner city," for that term has its own special connotations. The closest to a bullseye target in this Inner Area is the circle labeled Clothing, the focal point for what has become one of the largest metropolitan clusters of garment manufacturing in the USA.

16 Versions of this map appear frequently in the publications of Allen Scott. It is reproduced here from Scott and Soja eds., *The City: Los Angeles and Urban Theory at the End of the Twentieth Century*, Berkeley and Los Angeles: University of California Press, 1996: 13.

As in New York City and other major city-regions with large garment or apparel industries, the major cluster of manufacturers and workers tends to be highly centralized, typically abutting, as it does in the highly decentralized region of Los Angeles, the Central Business District and Civic Center. The Clothing Circle thus symbolically anchors the industrial geography. The smaller circles for Furniture and Jewelry, which in strict cartographic terms should overlap into the Clothing Circle for they too are concentrated relatively close to the downtown center, are displaced to its edge for the sake of visual clarity. The circle for Movies and TV is positioned more appropriately right over Hollywood, although much of the current action in the film-making industry has shifted to other areas such as Burbank, Culver City, and Santa Monica.

The inner circles serve a double purpose. They indicate both the tendency for such craft-based industrial districts (for that is what the circles represent) to be centripetal in the metropolitan geography; but also to suggest a concurrent centrifugal force, a tendency toward dispersal and decentralization from the established core agglomeration. This simultaneous pull-to and push-away from the center is perhaps the most fundamental geographical dynamic that arises from the interplay of industrialization and urbanization processes. It gives rise to a recurrent concentricity in the cartographic envisioning of industrial development over time and space, with centers being formed in an Inner Area then spinning off with an occasional jump or two in an ever-widening constellation of sites. Scott typically overlays his industrial geographies with a "basic annular structure" of concentric rings presumed to chart a distance decay pattern from the center, very much like the gradients of population density or land values in Chicago School models of urban form, which were built on a similar dialectic of centripetal–centrifugal forces.

Just such an annular structure is implicitly embedded in figure 6.1. All the mapped symbols can be seen as resulting from the same fundamental dynamic of concentric centralization and dispersal revolving around the largest core agglomeration. Look first at the cross-hatched area labeled Machinery-Metallurgical, the only areally extensive zone shown on the map. It is given such expansive coverage for it is not viewed as a postfordist industrial district but rather as a prominent residual from the Fordist industrialization of Los Angeles. Once containing what was reputed to be the second largest urban-industrial subregion in the world (after the Ruhr), it no longer has an identifiable nodal concentration but exists at residual sites dispersed over a wide area. Although not identified as such, this area, at least within Los Angeles County, defines the primary zone of deindustrialization and plant closures. In the 1960s, it contained the largest automobile assembly, tire and glass manufacturing, and iron and steel industries in the Western USA. Today, almost every one of these major production sites has closed down, leaving only a more scattered distribution of smaller establishments producing machinery and metallurgical products, such as transportation equipment.

The shape of the Machinery-Metallurgical blob is also quite revealing. Although not entirely accurate in depicting the current distribution of the major manufacturing establishments in this sector, it does indicate by its bulges and extensions the major pathways of decentralization from the Los Angeles downtown core to beyond the Inner Area. A long and thin finger, following rail and freeway routes, points into the San Fernando Valley, perhaps the most iconic space of American upper-working-class suburbia in the postwar era. Further south there are two bulges, one to the east toward the San Gabriel Valley and another to the west toward the Airport Area. The western bulge covers the old heavy industry zone that once contained another major concentration of the relatively well-off suburban working class, sharply divided between black and white by the Alameda Boulevard Cotton Curtain. Today, these bulging wings cover the core of Latino Los Angeles. The most prominent new extension of this industrial path, however, pushes to the southeast into Orange County and the Irvine Area. Indeed, the whole blob looks like a fat arrow pointing directly to Orange County, signaling obtrusively that it is here where the industrial decentralization from the city center of Los Angeles has proceeded furthest, and where the regional industrial geography has become most formidably recentered, deserving its own independent consideration.

Of all the major technopoles so boldly depicted on the map, Orange County's is the most heavily studied and most prototypical "new industrial space." Almost completely out of the picture of the industrial geography of the Los Angeles region in 1960, Orange County has emerged as the representative centerpiece and model of postfordist industrial development in California, rivaled only by Silicon Valley in Santa Clara County. The pioneering figure in presenting an industrial urbanist interpretation of this key site, as he has been for almost all of the sites shown on figure 6.1, is Allen Scott. His "New Frontiers of Industrial-Urban Development: The Rise of the Orange County High-Technology Complex, 1955–1984," chapter 9 of *Metropolis* (1988), has become a primary reference point and exemplary model for studying the development of industrial districts all over the world. Orange County, with its primary focus in the Irvine Area, has indelibly been put on the map of the industrial geography of metropolitan Los Angeles. It will reappear, viewed from different perspectives, in several of the subsequent discourses on the postmetropolis.

There are other major and minor technopoles shown on the map, although none has been studied as intensively as Orange County. Recently, however, Scott has reapplied his methodology to the northern tier of technopoles in the eastern and western San Fernando Valley, with an extension to the west in Ventura County. Through a series of characteristic mappings of the distribution of high-technology industrial establishments in 1955, 1973, and 1991, along with supplementary depictions of population distributions (including separate maps for Asians and Hispanics), Scott tells a story that virtually reproduces, with changing details, what was presented in his work on Orange County. The summary outcome of this story, represented in figure 6.2, centers another technopolitan bullseye target on the Chatsworth-Canoga Park area, a New Irvine emerging as the core of a Greater San Fernando Valley High Tech-

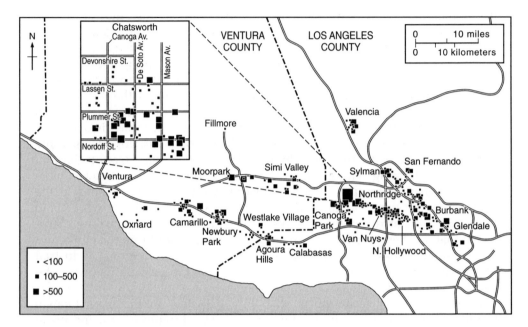

Figure 6.2 *Technopoles of the San Fernando Valley* (Source: Scott and Soja eds, *The City*, 1996: 292, figure 9.11)

nology Industrial Complex. A major technopole remains in the East Valley, with much older roots, while a minor one is budding off to the west, in what is called the Ventura Technology Corridor.

A few words need to be said about the remaining sites on figure 6.1. The Airport Area, once called "Aerospace Alley," continues to be a Major Technopole despite the recent decline in the defense-led aerospace industry. It has not been as thoroughly studied as the Orange County and San Fernando Valley technopoles, and does not seem to have developed its own autonomous "geographical dynamic" separate from the core Los Angeles agglomeration. Its presence on the map, however, may be better understood by connecting the technopole, via a series of specialized business service districts such as the complex of lawyers and other professionals in Century City, to the Movies and TV circle in Hollywood. This would create a "Westside" high-technology and craft-based industrial complex focused increasingly on the burgeoning entertainment industry. In his recent work on the "cultural economy of cities," Scott is zeroing in on this Westside complex of "cultural production," especially the rapidly growing multi-media industry, with its cyberspatial connections and computerized special effects studios.[17] In the emerging new map of the indus-

17　Allen J. Scott, *From Silicon Valley to Hollywood: Growth and Development of the Multimedia Industry in California*, Los Angeles (UCLA): Lewis Center for Regional Policy Studies, Working Paper 13, 1995; and "The Craft, Fashion, and Cultural-Products Industries of Los Angeles: Competitive Dynamics and Policy Dilemmas in a Multisectoral Image-producing Complex," *Annals of the Association of American Geographers* 86, 1996: 306–23.

trial geography of Los Angeles, a different symbol or icon needs to be developed that combines the Technopole "T" with the craft-centered circle, for it is here, in what Scott describes as a "multisectoral image-producing complex" and what local officials have recently dubbed the Digital Coast, part of a larger "Tech Coast" region stretching from Santa Barbara to San Diego, where much of the current "purposeful reflexive action" in Los Angeles is taking place.

Finally, there are the two almost forgotten outliers, the small technopoles located at Palmdale and the San Gabriel Valley. Here we can see some of the downside of technopolitan development. Both these sites were established fairly early, primarily as centers for the aerospace industry. This early development stimulated massive cheap housing booms in the Antelope Valley near Palmdale and Lancaster, and in the so-called Inland Empire (eastern LA and western San Bernardino and Riverside counties), where municipalities such as Moreno Valley mushroomed in the hopes that another Orange County was in bud. No such budding took place, and with the decline of the aerospace industry, hundreds of thousands of working families found themselves stranded, two hours' freeway driving from their old jobs or from similar employment opportunities in the growing industrial complexes. The small technopoles at Palmdale and the San Gabriel Valley thus signify promises unmet, anticipatory growth poles that never developed to regional expectations. More will be said about these areas in chapter 8.

Developmental dynamics of the industrial complex

The snapshot map of the regional industrial geography has deeper and more dynamic geohistorical roots, for nearly every one of the major nucleations of industrial production as well as the composite regional patterning has been framed by Scott and his students within a dynamic stages of growth model that represents another mode of synthesis in the local discourse on industrial urbanism. In this "ordered spatio-temporal process," as Scott calls it, two cycles of growth are identified, one dealing with the initial establishment of an industrial complex, the other with its post-establishment growth dynamics.

Roughly depicted, the first or "originary" cycle begins, Scott argues, with "a chaotic series of initiating events" and a set of "fortuitous circumstances" usually involving local "industrial pioneers" and spatially specific local circumstances. This purposeful vagueness reflects Scott's determination to avoid creating a general theory of locational origins, whether based on traditional Weberian models of efficient locational equilibria based on transport and other cost criteria or, worse, simplistic explanations emphasizing open space and climate, such as the constant sunshine model for the location of the motion picture industry in Los Angeles. Scott points instead to unpredictable local convergences of unique events, individuals, and institutions. Answering the classic question of why industries locate where they do – the question that has driven industrial location theory from its origins – is thus shifted away from an abstract spatial model of profit-maximizing behavior and generalized rational choice to the resourceful probing of idiographic historical geographies. It is here where Scott provides an opening for a very different and more powerful location theory based on softer factors such as the role of local conventions, untraded interdependencies, reflexivity, learning, and synekism.

Subsequent phases deal with what makes the initial development "stick" and grow, with many of the same softer factors continuing to play a major role. For the early industrialization of Los Angeles, Scott notes the importance of the network of activities created by "local power brokers," such as Harry Chandler of the *Los Angeles Times* and the Merchants and Manufacturers Association, and their ability to "mobilize critical resources and energies in support of local economic growth." Here Scott touches on what has become perhaps the most important planning and public policy recommendation derived from the industrial urban discourse, the need to create *regional industrial networks or councils* of businesses, labor, and public institutions to share information and learn from one another as a strategy for promoting efficient and equitable regional economic development. These networks, fostered by traded as well as untraded local interdependencies, are the basing points for what Scott defines as the third and fourth phases, the "breakthrough moment" when industrial production capitalizes on "a developing local complex of cultural and/or technological sensitivities and skills" to move beyond regional to national and international markets; and a "consolidation of the local production complex" arising from the growth of secondary networks of input providers and multifaceted local labor markets. The inductive conclusion we are drawn to is stated with Scott's characteristic qualified assertiveness: "regional industrial development often occurs not so much because of the presence of naturally-occurring endowments, but as a result of local social and political mobilization."

A second cycle picks up from the first. In its most simplified version, Scott appears to lessen his emphasis on local social and political mobilizations and networks, and wraps his descriptions in old-fashioned Weberian cost–distance modeling and geometries, aiming perhaps to reach a particular audience of economists. But placed in context, even these departures are useful. Here I summarize Scott's staging of the second cycle, with specific reference to the technopoles of Southern California:[18] (a) at some historical point, agglomeration economies and local labor market pressures bring about the formation of an initial technopole, or proto-technopole close to the city center; (b) as this initial technopole grows, land prices and labor costs begin to rise, inducing some decentralization of production units toward cheaper sites along the existing fringes of urban development; (c) eventually, the gravitational pull of agglomeration economies will induce these decentralizing units to form incipient technopoles in suburban areas; (d) the new suburban technopoles will

---

18   The list that follows as well as the quoted phrases in the previous paragraphs are taken from Allen J. Scott, "Industrial Urbanism in Southern California: Post-Fordist Civic Dilemmas and Opportunities," *Contention* 5-1, 1995: 39–65.

begin to grow ever more rapidly as overall industrial expansion proceeds, and in due course, the central technopole itself may begin to atrophy when agglomeration diseconomies and rising land prices pass a certain threshold; (e) so long as industrial growth continues, this cycle of events will repeat itself, with new technopoles budding off from the old and recurring yet further out in the urban field. Meanwhile those technopoles that had in the previous generation of events been identifiable as "suburban" now lie well within the frontiers of outward urban expansion.

These discursive observations on the dynamics of industrial complex formation and expansion are far from earth-shaking, but they represent a significant departure from traditional geographical locational theory. They also depart from an image of Scott's research as blindly and abstractedly "productionist." His breakthrough research on intra- and inter-firm transactions and the vertical disintegration of the production process into subcontracting networks and geographically clustered complexes of upstream and downstream input providers was criticized by urban scholars for being disconnected from urban politics and the pressing problems of housing, homelessness, gender, race, ethnicity, planning, social welfare, and other vital social issues. Rather than a dramatic shift in direction, however, Scott's now more explicit concentration on "social and political mobilization" and "postfordist civic dilemmas and opportunities" is a logical outgrowth of his confident and creative theorization of the postfordist transition. Following the path of the French Regulation School he has been influenced by, Scott has moved from a global focus on the "inner workings" of the emergent flexible "regime of accumulation" to concentrate on the more local and regional problems associated with the development of new "modes of social regulation" – the institutional structures, labor markets, social movements, community organizations, governance systems, industrial atmospheres, and ideological cultures that are being created to sustain, for better and worse, postfordist economic and metropolitan development.

Concluding in the realm of public policy

Scott's essay on "Industrial Urbanism in Southern California" (1995) ends significantly with intimations of the crises brewing in the intense social polarization, the "hotbed of social predicaments and tensions," "the never-ending downward spiral of wage-cutting," and the "huge deficit" in appropriate "institutional infrastructures," that, if left unchecked, "threatens to take Southern California . . . straight toward the bleak 'Blade Runner' scenario that Davis (1990) has so eloquently alluded to." The final section is entitled "Reinventing Southern California" and presents Scott's preferred social democratic future for the region, a vision based in a German/Japanese (as opposed to Anglo-American) model characterized by "relatively high levels of governmental direction of economic affairs, significant degrees of cooperation between private firms, and a corporatist social structure that tries to build solidarity by providing safety nets for all major constituencies in society." Two "main thrusts" are locally necessary in the move toward social democracy: "concerted institution-building so as to enhance the productivity and competitiveness of the region's main industrial clusters"; and "massive investment in social overhead capital so as to improve the quality of the work-force, and . . . foster re-incorporation of currently underprivileged groups (among whom women, African-Americans, the homeless, and unskilled migrant workers are significantly represented) into the mainstream of society."

Four "subsidiary lines of action" are presented fostering more cooperative information-sharing: inter-firm relations and transactional networks; regional technology development and labor training programs; efficient "steering mechanisms" aimed at expanding high-skill high-wage employment in such industries as entertainment, medical instruments, and biotechnology; and a "mediation" of development programs down to the community level, especially in the "more disadvantaged" parts of the region. The work being done to promote the development of the electric vehicle industry in Southern California is offered as an illustrative example.[19] The last sentence redescribes Scott's political and public policy perspective: "The analysis that I have tried to lay out, if correct, suggests that out of all the possible futures that the region now faces, there is at least one that can offer a better deal, economically and socially, than the future that will certainly come to pass if we simply pin our hopes on what Ronald Reagan used to call 'the magic of the market.' "

19 See Allen J. Scott and David Bergman, *Advanced Ground Transportation Equipment Manufacturing and Local Economic Development: Lessons for Southern California*, UCLA: Lewis Center for Regional Policy Studies, Working Paper No. 8, 1993. This report was one product of the first major research project of the Lewis Center, for which Scott served as the first Director.

Chapter 7
Cosmopolis: The Globalization of Cityspace

Representative Texts

- *Spaces of Globalization: Reasserting the Power of the Local* (Cox ed., 1997)
- *World Cities in a World-System* (Knox and Taylor eds., 1995)
- *Global Cities: Post-Imperialism and the Internationalization of London* (King, 1990)
- *The Global City: New York, London, Tokyo* (Sassen, 1991)
- *Cities in a World Economy* (Sassen, 1994)
- *Cities for Citizens: Planning and the Rise of Civil Society in a Global Age* (Friedmann and Douglas eds., 1998)
- *Urban World/Global City* (Clark, 1996)
- *The Informational City: Information, Technology, Economic Restructuring and the Urban-Regional Process* (Castells, 1989)
- *Regions and the World Economy: The Coming Shape of Global Production, Competition, and Political Order* (Scott, 1998)
- *After Modernism: Global Restructuring and the Changing Boundaries of City Life* (Smith ed., 1992)
- *Re-Presenting the City: Ethnicity, Capital and Culture in the twenty-first Century Metropolis* (King ed., 1996)
- *Global Culture: Nationalism, Globalization and Modernity* (Featherstone ed., 1990)
- *Culture, Globalization and the World-System: Contemporary Conditions for the Representation of Identity* (King ed., 1991)
- *Globalization: Social Theory and Global Culture* (Robertson, 1992)
- *Globalization and Territorial Identities* (Mlinar, 1992)
- *Modernity at Large: Cultural Dimensions of Globalization* (Appadurai, 1996)
- *Transnational Connections: Culture, People, Places* (Hannerz, 1996)
- *Transnationalism from Below* (Smith and Guarnizo eds., 1998)
- *Transnational Citizenship: Membership and Rights in International Migration* (Bauböck, 1994)
- *Global/Local: Cultural Production and the Transnational Imaginary* (Wilson and Dissanayake eds., 1996)
- *Global Shift: The Internationalization of Economic Activity* (Dicken, 1992)

- *The New Global Economy in the Information Age: Reflections on Our Chang-ing World* (Carnoy, Castells, Cohen, and Cardoso, 1993)
- *The Global Region: Production, State Policies, and Uneven Development* (Sadler, 1992)
- *Global Modernities* (Featherstone, Lash, and Robertson eds., 1995)
- *Global Capitalism: Theories of Societal Development* (Peet, 1991)
- *Spaces of Identity: Global Media, Electronic Landscapes and Cultural Bound-aries* (Morley and Robins, 1995)
- *The Borderless World* and *The End of the Nation State* (Ohmae, 1990 and 1995)
- *Global Financial Integration: The End of Geography* (O'Brien, 1992)
- *Losing Control? Sovereignty in an Age of Globalization* (Sassen, 1996)
- *Globalization and its Discontents: The Rise of Postmodern Socialisms* (Burbach, Núñez, and Kagarlitsky, 1997)
- *Globalization in Question* (Hirst and Thompson, 1996)
- *Democracy and the Global Order: From the Modern State to Cosmopolitan Globalism* (Held, 1996)

Globalization has become the compelling catchword of the *fin de siècle*, a mil-lenarian metaphor for practically everything that has been happening almost everywhere through the late twentieth century. In the academic world, some enthusiasts have gone so far as to suggest that globalization studies are now "the successor to the debates on modernity and postmodernity in the under-standing of sociocultural change and as the central thematic for social theory."[1] As an encompassing paradigm for all studies of the contemporary, globaliza-tion has become a particularly voracious trope, devouring and digesting a widening gyre of alternative discursive representations of what is new in our present world, while at the same time asserting itself as the necessary foun-dational concept for deciding what is to be done in response to this perva-sively global newness.

A look at the titles and subtitles of the representative texts listed above indi-cates the growing array of consequences that are becoming attached to the far-reaching impact of globalization. The rise of world cities in a world system heads the list and is the primary focus of this chapter, but the effects of glob-alization extend much further and deeper to shape global culture-society-economy-capitalism, social theory and societal development, economic restructuring and the urban-regional process, a new international division of labor, the formation of global regions, the representation of identity, transna-tional citizenship, and a reassertion of the power of the local. Additional asso-ciations are made with global media, electronic landscapes, post-imperialism, new modernities, the end of the nation-state, an increasingly borderless world, postmodern socialisms, the end of geography, and the expansion of a transna-tional imaginary. Everyone, from the radical community activist to the cor-porate entrepreneur, from the poet to the politician (not to mention the book

---

1 Mike Featherstone, Scott Lash, and Roland Robertson eds., *Global Modernities*, London: Sage, 1995: 1.

publisher) is being urged to "think global," or else miss out on all that is new and innovative in the contemporary world. What is this seemingly all-encompassing tropic of discourse and how does it shape our understanding of the postmetropolis, both in a general sense and within the particular context of Los Angeles?

Recomposing the Discourse on Globalization

Viewed most broadly, globalization is conceived as "the compression of the world and the intensification of consciousness of the world as a whole," bringing with it the deepening and widening of "worldwide social relations which link distant localities in such a way that local happenings are shaped by events occurring many miles away and vice versa."[2] The key word here is "intensification," for everything else being described has been happening to urban-based societies for at least the past thousand, if not ten thousand, years, ever since the origins of synekistic urbanism. What is distinctive about the contemporary era, then, is not globalization *per se* but its intensification in popular (and intellectual) consciousness and in the *scope and scale* of globalized social, economic, political, and cultural relations. In simple statistical terms, more of the world's total population than ever before are aware of a *globality* that stretches over the entire planet; and more of everyone's daily life is being affected by the circuits of human activity that operate specifically at this global scale.

Contemporary globalization can be interpreted simply as another round of a long-established historical process, but this simplification disguises more than it reveals. Over the last three decades, enough evidence has accumulated to suggest to many observers and analysts that a certain threshold has been passed. Virtually (and I use this term in both its old and new meaning) the entire earth's surface is now globalized, a claim that could not be so easily made fifty years ago. And even more significantly, the global scale of human life, the outermost level of the many materially relevant spatial scales in which each human body is nested, has accrued more power and influence than at any other moment in history. It is this forceful *empowerment of globality* and global consciousness as a source of human action and practice that underpins the emergence of globalization as the most widespread concept being used to understand the distinctiveness of the present and to rationalize and explain almost everything happening in the contemporary world.

Presenting the major features of the general discourse on globalization thus presents a formidable challenge, for the discourse itself has become so unwieldily inclusive (global?) in its scope, and its discursants, celebrant as well as antagonistic, are found in almost every field of study. Rather than attempting to summarize the vast literature on globalization, I will recompose

---

2 Roland Robertson, *Globalization*, London: Sage, 1992: 8; Anthony Giddens, *The Consequences of Modernity*, Cambridge: Polity, 1990: 64.

the discourse around a series of representative themes and concepts that sequentially build toward a new framework for understanding the impact of *globality, globalization, and globalism* on contemporary cityspaces and the formation of the postmetropolis.[3] Underpinning this recomposition is a continuing effort to demonstrate the particular insights and power of an *urban-centered geographical imagination* and *critical spatial perspective*; and to explore further the *spatialization of social theory* that has seemed to accompany the increasing empowerment of globality, globalization, and globalism in the late twentieth century.[4]

The globality of production and the production of globality

Shaping and focusing the globalization discourse, literally pinning it down to concrete empirical forms and expressions, is an argument that views intensified globalization and the empowerment of globality primarily as the product of a dramatic expansion in the scale and scope of capitalist industrial production. It is argued that we have entered an era of *global capitalism* that is marked by a *new international division of labor* (NIDL) in which industrial production (or what the first discourse would call industrial urbanism) has become more widely distributed over the inhabited world than ever before. The rise of the NICs (newly industrialized countries such as the "Tigers" of eastern Asia) and the creation of other *new industrial spaces* where there had never been any significant industrialization (including such exemplary places as Silicon Valley and the once-suburban technopoles of Southern California), in combination with the *deindustrialization* of many older manufacturing regions, are seen as signaling the emergence of a new and different world economic order, a restructured global space economy that demands to be studied on its own emphatically globalized terms.

In response to those who remind us that capitalism has always operated on a global scale, the production-oriented globalists argue that a qualitatively new level of globality is now operating. Significant continuities with the past remain prominent, but what is new and different about contemporary patterns of globalization demand greater theoretical and practical attention. The earliest capitalist world system began with the globalization of commercial or mercantile capital in the sixteenth century.[5] European merchants and traders,

---

3 These three terms are used very much like the triad of concepts and discourses they are allegedly replacing: modernity, modernization, and modernism (with and without the prefixing of *post-*). In each case, the suffix *-ity* represents the general condition, while *-ization* and *-ism* refer respectively to the material processes producing and reproducing this condition, and the conscious and assertive practices that arise from situated knowledge of the general condition as it is expressed in particular times and places.

4 Mike Featherstone and Scott Lash, "Globalization, Modernity and the Spatialization of Social Theory," an editorial introduction to *Global Modernities*, 1995: 1–24.

5 For an interesting look at the development of a pre-modern, pre-capitalist world system, see Janet Abu-Lughod, *Before European Hegemony: The World System A.D. 1250–1350*, New York: Oxford University Press, 1989.

based in "world cities" such as Amsterdam, Hamburg, and Venice, and sustained by absolutist monarchical states, exploited far-flung sources of wealth-producing raw materials, from gold and spices to slaves and indigenous technological knowledge. Later, in the age of imperialism, globalization and the capitalist world system were extended and "thickened" by the infusion and diffusion of financial capital, organized and at least partially controlled by industrialized nation-states and their dominant imperial "metropoles" such as London, Paris, and New York. In this world system of colonial domination and national development, investments from the core states and city-regions of Europe and North America in the colonial peripheries assured a more reliable supply of inputs for the burgeoning urban-industrial centers and also created a more tightly organized international division of labor, with its familiar regional divisions: core and periphery, metropole and satellite, and, after the rise of a socialist world region, the encompassing structure of First, Second, and Third Worlds.

It is precisely this ordered configuration of international relations, which has lasted in relatively stable form since the late nineteenth century, that is currently being substantially restructured in what some have called an era of flexible accumulation and "disorganized" capitalism. While the commercial and financial circuits of capital are playing a vital role in this restructuring, it is the expanding geographical scope of productive industrial capital that most distinguishes the present era of globalization. Formerly confined to the core industrial countries, urban-based industrial capitalist production has spread to many more parts of the world than ever before, exemplified most directly in the growing list of NICs. This has been associated with a breakdown of the old *international* (or interstate) capitalist world economy and its distinctive spatial (or territorial) division of labor based primarily on nation-states; and its reconfiguration as an intensified *global* or *transnational* capitalist economy with a "new world order" of networked flows and linkages that are no longer as confined by national boundaries as they were in the past.

Driving this deep restructuring process in a new Age of Globalism are many potent forces, every one of which can be seen as having a significant effect on the postmetropolitan transition. These forces include:

- the industrialization of major segments of the old Third World and the simultaneous deindustrialization of established cities and regions of Fordist industrial production;
- the creation of new forms of globally networked manufacturing, symbolized in such products as the "world car" and the many-colored Benetton sweater;
- the accelerated movement of people, goods, services, and information across national borders and the growth of global markets for labor and globally networked commodities;
- the reorganization of international trading systems and markets, from the European Union to the North American Free Trade Association

(NAFTA) and various Asian, African, and Latin American trading blocs;

- the propulsive emergence of the transnational corporation to rationalize and coordinate global investment, production, and capital accumulation;
- the space-spanning and networking effects of the telecommunications and information revolution;
- the emergence of powerful institutions to promote global financial integration, consolidating all three of the major circuits of capital (commercial, financial, industrial) at the global scale;
- the rise of the Pacific Rim as a competitive power bloc to the North Atlantic alliance;
- the concentration of political and economic power in a re-ordered hierarchy of global cities acting as command posts for controlling the changing financial operations of the world economy.

Each of these processes of change has provided a focal point in studying the geopolitical economy of globalization and is the subject of a large and growing literature. To simplify their representation here, they can be clustered around two encompassing categories, the *globalization of capital* and the *globalization of labor*. Seen as a process affecting national economies, as in the debates on globalization and public policy in the USA, the globalization of capital is typically measured by such indicators as increased foreign direct investment, the growth of foreign investment in the domestic economy, the increasing importance of import and export trade, and the intensification of other "flows" (of money, jobs, services, and workers) across national borders. This has resulted in, among other effects, the dramatic transformation of the USA from being the world's largest creditor nation in the early 1980s to the world's largest debtor nation just ten years later. These statistics, however, are only indirect measures of globalization and can often be misleading when taken as unequivocal signs of the empowerment of globality and the declining economic sovereignty of the nation-state.

Some of those critical of the emphasis being given to globalization and the allegedly impending "end of the nation-state" point out, for example, that each of these indicators, while registering a relatively increased proportion of global economic activity, also signify the continuing domination of the national economy and domestic production. In response to these critics, it is argued that, while the national economy has certainly not been eclipsed by global economic forces, the most rapidly globalizing activities have become the leading or most propulsive sectors in terms of employment growth, urban and regional development, and increasing Gross National Product. Furthermore, there now seems to be a world market for practically everything and these world markets appear to be expanding at a faster rate than those established at the national and local levels in almost every industrialized country. This means that the driving economic forces of competition and productivity growth in domestic industries are also becoming increasingly globalized in their scope of operation, making it more difficult than ever before to separate the domestic from the global economy.[6] The era of the nation-state has by no means come to an end, but it is equally certain that national economies are no longer what they used to be as recently as thirty years ago. That this difference matters and must be rigorously investigated and understood is a key assumption underpinning most studies of globalization.

When viewed more broadly than as statistical indicators, the globalization of capital has tended to be studied with respect to three interlocking circuits of capital flow: commercial trade, financial investment, and industrial production. As suggested earlier, it is the expansion, diffusion, and networking of industrial capital and industrial urbanism on a global scale that can be seen as the most distinctive feature of the current phase of globalization. It is here that most geopolitical economists have concentrated their attention. The general academic and policy discourse, however, has focused more heavily on either the commercial circuit, viewing globalization primarily in terms of the growth and repatterning of world trade; or the technology-led new phase of transnational financial integration and electronic networking that is reshaping the flow of money, credit, and investment in what some observers describe as an increasingly borderless world. One can crudely categorize the discourse on the globalization of capital according to which of these three emphases is given the greatest priority: Production, Trade, or Finance.

The other side of global capitalism, but given somewhat less attention, is defined by the *globalization of labor*. It has perhaps always been true that capital is more footloose than labor, better able to pack up and move to greener pastures when necessary. It is probably also true that in this Age of Globalism, capital has continued to be freer in its movements than has labor, which remains primarily locked in to nationally localized labor markets. By its very nature and geography, however, the globalization of production has induced an increased globalization of labor, a larger-scale movement of workers to the now more numerous major nodes of industrial production. Over the past thirty years, the volume of labor migration across national boundaries, as well as other forms of voluntary and involuntary migration (for example, refugees), has probably reached a higher level than in any earlier period. Moreover, the scope of this migration involves significant numbers from more countries and cultures than ever before. This may be producing, for the first time at this scale and scope, a truly global proletariat, but one that remains highly fragmented, difficult to organize, and not yet conscious of its potential global power.[7]

---

6 I mention these debates for they bring up again an interpretive contrast that is present in all contemporary discourses on restructuring and the postmetropolitan transition. On the one side are those who see no significant changes taking place, but rather more (or less) of the same thing: the persistent power of historical continuities. On the other side are those who focus on what is new and different, on the power that comes from the intensification and relative expansion of certain processes of change that outweigh in their contemporary relevance the continuing influences from the past. While it is important to continue to recognize the first position, at the very least as a check on excessive claims and overinterpretation of what is new, it is the second that guides the discussion here.

7 For a radical critique of the globalization discourse and especially its mixed implications for the workers of the world, see David Harvey, "Globalization in Question," *Rethinking Marxism* 8, 1995: 1–17.

As with all aspects of globalization, this intensified migration of people is geographically unevenly developed in its impact and intensity, as well as open to many different interpretations of its causes and consequences. But there can be little doubt that the globalization of labor is playing as significant a part as the globalization of capital in shaping and defining the contemporary postmetropolis. In such postmetropolitan regions as Los Angeles and New York, London and Paris, the influx of global capital and labor, as well as fashions, music, cuisines, architectural styles, political attitudes, and life-sustaining economic strategies from all over the world is not only creating highly differentiated capital investment and labor markets but also the most economically, politically, and culturally heterogeneous cityspaces that have ever existed. And cross-cutting this cultural and economic heterogenization, polarizing and fragmenting cityspace in new and different ways, is a significantly restructured set of *class relations* arising directly and indirectly from the new urbanization processes stimulated by globalization. How this heterogeneity and fragmentation has affected postmetropolitan cityspace will be discussed in more detail in chapters 8 and 9.

It is useful here to recall the discussion of the third Urban Revolution in chapter 3. Defining this dramatic transformation of cityspace was the entry into the urban fabric (i.e., the urbanization) of three major domestic or national population groupings, the industrial bourgeoisie, the industrial proletariat, and the standby reservoir of labor Marx called the lumpenproletariat. Accompanying this explosion in the size of the urban population and the implantation of a new urban class structure was an equally dramatic reorganization of the built environment to open up room for the factory system of industrial production and the residential, transit, and consumption needs of its workforce. Over the past thirty years, in large part through the globalization of production and the production of globality, the major metropolitan regions of the world have been experiencing what may very well be the beginnings of an equally dramatic transformation of urban society and cityspace. Global flows of capital investment, labor migration, information, and technological innovation are reshaping cityspace and local capital–labor relations, creating new industrial spaces, a reshuffling of class identities, different urban divisions of labor, and a repolarized and refragmented pattern of social and spatial stratification.

Again, new population groupings are being added to the urban fabric in large numbers. At least fifteen metropolitan regions today contain more than 10 million inhabitants and a few are growing beyond 25 million, a figure that would have been unimaginable thirty years ago. As charted out in the six major discourses on the postmetropolis, a very different kind of cityspace and urbanism is emerging as we enter the twenty-first century. Whether these changes represent the onset of a fourth Urban Revolution, only space and time will tell. At the very least, however, we must keep this possibility in mind as we continue to look at the most innovative spatial interpretations of the globalization process.

Regional worlds of globalization

The discursive emphasis on economic globalization and the worldwide diffusion of urban-industrial capitalism has developed in two broadly defined streams, one based largely in economics, international relations, strategic studies, and management science, the other in what I have been describing as a geopolitical economy perspective. Although there is some overlap between the two streams, it is primarily in the second where there is significant attention being given to the specific impacts of globalization on cities and regions and hence to the conceptualization and interpretation of the postmetropolitan transition. Centering our attention on the geopolitical economy of globalization opens up interesting connections to the first discourse. Indeed, this extension of the debates on economic restructuring, industrial urbanism, and postfordist flexible accumulation has produced some of the most insightful empirical research and most thoughtful theorizations of the globalization process. At the same time, this connection between the first and second discourses carries with it, usually as an unexpressed undercurrent of conceptual and methodological conflict, an earlier discursive division on the Left over what might broadly be described as the most appropriate way to theorize geographically uneven development and, as it was called in chapter 6, the geographical anatomy of industrial capitalism. As this debate has some bearing on how the postmetropolis is understood and interpreted, let us look at it more closely.

As in the 1970s, with the development of neo-Marxist theories of underdevelopment, dependency, and world systems analysis, the conflict arises primarily between endogenous or "internalist" and exogenous or "externalist" views of causality and explanation. The internalist view tends to focus on unraveling the inner workings of the capitalist economy as it is expressed in particular local contexts and sites; while the externalist view concentrates on the importance of global and other macroeconomic forces in shaping these inner workings and producing specific geographies. Stated differently, the first approach explains the development of the postmetropolis and engages with the larger theoretical challenge regarding geographically uneven development primarily from inside cityspace, and the second primarily from outside. This has led many urban and regional political economists wedded to endogenous development theory to be suspicious of the attention being given to macroeconomic globalization processes, either because they hide from view the local dynamics of class conflict or else divert attention away from the particular inner workings of local and regional networks, institutions, and conventions that are seen as the driving force of contemporary economic development and change. At the same time, those that emphasize globalization as the primary interpretive window often shy away from geopolitical economy because of its putative productionism, narrow microeconomism and localism, outdated Marxian orthodoxy, and failure to see the big picture.

In the 1970s, this conceptual conflict deeply split the debates on urban, regional, and international development. In the 1990s, however, a new and more balanced and "recombinant" perspective on geopolitical economy has been developing, in part derived from powerful postmodern critiques of modernist epistemologies, which dominated both endogenous and exogenous development theories. Especially pertinent here has been a growing sensitivity to the problems of binary thinking, through which the internalist and externalist emphases (as well as other such Big Dichotomies as bourgeoisie-proletariat, capitalism–socialism, core–periphery, man–woman, colonizer-colonized, agency–structure) are represented as a categorical either/or choice. Under such polarizing binary logic, there was a push to choose one side over the other, and to critically uphold this epistemological choice against its strongest opposition arguments. Let me make it clear that I am not saying that all geopolitical economists took a categorical either/or stance on the issue of internalist versus externalist approaches, but rather that the dominant discourse until very recently has tended to shape itself predominantly into two camps, one grounded primarily in unraveling the microanalytical and materially localized endogenous workings of geographically uneven development, including the effects of globalization; and the other focused more on the macroanalysis of larger-scale structural forces emanating from the capitalist world system and exogenously shaping local, urban, regional, and national development trajectories.

The best scholars in each of these two camps (Harvey, Scott, Castells, Gunder Frank, and Wallerstein come to mind) insistently argued that their work combined both internalist and externalist interpretations. Their particular positioning reflected not so much a categorical choice as a personal, political, and intellectual preference. What they chose to emphasize was an interpretive arena that they saw as significantly underexplored, especially within the prevailing Marxist and/or social science discourses. So pervasive was the tendency toward binary thinking, however, that their relative choice tended to be seen by their interpreters as absolute commitment. As more and more of these binarized categorical labels came to be pinned on individual scholars and their works, the literature was filled with defensive denials of an imputed categorical essentialism, of being narrow-mindedly structuralist, voluntarist, circulationist, spatialist, functionalist, historicist, Third Worldist, Eurocentrist, too Marxist or not Marxist enough. That someone could concentrate primarily on developing knowledge on one side of a Big Dichotomy without necessarily denying the importance of its alleged opposite was all too often deemed epistemologically or politically unacceptable.

Today, there are signs that a new epistemological and political mood is emerging in attempts to make theoretical and practical sense of globalization. The rigidities of either-or binarisms are breaking down, creating a recombinatorial alternative of the both/and also (rather than either/or) that opens new possibilities for a significantly different conceptualization of the original opposition.[8] One small but revealing example of this new twist on the globalization discourse has been the conception of an alternative viewpoint that emerges from and redefines both the internalist-localization and externalist-globalization perspectives. I refer here, with all its immediate awkwardness, to the composite term *glocalization*.[9] As Roland Robertson notes, the term has entered *The Oxford Dictionary of New Words* (1991: 34) as a "telescopic" blending of the global and the local, drawing heavily from the Japanese business strategy of *dochakuka*, a global outlook adapted to local conditions or the localization of globality. Glocalization scholars have extended this meaning to make glocalization a distinctive process in itself, with further extensions in such terms as glocal, glocality, and glocalism.

By literally interjecting the local into the global (and vice versa), the concept of glocalization triggers a disruptive challenge to the widespread view that globalization and localization, and their more ideological or advocative expressions as globalism and localism, are separate and opposing processes or ways of thinking.[10] From this alternative perspective, the global and the local, along with internalist–externalist epistemologies and related micro–macroanalytical approaches, are simultaneously rethought together through the assertion of a new and different concept that selectively breaks down the original opposition and opens up another mode of inquiry that was hitherto unseen or unexplored. In rethinking localization, for example, it is recognized that we always act (and think) locally, but our actions and thoughts are also simultaneously urban, regional, national, and global in scope, affecting and being affected by, if often only in the smallest way, the entire hierarchy of

8   In *Thirdspace*, I described this breaking down and opening up of binary oppositions as a "critical thirding-as-othering," and noted that this "thirding" was not just a positioning in-between two opposing terms but a distinctive "othering," the creation of a new and different way of understanding what was being described by the original binary opposition.

9   One of the first to use the term glocalization was Erik Swyngedouw, a Belgian geographer who teaches at Oxford University. See Swyngedouw, "The Mammon Quest: 'Glocalisation,' Interspatial Competition and the Monetary Order: The Construction of New Scales," in M. Dunford and G. Kafkalas eds., *Cities and Regions in the New Europe: The Global–Local Interplay and Spatial Development Strategies*, London: Belhaven Press, 1992: 39–68; and most recently, "Neither Global nor Local: 'Glocalization' and the Politics of Scale," in K. R. Cox ed., *Spaces of Globalization: Reasserting the Power of the Local*, New York and London: Guilford Press, 1997: 137–66. See also Roland Robertson, "Glocalization: Space, Time, and Social Theory," *Journal of International Communication* 1 (1994); and "Glocalization: Time–Space and Homogeneity–Heterogeneity," in *Global Modernities*, Featherstone et al. eds., London: Sage, 1995: 25–44. Also relevant here is Thomas J. Courchene, "Glocalization: The Regional/International Interface," *Canadian Journal of Regional Science* 18, 1995: 1–20.

10   For similar attempts to hybridize the global and the local from a more cultural studies perspective, see Rob Wilson and Wimal Dissanayake, *Global/Local: Cultural Production and the Transnational Imaginary*, Durham and London: Duke University Press, 1996. Chapter titles include such phrases as "Tracking the Global/Local" (editorial introduction), "The Global in the Local" (Arif Dirlik), "Localism, Globalism, and Cultural Identity" (Mike Featherstone), "Globalism's Localisms" (Dana Polan), and "Global/Localism in the American Pacific" (Rob Wilson). See also the other chapters in Kevin R. Cox ed., *Spaces of Globalization*, 1997, written primarily from the geographer's viewpoint.

spatial scales in which our lives are embedded. Similarly, rethinking global-ization leads to the recognition that it is not a process that operates exclusively at a planetary scale, but is constantly being localized in various ways and with different intensities at every scale of human life, from the human body to the planet. In this sense, every locality in the world today, be it in Los Angeles or Antarctica, is globalized – and also simultaneously urbanized, regionalized, and nationalized, albeit with very different intensities.[11]

Moreover, this nested hierarchy of scales, as integral parts of human spatiality, is not naively given but is socially constructed, as a vital part of what Henri Lefebvre described as the production of perceived, conceived, and lived spaces. Although one particular scale, such as that associated with the nation-state over the past two hundred years, can become conceptually reified and profoundly empowered in terms of its effects on daily life and geo-graphically uneven development, this too is a socio-spatial construct and can therefore be changed through human action. It is precisely this *breaking down and reconstitution of spatial scales*, from the most intimate spaces of the body, household, and home to the metropolitan region and the territorial nation-state, that is so deeply involved in the contemporary intensification of glob-alization. The innocent-sounding neologism of glocalization can thus be seen as one of the initial sparks for rethinking not just the relations between the global and the local or the competitive debates about internalist and exter-nalist approaches, but also the entire fabric of relations that define the spa-tiality of contemporary social life and, in particular, the spatial specificity of urbanism. Erik Swyngedouw summarizes his glocal view of the politics of scale in this way:

> The crux is not, therefore, whether the local or the global has theoretical and empirical priority in shaping the conditions of daily life, but rather how the local, the global, and other relevant (although perpetually shifting) geographical scale levels are the result, the product of processes, of sociospatial change. In other words, spatial scale is what needs to be understood as something that is pro-duced; a process that is always deeply heterogeneous, conflictual, and contested. Scale becomes the arena and moment, both discursively and materially, where sociospatial power relations are contested and compromises are negotiated and regulated.   (1997: 140)

11 That the entire world was becoming urban, at least since the early decades of the twentieth century, and that every potential political or economic revolution would have to be seen as a fundamentally *urban* revolution, was an argument Henri Lefebvre made in the 1960s, to the great confusion and consternation of even his closest Marxist and urbanist allies. Looking back now at his arguments, they can be seen as an attempt to reassert the fundamental importance of urbanism, rather than just the material form of big cities, in (urban-)industrial capitalism. He would later expand this "urban approximation" to a more encompassing *spatial* reconceptualization that cut across all spatial scales from the local to the global in *The Production of Space* (original French 1974, English 1991). For more on Lefebvre's reconceptualization of spatiality, see *Thirdspace* (1996) and the brief discussion in chapter 4 above. It is interesting to note that Erik Swyngedouw, a key figure in developing the term "glocalization," has been one of the most insightful interpreters of Lefebvre's work.

Use of the term glocalization has not yet entered very deeply into the globalization discourse, but many of the same recombinant arguments it induces have been developed in a different way by geopolitical economists concerned with the "resurgence of regional economies" and the explicit retheorization of localization-agglomeration-urbanization effects, a vital part of what I have called synekism. This regionalist approach, discussed in more detail in the previous chapter, tends to be critical of the overemphasis often given to globalization processes in the current literature, and especially the persistent dichotomy conventionally built around the global versus the local. Specifically focusing attention on urban-regional agglomerations, Michael Storper forcefully expresses this critical regionalist viewpoint:

> There is a dialectical dynamic of globalization and territorialization at work in the construction of city economies today, with many apparently paradoxical dimensions. The organization of reflexivity by local, regional, national, and global firms pushes all of them towards cities. Globalization is both the top-down force of organizing markets and production systems according to supra-national competitive criteria and resource flows, and the bottom-up pull of territorialization of both market penetration (a process requiring global firms to insert themselves in conventional-relational contexts of their markets, not a simple technocratic operation) and the effort to tap into geographically differentiated producer's capabilities . . . City economies are pulled simultaneously in both these directions by these forces and it is the interrelationship between the two that has to be appreciated in the study of a particular city's economy.   (1997: 248–9)

What Storper describes as territorialization can just as easily be labeled localization or regionalization. It is also closely linked to processes of urban agglomeration and synekism, given the rootedness of his concept of reflexivity in proximity, purposive action, innovation, and socio-spatial learning. What is most pertinent to the discussion of the second discourse, however, is the expanded definition of localization across all geographical scales so that it can be seen as operating very much like globalization itself, only from the "bottom-up" rather than the "top-down." How, then, is this dialectic of globalization and localization resolved or played out? And how can we avoid its formulation as another rigid dichotomy? For Storper, with his fixation on firm-based economic processes, the answer takes on several different forms. Most broadly, the playing out occurs as a "meso-level" resolution of macroeconomic (top-down) and microeconomic (bottom-up) forces, attaching his arguments to one of the most fundamental problems of economic analysis. More specifically, this meso-level synthesis-plus revolves around a whole string of interrelated concepts, including the resurgence of regional economies and regional worlds of production as fundamental forces shaping territorial development in global capitalism. In part to shift attention away from narrower definitions of globalization, Storper renames this meso-level regional resolution "reflexive capitalism."

Another example of a creative hybridization is emerging in the literature on "postcoloniality." As I argued in *Thirdspace*, the postcolonial discourse can be viewed as emerging from a disruptive and reconstructive critique of the two opposed metanarratives that have shaped how we study and interpret historically and geographically uneven development. The first emphasizes the positive side of capitalist development as an innovative force for continuous progress, economic growth, and *modernization*. The second and more fundamentally socialist metanarrative shifts attention to the negative consequences of capitalist development, especially with respect to *social justice*. A similar metanarrative split pervades the current literature on globalization, dividing its discursants into those who see globalization optimistically, as bringing new opportunities for development, modernization, and democracy; and those, the so-called "discontents," who see mainly the injustices and sociospatial cleavages being intensified in the rise of global capitalism. The best of the postcolonial critiques selectively accommodate both these perspectives, but build beyond their simple combination in new and innovative directions, particularly with respect to the progressive opportunities associated with the reassertion of the local, the power of place-based identities, the development of "counter-narratives of the nation" (see Bhabha, 1990), and more generally from what Smith and Guarnizo (1998) describe as "transnationalism from below."

To explore the postcolonial critique of globalization, however, takes us beyond the geopolitical economy literature and into the growing field of critical cultural studies, where a distinct subdiscourse on globalization has been developing. But before turning to this critical cultural approach, one additional area of thematic rethinking within the framework of geopolitical economy needs to be discussed.

New geographies of power

Here the discussion shifts gears from the economic to the political in the effort to understand the geopolitical economy of globalization. Unfortunately, the explicitly political discourse on globalization is not as well developed and conceptualized as the economic, and has tended to express itself more frequently in hyperbolic claims and conceptual clutter. The most prominent examples of such discursive excess can be gleaned from the titles of some of the representative texts listed at the head of this chapter: The Borderless World, The End of the Nation-State, and The End of Geography. I want to make it clear that I am not necessarily challenging the substance of the arguments developed by the authors of these texts, but using their titular phrases to stimulate a rethinking of the effects of globalization on the changing *political geography* of power in the contemporary world.

The discourse on the political effects of globalization has been centered on the *nation-state* and what some have called its "perforated sovereignty," its loss of "exclusive territoriality," and its new "legitimation crisis."[12] There is little doubt that globalization has been eroding many of the sovereign powers of nation-states over the past thirty years, but to conclude that this signals the end of the nation-state and the emergence of a borderless world is not just a gross exaggeration but a deflection away from making practical and theoretical sense of these significant changes. More appropriately, the changes in the sovereign powers of the territorial nation-state need to be seen first in the context of the geohistory of globalization and capitalist development; second, with specific reference to the dynamics of the profound restructuring processes that have been shaping the world over the past thirty years; and third, and perhaps most important, from a specifically geopolitical perspective that is sensitive to the multiple scales that characterize the spatiality and governmentality of political life.

I cannot go very deeply into the geohistory of the nation-state here, but a few brief comments are appropriate. The literature on the modern nation-state suggests that it began to take its distinctive form in late eighteenth-century Europe and North America, with the rise of liberal democracy in the Age of Revolution and the concurrent expansion of urban-industrial capitalism. As a real and imagined self-governing political community on a territorial scale above the city-state and below the state-empire, it was both ideologically democratic and substantively capitalist to begin with, creating tensions and contradictions that continue to fascinate theorists of the nation-state to this day. In its internal operations during the nineteenth century, this new kind of state was engaged in a process of nation-building, which consisted not only of promoting a national identity (or territoriality) within the more formally and legally defined borders of the state, but also of creating a reinforcing coincidence of three powerful spaces: the aforementioned mental space of territorial-national *identity*, or what Benedict Anderson (1983) called an "imagined community"; the jurisdictional and institutional space of state *authority* and control; and the fundamentally capitalist space defined by the power of the *market*. Through this induced territorial coincidence of identity, authority, and market that defined the successful nation-state, competing "subnational" sources of power in cities and regions were subordinated, but never entirely erased. They remained potent as spaces of alternative cultural identity, sites of resistance against national authority, and localized contexts for self-generated economic development and innovative synekism, although they tended to fade away in the larger and more "nationalized" theoretical discourse.

Beginning earlier but accelerated during the Age of Imperialism, the capitalist nation-state was globalized in at least rudimentary form as extensions to a global scale of these three national spaces of power. This imposed

12 Ivo D. Duchacek et al. eds., *Perforated Sovereignties and International Relations: Trans-sovereign Contacts of Subnational Governments*, New York: Greenwood Press, 1988; Saskia Sassen, *Losing Control? Sovereignty in an Age of Globalization*, New York: Columbia University Press, 1996; Jürgen Habermas, *Legitimation Crisis*, Boston: Beacon Press, 1973.

and consolidated a specifically *inter-state* network of global relations and a worldwide territorial division of labor and power that was structured around a dominant core of advanced industrial nation-states and a subordinated and "dependent" periphery of polities and economies conceptualized and imaginatively constructed as being at lesser levels of political and economic development.[13] Although shrouded in economic myths of comparative advantage and equal exchange as well as cultural myths of racial superiority and moral right, this inter-state and imperial geography of power was produced and sustained by simultaneous processes of induced capitalist development and underdevelopment. Here again, ideology (national patriotism), authority (the national state, with its military and police forces), and the market (especially via capital investments) worked together in the core countries to subordinate and subsume, without totally obliterating, competing sources of power, not just in the domestic arena but also in the cities, regions, and states of the periphery. In return for this subordination, there were promises of military protection, moral enlightenment, and economic modernization.

This globalized geography of power, inscribed in what today might be described as the old international division of labor, remained remarkably stable for nearly a century, despite anti-colonial uprisings in the periphery and destructive wars over ideology, territorial authority, and markets among the core states. By the 1970s, with the independence of most peripheral colonies, the nation-state had become so well entrenched as the most prodigious "container" of territorial power and community that alternative forms of governance seemingly disappeared from the global political imaginary. The capitalist world and even its incorporated socialist bloc was a world of nation-states or "destined to be" nation-states, each seen as a reified actor on a global stage, filling all possible roles.

What has been happening to the political geography of the world in the last third of the twentieth century can perhaps be best described as an opening up of the political imaginary as well as of the material realm of political possibility to "other" spaces and scales of governmentality and allegiance, triggered by an unprecedented U-turn in the evolving power and sovereign control of the core nation-states over territorial identity, authority, and markets. National control in these three territorial spheres has certainly not been lost, but has just as certainly been experiencing a significant restructuring.[14] It is useful to consider the old geography of power as operating pri-

---

13   This accelerated what Edward Said has called "Orientalism" and the bifurcation of the world into "imagined geographies" of the hegemonic colonizer and the subaltern colonized, the core and the periphery. Here, too, more contemporary debates are deconstructing and reconstituting this imposed binarism in the global geography of power.

14   A leading figure in conceptualizing this restructuring of the nation-state as a fundamental process of reterritorialization and rescaling, drawing heavily from the work of Henri Lefebvre, is Neil Brenner. See Brenner, "Globalisation as Reterritorialisation: The Re-scaling of Urban Governance in the European Union," *Urban Studies* 36, 1999: 432–51; and "Between Fixity and Motion: Accumulation, Territorial Organization and the Historical Geography of Spatial Scales," *Environment and Planning D: Society and Space* 16, 1998: 459–81.

marily at three levels or scales, the local, the national, and the global. The consolidation of the nation-state over the past two centuries has progressively penetrated and redefined the other two levels, that is, it has empowered all potential forms of governance above and below itself on its own terms, so that both the local and global spheres, with respect again to identity-authority-markets, were effectively subordinated and subsumed. For this reason, many continue to argue that globalization as well as local, urban, and regional development are primarily products of nation-states, and there are good reasons to believe that this is at least partially correct.

Nonetheless, the three-tiered geography of power has been significantly revamped over the past thirty years in several different ways. Most obvious perhaps is the growing strength and autonomy of *transnational globality*, a relative augmentation of the upper tier that is a primary effect of what is usually described as globalization. At the other end of the scale, some claim, there has also been an associated reassertion of the power of the local, both to accommodate and to resist the forces of globalization. Focusing on the nation-state itself, there has been at the very least a significant *pluralization* of the territorial bases of power. This has created what some commentators have identified as a new "crisis of the state," usually defined as arising from changing relative power relations between the nation-state and the scale above (the global) and the scale below (the local).

The conventional discourse on globalization has been almost entirely entrenched at these three scales. But in many ways the most interesting developments arising from globalization and postfordist economic restructuring can be found in the "in-between" spaces, the new geographies of power emerging between the national and the global and the national and local scales. The former primarily involves the development of *supra-national or supra-state regionalisms*, emerging forms of territorial identity, political authority, and market organization above the level of the nation-state. The most prominent example of such supra-national regionalism has been the formation of the European Union (EU), the first and as yet only serious attempt to politically confederate a large cluster of established and highly industrialized capitalist nation-states. A distinctive European identity still remains weakly developed, as does the effective authority of EU political institutions, although both are growing. The greatest advances have been made with regard to markets for labor and trade, leading some observers such as Manuel Castells to conclude that the EU today is little more than an expansive political cartel controlled by what he calls the "super nation-state."[15]

15 As Castells sees it, "The formation of the European Union . . . was not a process of building the European federal state of the future, but the construction of a political cartel, the Brussels cartel, in which European nation-states can still carve out, collectively, some level of sovereignty from the new global disorder, and then distribute the benefits among its members, under endlessly negotiated rules. This is why, rather than ushering in the era of supranationality and global governance, we are witnessing the emergence of the super nation-state, that is of a state expressing, in a variable geometry, the aggregate interests of its constituent members." Manuel Castells, *The Power of Identity*, volume II of *The Information Age: Economy, Society and Culture*, Oxford, UK, and Cambridge, MA: Blackwell Publishers, 1997: 267.

The European Union today may indeed be not much more than an extension of the nation-state at a larger scale, but its formation, along with the
related breakdown and reformation of the communist bloc, has been an
important stimulus to intensified supranational regionalism, at least in the
area of world trade and global flows of goods, services, people, and information. Shaped by the increasing globalization of capital, labor, and industrial
production, a system of overlapping regional trading blocs has emerged and
assumed increasing power in the world economy. Crudely but not inaccu-
rately pictured, the world economy is becoming increasingly organized in
three broad bands or zones stretching North–South from pole to pole, one centered on the USA and containing the entire Western Hemisphere; another, with
a Western European core, covering western Eurasia and Africa; and a third,
led by Japan, spanning eastern Eurasia, Australia-New Zealand, and most of
the Pacific basin (now often described as the Asian Pacific).

Although some of the multiple trading blocs that comprise each of these
longitudinal zones overlap into the other two, and the core areas of each continue to trade primarily with one another, trade, information, and migration
flows, and perhaps also geopolitical ties, within the North–South bands
appear to be increasing rapidly. Even more apparent, increasing intra-zonal
economic and political integration has been accompanied, if not led, by the
growing concentration of political and economic power in three specific postmetropolises that serve as the dominant "command centers" for each zone:
New York, London, and Tokyo, each the peak of a nested hierarchy of similar
"capitals of global capital." In many ways, this triadic supranational division
of the global political economy, with its internally structured geography of
power, is replacing the older international division of labor between First,
Second, and Third Worlds as well as that popular latitudinal metaphor for
core and periphery, the North–South divide. Kenichi Ohmae, in his business-
man's tour of the "borderless world," sees in this global reordering the rise of
the "regional state," described as "bigger than a continent" and emanating
from what he calls "the Interlinked Economy of the Triad (the United States,
Europe, and Japan)."[16]

Just as interesting and also controversial have been the developments in
between the national and local governmental scales. As described earlier,
globalization and economic restructuring have been associated with the
resurgence of regional economies in terms of both endogenously generated
development and discursive emphasis. In addition to this subnational economic regionalism, however, globalization has been accompanied by the
resurgence of subnational cultural and political regionalisms. The formation
of the European Union, for example, has not just had a supranational effect
but has also led to what has been described as a new "Europe of the Regions,"
in which many old regional identities and geopolitical and economic powers,

---

16 Kenichi Ohmae, *The Borderless World*, New York: Harper Business, 1990: x–xi. For a fascinating critique of Ohmae and other speculative regionalists, see Christopher L. Connery, "The Oceanic Feeling
and the Regional Imaginary," in Wilson and Dissanayake eds., *Global/Local*.

long submerged under the national state, are being reasserted. Catalunya in Spain, the Lombardy League in northern Italy, Scotland and Wales in Great Britain, are among the least disruptive examples of these regionalist movements, at least for the moment. Much more radical in its effects has been the disintegration of former Yugoslavia, resurrecting a term that has historically been one of the most fearful metaphors for threats to the territorial integrity and sovereignty of the nation-state: balkanization.

Balkanization is one way of describing the resurgence of subnational regionalisms in the contemporary era of globalization.[17] Much softer in its implications for the nation-state has been the revival and reinvigoration of the theory and practice of confederalism. In the writings of such nineteenth- and early twentieth-century anarchist (and regionalist) thinkers as Proudhon and Kropotkin, confederalism was a means of subverting all forms of centralized authority and especially the nation-state as it was developing at the time. Today, it carries with it a milder version of this fulsome anti-statism, built around what can be described as a movement for the territorial *decentralization* of power and authority and its *recentralization* at more local or regional scales. Far from balkanization, which was also part of the agenda for the nineteenth-century anarchists, decentralization or devolution has become another catchword in current discussions of the declining power of the nation-state. For the most part, however, this downward decentralization, much like the upward decentralization discussed for the European Union, remains attached to the nation-state itself. It can therefore be interpreted either as a tactical extension of the still-centralized state or as a significant restructuring and weakening of the state's subnational political power – or perhaps both.

Linked to these discussions of decentralization and recentralization, confederalism and balkanization, the resurgence of regionalism and the reassertion of the local, and the triadic zoning of geopolitical and economic power, has been a string of new terms to describe what globalization scholars speculate may be emerging in the intervening spaces between the national and the local state. Among the most interesting, especially for understanding the scope and scale of postmetropolitan political and economic power, are those that signal the resurrection of the *city-state* in one form or another. Riccardo Petrella, for example, speaks of "world city-states" and the reincarnation of a "New Hanseatic League" connecting them.[18] A web site (http://www.citistates.com) created by a pair of business consultants celebrates the emergence of what they call regional "Citistates" ("the focus of how our world is now organizing itself"). Looking forward rather than back in time, these subna-

---

17   Balkanization is also a term that is beginning to be used to refer to the political fragmentation of the postmetropolis. In the already highly fragmented postmetropolis of Los Angeles, for example, there are new or revived secessionary movements in the San Fernando Valley, the port area of San Pedro, the Westside, and elsewhere aimed at breaking off from the City of Los Angeles.

18   Riccardo Petrella, "World City-States of the Future," *New Perspectives Quarterly* 8, 1991: 59–64; and "Techno-Appartheid for a Global Underclass," *Los Angeles Times*, August 6, 1992.

tional entities might best be described as (globalized) *city-region states* to emphasize their resurgent regionality and their growing role as motors of the global geopolitical economy. My own preference is to combine their multi-scalar description into the notion of the postmetropolis itself, as an incipient form of the postmetropolitan region-state or polity.

Many postmetropolitan regions have already begun to take on some of the functions and authority of the old national state, such as diplomacy, negotiating trade relations and investment partnerships, even obtaining foreign loans to subsidize local government payrolls and pension funds. While far from autonomous in their political and economic operations, these subnational city-regions tend more than ever before to bypass the national state in their global ties, adding a significant political dimension to their growing roles as assertive motors of the global economy. In his most recent book, *Regions and the World Economy* (1998), Allen Scott adds a much more explicitly political dimension to his economic regionalism, opening up new challenges to the geopolitical economy of globalization. Here is a brief extract from the book's cover-notes.

> The steady globalization of economic activity over the past few decades has intensified the re-assertion of the region as a critical locus of economic order and as a potent foundation of competitive advantage. As a corollary, many regions in the modern world are also beginning to acquire an intense self-consciousness of themselves as socio-political and economic entities, and all the more so as they increasingly find themselves bound together in both competitive and collaborative relationships across national borders. The significance of these tendencies for new kinds of political mobilization is explored, and their potential impacts on substantive forms of democracy and citizenship in the new world order are assessed.

This expressly political turn in globalization studies has had two primary effects. First, it has begun to focus serious attention on the degree to which globalization is forcing us to rethink and perhaps redefine the foundations of democracy and citizenship in the contemporary world. And second, it has provided an unexpected bridge between geopolitical economy and critical cultural studies, especially around such crucial issues as expanding the definition of citizenship and residential "rights to the city," the new cultural politics of identity and representation, and struggles for explicitly *spatial justice and regional democracy* in the postmetropolis.

Adding culture to the global geopolitical economy

Thus far the discourse on globalization has been represented primarily from the perspective of geopolitical economy. As noted, however, there has also developed a distinctive cultural studies discourse on globalization, often with close connections to the work of geopolitical economists but just as often taking the discourse on globalization in significantly different directions. Especially influential here has been the work of the anthropologist and post-colonial critic Arjun Appadurai on the disjunctures, ironies, resistances, and complex spatial dynamics that are built into what he cogently defines as the new "global cultural economy."[19] "The central problem of today's global inter-actions," Appadurai argues, "is the tension between cultural homogenization and cultural heterogenization" (1996: 32). In his view, too much attention in the contemporary literature, especially on the Left, has been given to the view that the cultures of the world are becoming increasingly homogenized through an irrepressible force typically associated with commoditization and Americanization, and spread through the globally enmeshing networks of the market and the media. What this view misses are many countervailing forces of resistance, indigenization, syncretism, rupture, and "disjuncture" that reassert and often reorder cultural differences and reaffirm the power of heterogeneous political cultures and identities.

> The new global cultural economy has to be seen as a complex, overlapping, dis-junctive order that cannot any longer be understood in terms of existing center-periphery models (even those that might account for multiple centers and peripheries). Nor is it susceptible to simple models of push and pull (in terms of migration theory), or of surpluses and deficits (as in traditional models of balance of trade), or of consumers and producers (as in most neo-Marxist theo-ries of development). Even the most complex and flexible theories of global development that have come out of the Marxist tradition are inadequately quirky and have failed to come to terms with . . . disorganized capitalism. The com-plexity of the current global economy has to do with certain fundamental dis-junctures between economy, culture, and politics that we have only begun to theorize. (1996: 32–3)

In *Modernity at Large: Cultural Dimensions of Globalization*, Appadurai centers our attention around two major and interconnected "diacritics," *media* and *migration*, and explores their joint effect on the *"work of the imagination as a constitutive feature of modern subjectivity"* (1996: 3). His real-and-imagined discourse echoes many others trying to make sense of the restructured moder-nity or postmodernity being shaped by globalization.[20]

> The image, the imagined, the imaginary – these are all terms that direct us to something critical and new in global cultural processes: *the imagination as a social practice.* No longer mere fantasy (opium for the masses whose real work is else-

---

19   The key work by Appadurai is "Disjuncture and Difference in the Global Cultural Economy," *Public Culture* 2 (1990), 1–25. He elaborates his ideas further in "Global Ethnoscapes: Notes and Queries for a Transnational Anthropology," in *Recapturing Anthropology: Working in the Present*, R. G. Fox ed., Santa Fe, NM: School of American Research Press, 1991. Both these articles are reprinted and revised in *Modernity at Large: Cultural Dimensions of Globalization*, Minneapolis and London: University of Minnesota Press, 1996.

20   See, for example, Michael Storper's comment on the reality of constructed images in regional worlds of production, chapter 6, p. 178.

where), no longer simple escape (from a world defined principally by more concrete purposes and structures), no longer elite pastime (thus not relevant to the
lives of ordinary people), and no longer mere contemplation (irrelevant for new
forms of desire and subjectivity), the imagination has become an organized field
of social practices, a form of work (in the sense of both labor and culturally organized practice), and a form of negotiation between sites of agency (individuals)
and globally defined fields of possibility . . . The imagination is now central to
all forms of agency, is itself a social fact, and is the key component of the new
global order.   (1996: 31)

To make these claims meaningful, Appadurai outlines an "elementary framework" to explore "global cultural processes" based on five inter-related
cultural-economic landscapes, which he also calls, extending Benedict Anderson's work on nationalism, *imagined worlds*.[21] "The suffix scape," he writes,
"allows us to point to the fluid, irregular shapes of these landscapes, shapes
that characterize international capital as deeply as they do international clothing styles" (1996: 33). *Ethnoscapes*, his primary focus, are shaped by global
flows of people (tourists, immigrants, refugees, exiles, guest workers, and
other "moving groups"), now intensified to an unprecedented level of scale
and scope both in material terms and in the global imaginary. *Technoscapes* are
fluid global configurations of both high and low, mechanical and informational technology, being shaped and reshaped with unprecedented speed as
technology moves across hitherto impervious boundaries. *Finanscapes* focus
around the now more "mysterious, rapid and difficult to follow" landscape
of global capital, where "megamonies move through national turnstiles at
blinding speed."

Further "defracting" the deeply disjunctive relationships between these
first three scapes are two realms of created imagery. *Mediascapes*, based on
"image-centered, narrative-based accounts of strips of reality" electronically
disseminated by newspapers, magazines, television stations, film studios, and
other globalized media, provide "large and complex repertoires of images,
narratives, and ethnoscapes to viewers throughout the world, in which the
world of commodities and world of news and politics are profoundly mixed."
Ideoscapes, also concatenations of images, are more directly political, having to
do with "the ideologies of states and the counter-ideologies of movements
explicitly oriented to capturing state power or a piece of it." In the ideoscape,
the "master-term" democracy and the Euro-American "master narrative of the
Enlightenment" play a particularly important role, reflecting Appadurai's
reinsertion of the globalization discourse into the geohistorical debates
on modernity and postmodernity (as well as closely related discussions of
democracy, justice, and citizenship rights).

Appadurai's "transnational anthropology" of scapes and flows, along with
the work of other cultural critics such as Homi Bhabha, Edward Said, and

---

21 For Benedict Anderson, see his *Imagined Communities: Reflections on the Origins and Spread of
Nationalism*, London: Verso, 1983.

Gayatri Spivak, reflects the entry into the general discourse on globalization of a potent *postcolonial* cultural perspective that dwells more on the disruptive, conflict-filled heterogeneity of this disordered postmodern world than on the homogenizing effects of global interdependence and consciousness. They reconfigure the globalization discourse not in a simple dichotomy of homogenization–heterogenization but around what is described as *multiple scales of hybridity*, the places and people most embroiled in the tensions arising from simultaneous cultural homogenization and heterogenization processes, or what might be called cultural glocalization or transnationalism. Two of these scales feature most prominently in the postcolonial critiques: the nation-state and nationalism on the one hand and the production of locality and local identity on the other, but it is the interaction and hybridization across many different scales, from the most global to the most local and individuated, that is of primary importance.[22]

The key concept of hybridity is defined by Homi Bhabha as the "third space" that "enables other positions to emerge," that "sets up new structures of authority, new political initiatives." It works to create "something different, something new and unrecognisable, a new area of negotiation of meaning and representation."[23] In his essay on "Globalization as Hybridization," Jan Nederveen Pieterse, a self-proclaimed "critical globalist," sees hybridity as "part of a power relationship between centre and margin, hegemony and minority" that "indicates a blurring, destabilization or subversion of that hierarchical relationship." Noting that hybridity can also produce submission and alienation, he constructs a "continuum of hybridities" that has at one end "an assimilationist hybridity that leans over towards the centre, adopts the canon and mimics the hegemony" and at the other end "a destabilizing hybridity that blurs the canon, reverses the current, subverts the centre."[24]

These real-and-imagined glocal dynamics have foregrounded another dialectical pairing that, like deindustrialization–reindustrialization, decentralization–recentralization, and the metaphorical root of all such *de-re* pairings, deconstruction–reconstitution, suggests key modes of interpreting the pervasive restructuring processes shaping the contemporary world and, in particular, the formation of the postmetropolis. I refer here to what may be the most revealing window through which to understand the new global cultural economy and the new cultural politics of representation and identity that is

---

22 Contributing significantly to critical studies of transnationalism in an urban and regional context, as well as with specific reference to California, is the work of Michael Peter Smith. See Smith and Guarnizo eds., *Transnationalism from Below*, New Brunswick, NJ: Transaction Publishers, 1998; M. P. Smith, "Can You Imagine? Transnational Migration and the Globalization of Grassroots Politics," *Social Text* 39, 1994: 15–33; and "Postmodernism, Urban Ethnograpy, and the New Social Space of Ethnic Identity," *Theory and Society* 21, 1992: 493–531.

23 Homi Bhabha, "The Third Space," in J. Rutherford ed., *Identity, Community, Culture, Difference*, London: Lawrence and Wishart, 1991: 211. See also his *Location of Culture*, New York and London: Routledge, 1994. Bhabha's hybridity is also discussed in *Thirdspace*, 1996: 139–44.

24 The essay from which these quotes are taken appears in M. Featherstone, S. Lash, and R. Robertson eds., *Global Modernities*, 1995: 56–7.

so vital a part of it: the dynamic interplay between *deterritorialization* and *reterritorialization*.

What this pairing suggests is the complex simultaneity of two interwoven processes of restructuring. Deterritorialization involves the breaking down of Fordist worlds of production and related spatial divisions of labor, the long-standing political and discursive hegemony of the modern nation-state and traditional forms of nationalism and internationalism, and established patterns of real-and-imagined cultural and spatial identity at every scale from the local to the global. Reterritorialization is the critical response to globalization and postfordist restructuring, generating new efforts by individuals and collectivities, cities and regions, business firms and industrial sectors, cultures and nations, to reconstitute their territorial behavior, their fundamental spatiality and lived spaces, as a means of resisting and/or adapting to the contemporary condition. The discourse on globalization has helped significantly in understanding the first, but still has a long way to go in understanding the second. Here is where the cutting-edge research and most progressive social movements in the future are likely to be found.

The reconstruction of social meaning in the space of flows

The global economy emerging from informational-based production and competition is characterized by its *interdependence*, its *asymmetry*, its *regionalization*, the *increasing diversification within each region*, its selective inclusiveness, its *exclusionary segmentation*, and, as a result of all these features, an extraordinarily *variable geometry* that tends to dissolve historical, economic geography.

(Castells, 1996: 106)

The most comprehensive, assertive, empirically detailed, and increasingly influential conceptualization of the social and spatial impact of globalization on cities and regions has been developed by Manuel Castells. His representation of globalization reaches into and reinterprets nearly all the diverse literatures on globalization – economic, political, cultural – and focuses them on what he calls the "urban-regional process." Created in the wake of his synthesizing ambition is an extraordinarily far-ranging reconstitution of contemporary social and spatial theory, recently expanded to monumental proportions in his three-volume work on *The Information Age: Economy, Society and Culture.*[25] How his ideas have enhanced our understanding of the spatial specificity of urbanism, the postmetropolitan transition, and the conceptualization of the cosmopolis will be discussed later in this chapter. Here we look at the strengths and weaknesses of Castells's grand global synthesis.

25   Volume I, *The Rise of the Network Society* (1996), volume II, *The Power of Identity* (1997), and volume III, *End of Millennium* (1998), Oxford, UK, and Cambridge, MA: Blackwell Publishers.

Two major discursive focusings shape Castells's revisionary arguments. The first is the conceptual centrality of the *information technology revolution*, which he describes as his "entry point in analyzing the complexity of the new economy, society, and culture in the making" (1996: 5). In *The Informational City* (1989), Castells spoke of an "informational mode of development" arising from the convulsive restructuring of capitalism, and infused this "new technological paradigm" into practically every aspect of geopolitical economy, creating many interpretive bridges between the industrial urbanist and global urbanist discourses on the postmetropolis. At the heart of this new mode of development was *information-based production*, in essence a recomposition of what the industrial urbanists described as one of the leading sectors of postfordist flexible accumulation. A new mode of production in the Marxian sense had not appeared from the restructuring of capitalism, but rather a new *technological paradigm* for continued capitalist industrial production and reproduction. The microelectronics revolution was the cutting edge, emerging from and building sequentially on such key innovations as the transistor (1947), the integrated circuit (1957), the planar process (1959), and the microprocessor (1971). The production process remained the defining moment of the capitalist economy, as it did for most geopolitical economists, but for Castells capitalist production had entered an "organizational transition" from industrialism to *informationalism*, an assertion that would disturb many industrial urbanists.[26]

In looking at "the locational pattern of information-technology manufacturing and its effects on spatial dynamics" (chapter 2 in *The Informational City*), Castells presented his own version of the industrial urbanist discourse on the rise of new industrial spaces and the critical importance of "milieux of innovation," at least for the special case of high-technology manufacturing.[27] Castells moves next into the "dialectics of centralization and decentralization" reshaping the organization and technology of the services economy (chapter 3), the restructuring of capital–labor relationships and the rise of the "Dual City" (chapter 4); the transition from the "urban welfare state" to the "suburban warfare state" (chapter 5), and finally to the "internationalization of the economy" and its effects on new technologies and the "variable geometry" of the new urban-regional process (chapter 6). Running through all these chapters is his second discursive emphasis, on the rising power of the elusively

---

26 See, for example, Michael Storper's critique of Castells's informationalism in *The Regional World*, 1997: 236–41. The reaction of the industrial urbanists was in part a product of a suspicion of all claims that industrialism has come to an end, especially when promulgated by sociologists. Not only was the concentration on information-based industries likely to lead to overlooking the importance of craft-based and less high-technology-oriented industrial activities, it appealed too easily to the production-blind tenets of postindustrialism.

27 Castells writes "Although the concept of milieu does not necessarily include a spatial dimension, I will argue that, in the case of information-technology industries, spatial proximity is a necessary material condition for the existence of such milieux, because of the nature of interaction in the innovation process" (Castells, 1989: 82). See the preceding footnote for Storper's critique of Castells's concepts of milieu and innovation.

abstract *space of flows* versus the more grounded and socially congruent *space of places*.

In his conclusion to *The Informational City*, Castells wraps up his comprehensive revisioning under the potent title "The Reconstruction of Social Meaning in the Space of Flows."

> At the end of this analytical journey, we can see a major social trend standing out from all our observations: the historical emergence of the space of flows, superseding the meaning of the space of places. By this we understand the deployment of the functional logic of power-holding organizations in asymmetrical networks of exchanges which do not depend on the characteristics of any specific locale for the fulfillment of their fundamental goals. The new industrial space and the new service economy organize their operations around the dynamics of information-generating units, while connecting their different functions to disparate spaces assigned to each task to be performed; the overall process is then reintegrated through communications systems. The new professional managerial class colonizes exclusive spatial segments that connect with one another across the city, the country, and the world; they isolate themselves from the fragments of local societies, which in consequence become destructured in the process of selective reorganization of work and residence. The new state, asserting its sources of power in control and strategic guidance of knowledge, fosters the development of an advanced technological infrastructure that scatters its elements across undifferentiated locations and interconnected secretive spaces. The new international economy creates a variable geometry of production and consumption, labor and capital, management and information – a geometry that denies the specific productive meaning of any place outside its position in a network whose shape changes relentlessly in response to the messages of unseen signals and unknown codes. (1989: 348)

> The emergence of the space of flows actually expresses the disarticulation of place-based societies and cultures from the organizations of power and production that continue to dominate society without submitting to its control. In the end, even democracies become powerless confronted with the ability of capital to circulate globally, of information to be transferred secretly, of markets to be penetrated or neglected, of planetary strategies of politico-military power to be decided without the knowledge of nations, and of cultural messages to be marketed, packaged, recorded, and beamed in and out of people's minds . . . The flows of power generate the power of flows, whose material reality imposes itself as a natural phenomenon that cannot be controlled or predicted, only accepted and managed. This is the real significance of the current restructuring process, implemented on the basis of new information technologies, and materially expressed in the separation between functional flows and historically determined places as two disjointed spheres of the human experience. People live in places, power rules through flows. (1989: 349)

These dense passages represent both the major strengths of Castells's revisioning of the general discourse on globalization and its embedded weaknesses. The strengths lie in its empirically informed comprehensiveness, its rootedness in an integrative sociological and spatial perspective, and its creatively balanced treatment of many of the prevailing conceptual oppositions that have tended to split the globalization discourse into unnecessarily competitive and conflicting camps: production–consumption, capital–labor, manufacturing–services, globalization–localization, geopolitics–geoeconomics, internalist–externalist, society–spatiality. Unfortunately, the means by which Castells achieves this remarkable synthesis and revisioning – his discursive emphasis on the technological paradigm of informationalism and the apparently all-encompassing dynamics expressed in the space of flows versus the space of places – too often comes too close to producing its own iron cages of interpretation.

The most serious problems arise not so much from the informational emphasis, for in the future this may very well be looked back on as the defining feature of the new economy, society, and culture emerging in the late twentieth century, but more so from the overly dichotomized and totalizing conceptualization of the space of flows versus the space of places. Although his political intent is clearly aimed at mobilizing the progressive political power of the space of places, he tends to represent the opposing power of the space of flows as forebodingly overwhelming. It is here more than anywhere else where Castells's discourse can benefit from a critical thirding, informed by the hybridities of Appadurai's scapes and transnational anthropology, the dialectics of deterritorialization–reterritorialization, the recombinant concept of glocalization, the new regionalism of synekistic reflexivity promoted by Storper and others, and that insistent phrase used by Henri Lefebvre when faced with any overarching dichotomy: two terms are never enough . . . there is always an Other (*Il y a toujours l'Autre*).

Referring again to Lefebvre and my related arguments in *Thirdspace*, there are additional problems that arise from the particular way Castells conceptualizes spatiality and spatializes social theory, even in its latest improved version.[28] There is much more to the contemporary world than can be seen in the binary power play between flows and places. Hybridized and glocalized movements and practices are developing that recombine abstract flows and concrete places, opening up new and different real-and-imagined spatialities of resistance and contention at multiple scales. In *The Power of Identity* (1997), Castells recognizes some of these new movements and practices (the Mexican Zapatistas, the struggles for environmental justice and lesbian-gay liberation), but the overall impression remains that power rules exclusively and triumphantly in the space of flows and that the new cultural politics has little chance of making a significant difference in cities, regions, nation-states and the world at large. Whether intentional or not, Castells appears overly pessimistic about the rise of specifically place-based or territorial power in the spaces where people live, the power that is always embedded deeply in what Lefebvre called, in his effort to expand the scope of the geographical imagination, *lived spaces*. But even in noting these problems, it can be concluded that

---

28 See the discussion of "the social theory of space and the theory of the space of flows" in *The Rise of the Network Society*, 1996: 410–18.

in *The Informational City* and in his three volumes on *The Information Age*, Manuel Castells has produced the most far-reaching, insightful, and systematically argued statement on globalization and the urban-regional process currently available. It will remain the benchmark and target of debate well into the new millennium.

Globalized neoliberalism: a brief note

The discourse on globalization is seriously incomplete without some discussion of the rise of neoliberalism as perhaps the dominant glocal ideology and most influential "ideoscape" of the contemporary world. Building on simulations of traditional precepts of liberal democracy, neoliberalism has forged a new synthesis or hybrid that effectively rationalizes, celebrates, and promotes the globalization process and the increasing globality of industrial production, commercial trade, financial integration, and information flow. It has brought to the fore a new global class of economic and political entrepreneurs who operate not only transnationally but also at the national, regional, metropolitan, and local scales to foster those conditions that facilitate the freedoms of global capitalism: increasing privatization of the public sphere, deregulation in every economic sector, the breakdown of all barriers to trade and the free flow of capital, attacks on the welfare state and labor unions, and other efforts to reshape the power of established political and territorial authorities to control both the globality of production and the production of globality. And it is carried forward in a series of familiar spin-doctoring slogans having to do with the magic of the market, the ineffectiveness of Big Government, the triumph of capitalism, the emergence of a borderless world, and a whole slew of the "end ofs" – of history and geography, of socialism and the welfare state, of ideology itself.

The increasing empowerment of neoliberalism can be seen across all scales of territorial governmentality, but has been most complex and confusing in its effects on national politics and policies. In the USA, it has created deep divisions within the Democratic and Republican parties and blurred many of the distinctions between them, opening up political space for a new hybridized politics cultivating the middle ground between Democratic and Republican, Left and Right, pro-business and pro-labor, conservative and radical, and many other traditionally two-sided political oppositions. This middle ground has always existed in US politics, but today it seems to have become larger and more powerful. Its blurring effects are more evident and its ideological driving force has become more explicitly globalist than purely domestic. Indeed, even the differences between promoting national as opposed to global interests has become increasingly cloudy in this neoliberal hybridization. All this has had the peculiar effect of opening up a new kind of "centrist" politics, beyond rather than in-between the Left–Right polarity, seemingly amorphous, ambiguous, difficult to pin down but intrinsically globalized and perhaps also distinctively postmodern.

This association of neoliberalism with postmodern politics has led many on the Left to close down the possibility of developing a more progressive, if not radical, postmodernism. If neoliberalism is what postmodern politics is about, it is frequently thought, then it surely must be resisted.[29] Such ideological closure has generated a growing backlash against the new cultural politics perspectives, poststructuralist theories, and much of the feminist and post-colonial literatures dealing with issues such as identity, representation, other-ness, and hybridity that have also been closely associated with critical postmodernism.[30] Whatever stance one takes on these linkages, however, a strong argument can be made that the "center" of the established political spectrum is being significantly reconfigured, and that struggles over the directions that this reconstituted center will take are likely to be of major significance in the twenty-first century at every geographical scale, from the global to the local. Neoliberalism, postmodern or otherwise, has become a dominant force in the new globalized national politics of the moment, but it should not be seen as filling the entire realm of critical centrist possibilities or precluding the development of a more progressive and, if not entirely anti-capitalist then significantly pro-socialist postmodernism of the radical center.

A particularly well-informed and spatially relevant take on this new glob-alized national centrism can be found in the recent work of Anthony Giddens, currently an influential advisor to the New Labour government of Tony Blair via his position as Director of the London School of Economics and Polit-ical Science and one of the world's leading social and spatial theorists. He speaks of cultivating the "radical middle" between the traditional Left and Right, and developing a "third way" as a strategy to promote more pro-gressive national public policy in an age of globalization.[31] However one responds to this rethinking of radical politics and social democracy, it is im-portant to note that one of the first major projects of the Blair government was to begin reorganizing the intranational geography of power in Great Britain through referendums on increased regional autonomy for Scotland and Wales, as well as to make efforts to deal in a more open and balanced way with the problems of Northern Ireland. There has also been talk of reviving metro-politan regional governments and planning bodies, such as the Greater London Council, after their almost complete destruction by the previous Thatcher–Major governments. Here then are a few, still tentative, examples of how such concepts as critical regionalism, glocalization, reterritorialization,

29 In a strange alliance, a similar reaction to both neoliberalism and postmodernism has built up on the far Right, from Christian Coalitions to Islamic fundamentalism.
30 I disagree strongly with this "Left conservatism," as some have begun to call it, but will not elaborate a defense of my position in any detail here. Keeping open the possibility for a progressive and socialist postmodernism has been central to my writings, from *Postmodern Geographies* to *Postmetropolis*.
31 Anthony Giddens, *Beyond Left and Right: The Future of Radical Politics*, Stanford: Stanford Univer-sity Press, 1994; and *The Third Way: The Renewal of Social Democracy*, Oxford, UK and Malden, MA: Blackwell Publishers, Polity Press, 1998.

hybridity, and the new cultural politics have begun to enter the scene of national politics, as both adaptation and resistance to the diffusion of global neoliberalism.

Metropolis Unbound: Conceptualizing Globalized Cityspace

Much has already been said about how globalization affects cityspace, but mainly as an incidental aside. Beginning in the early 1980s, however, there has developed a body of literature that revolves specifically around the effects of globalization on cityspace, on patterns of uneven urban development, and on the spatial specificity of urbanism as a way of life. Let us look at this literature – again with a particular emphasis on learning from Los Angeles – and explore its relevance to enhancing our understanding of the postmetropolitan transition.

It is useful to begin by noting the conceptual and material *unbounding* of the modern metropolis, for it has been this breaking down of old boundaries that has generated new ways of looking at and interpreting cityspace. The dialectics of globalization–localization, and its accompanying restructuring of industrial production, the centralized political authority of the state, and patterns of territorial identity has brought about an extraordinary expansion in the scale and scope of the modern metropolis. Even such expansive terms as megalopolis and megacity no longer seem sufficient to define the outer limits of the globally restructured metropolitan region. Official estimates of the population size of some city-regions such as Mexico City and Tokyo have ballooned to over 25 million and, in the Pearl River Delta as well as around Shanghai, regional city systems now exist that are twice this size and growing. But even these mappings underestimate the reach of the postmetropolis. As Iain Chambers, our discursive tour guide, has argued, we can no longer be confident that we know how to map the new metropolis, "its extremes, its borders, confines, limits," for there has been a "loss in focus." What was once clearly "elsewhere" to the city is now being drawn into its "expanded symbolic zone" as the geohistory of cityspace has been "uprooted" and "rerouted" in the late twentieth century.

As a result of this unbounding and "reworlding" of cityspace, it has become more difficult than ever before to unravel its so-called "inner workings" – economic, social, cultural, political, psychological – *endogenously*, that is, from what is happening locally, inside its conventionally defined boundaries. The practices of daily life, the public domain of planning and governance, the formation of urban community and civil society, the processes of urban and regional economic development and change, the arena of urban politics, the constitution of the urban imaginary, and the way in which "the city" is represented, are all increasingly affected by global influences and constraints, significantly reducing what might be called the conceptual autonomy of the urban. The unbounding of the metropolis, its expanding scope and scale, in short its increasing globality, is a central feature of the postmetropolitan transition. How urbanists have conceptualized this globalization of the modern metropolis can be traced through four major lines of thought.

The world city hypothesis

The *world city* hypothesis is about the *spatial organization* of the new *international division of labor*. As such, it concerns the contradictory relations between *production* in the era of global management and the *political determination* of territorial interests. It helps us to understand what happens in the major global cities of the world economy and what much *political conflict* in these cities is about. Although it cannot predict the outcomes of these struggles, it does suggest their common origins in the *global system* of market relations.

John Friedmann, "The World City Hypothesis" (1986): 69–70; emphasis added

The first to crystallize academic discussion of the impact of globalization on cities was John Friedmann, working initially with Goetz Wolff, then a doctoral student in Urban Planning at UCLA, where Friedmann was a professor from 1970 until his retirement in 1996. The first product of their collaboration was a working paper that appeared in 1981 as part of a series on Comparative Urbanization Studies distributed by the Graduate School of Architecture and Urban Planning. It was called "Notes on the Future of the World City" and reflected Friedmann's longstanding interest in regional development planning in Latin America and Asia as well as his localized involvement in urban theory, especially as empirically expressed in the "urban field" of Los Angeles, a term he developed in the early 1970s. A second working paper with Wolff quickly followed, entitled "World City Formation: An Agenda for Research and Action." Published in 1982 in the *International Journal of Urban and Regional Research*, it was not just a conceptual rethinking but also a call for concerted social action to alleviate what was seen as an intensified racial and class polarization, symbolized in the face-off between the citadel and the ghetto, arising directly from globalization and world city formation.

These early studies were set within two more specialized discourses. The first was framed by Friedmann as "comparative urbanization studies" and sought to identify contemporary trends in urban development throughout the world as a means of reshaping the action agenda for urban and regional planning.[32] With his global perspective on regional and international development issues, Friedmann wove into these comparative studies the *world systems theory* that was pioneered by Immanuel Wallerstein and his colleagues at SUNY-Binghamton (at that time one of the leading centers for rethinking social theory in the eastern USA), as well as the related neo-Marxist work on under-

---

32 Friedmann was the chair of a short-lived Committee on Comparative Urbanization Studies for the Social Science Research Council in New York during the early 1970s. I first met John at that time, when I was teaching in the Department of Geography at Northwestern University. It was his invitation that resulted in my appointment in the Urban Planning Program at UCLA in 1972.

development and dependency theory.[33] By this time, a few world systems theorists had begun to explore the phenomenon of world cities.[34] Friedmann (now without Wolff, who had moved on to other issues) built on this work, along with the new literature on the changing international division of labor and its effects, to crystallize a more assertive and explicitly spatialized statement on world city formation. Described as *The World City Hypothesis*, it was originally published in the journal *Development and Change* (17-1, 1986: 69–84) and reprinted almost a decade later in *World Cities in a World System* (1995), edited by Paul L. Knox and Peter J. Taylor. This volume, with its summative title, was built around Friedmann's hypothesis-cum-paradigm and also included Friedmann's own retrospective, "Where We Stand: A Decade of World City Research."

The second discourse in which Friedmann's world city research was originally emplaced was more localized, or perhaps better put, glocalized. In the early 1980s, a group of urban studies scholars centered in the departments of Urban Planning and Geography at UCLA began to turn their attention to making both practical and theoretical sense of the unusually rapid changes taking place in the Los Angeles metropolitan region. In the two decades after the 1965 Watts Rebellion, the regional cityspace of Los Angeles was transformed dramatically and in ways that did not seem to fit very well into prevailing models of urban analysis, which in any case had usually treated Los Angeles as a rather bizarre exception in the historical development of cities. In what would eventually develop into what some have called a Los Angeles "school" of critical urban studies, this group of scholars set about building an empirical and theoretical interpretation of the changing regional cityspace, generating contributions that are relevant to all six discourses on the postmetropolis.[35] Friedmann's world city research was initially part of this group's

33 Friedmann himself was a major figure in the translation of underdevelopment and dependency theory into planning theory and practice. It is also interesting to note that one of the leading theorists of underdevelopment, Andre Gunder Frank, was a student colleague of Friedmann's at the University of Chicago in the early 1950s.

34 See, for example, Robert Ross and Kent Trache, "Global Cities and Global Classes: The Peripheralization of Labor in New York City," *Review* 6(3), 1983: 393–431. *Review* is the journal published by the Binghamton center at the State University of New York in Binghamton. See also John Walton, "The International Economy and Peripheral Urbanization," in Norman and Susan Fainstein eds., *Urban Policy under Capitalism*, Beverly Hills: Sage, 1982: 119–35.

35 Goetz Wolff would join with the present author and his then colleague, Rebecca Morales, in a project generated by a labor coalition organized to fight the multiplying plant closures in the old industrial heartland of Los Angeles, amidst what was at that time one of the world's most dynamic, job-generating regional economies. For our attempt to make practical as well as political sense of the paradoxical dynamics of deindustrialization and reindustrialization, see Edward Soja, Rebecca Morales, and Goetz Wolff, "Urban Restructuring: An Analysis of Social and Spatial Change in Los Angeles," *Economic Geography* 59, 1983: 195–230. At about the same time, Allen Scott was beginning his long-term project on industrial restructuring in Los Angeles. See his three-part series on "Industrial Organization and the Logic of Intra-Metropolitan Location," published in *Economic Geography*: "I: Theoretical Considerations" (1983: 233–50); "II: A Case Study of the Printed Circuits Industry in the Greater Los Angeles Region" (1983: 343–67); and "III: A Case Study of the Women's Dress Industry in the Greater Los Angeles Region" (1984: 3–27). Michael Storper would also join the UCLA faculty in

work, with Los Angeles featuring prominently in the first working papers and publications. By the time of the publication of "The World City Hypothesis," however, the spatial specificity of Los Angeles was much less prominent, and when Los Angeles was mentioned it was almost always paired secondarily with New York City.

Friedmann summarized his world city hypothesis in seven interrelated assertions. (1) The form and extent of a city's integration with the world economy, and the functions assigned to the city in the new spatial division of labor, will be decisive for any structural changes occurring within it. (2) Key cities throughout the world are used by global capital as "basing points" in the spatial organization and articulation of production and markets. The resulting linkages make it possible to arrange world cities into a complex spatial hierarchy. (3) The global control functions of world cities are directly reflected in the structure and dynamics of their production sectors and employment. (4) World cities are major sites for the concentration and accumulation of international capital. (5) World cities are points of destination for large numbers of both domestic and/or international migrants. (6) World city formation brings into focus the major contradictions of industrial capitalism – among them spatial and class polarization. (7) World city growth generates social costs at rates that tend to exceed the fiscal capacity of the state. Friedmann would conclude his essay with this observation: "The struggles of people, caught in the trap of relative territorial immobility and the mobility of international capital, are a part of the dynamic which will shape both the world cities and the capitalist world economic system."

The world city hypothesis was formulated with such a broad brush that today, at least from a progressive political perspective, it appears to be little more than an elucidation of the obvious. But at the time, it effectively crystallized a city-focused approach to globalization when there was none, and guided the research of a generation of "world city" scholars, mainly geographers and planners. Especially important in this Friedmann-led trajectory is its persistent urge to action in the form of critical planning practice and community-based social struggle. As it has developed, however, the Friedmann lineage of world city research has tended to move away from specific investigations of the impact of globalization on cityspace itself and toward the study of inter-urban linkages and debates about how best to identify and describe the *hierarchy* of world cities. In the larger picture of conceptualizing the postmetropolis, *World Cities in a World System* can be seen as marking the end of an era, for surpassing this trajectory was another line of research that would focus attention on the "social order" and "command functions" of *global* rather than world cities, and especially on the three peak points of the global hierarchy, New York, London, and Tokyo.

Urban Planning at about this time and develop his own take on restructuring in Los Angeles. See Michael Storper and Susan Christopherson, "Flexible Specialization and Regional Industrial Agglomerations: The Case of the US Motion Picture Industry," *Annals of the Association of American Geographers* 77, 1987: 104–17.

Commanding our attention: the rise of global cities

[T]he combination of spatial dispersal and global integration has created a *new strategic role* for major cities. Beyond their long history as centers for international trade and banking, these cities now function in four new ways: first, as highly concentrated *command points* in the organization of the world economy; second, as key locations for *finance* and for *specialized service* firms, which have *replaced manufacturing* as the leading economic sector; third, as sites of production, including the *production of innovations*, in these leading industries; and fourth, as *markets* for the products and innovations produced . . . Cities *concentrate control* over vast resources, while finance and specialized service industries have restructured the urban social and economic order. Thus a new type of city has appeared. It is the *global city*. Leading examples now are New York, London, and Tokyo.

Saskia Sassen, The Global City (1991): 3–4; emphasis added

A second lineage in conceptualizing urban globality has developed directly from and alongside the first. In particular, it hinges around Friedmann's second and third theses, on key cities as "basing points" and control centers for global capital, collapsing many other aspects of urban globalization around these commanding functions. Although her recent work extends well beyond this narrowed channel, Saskia Sassen has been the leading figure in bringing about this refocusing. Writing as Sassen-Koob, she began her work on global cities in the early 1980s, during which time she spent a brief period as a visiting professor in the Urban Planning department at UCLA. Influenced significantly by world systems theory as well as the work of Friedmann and others in the budding Los Angeles school, Sassen initially focused on one particular feature of urban globalization, the "peripheralization" of "core" cities, using terms that signaled the influence of world systems theory and the historical sociology of Immanuel Wallerstein.[36] At the heart of her research, both then and today, is an attempt to understand the "informal economy" (a term developed primarily in cities of the Third World) and the associated restructuring of urban labor markets, especially the changing work patterns of women, minorities, and the poor in an era of increasing capital mobility and mass labor migrations.

With the publication of *The Mobility of Capital and Labor: A Study in International Investment and Labor Flows* (1988) and then *The Global City: New York, London, Tokyo* (1991), Sassen reshaped the discourse on world cities and became recognized as one of the leading spokespersons on the economic, political, and sociological effects of globalization. In so doing, the Sassen line on global cities came to differ significantly from Friedmann's world cities

36   Saskia Sassen-Koob, "Recomposition and Peripheralization at the Core," *Contemporary Marxism* 5, 1982: 88–100; reprinted in M. Dixon, S. Jonas, and D. McCaughey eds., *The New Nomads: Immigration and the New International Division of Labor*, San Francisco: Synthesis Publications, 1982. See also "Capital Mobility and Labor Migration: Their Expression in Core Cities," in M. Timberlake ed., *Urbanization in the World System*, New York: Academic Press, 1984.

approach. There was a major shift in representative sites, for example, from Los Angeles and the Pacific Rim to New York City and the North Atlantic. In large part, this had to do with Sassen's then home base in Urban Planning at Columbia University in Manhattan. But it also reflected a deeper discursive split between prevailing scholarly modes of analysis between east- and west-coast scholarly styles and cultures. I do not want to make too much of this bicoastal division, but there are several interesting contrasts that are worth mentioning.

First, there is the continuing use in Sassen's writings and in the New York-focused discourse of the concept of postindustrialism and Daniel Bell's evocation of a postindustrial society. This has had the effect of focusing primary attention on the services economy, and especially on the "power-holding organizations" of the FIRE sector: finance, insurance, and real estate. These commanding financial, banking, and producer services define what Sassen calls the primary "postindustrial production sites" ordering the economy of global cities and shaping a "new urban regime" of capital accumulation. Always cognizant of the role played by FIRE-employment growth and its overspill in New York's recoveries from deindustrialization and fiscal crisis, research on New York has paid special attention to such issues as the impact of advanced telecommunication and information-processing technologies, the perturbations and transformations of global capital markets, and the localized emergence of a new elite of urban professionals led by brokers, bond sellers, securities dealers, and their affiliates. At the opposite pole in what some New York researchers call the new "Dual City" is the informal or underground economy and the welfare-dependent underclass of new migrants, minorities, and the poor, struggling for survival in the new sociology of power. Here is one of Sassen's summative statements on New York:

> These [restructuring] processes can be seen as [generating] distinct modes of economic organization and their corresponding uses of space: the postindustrial city of luxury high-rise office and residential buildings located largely in Manhattan; the old dying industrial city of low-rise buildings and family-type houses, located largely in the outer-boroughs; and the Third World city imported via immigration and located in dense groupings spread all over the city . . . Each of these three processes can be seen to contain distinct income-occupational structures and concomitant residential and consumption patterns, well captured in the expansion of a new urban gentry alongside expanding immigrant communities.[37]

Sassen, especially in her most recent work, brings a more sophisticated spatial perspective into her writings, but her earlier geographical imagination and that of most global city researchers working in New York has tended to be much weaker than among those studying Los Angeles or the Bay Area. In

---

37 Saskia Sassen, "New York City's Informal Economy," paper prepared for the Social Science Research Council Committee on New York City, 1988: 1; quoted in Manuel Castells, *The Informational City*, 1989: 215.

many subtle and not so subtle ways, the persistent presence of a postindustrial perspective in the scholarly writings on New York has privileged the sociological over the geographical imagination, leading to another Atlantic–Pacific contrast. This difference is characteristically displayed in how the manufacturing sector is treated in the study of urban globalization. In New York, attention is typically deflected away from manufacturing and the underlying principles of industrial urbanism that have been so central in Los Angeles research, especially the regionalist perspective on postfordist economic restructuring and the explicitly geopolitical economy of urbanism. The very nature of the global city is seen from New York as revolving almost entirely around the FIRE sector and its commanding control over global flows of capital investment and labor migration. In her short textbook, *Cities in a World Economy* (1994), published in a series on Sociology for a New Century, Sassen barely mentions the manufacturing sector, except to note its decline, and little reference is made to the industrial restructuring literature or to the globalization of industrial production.

It might be argued that postfordist is as inappropriate a label for New York as postindustrial is for Los Angeles, but this argument masks too much from view. Despite the massive decline of manufacturing employment in the five boroughs of New York City, there has been continued growth in the Greater New York region, paralleling a similar reindustrialization in the metropolitan regions of Boston and other eastern cities. This reindustrialization becomes magnified even further if *"producer* services" is taken literally, as services to manufacturing industries that now include the production not only of hamburgers and fried chicken but also of information, entertainment, and culture. When seen as a city-*region*, and not just as Manhattan, New York leaps out as the second or third largest postfordist industrial metropolis in North America, as well as the leading control center for the globality of production and the production of globality: a highly representative postmetropolis. Yet the postfordist regional landscape has remained relatively unexplored in Greater New York, with one great exception: the prodigiously powerful and flexibly specialized "industrial district" (or as Sassen calls it, the postindustrial production site) of Lower Manhattan.

The discursive pre-eminence of the FIRE sector and its extensions has also produced in New York what I once described as the "vanity of the bonFIRES," a tendency to condense the globalization and localization processes almost entirely around the Wall Street omphalos and its immediate sphere of influence.[38] This has led most local global city researchers and planning critics to

38 My play on Tom Wolfe's acrid allegory on the urban condition in New York City originally appeared in "Poles Apart: Urban Restructuring in New York and Los Angeles," a paper presented to the Dual City Working Group of the Social Science Research Committee on New York City. The paper was later published, with reference to the "vanity of the bonFIRES" deleted at the request of the editors, in John H. Mollenkopf and Manuel Castells eds., *Dual City: Restructuring New York*, New York: Russell Sage Foundation, 1991: 361–76. The editors introduce New York City as "the social laboratory for the New Society" and claim, "Just as Chicago was central to nineteenth-century urban industrialization, and the founders of modern social science studied it to understand these processes, New York can be viewed as central to understanding the late twentieth-century postindustrial transformation" (1991: 5).

limit their purview to the large-scale urban redevelopment projects in Lower Manhattan, such as Battery Park City, South Street Seaport, Times Square, and the World Trade Center, all located in and around Manhattan's financial core. This emphasis on the commanding FIRE stations also spills over into comparative studies of global cities, with New York's World Financial Center in Battery Park City and London's Canary Wharf project in the Docklands becoming the epitomizing discursive urban sitings of glocalization.[39] Even the pioneering work of Neil Smith on what he calls the "Revanchist City" and the "Satanic Geographies" of globalization remains somewhat narrowly rooted in the rowdy frontier of Tompkins Square Park, sitting at a leading edge of yuppie gentrification.[40] Similarly, the encompassing power of Manhattan's financial citadel also seems to hover in the shadows in Sharon Zukin's excellent portrayals of glocalized landscapes of power and despair, even when she ventures well outside its reach.[41] In all these works, the regional world beyond the pale of Manhattan and its most adjacent boroughs seems almost to disappear from view.

The writings of Neil Smith, Sharon Zukin, and other Manhattan-focused scholars such as E. Christine Boyer and Susan Fainstein, nonetheless represent some of the best research being done today on the global city. Their work is strongest, however, when it constructs bridges to other and larger discourses, ranging from geopolitical economy to critical cultural studies. In this sense, they may be described as departures from the strict Sassen line of global city research. But Sassen too, in her most recent writings, has also been moving in new directions, edging closer to what I will define below as the concept of cosmopolis.[42] But before discussing this conceptual turn, a brief look at the global city discourse as it has developed in Los Angeles provides a useful comparative view.

The global city discourse in Los Angeles has been much less "triumphant" than in New York City and somewhat more balanced in its attention to the globalizations of labor, capital, and world cultures. With what might be seen as its own city-centrism, the discursive emphasis has revolved primarily around the position of Los Angeles in the expanding Pacific Rim economy, its

39   For the best of these comparative studies, see Susan Fainstein, *The City Builders: Property, Politics, and Planning in London and New York*, Oxford, UK, and Cambridge, MA: Blackwell, 1994; and Susan Fainstein, Ian Gordon, and Michael Harloe eds., *Divided Cities: Economic Restructuring and Social Change in London and New York*, Oxford, UK, and Cambridge, MA: Blackwell, 1992.

40   See Smith, "New City, New Frontier: The Lower East Side as Wild West," in Michael Sorkin ed., *Variations on a Theme Park: The New American City and the End of Public Space*, New York: Hill and Wang 1992: 61–93; "After Tompkins Square Park: Degentrification and the Revanchist City," in Anthony King ed., *Re-Presenting the City: Ethnicity, Capital and Culture in the twenty-first Century Metropolis*, London: Macmillan, 1996: 93–107; "The Satanic Geographies of Globalization: Uneven Development in the 1990s," *Public Culture* 1997, 10–11: 169–89; and *New Urban Frontier: Gentrification and the Revanchist City*, New York and London: Routledge, 1996.

41   Sharon Zukin, *Landscapes of Power*, Berkeley and Los Angeles: University of California Press, 1991.

42   Saskia Sassen, *Losing Control? Sovereignty in an Age of Globalization*, New York: Columbia University Press, 1996; and "Whose City Is It? Globalization and the Formation of New Claims," *Public Culture* 8, 1996: 205–23.

attractiveness to foreign investment in both its inner and outer cities, the powerful role of its globally extensive military industrial complex and culture industry, and above all its expansive multiculturalism. Gentrification has not been a major theme in Los Angeles, largely because neighborhood change has been so rapid and intense, and so complex in its racial, ethnic, and class mix, that the simpler gentrification theories of "rent gaps" and yuppie incursions seem to shed little light on the more kaleidoscopic and heterogeneous local and regional patterns of residential restructuring.[43]

Although there have been few detailed studies of Los Angeles as a world financial center and there is nothing equivalent to Wall Street or the City of London as financial citadels, the more dispersed and polycentric FIRE sector is probably now of sufficient aggregate size for the Los Angeles conurbation to be considered among the many global candidates contending to join the ranks of the big three, behind Tokyo, New York, and London, with San Francisco and Chicago as its main North American competitors. As one of the preeminent capitals of global capitalism, however, Los Angeles is more closely comparable to Tokyo than to either London or New York in its more locationally dispersed financial services complex, its still very extensive manufacturing base, and especially the greater connectivity of the FIRE sector with the larger regional economy. This regional connectivity is difficult to measure, but with its greater specialization in savings and loan institutions, the real estate industry, and technologically innovative consumer banking services, as well as other local linkages (especially with manufacturing), the FIRE sector of Los Angeles probably has greater regional multiplier effects than the more globally specialized and tightly localized sectors of London and New York.[44]

Los Angeles's position as a world city is also significantly enhanced by its other specializations. In Ann Markusen's terms, Los Angeles has been the capital of the American "Gunbelt" and perhaps the world's largest arsenal for what Castells describes as "planetary strategies of politico-military power."[45] Los Angeles is also the world's leading manufactory of global culture and popular entertainment, and not far from the top in fashion and design.[46] Even

---

43 One of the best critiques of gentrification theories from a Los Angeles perspective, focusing on the many different definitions of the "West Adams Community," can be found in Sylvia Sensiper, *The Geographic Imaginary: An Anthropological Investigation of Gentrification*, unpublished doctoral dissertation, Urban Planning, UCLA, 1994. See also Allan David Heskin, *The Struggle for Community*, Boulder, CO: Westview Press, 1991, a revealing case study of a low-income, multi-ethnic, limited-equity housing cooperative that might be described as an almost oxymoronic example of gentrification by the poor.

44 For an interesting study of the commercial banking sector in Los Angeles, see Jane S. Pollard, *Industry Change and Labor Segmentation: The Banking Industry in Los Angeles, 1970–1990*, unpublished doctoral dissertation, Urban Planning, UCLA, 1995; reprinted Ann Arbor: University Microfilms International, 1995.

45 See A. Markusen, P. Hall, S. Campbell, and S. Dietrick eds., *The Rise of the Gunbelt*, New York: Oxford University Press, 1991.

46 For an excellent study of the design industries in Los Angeles and their regional multiplier effects, see Harvey Molotch, "L.A. as Design Product: How Art Works in a Regional Economy," in Scott and Soja eds., *The City*, 1996: 225–75.

more noteworthy perhaps, it has become the world's largest metropolis of global labor at both ends of the skills spectrum. It not only contains what is reputed to be the largest concentration of scientists, engineers, mathematicians, and computer analysts (a significant proportion of whom are foreign-born) but also one of the largest and most culturally heterogeneous urban pools of cheap, unskilled, and weakly organized workers the world has ever seen. Nearly 40 percent of the more than nine million people residing in Los Angeles County are foreign-born and, if we add in the domestic non-white minorities (Chicano/a, African American, Asian American), the total regional population with roots in what was formerly described as the Third World would reach close to seven million.[47]

It is no surprise, then, that the debate and discourse on Los Angeles as a global city has centered, in one way or another, around its multiculturalism and its role in the global cultural economy rather than on its FIRE stations and gentrifying elite. Put in another way, there has been a more eclectic approach to globalization, a more balanced exploration of the region's glocalized ethnoscapes, technoscapes, finanscapes, mediascapes, and ideoscapes (to refer back to Appadurai). The most interesting local studies of the impact of this extraordinary demographic and cultural heterogeneity, however, have not been couched specifically in the discourse on global cities, which remains relatively peripheral in comparison with New York. They will therefore be treated in more detail in the remaining four discourses on the postmetropolis. Continuing our genealogy of specifically urban concepts of globalization brings us next, or back again, to the work of Manuel Castells.

Urban dualism, the Informational City and the urban-regional process

[T]here is a new form of urban dualism on the rise, one specifically linked to the restructuring process and to the expansion of the informational economy. It relates, first of all, to the simultaneous processes of growth and decline of industries and firms, processes taking place most intensely at the nodal points in the economic geography, namely, the largest metropolitan areas where most of the knowledge-intensive activities and jobs are concentrated ... The transition from industrial to informational production processes overlaps with the rise of flexible production ... with de-institutionalized capital-labor relationships ... [and] the general demise of traditional labor ... The new dual city can also be seen as the urban expression of the process of increasing differentiation of labor into two equally dynamic sectors within the growing economy: the information-based formal economy, and the downgraded labor-based

47 Apparently stunned by the magnitude of this mass in-migration, one quick-visit New York journalist glibly dubbed Los Angeles the "capital of the Third World." See David Rieff, *Los Angeles: Capital of the Third World*, New York: Simon and Schuster, 1991. A more pragmatic and less moralizing approach to the globalization of Los Angeles, albeit one which is filled with optimistic boosterism, is taken by another journalist who is much more familiar with the local scene. See Joel Kotkin, *Tribes: How Race, Religion, and Identity Determine Success in the New Global Economy*, New York: Random House, 1993.

informal economy . . . The economy, and thus society, becomes functionally articulated but organizationally and socially segmented . . .

Manuel Castells, *The Information City*: 224–6

With these words, Castells outlines his conceptualization of the Informational City as a Dual City, dichotomized, fragmented, and rearticulated by the restructuring process and the emergence of a New Information Age in which the space of places becomes increasingly dominated by the space of flows. In many ways, Castells's conceptualization is not very different from Sassen's, but Castells tends to be more directly involved with the changing spatial specificities of his version of the global city, and thus offers a much richer picture of its changing social geography. I will quote Castells at length, for he provides a vivid portrayal of the social and spatial stratification of the postmetropolis and offers a comprehensive backdrop to what will be discussed in the subsequent chapters.

The vast majority of downgraded workers and new laborers share an excluded space that is highly fragmented, mainly in ethnic terms, building defensive communities that fight each other to win a greater share of services, and to preserve the territorial basis of their social networks, a major resource for low-income communities. Downgraded areas of the city serve as refuges for the criminal element of the informal economy, as well as reservations for displaced labor, barely maintained on welfare. Newcomers to the dual city often pioneer transformations of these areas [via gentrification], increasing the tension between conflicting social interests and values expressed in territorial terms. On the other hand, a large proportion of the population, made up of low-level labor forming the legions of clerical and service workers of the informational economy, insert themselves into micro-spaces, individualizing their relationship to the city . . . Structural dualism leads at the same time to spatial segregation and to spatial segmentation, to sharp differentiation between the upper level of the informational society and the rest of the local residents . . . , [and to] frequent opposition among the many components of restructured and destructured labor . . . The territorially based institutional fragmentation of local governments and of schools reproduces these cleavages along the lines of spatial segregation.

The social universe of these different worlds is also characterized by differential exposure to information flows and communication patterns. The space of the upper tier is usually connected to global communication and to vast networks of exchange, open to messages and experiences that embrace the entire world. At the other end of the spectrum, segmented local networks, often ethnically based, rely on their identity as the most valuable resource to defend their interests, and ultimately their being. So the segregation of space in one case (for the large social elite) does not lead to seclusion, except regarding communication with the other components of the shared urban area; while segregation and segmentation for defensive communities of ethnic minorities do reinforce the tendency to shrink the world to their specific culture and their local experience, penetrated only by standardized television images, and mythically connected, in the case of immigrants, to tales of the homeland. The dual city opposes, in traditional sociological terms, the cosmopolitanism of the new informational producers to the localism of the segmented sectors of restructured labor . . .

The fundamental contemporary meaning of the dual city refers to the process of spatial restructuring through which distinct segments of labor are included in and excluded from the making of new history.

(Castells, 1989: 227–8)

Castells builds these highly spatialized images from case studies of New York City and Los Angeles, and from the community of scholars based in the Bay Area and the University of California at Berkeley, where he has been a professor in the Department of City and Regional Planning (and later in Sociology) since 1979. He would develop them further, but with a significantly lessened spatial emphasis, in *Dual City: Restructuring New York* (1991), co-edited with John Mollenkopf. But here again the interpretation is constrained by the rigid dichotomization into the power of flows versus the power of places and by the master narrative of informationalism. To break from these constraints and others in the literature on urban globalization, an alternative term needs to be introduced.

The turn to cosmopolis

The use of the term *cosmopolis* to refer to the globalized and culturally heterogeneous city-region is a recent development. To begin to understand the appeal of this term, it is useful to turn to the work of the philosopher Stephen Toulmin, currently a member of the humanities faculty at the University of Southern California. Toulmin (with Allan Janik) was the author of one of the most brilliant urban-centered treatises on continental philosophy, *Wittgenstein's Vienna* (1973), in which the rich context and spatial specificity of the Austrian metropolis features almost as centrally as the ideas of the Viennese philosopher. In his more recent work, *Cosmopolis: The Hidden Agenda of Modernity* (1990), the city (as polis) is more distant historically and geographically, but there is much of contemporary relevance.

As used in classical Greece, the word "cosmopolis" referred to the interplay of two kinds of order, one (*cosmos*, the astronomical universe) embedded in Nature, and later the scientific understanding of natural phenomena; and the other (*polis*, the administration of cities) rooted in Society and our growing understanding of the practices and organization of human communities as political (and territorial) units, what I have also called phronesis. Toulmin traces philosophical thought about this interplay of Nature and Society from the origins of the "problem of modernity" (which he dates to the period from 1600 to 1650) to contemporary debates about postmodernity and "the way we live nowadays." In so doing, he reinserts the study of urban globalization and hence our understanding of the contemporary global postmetropolis back into the geohistorical discourse on modernity and postmodernity. For Toulmin, the cosmopolis represents the "hidden agenda of modernity," an urban-centered inquiry into the fundamental meaning of being alive in particular times and places. What has been discussed as the discourse on globalization can be seen not so much as a "successor to the debates on modernity and postmodernity," as noted in the first paragraph of this chapter, but as its recrystallization around the "hidden agenda" of *cosmopolitical cityspace*.

The term cosmopolis has recently been taken up again by two scholars, both of whom have been peripherally involved in the global cities debates and also feel comfortable in framing their cosmopolitan analyses in a critical post-modern perspective. In *Towards Cosmopolis: Planning for Multicultural Cities* (1998a), Leonie Sandercock builds on her work with students and faculty in the Department of Urban Planning at UCLA, and her longstanding experience in Australia, a personal-as-political vision of cosmopolis as achievable Utopia.

> Cosmopolis is my imagined Utopia, a construction site of the mind, a city/region in which there is genuine connection with, and respect and space for, the cultural Other and the possibility of working together on matters of common destiny, a recognition of intertwined fates. I will then outline the principles of this postmodern Utopia – new concepts of social justice, citizenship, community, and shared interest – and suggest a new style of planning which can help create the space of/for cosmopolis.   (1998a: 125)

Sandercock's "normative cosmopolis" is "a Utopia with a difference, a post-modern Utopia" that "can never be realized, but must always be in the making." (1998a: 163) Her focus is on the theory and practice of planning and her goal is a "paradigm shift" from "modernist planning wisdom" to "a more normative, open, democratic, flexible, and responsive style that is sensitive to cultural difference" (1998: 204). It is this "transformative politics of difference," building on the transition from metropolis to cosmopolis, that expands the political horizons of progressive planning theory and practice. She concludes her book with an ambitious look to the future:

> I want a city where my profession contributes . . . , where city planning is a war of liberation fought against dumb, featureless public space as well as against the multiple sources of oppression and domination and exploitation and violence; where citizens wrest from space new possibilities, and immerse themselves in their cultures while respecting those of their neighbours, and collectively forging new hybrid cultures and spaces.   (1998: 219)

In his geohistorical analysis of "the metropolis unbound," the Canadian geographer-planner Engin Isin also reconstitutes the contemporary debates on global urbanization around the shift from metropolis to cosmopolis.[48]

48   Engin F. Isin, "Metropolis Unbound: Legislators and Interpreters of Urban Form," in J. Caulfield and L. Peake eds., *City Lives and City Forms: Critical Urban Research and Canadian Urbanism*, Toronto: University of Toronto Press, 1996: 98–127; "Global City-Regions and Citizenship," in D. Bell, R. Keil and G. Wekerle eds., *Global Processes, Local Places*, Montreal: Black Rose Books, 1996: 21–34; and "Who is the New Citizen? Toward a Genealogy," *Citizenship Studies* 1, 1997: 115–32.

Drawing on the synekistic milieu of postmetropolitan Toronto as a "global city-region," Isin centers his attention on contemporary struggles over citizenship and the "rights to the city," but digs much deeper into the "history of the present" to trace a Foucauldian genealogy of citizenship and cityspace.

> Just as we marvel at the rise and fall of the Greek polis or the medieval city, future urban historians will perhaps marvel at the rise and fall of the modern metropolis in the twentieth century . . . [T]he period between 1921 and 1971 was the era of the metropolis: a dominant core city surrounded by several cities, towns and villages economically and socially integrated with it . . . By the 1990s most American and Canadian metropolises no longer focus exclusively on the original core cities . . . The twentieth century metropolis has become a polycentric urban region.   (1996a: 98–9)

> Whatever metaphor we choose to describe the metropolis unbound – the multi-nucleated metropolitan region, the polycentric urban region, the new techno-city, post-suburbia, the galactic metropolis, the city without, the postmodern urban form, the city-state – the new urban form is "marked by hitherto unimagined fragmentation; by immense distances between its citizens, literal, economic, cultural, social and political; and by novel planning problems, which raise the stakes for, and may very well demand changes in the way we think about urban planning itself" (Bloch 1994: 225). I suggest another metaphor for the metropolis unbound: the cosmopolis. This metaphor marks both the continuity and discontinuity with the metropolis . . . The cosmopolis also signifies the global character of the metropolis unbound . . . still a polis, albeit a fragmented, sprawling, and global one.   (1996a: 123)[49]

It is still too soon to gauge the significance of this budding convergence around the concept of cosmopolis, but it has the potential to lead the discourse on globalization and the postmetropolitan transition into significantly new directions in the future. In particular, it helps to recenter the specifically urban discourse not just on the negative impacts of globalization but also on the new opportunities and challenges provoked by globalization to rethink from a more explicitly spatial perspective established notions of citizenship and democracy, civil society and the public sphere, community development and cultural politics, social justice and the moral order (see, e.g., Friedmann and Douglas, 1998). To illustrate this rethinking and potential redirection with an example that relates directly to current developments in Los Angeles but resonates with relevance in every postmetropolis, I conclude with a brief reference to the work of Raymond Rocco, a transdisciplinary political scientist and specialist on the formation of Latino citizenship who teaches at UCLA.

---

49   The reference in this quote is to Robin Bloch, *The Metropolis Inverted: The Rise and Shift to the Periphery and the Remaking of the Contemporary City*, unpublished doctoral dissertation, Urban Planning, UCLA, 1994. It is indicative of a growing line of contact between scholars in Toronto and Los Angeles. Bloch's dissertation was written under the primary supervision of Michael Storper and John Friedmann, with additional advice from the present author, Allen Scott, and other faculty at UCLA.

In his contribution to a forthcoming book edited by Engin Isin, *Politics in the Global City: Rights, Democracy and Place*,[50] Rocco argues that "the spaces created by the complex and multidimensional processes of globalization have become strategic sites for the formation of transnational identities and communities and the corresponding emergence of new types of claims within these transformed spaces."[51] These claims to "associational rights" and the "networks of civic engagement" that promote them (borrowing from Putnam, 1993) are grounded in and derived from "situated practices" that are attuned to the specific geography of the globalized city-region, and especially to those "spaces of difference" theorized as "third space, hybridity, borders, the 'in-between,' or margins." They are thus inherently spatial claims, localized demands for increased rights to the city and explicit calls for greater spatial justice and regional democracy. These new urban spatial (rather than just social) movements are developing most forcefully from the dense agglomerations of immigrant populations and the working poor, as emblematic as anything else of contemporary urban globalization and transnational cultural adaptation. And finally, it is in these radically particularized and politicized spaces, Rocco argues, that the geopolitical, postcolonial, and related critical discourses come together to help us understand better the lived experience of the postmetropolis.

---

50   The original title was to be *Rights to the City: Citizenship, Democracy, and Cities in a Global Age*, after an international conference organized by Engin Isin and others at York University in Toronto in June, 1998. Routledge, the publisher, suggested a change, feeling that Rights to the City was too narrow and would restrict the audience.

51   Raymond Rocco, "Associational Rights Claims, Civil Society and Place," in Engin Isin ed., *Politics in the Global City: Rights, Democracy and Place*, London: Routledge, forthcoming. See also by Rocco, "The Formation of Latino Citizenship in Southeast Los Angeles," *Citizenship Studies* 3, 1999: 95–112; and "Latino Los Angeles: Reframing Boundaries/Borders," in Scott and Soja eds., *The City*, 1996: 365–89. The reference to Putnam in the next sentence is R. D. Putnam, *Making Democracy Work: Civic Traditions in Modern Italy*, Princeton, NJ: Princeton University Press, 1993.

Chapter 8
Exopolis: The Restructuring of Urban Form

Representative Texts

- *Edge City: Life on the New Frontier* (Garreau, 1991)
- *The 100 Mile City* (Sudjic, 1992)
- *Post-Suburbia: Government and Politics in the Edge Cities* (Teaford, 1997)
- *Postsuburban California: The Transformation of Orange County since World War II* (Kling, Olin, and Poster eds., 1991)
- *Magnetic Los Angeles: Planning the Twentieth-Century Metropolis* (Hise, 1997)
- *The Metropolis Inverted: The Rise and Shift to the Periphery and the Remaking of the Contemporary City* (Bloch, 1994)
- *The Reluctant Metropolis: The Politics of Urban Growth in Los Angeles* (Fulton, 1997)
- *Metropolis to Metroplex: The Social and Spatial Planning of Cities* (Meltzer, 1984)
- *The New Urbanism: Toward an Architecture of Community* (Katz, 1994)
- *The New Urbanism: Hope or Hype for American Communities* (Fulton, 1996)
- *The Fractured Metropolis: Improving the New City, Restoring the Old City, Reshaping the Region* (Barnett, 1995)
- *The Next American Metropolis: Ecology, Community, and the American Dream* (Calthorpe, 1993)
- *The Outer City* (Herington, 1984)
- *From City Center to Regional Mall* (Longstreth, 1997)
- *The Geography of Nowhere: The Rise and Decline of America's Man-Made Landscape* (Kunstler, 1993)
- *Dreaming the Rational City: The Myth of American City Planning* (Boyer, 1983)
- *Bourgeois Utopias: The Rise and Fall of Suburbia* (Fishman, 1987)
- *Crabgrass Frontier: The Suburbanization of the United States* (Jackson, 1985)
- *Since Megalopolis* (Gottman and Harper eds., 1990)
- *Suburbia Re-examined* (Kelly ed., 1989)

The combined discourses on globalization and economic restructuring provide a powerful conceptual framework for understanding and analyzing the major forces that have been generating the new urbanization processes. The next pair of discourses is concerned more directly with interpreting the concrete outcomes and effects of these new urbanization processes in post-metropolitan cityspace. In this chapter, the postmetropolis is represented primarily in terms of its reconfigured empirical geography, the new patternings and specificities of urban form, function, and behavior that have emerged in the wake of globalization and postfordist economic restructuring. In the following chapter, the focus shifts to the concurrent and interdependent reshaping of the urban social order and the new patterning of social stratification and socio-economic inequality.

The division between these two discourses is artificial, for, like the first two discourses, each is intrinsically intertwined with the other. They are best viewed in combination, as part of a socio-spatial dialectic from which new ideas and approaches are generated that often transcend overlapping fields of specialized interest as well as opposing points of view. Their separation here is not so much based on substance and meaning as on disciplinary emphasis and established interpretive traditions. Foregrounded first are the perspectives of the more explicitly spatial disciplines (geography, architecture, urban planning), to be followed in chapter 9 by more sociological or social scientific interpretations of the postmetropolitan transition.

Metropolis Transformed

That there have been pronounced changes in the spatial organization of the modern metropolis over the past thirty years, and that these changes are inducing significant modifications in the "urban condition" and the ways we interpret it is the provocative premise of the third discourse. Relatively little attention is given within the discourse to the causes of this deep and broad reorganization of cityspace, for such causality is either implicitly or explicitly imputed to the restructuring processes discussed in the preceding two chapters. What is emphasized here are the *geographical outcomes* of the new urbanization processes and their concrete effects on everyday life, the planning and design of the built environment, and the uneven patterning of intra-urban economic growth and development.

The impact of globalization and economic restructuring has generated an extraordinary array of new terms and concepts to describe the reconfigured spatial specificities of the postmetropolis, triggering increasingly heated debates about how best to capture the most important features of contemporary postmetropolitan geographies. More than in any of the other discourses, the debates on the restructuring of urban form have become embroiled in a naming game, with a multiplicity of metaphorical terms competing to capture the essence of what is new and different about cities today.

I will represent the discourse here through a series of these different yet related nominal encapsulations.

Megacities and metropolitan galaxies

The new global economy and the emerging informational society have indeed a new spatial form, which develops in a variety of social and geographical contexts: megacities . . . They are the nodes of the global economy, concentrating the directional, productive, and managerial upper functions all over the planet . . . Megacities concentrate the best and the worst, from the innovators and the powers that be to their structurally irrelevant people, ready to sell their irrelevance or to make "the others" pay for it . . . It is this distinctive feature of being globally connected and locally disconnected, physically and socially, that makes megacities a new urban form . . . Megacities are discontinuous constellations of spatial fragments, functional pieces, and social segments.
    Manuel Castells, *The Information Age* (1996): 403, 404, 407; emphasis deleted

Megacity, the first entry in the glossary of neologisms being used to characterize the spatial transformation of the modern metropolis, refers both to the enormous population size of world's largest urban agglomerations, and to their increasingly discontinuous, fragmented, polycentric, and almost kaleidoscopic socio-spatial structure. Castells describes these global megacities as the primary carriers and "constellations" of "third millennium urbanization," larger in size and more complex in their socio-spatial structure than their predecessors. In a more theoretically modest but equally epochal depiction, focused primarily on the built environment and urban planning, Deyan Sudjic uses the term *100 Mile City* to denote their expanded scale and galactic form, concluding that "the eighties were the decade in which the industrial city finally shook off the last traces of its nineteenth century self and mutated into a completely new species" (Sudjic, 1992: 3). While both Castells and Sudjic express their profound concern for the negative political, social, and cultural repercussions of megacity formation, they nonetheless agree that this new spatial form is here to stay and must be critically interrogated on its own terms if the growing problems associated with these mutated global cityspaces are to be effectively addressed.

    One of the characteristic features of the megacity is the difficulty of delineating its outer boundaries and hence of accurately estimating its population size. How many urban centers does one include within the megacity region? How far does the regional hinterland stretch? How far does one go to recognize the increasingly global reach of the megacity? On most lists of the world's largest urban agglomerations, Tokyo–Yokohama comes out on top, with a population of more than 25 million. Some estimates for Mexico City place it slightly higher. But if the multi-centered Chinese regional metropolises around Shanghai and the Pearl River Delta are considered as megacity-regions, or if Tokyo–Yokohama is combined with adjacent Osaka–Kobe–Kyoto, each would top the list at 40 million or more.

I give here two rankings of the megacities with greater than 10 million inhabitants, the first based on 1992 United Nations data cited in Castells (1996: 404) and the second providing United Nations estimates for the year 2000.[1] In 1950, only one city (New York) surpassed 10 million inhabitants. By the early 1990s, a dozen more cities entered the list, with only Tokyo, Los Angeles, and Osaka located in more advanced industrial countries. Estimates for the year 2000 project the addition of at least eight more megacities, all from what used to be called the Third World.

1. Tokyo	1. Tokyo–Yokohama
2. São Paulo	2. Bombay
3. New York	3. São Paulo
4. Mexico City	4. Shanghai
5. Shanghai	5. New York
6. Bombay	6. Mexico City
7. Los Angeles	7. Beijing
8. Buenos Aires	8. Jakarta
9. Seoul	9. Lagos
10. Beijing	10. Los Angeles
11. Rio de Janeiro	11. Calcutta
12. Calcutta	12. Tianjin
13. Osaka	13. Seoul
	14. Karachi
	15. Delhi
	16. Buenos Aires
	17. Manila
	18. Cairo
	19. Osaka
	20. Rio de Janeiro
	21. Dhaka

Looking just at the USA, there are now at least forty metropolitan areas with more than 1 million inhabitants. The ten largest, each with a population greater than 3 million, are, in approximate rank order:

New York – NY-NJ-CT
Los Angeles – CA
Chicago – IL-IN-WI
San Francisco-Oakland-San Jose – CA
Philadelphia – PA-NJ-DE-MD
Detroit – MI-CAN
Boston – MA-NH

1 The ranking for the year 2000 is taken from United Nations Department for Economic and Social Information and Policy Analysis, Population Division, *World Urbanization Prospects: The 1994 Revision*, 1995.

Washington DC-MD-VA
Dallas-Fort Worth – TX
Houston – TX

Signaling the rising importance of megacities, the 1990 census marked the first time in US history that the majority of the national population lived in these million-or-more metropolitan regions. With few exceptions, the most rapidly growing areas were in the suburban rings surrounding the defining central city or cities. Many US megacities sprawl over several states, and three (Detroit, San Diego, Buffalo) extend across national borders into Canada and Mexico. But even these border crossings underestimate the fragmented and increasingly polycentric nature of most megacity regions, as well as the inadequacy of conventional census criteria in accurately depicting this complexity. Take Los Angeles, for instance. The Greater Los Angeles Metropolitan Region is best represented as consisting of five counties with a total population of more than 15 million. The City of Los Angeles contains less than a third of this population, and there are at least a dozen other cities with more than 100,000 residents, led by Long Beach with nearly 500,000. And then there is Orange County, a polymorphous constellation of municipalities none of which contains much more than 300,000 people but, when taken together as an urbanized region, would comprise a "county-city" of 2.6 million.

The cityspace of Orange County does not seem to fit well into any of the standard census categories, often befuddling the presentation of accurate population data. There are times when it is left out of official population statistics for the Los Angeles megacity, while at other times it is included but not recognized as a composite city of its own.[2] It is almost as if a new category of city is being invented, one that does not fit any of the conventional definitions. Similar problems exist in the Bay Area, where the largest city is now San Jose in Santa Clara County, the core of Silicon Valley; in Dallas–Fort Worth, where the term *metroplex* was invented to describe the multi-centered urban region; as well as in older eastern megacities such as New York and Washington DC, where surrounding suburban regions have consolidated into peculiar proto-metropolises of their own yet are still absorbed into the official identity (and urban imaginary) of the dominant Central City. Trying to make sense of this "discontinuous constellation of spatial fragments, functional pieces, and social segments" takes us into more focused formulations of the new urban forms arising in the postmetropolis.

2   This is not just a statistical issue, for the confusion flows into more everyday problems of naming and urban identity in the megacity. Until recently, with the purchase by the Disney Corporation of the local hockey and baseball franchises, local professional sports teams in Orange County had the names "California" or, even more grating to the local population, "Los Angeles." It took the Disney imagineers to celebrate the local for the first time, with the renaming of the Anaheim Angels and the Anaheim Mighty Ducks, after one of the oldest and largest centers in the county-city and the major entrepot to Disneyland. Significantly, no one has as yet taken seriously the possibility of giving the name "Orange County" to any professional team.

Outer Cities, postsuburbia, and the end of the Metropolis Era

In 1976, a small monograph appeared with the title *The Outer City: Geographical Consequences of the Urbanization of the Suburbs*.[3] Written by Peter O. Muller, it consolidated an ongoing debate in the USA on the changing geography of urbanism and introduced several terms that continue to shape the discourse on postmetropolitan cityspace.[4] Although still steeped in the canons of traditional urban geographical analysis, this work was one of the first to demonstrate clearly that something very un-suburban was happening to American suburbia. By this time, suburbia had been recognized by academic writers and the popular media as a social and cultural milieu quite distinct from popular and academic notions of "the city." No longer just a commuting zone for the urban agglomeration, suburbanism had become its own way of life with its own spatial specificities, most revolving in one way or another around the automobile and the detached owner-occupied home and household. Suburbia was described by its leading historians as the product of the search for "bourgeois utopias" (Fishman, 1987) on the "crabgrass frontier" (Jackson, 1985), the new heartland of American culture and ideology. But as these historians and geographers noticed, suburbia was being significantly transformed in the second half of twentieth century in the development of a seemingly new form, perhaps most simply called the *Outer City*, arising from a process involving the *urbanization of the suburbs*, with both concepts literally and figuratively rife with oxymoronic connotations. If suburbs were becoming urbs, where are we then when we venture outside the city?

The urbanization of suburbia and the growth of Outer Cities has generated its own tracks of reconceptualization, not just of the erstwhile suburban milieu but of the modern metropolis as a whole. In recent years, *postsuburbia* has emerged as one of the catchall terms, with Orange County, the heartless center of postsuburban California (Kling et al., 1991), as its most representative case. There are other descriptive metaphors: "the metropolis inverted," the "city turned inside-out," "peripheral urbanization," and, in a more comprehensive sense, the term postmetropolis itself. What all these descriptions share, implicitly or explicitly, is the notion that *the era of the modern metropolis has ended*. I hasten to say that this does not mean that the modern metropolis has disappeared, only that its social, cultural, political, and economic dominance as a distinctive organizational form of human habitat is no longer what it once was;

---

3   Peter O. Muller, *The Outer City: Geographical Consequences of the Urbanization of the Suburbs*, Resource Paper 5: 7S–2, Washington, DC: Association of American Geographers, 1976. For a summary of the British debates on the same subject, see John Herington, *The Outer City*, London: Harper and Row, 1984.

4   At the time, the term that prevailed in describing this changing urban geography was *counter-urbanization*, coined by the University of Chicago geographer, Brian J. L. Berry. See Berry, "The Counter-Urbanization Process: Urban America since 1970," in Berry ed., *Urbanization and Counter-Urbanization*, Urban Affairs Annual Review 11, Beverly Hills: Sage Publications, 1976.

and that a new urban form and habitat is emerging, not as a total replacement but as the leading edge of contemporary urban development.

In our earlier discussion on the evolution of urban form in North America (chapter 4), the period following the First World War and extending into the 1970s was described in conjunction with the rise of Fordism and the effects of Keynesian state management on mass production, mass consumption, and urban development. It can also be seen retrospectively as the Era of the Modern Metropolis, a period in which the metropolitan region, with its distinctively dualized configuration of a monocentric urban world surrounded by a sprawling suburban periphery, consolidated as the dominant and defining habitat and source of local identity for the majority of the national population. Earlier roots and routes of the modern metropolitan region can be traced back to the urban restructuring that occurred in the last three decades of the nineteenth century, when major cities began to spawn satellite industrial centers and, closer by, "streetcar suburbs," reshaping what had been the earlier and simpler form of the more compact industrial capitalist cityspace.[5] But it was only in the 1920s, with the onset of what would later be described as Fordist mass production and mass consumption, that the regional metropolis began to take on its most representative form, marked by a distinct and cosmopolitan urban world concentrated in the core or central city, where the most important economic, political, and cultural activities (along with the positive and negative synekisms) were most densely packed; and by a more extensive and culturally homogeneous, administratively fragmented, and relatively disarticulated "middle-class" suburban world, drawing selectively on the attractions of both the central city and the more open spaces of the countryside, and increasingly dependent on the automobile to allow both city and countryside to be at least potentially accessible.

In the traditional discourse, the regional morphology of cityspace was seen most broadly as a product of the continuous interplay of centrifugal and centripetal forces emanating from a dominant and generative "central city." The center, as has almost always been the case for cities, was the translucent vortex of urban life, the defining node for concentric, radial, and other patternings of urban behavior and land use; for the stimulating but also often frustrating densities of urbanism as a way of life; and for the accretion of residential communities into an expanding cosmopolitan urban realm, defined by the official boundaries of what was generally recognized as *the* City. The taken-for-granted center, signified in such terms as "downtown" (curiously, never "downcity") or the CBD (central business district) was the focal point for concurrent processes of clustering and dispersal, for the simultaneous and systematic creation of urban and suburban life.

Fordism simultaneously accentuated centrality, with the concentration of financial, governmental, and corporate headquarters in and around the downtown core; and it accelerated decentralization, primarily through the subur-

5   Herington (1984) begins his first chapter, "The City Beyond the City," with a prescient quote from H. G. Wells, writing in 1902: "The country will take upon itself many of the qualities of the city."

banization of the burgeoning middle class, manufacturing jobs, and the sprawling infrastructure of mass consumption that was required to maintain a suburban mode of life. The literature on the development of the modern metropolis, not surprisingly, has focused primarily on suburban decentralization or dispersal, for in effect centralization was presumed to be given. Many metropolitan downtowns did not experience significant growth during this period and only a few developed the large and often downtown-adjacent heavy industrial zones of Fordist mass production. But every major metropolitan region experienced significant suburbanization, as growth by annexation slowed down and the formal boundaries of the central city became relatively stabilized.[6]

In the now classic works of urban historians, suburbia was viewed primarily as a product of voluntary residential decentralization, initially of a wealthy elite, but soon followed, closer to the city center, by working-class inner suburbs and further out by primarily white middle-class "pioneers" pushing ever outward the suburban "frontier," following the grand American tradition of civilizing frontier settlement. The search for better housing, backed by improved public transportation facilities and promoted by eager real estate developers, was seen as the major driving force behind suburbanization, and the end result was a sprawling dormitory landscape of detached and privately owned homes, a culturally homogeneous and "consumerist" suburbia where most jobs (and those proverbially satanic mills) remained outside the local milieu. Carried along with these histories was the old dichotomy of city and countryside, now reconstituted in the modern metropolis around the division between urban and suburban landscapes or worlds, each with their distinctive "ways of life."

That these contrasting worlds were inherently shaped by class, race, and gender relations spawned an early round of what today is called critical urban studies. Feminist urban scholars, for example, saw the construction of the metropolitan region as not only male-dominated in conception and implementation, but also as intensifying patriarchal power. In particular, it was argued that women as "housewives" were "trapped" in suburbia, subservient to the dominant male "breadwinner" and subsumed into unpaid household labor, with all its ostensibly labor-saving appliances. Although given less attention, the urban core was also seen as a masculinist space, a built environment designed to control, often through violence, women's access to the primary sites of male power. Parallel and occasionally connected arguments were made about how the spatial organization of the modern metropolis, and particularly its division into urban and suburban worlds, was shaped by discriminatory practices based on class, race, and ethnicity, producing in the

---

6 The slowdown in central city annexation has been given relatively little attention in interpreting the rise of the modern metropolis. In many ways, however, it both defined and accentuated the growth of suburbia. Had the central city continued to grow by absorbing the budding urban centers on its fringes, the officially suburban realm would have been much smaller and the statistical differences between "urban" and "suburban" population growth much less pronounced.

normal workings of the dualized metropolitan region two distinct systems for producing and reproducing social inequalities.

This simplified structure of the modern metropolis continues to dominate the urban imaginary of scholars, the media, and most popular discourse. It is becoming increasingly clear, however, not only that the metropolitan region today no longer fits the older model as much as it once did, but also that, when viewed from a contemporary perspective, significant modifications may have to be made in conventional historical interpretations of the Metropolis Era itself. In *Magnetic Los Angeles* (1997), for example, Greg Hise draws upon the new geopolitical economy to re-explore the historical relation between Fordism and the modern metropolis. He begins by challenging the very distinction between "city" urbanization and "countryside" suburbaniza-tion, arguing for a recombinant alternative that views urban and suburban development as a process of dispersed nucleation or *citybuilding* right from the start. Moreover, it is not housing and residential choice that drives this process so much as the decentralization of industrial production and employ-ment. This formative budding-off process is accompanied by the opportunis-tic actions of "community builders," private developers as well as public entrepreneurs, to attract residents and infrastructural investment to the nascent urban nucleations. The development of these multiple nuclei can be described as demand-driven, but the demand was not as much from house-holds as for labor.

Hise also argues that these citybuilding processes were most often highly planned and plotted, and that what has been called uncontrolled suburban sprawl was actually, for the most part, carefully organized and often fairly well designed and planned urban development. The target population for these Fordist "edge cities," as Hise describes them, was not primarily a homo-geneous white elite seeking exclusive enclaves but the working class seeking better jobs. There were many areas where speculative building arrived well before the local availability of attractive jobs, creating true "dormitory suburbs" occupied almost entirely by the white and predominantly white-collar middle class and frequently sustained by racially restrictive covenants and other regulations on entry. But where the employment nucleations did form and grow, labor demand was such that most of these restrictions were lifted or bypassed, producing more racially mixed populations than were usually assumed to exist in classic suburbia.

There are thus significant continuities between the Metropolis and Postmetropolis eras, just as there are between Fordism and postfordism, modernity and postmodernity. But again the discursive question revolves around whether a certain tipping point or threshold has been reached where the interpretive power of studying the "intensified" new forms and functions outweighs a revisioning of the continuities that link the present to the past. Emphasizing the new while recognizing the persistence of long-established geohistorical trends, it can be argued that during the past thirty years the growth of Outer Cities has both decentered and recentered the metropolitan landscape, breaking down and reconstituting the prevailing monocentric urbanism that once anchored all centrifugal and centripetal forces around a singular gravitational node. Deindustrialization has emptied out many of the largest urban-industrial zones and nucleations of Fordism, while postfordist reindustrialization has concentrated high-technology industries in new industrial spaces far from the old downtowns. These "green-field" sites, the urban equivalent of the Newly Industrialized Countries (NICs) in the global economy, are not just satellites but have become distinctive cities and gravitational nodes in their own right. The most successful have spawned and sustained the mall-centered hives of consumerism that are the popular hallmarks of the postfordist, postmetropolitan Outer City.

Although the decentralization of industrial production and employment began in the last half of the nineteenth century, it was only in the last third of the twentieth century that the regional balance of industrialization in many postmetropolitan areas was reversed, with the majority of production and jobs located in the outer rings rather than in the inner cities of the conurbation. As much as anything else, it is this *role reversal in the geography of industrial urbanism* that has led observers such as Sudjic to claim that the new urban form marks the moment when the industrial city "finally shook off the last traces of its nineteenth century self."

In a process that can no longer be simply described as sprawl, post-metropolitan cityspace has been both stretched out and pinned down to cover a much larger regional scale than ever before. It reaches out and connects to a network of interdependency that is now global in scope, a hierarchical hinterland that blurs the discreteness of both the city and the older metropolitan region, and dilutes the degree to which cityspace represents the "culmination of local and territorial cultures" (Chambers, 1990: 53). If sprawling suburbia is no longer what it used to be, the same is true for the urban core. In a strange contrapuntal movement, the densest urban cores in places like New York are becoming much less dense, while the low-rise almost suburban-looking cores in places like Los Angeles are reaching urban densities equal to Manhattan. What once could be described as mass regional suburbanization has now turned into *mass regional urbanization*, with virtually everything traditionally associated with "the city" now increasingly evident almost everywhere in the postmetropolis. In the Era of the Postmetropolis, it becomes increasingly difficult to "escape from the city," for the urban condition and urbanism as a way of life are becoming virtually ubiquitous.[7] And in the wake of these changes, the ways in which the metropolitan region is patterned by class, race, and gender relations have become more complex and opaque.

---

7 For some cinematic references, see the recent films *Escape from New York* and *Escape from Los Angeles*. Many other references can be made to the wave of illustrative films on the postmetropolis and the contemporary urban condition, but I will generally leave such textual enrichment to the reader.

Edge Cities and the optimistic envisioning of postmetropolitan geographies

Americans are creating the biggest change in a hundred years in how we build cities. Every single American city that *is* growing, is growing in the fashion of Los Angeles, with multiple urban cores. These new hearths of our civilization – in which the majority of metropolitan Americans now work and around which we live – look not at all like our old downtowns. Buildings rarely rise shoulder to shoulder . . . Instead, their broad, low outlines dot the landscape like mushrooms, separated by greensward and parking lots.

Joel Garreau, *Edge City* (1991): 3

No other book has captured the nominal imagery of the postmetropolis quite like Joel Garreau's *Edge City: Life on the New Frontier* (1991).[8] A senior writer for the *Washington Post* and author of *The Nine Nations of North America* (1981), a book that attempted optimistically to transfigure the regional makeup of the continent in much the same way that *Edge City* approaches contemporary urbanism, Garreau has become the Pied Piper of Postsuburbia, a guru to a mass national audience of businessmen, academics, and just plain folks trying to understand what has been happening to the cities of North America in the late twentieth century. Garreau's view of the restructuring of urban form emphasizes not just the increasingly polycentric nature of postmetropolitan cityspace but revolves specifically around its most visible landmarks, the shopping mall and office-centered developments he calls, and nimbly trademarks as, Edge Cities.

According to Garreau's defining criteria, the Edge City (1) has 5 million square feet or more of leasable office space – the workplace of the Information Age; (2) has 600,000 square feet or more of leasable retail space – the equivalent of a fair-sized mall; (3) has more jobs than bedrooms; (4) is perceived by the population as one place; and (5) was nothing like "city" as recently as thirty years ago (1991: 6–7). Southern California has the largest total number of existing (16) and "emerging" (8) Edge Cities, closely followed by Washington DC (16 and 7) and New York (17 and 4). According to the *Edge City News*, a newsletter published by the Edge City Group Inc. and subtitled "Tools for the New Frontier," there are nearly 200 Edge Cities already built in the USA, more than four times the number of comparably sized "old downtowns." They now contain two-thirds of America's office space, a huge jump from the approximately 25 percent that was there in 1970. The figures for the number of jobs located in Edge Cities against those for the old downtowns also show a dramatic increase.

8 *Edge City: Life on the New Frontier*, New York: Doubleday. See also Garreau's *The Nine Nations of North America*, Boston: Houghton Mifflin, 1981.

Garreau takes a few other rough cuts at categorizing different types of Edge Cities. "Uptowns" are built on the commercial renaissance of older, established nodes such as Pasadena CA or Stamford CT, and take on a wide diversity of forms and flavors befitting their more complex historical cityspaces. "Boomers" are "the classic kind of Edge City," centered on a mall at the intersection of freeways and etched into place in three different shapes: the Strip, the Node, and the Pig in the Python (multinodal strips). The "Greenfield" version "is increasingly the state of the art, in response to the perceived chaos of the Boomer." They are figuratively built "at the intersection of several thousand acres of farmland and one developer's monumental ego." Irvine, in California's Orange County, and the more recently Disneyed world near Orlando, in Florida's Orange County, are two prime examples.

For Garreau and many of his interlocutors, the Edge City becomes a frontier outpost of epochal proportions. Here are just a few of his discursive tropes: "in-between triumphant," "a vigorous world of pioneers and immigrants," "the third wave of our lives pushing into new frontiers," "places to make one's fame and fortune," "anchored by some of the most luxurious shopping in the world," "the crucible of America's urban future," "the forge of the fabled American way of life well into the twenty-first century," a release "from the shackles of the nineteenth-century city," "another Garden . . . the best of both worlds," "the philosophical ground on which we are building our Information Age society," "the most purposeful attempt Americans have made since the days of the Founding Fathers to try to create something like a new Eden," "the result of Americans striving once again for a new, restorative synthesis," "the search for Utopia at the center of the American Dream." I think you get the idea.

Garreau fundamentally ignores the explanatory arguments of the industrial urbanism discourse and rarely speaks of globalization except to intone connections to the New Information Age.[9] Instead, he invents his own causal nexus for the emergence of Edge Cities, beginning, promisingly enough, with what he calls "the empowerment of women." What was once suburban entrapment for women is inverted by Garreau into Edge City liberation.

> Edge Cities doubtless would not exist the way they do were it not for one of the truly great employment and demographic shifts in American history: the empowerment of women . . . It is no coincidence that Edge Cities began to flourish nation-wide in the 1970s, simultaneous with the rise of women's liberation . . . they were located near the best-educated, most conscientious, most stable workers – underemployed females living in middle-class communities on the fringes of the old urban areas.   (1991: 111–12)

9 Industry in *Edge City* is equated to commerce and office space. Garreau hardly speaks of manufacturing at all, and when he does (briefly, in the chapter on New Jersey) he claims that "Industrial and warehouse space does not create anything urbane. No dense centers ever evolve" (1991: 31). Garreau's failure to see the important and continuing links between urbanization and industrialization (see chapter 6 and the discussion of Greg Hise's work in the preceding section) significantly weakens his conceptualization of Edge Cities.

In a long chapter on Atlanta, Garreau also enlists another "revolutionary" development: the emergence of a new black middle class. Here again, his fixation on selected success stories blinds his vision of the downside of the postmetropolitan transition.

> The rise of Edge Cities contained a nightmare possibility for America: that because so many jobs were moving out to the fringe, frequently into what had been lily-white suburbs, an entire race would be left behind, trapped, in the inner city, jobless, beyond reach of the means of creating wealth. Such fears, however, have not been confirmed, despite the plight of the black underclass. A black suburban middle class is booming, statistics show. And it is emerging at the same time and in the same places as Edge Cities.   (1991: 144)

He uses these statistics to argue that "the rise of Edge Cities is primarily a function of class – not race" (1991: 152). "Karl Marx was right," he writes, "issues of class are what control" (1991: 165), a progressive-sounding but inadequately explored causal argument.

Los Angeles looms large in Garreau's *Edge City*, and vice versa. Garreau has become well connected to a local network of journalists and others who are similarly spin-doctoring optimistic pictures of paradigmatic Los Angeles and life on its "new frontier" in local and national newspapers. One particularly influential contact has been Christopher B. Leinberger, author (with Charles Lockwood) of "How Business is Reshaping America" (*Atlantic*, October 1986), an article which perhaps more than any other drew the popular attention of the East Coast to the emergence of Los Angeles as the leading edge of American urban trends. Leinberger's notion of "urban villages" is closely akin to Garreau's Edge Cities. Both are filled with allusions to the original Garden City concept of Ebenezer Howard (and also to an even earlier Edenic garden), where one can obtain the best of both worlds, city and countryside wedded together by the electronic possibilities of the new Information Age and a radically optimistic vision of the coming together of gender, race, and class divisions.

Another important local contact is Joel Kotkin, a former colleague at the *Washington Post* and currently a contributing editor to the Opinion section of the *Los Angeles Times*, senior fellow at the Center for the New West in Ontario and the Pepperdine University Institute for Public Policy in Malibu. Kotkin and his colleague David Friedman have become the leading entrepreneurial spin-doctors of the new Los Angeles. Unlike Garreau, they pay particular attention to the restructured postfordist geopolitical economy and the local and global literature on industrial urbanism in their rosy localized reconstitutions of the Edge City idea.[10] Often capturing the attention of local decision-

---

10   See, for example, the glossy report by Kotkin and Friedman, *The Next Act: Southern California's New Economy*, Ontario, CA: Center for the New West, 1994. The report concludes with the following admonition: "But upon one thing all else depends: the restoration of public confidence and faith in the region's long term prospects . . . Southern Californians must realize – and communicate to the world – that this region still possesses a remarkable economic, cultural and creative dynamism unmatched by any major urban region in North America" (1994: 24).

makers involved in citybuilding (mayors, architects, developers) as well as the popular urban imaginary in Los Angeles, Kotkin in particular has launched a crusade against all those who speak of a downside to the contemporary globalized multicultural postfordist metropolis. Included here as special targets are the critical urban planners, geographers, and sociologists of UCLA who featured so prominently in the previous two chapters. They are seen by Kotkin as the leading purveyors of the "declinism," "unmitigated negativity," and "loss of confidence" allegedly plaguing and biasing the contemporary image wars over the region's future. These occasionally Red-baiting attacks feed into and on the confused public realm, desperate for good news and easy solutions to the current concatenation of crises facing the edgy postmetropolis of Los Angeles.

Like Ronald Reagan's hyperreal interpretation of the causes of stagflation in the 1980s ("it's all in the mind of the beholder"), the new-wave boosters locate the problems of the 1990s in Los Angeles (and by paradigmatic implication, everywhere else in urban America) in the popular state of mind, in downside thinking, in the wrong attitudes. Factuality is subordinated to image-making and appropriate faith in the economic system, critics are admonished as destructive doomsayers, and the future is hinged on getting the right and proper spin. They have become the latest entry in a long line of public–private interfacers attempting to boost a new Los Angeles by sublimating its darker geohistory.[11] Similar booster-entrepreneur journalists, often backed by affiliations with local universities, now exist in almost every urban region, making a living by promoting a soothing vision of exaggerated optimism over the contemporary restructuring of urban form.

City Lite and postmetropolitan nostalgia

The transformation of the modern metropolis has stimulated a distinctive subdiscourse that is concerned not so much with what is emerging but with what is being lost in this expansive restructuring of urban form. In its most acerbic scholarly expressions, it elicits an urban nostalgia, a longing for what is called the "historical city," a once more clearly definable urbanism that is believed to have been civilized, urbane, and richly creative. An excellent recent representation of this nostalgic longing appeared in the Opinion section of the Los Angeles Times (December 22, 1996), written by Thomas Bender, a professor of humanities at New York University. Bender adds to our repertoire of descriptive terms for the postmetropolis the flavorless notion of City Lite. Here are some selections from his deeply historical narrative.

11 For a very perceptive history of this tradition of spin-doctoring time and place in Los Angeles, see Norman M. Klein, *The History of Forgetting: Los Angeles and the Erasure of Memory*, London and New York: Verso, 1997.

As we approach the end of both a century and a millennium, a century of cities in the United States and a millennium of cities in the West, those of us who love the historical city wonder whether it will survive into the next era of American life . . .

Today . . . the city lacks . . . clear definition. There seem to be more boundaries within the city than between the city and the larger metropolitan landscape . . . [V]ast, centerless and borderless areas are laced with invisible electronic connections to the global Internet. How can such an agglomeration be a city? Can such a human settlement focus and intensify human life, as city life has done in the past?

. . . It seems as if our best middle-class vision of the city today is that of an entertainment zone – a place to visit, a place to shop; it is no more than a live-in theme park . . . This amounts to Urbanism Lite. This new urban recipe is insidious, for it pretends to offer what it is not. Such pseudo-city culture offers scenes of city life, not the city itself. The City Lite is safe, orderly, simplified. It demands little – and gives little . . .

Advocates of City Lite reject the gifts of the historic city: juxtaposition of peoples and events, engagement with and recognition of the unfamiliar, the risk of understanding and the excitement of invention. The City Lite is a place of easy entertainment . . . It devotes itself to consumption, not creativity . . .

For a millennium, cities have carried history and sustained our cultural traditions, through their universities, museums and libraries and in their physical fabric, with its traces of social succession. "In a city," Lewis Mumford has written, "time becomes visible." The complexity of that history, like the social and physical complexity of the city more generally, nourishes the human spirit, even as it tries it. Life in the Lite City reveals no passage of time, no history. The City Lite does not age; it is consumed and replaced. It is any time and any place – it no longer holds culture nor provides an orientation to past and present for its residents.

For Bender, the first half of the twentieth century "marked the triumph of city culture," when cities such as New York were "engines of wealth and incubators of creativity." After mid-century, suburbanization and its "cluster of values celebrating the privatization of life," devoured the spirit of urbanity and undermined the "civic obligation to nourish a common life." Only the "gritty city" survives under the glitter, offering perhaps the only hope for a recovery of "a sense of time, of place and of civic purpose."

This very different reading of the contemporary metropolis offers a refreshing antidote to the cheerful optimism of the Edge City entrepreneurs, although here too there is exaggeration and hyperbole, based largely on a romancing of an urban past that may never have been so dichotomous with the urban present. There has always been a deep streak of nostalgia running through twentieth-century urban studies, a retrospective longing for the alleged spiritual glories of the "democratic" Athenian polis, ancient Rome, the great

Renaissance cities of Italy, the medieval Hanseatic league of cities and its famous motto, *Stadt Luft macht frei* (city air makes one free), and now, it would seem, the early modern metropolis. Whatever emphasis one wishes to give to this remembrance of things past, it must be layered into any comprehensive account of the contemporary restructuring of urban form.

Simulating the New Urbanism

Also arising from the contemporary discourse on urban form has been a peculiar postmodern combination of historical urban nostalgia and present-day postsuburbia. I refer here to the growing movement in the citybuilding professions that is called by the British Neotraditional Town Planning (NTP), and in the USA, with deliberately ambitious vagueness, the New Urbanism. In Britain, the movement was built primarily on the collaboration between Prince Charles and the "visionary architect" Leon Krier, who together dreamed of recreating pre-industrial cities in postindustrial Europe. In the USA, the leading figures of the New Urbanism have been Andreas Duany and Elizabeth Plater-Zyberk, a husband-wife team whose projects, like Garreau's Edge City formulations, are filled with historical allusions to Founding Fathers, the American Dream, and Edenic fantasies rooted not just in Ebenezer Howard's Garden City but in even more ancient urban sites and spirits.

The fountainhead of the New Urbanism in America is located at Seaside, Florida, a second-home resort and "revival town" designed by Duany and Plater-Zyberk. Krier's Greek Revival "tower house" in Seaside symbolizes the strong trans-Atlantic ties and the shared effort to recreate the urban character of the premodern era through what they call "controlled heterogeneity."[12] Another flagrant extension of the New Urbanism can be found in Los Angeles. The 1,000-acre Playa Vista project, located on a broad sweep of land north of Los Angeles International Airport and encompassing one of the few remaining wetland areas in Southern California, is one of the largest urban development projects in the western USA. Once the property of Howard Hughes and the site for his construction of the Spruce Goose, the biggest airplane ever built, the land is reputed to be the largest undeveloped parcel in the built-up urban fabric of the City of Los Angeles.

The controversial project, initially conceived more than ten years ago, has become the focal point for competing visions of urban development and planning from a string of developers, architects and urban designers, community groups and environmental activists, the Los Angeles City Council, and most recently DreamWorks SKG, the huge new entertainment conglomerate led by

---

12   Seaside was recently used as the setting for *The Truman Show*, a film in which the lead character is born and lives his entire life within an elaborate stage set for a long-running television series. Until the very end, Truman is unaware that he lives within an entirely simulated community in which his family, friends, and workmates are played by actors. The lead character is played by Jim Carrey, whose earlier films include *Liar, Liar* and *Dumb and Dumber*.

Steven Spielberg that had planned to build its headquarters in Playa Vista (with substantial subsidies from the City of Los Angeles), until its withdrawal in 1999. All that exists at present is the high-rise Howard Hughes office center on its eastern flank (complete with a new freeway exit) and a few office buildings on the cliffs overlooking the site near the Ballona Creek wetlands. But under the current compromise plan, there are proposals for more than 13,000 residential units and 6.1 million square feet of commercial space, making Playa Vista, should it be completed, the largest single building project in Los Angeles history.[13]

As devised by Duany/Plater-Zyberk and their local exponents, the New Urbanist plans for Playa Vista include a small nature preserve, with pedestrian walkways and bird-watching paths, and some affordable housing planted amidst courtyard-style compounds in a Spanish red-tile-roofed motif, designed to recapture historic illusions and allusions. It is all very pleasant-looking on paper, so much so that a team of New Urbanists was recently hired to help replan downtown Los Angeles as a "livable" community/urban village, no doubt complete with its own fictional history. Such fictional histories are common features of the projects inspired by the New Urbanism. For example, the promotional brochure for Montgomery Village outside Princeton, New Jersey, presents the following hypersimulation:

> Once upon a time, a Dutch family settled in what is now Somerset County, New Jersey. They built a thriving farm and as the family prospered, so did the area. Other families moved nearby and businesses flourished. Over the next two centuries, the area grew to become today's Montgomery Village.[14]

The New Urbanism is essentially a contemporary historicist transmogrification of the New Town ideal, packaged with nostalgic references to the small towns-cum-urban villages of early America and poured into the Outer and Inner Cities of today.[15] Added to the olio are the peopled public spaces and car-less pedestrian life romanticized by Jane Jacobs in her old Greenwich Village neighborhood, the anti-crime "defensible space" designs of Oscar

---

13 Playa Vista is perhaps the closest new development in Los Angeles to such huge projects as Battery Park City in New York and Canary Wharf in London. But whereas these projects, as well as the more humanely scaled developments in the old docklands of Amsterdam, primarily serve the needs of a new "gentry" based in the financial sector (brokers, stock dealers), in Los Angeles the entertainment industry is the center of attraction.

14 Cited in Ruth Knack, "Repent Ye Sinners, Repent," *Planning* (1989: 10), and in an unpublished paper by Mark Garrett, "Neotraditional Town Planning and the Postmodern," Department of Urban Planning, UCLA, 1994.

15 Another group of New Urbanists has recently been chosen to redevelop a middle-income African American residential enclave in South Central Los Angeles. The proposed project, with its small business "incubators" and cluster of picturesque apartments, stirred controversy among local community leaders, who favored more commercial development to restore the burnt-out shops and businesses along Vermont Avenue, an area severely affected by the Spring 1992 Justice Riots. This and other controversies over the New Urbanism bring up some interesting questions, such as whose history is to be remembered, and for what purpose?

Newman and others, and the soft environmental socialism of Ebenezer Howard's old-New Towns. Like Garreau's Edge Cities, NTP, and the New Urbanism, can be easily dismissed as opportunistic interventions marketing hypersimulations of urban utopia to a middle-class population battered by economic restructuring, fearful of crime, and hungry for new and better images of postmetropolitan life. But also like Edge Cities, it is increasingly capturing the contemporary popular and professional urban imaginaries and affecting the practices of citybuilding in nearly every postmetropolis. It must continue to be critically evaluated to help preserve some of its most positive possibilities, for in many ways the New Urbanism represents a better future for the postmetropolitan built environment than many of its "default" alternatives.

Exopolis as synthesis

In trying to weave together the various strands of the discourse on the restructuring of urban form, I have decided to enter the naming game with my own preferred choice: *Exopolis*. I defined and explored the Exopolis within the specific confines of Orange County in chapter 8 of *Thirdspace* and will not repeat these formulations here, except to recapture the term's multi-sided meanings. The prefix *exo-* (outside) is a direct reference to the growth of "outer" cities, and also suggests the increasing importance of exogenous forces shaping cityspace in an age of globalization. Perhaps never before, short of military invasion, has endogenous development and localized synekism been as intensely affected by global constraints and opportunities. The prefix can also be seen as denoting a hint of the "end of," as in the ex-city, the rise of cities without the traditional traits of cityness as we have come to define them in the past. Hence, there are implications of a significantly reconstituted cityspace, urbanism, and polis/civitas.

I also use the term Exopolis to signify a recombinant synthesis and extension, a critical thirding, of the many oppositional processes and dualized arguments that have shaped the general discourse on urban form. The new geography of postmetropolitan urbanism is thus seen as the product of both a decentering and a recentering, deterritorialization and reterritorialization, continuing sprawl and intensified urban nucleation, increasing homogeneity and heterogeneity, socio-spatial integration and disintegration, and more. The composite Exopolis can be metaphorically described as "the city turned inside-out," as in the urbanization of the suburbs and the rise of the Outer City. But it also represents "the city turned outside-in," a globalization of the Inner City that brings all the world's peripheries into the center, drawing in what was once considered "elsewhere" to its own symbolic zone (to refer back to Iain Chambers's allusive phrase). This redefines the Outer and the Inner City simultaneously, while making each of these terms more and more difficult to delineate and map with any clarity or confidence.

In the spatially reconstituted postmetropolis, there is room for optimism and pessimism, nostalgia and exuberance, despair and hope for the future. There are complex utopian and dystopian ramifications for social justice and economic development, and for the amelioration of ethnic, class, and gender inequalities. And as a new form of lived space, it is open to a multiplicity of interpretive approaches, challenging all attempts to reduce explanation to narrowed causes and consequences. Hence the need to keep the scope of critical interpretation radically open to many different perspectives, while at the same time being guided by a political project, by interpretations of the postmetropolis that can best assist in the praxis of achieving greater social and spatial justice. Continuing this political project, I turn next to the exemplary geography of Los Angeles to illustrate some of the more concrete expressions of the exopolitan restructuring of urban form.

Representing the Exopolis in Los Angeles

The maelstrom of globalization, economic restructuring, and mass regional urbanization in Southern California has produced a cartography of everyday urban functions and spatial practices that is filled not just with social polarizations of increasing magnitude (the subject of the next chapter), but also with intensified *spatial polarizations* and a growing multiplicity of what have been called *spatial mismatches*. Receiving the most attention from local planners and urbanists has been the *jobs–housing imbalance*, a mismatched geography of affordable housing and available employment opportunities that has always been a part of urban life but has grown to unusual proportions in the increasingly kaleidoscopic geography of the Exopolis. More than just a matter of reducing the journey to work or simply adding more housing, the challenges raised by such spatial discordance reach deeply into questions of transportation planning, industrial policy, environmental regulation, regional governance, community development, social welfare, urban politics, and the wider struggle for social and spatial justice. The imbalanced geography of jobs and housing thus forms a revealing window through which to explore a few representative sites in the restructured geography of postmetropolitan Los Angeles.

Starting in the New Downtown

Thirty years of globalization and economic restructuring have recentered the Los Angeles postmetropolis, as well as the local urban imaginary, around a materially and symbolically assertive downtown. Superseding the Hollywood sign and the palm-fronded beach as the most popular postcard icons, the new downtown skyline symbolizes Los Angeles as never before. Viewed from the air, its skyscrapers, government offices, and corporate complexes seems to float above the urban flatlands surrounding it, like volcanic Hasan Dag above

Figure 8.1   *Air view of Downtown Los Angeles*   (Source: *Los Angeles Times* photo by Ken Lubas, February 21, 1998)

the ancient settlement of Çatal Hüyük (see figure 8.1). But viewed from below, it takes on a different character and flavor.

On the ground, competing territorialities position themselves in the micro-geography of the downtown core, creating an assemblage of enclaves that materialize and make visible all that has been happening in the past three decades. With regard to jobs and housing in particular, this enclaved down-town is the site of two striking agglomerations representing the extremes of presence and absence. In the western half, consisting of the Civic Center complex of city, county, state, and federal offices, and the corporate towers of the Central Business District and its southern extension around the Conven-tion Center, is the densest single cluster of jobs in the polycentric post-metropolis. In the middle of the tiered enclaves that comprise the eastern half is Skid Row, on any given night the largest concentration of homeless people in the region if not the entire USA. With cruel irony, the homeless, with neither good jobs nor housing, probably outnumber the housed and employed residential population in the downtown core, despite concerted public efforts to induce middle-class residents to live in the area and to control if not erase Skid Row.

The streetscape and daily life downtown take on some distinctive rhythms as a result of these peculiar presences and absences of jobs and housing. For five days a week during the daytime working hours, the westside population may reach above 100,000, counting tourists and visitors as well as workers. In the evening and on most weekends, the westside empties out into a virtual urban desert. Audiences rush in and out of the Music Center and the Museum of Contemporary Art without appearing in any significant numbers on the streets or in the very few public spaces. When all is most quiet, usually at night but also in the daylight on Sundays, the homeless move out of their eastside shelters to reoccupy the abandoned west, at least as far as the sparse local police will allow them to roam.

Meanwhile, beyond the wall of high-rise apartment blocks that separates the two halves of downtown, the eastside bustles all week long, especially on Broadway, the busiest and, according to some estimates, the most profitable commercial street in the region. Broadway serves as the central commercial and cultural axis of Latino Los Angeles, connecting on the north to the old Plaza and El Pueblo area where the city was born more than 200 years ago, and stretching south to the Garment District, where thousands of Latinos work in what has become the core of the largest apparel manufacturing industry in the USA. Few Latinos actually live in the downtown core, although they form an increasing proportion of the homeless, especially women and children. But to the east, south, and west of downtown, just beyond the triangle of freeways that defines its borders, are the most densely populated *barrios*, where at least a million Mexican and Central American immigrants have clustered over the past thirty years in low- to mid-rise buildings that are now among the most overcrowded in the country. On bustling Broadway, one is aware of another reoccupation of the most central place of the Los Angeles conurbation.

There is also a significant and growing Asian presence on the eastside of downtown. Although there are relatively few Asians in Skid Row, they shop on Broadway, work and own establishments in the Garment and Jewelry districts, and occupy their own residential and commercial enclaves in Chinatown and Little Tokyo. The most unusual Asian enclave, however, is Toy Town, a zone of warehouses for toys and other cheap consumer goods from mainland China, Hong Kong, Taiwan, Thailand, and other East Asian countries. Located between the upscale Little Tokyo to the north and down-and-out Skid Row to the south, Toy Town has its own peculiar rhythms linked to the microgeography of jobs and housing. It acts as a buffer against the northward spread of the homeless into Little Tokyo, with its tourist attractions and hotels and other services for visiting Japanese businessmen. Several of the warehouses, for example, have water sprinkling systems at the entrances which work only at night, to prevent the homeless from finding a dry niche to sleep. But the aim is not to repel the homeless entirely, for there is need for their cheap and timely labor during peak moments of loading and unloading. Here the jobs–housing imbalance takes on a very different spin.

There is no better way to enter the globalized exopolis of Los Angeles than through a walking tour of its downtown archipelago of enclaves. Despite its sprawling polycentricity, the urban region has always been centered here and this centrality continues to hold as both a pole of attraction and a node of dispersal. Few other downtowns today contain such a distillation of contrasts and extremes in so small a space, so much evidence of centrifugal and centripetal forces, the city turned inside out and outside in, the core and the periphery entwined together in the same time and place.

Inner City blues

Sweeping outward from the New Downtown in a half circle that runs from East Los Angeles around the south of downtown to Koreatown and the primarily Central American *barrio* of Pico-Union to the west, is what might be described as the New Inner City. At its geographical and symbolic core is South Central Los Angeles, located astride the old industrial zone that once stretched from downtown to the twin ports of San Pedro and Long Beach. Over the past thirty years, plant closures and white flight have emptied this area of its manufacturing jobs and resident Anglo population, devastating many neighborhoods and creating the formative conditions for what the neo-Chicago School sociologist William Julius Wilson (see chapter 9) described as the welfare-dependent "permanent urban underclass." Wilson locates the underclass in primarily African American communities geographically stranded in deindustrialized inner cities, epitomized in Chicago and repeated in many other major cities in the eastern USA. The problem in these "new American ghettoes," as Camilo Vergara calls them, is not so much a jobs–housing imbalance but the relative absence of both decent jobs and adequate housing conditions, as well as the vicious circle of poverty this produces.[16] Just such a process of deepening impoverishment has affected the African American community of Los Angeles over the past thirty years, creating conditions that in some areas have significantly worsened since the Watts Rebellion of 1965.

In terms of statistical measures of job accessibility, Watts was once in a highly favorable location, adjacent to (although often racially excluded from) the region's largest concentration of unionized manufacturing jobs. Most of these high-paying jobs have disappeared, resulting in the outmigration of most of the once job-secure white working class and many African American

---

16 Camilo Vergara, *The New American Ghetto*, New Brunswick, NJ: Rutgers University Press, 1995. Vergara is a photo-sociologist whose photography traces the transformation of the built environment in the ghettoes of New York, Newark, Detroit, Chicago, and Los Angeles over the past thirty years.

families as well. This has reshaped the iconic Black Ghetto of South Central Los Angeles in at least two ways. It has pumped large numbers of the most destitute and welfare-dependent African Americans into downtown's expansive Skid Row. In addition, Latino populations have not only replaced the predominantly southern white working class that occupied much of the southeastern quadrant of Los Angeles County (more on this in chapter 9), but have spilled over to become the majority in Watts and other South Central communities. This has pushed the core of African American Los Angeles westward, further compacting the ghetto and bringing the poorest and wealthiest African Americans into even closer proximity than they were before.[17]

The eastern formulations of spatial mismatch theories and the welfare-dependent urban underclass thus have some resonance in Los Angeles, but the metropolitan geography of jobs and housing has always been more complex and polynucleated than in eastern cities. For example, the westward shift of the core African American residential area has brought the population closer to the major job concentrations of the LAX airport complex and the rapidly growing multi-media entertainment centers of Santa Monica and Culver City. Although racial job discrimination is still intense, it cannot be argued empirically that African American job-seekers are geographically stranded from available opportunities to the degree they are in other postmetropolitan areas. Simple models of Inner versus Outer City employment patterns do not work as well in Los Angeles as they might do in Chicago.

Complicating the picture further has been the Latinoization of poverty in Los Angeles and the emergence of what local scholars have called, in contrast to the welfare-dependent underclass, the *working poor*. Far from welfare-dependent, jobless, or homeless, the mainly immigrant and largely Latino working poor have grown on the massive expansion of low-wage and/or part-time jobs that have traditionally been unattractive to most African American, Anglo, and Chicano/a workers. Combined with the underclass and joined by other immigrant entrepreneurs, they have created an extraordinary milieu of adaptive survival in the New Inner City. Attempting to make the best of the "surge of inequality" and deepening poverty that has been so characteristic a part of the postmetropolitan transition, the working poor and others have become part of a vast and growing informal or underground economy of swap meets, bartered personal services, street vending, day labor, drug distribution, and other specialized legal and illegal activities. And here too, in these peak population densities of the "gritty city," as Bender called it, innovative new strategies for community-based struggles for a better life are emerging, evoking another variation on the theme of synekism, the stimulus of urban agglomeration.

The survival economy of the New Inner City, despite deepening poverty and the absence of a sufficiently responsive public realm, has produced in the

17 Los Angeles County is reputed to have the wealthiest and the poorest predominantly African American municipalities in America.

real-and-imagined space of South Central Los Angeles a paradigmatic postmetropolitan icon of the contemporary urban condition. At once the epitome of despair and the source of creative energy in nearly all aspects of contemporary popular culture, the gritty spaces of South Central, along with the barrios of East LA and Pico-Union, have become the focal points for a growing public discourse and concerted community activism aimed at increasing political empowerment for the expanded and multicultural underclasses. And what has been developing in this real-and-imagined realm of "greater" South Central affects more than Los Angeles. If only for a fleeting moment, all the world heard the resounding demand that emanated from these lived spaces in 1992: *NO JUSTICE – NO PEACE*. As much as in any other place in the postmetropolis today, it is here where, to recall Lewis Mumford un-nostalgically, "time becomes visible" to invigorate new sources of solidarity and new strategies in the struggle for social and spatial justice.

Exemplifying the creative solidarities of the working poor are a number of post-1992 coalitions that have consciously used the specific geography of the postmetropolis as a staging point for renewed political struggles over explicitly *spatial* justice, especially with respect to the far-reaching implications of the jobs–housing imbalance. Although beginning well before 1992, community struggles over the siting of noxious facilities and the geographical distribution of environmental hazards with respect to the location of minorities and the poor have generated a particularly vigorous *environmental justice* movement in Los Angeles. Increasingly allied with other movements, such as those for a living wage and for growth-with-equity (discussed further in chapter 14), the now regionalized environmental justice movement is richly conscious of the restructured postmetropolitan geography, and uses its discordant inequities as a mobilization strategy. From the siting of hazardous facilities to the geographical distribution of the worst health effects of air pollution, it is being made clear (a) that poor and immigrant communities suffer disproportionately; (b) that these environmental effects are, to a significant degree, socially constructed; and (c) that therefore the conditions can be changed through concerted social action.

There are also signs that the environmental justice movement is expanding into a wider collective struggle over explicitly spatial justice and what can be called regional democracy. One particularly important example that creatively illustrates the potential public power that can arise from a critical geographical consciousness and new forms of urban cultural politics is the recent court case involving a new alliance of the working poor called the Bus Riders Union (*Labor/Community Strategy Center v. Los Angeles Metropolitan Transit Authority*). The Bus Riders Union (BRU) was created under the leadership of Eric Mann and the Labor/Community Strategy Center (LCSC), a broad-based and multiracial organization that grew out of struggles against factory closures in the 1980s. The LCSC has used its labor-organizing base to reach into a wider variety of community issues revolving around class, race, and gender, and more general questions of social and spatial justice.[18] In the mid-1990s, Mann and the LCSC, through the newly created Bus Riders Union, turned specifically to the needs of the "transit-dependent," consisting primarily of poor immigrant populations concentrated most heavily in the New Inner City.

In a lawsuit against the Metropolitan Transit Authority, the BRU and its lead counsel, the NAACP Legal Defense Fund, linked civil rights legislation to the geography of transit use in Los Angeles to argue that a particular population of transit-dependent bus-riders were being discriminated against by the policies and investment patterns of the MTA, which clearly favored wealthy, white, and predominantly male suburban users of the expensive new fixed-rail system being constructed, as well as by existing bus services, which studies showed subsidized wealthy bus riders more than the poor. Certified as a class action suit on behalf of 350,000 bus riders, the case was resolved in late 1996 through a Consent Decree that, while still being worked out in detail, has contributed significantly to forcing a dramatic shift of attention and resources in the MTA from fixed-rail construction to the improvement of bus services, especially for the transit-dependent.[19]

The impact of this still tentative victory is difficult to gauge, but in combination with many other events it has (temporarily) stopped the multi-billion-dollar construction of the planned fixed-rail transit system and induced a potentially massive reallocation of funds to serve the primarily poor, minority, immigrant, female, and Inner City transit-dependent population. The BRU has committed itself to "the fight against racism, class oppression, sexism, and the oppression of immigrants" and to an ambitious program, "Billions for Buses," that could play a significant role in the economic development of the New Inner City in the future. Never shy in proclaiming his victories, Eric Mann is completing a book entitled *Driving the Bus of History: The LA Bus Riders Union Models a New Theory of Urban Insurgency in the Age of Transnational Capitalism.*

At the very least, the BRU represents an important example of coalition-based movements arising at the spatially specific intersections of race, class, and gender, and having a socially beneficial effect on the geography of the postmetropolis. Viewed more ambitiously, it can be seen as opening traditional notions of civil rights to a more specifically spatial politics revolving around new visions of democratic citizenship and the rights to the city, the

18   The LCSC publication, *LA's Lethal Air: New Strategies for Policy, Organizing, and Action* (Mann et al., 1991) remains a key document in the growing environmental justice movement, and its comparative analysis of service workers' wages helped to spur one of the most effective labor struggles affecting poor and minority communities, Jobs for Janitors.

19   Eric Mann et al., *A New Vision for Urban Transportation: The Bus Riders Union Makes History at the Intersection of Mass Transit, Civil Rights, and the Environment,* a report of the Labor/Community Strategy Center, 1996. For another view of the BRU case, see Jeffrey Brown, "Race, Class, Gender and Public Transportation: Lesson from the Bus Riders Union Lawsuit," *Critical Planning* (Journal of the UCLA Department of Urban Planning) 5, 1998: 3–20.

rights – and responsibilities – of all urban dwellers to participate effectively in the social production of their lived cityspaces.

The middle landscape

Tucked away in the affluent Westside Outer City, just east of the LAX airport complex, is Lennox, a tiny residual plot of unincorporated county land with a population of 23,000 and an area of 1.1 square miles. Nearly 90 percent of the population is Latino and more than 60 percent are foreign-born (as against around 40 percent for Los Angeles County). Unemployment rates are not particularly high but household income is well below surrounding areas, for Lennox has become a highly specialized Outer City enclave of the immigrant working poor, a ghetto of hotel and restaurant workers cheaply servicing the three Edge Cities Garreau defines for this area: Marina Del Rey-Culver City, Los Angeles International Airport-El Segundo, and the South Bay-Torrance-Carson-San Diego Freeway area. The problem here is not so much a mismatch between jobs and housing but an immiserating concentration of the worst of both. And the problems are compounded by glocalization. The recent devaluation of the Mexican peso and the general decline of the Mexican economy has had a particularly devastating effect on Lennox, where much of the population maintains binational households. Such specialized pockets of poverty are embedded in, and play a key role in sustaining, the expansive development of the Outer Cities.

Thirty miles east is another example of what Mike Davis, the noirest of the local explorers of the dark side of the Exopolis, calls "The Suburban Nightmare" that is nestled in the "political middle landscape," the in-between zone of older and newer urbanized suburbs where Inner and Outer City mix together. He looks in particular at Pomona, a municipality of around 150,000 residents on the eastern edge of Los Angeles County and the gateway to the Inland Empire, the name given to the "anticipatory" Outer City of San Bernardino and Riverside counties.

> Once upon a time a placid town basked in the golden glow of its orchards. In the 1920s, it was renowned as the "Queen of the Citrus Belt." In the 1940s, it served as one of Hollywood's models for Andy Hardy's hometown. In the 1950s, it became a commuter suburb for thousands of Father-Knows-Bests in their starched white shirts. Now, its nearly abandoned downtown is surrounded by acres of vacant lots and derelict homes. Its major employer, an aerospace corporation, pulled up stakes and moved to Tucson. The 4-H Club has been replaced by local franchises of the Crips and Bloods. Since 1970, nearly 1 percent of its population has been murdered. This town is, of course, Pomona, Los Angeles County's fourth largest city.
>
> Although geographically a suburb, Pomona now displays pathologies typically associated with a battered inner city. Its incidence of poverty, for example, exceeds Los Angeles' and its murder rate, in bad years, approaches Detroit's. Its density of gang membership, as a percentage of the teen-age male population,

is one of the nation's highest. Unfortunately, Pomona is not unique. Across the nation, hundreds of aging suburbs are trapped in the same downward trajectory, from garden city to crabgrass slum. This silent, pervasive crisis dominates the political middle landscape . . . America seems to be unraveling its traditional moral center: suburbia.[20]

In his own reclassification of Garreau's Edge Cities, Davis devises a geographical class war between the "new pariahs," older suburban cities such as Pomona and those around Minneapolis, Chicago, and in the Bay Area; against the "predatory" edge cities "further out on the spiral arms of the metropolitan galaxy." What results, he contends, is "an unstable mosaic" of new polarizations, an emerging second round of urban crises, expressed in Southern California in "the widening divides between northern and southern Orange County, the upper and lower tiers of the San Gabriel Valley, the east and west sides of the San Fernando Valley or the San Fernando Valley as a whole and its 'suburbs-of-a-suburb' – like Simi Valley and Santa Clarita."

Davis adds to his darkside revisioning of the Exopolis an almost apocalyptic picture of the environmental devastation that arises from the unbalanced geography of well-paying jobs, affordable housing, and shorter and less automobile-dependent journeys to work. In his view, Los Angeles has become a "Cannibal City," a fountainhead of "ecocide" that continues insatiably to devour natural and human landscapes, especially in this middle zone. In "How Eden Lost Its Garden," Davis lists the "lost landscapes" of Los Angeles, from the nineteenth-century destruction of native grasslands and the oak savannah to the late twentieth-century elimination of the remaining tidal marshes and coastal sage scrub, an intentional reference to the Playa Vista project of the New Urbanists.[21] Although framed by historical continuities, there is a clear intimation that recent developments have accelerated these processes, adding a potent environmental critique to the discourse on the restructuring of urban form, one that is sure to expand in the future.[22]

Off-the-edge cities

Further out, on the distant borderlands of the megacity, the jobs–housing imbalance takes on still another distinctive form. Flushed by the success of Orange County, the Westside, and more recently the West San Fernando

20   Mike Davis, "The Suburban Nightmare: While Older Suburbs Experience Many Problems of the Inner City, "Edge Cities" Now Offer a New Escape," *Los Angeles Times*, Opinion, October 23, 1994.
21   See Mike Davis, "Cannibal City: Los Angeles and the Destruction of Nature," in R. Ferguson ed., *Urban Revisions*, 1994; and "How Eden Lost its Garden: A Political History of the Los Angeles Landscape," in Scott and Soja eds., *The City: Los Angeles and Urban Theory at the End of the Twentieth Century*, 1996: 160–85. For another look at the "Apocalypse Themepark" of Los Angeles, see Davis, "Los Angeles After the Storm: The Dialectic of Ordinary Disaster," *Antipode* 27 (1995), 221–41.
22   For a compilation and expansion of this apocalyptic environmental critique, see Davis's most recent work, *Ecology of Fear: Los Angeles and the Imagination of Disaster*, New York: Metropolitan Books, Henry Holt, 1998.

Valley, and intensified by fear of the New Inner City, a remarkable anticipatory building boom has taken place in the outer fringes of the LA Exopolis
over the past two decades. In the 1990 census, more than half of the fastest-
growing small cities in the USA were found in this region. Where jobs were
relatively abundant and accessible, such as in Irvine and Mission Viejo in
Orange County, and somewhat later in places such as Thousand Oaks, Westlake Village, and Simi Valley straddling the Los Angeles-Ventura county
border, thriving middle-class communities were formed. In other areas, where
Outer City industrialization and job growth stalled, whole cities were left
stranded, creating a socio-spatial crisis of outlandish proportions. Two of these
areas, Moreno Valley east of Riverside and Palmdale and Lancaster in the
Antelope Valley in the high desert of northern Los Angeles County, deserve
special attention, for they illustrate well an argument that underlies and spins
off from all the discourses on the postmetropolis, that thirty years of crisis-
generated restructuring are currently leading to the onset of a period of
restructuring-generated crises that are not located only in the ghettoes and
barrios of the old inner city.

In Moreno Valley, located about sixty miles east of downtown Los Angeles
and almost as distant from Irvine, the jobs–housing mix has become disas-
trously out of whack. The 1990 census listed Moreno Valley as the fastest-
growing city over 100,000 in the entire country. Attracted by affordable
housing, mainly young lower-middle working-class families flocked to the
area, in part also to escape the real and imagined problems of the old and new
inner city. Population boomed from 45,000 at the time of incorporation in 1984
to almost 120,000 in 1990. Today, the city is described as "solidly middle-class"
with a population of about 135,000, a median family income close to $45,000,
and a racial mix of 57 percent Anglo, 23 percent Latino, 13 percent African
American, and 6 percent Asian and Pacific Islanders. Beneath the appearances
of comfortable suburban life, however, there are unforeseen problems of social
pathology and personal despair as intense and disruptive as those seemingly
left behind.

With local employment growth far below what was promised by the optimistic community developers greedily driven by the development of adjacent
Orange County, the journey to work (as well as an unemployment rate higher
than 12 percent) has become an unusual burden. Many working residents are
forced to rise well before dawn to drive or to be taken by a fleet of vans and
buses, often for more than two hours, to the places of employment they held
before moving to their affordable housing. Without a large commercial or
industrial tax base, public services are poor, schools are overcrowded, freeways are gridlocked, and family life is deeply stressed as residents contend
with their location in a wannabe Edge City.

Advertised as "A City of Promise . . . Poised for the twenty-first Century,"
Moreno Valley boomed on what a local observer likened to a Ponzi scheme,
based on the flow of developers' permit fees. Aggravated by the closure of the
nearby March Air Force Base and reductions in the flow of permit fees, Moreno
Valley recently elicited other headline descriptions – "Bad Time for a Boom

Town" and "Boom Town Going Bust" – as it plunged into a budget crisis, unable to maintain basic police, fire, and even school crossing guard services without a substantial increase in local taxes.[23] The plight of Moreno Valley reached national attention in leading eastern newspapers and on television's multiplying "newsmagazine" programs, where the remarks of happy valley residents were contrasted with demoralizing stories of broken marriages, delinquent children, disruptive van romances, and spousal abuse, further evidence for many of the California Dream-become-Nightmare.

Locally, as is typical in these off-the-edge cities, all problems were blamed on incompetent municipal leadership and the failures of planning, ignoring the inherent dynamics of exopolitan restructuring and the need for effective regional coalition-building among similarly affected areas. Both views are seriously short-sighted, for such enclaves of "invisible" middle-class immiseration are a characteristic feature of postsuburban landscapes all over the country, as much a part of the Exopolis as the new American ghettoes of the underclass and the working poor or the burgeoning technopoles and successful edge cities. The restructuring of urban form, in combination with mass movements against increasing taxes and for smaller government, is creating a new round of fiscal crises in postsuburbia, leading an increasing number of the constellation of local governments that comprise the postmetropolis to the edge of bankruptcy, and beyond, as occurred in Orange County in 1994. But the crises that are affecting the off-the-edge cities are even deeper and more difficult to address.

The 100 Mile City and the notion of spatial polarity take on a new meaning in places such as Moreno Valley, located roughly a hundred miles east of its postsuburban antipode at Malibu, also recently incorporated as a municipality. Located a similar distance apart, but North–South rather than East–West, is another pairing of even more extreme socio-spatial polarities: the peninsula of Palos Verdes, where the tiny incorporated and gated community of Rolling Hills recently topped *Worth* magazine's list of the most wealthy communities in America (with an average household income of more than $300,000), and Palmdale, located in the high desert of northern Los Angeles County. The development of Palmdale and the entire Antelope Valley was given an even greater push to excess than Moreno Valley, as the area contained both the site for a proposed international airport and a cluster of big aerospace firms associated with sprawling Edwards Air Force Base, a major cog in the NASA network of space stations.[24] In the 1980s, the rolling brown hills and sage-brushed sands of the Antelope Valley, pictured at the Palmdale freeway exit by David Hockney in one of his most famous photo-collages (see figure 8.2) became covered by a sea of peach and beige stucco houses with red-tiled roofs

---

23 See Tom Gorman, "Moreno Valley: Boom Town Going Bust Turns to Voters," *Los Angeles Times*, October 28, 1996; and "Bad Times for a Boom Town," *Los Angeles Times*, January 12, 1994.

24 The area also contains the barely visible ruins of Llano del Rio, the socialist utopian community founded in the early decades of the century and celebrated by Mike Davis in the introduction to his *City of Quartz* (1990).

Figure 8.2 David Hockney, *Pearblossom Highway, 11–18 April 1986*, 2nd version, photographic collage, $71\frac{1}{2}\times107$ inches; © David Hockney   (Source: The J. Paul Getty Museum, Los Angeles)

selling at bargain basement prices, at least in comparison to the city far away to the south.

With the end of the Cold War and the steep decline of the region's aerospace industry, as well as the ensuing real estate crisis and economic recession of the early 1990s, the booming Antelope Valley became the site of what one reporter called a "middle-class implosion." In a pair of richly detailed articles, *Los Angeles Times* reporter Sonia Nazario painted an agonizing picture of roadblocked dreams and the unfolding of what she described as a new "class struggle."[25] Even more so than in Moreno Valley, excessively long journeys to work were having pathological effects on family life and personal health. In the mid-1990s, nearly 40 percent of work commutes in Palmdale and 30 percent in the entire Antelope Valley took two hours or more, compared with 15–17 percent in Los Angeles, Ventura, and Orange Counties, 25 percent in Riverside and San Bernardino Counties, and 6 percent for the USA as a whole. Many workers spend more than five hours a day in their cars and young children are often

25   Sonia Nazario, "Suburban Dreams Hit Roadblock," *Los Angeles Times*, June 23, 1996; and "Class Struggle Unfolds in Antelope Valley Tracts," *Los Angeles Times*, June 24, 1996.

left for more than twelve hours in day-care centers that open before dawn. Suicide rates are unusually high in Palmdale and nearby Lancaster; the local Sheriff's Office reports that domestic violence felony arrests are above those of any of their other 16 stations, and there are more child abuse reports than almost anywhere in California. The Antelope Valley psychological center that specializes in domestic violence is reputed to be the largest in the USA. The number of violent juvenile crimes and gang membership has increased precipitously and some shopping malls have prohibited entry to anyone wearing a baseball cap backward or to one side. In one recent period, over a hundred teenagers a day were arrested for truancy.

With plummeting land values, mortgage foreclosure rates (at around 10 percent) are now among the highest anywhere in the country, and many of the empty homes are becoming filled with underclass squatters from the inner city, still another example of the metropolis inverted. In recent years, Nazario reports, 25,000 public assistance cases have been transferred from the City of Los Angeles to the Antelope Valley. She also states that nearly 50 percent of those receiving public assistance are white, 32 percent Latino, 17 percent African American, and 2 percent Asian. Sweatshops have been set up in the area and crackhouses have been raided by police battering rams. There are some who still maintain their middle-class dreams amidst this implosion. "Here we are really content," says one resident, an LAPD officer, but most would agree with the conclusion of a local Lutheran priest: "This way of life is destructive." Some academic analysts might argue that these conditions are only temporary growing pains, but temporary or not, the present day reality of the Antelope Valley stands out as one of the darkest outcomes of exopolitan restructuring.

Chapter 9

Fractal City: Metropolarities and the Restructured Social Mosaic

Representative Texts

- *The Ethnic Quilt: Population Diversity in Southern California* (Allen and Turner, 1997)
- *The Widening Divide: Income Inequality and Poverty in Los Angeles* (UCLA Research Group on the Los Angeles Economy, 1989)
- *Ethnic Los Angeles* (Waldinger and Bozorgmehr eds., 1996)
- *The New Asian Immigration in Los Angeles and Global Restructuring* (Ong, Bonacich, and Cheng eds., 1994)
- *Caught in the Middle: Korean Merchants in Multiethnic America* (Min, 1996)
- *Politics in Black and White: Race and Power in Los Angeles* (Sonenshein, 1993)
- *The First Suburban Chinatown: The Remaking of Monterey Park, California* (Fong, 1994)
- *Irangeles: Iranians in Los Angeles* (Kelley, Friedlander, and Colby eds., 1993)
- *The Politics of Diversity: Immigration, Resistance, and Change in Monterey Park, California* (Horton, 1995)
- *Multiethnic Coalition Building in Los Angeles* (Yu and Chang eds., 1995)
- *Los Angeles – Struggles Toward Multiethnic Community: Asian American, African American, and Latino Perspectives* (Chang and Leong eds., 1993)
- *Separate Societies: Poverty and Inequality in U.S. Cities* (Goldsmith and Blakeley, 1992)
- *American Apartheid: Segregation and the Making of the Underclass* (Massey and Denton, 1994)
- *The Truly Disadvantaged: The Inner City, the Underclass, and Public Policy* (Wilson, 1987)
- *The Urban Underclass* (Jencks and Peterson eds., 1991)
- *The Homeless* (Jencks, 1994)
- *When Work Disappears: The World of the New Urban Poor* (Wilson, 1996)

- *Immigration and Ethnicity: The Integration of America's Newest Arrivals* (Edmonston and Passel eds., 1994)
- *White Racism: The Basics* (Feagin and Hernán, 1994)
- *Black Wealth/White Wealth* (Oliver and Shapiro, 1995)
- *Friends or Strangers? The Impact of Immigrants on the U.S. Economy* (Borjas, 1990)
- *Race, Ethnicity, and Entrepreneurship in Urban America* (Light and Rosenstein eds., 1995)
- *The New Urban Reality* (Peterson ed., 1985)
- *Immigrant America* (Portes and Rumbaut, 1990)
- *Dual City: Restructuring New York* (Mollenkopf and Castells eds., 1991)
- *Still the Promised City? New Immigrants and African-Americans in Post-Industrial New York* (Waldinger, 1996)

Interwoven with the jumbled *spatiality* of the globalized postfordist exopolis is a recomposed *sociality* that has become similarly fluid, fragmented, decentered, and rearranged in complex patterns that are only beginning to be recognized, understood, and effectively studied. Although significant continuities persist and must not be ignored, the contemporary urban social order can no longer be defined effectively by such conventional and familiar models of social stratification as the class-divided Dual City of the bourgeoisie and proletariat; the neatly layered Hierarchical City of the wealthy, the middle class, and the poor; or the "two Americas" Racially Divided City of black versus white that was described in the aftermath of the 1960s urban insurrections. *These older polarities have not disappeared*, but a much more polymorphous and fractured social geometry has taken shape from the far-reaching restructuring of the social boundaries and categorical logics of class, income, occupation, skill, race, ethnicity, and gender that characterized the modern metropolis up to the early 1970s.

   A distinctive discourse has emerged attempting to describe and interpret this *restructured social mosaic* and its more complex patterning of what I will describe as *metropolarities*, the multiple axes of differential power and status that produce and maintain socio-economic inequality. Its main thematic emphases are tersely captured in the titles of the representative texts: the new ethnic quilt, the widening divide, income inequality and poverty, race and power, the truly disadvantaged, black wealth/white wealth, the urban underclass, American apartheid, separate societies, immigration and ethnicity, immigrant America, the new urban reality. Underlying these indicative themes is one of the most important and challenging findings arising from all the discourses on the postmetropolis, *that inherent in the new urbanization processes has been an intensification of socio-economic inequalities*. A forceful reassertion of this profound and disturbing conclusion, and a look at the theoretical, empirical, and policy debates that have evolved around it is an appropriate way to begin discussion of the fourth discourse.

Manufacturing Inequality in the Postmetropolis

The U.S. has the largest gap between wealth and poverty in the developed world and the ratio is widest in New York and Los Angeles, comparable to Karachi, Bombay, and Mexico City.[1]

This stunning observation, taken from a United Nations report, appeared in the *Los Angeles Times* in May 1992, just after the Justice Riots that followed the original Rodney King verdict. The UN report argued that the 1992 riots were part of "an urban revolution taking place on all six inhabited continents, brought about by conditions very similar to those in Los Angeles: crime, racial and ethnic tension, economic woes, vast disparities of wealth, shortages of social services and deteriorating infrastructure." It went on to predict that "urban poverty will become the most significant and politically explosive problem of the next century." It is worth while noting not just the globality of this observed association of social unrest with deepening poverty, ethnic and racial tensions, and growing disparities of wealth, but also the explicit grounding of this explosive problem in a specifically urban context, in the particular contemporary conditions embedded in cityspaces and characterizing urbanism as a way of life everywhere in the inhabited world. Even more pertinent to our present discussion is the identification of Los Angeles and New York, the premier postmetropolitan regions of the USA, as the extreme cases of the polarization of wealth and poverty in the advanced industrial countries.[2]

Nearly every day further evidence accumulates to reinforce the conclusion that socio-economic inequality and polarization in American society have been increasing over the past thirty years. A recent report by the Milton S. Eisenhower Foundation issued in 1998, thirty years after the landmark Kerner Commission delivered its conclusion that the USA was "moving toward two societies, one black, one white – separate and unequal," not only argued that this racial divide persists but that it has widened in scope to include new immigrant populations and was also becoming increasingly *urban* in its expression. Between 1968 and 1998, the proportion of the US population living in poverty increased from 12.5 to 14 percent. Nearly a third of all African American and Latino families now live below the poverty line, three times the

---

1　Robin Wright, "Riots Called Symptom of Worldwide Urban Trend," *Los Angeles Times*, May 25, 1992. There was no specific mention of which UN report this referred to.

2　The surge in inequality has been much less pronounced in Europe, where stronger welfare states continue to be centrally concerned with widening income gaps and the problems of the poor. In Europe, the key policy issues regarding economic prosperity revolve more around the problems of unemployment, for European national and regional economies have been unable to match the extraordinary capacity of the US economy to generate jobs. This has created not only a major contrast between Europe and North America, but also a potential complementarity in which the west side of the North Atlantic divide can learn about dealing effectively with poverty and inequality from the east side, while Europe, in return, learns how better to stimulate job generation and reduce unemployment. This potential complementarity of policy knowledges and experiences, despite the many problems involved on both sides, may be one of the most interesting arenas of international learning in the twenty-first century.

rate of non-Latino whites. Similarly, median incomes for these families are around 55 percent of their non-Latino white counterparts. And while thirty years ago only about half the poor lived in metropolitan areas, 77 percent do so today, a remarkable 50 percent increase.[3] Other studies have shown that beginning in 1990, the "fortunate fifth" of American income earners took home more money than the other four-fifths combined, the highest proportion in postwar history. Moreover, in terms of taxes paid, proportion of income given to charity, local political participation rates, and choices of residential environments, larger numbers of the "fortunate fifth" seem to be seceding from civic life and its public responsibilities, creating new kinds of privatized postmetropolitan enclaves and new ways of reinforcing and securing their isolation.[4]

What has caused this pronounced surge in socio-economic and spatial inequalities? Why does it seem to be especially concentrated in the USA? More specifically, why has it been linked so closely to the postmetropolitan transition and why does it reach its highest intensity in Los Angeles and New York? Let us try to unravel some of the ways these questions have been addressed.

Normalizing inequality: the extremes at both ends

Social inequality as a moral problem and as a target for public policy intervention has been a core issue in all liberal democracies and in liberal social science and philosophy for at least the past two centuries. Consequently, one might expect that the accumulated evidence of deepening poverty and resurgent inequality over the past thirty years would have generated an equivalent resurgence of interest in and attention to addressing this core issue, and trying to explain, in particular, why social inequality has been intensified by the new urbanization processes, especially in the USA. To some degree, this has occurred and these debates form the focus for the fourth discourse. But at the same time, the magnitude and meaning of this recent surge in inequality and its embeddedness in urban restructuring processes has been obscured in both the academic and public arena by what can be described as a reactivated counter-discourse that insistently normalizes social inequality and represents it as an intrinsic part of all contemporary capitalist societies.

Both left- and right-wing versions of this counter-discourse can be identified, and they are curiously united around a shared belief that capitalism, by its very nature, perpetually produces and reproduces inequalities of wealth and power as part of its inner workings, indeed as one of its primary motors of socio-economic development. What we see today, viewed from this essentially historical if not historicist perspective, is therefore just more of the same

---

3   Reported in Alissa J. Rubin, "Racial Divide Widens, Study Says," *Los Angeles Times*, March 1, 1998.
4   Robert Reich, "Secession of the Successful," *New York Times Magazine*, January 27, 1991. For a more detailed elaboration of his argument, see Robert Reich, *The Work of Nations: Preparing Ourselves for 21st-Century Capitalism*, New York: Alfred A. Knopf, 1991.

thing, another accelerated round of "creative destruction" and/or crisis-generated restructuring not greatly different from similar stressful periods in the past. There is little that is new and different, except perhaps an unusual speeding up of the processes of change, what David Harvey (1989) has called "time-space compression," linked primarily to the new technologies of the Information Age and the intensified economic competition associated with globalization. The major contrast between these two positions is that the traditional Right tends to see increasing inequality as a temporary and probably necessary accompaniment (or unavoidable cost) to economic recuperation, innovation, and growth; while the more orthodox Left views it as a nefarious reflection (and permanent accompaniment) of deep structural forces that have always been intrinsic in class-divided capitalist societies.

In both cases, there might be a tacit acceptance of the need to intervene and address the problems arising from increasing socio-economic disparities, but behind this democratic altruism is all too often a stubborn conviction that "this is the way it is – there is nothing much that can be done about it." For the purists on the Right and increasingly in the neoliberal center, there is only one ultimately reliable solution, continued reliance on the magical powers of the free market and its allegedly eventual trickle-down effects. Purists on the Left also have only one ultimately reliable solution, insurgency to social revolution. Both these positionings have their appeal and can be buttressed by abundant historical evidence and argument. But their combined effect is to divert immediate attention away from concerted efforts to ameliorate the explosive problems associated with increasing inequalities and to reduce the political and interpretive significance of the extraordinary contemporary surge in inequality.[5] While they hover in the background of the fourth discourse, perhaps usefully checking its excesses and immediate fixations on the present, they must be set aside to further the discussion.

Variations on the theme of intrinsic causality

Perhaps the simplest and most widely adopted explanation of the surge in inequality over the past thirty years relies on a logic that, while often implicitly assuming a certain degree of constancy or inevitability to societal inequalities, assigns causality for the recent surge to generically defined restructuring processes, such as globalization, the rise of new information technologies, and the transition to a postindustrial or postfordist society. Three variants of this approach can be identified, the first being the most superficial, straightfor-

---

5   Further confusing the issue of what is to be done with regard to increasing social and economic inequalities is the fact that empirical data on income patterns, unemployment rates, and household poverty can be adeptly manipulated to submerge the contemporary resurgence of inequality, especially in an age when it is more difficult than ever before to distinguish between the real and the imagined or between fact and fiction. See chapter 11 for further discussion of this contemporary confusion of the real and the imagined.

ward, and popular in the public arena. From this first viewpoint, the rich have become richer over the past thirty years primarily because of both traditional and new strategies connected to technological innovation, corporate reorganization, governmental deregulation, and geographical location. There are more millionaires and billionaires in the USA today because more entrepreneurs have been able to profit significantly from global, national, regional, and local restructuring processes. Building on already established agglomerations of wealth, the largest concentrations of the most successful rich, not surprisingly, reside in the largest and most expansive global cities. Here, they are able to maximize utility to profit from the new urbanization processes and, through their more footloose and "reflexive" locational choices, escape from most of the negative spillover effects of the postmetropolitan transition in protected residential enclaves and globalized financial and investment networks stretching out from their multilocational home bases.

On the flip side of the widening gap has been a massive influx of poor immigrants providing cheap and weakly organized labor supplies, also decidedly concentrated in New York, Los Angeles, and other major postmetropolitan regions. The immigrant poor, by their very survival, not only reduce average income levels for the bottom 10 percent, they are seen as dragging down income levels for the native-born poor by taking up the lowest-paying jobs and absorbing a significant part of the reduced pool of welfare expenditures. This intrinsically conservative view thus explains rising inequalities as a statistical product, if not artifact, of successful *entrepreneurialism* plus intensified *immigration* from poor countries. As these two poles swell, the middle class is proportionately reduced in size, giving at least the appearance of decline if not a true income "squeeze." Given the logical simplicity and popularity of this explanation of the widening gap, it is easy to understand why so many Americans, from the native-born poor to the middle classes and even the "fortunate fifth," blame mass immigration and the new immigrants for whatever economic problems they are facing. Often disguised under guileless arguments of overpopulation – too many people for too few resources – an anti-immigrant movement has also been growing in the academic and public policy discourse, especially in response to the increasing ethnic and racial tensions that have been so evident in Los Angeles, New York, and other major urban regions in the 1990s.[6]

---

6   See, for a very recent example, an editorial published in the *Los Angeles Times* on the ides of March (March 15, 1998) by Ben Zuckerman, an astronomer and member of the Institute of the Environment at UCLA. Under the title "Cut Immigration, Save the Environment," the author urges the Sierra Club to join the Wilderness Society and a few other environmental groups to publicly state "that ecological sustainability requires lower immigration rates" and to work together to change current immigration laws. Blaming the "liberal media" and such "environmental politicians" as Vice President Al Gore, and sidestepping the barely mentioned issue of "inequity," Zuckerman calls for "an effective policy that will stabilize the U.S. population." "While individuals deserve compassion," he states, "the media should also illuminate how so very many millions of immigrants, eager to embrace the highly consumptive American lifestyle, impact the environment both here and abroad." He emphasizes his point with a literary flourish: "In an avalanche, each unique, beautiful snowflake pleads not guilty."

There are also much less conservative views which similarly attribute causality to business as usual, modified only by certain intensifications associated with global economic restructuring. A particularly incisive and specifically urban explanation of the generation and persistence of inequalities in the capitalist city can be derived from David Harvey's liberal formulations in *Social Justice and the City* (1973). As discussed briefly in chapter 4, Harvey argued that the normal workings of the urban system under capitalism always tend toward a redistribution of real income in favor of the rich. Market forces as well as the conventional operation of public decision-making and urban planning create a specific urban geography that constrains concerted attempts to achieve greater equality of real incomes. Greed, corruption, racism, and such tactics as investment "red-lining" and charging higher retail prices in poor neighborhoods, may reinforce this redistributive tendency, but even in their absence urban business-as-usual will continue to generate widening income gaps. There are some limits to this process, and effective planning and public intervention into housing, land, and labor markets can alleviate some of the problems arising from disparities of wealth in a few target areas, but the fundamental inequalities associated with the uneven development of city-space will persist indefinitely, declining during some periods, growing in others. That there has been a surge in inequality over the past thirty years, with significantly reduced government intervention, extensive deregulation and privatization, and the severe weakening of the welfare state, therefore comes as no surprise.

Harvey would later argue forcefully that true social and territorial justice can only be obtained through socialism. But even in the absence of this socialist transformation, his arguments can be usefully applied to the accentuated surge of inequalities in Los Angeles and New York. These are the most globalized cities in the USA in terms of capital, labor, and cultural heterogeneity; they are in postmetropolitan regions where at least one if not all of the three most propulsive sectors of the flexible postfordist economy (high-technology industry, craft-based and design-intensive production, and finance-insurance-real estate and related business services) are heavily concentrated; and their huge size and exopolitan geography accentuates even further the generation of new kinds of social and economic inequalities, environmental injustices, and what I have been calling metropolarities. Again, there is no surprise that the greatest disparities between wealth and poverty in the developed world today are found in these two urban regions. For the most part, this interpretation of the widening gap has not generated a wide following outside the field of radical geography and geopolitical economy, but it remains one of the most potent critiques of globalization, postfordist industrial restructuring, and the social and spatial effects of the postmetropolitan transition.

A third variant on the theme of intrinsic causality is exemplified best by the influential work of William Julius Wilson, an African American sociologist who, while currently on the faculty of Harvard University, spent most of his academic career at that wellspring of urban studies, the University of Chicago. Wilson has deeply shaped the discourse on the "new poverty" in America in both the academic and public policy arenas, bringing needed attention to the plight of those he has described as the *truly disadvantaged*, and especially the welfare-dependent *permanent urban underclass* produced, consolidated, and geographically concentrated by the creative destruction arising from deindustrialization, globalization, and other aspects of economic restructuring.[7] Wilson's liberal formulations have defined and monopolized the contemporary extension of the old Chicago School of urban sociology and injected the discourse on metropolarities with vivid representations derived directly from the midwestern postmetropolis. Chicago has always had a very simple social and spatial structure in comparison to Los Angeles, New York, or the San Francisco Bay Area. These simplicities are reflected in Wilson's broad theorization of "the declining significance of race" and in his mode of explaining the formation of the overwhelmingly African American urban underclass through old-fashioned location theories and a modified Schumpeterian "creative destruction" approach to economic restructuring, an approach which normalizes restructuring as both inevitable and efficient.

Wilson's location theory explanation hinges around the notion of a *spatial mismatch* in which new technologies and the availability of cheap land accelerate the suburbanization of industry and jobs, leaving African Americans in particular "anchored" in the deindustrialized inner city, socially trapped and isolated from mainstream society in a process others have called "hyperghettoization." The shift to knowledge-intensive and information processing industries aggravates this spatial mismatch with a related educational and skills mismatch that further marginalizes and isolates the underclass in concentrated enclaves of poverty. Wilson's attention to the spatial specificities of contemporary urbanism, reflecting the old Chicago School heritage, has significantly influenced sociological research on racial, ethnic, class, and gender inequalities in the USA, a noteworthy accomplishment given the weakening of a specifically spatial perspective in mainstream American sociology and the particularly dramatic decline of the subfield of *urban* sociology.[8]

---

7   William Julius Wilson, *The Truly Disadvantaged: The Inner City, the Underclass, and Public Policy*, Chicago: University of Chicago Press, 1987; "The American Underclass: Inner-City Ghettoes and the Norms of Citizenship," Godkin lecture, John F. Kennedy School of Government, Harvard University, 1988; "Social Theory and Public-Agenda Research: The Challenge of Studying Inner-City Social Dislocations," Presidential address, annual meeting of the American Sociological Association, 1990. The prelude to these studies was Wilson, *The Declining Significance of Race: Blacks and Changing American Institutions*, Chicago: University of Chicago Press, 1980.

8   Although it is difficult to quantify, it does appear as if the status, popularity, and number of courses taught in urban sociology has declined significantly in the past decade. Part of this decline may be due to the harsh reaction among more conservative (or formerly radical) sociologists to the insurgent radicalism of the neo-Marxist "New Urban Sociology" that developed in the 1970s. See, for example, the reactionary diatribe of Irving Louis Horowitz, *The Decomposition of Sociology*, New York and Oxford: Oxford University Press, 1994. But another factor has been the relative weakness of the New Urban Sociology (as it is still called today with some irony) in dealing with the new urbanization processes and their specifically spatial manifestations. Many sociologists have shifted their interests from urban sociology *per se* to the more rapidly growing fields of ethnic, racial, gender, and immigration studies, where they are distanced from the major theoretical and interpretive debates about globalization, economic restructuring, and the reconfiguration of cityspace. It is also interesting to note that many of the sociologists who have been leading figures in these latter debates, such as Manuel Castells and Saskia

Wilson never denies the importance of racism in these developments, as some of his critics (as well as proponents) have claimed he does. Instead, he argues that race and racism are much less important than the normal dynamics of class and capitalist development during this contemporary phase of crisis-generated but presumably functionally efficient restructuring. Unfortunately, the images and explanations projected from his work are too easily co-opted and ideologically "spin-doctored," not just as a means of submerging the critical debates on racism in America but also as a camouflage that makes all of the new metropolarities appear to be normal and "natural" outgrowths of urban and economic restructuring and the productive rebuilding of the American economy in the New Information Age. Wilson has devoted great effort to counter the misrepresentation of his work from those both to his Left and his Right, especially with regard to affirmative action, which he clearly favors as part of a larger policy to deal with the new poverty. In *When Work Disappears* (1996), Wilson backs significantly away from his earlier concept of the permanent urban underclass, which seemed too easily co-optable by arch-conservative scholars such as Charles Murray to feed their simplistic and normalizing "culture of poverty" explanations of persistent inequality.[9] Instead, he speaks more broadly of the "new urban poor" and expands his attention to the effects of globalization, to the need for explicitly *regional* policies for dealing with the new poverty, and, without directly describing it as such, to the new and more subtle racism that has been emerging in both academic and public policy debates.

These three modes of understanding the surge of inequality in the USA, for all their shortcomings, at least try to develop a conceptual framework for explaining the changes that have been taking place in the urban social mosaic over the past thirty years. I emphasize this point, for the core of the fourth discourse has tended to shy away from theorizing the persistence of inequality except as a broad-brush outcome of globalization and economic restructuring. This has shifted attention away from explanation and critical theory-building, and from the spatial specificity of urbanism, to detailed empirical *descriptions* of the particular sociological outcomes that can be statistically measured (and perhaps also mapped) within the confines of specific urban regions.

Describing metropolarities: empirical sociologies and labor market dynamics

Perhaps not unexpectedly, the contemporary discourse on the restructuring of the social order of the postmetropolis has been dominated by sociologists and

Sassen, have their primary appointments in departments of urban planning. Even William Julius Wilson is now part of the faculty of the Kennedy School of Government at Harvard, where urban planning has been primarily housed.

9   See Charles Murray, *Losing Ground: American Social Policy, 1950–1980*, New York: Basic Books, 1984.

by a model of sociological inquiry that is primarily concerned with the statistical correlates of social stratification; that is, with empirical investigations of how such variables as race, ethnicity, gender, age, family composition, education level, occupation, and other census-measurable attributes, are associated with levels of status, income, and power in society, and therefore with the production and reproduction of social inequalities. In its most basic form, the core discourse attempts to trace and chart the changing structure of socio-economic inequalities over the past thirty years, whatever their causes or explanation. For the most part, American versions of this empirical and inductive sociology of urbanism tend to draw upon theories of economic restructuring that are more closely tied to the concept of postindustrial society than to the postfordist, flexible accumulation, and regional approaches of the more spatially minded industrial geographers and geopolitical economists.

A similar disciplinary preference exists with respect to the urban social impacts of globalization and world city formation, which tend to be seen primarily as generalized "world systems" effects, intensifying the new postindustrial social polarizations. At one extreme, the influx of global capital expands the superstratum of knowledge-intensive, professional-managerial, and producer-services jobs that coordinate and control the Informational City (another heavily sociologized concept); while at the other extreme, an even more massive in-migration of global labor balloons the growing postindustrial underclass and the informal, underground, or "black" economy. In between, the domestic middle class is squeezed from both sides after a century or more of almost continuous expansion, a favored few floating up the hierarchy to its highest rungs, a much larger cohort filtering downward into the ballooning lower tier.

The resultant urban sociology is thus represented as a product of many different processes of social stratification, segmentation, and segregation that lead to a layered mosaic of uneven socio-economic development and polarized positionings of status and power. Like Lefebvre's conceptualization of geographically uneven development, there are simultaneous tendencies that work toward both equalization and differentiation, expressed primarily in patterns of social mobility up and down the hierarchical layers. But full equality is never reached in any society. What occurs instead, especially in such periods of rapid social change as we have been experiencing over the past thirty years, is a reshuffling of social hierarchies, a new tesselation of the social mosaic that today seems to many to have become more complex and kaleidoscopic than ever before. This translates politically, as has always been the case, into struggles for greater equality within a series of (postindustrial) social movements organized around what have become today much more pluralistic axes of inequality formation: class, race, ethnicity, gender, sexuality, age, residential location, immigrant status, housing, environmental justice, cultural identity, and so on.

The new sociology of urbanism is thus not yet very different from either the radical New Urban Sociology that developed to make sense of postwar (Fordist) urbanization and the urban crises it generated; or the mainstream "analytical" sociology that displaced and despecified its urban spatial focus in reaction to the perceived ecological spatialism of the early Chicago School.[10] In the USA, at least, urban sociology seems either to have been caught by surprise by the crisis-generated urban restructuring or to have accommodated these restructuring processes under an extension of the postindustrial society thesis. As a result, specifically urban sociologists, in addition to being reduced in number, have participated only marginally in the more recent development of postmodern critical urban and regional studies and in theorizing the dramatic socio-spatial changes that have been taking place in the city and in urbanism as a way of life over the past several decades.

The most significant sociological contributions to the postmetropolitan discourse in the USA have come from carefully measured empirical studies and statistical descriptions of the social restratification of highly globalized *urban labor markets*, such as those in New York, Los Angeles, Chicago, and Miami. The urban labor market, with its defined occupational categories, has served as the major grid through which stratification patterns based on class (income, status, power), gender, race, and ethnicity are represented and analyzed. Paralleling the interpretation of the restructuring of urban spatial form discussed in the previous chapter, the restructuring of urban social form is interpreted through the changing social configurations that arise from the impact of globalization and postfordist (although more typically postindustrial) economic change. Of particular importance in these studies has been the infiltration into the labor market of immigrant populations and the impact this has on the native-born workforce. And also paralleling the third discourse, the discourse on the restructured social mosaic has over the years generated a host of new terms to describe the contemporary dynamics of social restructuring. Not surprisingly, these new terms have been concentrated on the population segments that have contributed most to increasing metropolarities and the widening gap in incomes: the yuppie-fed overseer class of Upper Professionals and the immigrant-gorged underclass of the truly disadvantaged and the working poor.

Analyzing the restructuring of urban labor markets has become as much an emblematic research focus for the fourth discourse as the industrial or sectoral case study has been in the discourse on industrial urbanism. Earlier analysts posited a relatively simple structure to labor markets, usually looked at mainly at the national rather than the urban scale. Based on skill levels, education, occupation, and income (assuming direct returns to human capital), the workforce was seen as reflecting the general pattern of American society. The vast majority of the population, assumed by most to be larger in size than

---

10   I use the terms "displaced" and "despecified" here to describe a long-term trend in the discipline of sociology that has loosened its attachments to the specific material contexts and geographies of the city, reducing them to reflections of larger, often aspatially represented *social* processes. In its extreme expressions, this trend virtually sublimates the "urban" of urban sociology into pure sociality, making the spatiality (and at times also the historicity) of the city merely backdrops or reflections of sociologically conceived and universalized "societal" processes, such as stratification.

in any other country, was classified as middle-class, with upper (professionals, managers), middle (mainly white-collar), and lower (largely blue-collar) subdivisions. Above and below on the income ladder were the rich and the poor, the former often not considered true workers and the latter also falling off the bottom edge of the formal or defined labor market. Keeping this hierarchical structure together was the hope for mobility, the possibility of rising higher up the ladder.[11]

This simple structure was modified slightly by the recognition of a significant internal barrier dividing what was called the "primary" and "secondary" labor markets, with the secondary market experiencing much greater constraints on social mobility. This labor market *dualism* was made more complicated by models of labor market *segmentation*, which recognized not just a bipartite division but a more complex *compartmentalization* based on race, ethnicity, gender, and other distinguishing characteristics. Mobility "ceilings" of various sorts were identified and studied for many different occupational, racial, ethnic, and gender segments. These studies raised important questions about discrimination as a seedbed for generating "unnecessary" and more easily eradicable inequalities, especially with regard to women and African Americans; but they also identified specialized ethnic and gender *enclaves* or *niches* where such compartmentalization provided some added opportunity for social mobility. In effect, the labor market as a whole was seen as being overlaid by many different *divisions of labor* based not just on skill, education, and income but also, and especially, on gender, race, and ethnicity. These patternings, and especially the discovery of ceilings and other forms of discriminatory labor practices, fostered and fed the growth of what has been described as *equality politics*, based in feminist, black nationalist, ethnic, gay and lesbian, and other struggles aimed at achieving greater job opportunities, income, and mobility. I will return to these struggles for greater equality in the next section.

The most recent developments and most of the new descriptive language used in labor market studies today revolve around the restructuring of the three fundamental strata defined previously around the wealthy, the middle class, and the poor. Looking first at the top of the income ladder, we can see an extraordinary expansion in the number of millionaires in America and an unusually diverse composition of what used to be called the *nouveau riche*. Drawing on a still older concept, I am tempted to describe the upper 10 percent as containing a sort of reserve army of the wealthy, a "lumpenbourgeoisie" consisting not just of the barons of industry and finance but increasingly of rock stars and baseball players, computer software specialists and real estate agents, celebrity hairdressers and employment headhunters, drug dealers and dentists, stockbrokers and fashion designers, and thousands of homeowners who were lucky enough to buy at the

11   This was true despite the fact that one of the most persistent empirical findings of labor market analysts was that a person's class position was most directly correlated with his/her father's class position, a sign of extraordinary cross-generational stability in the system of social stratification.

right time in the right place. Never before perhaps have the top percentiles of the income ladder been so heterogeneous, so internally divided, so *déclassé*, and, like Marx's original concept of the lumpenproletariat, so politically unpredictable.[12]

The fastest track between the middle and upper classes has been trail-blazed by a group whose name has become synonymous with rapid upward mobility. *Yuppies*, or young urban professionals, have come to symbolize the main newcomers to the growing executive-professional-managerial class of overseers that Daniel Bell called the "new dominant class" of the postindustrial city. Such Upper Professionals, another frequently used term, may not constitute a cohesive class and probably do not control the highest peaks of economic and political power in the postmetropolis, but they increasingly influence daily life in the city and the look of the urban landscape through their control over the information-bloated urban imaginary. Upper Professionals and their families today probably make up close to one-third of the population in Los Angeles and New York, a much higher percentage than existed thirty years ago. In Los Angeles, their leading edge springs primarily from the entertainment industry and the new technocracy associated with high-technology electronics, biomedicine, and aerospace production; while in New York stockbrokers, bond dealers, and other FIRE-men and women tend to lead the way.

In almost every postmetropolis, the Upper Professionals have become the most aggressive territorial in-fighters in the public domain of planning and urban policy, forming an army of "gentrifiers" struggling to establish and maintain their distinctive lifestyles and lived spaces in the literal and figurative heart of the city. They tend to be younger and more central city-focused than their Fordist predecessors, who typically moved quietly to the suburbs in privatized households far from the (usually male) breadwinner's place of work. The present generation demands much more and has the public and private power to make its demands fit into the crowded, edgy, and fragmented built environment, increasingly shaping the citybuilding process to their own image. As Christine Boyer notes for New York City: "Luxury neighborhoods, food shops, boutiques, entertainment zones, and television and information nodes are commanding more and more territory and displacing many of the city's former residents, functions, and services."[13]

The dominant metaphor used to describe what has been happening to the once-swollen middle classes is a *squeeze*, a societal belt-tightening that has

---

12   Marx defined the lumpenproletariat as a "free floating mass" rather than a clearly defined social group with a well-articulated political stance. The lumpenproletariat tends to become important, he argued, only in times of crisis and social disintegration, when the free floating mass becomes particularly vulnerable to "reactionary ideologies" such as fascism. Turning Marx on his head, if not over in his grave, the notion of a lumpenbourgeoisie as used here also implies a politics susceptible to both radical and reactionary ideologies, to a confusing mix of Left and Right.

13   M. Christine Boyer, "The Return of Aesthetics to City Planning," *Society* (1988), 49–56. See also the work of Sharon Zukin, especially *Landscapes of Power: From Detroit to Disney World*, Berkeley and Los Angeles: University of California Press, 1991.

changed the overall shape of the labor market. Some analysts speak of the "missing middle" or a new "dumbbell" shape to urban labor markets arising from a pronounced polarization that has allowed a fortunate few to rise to the highest income levels while a much larger segment has suffered significant downward mobility. The industrial urbanists have attributed this middle-class squeeze to technological, institutional, and geographical forces intrinsic to postfordist and flexibly specialized industrial economies and intensified by the declining role of unions and the weakening of the welfare state. Most comprehensive statistical studies, however, have not shown as prominent a squeeze as expected from the arguments of the deindustrialization-reindustrialization theorists, especially when household income data are used. This apparent contradiction is explainable in large part because the undoubted squeeze on the middle class has been responded to, at least in the USA, by a profound change in household economies and attendant family life. A key part of this response has been an unprecedented increase in women's participation in the labor market, particularly for women with children. Accompanying this influx has been a rapid rise in the number of multi-job households, a lengthening of the workday that has reversed the trend of the past century and a half, and an explosion of part-time work and "contingency" jobs (seasonal, temporary, specific task-oriented) that has made Manpower Inc. the largest employer in the country.[14]

Income maintenance for the stressed middle class has become a very different process from what it was thirty years ago. Job security is less dependable, benefits are often curtailed, employee pension funds are much less reliable, and the one-job family is fast becoming a tiny minority at almost every level of the income ladder. DINK households (double income, no kids) have become more common, as have households where women are the primary breadwinners. Young adult children tend to reside longer at home and increasing numbers of divorced or unemployed adults return to live with their parents. These efforts to offset what has been a long decline in real personal salaries and wages has enabled average household incomes to continue to rise over the past thirty years of crisis-generated restructuring, union-busting, the disintegrating welfare state, privatization, deregulation, and rising rates of poverty. Focusing attention on rising household incomes has thus become a way of obscuring the profound income squeeze that has affected the American middle class over the past thirty years.

As much as anything else, what has made continued growth of household incomes possible has been the spectacular success of the American job machine, with its primary motors located in Los Angeles, Houston, Miami, New York, and other leading postmetropolitan regions. Critics have argued that most of the jobs generated are at low wages, with few benefits and often with little chance for upward mobility. But many are also high-end and very

14 For an analysis of the lengthening of the working day, see Juliet B. Schor, *The Overworked American: The Unexpected Decline of Leisure*, New York: Basic Books, 1991.

well paid. The most serious problem may not be the quality of the jobs *per se* as much as the social and psychological costs associated with the new household employment strategies. The continued generation of jobs in the American economy is very much a major factor shaping the globalized postfordist postmetropolis. It can be linked to the growth of Outer Cities and Garreau's most successful Edge Cities, reflecting the Exopolis turned inside-out; and it is also related to the "peripheralization" of the inner cities, with their pools of unskilled labor, immigrant entrepreneurs, and the working poor, evoking the Exopolis turned outside-in. But it is in such places as Lennox, Pomona, Moreno Valley, and Palmdale where its negative effects are most pronounced, not because there is a lack of jobs but because of the costs involved in maintaining established income levels and lifestyles. These cases represent many of the hidden dimensions of the surge of inequality in the USA. They can be easily buried under aggregate data analyses or excessive attention to the success stories of restructuring, but they are an intrinsic part of the postmetropolitan transition.

Also intrinsic to the postmetropolitan transition is what has been happening to the bottom end of the social hierarchy, underneath the middle-class squeeze. Downward mobility and the new poverty have generated another set of neologisms, as representative of the restructured social mosaic as yuppies and the DINKs. Once well-off workers are described as having been "K-Marted" or "Burger Kinged" as their income is cut in half in their forced move from manufacturing to the burgeoning services economy. A growing population of "new orphans" fills the streets with children abandoned by (or voluntarily abandoning) their parents and with the elderly poor (as opposed to "woopies," well-off older people) abandoned by their children. Bands of homeless runaway youth compete for living space in desolated "landscapes of despair" and "welfare-dependent ghettoes";[15] while older forms of domestic and industrial slavery and peonage have re-emerged in new guises, as immigrants from Indonesia, Thailand, China, and Central America are imported and sold to wealthy households as live-in domestic servants, their passports held by their "owners" in return for limited room and board. A "sweatshop economy" of Dickensian proportions gathers other immigrants, often undocumented and mainly women, into hazardous worksites toiling for sub-minimum wages backed by constant threats of deportation. And huge homeless populations overflow from Skid Rows to form their own geographies throughout the urban fabric, with their largest concentrations unhoused in Los Angeles and New York, the homeless capitals of America.[16]

15 Susan M. Ruddick, *Young and Homeless in Hollywood: Mapping Social Identities*, New York and London: Routledge, 1996.
16 For more detailed statistics on the working poor and homeless in Los Angeles, see Paul Ong and Evelyn Blumenberg, "Income and Racial Inequality in Los Angeles," and Jennifer Wolch, "From Global to Local: The Rise of Homelessness in Los Angeles During the 1980s," both in Scott and Soja eds., *The City: Los Angeles and Urban Theory at the End of the Twentieth Century*, 1996: 311–35 and 390–425.

Moving beyond equality politics

The accumulating evidence of deepening and widening metropolarities has reinforced the need for a vigorous and strengthened politics aimed specifically at reducing rising socio-economic inequality. At the same time, however, potent counterforces have developed from a wide variety of sources to blunt the impact of social movements built specifically around categorically defined "binary" politics. In other words, just when the polarizations built around class (labor versus capital), race (black versus white), and gender (women versus men), the three most entrenched axes of inequality in contemporary American society, have become intensified, it has become increasingly difficult to mobilize around each of these separate channels of political struggle. But it is not just the intensified opposition to a more radical equality politics that is blunting its effect. The postmetropolitan transition itself has created a significantly altered context for the struggles to achieve greater social and spatial equality and justice. In particular, the axes or categories around which inequality is defined have changed significantly, becoming more complex, multi-sided, and intertwined. In this restructured urban milieu, equality politics in its conventional forms may be increasingly necessary, but at the same time many of the traditional practices of equality politics have also become increasingly limiting and ineffective.

This has given rise to attempts to move beyond equality politics to new strategies for achieving social and spatial justice that are more adaptive to the specificities of the globalized, postfordist, exopolitan, and culturally heterogeneous contemporary urban society. In *Thirdspace*, I linked these adaptive strategies to the development of a *new cultural politics* that approaches the problems of inequality not by focusing political struggles solely around the rigidly defined and often exclusionary channels of resistance based on class, race, and gender; but also around more cross-cutting and inclusive foundations of solidarity, collective consciousness, and coalition building. Drawing on the literature in critical cultural studies, and especially the work of radical women of color, whose lived experience most effectively combines the oppressions of class, race, and gender, I described the new cultural politics as building on three converging discursive "turns" in critical theory and practice: cultural, postmodern, and spatial.

The *cultural turn* has been most widely recognized and forms the basis for the terminological shift from an equality politics defined primarily around socio-economic status and power to a specifically cultural politics where the aim is not just to reduce inequalities but also to redefine on a much broader scale how inequalities of power and status are used to foster economic exploitation, cultural domination, and individual oppression. Attacking inequality remains central to the political agenda, but the agenda is also opened up to more encompassing questions of *identity, representation,* and *difference*; in other words, to how differences between people are intrinsically created, externally imposed, and culturally represented through a politically charged process of identity formation and what cultural scholars call the construction of the subject, with its double-barreled meaning of assertive (subjective) identity and imposed subjection. What is new and different about this cultural politics is captured by Cornel West:

> Distinctive features of the new cultural politics of difference are to trash the monolithic and homogeneous in the name of diversity, multiplicity, and heterogeneity; to reject the abstract, general, and universal in light of the concrete, specific, and particular; and to historicize, contextualize, and pluralize by highlighting the contingent, provisional, variable, tentative, shifting and changing . . . To put it bluntly, the new cultural politics of difference consists of creative responses to the precise circumstances of our present moment . . . in order to empower and enable social action.[17]

Note that this new cultural politics is not defined around erasing inequalities *per se* but rather around the reassertion of *difference*, diversity, multiplicity, heterogeneity. The intent here is to avoid being confined to those narrow and often exclusionary channels of resistance built specifically around the categories of class, race, gender, sexual orientation, age, nation, nature, region, etc.: an avoidance that often creates significant conflicts between the new cultural politics and more conventional social movements separately defined around each of these categories. Rather than seeing difference, including the difference associated with intergroup inequalities, only as something to be erased, the *right to be different* is asserted as the foundation of the new cultural politics. Hence the description of the new cultural politics as a politics of difference rather than of equality. This results in a marked contrast between the old and the new politics with respect to the strategic significance of fragmentation, or the multiplication of progressive social movements. Whereas in the past such multiplicity was seen as almost inevitably weakening the political power of channeled struggles, in the new cultural politics it becomes both a danger and an *opportunity*, a heterogeneous reality that must be recognized and used to mobilize a more open, adaptively recombinant, coalition-building politics.

The cultural turn has been integrally related to the development of a powerful postmodern epistemological critique of modernist theories and political as well as aesthetic practices. This postmodern turn has been particularly effective in attacking the limitations of binary thinking and its prominent application in what can now be defined as the old modernist equality politics. Rather than simply rejecting the importance of such binaries as labor–capital, black–white, woman–man, gay–straight, the postmodern cultural critique seeks to re-articulate them in combinatorial and inclusionary networks that are more adaptive to "the precise circumstances of our present moment," to a politics that can respond more effectively to the conditions of postmodernity and the specificities of the postmetropolitan transition. As a quick summation

17 Cornel West, "The New Cultural Politics of Difference," in R. Ferguson et al. eds., *Out There,* Cambridge, MA: MIT Press, and New York: New Museum of Contemporary Art, 1990: 19–20.

of both the cultural and postmodern turns and as a connecting link to the increasing spatial turn that is currently being infused into the new cultural politics, I look again to bell hooks:

> Postmodern culture with its decentered subject can be the space where ties are severed or it can provide the occasion for new and varied forms of bonding. To some extent, ruptures, surfaces, contextuality, and a host of other happenings create gaps that make space for oppositional practices which no longer require intellectuals to be confined to narrow separate spheres with no meaningful connection to the world of the everyday . . . A space is there for critical exchange . . . [and] this may very well be "the" central future location of resistance struggle, a meeting place where new and radical happenings can occur.[18]

The *spatial turn* has been the most recent addition to the specialized discourse on the new cultural politics, and it is also the conceptual underpinning and critical driving force behind every chapter in *Postmetropolis*. What it has done is to energize the new cultural politics around a shared consciousness of the interrelations of space, knowledge, and power; and how the social production of human spatiality, from the global to the most local scales, is an active part of the creation and maintenance of inequality and injustice, of economic exploitation, cultural domination, and individual oppression. If traditional equality politics mobilizes its radical subjectivity most expansively around taking collective control over the "making of history," then the new cultural politics of difference, identity, and representation, without lessening the power of its historically inspired strategies, adds a new source of mobilized consciousness rooted in the more immediate collective struggle to *take greater control over the "making of geography" – the social production of human spatiality*. This involvement in producing and in already produced spaces and places is what all those who are oppressed, subordinated, and exploited share, and it is this shared consciousness and practice of an explicitly spatial politics that can provide an additional bonding force for combining those separate channels of resistance and struggle that for so long have fragmented modernist equality politics.

Although the spatial turn has deeper intellectual roots, it was only in the late 1990s that its impact extended beyond academic discourse to affect postmetropolitan politics in a significant way. Open-ended coalitions aimed specifically at addressing the multiple oppressions of race, class, gender, sexuality, and other individual and collective sources of marginalization and inequality are increasingly being mobilized in many postmetropolitan regions around a shared spatial consciousness, an awareness that oppression, marginality, and inequality are produced and reproduced to a significant degree through the new urbanization processes and the restructured socio-spatialities of urbanism. One small but important example, the Bus Riders Union, was mentioned in the previous chapter. The growing movement for environmen-

18   bell hooks, *Yearning: Race, Gender, and Cultural Politics*, Boston: South End Press, 1990: 31.

tal justice provides many more examples of fundamentally spatial struggles, as do the new movements redefining postmetropolitan citizenship and the "rights to the city," mentioned in chapter 7 on the globalization of cityspace. A more inclusionary feminism, moving beyond older boundaries of gender, race, class, and sexual preference, is beginning to reshape postmetropolitan cityspace, as are new *intercultural* coalitions that consciously combine formerly separate and often antagonistic racial and ethnic groupings, such as African Americans and Koreans in Los Angeles. The urban social movements of the past are becoming more explicitly *spatial* movements as well, responding directly to the geographically uneven effects of globalization, postfordist economic restructuring, and the reconfiguration of urban form. To use an increasingly popular trope, these political movements are beginning to open up new "spaces of resistance" in the postmetropolis, not just as figures of speech but also as concrete sites for progressive political action.

This brief discussion of the new cultural politics of space and place provides only a fleeting glimpse of a much larger and more complex development that cannot be effectively summarized in a few paragraphs. It serves more as an invitation to the reader to think differently about contemporary urban politics and to look for similar examples of explicitly spatial movements and struggles in other cities and regions. I specifically make this invitation here, however, in a discussion of the restructured social mosaic of the postmetropolis, for this fourth discourse has evolved with perhaps the least attention of all the discourses to the impact of the cultural, postmodern, and spatial turns. The relative absence of a critical cultural, postmodern, and spatial perspective has significantly weakened the theoretical, empirical, and practical discourses on the restructuring of sociality in the postmetropolis as well as on the problems arising from the dramatic surge of inequality that has been associated with the postmetropolitan transition. All that has preceded this chapter and all that will follow is in large part an attempt to reassert what has been missing, or only weakly developed, in the fourth discourse itself.

Remapping the Fractal City of Los Angeles

In keeping with the practice of heading each chapter in Part II with an emblematic name that would effectively capture the focus of the represented discourse, I have chosen the term *fractal city* to describe the restructured social mosaic of the postmetropolis. This was not an easy choice, nor am I completely comfortable with it. Initially, this chapter was simply titled "Metropolarities" to configure the discourse around the multiplying and cross-cutting social polarizations that have developed in cityspaces such as Los Angeles and New York. For a time, I settled on the term heteropolis, borrowing from a book on Los Angeles by the architectural historian and critic Charles Jencks. Heteropolis captured the extraordinary diversity and cultural heterogeneity being produced by the new urbanization processes, but there seemed to be a greater complexity and instability to the restructured social mosaic, a kaleidoscopic quality that was not quite captured in this term. Finally, the concept of fractals came to mind as a useful description of the combined and interactive spatiality and sociality of the postmetropolis.

Very broadly defined, a fractal is anything that contains in its parts self-similar images of the whole. One common example is the blood vessels in your hand, which resemble the entire circulatory system of the body. This was an appealing quality, suggesting that each piece of the restructured sociospatial mosaic can be seen as a kind of social hieroglyph representing and revealing all the complex dynamics of the postmetropolitan transition, much as Marx used a simple commodity such as a pin or a pair of shoes to open up a critical discussion of the inner workings of the whole capitalist economy. There is also a compelling analogy here to my arguments about *lived space*. Adapting a critical thirdspatial perspective allows us to see in every empirical site, from the body to the global sphere, the fundamental nature of the spatiality of human life in all its richness and complexity, much as an individual biography or a social history opens up possibilities to consider all aspects of the general human condition.

The theory of fractals has another appealing feature, one which both constrains and enables a deeper understanding of localized geographies. It has developed in close association with chaos theory, an attempt to make sense of extraordinary complexity, to uncode what appears to be disordered and chaotic in ways that make the resplendent chaos a little more comprehensible. Postmetropolitan cityspace is probably as chaotic in its social and spatial configuration as any other in the long history of cities. Yet there are some significant patternings to be discovered if one looks at cityspace in new ways, with a different set of interpretive lenses from those traditionally used by urbanists in the past (and many in the present as well).

What follows, then, is an attempt to map the Fractal City that is embedded in and activates the restructured social and spatial mosaic of Los Angeles. Although built upon a discoverable orderliness and a presumed representative relation between the parts and the whole, the fractal city is also streaked through with unsettled complexity and instability, placing significant constraints on confident generalization and accurate cartography. Accepting these constraints, let us look at the representations of Los Angeles as a heterogeneous mosaic of new and old ethnicities.

An overview of the ethnic mosaic

Four to five million immigrants, perhaps more if we count those missed by census enumerators, now live in the Los Angeles metropolitan region, about 20 percent of all immigrants in the USA. The densest concentrations are in the City and County of Los Angeles, where the proportion of foreign-born residents comes close to matching the 40 percent peak achieved in turn-of-the-century New York. When the domestic Asian, Latino, and African American populations are added, the urban region can be described as having a "majority of minorities," another of those provocative oxymorons that describe the postmetropolis. When it is remembered that the regional population in 1960 was about 80 percent Anglo, the magnitude of the demographic and cultural transformation becomes even more impressive.

Furthermore, there is growing evidence that the urban minorities, domestic and foreign-born, in postmetropolitan Los Angeles have some of the highest levels of intra-ethnic inequality in the industrialized world. A recent national survey has shown, for example, that Los Angeles contains both the richest and the poorest predominantly African American communities in urban America and my guess is that similar results would be found for Mexican-American and some Asian American ethnic groups as well. In the early 1990s, Jeffrey Reitz, a Canadian sociologist, arrived in Los Angeles with some comparative statistics he had collected on levels of income inequality among recent immigrant populations in US, Canadian, and Australian cities. His data had surprised him, for of all the metropolitan areas he surveyed, the three with the highest levels of immigrant inequality were Los Angeles-Long Beach, Orange County, and San Bernardino-Riverside.[19] That they were among the fastest-growing of all the urban areas surveyed was also significant.

How this majority of minorities has etched itself into the social and spatial orders, and especially into the regional labor market, has generated an expansive local literature. Of the many published resources currently available for studying the restructured social mosaic, three stand out for their comprehensiveness and empirical richness. *The Ethnic Quilt: Population Diversity in Southern California* (1997), written and mapped by James P. Allen and Eugene Turner, and published by the Center for Geographical Studies, California State University-Northridge, presents an expansive tapestry of maps, text, and tables that can be pored over endlessly for the information it offers and the reinterpretations it stimulates.[20] This remarkable atlas-text provides a valuable introduction to the specific geography of ethnic Los Angeles and a stimulating benchmark for comparative studies with other urban regions.

A product of a collaborative research project by students in Urban Planning at UCLA, *The Widening Divide: Income Inequality and Poverty in Los Angeles* (1989) draws from the new literature on urban and industrial restructuring to explore in more detail the intensified polarizations of race, ethnicity, and gender being generated in Los Angeles.[21] Organized and edited by the urban planner and labor economist Paul Ong, also a specialist in computer mapping and geographical information systems (GIS), *The Widening Divide* received widespread attention in local and national news media, and added the concept

---

19 Personal communication. These surveys were eventually incorporated into Jeffrey G. Reitz, *Warmth of the Welcome: The Social Causes of Economic Success in Different Nations and Cities*, Boulder, CO: Westview Press, 1998.

20 See also Eugene Turner and James P. Allen, *An Atlas of Population Patterns in Metropolitan Los Angeles and Orange Counties 1990*, published by the Center for Geographical Studies, Department of Geography, California State University-Northridge, 1991.

21 Authored by the Research Group on the Los Angeles Economy, unpublished report, Urban Planning, UCLA (1989).

of the predominantly Latino and largely female "working poor" to the national scholarly and policy debates on poverty in America. In contrast to the national discourse, which was focused on Frostbelt deindustrialization, a primarily African American urban underclass, and "postindustrial society" explanations, Ong and his students offered a Southern Californian perspective, showing that even greater levels of income inequality and poverty can be generated in the most successfully reindustrialized region in the country and among populations with relatively low levels of unemployment and welfare dependency.[22]

The third notable contribution is *Ethnic Los Angeles* (1996), co-edited by Roger Waldinger and Mehdi Bozorgmehr.[23] Written from a primarily sociological perspective (fifteen of the contributors are sociologists), the book also contains chapters by geographers (William A. V. Clark and Allen Scott), urban planners (Paul Ong and Abel Valenzuela), a historian (John Laslett), and an ethnic studies specialist (Philip Yang). All except Yang were either students or faculty at UCLA. Roger Waldinger, formerly based in New York City where he was a leading scholar studying New York's immigrant populations and ethnic division of labor, is the key figure behind *Ethnic Los Angeles*.[24] His work has focused on networking strategies, niche formation, and patterns of social stratification within the changing ethnic division of labor in Los Angeles.

Drawing on these and other sources, a finer-grained mapping of the changing ethnic mosaic can be constructed. In 1990, the population of the five-county Los Angeles CMSA (Consolidated Metropolitan Statistical Area) was 14.5 million, with the following breakdown by major ethnic category:

Non-Hispanic White	7.2 million (49.8 percent)
Black	1.2 million (8.5 percent)
Hispanic	4.8 million (33.0 percent)
Asian/Pacific Islander	1.3 million (9.2 percent)

The dramatic demographic transformation of the region is exemplified best in Los Angeles County, where the proportion of non-Hispanic whites or Anglos, to use the local term, was cut in half (from 80.8 in 1960 to 40.8 percent in 1990),

22   Ong and his colleagues have also produced some of the best work on social polarization within Asian American populations. See Paul Ong, Edna Bonacich, and Lucie Cheng, *The New Asian Immigration in Los Angeles and Global Restructuring*, Philadelphia: Temple University Press, 1994. Distinguishing Ong's work is his strong concern for planning and public policy responses to increasing metropolarities.

23   Roger Waldinger and Mehdi Bozorgmehr eds., *Ethnic Los Angeles*, New York: Russell Sage Foundation, 1996. See also Roger Waldinger, "Immigration and the Los Angeles Economy," paper presented at a conference on "Los Angeles: Economic Challenges and Opportunities," Lewis Center for Regional Policy Studies, UCLA School of Public Policy and Social Research, December 1994.

24   Roger Waldinger, *Through the Eye of the Needle: Immigrants and Enterprise in New York's Garment Trades*, New York: New York University Press, 1986; Thomas Bailey and Roger Waldinger, "The Changing Ethnic Division of Labor," in John Mollenkopf and Manuel Castells eds., *Dual City: Restructuring New York*, New York: Russell Sage Foundation, 1991: 43–78.

while the Hispanic population (henceforth Latino) grew from 577,000 (9.6 percent) to 3,350,000 (37.8 percent). All current estimates suggest that Latinos are now the largest ethnic group in the county. The county's black population doubled over these thirty years, but there are indications that its numbers peaked in the early 1990s and have now begun to decline. The largest percentage increase (from 1.9 to 10.8) was for Asians and Pacific Islanders, who outnumbered blacks in the CMSA in 1990 and today probably outnumber them in Los Angeles County as well.

The white population has also decreased proportionately in the outer four counties (Orange, Riverside, San Bernardino, and Ventura), but at the same time there has been a significant growth in population numbers, suggesting a large intrametropolitan shift from Inner to Outer cities, partially induced by the phenomenon known as white flight. While Los Angeles County had a net decrease in whites (1960–90) of 1.3 million, mainly from the more densely populated southern half of the county, this was matched by a net increase of 2.1 million in the outer counties. The other three ethnic groupings also participated in this intrametropolitan shift, with the black population increasing by over 200,000 (mainly in San Bernardino County), Asians by 370,000 (heavily concentrated in Orange County), and the more widely dispersed Latinos by nearly 1.25 million.

Decomposing these aggregate figures for the region, a more detailed picture of Ethnic Los Angeles can be constructed. The following is a list of the largest ethnic populations in 1990 by country of origin, with additional data for median household income and percent foreign-born over the age of 25, drawn from Allen and Turner, *The Ethnic Quilt*.

Population by of origin country	*Population 1990*	*Median household income ($)*	*Percent foreign-born over age 25*
1. Mexican	3,751,278	29,160	62.7
2. African	1,229,809	26,350	7.5
3. English	993,735	43,000	7.4
4. Chinese	304,588	39,600	90.0
5. Filipino	291,618	48,000	92.0
6. Salvadoran	274,788	22,200	99.0
7. Russian	196,467	51,000	13.3
8. Korean	194,437	32,000	97.9
9. Japanese	173,370	46,000	37.1
10. Vietnamese	148,217	34,700	99.0
11. Guatemalan	139,650	22,650	98.1
12. Armenian	111,138	30,300	81.4

The numbers for each of these groups, except perhaps African Americans, have increased significantly since 1990. In terms of population size, the group that stands out most clearly is of Mexican origin, split roughly two-thirds/one-third into foreign- versus native-born, the latter comprising the large (more than 1.2 million) Chicano/a population. The African- and English-origin populations have by far the smallest percentage of foreign-born, but the figures for the Japanese also indicate a high proportion of native-born Japanese Americans, who, like Chicano/as, have developed a distinctive localized identity. Each of these ethnic groupings homogenize significant differences in country or region of origin. The Chinese foreign-born, for example, come primarily from the People's Republic of China and Taiwan, but there are also large numbers from Vietnam, Hong Kong, and Malaysia, with each group maintaining its distinctive traditions.[25] Such intra-ethnic group differences represent an important but understudied aspect of the Los Angeles cosmopolis.

The median household income data provide a first glimpse at some of the ethnic polarities of wealth and poverty in Los Angeles. The highest income groups are Russian (a large proportion of whom are Jewish) and Filipino, a population that is frequently fluent in both English and Spanish and also disproportionately made up of professionals specializing in particular in nursing and medicine. Interestingly, the Russian-origin population has the greatest gap of any group between the personal incomes of the native- and foreign-born, with the former earning nearly twice as much as the latter. On a longer list of 34 ethnic groups, Asian Indians come next (MHI = $47,000), followed by the Japanese, English, Israeli, Pakistani, Iranian, and Turkish populations, all of whom have median household incomes of $40,000 or higher. At the opposite end of the income ladder are the nearly 35,000 Cambodians ($20,160), followed closely by Salvadorans and Guatemalans. What these data show is that the greatest income polarities *within* the four major ethnic groupings are found among Asian-Pacific Islanders and, in particular, between two populations originating from Southeast Asia, Filipino and Cambodian. Such unexpected income inequalities pepper the ethnic mosaic.

The Ethnic Quilt also contains a rich depiction of ethnic niches within the greater Los Angeles labor market, and these occupational specializations add another dimension to the fractal city. Here is a listing of the strongest ethnic niches, with the number indicating the percentage of all workers in that occupation who are in the ethnic group (*The Ethnic Quilt*: table 8.4, pp. 211–12).

Lawyer	White men	88.5
Actor, director	White men	86.1
Actor, director	White women	85.1
Marketing, advertising	White men	83.5
Farm worker	Mexican women	78.4

25 One example of these intra-ethnic differences arose when Hong Kong Chinese developers revealed plans to build a high-rise apartment complex in the old Chinatown, reminiscent of their crowded island urbanism back home. They were resisted by other Chinese for not fitting into the local cultural landscape. As the new suburban Chinatown has developed in the area around Monterey Park, similar clashes have occurred over the built environment between the majority of Taiwanese and other Chinese groups.

Textile sewing machine operator	Mexican men	68.4
Groundskeeper	Mexican men	60.3
Busboy, kitchen assistant	Mexican men	57.0
Textile sewing machine operator	Mexican women	56.7
Assembler	Mexican men	52.2
Cook	Mexican men	52.0
Assembler	Mexican women	51.6
Construction laborer	Mexican men	49.8
Electronic equipment assembler	Mexican men	43.9
Electronic equipment assembler	Mexican women	41.9
Postal clerk	Black women	40.3
Janitor, cleaner	Black women	38.0
Bus driver	Black women	35.6
Private household servant	Black women	35.2
Bus driver	Black men	33.5
Postal clerk	Black men	28.4
Guard, police (private)	Black women	23.7
Licensed vocational nurse	Black women	22.5
Nursing aid, orderly	Black women	22.3
Guard, police (private)	Black men	21.5
Social worker	Black women	20.9
Private household servant	Salvadoran women	20.8

Other "ethnic specializations," where a group's representation is more than five times their labor market average, include for MEN: food service, lodging manager (Chinese), accountant (Filipino), electrical engineer (Chinese), physician (Russian, Chinese), lawyer and actor, director (Russian), clinical laboratory technician (Filipino, Chinese), electronic technician (Vietnamese), cashier (Korean), computer operator (Filipino), bookkeeper, accounting clerk (Filipino), postal clerk (Filipino), mail carrier (Black, Filipino), general office clerk (Black, Filipino), cook (Chinese), nursing aid, orderly (Black, Filipino), painter (Salvadoran), electronic equipment assembler (Vietnamese), and textile sewing machine operator (Salvadoran, Guatemalan). Ethnic specializations for WOMEN include accountant (Chinese), aerospace engineer (Chinese), electrical engineer (Chinese), computer systems analyst (Chinese), physician (Filipino, Russian, Asian Indian), registered nurse (Filipino), pharmacist (Chinese, Korean, Vietnamese), lawyer and actor, director (Russian), clinical laboratory technician and licensed vocational nurse (Filipino), electronic technician and electronic equipment assembler (Vietnamese), computer programmer (Chinese), computer operator (Black), postal clerk (Chinese), household childcare worker (Salvadoran, Guatemalan), private household servant (Guatemalan), janitor, cleaner (Black, Salvadoran), hairdresser, cosmetologist (Vietnamese), and textile sewing machine operator (Salvadoran, Chinese).

This tableau of ethnic occupational niches presents a vivid picture of everyday life in contemporary Los Angeles. For those who live here, it is both familiar and fascinating. For those who do not, it is a complex ethnic patterning of work that calls out for comparative study in other postmetropolitan regions. The empirical patterning of the restructured social mosaic is effectively summarized in a representatively sociological language by Roger Waldinger in his concluding chapter to *Ethnic Los Angeles*, "Ethnicity and Opportunity in the Plural City." I have added emphasis to Waldinger's discursive terms and phrases.

Los Angeles is now profoundly, irremediably ethnic. The issue confronting the region is whether this newly *polyglot metropolis* can work. And that is not a question for the region alone. In L.A., late twentieth-century America finds a mirror to itself. Los Angeles, after all, is not an old, decaying inner city. Instead, it is America's *quintessential suburb*, the dynamic product of postwar U.S. capitalism at its most robust, and for that reason, as the writer David Reid noted, "the American city the world watches for signs and portents." (1996: 447)

The region's pattern of ethnic specialization also constitutes a *system of inequality*. Even the most fortunate of the new Angelenos are some distance from the top of the hierarchy, as can be seen from a comparison with native-born Russians/Jews, the one persistently ethnic European-origin group . . . Chinese and Japanese Americans have moved into advantageous specializations, where they find ample opportunity to work in white-collar jobs and do better in *industries of lower ethnic density*. Other groups – African and Mexican American, as well as Korean, Filipino, and Vietnamese immigrants, for example – occupy the *middle ranges of the continuum*, sometimes doing better in *industries of high ethnic density*, sometimes doing worse. Mexican, Salvadoran, and Guatemalan immigrants – the most concentrated of all – do the very worst, crowding into menial employment where the *wage ceiling* is extremely low.

(1996: 449)

Niching is pervasive, but not every niche proves rewarding. Some do, notably those concentrations that provide opportunities for self-employment; ethnic Angelenos who work on their own earn a considerable *self-employment bonus*, which holds even when taking *human capital factors* into account. One could add a public-sector difference comparable to the self-employment bonus; for African Americans, government is an advantageous niche because it reduces exposure to employers who might discriminate as well as to immigrants who might compete for jobs that blacks have until recently held. By contrast, Mexicans and Central Americans seem to have been herded into niches that constitute *mobility traps*; in these cases, concentration in an *ethnic specialization* saturates supply and thus increases the potential for competition with one's own kind.

(1996: 451)

Thus, the economic complexities of L.A.'s *ethnic order* cannot be reduced to the antinomies of conventional academic views. While the region's ethnic transformation has been accompanied by a *growing gap between rich and poor*, that division does not organize *the ethnic map* of contemporary L.A. The march toward greater social distinction has occurred most rapidly *within* the region's African American population; whether one looks at earnings, family patterns, or residence, better-educated African Americans are far more distant from their less-fortunate brethren today than they were in 1970. And while keeping in mind the defects of the *model minority* view, it is worth noting that native-born Asian families do better than native whites on not one but several significant indicators.

(1996: 451)

In the end, the demographic transformations of the past twenty years have created a *new ethnic division of labor* in which *ethnicity intersects with class*. The region's Chinese and Japanese Americans make up a professional middle-class integrated into the region's core industries in manufacturing and professional services. Koreans, Iranians, and Chinese immigrants make up a diversified business grouping, with Koreans struggling as an embattled *petite bourgeoisie* and Iranians and Chinese on the road to high-tech, high-skill entrepreneurship. African Americans divide into two groupings, an emergent middle-class component linked to government and other large employers and an impoverished, lower-skilled segment increasingly extruded from the employment system itself. Mexicans are likewise divided into a native-born, working/lower middle class of skilled laborers and lower-level bureaucrats that overlaps little with foreign-born ranks and an isolated immigrant proletariat confined to the bottom tiers of the region's economy where they are joined by Central Americans, the latest addition to the region's low-wage labor pool.   (1996: 454–5)

These observations derive primarily from what might be described as a discrete "matrix" view of the social mosaic. Although words such as "map" and "distance" are used, they do not refer specifically to geographical space but to an abstracted social space defined by the compartmental structure of the labor market.[26] Some attention is given to intra-ethnic differences, but each ethnicity referred to tends to be seen as a homogeneous statistical grouping that can be arrayed in comparable columns intersecting rows of selected variables. This well-established model for empirically inductive social science research has its ample virtues and in *Ethnic Los Angeles*, supplemented with more detailed ethnic case studies, it has been handled well and has generated a wealth of comparative information. So much information in fact that it is difficult to see not just the intra-ethnic patterns but also two other critical dimensions of the restructured social mosaic: the specifically spatial expression of the new social order (very little of what was discussed in the third discourse, for example, appears in *Ethnic Los Angeles*) and the emerging pattern of inter-ethnic or multicultural relations that are also an important part of the postmetropolitan transition in Los Angeles. Drawing further on the information contained in Allen and Turner's *The Ethnic Quilt* and other more geographical sources, it is possible to open up to view these additional dimensions of Los Angeles's restructured social mosaic.

26   For an excellent critique and creative spatialization of labor market studies, see Jamie Peck, *Work-Place: The Social Regulation of Labor Markets*, New York and London: Guilford Press, 1996.

Mono-ethnic geographies: segregating cityspace

Using data from the 1990 census, a base mapping can be constructed of mono-ethnic Los Angeles, portraying census tracts in which one of the four major ethno-racial groupings (African American, Asian and Pacific Islander, Latino, and non-Hispanic white) surpasses their county average percentage, one of the classic sociological indices of spatial concentration/segregation. Almost 54 percent of the *white population* of Los Angeles County, by far the highest percentage, live in such "concentrated" census tracts, and it is probable that the percentage is even higher in other surrounding counties. The most pronounced geographical concentrations (over 80 percent of tract population) occur in the wealthy Westside wedge that straddles the slopes of the Santa Monica Mountains, extending from Beverly Hills and Studio City through the elite LA City suburbs of Belair, Brentwood, and Pacific Palisades, to the newly incorporated cities of Malibu and Westlake Village, lapping over to Thousand Oaks in Ventura County.

A southern extension of this heavily white and wealthy zone clings to the Pacific shoreline (peaking in Manhattan Beach) and reaching into the Palos Verdes Peninsula, with its cluster of gated communities in Rancho Palos Verdes and Rolling Hills Estates. After a break at the port of Los Angeles and downtown Long Beach, the beachfront concentration continues into Orange County and swells inland to cover nearly all of the southern half of the county. Strung along the Pacific shores are the whitest municipalities in the region, listed in order of their Entropy Index: Newport Beach, Laguna Beach, Manhattan Beach, Seal Beach.[27] This pattern is colorfully mapped in *The Ethnic Quilt* (*EQ*) in figure 3.3 (Non-Hispanic White: Percentage of Population 1990, page 53) and in the blue sea that surrounds the inner core of non-white ethnic Los Angeles in figure 9.1 (Leading Ethnic Population, page 233).

A very different white zone stretches across the northern tier of the region, along the foothills of the San Bernardino Mountains and the High Desert Country to Ventura County, the major location for what some have described as white flight suburbs, the best-known being Simi Valley, the site of the first trial of the policemen who beat Rodney King. Two additional maps in *EQ* highlight this white flight. One shows Major Shifts in Ethnic Populations (figure 3.1, page 51), with fat white arrows emanating in all directions from the center portraying the magnitude of the centrifugal shift of white populations from Inner to Outer cities. A small map, depicting the distribution of Police and Detectives (*EQ*: figure 2.13) shows this northern white redoubt more clearly, with its peaks of concentration in Santa Clarita, the Antelope Valley, Simi Valley, and Rancho Cucamonga. These two contrasting zones of predominantly white Los Angeles represent a marked polarity of lifestyle as

27 See table 9.4 (Most and Least Ethnically Diverse Urban Places, 1990), *The Ethnic Quilt*, 1997: 243.

well as income that is not often noticed in studies of the restructured social mosaic.[28]

Densely *Latino* census tracts, in which more than 37 percent of the county's Latino population lives, are located in a remarkably obverse relation to the densest white census tracts, a spatial polarity that dominates the map of mono-ethnic Los Angeles. People of Mexican origin, by far the largest Latino population, have their densest clusters (in some places reaching close to 100 percent) in the huge *barrio* of (still unincorporated) East Los Angeles and the adjacent Boyle Heights community (once a center of the county's Jewish population), with almost continuous extensions east to Pico Rivera and Santa Fe Springs; northeast into such San Gabriel Valley communities as El Monte and Duarte, and most recently south into communities that were once the heartland of (predominantly southern) white working-class suburbia (Huntington Park, South Gate, Downey, Lynwood, Cudahy, Bell). This expanding southward wedge has experienced one of the most rapid demographic transformations in urban history, shifting from 80 percent white in 1965 to, in many areas, over 90 percent Latino today. This torrential demographic wave has virtually erased the old white–black "Cotton Curtain" that once extended north–south along Alameda Boulevard, and is now flowing rapidly into nearby areas where African Americans were once the majority (for example, Watts, where today Latinos are the largest population group). Long Beach, the often neglected second largest city in the region, has its own densely settled *barrio*, as does Santa Ana, the county seat and second largest city of Orange County. Smaller Latino barrios exist in the north San Fernando Valley in the municipality of San Fernando and the adjacent LA City community of Pacoima, on the Westside in and around Lennox, and to the east in Pomona, Ontario, and Corona.

A distinctively Central American *barrio* has developed immediately west of downtown in the communities of Westlake and Pico-Union. Located in what many local observers expected to be the major zone of expansion for the city center of Los Angeles, this still low-rise and intensely overcrowded area now reportedly contains population densities comparable to Manhattan or Calcutta. Refugees from war-torn El Salvador, post-revolutionary Nicaragua, and the repressive regimes of Guatemala have given this area a more rebellious political flavor than most other immigrant enclaves. Pico-Union was a major center of the 1992 Justice Riots and its residents provided most of the more than 1,000 allegedly undocumented persons deported by the INS (with the support of the local police despite Los Angeles's official policy of not becoming involved in deportation activities). Another polarity thus emerged in 1992, a significant contrast in political activism between predominantly Central American and Mexican *barrios*, as East Los Angeles remained relatively quiet throughout the days of conflagration.

---

28 Within the white population there are also some specialized ethnic enclaves, such as those of Armenian ancestry (population: 111,000) in Glendale and Montebello, Russian ancestry (196,000) and Israelis (13,000) in the Fairfax District and parts of the south San Fernando Valley, and the large English ancestry population (994,000) in scattered coastal and foothill areas.

The core *black* ghetto of Los Angeles has experienced a significant contraction and a definite push westward. The number of cities and communities with more than 60 percent African Americans has shrunk to five: the large (169,000) West Adams-Baldwin Hills-Leimert district within the City of Los Angeles and four small pockets of unincorporated county land (Westmont, West Compton, West Athens, and View Park-Windsor Hills), with a total population of about 55,000. The very names of these areas signal the pronounced westward shift, as well as the overall shrinkage, of the core of black Los Angeles to the area in and around the Crenshaw District. With the growth of Koreatown, and Anglo gentrification pushing from the north and the Latino wave spilling in from the east, black Los Angeles has become increasingly compacted as well as more internally polarized by income and lifestyle differences. And still further west, across the San Diego Freeway, a new racial barrier looms in the great Anglo redoubt that runs along the Pacific shores south of Los Angeles International Airport. In this prime stretch of "surfurbia," as Reyner Banham (1971) once called it, barely 1,600 African Americans were counted in the 1990 census in five beach cities with a total population of nearly 140,000. The number of LA County census tracts with no African American residents has dropped, however, from nearly 400 in 1960 to as few as four in 1990, in large part due to successful anti-racist legal struggles in the regional housing market.

This compacting of black Los Angeles has led many resident African Americans to feel a deep sense of loss. Here are some extracts from "Lost Soul: A Lament for Black Los Angeles," by Erin J. Aubry:

> The seven square-mile Crenshaw District is the only predominantly black area of Los Angeles left, and the strongest argument against cultural annihilation. The storefront churches, screen-door restaurants and itinerant nightclubs may be weary, but they're still standing, and the area is the base of operations for a hefty percentage of black businesses and institutions . . . Yet for all its activity, Crenshaw has the feel of an island, a bunker. Lifetime resident and activist Valerie Shaw [feels] "There is a tremendous sense of loss in the black community – a loss of political status, loss of neighborhoods, loss of history . . . What people are dealing with is the breaking of a continuum" . . . The black side of town is no longer a given; as a recent United Way study observed, in flat but ominous bureaucratese, "What we commonly knew of the black community over the last 20 to 30 years was geographically presented, based on a cluster of neighborhoods with a concentrated majority of the city's black population . . . However, the notion of a geographically determined black community is no longer correct or viable."[29]

Mere statistical representations can never capture these more emotional repercussions of urban restructuring, but we must move on nevertheless.

Asians, along with Pacific Islanders (who have their largest continental North American concentrations in Los Angeles) are statistically the least geo-

---

29   Erin J. Aubry, "Lost Soul: A Lament for Black Los Angeles," *LA Weekly*, December 4–10, 1998.

graphically concentrated of the four major groupings. Whereas 54 percent of whites, nearly 40 percent of African Americans, and 37 percent of Latinos in Los Angeles County live in census tracts dominated by their ethnic group, only 17 percent of Asians do. They are in the majority only in the old China-town north of downtown, in Monterey Park and some surrounding areas in the San Gabriel Valley (now dubbed the first suburban Chinatown), and in some tracts in Gardena, Cerritos, and Long Beach.[30] Somewhat lesser concen-trations exist in Koreatown, Carson, and Orange County's Little Saigon. New migrations since 1990, especially of Chinese, have probably expanded the majority Asian areas, most prominently in the San Gabriel Valley, where the largely Taiwanese concentration in Monterey Park has spilled over to adjacent communities and expanded eastward to connect with heavy Asian concen-trations in Walnut, Diamond Bar, and Hacienda Heights.

Although these mono-ethnic geographies show the persistence of volun-tary and imposed forms of residential segregation, there are also signs that spatial segregation by race and ethnicity has declined statistically over the past thirty years. This is due in part to vigorous struggles to erase restrictive covenants and reduce the impact of less institutionalized racism in the housing market, especially for African Americans. But an even greater factor has been the mass Latinoization of Los Angeles and the cross-class settlement by the Asian population. Nearly every community, including Beverly Hills and Belair, has at least 5 percent Latino residents (even if many may be live-in servants, nannies, and gardeners). As noted earlier, the Asian population more than any other spans the extreme range of wealth and poverty, living in the richest and poorest areas of the county. But even with these changes, Los Angeles remains one of the most segregated urban regions in the country. No amount of data manipulation can disguise this fundamental fact.

Multicultural geographies: mapping diversity

What happens if we look at the opposite side of mono-ethnic concentration and explore the patterning of inter-ethnic or multicultural Los Angeles? Are there areas of exceptional diversity and dense inter-ethnic contacts, where no one group dominates the local scene? Where are these most cosmopolitan areas located? Using the traditional Entropy Index (measuring deviations

30 Timothy P. Fong, *The First Suburban Chinatown: The Remaking of Monterey Park, California*, Philadel-phia: Temple University Press, 1994. Monterey Park, reputed to be the first majority Asian American city in the continental USA, received national attention in the 1980s for its inter-ethnic struggles over language use, with Latinos and Anglos often combining to stop the exclusive use of Chinese on signs and elsewhere, and to declare English as the "official language." For more on these struggles, see John Horton, "The Politics of Ethnic Change: Grass-Roots Responses to Economic and Demographic Restructuring in Monterey Park," *Urban Geography* 10 (1989), 578–92; "The Politics of Diversity in Mon-terey Park, California," in Louise Lamphere ed., *Structuring Diversity: Ethnographic Perspectives on the New Immigration*, Chicago: University of Chicago Press, 1992; and *The Politics of Diversity: Immigration, Resistance, and Change in Monterey Park, California*, Philadelphia: Temple University Press, 1995.

from homogeneity) for the four major ethnic groups plus American Indians, Allen and Turner (*EQ*: 243) list the following urban places of more than 10,000 residents as the most diverse in the region in 1990:

Carson	0.876	Walnut	0.789
Gardena	0.867	West Covina	0.789
Hawthorne	0.836	Long Beach	0.784
West Carson	0.797	Rowland Heights	0.784
Alondra Park	0.792	Los Angeles	0.782

Using a variation on this index for 1980, Allen and Turner in an earlier article developed a list of the 100 most diverse urban areas in the USA.[31] More than half of these places were located in California, with twenty in Los Angeles County alone.[32] Here is a list of the twenty highest, with those in Los Angeles County underlined:

Gardena CA	2.00	Langley Park MD	1.74
Carson CA	1.99	Pittsburg CA	1.72
Daly City CA	1.85	San Francisco CA	1.71
Union City CA	1.80	*Pomona* CA	1.70
National City CA	1.77	Oakland CA	1.70
Marina CA	1.76	Gallup NM	1.68
Seaside CA	1.75	*Cerritos* CA	1.67
Los Angeles CA	1.75	Passaic NJ	1.67
West Carson CA	1.75	Jersey City NJ	1.66
Monterey Park CA	1.74	Richmond CA	1.64

At the top of both of the above lists are the cities of Gardena and Carson. With a combined population of over 150,000, these two cities are closely approaching a demographic diversity that has probably never before been achieved in any urban area of comparable size in the history of cities: a perfect quartering of the population into white, black, Asian, and Latino. Moreover, this quartering process has been developing over thirty years and shows no signs of being significantly reversed.[33]

Since at least the 1920s, the Gardena area has contained a large resident Japanese population and a distinct cluster of Hawaiians, also mainly of Japanese origin. The combined Korean and Chinese populations have increased in

31 James P. Allen and Eugene Turner, "The Most Ethnically Diverse Urban Places in the United States," *Urban Geography* 10, 1989: 523–39.

32 In *The Ethnic Quilt*, the authors also calculated entropy indexes for the 3,100 counties in 1990. Los Angeles County came in fourth place, after Queen's in New York City, an Aleutian Island borough in Alaska, and San Francisco.

33 The following discussion of Gardena and Carson has been greatly informed by the research assistance of Nari Rhee and, especially, Alfonso Hernandez-Marquez, who is currently investigating for his doctoral dissertation the impact of diversity on everyday life in the region stretching from Gardena and Carson to Cerritos.

recent years almost to the size of the Japanese, and there are growing numbers of Filipinos as well, giving the city of over 50,000 a distinctive "Pan-Asian" flavor. Gardena's Japanese heritage made it an important service center for businessmen traveling to the more than 300 Japanese firms that clustered in the larger South Bay area, including at one time the US headquarters of Honda, Toyota, and Nissan. Even today, Gardena is considered to have some of the best sushi restaurants in the region. Gardena was also one of the earliest centers of legalized gambling in the Los Angeles region and its large casino continues to thrive in large part on the patronage of Asian residents as well as visitors. The Latino population has grown most rapidly in recent decades, while the resident Anglo population has declined significantly. Both the Anglo and the black populations, however, seem to have stabilized at just under one-quarter of the total.

In part based on its extraordinary cultural diversity, the city government of Gardena has become one of the most progressive in the USA. In 1980, it received the All-America City award from the National Municipal League for the "active involvement of its citizens in initiating action and working with local officials to help resolve significant community problems"; it was named Model City of the Year in both 1985 and 1995 by WeTIP, a national crime-fighting organization; it won the Southern California Municipal Athletic Federation Golden Shield Award in 1976 and 1992 for promoting youth and adult sports programs; it was recognized with a national award in 1986 from the US Conference of Mayors for its Employee Assistance Program, Sick Child Care Project, Computerized Child Care Referral System, Senior Citizens' Day Care Center, and other programs "to support working families"; and in 1982 it was one of five cities to receive the Save the Children award from the US Conference of Mayors and the Save the Children Foundation. Active Sister City relations have been established with Japan and Mexico, and attempts are under way to add a West African counterpart. Clearly Gardena takes its diversity seriously and, while significant mono-ethnic residential segregation persists, there are sufficient signs that its multi-ethnic population has created an unusually innovative urban milieu.

Nearby Carson, with its almost perfectly quartered population of nearly 100,000, also reflects its diversity in interesting ways. Filipinos are probably the largest Asian group and there are more than 3,500 Samoans. Besides being a thriving business center (Nissan, Mercedes-Benz, TRW, Sony, Pioneer Electronics, Rockwell Medical, IKEA, Goodyear, ARCA, Shell, Yoplait, Herbalife, Kenwood, United Airlines, Mikasa, and Siemens all have offices here), Carson is the site of California State University Dominguez Hills, recently identified as having the most diverse student body in the Western USA and tied for second in the entire country, behind only Baruch College of the City University of New York. *Forbes* magazine also recognized CSUDH as one of the top ten "cyber-universities" in the country. Carson's awareness of its unusual cultural heterogeneity has led to the creation of the country's first Museum of Cultural Diversity, described as a Forum for Cultural Collaborations Through the Arts.

Anchored in Gardena-Carson is an arc of ethnic and cultural diversity that begins to the north in such places as Hawthorne, extends to the southeast in some of the older central census tracts in Long Beach, and curves back north to Cerritos and adjacent La Palma. Using a longer list of fourteen ethnic groups, including six from the category of Asian and Pacific Islander, Allen and Turner identified Cerritos as the most diverse urban area in the USA in 1990, a position it also held in 1980 and, from all signs, will likely continue to hold in the 2000 census. Cerritos has become a major center for the region's South Asian population and is the site of the Cerritos Center for the Performing Arts, one of the largest sites for music, dance, and theater performances in Southern California. This ethnically heterogeneous zone appears to follow major freeway routes that run on the western flank through the shifting borderlands of black and white Los Angeles, then cuts through the old industrial zone and oil refineries in Long Beach and its immediate hinterland, and ends near the boundary with Orange County. There is a second arc of high diversity that stretches, with more interruptions (see the Ethnic Diversity map, *EQ*: figure 9.3, page 235), north of downtown Los Angeles from around Culver City, through Koreatown and Glassell Park to the San Gabriel Valley and such high-diversity cities as Monterey Park, West Covina, Rowland Heights, Pomona, Diamond Bar, and Walnut, second to Cerritos on the 1990 list of the most diverse US cities using the extended list of fourteen ethnic groups.

Whether such statistical measures of diversity translate directly into significant inter-cultural mixing is an open question. Turner and Allen (*EQ*: 248–52) explore one way of beginning to answer this question through an analysis of ethnic intermarriage rates in Los Angeles County. Their findings suggest that ethnic intermarriage is increasing fairly rapidly but unevenly across different ethnic groups. The least likely to be married outside their ethnic group are, in order, Cambodians, Vietnamese, non-Hispanic whites, Koreans, and blacks, with rates ranging from 3.6 to 6.7 percent in 1990. The most likely to intermarry are American Indians (79 percent), Puerto Ricans (58 percent), Cubans (34 percent), and Thais (31 percent). In every case, however, married persons under the age of 35 are much more likely to marry outside their ethnicity, with particularly large differences found among Cubans, Japanese, and Samoans. Whether intermarriage rates are highest in the two arcs of maximum statistical diversity is not discussed. It remains one of the many open questions involved in studying the development of these diverse intercultural and *transnational* geographies of the postmetropolis.

Chapter 10
The Carceral Archipelago: Governing Space in the Postmetropolis

Representative Texts

- *City of Quartz: Excavating the Future in Los Angeles* (Davis, 1990)
- *Beyond Blade Runner: Urban Control and the Ecology of Fear* (Davis, 1992)
- *Building Paranoia: The Proliferation of Interdictory Space and the Erosion of Spatial Justice* (Flusty, 1994)
- *Policing Space: Territoriality and the Los Angeles Police Department* (Herbert, 1997)
- *To Protect and Serve: The LAPD's Century of War in the City of Dreams* (Domanick, 1994)
- *Power in Los Angeles: Neighborhood Movements, Urban Politics, and the Production of Urban Space* (Purcell, 1998)
- *City of Walls: Crime, Segregation, and Citizenship in Sao Paulo* (Caldeira, 1999)
- *Law, Space, and the Geographies of Power* (Blomley, 1994)
- *Discipline and Punish: The Birth of the Prison* (Foucault, 1977)
- *Defensible Space: Crime Prevention through Urban Design* (Newman, 1972)
- *The Malling of America: An Inside Look at the Great Consumer Paradise* (Kowinski, 1985)
- *Fortress America: Gated Communities in the United States* (Blakely and Snyder, 1997)
- *Common Interest Communities: Private Governments and the Public Interest* (Barton and Silverman, 1994)
- *Privatopia: Homeowner Associations and the Rise of Residential Private Government* (Mackenzie, 1994)

The first pair of discourses on the postmetropolis revolved around attempts to identify, conceptualize, and explain the most powerful general forces of change affecting the contemporary world in the last three decades of the twentieth century. In the second pair of discourses, the emphasis shifted to identifying, conceptualizing, and interpreting the more concrete social and geographical outcomes or consequences of these restructuring processes within the confines of postmetropolitan cityspace. The third pair of discourses is both more focused on the particularities of everyday life in the post-metropolis and more far-ranging in its interpretive scope.

Whereas the first four discourses can be seen together as defining a new *regime* of urbanization, a distinctively postmetropolitan mode of urban development, the fifth and sixth discourses explore the emerging institutional, behavioral, and ideological changes that are reorganizing what can be called a postmetropolitan *mode of social and spatial regulation*. At the heart of these discourses is a straightforward question. Given the exceedingly volatile cityspace produced by the new urbanization processes, with its unprecedented cultural heterogeneity, widening social and economic disparities, and multiplying points of tension and confrontation based on differences in race, ethnicity, gender, income, sexual preference, age, and other social and spatial attributes, *what has prevented the postmetropolis from exploding more frequently and more violently than it has over the past decade?*

In this chapter, the question is addressed by looking at the *intensification of social and spatial control* brought about by new developments in the privatization, policing, surveillance, governance, and design of the built environment and the political geography of cityspace. Responding to what Mike Davis (1992a and 1998) has described as an endemic *ecology of fear*, the postmetropolitan landscape has become filled with many different kinds of protected and fortified spaces, islands of enclosure and anticipated protection against the real and imagined dangers of daily life. Borrowing from Foucault, the post-metropolis is represented as a collection of *carceral cities*, an archipelago of "normalized enclosures" and fortified spaces that both voluntarily and involuntarily barricade individuals and communities in visible and not-so-visible urban islands, overseen by restructured forms of public and private power and authority. In chapter 11, the mode of regulating urban life and maintaining internal peace in the postmetropolis shifts from the hard edges of enforcement and enclosure to the softer manipulations of ideology and the reshaping of the urban imaginary.

Conceptualizing the Carceral Archipelago

No one writer or one book has so dominated and defined any of the six discourses as Mike Davis and *City of Quartz* (1990) has done for the representation of the postmetropolis as a Carceral Archipelago, both in more general terms and specifically for the Los Angeles urban region. Compelling depictions of what he calls the "proliferation of new repressions in space and movement," and the "security-obsessed urbanism" that feeds off the spreading "ecology of fear," fill the pages of *City of Quartz*, from its fiercely iconic front-cover photo by Robert Morrow of the eerily gleaming Metropolitan Detention Center hidden away in a corner of the downtown Civic Center of Los Angeles to the back-flap picture of the author standing tough and angry, arms hugging himself straitjacket-like in a foreboding concrete bunker under what looks like a freeway overpass.[1] There can thus be no better way to introduce and outline the conceptual territory of the fifth discourse than through the telling narrative of *City of Quartz*, possibly the best and unquestionably the most widely read critical geohistory of contemporary American urbanism. The discussions that follow draw heavily from the rich collection of rhetorical phrases that punctuate the pungent prose of *City of Quartz*. Representative quotations from the text guide the discussion and open its scope to elaborations, extensions, and critical reinterpretations of Davis's paradigmatic narrative.

Fortress L.A. and the rhetoric of social warfare

Welcome to *post-liberal Los Angeles*, where the *defense of luxury lifestyles* is translated into a proliferation of *new repressions in space and movement*, undergirded by the *ubiquitous "armed response"*. This *obsession with physical security systems*, and, collaterally, with the *architectural policing of social boundaries*, has become a *zeitgeist of urban restructuring*, a *master narrative* in the emerging built environment of the 1990s . . .

[T]oday's pharaonic scales of residential and commercial security supplant residual hopes for urban reform and social integration . . . we live in *"fortress cities"* brutally divided between *"fortified cells"* of affluent society and *"places of terror"* where the police battle the *criminalized poor*. The *"Second Civil War"* that began in the long hot summers of the 1960s has been institutionalized into the very structure of urban space. The *old liberal paradigm of social control*, attempting to balance repression with reform, has long been superseded by a *rhetoric of social warfare* that calculates the interests of the urban poor and the middle classes as a zero-sum game. In cities like Los Angeles, on the *bad edge of postmodernity*, one observes an unprecedented tendency to merge urban design, architecture and the police apparatus into a single, comprehensive security effort.

This *epochal coalescence* has far-reaching consequences for the social relations of the built environment. In the first place, the market provision of "security" generates its own *paranoic demand*. "Security" becomes a *positional good* defined by *income access* to private *"protective services"* and membership in some *hardened residential enclave* or *restricted suburb*. As a *prestige symbol* – and sometimes as the *decisive borderline* between the merely well-off and the "truly rich" – "security" has less to do with the degree of personal safety than with the degree of *personal insulation*, in residential, work, consumption and travel environments, from "unsavory" groups and individuals, even crowds in general . . .

Today's *upscale, pseudo-public spaces* – sumptuary malls, office centers, culture acropolises – are full of *invisible signs warning off the underclass "Other"*. Although architectural critics are usually oblivious to how the built environment con-

---

1 Mike Davis, *City of Quartz: Excavating the Future in Los Angeles*, London and New York: Verso, 1990. On the same backflap, Robert Morrow describes himself as a native Minnesotan compensating for the absence of ice-fishing in Southern California by "taking photographs of rifle ranges, barbed wire, bullet-ridden police cars, derelict factories, big dogs, and other symbols of daily life in Los Angeles's suburban badlands."

tributes to segregation, *pariah groups* – whether poor Latino families, young Black men, or elderly homeless white females – read the meaning immediately. (Davis, 1990: 223–6, emphasis added)

These excerpts from the introduction to "Fortress L.A.," the keystone middle chapter of *City of Quartz*, take us vividly into the heart of the fifth discourse. Reflecting the book's teleological subtitle, *Excavating the Future in Los Angeles*, Davis digs deeply into the particularities and virulent metropolarities discoverable in the localized scene to portray a foreboding vision of the future – and of the past and present – that extends well beyond local boundaries. Without belaboring the explicit connection, Davis ties the fortressing of Los Angeles to all the other discourses on the postmetropolis, incorporating their substance and meaning into his own discursive framing.

The formation of fortress cities, for example, is described as "a zeitgeist of urban restructuring" and "a master narrative" of the 1990s, a product of the crisis-generated changes arising from the "Second Civil War" that followed the "long hot summers of the 1960s." This "epochal coalescence" is locally exemplified in the unprecedented merging of architecture, urban design, and the police apparatus, the three primary targets of Davis's frontal attack on urban incarceration. Such unprecedented mergings are presented as part of a much more extensive transformation of the spatial specificities of urbanism that is affecting many other cities and regions, making the harsh particularities of the Los Angeles case relevant to a more general and comprehensive understanding of contemporary urban life everywhere. Ever cognizant of these wider implications, Davis positions Los Angeles "on the bad edge of postmodernity," implicitly accepting at least the material impact of what has been called the postmodern turn, although still begging the question of whether there is a good edge as well to the postmodern condition.

Although Davis always remains a critical historian, *City of Quartz* also marks the beginning of a consciously spatial turn to his historiography, a path he has continued to pursue, especially in his critique of architects, urban designers, planners and others in the citybuilding professions, his interpretations of the 1992 Justice Riots, and his more recent writings on environmental injustice and the disasters of "ecocide."[2] Globalization and postfordist economic restructuring, although never addressed directly in any detail, form the backdrop to Davis's explorations of security-obsessed urbanism, and its concrete expressions are filled with allusions to the radical restructuring of

---

2 Mike Davis, *Beyond Blade Runner: Urban Control and the Ecology of Fear* and *L.A. Was Just the Beginning – Urban Revolt in the United States: A Thousand Point of Light*, Westfield, NJ: Open Magazine Pamphlet Series, 1992; "Who Killed Los Angeles? A Political Autopsy, *New Left Review* 197 (1993), 3–28; "Who Killed Los Angeles? The Verdict is Given," *New Left Review* 199 (1993), 29–54; "Dead West: Ecocide in Marlboro Country," *New Left Review* 200 (1993), 49–73; and "How Eden Lost Its Garden: A Political History of the Los Angeles Landscape," in Allen Scott and Edward Soja eds., *The City: Los Angeles and Urban Theory at the End of the Twentieth Century*, Berkeley and Los Angeles: University of California Press, 1996: 160–85. As noted earlier (ch. 8, footnote 22), his most recent book is *Ecology of Fear: Los Angeles and the Imagination of Disaster*, published by Henry Holt in 1998.

urban form in what I have described as the Exopolis, as well as the widening disparities of wealth and poverty being generated in the Fractal City.

It is relatively clear then that Davis presents the fortressing of urban space as an integral part of the latest phase in the geohistory of capitalist urban development, a period of epochal transition that was generated by the urban crises of the 1960s, expanded through three decades of profound societal and spatial restructuring, and, as we entered the last decade of the twentieth century, was showing abundant signals of imminent explosion and disintegration. While it did not make a specific prediction, *City of Quartz* was nevertheless prophetic in its apocalyptic warnings of what would take place in the hot spring of 1992 in Los Angeles, and of what I have been describing, with the advantage of hindsight, as the beginnings of a restructuring-generated crisis, a series of social and spatial upheavals rooted in the new urbanization processes that have been shaping the postmetropolitan transition.

Davis wraps his insightful picture of the "pharaonic" expansion in the scale of residential and commercial security (and in the ecology of fear) around a major shift in political culture that has accompanied this transition. Under the "old liberal paradigm" that prevailed during much of this century, Davis argues, there was at least the attempt to mix repression with social and spatial reform. What others have described as a Fordist and/or Keynesian mode of social regulation left some openings for modernist social movements and the continuing force of organized labor to press for progressive changes in the urban environment. As Davis (and many others) recognize, this old liberalism and its mode of regulating urban society are no longer in force. In its stead is a new post-liberal, or to use today's more common term, neoliberal political culture that closes off progressive reform through what Davis calls a "rhetoric of social warfare" rather than welfare, a more militant rhetoric backed by a political calculus that demonizes the poor in a zero-sum game they cannot possibly win. All that is left as a residual is the magic of the market and its trickle-down promises that are even more illusory and cruelly deceptive than they have been in the past.

This hard-line and ominous interpretation of the contemporary urban condition appeals strongly to the more orthodox Left as well as to despairing and nostalgic liberals, who make up some of the most ardent readers and exponents of Davis's work. But as a framework for interpreting and acting politically within the contemporary urban context, this piling of blame on neoliberalism as the all-powerful right arm of the new capitalism has some serious shortcomings. Faced with the seemingly overwhelming power of neoliberalized states and markets, the dwindling "residual hope" for significant reform all too easily can lead to despondency and withdrawal, or to an inactive waiting for a cleansing apocalypse. In either case, attention is diverted away from the new opportunities for progressive change built in to the fortressed and reterritorialized geographies of the postmetropolis. A wide range of politically significant socio-spatial movements have emerged over the past two decades in Los Angeles and in other urban regions. Recharged with active attachment to location and neighborhood, these "hybridized" move-

ments and coalitions consciously cross racial, ethnic, class, and gender boundaries to mobilize an intercultural politics of space and place that is significantly
different from the rigidly polarized politics of capital–labor relations that
structures Davis's discourse.

Davis closes too many doors in *City of Quartz* by enveloping his underlying political narrative too tightly around his own all-encompassing rhetoric of
social warfare and a backward-looking vision of radical subjectivity and class
struggle. Despite his often brilliantly turned appropriations of the language
of critical cultural and spatial theory, Davis walls off his City of Quartz from
the new cultural politics and the most insightful feminist, postcolonial, and
postmodern critiques, subsuming patriarchy, racism, and explicitly spatial
politics into a mixture of radical rage and conventional Marxian essentialism.
In too many ways, this weakens rather than strengthens the ability of progressive coalitions to respond effectively to the eclectic challenges arising from
the growing restructuring-generated crises, and especially to the events of
1992 in Los Angeles.

There is, however, so much to be learned from *City of Quartz* despite – or
perhaps even because of – its tightly focused political philosophy of angry
Marxian anti-neoliberalism. In contrast to most other representative texts of
the fifth discourse, which tend to focus on the most obvious artifacts of spatial
fortification such as gated communities and walled-in shopping malls, *City of
Quartz* views the Carceral City much more broadly as an encompassing *zeitgeist* – and *raumgeist* – of postmetropolitan cityspace.[3] Its effects are felt everywhere and, even more insightfully, every representative site is connected to
the others in a web of real and imagined spatial causality and contingency.
Such totalizing inclusiveness may close off some useful alternative interpretations and isolate Davis's particular and general interpretation of the
fortressed city from the most important arguments of the other five discourses
on the postmetropolis, but at the same time it opens up many revealing pathways to explore the security-obsessed urbanism that forms so vital a part of
postmetropolitan daily life.

The destruction of public space and the architectonics of security-obsessed urbanism

The American city, as many critics have recognized, is being systematically
turned inside out – or, rather, outside in. The valorized spaces of the new megastructures and super-malls are concentrated in the center, street frontage is
denuded, public activity is sorted into strictly functional compartments, and circulation is internalized in corridors under the gaze of private police . . . In Los
Angeles, once-upon-a-time a demi-paradise of free beaches, luxurious parks, and
"cruising strips", genuinely democratic space is all but extinct. The Oz-like archipelago of Westside pleasure-domes – a continuum of tony malls, arts centers and

---

3 My thanks to Barbara Hooper for the term *raumgeist*, the spatial expression of the spirit of the times.

gourmet strips – is reciprocally dependent upon the social imprisonment of a third-world service proletariat who live in increasingly repressive ghettoes and barrios. In a city of several million yearning immigrants, public amenities are radically shrinking, parks are becoming derelict and beaches more segregated, libraries and playgrounds are closing, youth congregations of ordinary kinds are banned, and the streets are becoming more desolate and dangerous.

(Davis, 1990: 226–7)

Significantly, Davis begins his chapter on "Fortress L.A." with a stirring attack on the disappearance of "genuinely democratic" public space under the thickening blanket of privatization and the declining welfare state. Packaging his expressive prose in unflinching binary oppositions (fortified cells of affluence versus places of terror for the criminalized poor, Oz-like pleasure domes versus repressive ghettoes and barrios), Davis links the destruction of public space directly to a conspiratorial "security offensive" on the part of public officials, developers, and the citybuilding professions to meet "the middle-class demand for increased spatial and social insulation." This market-driven and class-orchestrated effort is buttressed by post-liberal tactics of privatization and deregulation, insidious welfare reforms, new electronic technologies for controlling spatial access and mobility, and the knowing participation of policing power.

Davis elaborates his and Los Angeles's fixation on security and surveillance later in the chapter on "Fortress L.A." in a section entitled "From Rentacop to *Robocop,*" another of his many references to films and the film industry. The "voracious consumption of private security services" is seen here as propelling the "enclavization" of Los Angeles, embedding into the urban landscape such repellent features as "high-tech castles," "belligerent lawns," and a "mansionizing mania" for terrorist-proof residential bunkers. As Davis notes, the security services industry is one of the fastest-growing in the USA and has been expanding especially rapidly in the Los Angeles region, today almost surely the densest cluster of activist home owners' associations (HOAs) and heavily guarded and gated communities anywhere in the world. It is also no surprise that the main security companies in Los Angeles are part of larger corporate conglomerates profiting handsomely from the ecology of fear. Westec, for example, was a subsidiary of Japan's Secom Ltd when *City of Quartz* was written, while its local rival, Bel-Air Patrol, was part of the Borg-Warner family of security companies that included Burns and Pinkerton. The reference to the Paul Verhoeven film *RoboCop* comes from the similar worldview of one of its entrepreneurial characters and that of a Westec president who is quoted as saying, "We are not a security guard company. We sell a *concept* of security." Today, the little signs announcing armed patrols, neighborhood watches, guarded communities, and occasionally that "trespassers will be shot" are atmospherically ubiquitous in the thickened carceral landscape of Los Angeles.

Digging ever deeper into the architectonics of security-obsessed urbanism, Davis rivets our attention to what he calls "Sadistic Street Environments."

The conscious "hardening" of the city surface against the poor is especially brazen in the Manichaean treatment of Downtown microcosms . . . [T]he city is engaged in a merciless struggle to make public facilities and spaces as "unliveable" as possible for the homeless and the poor. The persistence of thousands of street people . . . sours the image of designer Downtown living and betrays the laboriously constructed illusion of a Downtown "renaissance". City Hall then retaliates with its own variant of low-intensity warfare. (1990: 232)

Here he focuses on the "urban cold war" being fought to contain the homeless in Skid Row, using "architectural policing" to systematically transform the area into a controllable "outdoor poorhouse." Many "ingenious design deterrents" keep the persistent street people in their proper place. Barrel-shaped or in some cases metal-spiked benches make sleeping impossible and even sitting uncomfortable; sprinkler systems installed in a local park go on randomly through the night to serve a similar purpose; restaurants protect their refuse bins in "ornate enclosures" and "bag-lady proof trash cages" topped with spikes or razor wire. Public lavatories are generally hard to find anywhere in Los Angeles, but are virtually absent in the "toiletless no-man's-land east of Hill Street," which is also "barren of outside water sources for drinking or washing." On the other side of Hill Street, smart office buildings are moated with armed guards, locked gates, and security cameras to serve and protect their hermetically sealed inhabitants.

Over the past ten years, the containment of the homeless on Skid Row has advanced through an apparently more benign "gilding" of the fifty-block area. City, federal, and private investments amounting to around $300 million have restored more than forty small Single Room Occupancy (SRO) hotels (managed by new nonprofit institutions such as the Skid Row Housing Trust) and rebuilt in high modern architectural style the premier anchors of the themed mall that Skid Row has become, the Los Angeles Mission and the Union Rescue Mission (the latter moved from its slightly peripheral or "off the reservation" location to a more central site). Trees have been planted along some streets, and two tiny parks, along with a police and a fire station, have been added. As a founder of Las Familias del Pueblo, one of the area's children's centers, recently stated: "Skid row has become a permanent, stable neighborhood. No one's going to mow it down. Where else are you going to put 11,000 people?" But there is much that remains the same.

Dozens of men with thousand-yard stares occupy the small parks and lobbies of hotels . . . They operate under an intricate set of rules. If they leave the safety of the parks and hotels, the cops will harass them back into their enclaves. Skid row is one of the few places in the city where stopping on the sidewalk and talking to your friends can get you cited for loitering . . . "If you're visible, you're a problem," says [the Las Familias founder]. That's why police harass those who gather on sidewalks . . . It also explains the subtle interplay that keeps skid row contained between 3rd Street on the north and 7th Street on the south . . . In a sense, you could think of skid row these days as a lavishly financed, minimum security prison. A prison without physical walls, surely, but nonetheless a place that's hard to leave.[4]

Building (paranoically?) on Davis's sadistic street environments, Steven Flusty has elaborated his own architectural detailing of what he calls *Building Paranoia: The Proliferation of Interdictory Space and the Erosion of Spatial Justice.*[5] Flusty defines interdictory spaces as those specifically designed to intercept and repel would-be users. These spaces can be "stealthy" (hidden or camouflaged behind view impediments, intervening objects, or grade changes); "slippery" (unreachable or seemingly inaccessible due to missing or contorted approach paths); "crusty" (protected by harder obstructions such as walls, gates, and checkpoints); "prickly" (difficult or uncomfortable to occupy because of sprinkler systems, bum-proof resting surfaces, and other repellent design features); or "jittery" (monitored by roving patrols and/or remote sensing technologies connected to security stations). Combining various of these features are unfriendly "mutant typologies" in the carceral built environment. The "Blockhome" is a residence "with a crusty core of thick blank walls, often embedded in an extended jittery perimeter of alarms, video observation cameras and motion-sensitive security lighting." The "Luxury Laager" is "a relatively affluent residential community sealed behind a crusty perimeter, fenced off or built within walls sometimes reinforced by a stealthy periphery of densely landscaped berms." The "Pocket Ghetto" is "a public housing project or low-income area retrofitted with street barricades and patrolled by police garrisoned on-site."

In another subsection of Fortress L.A., Davis adds an additional variation on the theme of designed deterrence and containment, "The Panopticon Mall." After a segment on "Frank Gehry as Dirty Harry," an all-out attack on the prominent local architect for leading the way in "bunkering" urban space, "upgrading the region into a glitzy theme park for international tourism," and turning public architecture inside out "in the service of 'security' and profit," Davis notes that the "fortress" is also being used to "recapture the poor as consumers" (1990: 240). He calls this the "Haagenization" of South Central Los Angeles, silently using the mall-developer Alexander Haagen in alliterative allusion to the nineteenth century and the similarly security-driven Hausmannization of Paris. Another epochal "designer" figures prominently here: Jeremy Bentham, whose late eighteenth-century panopticon prison persists today as the iconic model of origin for the creative systems of surveillance and oversight that are being infused throughout the Carceral City. At several sites in South Central, shopping malls have been constructed behind high security fences, with tightly controlled access and all-seeing closed-circuit video (and often audio) surveillance. Visually prominent observatories

4   Robert A. Jones, "Rebuilding the Nether World," *Los Angeles Times*, August 2, 1998. You can be sure that Jones has read *City of Quartz*.
5   Steven Flusty, *Building Paranoia*, West Hollywood, CA: Los Angeles Forum for Architecture and Urban Design, Publication No. 11, 1994.

tower over the malled space, while inside equally prominent police substations stand forth "to protect and serve" the consumer, echoing the well-known motto of the Los Angeles Police Department (LAPD). As Davis notes, such Haagenization has been extended to housing throughout the New Inner City, with the "housing-project-as-strategic-hamlet" now mimicking the "mall-as-panopticon-prison" in many of the run-down public housing estates built in the 1950s, complete with steel fence fortifications, LAPD substations, armed surveillance of entry and exit, and even obligatory identity passes for the incarcerated tenants.

Policing space: doing time in Los Angeles

. . . the LAPD's pathbreaking substitution of technological capital for patrol manpower . . . was a necessary adaptation to the city's dispersed form . . . Technology helped insulate [a] paranoid *esprit de corps* . . . [and] virtually established a new epistemology of policing, where technologized surveillance and response supplanted the traditional patrolman's intimate "folk" knowledge of specific communities . . . But the most decisive element in the LAPD's metamorphosis into a technopolice has been its long and successful liaison with the military aerospace industry.

Under [former police chief] Parker, ever alert to spinoffs from military technology, the LAPD introduced the first police helicopters for systematic aerial surveillance. After the Watts Rebellion of 1965 this airborne effort became the cornerstone of a policing strategy for the entire inner city. As part of its "astro" program LAPD helicopters maintain an average nineteen-hour-per-day vigil over "high-crime areas," tactically coordinated to patrol car forces, and exceeding even the British Army's aerial surveillance of Belfast. To facilitate ground–air synchronization, thousands of residential rooftops have been painted with identifying street numbers, transforming the aerial view of the city into a huge police grid.

The fifty-pilot LAPD airforce was recently updated with French Aerospatiale helicopters equipped with futuristic surveillance technology. Their forward-looking infra-red cameras are extraordinary night eyes that can easily form heat images from a single burning cigarette, while their thirty-million-candlepower spotlights, appropriately called "Nightsun," can literally turn the night into day. Meanwhile the LAPD retains another fleet of Bell Jet Rangers capable of delivering complete elements of SWAT personnel anywhere in the region. Their training . . . sometimes includes practice assaults on downtown highrises.

(Davis, 1990: 251–2)

In "The L.A.P.D. as Space Police," Davis shifts his attention from the deterrent designs of the built environment to that other vital pillar of the Carceral Archipelago, the police. The term *Space Police* here has multiple meanings. At one level, it refers to the attachment of the City of Los Angeles Police Department to "outer" space age technology and aerospace imagery, from its fleet of jet airplanes, Aerospatiale helicopters, and Nightsun spotlights to its NASA-inspired Emergency Command Control Communications System, whose

Central Dispatch Center is "bunkered in the earthquake proofed and security hardened fourth and fifth sublevels of City Hall East (and interconnecting with the Police pentagon in Parker Center)," the latter site being the LAPD headquarters. The Space Police is thus also very much down to earth, actively overseeing and controlling the outer and inner lived spaces of the post-metropolis. The spatial logic behind the "historical world view and quixotic quest of the postwar LAPD" is clearly identified by Davis: "good citizens, off the streets, enclaved in their high-security private consumption spheres; bad citizens, on the streets (and therefore not engaged in legitimate business), caught in the terrible, Jehovan scrutiny of the LAPD's space program."[6]

Even more down to earth in detailing the spatial practices of the LAPD is Steve Herbert's *Policing Space* (1997), a detailed firsthand account of one patrol division's everyday operations to define, mark, and control territory.[7] Studiously avoiding the angry one-sidedness of Davis's approach to the Space Police, Herbert weaves together the work of Weber, Foucault, Giddens, and others on the "microgeopolitics of state power," to chart out what he calls "the normative orders of police territoriality": Law (preserving legal regulations), Bureaucratic Control (maintaining internal order through chain of command and differentiation of responsibilities), Adventure/Machismo (demonstrating courage and strength), Safety (preserving life), Competence (demonstrating capability and worthiness of respect), and Morality (demonstrating goodness by triumphing over evil). Each of these orders is presented as contributing "to the ways that police officers conceptualize the areas they patrol and how they mobilize to control those areas, how they *make* and *mark* space" through "the centrality of territorial action to everyday police behavior" (1997: 5).

Beginning and ending *Policing Space* with the beating of Rodney King and its denouement in the events of Spring 1992, Herbert traces the impact of racism as well as masculinism on these normative orders and more generally on the microgeopolitics of state power, providing additional psycho-behavioral insight into the architectonics of security-obsessed urbanism. Here are his conclusions:

> The control of space is a fundamental constituent of social power. In attempting to exercise their power, police officers seek to act territorially, to enact meaningful boundaries to restrict and control the flow of action across space. But officers are not the only ones for whom the definition and control of space is crucial. Space is important to the identity and power of a variety of social groups, a fact

6   For an up-to-date critical history of the Los Angeles Police Department, see Joe Domanick, *To Protect and Serve: The LAPD's Century of War in the City of Dreams*, New York: Pocket Books, 1994. Domanick presents the LAPD's "sacred credo" as: "Give no slack and take no shit from anyone. Confront and command. Control the street at all times. Always be aggressive. Stop crimes before they happen. Seek them out. Shake them down. Make that arrest. And never, never admit the department has done anything wrong."

7   Steve Herbert, *Policing Space: Territoriality and the Los Angeles Police Department*, Minneapolis and London: University of Minnesota Press, 1997.

that ensures that a complicated politics of spatial control persists across the variegated landscape of cities such as Los Angeles. That these geopolitics are important is but one lesson of the urban uprisings that engulfed Los Angeles.

(1997: 175)

As suggested here, the policing of space and the geopolitics of urban territoriality extend well beyond the police force and the professionals designing
the built environment. In Los Angeles, the local Space Police is powerfully
augmented by the quieter presence of what may be the most extensive
network of military installations around any major city, a global strike force
allegedly prepared to take on any challenge anywhere in the universe. In the
last chapter of *Postmodern Geographies* (1989), I described a circumferential
aerial tour above a simulated sixty-mile circle centered in Downtown LA
that sighted seven major military installations on the ground below, enclosing
the postmetropolis in an all-seeing but invisible wall of defensive and offensive ramparts. Several of these military installations closed down in the 1990s,
but their abundance and versatility virtually guarantees a continuing impact
even if converted to peacetime functions. To illustrate, during the Persian Gulf
War specialized training exercises were conducted in the deserts of Southern
California to simulate expected battle conditions. Especially attractive as a site
for maneuvers was a tiny desert hamlet made famous in a popular cult film.
The hamlet's name is Bagdad, missing only the "h" (for Hussein?) in the
middle.

At a much more intimate scale in the Carceral Archipelago is a household
militia of extraordinary proportions. Lethal weapons are kept in most homes
and in an increasing number of automobiles, creating a heterogeneous, fragmented, and highly mobile civilian armed force capable of shooting all trespassers on sight, wherever they may roam. Patrolling the private turfs, edges,
and transgressions of the carceral postmetropolis, this localized army aims
also to make and mark space, and contributes to keeping everyone in their
proper place, whether it be not-in-my-back-yard or not-in-my-freeway-lane.
The potential for everyday violence is thus raised to new heights, triggering
often-fatal attractions to a disciplinary technology of security and surveillance
that patrols the region with endless eyes.

Entering the Forbidden City: the imprisonment of Downtown

. . . a de facto urban renewal program, operated by the police agencies, . . . threatens to convert an entire salient of Downtown-East Los Angeles into a vast penal
colony. Nearly 25,000 prisoners are presently held in six severely overcrowded
county and federal facilities – not including Immigration and Naturalization
(INS) detention centers – within a three-mile radius of City Hall – the largest
incarcerated population in the nation . . . Jails now vie with County/USC Hospital as the single most important economic force on the Eastside.

(Davis, 1990: 254)

> If buildings and homes are becoming more prison- or fortress-like in exterior appearance, then prisons ironically are becoming architecturally naturalized as aesthetic objects. Moreover, with the post-liberal shift of government expenditure from welfare to repression, carceral structures have become the new frontier of public architecture. As an office glut in most parts of the country reduces commissions for corporate highrises, celebrity architects are rushing to design jails, prisons, and police stations.   (Davis, 1990: 256)

The physical embodiments of incarceration and policed space are nowhere more evident than in the City Center. Continuing his broadside attack on the architecture and design professions, Davis concentrates his unyielding attention on what he calls "the flagship of an emerging genre," the Metropolitan Detention Center. Featured on the cover of the more than 100,000 copies of *City of Quartz* now in circulation, the facility designed by Welton Becket Associates is the jewel in the crown of the carceral downtown.

> Although this ten-story Federal Bureau of Prisons' facility is one of the most visible new structures in the city, few of the hundreds of thousands of commuters who pass by it every day have an inkling of its function as a holding and transfer center for what has been officially described as the "managerial elite of narco-terrorism" ... This postmodern Bastille – the largest prison built in a major USA urban center in generations – looks instead like a futuristic hotel or office block, with artistic charms (like the high-tech trellises on its bridge-balconies) comparable to any of Downtown's recent architecture. But its upscale ambience is more than mere facade. The interior of the prison is designed to implement a sophisticated program of psychological manipulation and control: barless windows, a pastel color plan, prison staff in preppy blazers, well-tended patio shrubbery, a hotel-type reception area, nine recreation areas with nautilus workout equipment, and so on. In contrast to the human inferno of the desperately overcrowded County Jail a few blocks away, the Becket structure superficially appears less a detention than a convention center for federal felons.
>
> (1990: 257)

Noting the insidious psychic cost of such attention to prison aesthetics, Davis recalls the whispered comment of an inmate during his guided tour of the Center: "Can you imagine the mindfuck of being locked up in a Holiday Inn?"

With the "postmodern Bastille" as its anchor, an entire panopticon mall of federal government offices and tightly controlled and aestheticized pedestrian spaces has been constructed since the publication of *City of Quartz*. Featured most prominently are two artistic set-pieces, a central rotunda designed by Tom Otterness called The New World and a soaring silvered statue by Jonathon Borofsky called *Molecule Man*. The New World rotunda and its embedded bronze statuary brilliantly hides from short-sighted federal eyes (which fixed solely on the exposed genitals of the female bronzes) a vision of anarchic disintegration of the state by swarms of naked women and men challenging the microgeopolitics of state power. Located across from the Parker Center headquarters of the LAPD, *Molecule Man* stands tall despite being punctured by (bullet?) holes, leading to its local name: "The Drive-By Shoot-ing." As I attempted to show in my own tour of this little corner of the Down-town Citadel (*Thirdspace*, 1996: 228–36), the Roybal federal complex thus exposes additional viewpoints on the carceral city and illustrates the Fou-cauldian admonition that power, especially as it is expressed in the control over space, is not only repressive but also potentially enabling and liberatory, an argument that is often lost when our visions of its enforced enclosures become too monolithic and totalizing.

Returning to Davis's depiction of the Forbidden City, brutality reigns.

[W]hen Downtown's new "Gold Coast" is viewed en bloc from the standpoint of its interactions with other social areas and landscapes in the central city, the "fortress effect" emerges, not as an inadvertent failure of design, but as deliber-ate socio-spatial strategy . . . The goals of this strategy may be summarized as a double repression: to raze all association with Downtown's past and to prevent any articulation with the non-Anglo urbanity of its future. Everywhere on the perimeter of redevelopment this strategy takes the form of a brutal architectural edge or glacis that defines the new Downtown as a citadel vis-a-vis the rest of the central city.   (1990: 229–30)

Davis is never more biting and barbed than when he writes about what he calls Los Angeles's new "postmodern" Downtown. Described as one of the largest postwar urban design projects in North America, he uses it as the fulsome microcosm for all that has gone wrong in the American city, the nadir of security-obsessed urbanism. In what reads like a radical inversion of Joel Garreau's soppy Edge City optimism, Davis paints Downtown in the bleak-est of noir shades. It is described as "a megalomaniac complex," a "demoni-cally self-referential hyperstructure," "a Miesian skyscraper raised to dementia," a "post-Holocaust fantasy" that is "fragmented and desolated," enmeshed in a "massively reproduced spatial apartheid" with its own "local Berlin Wall" and "Gucci precincts," a "totalitarian semiotics of ramparts and battlements" representing "the archisemiotics of class war." What lies behind this exceedingly vitriolic portrayal?

First of all, it is important to recognize the long and continuing local dis-course and formidable citybuilding efforts that have revolved around down-town Los Angeles. More than in most other cities, there has developed in Los Angeles an abiding civic inferiority complex, a sort of downtown-envy that revolves around the size, shape, and visual presence of the metropolitan region's pinnacle agglomeration especially, it seems, among the male leader-ship. Intrigue and corruption that would make the film *Chinatown* pale by comparison have been added to spirited citizenship and creative city plan-ning over and over again in the effort to create a symbolic and liveable downtown commensurate with the city's size and global importance. In purely land-value terms, for the past fifty years downtown Los Angeles has probably had one of the widest profit gaps between actual and potential development of any place on earth. When in the 1970s it was proposed that tax increments from local development might be used to finance urban renewal, it was discovered that with just average growth over a ten-year period the coffers of the agency responsible for the Downtown development project would be filled with more than ten billion dollars, making it one of the largest public works projects in human history, rivaling the Alaska pipeline if not the pyramids of Egypt.

Today, thanks largely to the influx of foreign capital keenly aware of the profit gap, there is a more visible downtown presence in Los Angeles and it increasingly is becoming the dominant postcard image for the region, replacing such icons as the palm-treed beach and the Hollywood sign. What better target then for the hard-line excavator of the region's future than downtown's image-hidden reconstitution as a Forbidden City of redoubled oppression, ingeniously designed to make history invisible and to materially and mentally partition the center along the "brutal architectural edge" of race and class. But there are other targets behind Davis's depiction of the Downtown Dual City of citadel and ghetto.

Throughout *City of Quartz*, Davis wages an epistemological war against virtually all alternative critical interpretations of the postmodernized downtown of Los Angeles, especially those arising from the postmodern Left, which hard liners such as Davis tend to see as a political oxymoron. The most iconic site for this interpretive struggle has been the Bonaventure Hotel, on the opposite side of the Civic Center from the Metropolitan Detention facility. When Fredric Jameson, America's leading Marxist literary critic, first used the Bonaventure in 1984 to symbolize the hyper-spatial effects of postmodernism as the "cultural logic of Late Capitalism," Davis responded with a scathing critique of Jameson's historiography, his penchant for a presentism that erases the past, and his consequential misreading of the "true history" of what is hidden behind the hotel's glassy reflections.[8] Davis continues his attack in *City of Quartz*, noting that "despite the claims of some theorists of the 'hyperreal' or the 'depthless present' . . . the past is not completely erasable, even in Southern California" (1990: 376).[9] Again, too much is being closed off here in Davis's militant anti-postmodernism, but at the same time his tough stance on the dual incarcerations of downtown Los Angeles serves both as an effective antidote to simplistic local boosterism and as an invitation to rigorous comparative analysis of other recentered downtowns.

Homegrown Revolution: HOAs, CIDs, gated communities, and insular lifestyles

The security-driven logic of urban enclavization finds its most popular expression in the frenetic efforts of Los Angeles's affluent neighborhoods to insulate home values

8 See Fredric Jameson, "Postmodernism, or, the Cultural Logic of Late Capitalism," *New Left Review* 146, 1984: 53–92; and Mike Davis, "Urban Renaissance and the Spirit of Postmodernism," *New Left Review* 151, 1985: 53–92.
9 For those who wish to return to this particular confrontation, I refer you to my discussion of the Bonaventure debates in chapter 7 of *Thirdspace*, "Remembrances: A Heterotopology of the Citadel-LA," 1996: 195–204.

and lifestyles . . . [N]ew luxury developments outside the city limits have often become fortress cities, complete with encompassing walls, restricted entry points with guard posts, overlapping private and public police services, and even privatized roadways. It is simply impossible for ordinary citizens to invade the "cities" of Hidden Hills, Bradbury, Rancho Mirage or Palos Verdes Estates without an invitation from a resident . . . Meanwhile, traditional luxury enclaves such as Beverly Hills and San Marino are increasingly restricting public access to their public facilities, using baroque layers of regulations to build invisible walls . . . Residential areas with enough clout are thus able to privatize local public space, partitioning themselves off from the rest of the metropolis, even imposing a variant of neighborhood "passport control" on outsiders.

Mike Davis, *City of Quartz* (1990): 244–6

Centrifugally spinning ever outward from the Forbidden Downtown is a growing constellation of luxury island sanctuaries, residential areas with "clout" enough to partition themselves off fearfully from the real and imagined spaces of the criminalized poor. Revealing glimpses of daily life in these fortressed enclaves appear frequently in the local press. Here is one particularly telling example.

On "the Island," in the center of a 160-acre man-made lake, life is a sublime existence of morning tennis matches, cocktail hours on drifting pleasure boats and midnight strolls, a world apart from America's daily deluge of crime. But even here, from the other side of the fairy tale moat, fear seeps in like a baleful tide . . . To most of the wealthy homeowners who live on this comb-shaped spit of land in the heart of Westlake Village, the Island is the only true haven from crime that they have ever known. Murder, drug crimes, assaults, common burglaries – the encroaching furies of a nation's urban anarchy – are simply not found here . . . Yet even on the Island, as newcomers from crime-racked Los Angeles and tense Southern California suburbs marvel at their newfound freedoms, many remain unable to shake a nagging sense of vulnerability. If the Island is a sanctuary from crime's realities, it is also a marker of fear's distant reach . . . Perhaps that is why one waterfront mansion bristles with video surveillance cameras and electronic listening devices. Neighbors debate endlessly whether to upgrade the 30-year old gatehouse where private guards watch the only road inside. Roving security patrols remind residents to keep their garages closed. Driving off the Island into the real world, "all our shields go right up," says one resident . . . "I don't go downtown (Los Angeles). Ever," said [another] Island resident . . ." And if I need to go into the (San Fernando) Valley, I hire a van to take me. It's just not safe. The less we have to deal with those places, the better" . . . Two years ago, when riots swept Los Angeles, 40 miles to the southeast, the guardhouse at the Island's gate was deluged with calls from residents convinced armed gang members were on their way . . . "We wanted more glass so the guards can see everyone coming in . . . and tire spikes so they can catch anyone trying to drive in the wrong way."[10]

10 Stephen Braun and Judy Pasternak, "Even an Island Sanctuary Can't Stem Fear of Crime," *Los Angeles Times*, December 31, 1994.

Davis explains the formation of these new walled cities not just as a reflection of security-obsessed urbanism but also as a product of what he describes as a "Homegrown Revolution," the title of chapter 3 in *City of Quartz*. Everything comes together in this fortified revolution: the rising power of homeowner's associations, the slow-growth movement, the multiplication of gated communities, the inflation of land values, the patterning of municipal incorporations, the California taxpayers' revolt, the restructuring of zoning ordinances, white flight, downtown urban renewal, the refabrication of urban politics, the "new urban environmentalism," and more. The chapter subheadings are exceptionally graphic and convey his arguments better than a lengthy quote: Sunbelt Bolshevism, The White Wall, Suburban Separatism, Defending the Fat Life, Revolt Against Density, The Big Bang (in which the revolution is described as "the Watts Riot of the Middle Classes"), Highrises Versus Homesteads, Homeowners Soviets?, Nimbys and Know-Nothings.

Davis argues that the homeowners' movement has been a "protest against the urbanization of suburbia," a form of resistance to the exopolitan restructuring of urban form that has as its primary aim "the reassertion of social privilege." Although he did not describe it as such, it can also be seen as another contributing cause and exemplary instance of the restructuring-generated crises of the 1990s, as much a response to the postmetropolitan transition as the Justice Riots of 1992. But rather than looking forward to the broader future implications of the profound changes in local consciousness, democracy, and governmentality brought about by this Homegrown Revolution, Davis instead searches the past for ways to contain, at least rhetorically, its rising social power.

> In a famous passage of the *Eighteenth Brumaire* Marx depicted the French peasantry as a "sack of potatoes", constitutionally incapable of any large-scale coherence of interest or social action except as mobilized by a charismatic leader. From our foregoing account, it is hard to avoid a similar judgement about Southern California homeowners. Try as hard as they might to become "sunbelt Bolsheviks", the slow-growthers remain basically peasant potatoes whose "natural" scale of protest is disaggregated nimbyism; or would "residential anarchosyndicalism" be a better term?   (1990: 209–10)

Many softer and more narrowly focused extensions of Davis's incisive narrative on homeowners' associations (HOAs), common interest developments (CIDs), and gated communities have appeared since the publication of *City of Quartz*, adding new insights to the continuing "revolution." Dennis R. Judd, for example, begins his essay on "The Rise of the New Walled Cities" as Davis does in his chapter on "Fortress L.A.," with a historically rooted discussion of the erosion of public space as the necessary starting point for understanding these fortressed developments.[11] Under the heading "Appropriating the

11 Dennis R. Judd, "The Rise of the New Walled Cities," in Helen Liggett and David C. Perry eds., *Spatial Practices: Critical Explorations in Social/Spatial Theory*, Thousand Oaks, CA: Sage Publications, 1995: 144–66. The title of this collection of essays is a specific reference to the work of Henri Lefebvre on the social production of space. See also the chapter by Perry, "Making Space: Planning as a Mode of Thought: 209–42.

Symbols of Public Space," Judd notes how contemporary architects and developers are using the ancient public imagery of the marketplace and the voluntary residential community to refashion the urban fabric around tightly enclosed, privatized, and monitored commercial and residential spaces. Following up on Kowinski's pithy description of *The Malling of America* (1985), Judd first traces the transformation of shopping malls into enclosed fortresses of pseudo-urbanism, complete with community centers, entertainment zones, street carnivals, and magnetic nodes for hyperconsumption. Referring to Davis, he describes these "new megastructures" as "fortified cells of affluence" and "gilded private enclaves" that seal off the enclosed city from the city outside the walls. He then draws on Umberto Eco's *Travels in Hyperreality* (1986) to compare the contemporary with the medieval enclosed marketplace, hinting at the restructuring of citizenship that is going on behind the new urban enclosures: "One way in which modern cities differ from the medieval cities described by Eco is that the maleficent presences of the Middle Ages were often identified with nature. In contemporary cities they have become one's fellow citizens" (Judd, 1995: 154).

Continuing his longstanding interest in how private power affects public policy, Judd turns next to the enclosure of residential community in the *common interest development* (CID), typically advertised as a "community" in which the residents own or control common areas and shared amenities while also having "reciprocal rights and obligations" enforced by a private governing body or "community association." CIDs, which include single-family housing estates built by a single developer and whole New Towns as well as cooperative apartments and condominiums, numbered little more than 1,000 in the early 1960s, before the American city (and others elsewhere) would explode under the stifling pressures of postwar economic expansion. By the mid-1980s, there were more than 80,000 CIDs, and today they have probably become the principal form of new home ownership in almost every metropolitan area in the country. Again referring to Davis and to Los Angeles as a possible "harbinger of the urban future," Judd argues: "The boundaries of CIDs separate the private from the public world both physically and symbolically. The relative affluence and security of the protected realms creates a stratified culture of separation that makes public space less and less desirable" (1995: 162).

Before amplifying further, it is useful to get our often acronym-filled terminology straight, especially since the literature uses many different terms interchangeably. As defined above, CIDs are formed by contractual agreements that bind residents to certain rights and obligations. In some but not all cases, the contracts are "themed" around a chosen image for the community: New England Village, Greek Island Villa, Hawaiian Resort, Golfer's Paradise, Leisure World. Here the contracted rights and obligations are even thicker and more restrictive for they must maintain the official community image at any cost. Extremely revealing is the term some lawyers use for CIDs: *association-administered servitude regimes*, a trigger for those who claim that the CID represents a form of oppressive "private socialism." All CIDs thus have homeowners' or community associations of some type, but not all HOAs (homeowner's associations) or RCAs (residential community associations as defined by the CAI, the Community Associations Institute) are CIDs. There are around 200,000 RCAs currently registered with the CAI, including most HOAs and nearly all CIDs. Cutting across all of these is the specialized category of *gated communities*, which, as Davis notes so well, can be found in both the poor Inner as well as wealthy Outer Cities. As they are so widespread, it is difficult to estimate just how many gated communities there are in the US. Using data from the CAI, Blakely and Snyder in their recent work, *Fortress America* (1997), estimate that there are at least 20,000, with more than 3 million households and 8.4 million residents.[12] Other estimates push the current number of gated communities over 30,000.

All these forms of privatized community are implicated in the deep erosion of public space and the fortressing of the American city. More subtle and less visibly expressed in CIDs and HOAs, this erosive fortressing reaches its most obvious peak in the gated community. Blakely and Snyder identify three types of these privatized and guarded worlds: Lifestyle Communities (retirement communities, golf and leisure communities, and the suburban new town), Prestige Communities (preserves for the rich, the famous, the executive, and more generally the "fortunate fifth" of the income ladder), and Security Zone Communities (built primarily on the fear of crime and outsiders, divided by the authors into three different "perches," city, suburban, and barricade, the latter concentrated primarily in the poorest areas). Here is their comprehensive definition of the typical gated community:

> Gated communities are residential areas with restricted access in which normally public spaces are privatized. They are security developments with designated perimeters, usually walls or fences, and controlled entrances that are intended to prevent penetration by nonresidents. They include new developments and older areas retrofitted with gates and fences, and they are found from the inner cities to the exurbs and from the richest neighborhoods to the poorest. Their gates range from elaborate two-story guardhouses staffed twenty-four hours a day to roll-back wrought-iron gates to simple electronic arms. Guardhouses are usually built with one lane for guests and visitors and a second lane for residents, who may open the gates with an electronic card, a code, or a remote control device. Some communities with round-the-clock security require all cars to pass the guard, issuing identification stickers for residents' cars. Others use video cameras to record the license plate numbers and sometimes the faces of all who pass through. Entrances without guards have intercom systems, some with video monitors, that residents may use to screen visitors. (Blakely and Snyder, 1997: 2)

As they note, California, Florida, and Texas are home to the most gated communities, but they are growing rapidly around New York, Chicago, and other

---

12 Edward J. Blakely and Mary Gail Snyder, *Fortress America: Gated Communities in the United States*, Washington, DC: Brookings Institution Press, and Cambridge, MA: Lincoln Institute of Land Policy, 1997: 7.

large metropolitan areas, as well as in other non-Sunbelt regions. In Southern California, where the densest concentrations are found, there are three major swarms of gated communities: the Palos Verdes peninsula near the Port of Los Angeles, where several whole municipalities are gated; coastal and southern Orange County, home to the archetypal retirement community at Leisure World; and more recently, the west San Fernando Valley and adjacent Ventura County, with its most telling site being the city of Hidden Hills, where white picket fences are mandatory.

Under all these association-administered servitude regimes, microgovernance and "civic secession" revolve around what Foucault once called the "little tactics of the habitat." To give some idea about the burning issues driving these so-called experiments in private local democracy, here is a list of what residents consider the major problems facing RCAs in the US. In order of frequency, they are parking restrictions, inoperable junk vehicles, signs, commercial vehicles, illegal vehicles (trucks), common property use, campers, paint, pet size, holiday decor, satellite dishes, plantings, basketball hoops, mailboxes, play equipment, flag flying, and last on the list, security guards and gates.[13]

In *Privatopia: Homeowner Associations and the Rise of Residential Private Government* (1994), Evan MacKenzie provides a particularly well-balanced assessment of the potential repercussions of the rising private and public empowerment of HOAs, CIDs, and RCAs.[14] In "Reflections on Privatopia and the City," his concluding chapter, he begins where he started the book, with Ebenezer Howard's prediction nearly a century ago that the traditional city would die and be replaced by a new form of planned community, represented by his notion of the semi-socialist and utopian "Garden City." While not quite what Howard intended, many today see a "new city" emerging Phoenix-like (my pun) "from the ashes of the old." Take, for example, the projections seen by Robert H. Nelson, an economist in the US Department of Interior, whose words MacKenzie quotes at length.

> The provisions of RCAs could be extended to the private governance of existing neighborhoods that consist now of individually owned properties. Using the RCA model, the concept would be to establish the private neighborhood as a building block for metropolitan political and economic organization . . . If RCAs were to become the prevailing mode of social organization for the local community, this development could be as important as the adoption in the United States of the private corporate form of business ownership. We would have two basic collective forms of private property ownership – the condominium (or RCA) form for residential property and the corporate form for business property. (MacKenzie, 1994: 177)

13 See figure 1–6, Blakely and Snyder 1997: 23. The bar graph presented there was adapted from Doreen Heisler and Warren Klein, *Inside Look at Community Association Ownership: Facts and Perceptions*, Alexandria, VA: Community Association Institute, 1996.

14 Evan MacKenzie, *Privatopia: Homeowner Associations and the Rise of Residential Private Government*, New Haven and London: Yale University Press, 1994.

As MacKenzie himself notes, CID housing represents more than just the privatization of a few local government services. It "constitutes and facilitates privatization of the land planning function itself and of the process by which it is decided where and how people will live in American urban areas" (1994: 182). For another, very different, view of the future, MacKenzie turns to Robert Reich, who was cited earlier, in chapter 9, for his views on the current surge in social and economic inequality, and to Charles Murray, a much more conservative voice on the same issues.

> Robert Reich connects the privatization inherent in CID housing with a trend he calls "the secession of the successful": "In many cities and towns, the wealthy have in effect withdrawn their dollars from the support of public spaces and institutions shared by all and dedicated the savings to their own private services ... Condominiums and the omnipresent residential communities dun their members to undertake work that financially strapped local governments can no longer afford to do well – maintaining roads, mending sidewalks, pruning trees, repairing street lights, cleaning swimming pools, paying for lifeguards, and, notably, hiring security guards to protect life and property."
>
> From the other end of the political spectrum comes a similar observation by Charles Murray, who sees the growth of CIDs as a symbol of America's becoming a "caste society." He anticipates that privatized local government services will facilitate the emergence of a new caste as a powerful political force. "I am trying to envision what happens when 10 or 20 percent of the population has enough income to bypass the social institutions it doesn't like in ways that only the top fraction of 1 percent used to be able to do ... The Left has been complaining for years that the rich have too much power. They ain't seen nothing yet." (MacKenzie, 1994: 186–7)[15]

MacKenzie ends *Privatopia* by considering a "new possibility" in CID politics: the active mobilization of CID residents for mass political action not just at the local but also the national level. A lobbyist for California ECHO (Executive Council of Home Owners) has argued that such a mass constituency "could dwarf such legislative powerhouses as the public employee unions and trial lawyers organizations." That such a mobilization has already been occurring at the state and local levels is clear. In some areas such as Orange County, experience in RCAs is a key stepping stone for running for local public office and, as noted by a local assemblyman, Presidents Reagan, Bush, and Clinton have all included stops at Leisure World in their election campaigns. In a recently completed study of the San Fernando Valley, Mark Purcell examines the impact of HOAs on a series of major state and local issues, including the California Tax Revolt that led to the passage of Proposition 13 and current campaigns for dismantling the Los Angeles Unified School District and encouraging the secession of the Valley (and possibly other areas)

15   The Reich quote is from "Secession of the Successful," *New York Times Magazine*, January 20, 1991: 42. Murray's comments are quoted in Irwin M. Stelzer, "The Shape of Things to Come," *National Review*, July 8, 1991: 29–30.

from the City, which if successful would be the first time any major US city literally dis-annexed a major portion of its territory.[16] There can be little doubt that these "private governments" will be playing an increasingly important *public* role in the future.

Beyond the Blade Runner *scenario: the spatial restructuring of urban governmentality*

Despite his own attempts to transcend its limitations, a *Blade Runner* scenario has become indelibly attached to Davis's depiction of the *City of Quartz*. Drawing both on the novel of Philip K. Dick and the popular film directed by Ridley Scott, the scenario depicts a post-apocalyptic future city which has pushed the carceral exopolis to its ultimate extremes. All the cultures of the world appear to be packed together in a smoky urban core throbbing with impending violence. Ethnic and racial boundaries have seemingly melted away in a fractal chaos where there are no longer any safe places or stable identities. It is difficult to tell the difference between citizen and alien, even human and android, for every peripheralized group on earth now lives in the center, melded together in homogenized heterogeneity. At the same time as the Inner City has been globally introverted, the Outer City has moved even further outward into monolithic, barricaded, and isolated worlds that in the novel are described as being "Off-Earth." The bifurcation of cityspace is thus virtually complete.

Davis paints a premonitory picture of just such a rigidly binarized metropolis in his *City of Quartz* and continues to inflame it with apocalyptic disasters in *Ecology of Fear*. All the warning signals are identified: the destruction of democratic public space, a rampant sense of foreboding and fear that breeds security-obsessed urbanism, a built environment increasingly filled with paranoic architecture and deterrent designs, a technopolice upholding the microgeopolitics of the local state, a Third World service proletariat of the immigrant poor trapped in inner-city squalor, the enclavization of the affluent in fortified islands of privilege, the spread of sunbelt bolshevism and the privatized homeowners' revolution. What Davis sees and foresees is undoubtedly there in late twentieth-century Los Angeles and he must be applauded for his foresight and insight. But there is more to the story of Los Angeles and the Carceral Archipelago it has become. In this final section, I try to move the fifth discourse beyond the formative dichotomies of *City of Quartz* and the *Blade Runner* scenario that enshrouds it through an attempt to break open these entrenched oppositions to alternative possibilities of analysis and interpreta-

---

16   Mark Purcell, *Power in Los Angeles: Neighborhood Movements, Urban Politics, and the Production of Urban Space*, doctoral dissertation, Department of Geography, UCLA, 1998. See also by Purcell, "Divorce, California Style," *In These Times* 21, 1996: 18–20, 36; and "Ruling Los Angeles: Neighborhood Movements, Urban Regimes, and the Production of Space in Southern California," *Urban Geography* 18, 1997: 684–704.

tion. This is not meant to deny the validity of Davis's dominating discourse, but rather to avoid some of its discursive rigidities and enclosures.

Take, for example, the notion that public (versus private) space is being destroyed in the carceral postmetropolis. There is abundant evidence to suggest that this is indeed true, but there are also many who argue that the very distinction between public and private space has never been clear-cut and that what is happening today is more accurately described as a restructuring of both private and public spaces, accompanied by a reconceptualization of the categorical distinction between them. Referring specifically to the notion of homeowner's associations (HOAs) as "residential private governments," Evan MacKenzie makes the point that "the words *public* and *private* may seem distinct enough – and they are used in popular and political discourse as if they were – but they are not" (1994: 123–4). When seen in strictly dichotomous terms, there is a tendency to see changes in public space simply as a kind of undemocratic transfer to the private domain, resulting in an incontrovertible loss of civic freedom. Such thinking universalizes and homogenizes the public realm – as well as the privatization process – and protects them both from critical examination of how each is also affected by other processes of differentiation and change. From the ancient agora and forum of the Athenian *polis* to the present-day postmetropolis, public space has been divertingly romanticized and mythologized in Western urban theory and practice to such an extent that it is difficult to see that it is a fully *lived space*, subject to being shaped – and reshaped – not only by class conflicts but also by gender, race, ethnicity, and other relations of differential social and spatial power.

In other words, the simple dichotomy of public versus private space may be blocking from view a more comprehensive critical analysis of the spatial specificities of urbanism, an analysis that approaches every space in the city as simultaneously perceived, conceived, and lived, the central argument of *Thirdspace*. In so doing, it may also be impeding the growth of a consciously spatial politics able to search across all of the city for spaces and places of mobilization, resistance, and solidarity. Such potential spaces of resistance and progressive social change are largely occluded from Davis's *City of Quartz*, in part because of his entrenched binary logic but also due to his thick protective armor against the postmodern Left and the new spatial feminist, postcolonial, and anti-racist critiques closely tied to it. I have identified a few examples of these spatialized cultural politics in the preceding chapters and will add more in those that follow. To illustrate briefly one additional example of these alternative critical spatial viewpoints specifically focused on the Carceral Archipelago, I refer to the work of Thomas L. Dumm.

In "The New Enclosures: Racism in the Normalized Community," Dumm bounces off both *City of Quartz* and the 1992 Justice Riots in Los Angeles to argue that a "strategy of normalization," backed by the "representational power" of "scientific" racism and monitoring, has operated effectively to "encourage the internment of black minorities" as well as the protective fortressing of white, suburban, middle-class, male, straight, and law-abiding citizens.[17] Following Foucault more closely than Davis, Dumm criticizes the "Marxist critical tradition" for tending to reduce race and patriarchy to class and economics, and for closing off too many possibilities for resistance in the restructured governmentality of cityspace. He concludes hopefully with a call for a more spatialized cultural politics of *resistance* and *reconnection*.

> The new Enclosures cannot endure because they cannot sustain themselves. While suburban life is not yet an oxymoron, it will become one if those excluded from its peace are given only the miserable and incommodious lives of exclusion to live. The alternative future is upon us in the United States. It can and will result in the replication of the Los Angeles riot. But at the same time it is possible for the emergence of a politics of deterritorialization and reconnection, a politics in which arguments over space – its enclosures, exclusions, and internments –become subjects for debate and discussion, and more important, for resistances and transgressions.

While nearly all writings on CIDs, HOAs, and gated communities emphasize decreasing attachment to public institutions and the restrictions on representative and participatory democracy implicit in the transformation of public to private space, there is also developing a more balanced critical discourse that explores not just the perils to democracy but also the new possibilities arising from the homegrown revolution and the new spatial apartheid. Across the country, and in Los Angeles in particular, there have been spillover effects from the homeowners' movement and indeed from the renewed political emphasis on microgovernance and the "little tactics of the habitat." Perhaps never before have the poorer communities of Los Angeles, once described as the quintessential non-place urban realm, become so politically involved in their immediate neighborhoods and localities. This has begun to generate a grassroots, cross-class, and intercultural spatial consciousness and activism that is focused on many of the same issues promoted by homeowners' associations: greater self-governance, improved quality of life, controls over speculative private development, increased protection against environmental hazards, greater representation in planning decisions, better protection against crime and violence, improved and affordable housing, and more generally the *reassertion of the local* against the growing external forces of globalization and urban restructuring.

Many of the most interesting examples of these hybridized local movements in Los Angeles have grown out of the "new urban environmentalism" that Davis, at least in *City of Quartz*, confines almost entirely to middle-class homeowners. These include the successful campaign of the Concerned Citizens of South Central, supported by several wealthy HOAs, to fight against the LANCER (Los Angeles City Energy Recovery) Project's proposed location of a regional solid waste incinerator in their area; the efforts of Neighbors in

17 Thomas L. Dumm, "The New Enclosures: Racism in the Normalized Community," in Robert Gooding-Williams ed., *Reading Rodney King/Reading Urban Uprising*, New York and London: Routledge, 1993: 178–95.

Action in Riverside County to challenge clean-up strategies for the Stringfellow Acid Pits Superfund site; the work of Mothers of East Los Angeles struggling against the construction of new prisons and another incinerator in their area; Heal the Bay's efforts to force compliance with the Clean Water Act in Santa Monica Bay; and many other organizations, some mobilized entirely within specific ethnic communities but most significantly involving progressive middle-class Anglos and other "outside" communities.[18] Here and elsewhere in the country, the new urban environmentalism has helped to trigger a growing *environmental justice* movement that is embedding problems associated with race, class, gender, and the physical environment in a new spatial politics and innovative strategies of place-making. Even more representative of the expanding power of residential community associations is Route 2, a multi-racial, multi-ethnic, and politically progressive RCA that has created a thriving limited-equity low-income housing cooperative not far from downtown Los Angeles.[19]

I must be careful not to exaggerate the empowerment of this new wave of assertive spatial coalitions, for they still exist within a crusty local, state, and federal governmental structure and they must continue to contend with entrenched conservative private forces in the Carceral Archipelago. But neither should these movements be disempowered by an overly rigid and narrowed discourse that excludes them from view. In closing this chapter with some optimism, I am reminded again of Engels writing on Manchester and of the remarkably peaceful transition of contemporary South Africa from one of the most inflexible and determined regimes of territorial separation, partitioning, and fortressing the world has ever known. In both cases, formidable "disciplinary technologies" produced extraordinary "repressions on space and movement." But at the same time, such apartness also created a new synekism of identity, resistance, and struggle in the concentrated enclosures of the poor. Let us not abandon all hope that this can occur again in the Carceral Archipelago.

18 For further discussion of these movements, see Margaret FitzSimmons and Robert Gottlieb, "Bounding and Binding Metropolitan Space: The Ambiguous Politics of Nature in Los Angeles," in Scott and Soja eds., *The City*, 1996: 186–224. For a more recent discussion, see *LA Weekly*, October 2–8, 1998, which reports on the Progressive L.A. Conference: Uncovering Our Past and Envisioning our Future, held at Occidental College. Included here is an article by Robert Gottlieb and Peter Dreier, "From Liberty Hill to the Living Wage: A Brief History of Progressive Los Angeles." Gottlieb, who along with FitzSimmons taught for more than a decade in the Urban Planning Department at UCLA, is also the author of *Forcing the Spring: The Transformation of the American Environmental Movement*, Washington, DC: Island Press, 1993.

19 See Allan David Heskin, *The Struggle for Community*, Boulder, CO: Westview Press, 1991.

Chapter 11
Simcities: Restructuring the Urban Imaginary

Representative Texts

- *Simulations* (Baudrillard, 1983)
- *America* (Baudrillard, 1988)
- *Megalopolis: Contemporary Cultural Sensibilities* (Olalquiaga, 1992)
- *Travels in Hyperreality* (Eco, 1986)
- *The Geography of Nowhere: The Rise and Decline of America's Man-Made Landscape* (Kunstler, 1993)
- *The Theming of America: Dreams, Visions, and Commercial Spaces* (Gottdeiner, 1997)
- *Invisible Cities* (Calvino, 1974)
- *Postmodern Urbanism* (Ellin, 1996)
- *When Government Fails: The Orange County Bankruptcy* (Baldassare, 1998)
- *Popular Culture: The Metropolitan Experience* (Chambers, 1986)
- *Neuromancer* (Gibson, 1984)
- *Virtual Light* (Gibson, 1993)
- *CyberCities: Visual Perception in the Age of Electronic Communication* (Boyer, 1996)
- *Cyberspace: First Steps* (Benedikt ed., 1992)
- *Virtual Reality: A Revolutionary Technology of Computer-Generated Artificial Worlds – and How It Promises to Transform Society* (Rheingold, 1991)
- *The Virtual Community: Homesteading on the Electronic Frontier* (Rheingold, 1993)
- *City of Bits: Space, Place, and the Infobahn* (Mitchell, 1995)
- *Telecommunications and the City: Electronic Spaces, Urban Places* (Graham and Marvin eds., 1996)
- *Sim City: The Original City Simulator*, User Manual (Bremer, 1993a)
- *Sim City 2000: The Ultimate City Simulator*, User Manual (Bremer 1993b)
- *Cyberspace/Cyberbodies/Cyberpunk: Cultures of Technological Embodiment* (Featherstone and Burrows eds., 1995)

- *Simians, Cyborgs, and Women: The Reinvention of Nature* (Haraway, 1991)
- *Virtual Realities and Their Discontents* (Markley ed., 1996)

The sixth discourse on the postmetropolis revolves around still another late twentieth-century restructuring, another ongoing (partial) deconstruction and (tentative) reconstitution of our contemporary lifeworlds, worldviews, and lived spaces. Here the primary focus is on the restructuring of the *urban imaginary*, our situated and city-centric consciousness, and how this ideological refabrication affects everyday life in the postmetropolis. Also of concern is how this restructured city-centered consciousness extends its sphere of influence to shape the way urban space and society are regulated and controlled, how they are kept together in the face of powerful disintegrative forces. Whereas the preceding chapter concentrated on more overt disciplinary technologies of surveillance, enclosure, incarceration, and policing space, the sixth discourse explores a different and more subtle form of social and spatial regulation, one that literally and figuratively "plays with the mind," manipulating civic consciousness and popular images of cityspace and urban life to maintain order.

The urban imaginary, as it is used here, refers to our mental or cognitive mappings of urban reality and the interpretive grids through which we think about, experience, evaluate, and decide to act in the places, spaces, and communities in which we live. Postfordist economic restructuring, intensified globalization, the communications and information revolution, the deterritorialization and reterritorialization of cultures and identity, the recomposition of urban form and social structures, and many other forces shaping the postmetropolitan transition have significantly reconfigured our urban imaginary, blurring its once much clearer boundaries and meanings while also creating new ways of thinking and acting in the urban milieu. We live as never before in instantaneously global cityspaces where the frictions of distance appear to be receding and once impenetrable barriers to human communication are becoming more permeable and open. Drawing from the titles of the representative texts, we seem to have entered a new urban "hyperspace" of invisible cities, postmodern urbanism, electronic webs, virtual communities, nowhere geographies, computer-generated artificial worlds, Cybercities, Simcities, Cities of Bits. How scholars and others have tried to make theoretical and practical sense of these real-and-imagined cities and the accompanying reconstitution of the urban imaginary defines the broad scope of the sixth discourse.

Re-imagining Cityspace: Travels in Hyperreality

The city exists as a series of doubles; it has official and hidden cultures, it is a real place and a site of imagination. Its elaborate network of streets, housing, public buildings, transport systems, parks, and shops is paralleled by a complex of attitudes, habits, customs, expectancies, and hopes that reside in us as urban subjects. We discover that urban "reality" is not single but multiple, that inside the city there is always another city.

> Iain Chambers, *Popular Culture: The Metropolitan Experience* (1986)

. . . the logical distinction between Real World and Possible Worlds has been definitively undermined.

> Umberto Eco, *Travels in Hyperreality* (1986): 14

Involved in almost every aspect of the changing urban imaginary has been the realization that it has become more difficult than ever before to tell the difference between what is *real* and what is *imagined*, what can reliably be identified as fact as opposed to what must clearly be labeled fiction. This ambiguous blurring has spawned a new vocabulary aimed at capturing one fundamental premise: that reality, the Real World referred to by Eco, is no longer what it used to be. We hear of books described as "faction," of "reality TV" and simulated news events, of spin-doctors weaving reality on demand in digestible "sound-bites" and artful images. In Eco's words, we are increasingly immersed in a sea of "real-fakes" and "absolutely fake cities," reconstructed fantasy worlds that are "more real than reality." Whole new cyber-worlds are being created out of "virtual reality" and "artificial intelligence" and "digital community." Foreign policy, political campaigns, controversial court cases, even wars are being conducted with increasing attention to public and private imagery, vicarious impressions of what is happening as opposed to accurate knowledge of the actual facts.

The term that has come to be widely used to define and conceptualize this growing confusion and fusion of the realandimagined is *hyperreality*. There is an interesting relation between the prefixes of the terms hyperreality and postmodernity. Both *post-* and *hyper-*, as well as the related prefixes *meta-* and *trans-*, carry with them the notion of a movement *beyond* an existing state, although each takes on additional meanings with regard to this movement. *Post-* and *meta-* connote "after" and also a significant change in location, position, condition, or nature. *Trans-* is more strictly "across" but can refer to a change in condition as well. *Hyper-* adds to this a sense of speeding up, often with the hint of excess. In the debates on the new modernity of the contemporary period, each one of these prefixes has been used (postmodernity, metamodernity, hypermodernity, transmodernity) to connote subtle variations on the same theme. Similarly, arguments can be made to use such terms as postreality, metareality, and transreality instead of hyperreality. But like postmodernity, hyperreality has entered into popular and academic usage (and misusage) and remains the generally preferred term.

There are various pathways into the sixth discourse and its practical and theoretical explorations of how hyperreality is affecting the urban imaginary. Many of these "travels in hyperreality" provoke a sense of *déjà vu*, for much that is contained within them has already been discussed in this book (for example, in the Introduction to Part II) and in its companion volume, *Thirdspace* (especially in chapters 7 and 8). In these linkages to what has come before, there is also a recentering of the discourses on the postmetropolis around the perspectives and representational style of critical cultural studies. Whereas an explicitly cultural critique was introduced only obliquely in the preceding chapters, here it becomes pivotal.

Jean Baudrillard and the precession of simulacra[1]

Abstraction today is no longer that of the map, the double, the mirror or the concept. Simulation is no longer that of a territory, a referential being or a substance. It is the generation by models of a real without origin or reality: a hyperreal. The territory no longer precedes the map, nor survives it. Henceforth it is the map that precedes the territory – PRECESSION OF SIMULACRA – it is the map that engenders the territory . . . the territory whose shreds are slowly rotting across the map, whose vestiges subsist here and there, in the deserts which are no longer those of the Empire, but our own. *The desert of the real itself.*

Jean Baudrillard, *Simulations* (1983): 1–2

The world in which we once confidently spoke of change and renewal, of trends and directions, was a solid one in which we could tell the difference between an idea and its referent, a representation and what is represented, the image and the reality. But now the two things are hopelessly confused, says Baudrillard . . . Take the most important of his concepts: that of simulation ("feigning to have what one hasn't"). Simulation, you might think, consists in pretending that something is not what it in fact is; this does not alarm us because we feel that we know how to tell the pretence from reality. Baudrillard's simulation is not like that, however; it effaces the very difference between the categories true and false, real and imaginary. We no longer have any means of testing pretence against reality, or know which is which. Nor is there any exit from this quandary. To report the change involved, we must say that "from now on" the "relationship has been reversed", that the map, as it were, precedes the territory, or the sign the thing. Yet such talk is itself illegitimate, for with simulation rampant, even the words that we use "feign to have what they haven't", ie, meanings or referents. In fact we do not know the difference between the map and the territory, and would not know it even if we had our noses pressed up against the thing itself.

Zygmunt Bauman, "Disappearing into the Desert" (1988)[2]

Jean Baudrillard, the French sociologist and philosopher, is perhaps the best-known theoretician and interpreter of the expanding sphere of hyperreality and its induced blurring of the boundaries between the "real" and the "imagined." His hyperreal travels hinge around what he calls "the precession of simulacra," the cumulative replacement of the real (world) by its simulated representations or images, a process which he claims has

---

1 Parts of this section are taken directly from chapter 8 of *Thirdspace*, 1996: 239–44.
2 Zygmunt Bauman, "Disappearing into the Desert," *Times Literary Supplement*, December 16–22, 1988; a review of Jean Baudrillard, *America*, London and New York: Verso, 1988.

reached its highest stage in places such as Southern California, where virtually all reality is now realistically simulated.[3] In the first half of *Simulations* (1983), a small book in which he discusses this precedent-shattering precession in detail, he begins with a passage from *Ecclesiastes*, reminding us of the biblical use of the term *simulacrum* (a perfect copy of an original that may never have existed) to refer to the belief that the host and wine of communion *really* are the body and blood of Christ, that the alcove statue *really* is the Virgin Mary: "The simulacrum is never that which conceals the truth – it is the truth which conceals that there is none. The simulacrum is true." That is, the simulacrum "precedes" or comes before or ahead of the truth, the reality, and indeed defines the real *as itself*, at least for those who faithfully believe. Baudrillard secularizes the biblical notion of the simulacrum as a motive source for understanding more concrete contemporary themes, especially the expanding domain and dominion of the hyperreal.

In his best-known spatial allusion, inspired by the magical realism of Jorge Luis Borges, Baudrillard argues that today the map, the cartographic representation or image, increasingly takes precedence over the real territory it is meant to represent. In other words, the representation becomes the real, with nothing else left "behind" it. For Baudrillard, there are no longer any doubles, any hidden territories or cities to be found beneath the surface. Everything, including the urban imaginary, is now condensed around simulations and simulacra. He batters home his point in many different ways. "Law and order," and along with it all forms of incarceration and regulation, "might really be nothing more than a simulation" (1983: 39). It is now "impossible to isolate the process of the real, or to prove the real," for "the hyperrealism of simulation is expressed everywhere by the real's striking resemblance to itself" (1983: 41, 45). Even our worlds of production are being transformed. "What society seeks through production, and overproduction, is the restoration of the real which escapes it. That is why *contemporary 'material' production is itself hyperreal*" (1983: 44).[4]

---

3   Even before his rousing tour of *America*, cited above, Los Angeles was on Baudrillard's mind. In *Simulations* (New York: Semiotext(e), 1983: 26), he describes Los Angeles as encircled by "imaginary stations" which feed "reality-energy" to a place that is nothing more than "a network of endless, unreal circulation," an "immense script" and "perpetual motion picture" that pumps "childhood signals and faked phantasms" into its old urban imaginary.

4   This observation on production and overproduction lies at the heart of Baudrillard's critique of conventional Marxist theory and analysis. In his earlier work on the "mirror of production," "the political economy of the sign," and the importance of "symbolic exchange," he tried to stretch Marxism as far as it would go away from its fixation on material production and the locked-in simultaneity of such concepts as use value and exchange value to encompass wider cultural and symbolic production processes. In *Simulations*, he symbolically breaks his ties with Marxism and related forms of historical materialist and structuralist analysis by reconstituting the entire material base of production and overproduction (the built-in source of capitalist crises) first as "superstructure" and then as hyperreal. For his earlier work, see *The Mirror of Production*, tr. and intro. by Mark Poster, St. Louis: Telos Press, 1975; and *For a Critique of the Political Economy of the Sign*, tr. and intro. by Charles Levin, St. Louis: Telos Press, 1981.

Distinguishing between simulation and dissimulation (simply prevarication or lying), he argues:

> To dissimulate is to feign not to have what one has. To simulate is to feign to have what one hasn't. One implies a presence, the other an absence. But the matter is more complicated, since to simulate is not simply to feign ... [for] feigning leaves the reality principle intact: the difference is always clear, it is only masked; whereas simulation threatens the difference between "true" and "false", between "real" and "imaginary".   (1983: 5)

Pushing his argument into even more contemporary issues, Baudrillard urges us to recognize the degree to which the "real" Gulf War, for example, was not actually fought in the Middle East but rather in the trenches of CNN and the global media. The Gulf War (and by implication, almost every other major event of the past two decades) was about images, representations, and impressions at least as much as it was about guns and oil and other "underlying" material conditions. He looks back to the Watergate break-in the same way, stating that "before, the task was to dissimulate scandal," that is, lie about it, while today "the task is to conceal the fact that there is none," that what appears to be scandal is actually the normal workings of American government (1983: 28). As always, Baudrillard (hyper)flamboyantly overstates his point to drive home the importance of his overriding argument, that something profoundly different is happening today in the relation between the real and the imagined, creating an epochal change in how we comprehend the world and act within it. However one sees it, *reality is no longer what it used to be.*

Baudrillard's persistent and often purposeful exaggeration has angered and frustrated many of his readers. Many, especially on the Left, dismiss his work for its seemingly stultifying political implications, its apparent call to sit back and live with the irresistible world of simulations rather than struggle against it. But underlying his more fanciful flights is a powerful critique of contemporary epistemology (the study of how we know that our knowledge is true and useful) that deserves notice for the new insights it brings to an understanding of the restructured urban imaginary and to the postmetropolitan transition. Before dismissing Baudrillard too abruptly (or embracing his writings completely), it is useful to recapture these epistemological arguments.

Baudrillard develops his critique through what he calls "the successive phases of the image," a philosophical timeline whose periodization can be interpreted as a sequence of critical *epistemes* (key ways of knowing) in the development of post-Enlightenment Western modernity, or more simply, a series of different models for making practical sense of the world. The first episteme or phase is captured in the metaphor of the *mirror*, with the image being seen as "the reflection of a basic reality." Practical knowledge is derived from our ability to comprehend in rational thought the sensible "reflections" from the real empirical world, sorting out the accurate, good, useful information from the accompanying noise and distortion. This is essentially the epistemology of modern science and the scientific method. It continues in force to this day in the human, biological, and physical sciences as the dominant epistemology, and is still recognizable, despite its detractors, as an important foundation for critical thought and practice, that is, for making practical sense of the world in order to change it for the better.

A second critical episteme was developed most systematically in the nineteenth century, although, as for the first, predecessors can be found much earlier. Its metaphorical embodiment was not the mirror but the *mask*, a belief that the "good" reflections potentially receivable from the empirical world of the real are blocked by a deceptive shroud of false or counterfeit appearances. In Baudrillard's words, the image "masks and perverts a basic reality." Practical knowledge and critical understanding thus require an unmasking, a demystification of surface appearances, a digging for insight beneath the empirical world of directly measurable reflections. The systematic exposition of this mode of critical discourse is closely related to the development of various forms of structuralism, from Marx, Freud, and de Saussure to more contemporary cultural criticism in art, literature, and aesthetics (where some might say that an untheorized form of exploring what is hidden behind appearances, as in a painting, a poem, or a historical text, has always existed). This alternative episteme has probably been the dominant counterepistemology for explicitly critical theory and practice throughout the twentieth century.

For Baudrillard, a third episteme could be seen emerging alongside the others in the late twentieth century, ushering in a new critical epistemology metaphorized around the *simulacrum*. Here the image begins to mask "the *absence* of a basic reality," indicative of a transition from simple dissimulation (feigning not to have what one really has, the lies or deceptions that arise from the surface appearance of things) to the increasing "liquidation of all referentials," the substitution of signs and simulations of the real *for the real itself*. This precession of simulacra threatens the very existence of a difference (and hence of our ability to differentiate) between the true and the false, the real and the imaginary, the signifier and the signified. Even the best forms of materialist science and critical theory cannot capture the impact and meaning of this precession of simulacra, with its erosion of traditional referentials and muddled significations of what is real and what is not.

Baudrillard does not stop there, however. He adds a fourth phase, a kind of ultimate endstate where the image "bears no relation to any reality whatever; it is its own pure simulacrum," an "uninterrupted circuit without reference or circumference." Although an argument can be made that Baudrillard presents this fourth phase strategically as an impending possibility – his own version of the apocalypse of postmodernity, one that calls for an immediate politics of action and resistance – it is equally possible to read everything Baudrillard has written since *Simulations* as a reaction to a *fait accompli*, a world in which a basic reality has completely disappeared and all that is left is the "ecstasy of communication," a phrase which has helped make him a cult figure and guru to net surfers and cyberspaceniks everywhere. I prefer to imagine the former argument, for to accept the latter would close off too many opportunities for progressive resistance and reaction to the prevailing conditions of postmodernity and the contemporary postmetropolis. As both a conclusion to this section and an introduction to the next, I defer to Celeste Olalquiaga.

> ... the postmodern debate has not transcended what Umberto Eco dubbed a couple of decades ago "apocalittici e integrati," referring to the raging polemic about mass media's goods and evils. In the United States this has taken on several nuances of its own, in particular a very postmodern schizophrenia whereby theorists simultaneously love and hate postmodernism. Perhaps its most interesting representative is that peculiar cosmic prophet Jean Baudrillard, the mere mention of whose name produces among debaters an effect similar to that of Moses on the Red Sea. Personally, I confess to an ambiguous relationship, since despite being influenced by Baudrillard's gaze and believing that simulation is fundamental to the understanding of postmodernism, I disagree completely with his final analysis on the disappearance of the referent.
>
> (Olalquiaga, 1992: xv)

Celeste Olalquiaga and postmodern psychasthenia

> Bodies are becoming like cities, their temporal coordinates transformed into spatial ones. In a poetic condensation, history has been replaced by geography, stories by maps, memories by scenarios. We no longer perceive ourselves as continuity but as location, or rather dislocation in the urban/suburban cosmos. Past and future have been exchanged for icons: photos, postcards, and films cover their loss. A surplus of information attempts to control this evanescence of time by reducing it to a compulsive chronology. Process and change are now explained by cybernetic transformation, making it more and more difficult to distinguish between our organic and our technological selves. It is no longer possible to be rooted in history. Instead, we are connected to the topography of computer screens and video monitors. These give us the language and images that we require to reach others and see ourselves.   (1992: 93)

> The postmodern confusion of time and space, in which temporal continuity collapses into extension and spatial dimension is lost to duplication, transforms urban culture into a gigantic hologram capable of producing any image within an apparent void. In this process, time and space are transformed into icons of themselves and consequently rendered into scenarios.   (1992: 19)

Olalquiaga paints an-Other picture of the hyperreality of everyday life in the new Information Age, one that is more specifically urban and more explicitly spatial than Baudrillard's. In *Megalopolis: Contemporary Cultural Sensibilities* (1992), she writes about a growing psychological malaise brought about by the communications revolution and many other factors influencing how we relate to our habitat, to the places and spaces in which we live. She calls this malaise psychasthenia and associates it with what many have described as the "postmodern condition," with being literally and figuratively "lost in space." As quoted in the Introduction to Part II, Olalquiaga defines psychasthenia as "a disturbance in the relation between self and surrounding territory," a troubling inability to locate the boundaries of our own bodies. The normal spatial parameters of the body, that "geography closest in," are increasingly confused with *represented spaces*, leading us to abandon our own identity "to embrace the space beyond," to camouflage ourselves into the larger milieu, thus appearing to vanish as a differentiated entity (1992: 1–2).

This virtual and spatial identity crisis is thus associated with a blurring of the distinctions between the body, the self, the city, and each of their represented spaces, their imagined or simulated forms. Increasingly our imaginary maps of the real world appear to "precede" and fuse with, rather than simply mirror or mask, the real geographies of everyday life, to refer back to Baudrillard's terms. These representations or images, in turn, affect everything we do, from where we shop to how we vote, from our opinions on global issues to who we choose as sexual partners. Inhabitants increasingly camouflage themselves into the milieu of spatial representations and simulations. Location and site imagery are substituted for memory, experience, history; and connections with the "topography of computer screens and video monitors" provide the immediate language and images necessary to "reach others and see ourselves."

Such spatial psychasthenia is not unique to postmodern culture. Cities and other spatialities of social life have always had the power to absorb and represent consciousness and identity. What is so different today is the epidemic scale and scope of these simulated spatialities and their infectious power to shape the substance and meaning of our contemporary lifeworlds, world views, and lived spaces. But Olalquiaga does not just present this as an entirely negative or wholly immutable force, and this is of crucial importance. As she suggests, we have a critical choice to make. We can simply enjoy the undoubted enchantments of a psychasthenic dissolution into space, changing our costume to affix ourselves to each tempting new scenario, be it Disney World or the electronic internet. Or we may turn the process around, taking advantage of its expanded spatial scope, its blurred boundaries, its breakdown of rigid hierarchies, its flexibility and fragmentation, to engage in a more creative *spatial praxis of transgression, boundary crossing, border work, and commitment to the right to be different* that can redirect the diffusion of hyperreality from its primarily conservative channels to more progressive objectives.

In contrast to Baudrillard's doomsday scenario of postmodern culture, where there seems no way out, or alternative moralistic liberal-Left versions which wallow in nostalgia and mourn for all that has been lost in postmodernity, Olalquiaga identifies and celebrates the new possibilities for creative resistance and subversion opened up by the precession of simulacra, the spread of hyperreality. Focusing in on contemporary Latin Amercan "culturescapes" and their influence on the "Latinization of the United States," she derives her own postcolonial megalopolis, dubbed Tupinicópolis, after a "retrofuturistic" group of Tupi Indians who competed for the best "samba" in the 1987 Brazilian carnival driving "supersonic Japanese motorcycles, wearing brightly colored sneakers and phosphorescent feathers, and carrying with them a "high-tech urban scenario" of expressionistic diagonals and spirals containing highways, skyscrapers, neon signs, shopping centers, the Tupinocopolitan Bank, the Tupy Palace Hotel, and a disco. Using this and other Latin American examples, such as the Chilean punk movement and Superbarrio, a cult figure who emerged from the slums of Mexico City in the late 1980s to fight against police corruption, pollution, and poverty, Olalquiaga opens up a distinctly postcolonial, postmodern, and postmetropolitan rendering of the new cultural politics of difference, representation, and identity, Latin American style.

> Latin America's own version of international culture tends toward a hyper-realism of uniquely parodic attributes. This "magical hyperrealism" often inverts the image of a colonized people humbly subservient to metropolitan discoveries into one of a cynical audience rolling over with laughter at what it perceives as the sterile nuances of cultures with very little sense of their own self-aggrandizement.   (1992: 75)

She finds this hybridized "iconic radicalism," with its parodic desire to "overturn the paradigms produced by the First World," to be the place where

> ... the most exciting cultural proposals of the moment can be found. Leaving behind postindustrial melancholia and identity nostalgia, and to the side market globalization of ethnicity, the humorous overturning of mass media images, like the artistic exposure of scientific disciplines ... works exclusively within the iconic realm to proclaim it a flexible language that may be bent, twisted, and turned to satisfy far more needs than the ones that produced those icons in the first place. Trained by a long history of intertwining codes and spectacular roles, postcolonial cultures show in this reversal how the world can also be a scenario for their own directorial and spectatorial delight.   (1992: 91)

Here again we have allusions to what bell hooks has described as "choosing the margins as a space of radical openness," a place of traditional oppression to be sure, but also one that can be transformed to create subversive simulations and eclectic communities of resistance.[5] Such spaces of radical openness must be kept open and active, against both the nihilistic closures of *baudrillardism* and the voracious power of cyberspace, the next pathway we will take into contemporary hyperreality, to suck everything, positive and negative, into its controlling realm.

---

5 This seriously playful tradition of transgressive "magical hyperrealism" is particularly rich in Latin America and reaches deeply into contemporary chicano/a literature, often with a focus on Los Angeles. See, for example, Guillermo Gómez-Peña, *Warriors for Gringostroika*, St. Paul: Graywolf Press, 1993.

Cyberspace and the electronic generation of hyperreality

Carrying the philosophical and epistemological debates on hyperreality into the lifeworlds of the postmetropolis requires a passage through an intermediating subregion of the sixth discourse, one that represents itself as defining the primary causal medium for the production and reproduction of hyperreality. This subregion reeks with as many neologisms and invented vocabularies as any of the others that have been discussed, but one term has emerged from the logo-sea of popular consciousness and culture to become nearly hegemonic. The term is *cyberspace*, another Greek-Latin combination form like television or heterosexual. A critical tour of this embracing world of electronically-generated hyperreality provides another entry point into the restructured urban imaginary.

The prefix *cyber-* is derived from the Greek verb meaning to steer or, more pointedly, to *govern*. It came into English usage most prominently over forty years ago to define a new science of "cybernetics," the study of control and communications in both living organisms and machines through what was called "information theory." In the subsequent evolution of the cyber-discourse, cybernetics began begetting a whole extended family of terms signifying the opening up of a technologically-generated new world of CMC (computer-mediated communications) that came increasingly to be linked to notions of hyperreality (with frequent philosophical nods to Baudrillard).[6] With the conjoining of *cyber-* and space, however, cybernetics was explicitly and assertively spatialized in more than merely metaphorical terms. While cybernetics is rarely mentioned these days, cyberspace has captured the very core of popular consciousness and is deeply shaping the contemporary culture of space and time emerging at the turn of the twenty-first century.[7]

The first use of the term cyberspace is generally attributed to the novelist William Gibson. In his 1984 book *Neuromancer*, a science fiction–or magical hyperrealist?–tale filled with computer "cowboys" (later "cybernauts") "jacking in" their nervous systems to "the Matrix," Gibson created an original model for what has now been spun into the "artificial" world of *virtual reality*, the most widely used contemporary synonym for cyberspace.[8] Gibson presents cyberspace as "A consensual hallucination experienced daily by billions of legitimate operators, in every nation . . . a graphic representation of data abstracted from the banks of every computer in the human system. Unthinkable complexity. Lines of light ranged in the nonspace of the mind,

---

6   To surf "Baudrillard on the Web," plug into *http://www.edu/english/apt/collab/baudweb.html*. The site contains a long list of "links to works about and by Jean Baudrillard," including an essay by Mark Nunes, "Baudrillard in Cyberspace: Internet, Virtuality, and Postmodernity," originally published in *Style* 29, 1995: 314–27.

7   The remarkable persistence of the term *cyberspace* is, I would argue, at least partly due to the wide impact of the so-called spatial turn both in the human sciences and in the popular imaginary.

8   William Gibson, *Neuromancer*, New York: Ace Books, 1984; and *Virtual Light*, New York: Bantam Books, 1994.

clusters and constellations of data. Like city lights receding . . ." (1984: 51), city lights which in the novel's context evoke Los Angeles from the air. In his later "cyberpunk" novel, *Virtual Light* (1994), Gibson takes us further into those receding city lights to explore the San Francisco postmetropolis, with side excursions to Los Angeles via Mike Davis's *City of Quartz*, praised in Gibson's Acknowledgments for its "observations regarding the privatization of public space" (1994: 351–2). Here is a brief quote to help situate *Virtual Light*.

> Yamazaki stopped. He stood very still, one hand on a wooden railing daubed with hyphens of aerosol silver. Skinner's story seemed to radiate out, through the thousand things, the unwashed smiles and the smoke of cooking, like concentric rings of sound from some secret bell, pitched too low for the foreign, wishful ear.
>
> *We are come not only past the century's closing*, he thought, *the millennium's turning, but to the end of something else. Era? Paradigm? Everywhere, the signs of closure.*
> Modernity was ending.
> Here, on the bridge, it long since had.
> He would walk toward Oakland now, feeling for the thing's strange heart.
> (1994: 105)[9]

Two books by Howard Rheingold, editor of *Whole Earth Review*, flesh out the wider discourse that has been emanating from Gibson's fantastically real cyberspatial journeys.[10] In a chapter on "Cyberspace and Serious Business," in *Virtual Reality* (1991), Rheingold traces the development of the "cyberspace market" via the saga of the "Cyberia Project" organized by Autodesk, a large California software vendor. Autodesk defined "cyberias" as "places one goes to experience cyberspace." To its president, John Walker, cyberspace was the preferred term, much better than the "oxymorons" of "virtual reality" and "artificial reality." So enchanted was Autodesk with cyberspace that its lawyers actually tried to copyright the term in the name of one of its leading programmers, Eric Gullichsen, only to receive a letter from William Gibson's attorneys hinting that Gibson was cheekily preparing to trademark for himself the name "Eric Gullichsen" (1991: 184). Ah, the wonders of postmodern metonymy!

In *The Virtual Community* (1993), Rheingold delves deeper into "daily life in cyberspace" through "the WELL" (Whole Earth 'Lectronic Link), a "virtual village" networked in the San Francisco Bay area that he uses for information as well as funerals, picnics, parenting, and "barn raising." In a metaphorical spin from spatiality to biology, Rheingold enlivens the debate on "cyberculture":

9   Oakland was the original site for Gertrude Stein's famous statement on contemporary urbanism, "there is no *there* there," an aphorism that has probably been most frequently applied to Los Angeles.
10   Howard Rheingold, *Virtual Reality: A Revolutionary Technology of Computer-Generated Artificial Worlds – and How It Promises to Transform Society*, New York: Simon and Schuster, 1991; and *The Virtual Community: Homesteading on the Electronic Frontier*, Reading, MA: Addison-Wesley, 1993.

Although spatial imagery and a sense of place help convey the experience of dwelling in a virtual community, biological imagery is often more appropriate to describe the way cyberculture changes. In terms of the way the whole system is propagating and evolving, think of cyberspace as a social petri dish, the New as the agar medium, and virtual communities, in all their diversity, as the colonies of microorganisms that grow in petri dishes. Each of the small colonies of microorganisms – the communities on the Net – is a social experiment that nobody planned but that is happening nevertheless.

(1993: 6)

I bring Rheingold into the present discussion not to promote his visionary and hallucinatory experiences of cybernated utopia but to recognize his occasional cautionary critiques of plunging blindly into its power-enhancing enchantments. He does so, interestingly enough, by calling upon the "Hyper-realists."

Hyper-realists see the use of communications technologies as a route to the total replacement of the natural world and the social order with a technologically-mediated hyper-reality, a "society of the spectacle" in which we are not even aware that we work all day to earn money to pay for entertainment media that tell us what to desire and which brand to consume and which politician to believe. We don't see our environment as an artificial construction that uses media to extract our money and power. We see it as "reality" – the way things are. To hyper-realists, CMC, like other communications technologies of the past, is doomed to become another powerful conduit for disinfotainment [and, as Rheingold describes it earlier, "disinformocracy"]. While a few people will get better information via high-bandwidth supernetworks, the majority of the population, if history is any guide, are likely to become more precisely befuddled, more exactly manipulated. Hyper-reality is what you get when a Panopticon evolves to the point where it can convince everyone that it doesn't exist; people continue to believe they are free, although their power has disappeared . . .[11]

Televisions, telephones, radios, and computer networks are potent political tools because their function is not to manufacture or transport physical goods but to influence human beliefs and perceptions. As electronic entertainment has become increasingly "realistic," it has been used as an increasingly powerful propaganda device. The most radical of the hyper-realist political critics charge that the wonders of communications technology skillfully camouflage the disappearance and subtle replacement of true democracy – and everything else that used to be authentic, from nature to human relationships – with a simulated, commercial version. The illusion of democracy offered by CMC utopians, according to these reality critiques, is just another distraction from the real power play behind the scenes of the new technologies – the replacement of democracy with a global mercantile state that exerts control through the media-assisted manipulation of desire rather than the more orthodox means of surveillance and control. Why torture people when you can get them to pay for access to electronic mind control?   (1993: 297–8)

---

11   Baudrillard writes about the "end of the panopticon system" and the "very abolition of the spectacular" as a process of electronic "implosion" in *Simulations*, 1983: 49–58.

Rheingold's cautions and Gibson's neuromancing are not just intrinsically spatial in their rhetoric and referencing, they are also peculiarly urban.[12] I say peculiarly because so much of the discourse on cyberspace, virtual reality, and computer-mediated communications (as well as much of the globalization discourse) has been couched in projections of spatial ubiquity, the increasing elimination of distance friction, locational particularity, and regional differences in the homogenizing hum of the Internet, the super-network that escaped from its original cocoon in the Department of Defense in that strangely fateful year of 1984. Now, it is often proclaimed, we have "conquered" space. We can not only now/here be at two places at the same time, we can be everywhere . . . and no/where too. Space and place, distance and relative location, and perhaps also synekism, that vital stimulus of urban agglomeration, seem therefore to no longer be as important as they have been in human history, portending what some have called "the end of geography." In the more critical cyberspace discourse, however, these literally and figuratively utopian (in Greek, *ou-topos* meaning no-place) claims are literally and figuratively challenged by a persistent grounding in urban and, most characteristically, postmetropolitan milieux: Los Angeles and the Bay Area, New York, Washington DC, Miami, Chicago, Vancouver, London, Tokyo, Paris, etc. Location continues to matter and geographically uneven development continues to make a significant difference. Even when "surfing the Net" or "cruising the Web," we remain in a persistent urban nexus (restructured, to be sure) of space, knowledge, and power.

It is no surprise then that cyberspace is increasingly becoming a contested political space, with its own brand of electronic anarchism (led by the "hackers") and new (virtual?) social movements struggling actively to guarantee on-line accessibility for the poor, the elderly, disadvantaged minorities, and others left out of the Net. In this contested space there are not only the dystopian possibilities of accentuated social and spatial inequality and intensified forms of political and ideological control, there is also the promise of a non-hierarchical, multi-centered, and more open and democratic community, informed and active, multicultural and postcolonial, transcending the divisive forces of race, class, and gender. These cyberstruggles are now, and will continue to be, an integral part of the politics of the postmetropolis.[13] And it is also no surprise that cyberspace has become a fertile field for critical urban studies, especially in the articulated zone of criticism that connects architecture and urban planning. One of the most insightful explorers of this zone is M. Christine Boyer, whose major writings creatively draw together the critical spatial perspectives of both Henri Lefebvre and Michel Foucault to re-

---

12   For a wonderful tour of the cyberspatial urbanities of Singapore, designed to discover whether "that clean dystopia represents our techno future," see William Gibson, "Disneyland with the Death Penalty," *Wired* 1.4 (1993), 51–5, 114–16.

13   See, for example, Jube Shiver Jr., "Bursting the Barriers to Cyberspace – On-line activists fight to keep the poor, the elderly and minorities from being left out of the Information Age," *Los Angeles Times*, Column One, March 29, 1995.

envision the history of the citybuilding professions.[14] Let us add Boyer's travels in hyperreality to our itinerary.

M. Christine Boyer and the imaginary real world of Cybercities

From the moment William Gibson announced in his dystopian science-fiction account *Neuromancer* (1984) that the new informational network or computer matrix called cyberspace looks like Los Angeles seen from five thousand feet up in the air, there had been a predilection for drawing a parallel between the virtual space of computer networks and post-urban places of disorder and decay. Cyberspace has also been called a huge megalopolis without a center, both a city of sprawl and an urban jungle . . . This unwieldy mixture of urban dystopia and cyberspace-here called CyberCities-turns the reality of time and place into an imaginary matrix of computer nets electronically linking together distant places around the globe and communicating multilinearly and nonsequentially with vast assemblages of information stored as electronic codes . . . This transformation, it is said, replaces the traditional western space of geometry, work, the road, the building, and the machine with new forms of diagramming . . . and networks expressive of "a new etherealization of geography" in which the principles of ordinary space and time are altered beyond recognition.

M. Christine Boyer, CyberCities (1996): 14–15

In "The Imaginary Real World of CyberCities" and other chapters of *Cyber-Cities: Visual Perception in the Age of Electronic Communication* (1996), Boyer takes us on a caustic tour of the transformation of the Machine City of modernism to the Informational Cybercity of postmodernism, collecting *en route* a remarkable series of epigrammatic descriptions of urban cyberspace.[15] From Michael Benedikt's edited collection, *Cyberspace: First Steps* (1992), she takes the phrase "a new etherealization of geography" (1992: 22); and from Michel Heim's chapter in the same collection the notion of cyberspace's "erotic ontology" seducing the architect and planner into the formal laws of information management. Using Gilles Deleuze, Boyer begins a deeper disciplinary critique:

> Gilles Deleuze has recently suggested that Foucault's spaces of enclosure are increasingly strained. Thus the family, the factory, the school, the de-

14   M. Christine Boyer, *Dreaming the Rational City: The Myth of American City Planning 1893–1945*, Cambridge, MA: MIT Press, 1983; *Manhattan Manners: Architecture and Style, 1850–1900*, New York: Rizzoli, 1985; and *The City and Collective Memory: Its Historical Imagery and Architectural Entertainments*, Cambridge, MA: MIT Press, 1994.

15   M. Christine Boyer, *CyberCities*, New York: Princeton Architectural Press, 1996. The chapter on "The Imaginary Real World of CyberCities" was originally published in *Assemblage* 18 (1992), 115–28. The quotes that follow refer to Michael Benedikt ed., *Cyberspace: First Steps*, Cambridge, MA: MIT Press, 1992; Michael Heim, "The Erotic Ontology of Cyberspace," in Benedikt ed., *Cyberspace*, 1992; Gilles Deleuze, "Postscript on Societies of Control," *October* 59 (1992), 3–7; and Homi K. Bhabha, "Race, Time, and the Revision of Modernity," *Oxford Literary Review* 13 (1991), 193–219.

industrialized city, and certainly the process of city planning are in various stages of dissolution, reflective of the disciplinary breakdown that CyberCities entail. So, Deleuze maintains, disciplinary societies that have molded behavior are giving way to numerical societies of modulating control facilitated by computer technology. We have evolved from using machines of production that require a disciplined labor force and an efficiently planned and organized city to inhabiting what is known as a space of flows defined by global networks of computers-a free-floating membrane of connectivity and control encircling the globe in ultra-rapid fashion and enabling a new economic order of multinational corporations to arise. In this new order, control acts like a sieve (a computer matrix) whose mesh transmutes from point to point, undulating and constantly at work. The code, not the norm, becomes the important device; now it is the password, not the watchword, that provides or inhibits access.   (1996: 18)

Drawing on Homi Bhabha, Paul Virilio, and others, Boyer develops an argument about the "lag-times," temporal disjunctions, and colonial "non-places" that now fill the "disappearing" centers of the postmetropolis and shape the emerging new urban imaginary.

In the late twentieth century, unknown and threatening territories lie inside the boundaries of the metropolis, where there are many lag-times, temporal breaks in the imaginary matrix, and areas of forced delay put on hold in the process of postmodernization. These partitions, cuts, and interruptions in the urban imaginary allow us to deny our complicity in the making of distinctions between the well-designed nodes of the matrix and the blank in-between places of nobody's concern. Disavowed, overlooked, marginalized, left out of our accounts, these are the center's truly invisible places-the inexpressible, the incomplete, the unattended-that have been rendered absent and forgotten . . .

[T]he imaginary matrix performs spatial and temporal disjunctions that enable us to think of city centers as if they were natural bipolar places of uneven development, rather than effects of a willful dismemberment that place certain lives and locations outside of, and only sometimes beside, the main events of contemporary cities. It is this splitting that the binary logic of the computer matrix allows us to achieve with relative ease. Such an arrangement, for example, provides Paul Virilio with his images of the disappearing city – where chronological topographies replace constructed geographical space, where immaterial electronic broadcast emissions decompose and eradicate a sense of place.
(1996: 118–19)

In later chapters, Boyer ventures into her own New York-focused and noir feminist version of the Carceral as well as the Cybercity, complete with references to *Blade Runner*, *Chinatown*, *RoboCop*, detective stories, technologies of violence, surveillance systems, the militarization of space, the rise of privatized enclaves, imposed safety zones, the sprawling and malling of American cities, CIDs and HOAs, urban boosterism, and the destruction of public space. What Boyer effectively captures is a hard-hitting late modern (rather than postmodern) radical critique of the dystopian imprint of cyberspace on contemporary cities and citybuilding, a less truculent and more architecture-friendly transcription of Mike Davis's *City of Quartz*. This is a welcome accomplishment, adding a significantly spatialized urban perspective to the more typically aspatial and historicist "pomo-bashing" that characterizes most leftist responses to "cyberhype." But like so much of this radical anti-postmodernism, the forced choice between utopia and dystopia, the rosy and the noir, too tightly confines the political debates about cyberspace to totalizing moral choices, to the binary 0 = bad versus 1 = good.[16]

In the end, Boyer closes off too many paths of potentially effective resistance by historically recasting the Cybercity as not much more than a historical extension of the Machine City, creating more of the same rather than something significantly different. This stance virtually dismisses all potentially progressive cyberspatial possibilities (including those relating to race, gender, and class) as hallucinatory promises. Her last words in the chapter on "The Imaginary Real World of Cyberspace" encapsule the blinkered cynicism and unquestioned historicism that so often accompany the best of late modernist critiques of postmodernity: "Let the *cortège* pass by!" (1996: 38). She concludes the entire book by offering another possible response. After asking whether the Cybercity represents the "final and irreversible erasure of the spatial containers that once stored our icons and images, the dematerialization of the wax into which our memories were once impressed ... symbolically bombed into nothingness [as] the sacrificial sites of cyberspace," she suggests that perhaps these fears are "yet another fiction" (1996: 244). The immediate result of these two options is either "let's do what we have always been doing" and not worry about what's new, or else a sneering and stolid cynicism with regard to the present urban scene that rivals the bovine immobility of extreme baudrillardism.

Simcities, Simcitizens, and hyperreality-generated crisis

Drawing on all the preceding approaches to understanding the restructuring of the urban imaginary, I present still another pathway into the sixth discourse, one that digs more deeply into the increasing hyperreality of everyday urban life and those "little tactics of the habitat" that bring hyperreality closer to home. This pathway also takes me closer to home as well, for while Los Angeles iconically hovered over the previous pathways, it grounds the discussion here and leads us in some new interpretive directions. As I have done for most of the earlier discourses, I have selected my own descriptive term to draw together and represent the various conceptualizations of the postmetropolitan transition discussed in this chapter. To define the composite product of the restructured urban imaginary, I use the term *Simcities*, an adaptation of the title of one of the world's most popular computer games.

---

16 For one recent example of such dystopian cybertrashing from the late modernist Left, see Julian Stallabrass, "Empowering Technology: The Exploration of Cyberspace," *New Left Review* 211 (1995), 3–32.

Conceived and designed by Will Wright, the game of *SimCity* comes in two versions, the "Classic," also called The Original City Simulator, and *SimCity 2000*, billed more boldly as The Ultimate City Simulator.[17] The Classic's *User Manual* (Bremer, 1993a), complete with a lengthy essay on the "History of Cities and City Planning" written by Cliff Ellis, introduces the simulation games:

> When you play SimCity, you design, build, and manage cities. You can design your own dream city from the ground up, or take over existing cities such as San Francisco, Tokyo, and Rio de Janeiro. Along the way you will deal with the planning and environmental issues of today, as well as disasters like fires, floods, earthquakes, air crashes, and an occasional monster. Your cities are populated by Sims – Simulated Citizens. Like their human counterparts, they build houses, condos, churches, stores and factories. And, also like humans, they complain about things like taxes, mayors, taxes, city planners, and taxes. If they get too unhappy, they move out, you collect fewer taxes, and the city deteriorates.
> (Bremer, 1993a: 4)

A more moralizing tone is added in *SimCity 2000's User's Manual* (Bremer, 1993b). You are immediately admonished with a lead quote that "To search for the ideal city today is useless . . . a waste of time . . . seriously detrimental. In fact, the concept is obsolete; there is no such thing." From the Introduction that follows this quotation your challenge is given:

> You're in charge . . . If your city is a nice place to live, your population will increase. If it's not, your Sims will leave town. And be assured that they'll let you know what they think about you and your policies . . . One of the toughest challenges of SimCity 2000 is to maintain a huge city without sacrificing your Sim's quality of life, without going broke maintaining the infrastructure, and without raising taxes so high that businesses relocate. SimCity 2000 lets you face the same dilemmas that mayors all over the world are facing. We've all said it at one time or another that we could do a better job than our elected officials – here's your chance to prove it . . . Sim City 2000 is primarily a "building" game, where you create and try to increase the size of your cities – but you also have plenty of opportunities to destroy. From bulldozers to earthquakes to air crashes, the implements of destruction are only a mouse-click away. But remember, it's a lot more challenging to build than to destroy, and the lives, hopes and dreams of millions of Sims are in your hands. (1993b: 2)

The User's Manuals provide rich fodder for a deconstructive discourse analysis, but I will leave that to others who wish to play the game more seriously. For present purposes, *SimCity* provides a useful cyberspatial launching pad into the actual hyperrealities of everyday life in the Los Angeles postmetropolis, itself perhaps the "ultimate" city simulator, the place where more designers, planners, elected officials, businesses, and citizens than anywhere else are actively *replacing reality* with insidiously diverting simulations.

17   A *SimCity 3000* has recently appeared, but I have not had the chance to check it out.

This process of replacing reality has, among many other effects, disney-worlded the postmetropolis. To echo the title of a recent book, the "New American City" is being increasingly recomposed into "Variations on a Theme Park," divertingly packaged hyperreal worlds of simulated cultures, urban communities, lifestyles, and consumer preferences.[18] Simcitizens of the theme-parked city select their place of residence not just on the basis of conventional standards of affordability, proximity to work, or access to good public facili-ties, those rational options of what the urban geographers call residential search behavior. They also choose, if they can afford to, a symbolic site that simulates a particular theme or site-image package. Searching for a place to live and to participate in the creation of community increasingly mimics a visit to Disneyland, where one can choose to enter Fantasyland, Adventureland, Frontierland, Tomorrowland, Toon Town; or to Disney World, with its addi-tional options: EPCOT (the experimental community of tomorrow), ersatz Germany, Thailand, Mexico, etc. Once the decision is made, however, the sim-ulated freedoms of choice disappear. An array of formal and informal regu-lations and covenants enforce commitment to the imagery chosen, creating another type of residential enclosure and "community" akin to what the lawyers call an "association-administered servitude regime."

The patchwork quilt of specialized residential communities this produces is much more fine-grained in its territoriality than the race- and class-segregated cities of the past, for it contains not only the older segregations but many new ones as well. Within the urban fabric of the Los Angeles post-metropolis, for example, there are multiple Leisure Worlds and Sun Cities for different lifestyle groupings of the elderly; apartment-blocked marinas for the swinging singles set; gay and lesbian communities and a "gay and gray" city (West Hollywood). There are cities like Simi Valley, filled with active and retired policemen and women defending their turf; a dense concentration, almost a ghetto, of engineers in the beach cities south of LAX, the interna-tional airport; special places and spaces for families committing their children to Olympic competition (Mission Viejo), or to an ecotopian environment, or to the California Promise. There are residential developments and "urban vil-lages" for those who may wish to live in replicas of Cervantes's Spain, a Greek Island ("Welcome to Mykonos," one advertisement proclaims), Nashville or New Orleans, lily-white suburbia, old New England, or any number of Spanish Colonial revivals.

Inverted versions of this residential hyperreality can also be found in the New Inner City, where creative reproductions and cosmopolitan tableaux vivants of all the world's cultures come together in a glocalized ethnic theme

18 Michael Sorkin ed., *Variations on a Theme Park: The New American City and the End of Public Space*, New York: Hill and Wang-Noonday Press, 1992. This book contains my chapter, "Inside Exopolis: Scenes from Orange County," which was reprinted in revised and expanded form as chapter 8 in *Third-space* (1996) and which is drawn upon again in this chapter of *Postmetropolis*. Also included here are chapters by Mike Davis ("Fortress Los Angeles: The Militarization of Urban Space") and M. Christine Boyer ("Cities for Sale: Merchandising History at South Street Seaport").

park of extraordinary proportions. As a site for the vicarious experience and delight of millions of itinerant visitors, the Inner City may be the "original" model for Florida's Disney World, the most popular (and most postmodern) of all traditional theme parks. In both places, one can visit Thailand or Germany or Mexico without having to travel long distances. In Los Angeles, however, the itinerary is much larger. One can taste the food, observe the customs, hear the language, and sense the traditions of nearly every culture on earth without leaving Los Angeles County. Amplifying a bit, it takes only a little flight of fancy to imagine the day when every tourist entering the Cosmopolis might be provided with a visitor's passbook to hundreds of cultural worlds, with rights to one meal in an appropriately "ethnic" restaurant, an authentic cultural encounter, a musical event, and a brief language lesson.

Simulated urbanism through theme-parking is not only redrawing the map of the residential geography of the postmetropolis, it is also being condensed into a constellation of specialized commercial sites, from "renaissance centers" to the Mall of America, from bustling "boiler rooms" for telemarketing to artfully boutiqued streetscapes.[19] Among the thousands of examples of these hypersites that now densely dot every postmetropolis, one recent development in Los Angeles deserves particular attention. It is CityWalk, located on a hill above the Hollywood Freeway in the so-aptly named "community" of Universal City. Described by its architects and developers as an "idealized reality, LA style" and an attempt to "deliver the unkept promise of Los Angeles," CityWalk aims at capturing and condensing the "real" feel of an LA street, complete with facades borrowed from Melrose Avenue boutiques, 3D billboards (with moving parts) copied from the Sunset Strip, and a tiny replica of Venice Beach, made more real with a ton of sand, simulated waves, and strolling troubadours. There is even a branch of UCLA Extension, attached to a much larger "students store" selling clothing and knick-knacks with the world-famous and copyrighted UCLA (ook-la) label.

The original idea for CityWalk also included an attempt to prefabricate history, with buildings painted "as if they had been occupied before" and candy wrappers and chewing gum embedded into the terrazzo flooring to give what was described as "a simulated patina of use." The project's market researchers eventually dispensed with history, however, to sell instead a new present. A "new and improved Los Angeles" is urgently needed, they claimed, because "reality has become too much of a hassle."[20] The 1992 Justice Riots forced a more pragmatic turn to CityWalk. Surveillance machinery multiplied and security forces became more visible in an attempt to assure that the "real" Los Angeles would not be let into its hyperreal simulation, even to the point of prohibiting black teenagers from entering the multiplex cinema's presenta-

19 For a discussion of the telemarketing "boiler room," see *Thirdspace*, 1996: 275–6.
20 The quoted material comes from a report on CityWalk contained in the *Los Angeles Times*, February 29, 1992.

tion of such films as *Colors* and *Boyz N the Hood*. A small riot followed these restrictions and the policy was seemingly reversed, although CityWalk remains a tightly controlled space successfully isolated from the rest of Los Angeles. It exists today as a highly popular annex to that bulging world of ticket-required hypersimulations, the Universal Studios tour.

The theme-parking of the metropolis is spatially intertwined with another form of the "habitactics of make-believe," as I called it in chapter 8 of *Third-space*. I named this articulated zone where actual urban life is being replaced by especially thick layers of simulations the *scamscape*, and explored its tangible effects in Orange County. Perhaps more than in any other place, daily life in this postsuburban county-city is increasingly being played out as if it were a computer game of "ultimate" simulation. This has produced not only the "artificial paradise" and "primitive community of the future" that Baudrillard found in Orange County, but also a new set of problems growing out of the habitactics of make-believe and the restructured urban imaginary. One of the earlier examples of what I have described more generally as restructuring-generated crises was the Savings and Loan fiasco that was creatively centered in the scamscape of Orange County and may have eventually cost USA taxpayers as much as $500 billion to "resolve." In 1994, the cracks in the scamscape opened even wider with the county's peculiarly postmodern local government bankruptcy.[21]

The Orange County bankruptcy is a particularly vivid window from which to observe the Simcity in crisis and the degree to which federal, state, and local government in the USA has come to revolve around what might best be called Simpolitics, Simgovernance, Simcitizens, and SimAmerica. What occurred in 1994 differed significantly from the urban financial crises of New York City and other urban areas in the 1970s and early 1980s. The latter were caused primarily by cash flow problems arising from rapidly increasing expenditures on welfare, social services, and infrastructure, and city budgets that could not keep pace with these increases. Like corporations facing decreasing profits or potential losses, the response was to restructure, to get leaner and meaner by reducing payrolls, eliminating programs, and laying off workers. Unlike corporations, however, sessile city governments could not choose that other restructuring strategy, to close down and relocate somewhere else.

The fountainhead of the taxpayers's rebellion that culminated in the passage of Proposition 13 in 1978 and paragon of "small government is better government" ideology, Orange County by the early 1990s was a much-copied

---

21   For a thorough, informative, and critical policy analysis of this event, see Mark Baldassare, *When Government Fails: The Orange County Bankruptcy*, Berkeley and Los Angeles: University of California Press (with the Public Policy Institute of California), 1998. Baldassare roots his interpretation of the causes of the Orange County bankruptcy in political fragmentation (lack of central authority, too many local governments), voter distrust (opposition to tax increases, welfare expenditures, and spendthrift government, except for middle-class services), and state fiscal austerity shifting burdens to the local, revenues to the state). I try to add another dimension to these causes.

model of administrative efficiency and fiscal well-being. Proposition 13 had imposed strict limits on property tax increases and thus also on the ability of local governments to raise additional taxes. Faced with such constraints, municipal finance and county government increasingly came to mimic the simulation game of *SimCity*, whose software, as those who play it will know, is primarily geared around setting appropriate tax rates to assure growth while preventing Simcitizens from rebelling or monsters from gobbling up the city. With little possibility for increased property tax receipts and a dominant ideology that forbade any other kind of tax increase or dependency on the federal government for public funding (especially given the largesse of the Department of Defense in Southern California), Orange County's Tax Collector plunged into financial cyberspace to find new ways to finance the dozens of municipalities, school districts, transit authorities, water boards, police forces, prisons, freeways, and other public services.[22]

Leveraging the county's revenues, the Tax Collector entered that brave new deregulated world of exotic derivatives and leveraged synthetics that was being creatively reshaped by the "science of complex systems," a cybernetic theory which had long shifted its earlier attention from chess to financial markets in order to test complicated theories of neural nets and genetic algorithms. For more than a decade, the neuromancing Tax Collector, Robert Citron, was enormously successful, the envy of tax collectors around the country, betting the people's money on speculative expectations of decreasing federal interest rates. No tax shortfalls here in SimCounty, only happy faces. The modest and non-interfering Simgovernment of the Board of Supervisors as well as the county's Simcitizens, knowing little about the financial games being played, repeatedly expressed their pride in the lone Democrat's achievements, at least until the game crashed in December, 1994.

Unfortunately, this game of SimCounty could not simply be rebooted and played again, although one can almost imagine it being tried. What has happened since the bankruptcy has been a mixture of continuing disbelief and denial, manic attempts to find the evil perpetrators and throw them in prison, knee-jerk restructuring programs aimed at cutting back social services and laying off county workers, and, in a nightmare of contradictions, even a (failed) referendum to raise sales taxes a fractional percent to pay the $1.64 billion debt. Despite these efforts to wipe out the very real simulated loss (no one seemed to know where the lost money actually went to) and indeed to reboot the game of SimCounty, Orange County today is no longer what it used to be, although the large local army of spin doctors is actively trying to restore its former image.

---

22 The title "Tax Collector" in Orange County is a little like that of "Resident Pederast" in a playschool. The aptly named Robert L. Citron, a Democrat who lived very modestly, held this title for 24 years in this bastion of Republican fortitude. He survived in part by reportedly sending happy-face personal messages on the property tax forms his office distributed each year. His first response after the bankruptcy exploded in world headlines (*The Economist* led its story with the banner "Citron pressé") was "I did nothing irresponsible in any way, shape, or form," probably as accurate and honest a claim as can be found in the scamscapes of SimCounty.

SimAmerica: a concluding critique

To place the volatile scamscapes and Simcities of Southern California in a wider perspective, it is useful to turn to the national scale and look back briefly to the highly specialized and politically successful production of hyperreality that was practiced in the Reagan-Bush years. Without resorting to any conspiracy theory or demeaning the patriotic intent of its primary leaders, it can be argued that a reactionary form of postmodern politics, already in motion in the late 1960s, accelerated rapidly after the election of a Hollywood actor and ex-California governor as president in 1980. The Republican majority had already been constructed around a "southern strategy" that thinly veiled an appeal to white racism in the Sunbelt and in the suburbs that bulged with a fearful population fleeing the darker recesses of the inner cities and the urban riots of the late 1960s. In power, the Reagan regime acted boldly to consolidate its support from the so-called "silent majority," one of a dazzling array of hypersimulations used to sell postmodern neoconservatism to the American public. It is useful to recall here the difference between simulation and dissimulation. To dissimulate is to pretend that you do not have what you really have, to lie or to cover up. Watergate, at least initially, was good old dissimulation, as was the "disinformation" programs associated with the Vietnam War, although both served as effective training grounds for future innovations in informational spin-doctoring. In contrast, to simulate is to pretend to have something that you really do not have. When such simulation becomes so believable that you can no longer tell the difference between the simulated and the real, then you have genuinely edged into full-blown hyperreality.

Among the most convincing hypersimulations of the Reagan years was the crusade against "Big Government," a political scam that restructured the national ideology and, along with it, what I have called the urban imaginary. The spin-doctored ideology of small-is-better government was used as a potent weapon to attack the Keynesian welfare state, to dismantle many anti-poverty programs under the guise of a hyped-up New Federalism, to resimulate the civil rights movement through cleverly recomposed imagery that associated its accomplishments with "reverse racism" and "political correctness," to root recession in negative thinking and rationalize the need for a downsizing new austerity, and to virtually deconstruct and reconstitute the meaning of liberal democracy and representative government. Family values (during a period when the number of "traditional" households of one breadwinner, a wife, and two children may have declined more rapidly than ever before in USA history), Sunbelt and suburban virtues (including the open shop, union-bashing, and the patriotic promotion of xenophobic whiteness), and, above all the mythic power of the free market and legendary American entrepreneurial skills were all combined into a hyperreal substitute for Big Government. Backed by metafrauds that put the Savings and Loan scandal to shame, such as trickle-down (or voodoo) economics, deregulation as a development strategy, and privatization as a means of rescuing the public sector from debt and inefficiency, one of the most undertaxed of all industrial nations rationalized and supported one of the biggest government programs to subsidize the wealthy, that "fortunate fifth," in recent history. That all this could occur during a decade of deepening poverty, declining real wages, devastating deindustrialization, and the gargantuan ballooning of the national debt is a testimony to the real-and-imagined power of simulacra.

Behind the simulated retreat from Big Government was increased federal and local intervention into the economy and into everyday life across the country, a scam of such proportions that it had to be imagineered by another, more global, hypersimulation. During the Reagan years, a growing tide of factual disinformation reconstructed the already hypersimulated Cold War threat into what would eventually be named a New World Order, with a now economically weakened and polarized SimAmerica as its postmodern RoboCop and the mass media of the New Information Age as its primary battlefield. This very American and highly cinematic/televisual hypersimulation, punctuated by events in Grenada, Libya, Panama, Nicaragua, and that most postmodern and telematic of military spectaculars, Operation Desert Storm, legitimated the domestic reorganization of the welfare state into the more narrowly specialized warfare state. A sort of military Keynesianism fueled the economy, especially in Southern California, with many billions of dollars for national defense and related "strategic defense initiatives" such as Star Wars, all seemingly designed to protect the country against imminent Communist invasion.

Far more costly than drilling schoolchildren to "take cover" or constructing bomb shelters, an earlier model for simulating the threat of Cold War attacks, the New World Order ideology became the most effective force shaping urban and regional development in the USA, and another linchpin in the Republican southern or Sunbelt strategy. But on the domestic front, this was not enough. Continuing to feed off the fears of its majority constituencies, the hypersimulation-addicted neoconservative regime, by now also donning the label neoliberal in another of those postmodern twists, opened a new offensive against the inner cities, which were perceived to hold the most serious domestic threats to Republican hegemony and the militant new Pax Americana. The old war on poverty was spun into a war against the urban poor. Under the appealing banner of law and order, local and federal police forces were mobilized and militarized to lead the struggle against drugs, gangs, crime, illegal immigrants, unemployed black youth, and other inner city targets that symbolically defined a reconstituted and decidedly urban "enemy within."

This trajectory of hypersimulations remained in force after the Clinton victory and Los Angeles riots of 1992. Although the new administration began with more radical intentions, especially with regard to health care and the needs of workers, it quickly became swept up in the neoconservative-neoliberal tide. Fixated on images of economic recovery and job growth, the

national imaginary shifted in the late 1990s to a modified version of mytho-
logical Reaganism, a "new prosperity" in which an upswing of productivity
growth and GNP was built on continued reductions in real wages, severe cut-
backs on welfare, intensified disparities between the rich and poor, and
another round of lean and mean downsizing and austerity for the working
poor. There were a few progressive twists added under the Clinton administration, but not enough to suggest any major reversal of trajectory of the previous two decades.

What can be seen in these quick glimpses of emergent SimAmerica is a place
where conventional politics is being increasingly emptied of substance and
any presumption of factuality or objectivity; where a powerfully conservative
hyperreality absorbs the real-and-imagined in its own skein of simulations;
where representative democracy is rechanneled into a politics of strategic representation, dissembling reality into competitive image-bites and electronic
populism; where trickle-down economics is practiced without blush or question despite all the empirical evidence of its failures; and where "political
correctness" and other brilliantly devised hypersimulations are spun into
ever-absorptive and appealing metafrauds. For a large segment of the
American electorate today, these hypersimulations are continuing to affect
national and local politics. Affirmative action, for example, has seemingly
been successfully spun into an un-American and racist evil, the cause of
African American, Latino, and women's poverty rather than a potential solution. Similarly, feminism and homosexuality are persistently associated with
the destruction of god-fearing family values, labor unions and radical envi-
ronmentalists continue to be assigned primary responsibility for all signs of
economic decline, and the magic of free, open, and totally unregulated
markets is turned to with renewed faith, despite the fact that, like most simulacra, such markets have never actually existed. Increasingly in recent years,
immigrants and young African Americans are being symbolically reconstituted as the internal enemy and targeted for attack in vicious post-Cold War
games of renewed brutality, while the worst levels of social inequality in the
developed world are either ignored or, more cruelly, blamed on the poor and
truly disadvantaged.

These and other hypersimulations are genuinely believed by many, if not
most, Americans to be the true reality. How then might more progressive
forces respond to this empowerment of hyperreality and the precession of simulacra? Simply stripping away the imagery to unmask the "truer" material
realities hidden behind them – the most powerful strategy of radical modernism – may no longer be enough to present an effective challenge or an
appropriate critical response. Modernist politics of the Left traditionally builds
on the presumption of historical continuities, such as the persistence of essentially exploitative relations of capitalist production and the revolutionary
potential of the working class. These conditions continue to be part of the
present as much as they were in the past. But this unmasking or demystification tells us little more than that capitalism still exists. While Marxist critiques
remain insightfully relevant in helping us understand what is the *same* today

as it was in the past, they provide much less insight into helping us understand – and respond effectively to – what is *new and different*.

For these and other reasons, I have been arguing throughout this book that another and strategically postmodern radical politics needs to be developed that goes beyond demystification and unmasking the continuities of capitalism to confront and contend more directly with the now entrenched successes of neoconservative and neoliberal postmodernism and the other new forms of contemporary global and local capitalist development. This will involve in part the creation of alternative and transgressive new imagery that can help to resist and subvert the established conditions of postmodernity, for so much now depends on these image wars. In particular, new spaces must be opened in SimAmerica and in the postmetropolis to practice a strategically postmodern politics of social and spatial justice, building on the insights and actions of intercultural and hybridized coalitions that cross the boundaries of race, class, gender, and geography rather than being confined by them to separate channels of resistance.

These are not easy tasks, and simply intoning the need to pursue them is not enough. Keeping the challenge in mind, however, does help in understanding the pervasive implications of the sixth discourse on the postmetropolis. Hyperreality is here to stay. It will not pass by, and therefore it must be thoroughly understood and contended with as a vital part of contemporary political culture. In interpreting its meaning, it is also clear that we need to go beyond the rigid utopian–dystopian dualisms that have thus far marked so many of the interpretations of the changing urban imaginary. The postmetropolis is neither utopia nor dystopia *tout court*, but both in heavy doses . . . and more. All of its darkside emanations as well as the many new opportunities it offers for greater social and spatial justice need to be recognized in their complex interweavings. But before we feel too confident in our practical and theoretical understanding of the postmetropolitan transition, it must also be recognized that the postmetropolis may have turned a significant corner in the 1990s. What has for the past thirty years been describable as a complex process of crisis-generated restructuring may now be more cogently understood as the beginning of a period of multiplying crises emanating directly from the new urbanization processes themselves. This makes the need to develop a progressive if not radical response that is adapted to the particularities of the postmetropolis and postmodern urbanism even more urgent. Continuing to use Los Angeles as a window onto the contemporary urban condition, let us examine this shift from crisis-generated restructuring to restructuring-generated crisis through the real-and-imagined events associated with the Justice Riots of 1992.

Part III
Lived Space: Rethinking 1992 in Los Angeles

Introduction

If there is a general thread that runs through every chapter in this book, it is an interpretive foregrounding of a critical spatial perspective, one that seeks to understand the spatiality of human life as it is simultaneously *perceived, conceived*, and *lived*. This trialectic of spatiality, as I have called it, tilted more toward an emphasis on perceived empirical spaces and material spatial practices, past and present, in Part I: Remapping the Geohistory of Cityspace. In the Six Discourses on the Postmetropolis that comprise Part II, the primary emphasis shifted to conceived or imagined spaces, in particular to the scholarly representations and conceptualizations of the new urbanization processes and how they help to understand the formation of specifically postmetropolitan cityspace. In Part III, understanding fully lived space comes to the fore, combining the perceived and the conceived, the objectively real and the subjectively imagined, things in space and thoughts about space, in an expanded interpretive scope that I have described as a thirdspace perspective. To some degree, every preceding chapter has been informed by a thirdspace perspective and each has contributed in one way or another to our understanding of the lived spaces of Los Angeles and other postmetropolitan city-regions. Here, however, the problems as well as the new possibilities associated with a thirdspace perspective and epistemology become more immediately explicit and challenging.

Looking at lived space both broadens and narrowly focuses the discussion in the three concluding chapters. Viewed as an encompassing lifeworld of individual and collective experience, any fully lived space can be compared to your or my biography, our "lived time," or to a similar biography of a city or society in all its complexity. A thousand of the best specialists working for decades could never hope to produce anything near complete knowledge and understanding of these subjects, their intricacy and nuances. There is too much that is unknowable, incomprehensible, inaccessible, even with the best methods of analysis and interpretation. In adopting a thirdspace perspective, one is therefore forced to be selective, to focus on what is most likely to be revealing not in some abstract or universal sense but with regard to a particular purpose and commitment, a specific project that guides the search for knowledge and understanding. This often involves experimentation with new ways of increasing our knowledge and understanding beyond what is already known and accepted.

My project throughout this book has been to encourage better ways of thinking and acting to resolve the major problems facing contemporary societies throughout the world, an emancipatory project which I share with critical scholars everywhere. Distinguishing my emancipatory objective from most others is an assertive advocacy – call it affirmative action if you wish – of a critical spatial imagination and praxis that sees opportunities in the encompassing spatiality of human life and in an explicit consciousness of this spatiality to actively struggle against economic exploitation, cultural domination, and individual oppression, whether based on class, race, gender, or any other axis of differential power and inequality in society. At the heart of this advocacy is an intentional and strategic process of *spatialization* that reconstitutes all social struggles and the historical contexts in which they are contained as inherently spatial, continuously involved in the construction of social spatiality. Hence my assertion and use of such terms as spatial praxis, spatial politics, cityspace, geohistory, the spatial specificity of urbanism, synekism, regionality, regional democracy, the rights to the city, and, above all, *spatial justice*. I do not mean to substitute spatial justice for the more familiar notion of social justice, but rather to bring out more clearly the potentially powerful yet often obscured spatiality of all aspects of social life and to open up in this spatialized sociality (and historicality) more effective ways to change the world for the better through spatially conscious practices and politics.

The goal of achieving greater spatial justice has implicitly shaped every chapter of *Postmetropolis*, even when reaching back to Jericho, Çatal Hüyük, and Ur. It ties my commentary on the geohistory of synekistic cityspace and the more recently evolving postmetropolitan transition to a cluster of approaches to urban studies that have similarly emphasized and advanced a vividly critical spatial imagination: geopolitical economy and the new regionalism, spatial feminism and the postcolonial critique, and related extensions of postmodern cultural and geographical studies. In the next three chapters, everything comes together, so to speak, in the microcosm of what I have purposefully chosen to call the Justice Riots that literally and figuratively "took place" in Los Angeles in the early spring of 1992.

The year 1992 was especially memorable. Looking back half a millennium, it marked the quincentennial of Columbus's footfall in the New World and the onset of a Spanish conquest and colonization that would, along with other subsequent European incursions, destroy long-established indigenous civilizations and install a lasting Old World presence in their wake. Two centuries ago, in 1792, the French Revolution was in full flow, with the proclamation of the French Republic under the Jacobins and the initial use of both the revolutionary calendar and the guillotine. In the USA in the same year, dollar coinage was first minted, Part Two of Thomas Paine's *Rights of Man* was published, and both the Republican and Federalist parties were founded. Two hundred years later, not only did Los Angeles explode but William Jefferson Clinton would be elected President, appearing to end an era of Republican ascendancy under Ronald Reagan and George Bush.

In the conurbation of Los Angeles, the fall of the Berlin Wall, the attendant beginning of the end of the Cold War, and the disintegration of the Communist arch-enemy had contributed to what, by 1992, had clearly emerged as one of the worst economic recessions in the region's history. Accustomed if not addicted to boom, the regional economy seemed to be in an uneasy state of denial as arguably the most active job machine in the Western world ground virtually to a halt. After peaking in 1989, the year the Berlin Wall fell, manufacturing employment in Los Angeles County would decline by nearly a third over the next five years, much faster than almost anywhere else in the country. Nearly every sector felt the recession, but the impact was particularly severe on African Americans and the Latino working poor, compressed as they were into tight niches within the restructured labor market of the postfordist industrial metropolis. The mood of the population, across all class, ethnic, and gender boundaries, was unusually tense and filled with new fears and frustrations.

This tension was aggravated still further, especially but not only in Black Los Angeles, by two events that occurred in the previous year. First was the murder of 15-year-old Latasha Harlins by an elderly Korean woman grocer who was subsequently acquitted of any major crime. The second was the now infamous beating by a covey of LAPD officers of Rodney King during a routine stop for erratic driving. Filmed by a bystander, the recorded images of the beating would send shockwaves around the world and, eventually, through the trial of the police officers involved, prepare the way for the most violent and destructive urban uprising in twentieth-century America. This is the backdrop from which we move into Rethinking 1992 in Los Angeles.

This interpretive rethinking begins with two chapters in which I experiment with an alternative mode of writing about lived space. In chapters 12 and 13, I present no text of my own except through a running commentary in the footnotes. The chapters are composed instead of a purposeful selection of excerpts from the literature on the Justice Riots and their geohistorically wider and deeper implications. My intent, in part, is to orchestrate a multiplicity of voices and interpretations, but with a continuing bias toward those observers and observations that enhance a critical spatial perspective on the events and their aftermath. Especially prominent among these observers is Barbara Hooper, whose essay "Bodies, Cities, Texts: The Case of Citizen Rodney King," features prominently in chapter 12 and from whose unruly critical spatial imagination I have learned so much.

I have taken as my textual and contextual model and inspiration for these chapters the poetically scripted text, *Twilight – Los Angeles, 1992*, composed as a book and performed as a prize-winning play by the documentary theater artist Anna Deveare Smith. As she has done before and since on different but related subjects, Smith collected interviews with key individuals involved in one way or another with the events of 1992, scripted these interviews in loose verse form in a written text, and then performed all the parts herself on stage in a one-woman show that reflected her "search for the character of Los Angeles in the wake of the initial Rodney King verdict" (1994: xvii). I cannot hope to achieve the power of Smith's performative artistry, but try to follow her lead in scripting chapters 12 and 13 around selected passages from her work, from the equally performative essay of Barbara Hooper, as well as from many other sources of potential insight into what happened in Los Angeles in 1992 and in the years that have followed.

In the final chapter, I use no lengthy quotes from other sources but instead try to present in my words alone an open-ended conclusion to *Postmetropolis*. Drawing on what has been happening in Los Angeles since that eventful year, I focus on two "new beginnings" locally emerging in the aftermath of the Justice Riots. The first inflects upon what I have persistently argued throughout this book, that the postmetropolitan transition has moved from a period of crisis-generated restructuring to one of restructuring-generated crises. The second centers on the very recent development of significant spatially-conscious and broad-based movements aimed at redirecting the new urbanization processes toward greater spatial justice and regional democracy. These new beginnings both build on existing interpretations of the postmetropolitan transition and present additional challenges to our practical and theoretical understanding of the contemporary moment.

Chapter 12
LA 1992: Overture to a Conclusion

Revisionings

This twilight moment
is an in-between moment.
It's the moment of dusk.
It's the moment of ambivalence
and ambiguity
The inclarity,
the enigma,
the ambivalences,
in what happened in the L.A.
uprisings
are precisely what we want to get hold of.
It's exactly the moment
when the L.A. uprisings could be something
else
than it was seen to be,
or maybe something
other than it was seen to be . . .

(Homi K. Bhabha)[1]

And Polo said: "The inferno of the living is not something that will be; if there is one, it is what is already here, the inferno where we live every day, that we form by being together. There are two ways to escape suffering it. The first is easy for many: accept the inferno and become such a part of it that you can no longer see it. The second is risky and demands constant vigilance and apprehension: seek and learn to recognize who and what, in the midst of the inferno, are not inferno, then make them endure, give them space."

(Italo Calvino)[2]

---

1 Homi K. Bhabha, "Twilight #1," from a telephone conversation with documentary theater artist Anna Deveare Smith, in Deveare Smith, *Twilight – Los Angeles, 1992*, New York: Doubleday Anchor Books, 1994: 232–4. Her richly performative text was enacted as a prize-winning play in which she played all the characters, drawing on the scripts contained in *Twilight*.
2 Italo Calvino, *Invisible Cities*, tr. W. Weaver, New York: Harcourt Brace Jovanovich, 1974: 165. Calvino's writings, especially *Invisible Cities*, have been an especially rich source of insightful quotations for contemporary urban and cultural studies scholars. This particular quote, taken from the concluding paragraph of this wonderful book, kindles new kinds of remembrances arising from the

On thinking about Hell, I gather
My brother Shelley found it was a place
Much like the city of London. I
Who live in Los Angeles and not in London
Find, on thinking about Hell, that it must be
Still more like Los Angeles.

(Bertolt Brecht)[3]

And here we are, at the center of the arc, trapped in the gaudiest, most valuable, and most improbable water wheel the world has ever seen. Everything now, we must assume, is in our hands: we have no right to assume otherwise.

(James Baldwin)[4]

we learn three things:
one, we learn that the hard outlines of what we see in
    daylight
that make it easy for us to order
daylight
disappear.
So we begin to see its boundaries in a much more faded
    way.
That fuzziness of twilight
allows us to see the intersections
of the event with a number of other things that daylight
    obscures for
us,
to use a paradox.
We have to interpret more in
twilight,
we have to make ourselves
part of the act,

infernal ashes of 1992, and also looks forward in their twilight residue with a call that effectively captures the contemporary political moment: find who and what are not inferno and make them endure, *give them space*. This is what I try to do with the collage of reflections that compose and comprise this and the next chapter.

3 Bertolt Brecht, "On Thinking about Hell," *Poems, 1913–1956*, John Willett and Ralph Manheim eds., New York: Methuen, 1979; lead quote in Michael Omi and Howard Winant, "The Los Angeles 'Race Riot' and Contemporary USA Politics," in *Reading Rodney King/Reading Urban Uprising*, Robert Gooding-Williams ed., New York: Routledge, 1993: 97–114. Brecht was among the many European intellectuals who settled for some time in Los Angeles after fleeing from fascism. His comments about Los Angeles as Hell, as inferno, attach to a long tradition, one that harks back at least to the violent post-conquest period of the late nineteenth century, when the new American city was actually described as Hell Town for its unusually high incidence of violence and murder.

4 James Baldwin, *The Fire Next Time*, New York: Dell, 1981: 41. The incendiary theme continues with one of the most powerful African American voices of the twentieth century, drawing from a book whose title was in part a reflection of the urban crises of the 1960s, and in part a prediction of what was to come in 1992. The brief excerpt is as apt as ever, even if one does not take the most gaudy, valuable, improbable water wheel trap to be centered only in Los Angeles.

we have to interpret,
we have to project more.
But also the thing itself
in twilight
challenges us
to
be aware
of how we are projecting onto the event itself.

(Homi K. Bhabha, continued)[5]

[R]ecent apertures in critical thought instigated by certain internal displacements in the hearth of the West (feminism, deconstructionism, psychoanalysis, post-metaphysical thought) have been increasingly augmented by the persistent question of a presence that no longer lies elsewhere: the return of the repressed, the subordinate and the forgotten in "Third World" musics, literatures, poverties and populations as they come to occupy the economies, cities, institutions, media and leisure time of the First World. Such a highly charged punctuation of the cosmopolitan script destined finally to be recognised as a part of our history and be televised in future riots of the metropolitan dispossessed, compels us to recognise the need for a mode of thinking that is neither fixed nor stable, but is one that is open to the prospect of a continual return to events, to their re-elaboration and revision. This retelling, re-citing and re-siting of what passes for historical and cultural knowledge depend upon the re-calling and re-membering of earlier fragments and traces that flare up and flash in our "present moment of danger" as they come to live on in new constellations. These are fragments that remain as fragments: splinters of light that illuminate our journey while simultaneously casting questioning shadows along the path. The belief in the transparency of truth and the power of origins to define the finality of our passage is dispersed by this perpetual movement of transmutation and transformation. History [ES: and Geography] is harvested and collected, to be assembled, made to speak, remembered, re-read and rewritten, and language comes alive in transit, in interpretation.

(Iain Chambers)[6]

We are part of
producing the event,
whereas, to use the daylight
metaphor,
there we somehow think
the event and its clarity

---

5   If I were to underscore anything in this continued conversation with Homi Bhabha, it would be his admonition that we have to make ourselves part of the act and become more aware of how we are projecting ourselves onto the events if we are to interpret the twilight moment.

6   Iain Chambers, *Migrancy, Culture, Identity*, London: Routledge, 1994: 3. Chambers's vivid prose has guided us through many chapters of *Postmetropolis*. Here he compels us to a continual return to events, to their re-elaboration, revision, retelling, re-citing and re-siting. I am sure he would not mind my adding Geography to History in defining what is being rewritten.

as it is presented to us,
and we have to just react to it.
Not that we're participating in its clarity:
it's more interpretive,
it's more creative.

(Homi K. Bhabha, continued)

I think there is an expectation that in this diverse city, and in this diverse nation, a unifying voice would bring increased understanding and put us on the road to solutions. This expectation surprises me. There is little in culture or education that encourages the development of a unifying voice. In order to have real unity, all voices would have to first be heard or at least represented. Many of us who work in race relations do so from the point of view of our own ethnicity. This very fact inhibits our ability to hear more voices than those that are closest to us in proximity. Few people speak a language about race that is not their own. If more of us could actually speak from another point of view, like speaking another language, we could accelerate the flow of ideas.

(Anna Deveare Smith)[7]

Let us hope and pray that the vast intelligence, imagination, humor, and courage of this country will not fail us. Either we learn a new language of empathy and compassion, or the fire this time will consume us all.

(Cornel West)[8]

We are much more recent than we think.

(Michel Foucault)[9]

We're all stuck here for awhile . . .

(Rodney King)[10]

7   Anna Deveare Smith, "Introduction," *Twilight – Los Angeles, 1992*, 1994: xxiv–xxv. What Deveare Smith says for race and ethnicity holds true for class, gender, sexuality, and other axes of unequal power: we must not only make sure that all voices are heard and represented, we must also learn to speak from another point of view, one that is not necessarily inscribed in our own personal identities. For those who speak from a position of privilege, like so many of us, it is useful to recall Gayatri Spivak's provocative urging that we "unlearn our privilege as our loss," a very difficult challenge, for indeed we have so much to lose.
8   Cornel West, "Learning to Talk of Race," *New York Times Magazine*, August 2, 1992. Here again there is a call for a new language that is radically open and filled with a multiplicity of voices. And there is a new urgency, arising from the immediacy of crisis, that recalls Baldwin's earlier warnings that the fire next time is upon us *now* and *here*.
9   Michel Foucault, *Politics, Philosophy, Culture: Interviews and Other Writings*, Lawrence D. Kritzman ed., tr. Alan Sheridan, New York: Routledge, 1988: 156.
10   Rodney King, after his more publicized question: "Can we all get along?"

Bodies, Cities, Texts: The Case of Citizen Rodney King
(by Barbara Hooper)[11]

Inscriptions[12]

Many questions were troubling the explorer, but at the sight of the prisoner he asked only: "Does he know his sentence?"
"No," said the officer, eager to go on with his exposition . . .
"He doesn't know the sentence that has been passed on him?"
"No," said the officer again . . . "There would be no point in telling him. He'll learn it on his body."

(Franz Kafka)[13]

The whole of (social) space proceeds from the body.

(Henri Lefebvre)[14]

In the production room that was the Simi Valley Courthouse, power was made, displayed, in the torture/beating of Rodney King – "a grotesque piece of compensatory drama" that produced the LAPD, America, democracy, the new world order, as regime, and the pain of Rodney King as its power. This "obsessive display of agency" . . . occurred in stark opposition to the display of King's silence.[15]

---

11   What follows has been extracted from Barbara Hooper, "Bodies, Cities, Texts: The Case of Citizen Rodney King," unpublished manuscript, February 1994, 80pp. A preliminary version of the manuscript was presented at the annual meetings of the Association of American Geographers, Atlanta, 1992. Hooper's work on Rodney King is part of a larger dissertation/book project under the working title *Performativities of Space: Bodies, Cities, Texts,* in which she also explores bodies, cities, and texts in the Athenian polis and in nineteenth-century Paris. See Hooper, "Corporeal Democracy: The Production of the Citizen-Body in Classical Athens," unpublished manuscript, presented at the annual meetings of the Association of American Geographers, San Francisco, 1994; and "The Poem of Male Desires: Female Bodies, Modernity, and 'Paris, Capital of the Nineteenth Century,'" in Leonie Sandercock ed., *Making the Invisible Visible: A Multicultural Planning History,* Berkeley and Los Angeles: University of California Press, 1998: 227–54. I want to thank Barbara for letting me use her 1994 text to illustrate the new interpretive languages of critical spatial analysis that are developing in the 1990s to make practical and theoretical sense of the contemporary moment, and, in particular, to help rethink what can be learned from the events of 1992 in Los Angeles.
12   The material that follows under *Inscriptions* collects together brief excerpts from Barbara Hooper's entire essay, plus a few additional commentaries I have added. In this section as well as in *Somatography: The Order in Place,* the added material appears in square brackets [ ].
13   Franz Kafka, *The Metamorphosis, the Penal Colony, and Other Stories,* New York: Schocken Books, 1975: 197. Lead quote in Hooper, *Inscriptions.*
14   Henri Lefebvre, *The Production of Space,* Oxford, UK, and Cambridge, MA: Blackwell, 1991. Lead quote in Hooper, *Somatography.*
15   Barbara Hooper, 1994: 62. The material in quotation marks refers to Elaine Scary, *The Body in Pain: The Making and Unmaking of the World,* New York: Oxford University Press, 1985: 27–8. What Scary describes as "a grotesque piece of compensatory drama" is torture, "the conversion of absolute pain to absolute power." Drawing on Scary, Hooper writes: "Hence, the rooms in which torture occurs have been named accordingly: 'the production room' in the Philippines; 'the cinema room' in South Viet Nam; the 'blue lit stage' in Chile."

[In the white world the man of color encounters difficulties in the development of his bodily schema. Consciousness of the body is solely a negating activity. It is a third person consciousness. The body is surrounded by an atmosphere of certain uncertainty ... movements are made not out of habit but out of implicit knowledge. A slow composition of my *self* as a body in the middle of a spatial and temporal world – which seems to be the schema ...

Below the corporeal schema [is] a historico-racial schema. The elements I had used had been provided for me ... by the other, the white man, who had woven me out of a thousand details, anecdotes, stories. I thought that what I had in hand was to construct a physiological self, to balance space, to localize sensations, and here I was called on for more.

"Look, a Negro!" It was an external stimulus that flicked over me as I passed by. I made a tight smile. "Look, a Negro!" It was true. It amused me.

"Look, a Negro!" The circle was drawing a bit tighter. I made no secret of my amusement. "Mama, see the Negro! I'm frightened!" Frightened! Frightened! Now they are beginning to be afraid of me. I made up my mind to laugh myself to tears but laughter had become impossible.

(Frantz Fanon)[16]]

[The visual field is not neutral to the question of race; it is itself a racial formation, an episteme, hegemonic and forceful ... In Fanon's recitation of the racist interpellation, the black body is circumscribed as dangerous, prior to any gesture, any raising of the hand, and the infantilized white reader is positioned in the scene as one who is helpless in relation to the black body, as one definitionally in need of protection by his/her mother or, perhaps, the police. The fear is that some physical distance will be crossed, and the virgin sanctity of whiteness will be endangered by that proximity. The police are thus structurally placed to protect whiteness against violence, where violence is the imminent action of the black male body. And because with this imaginary schema, the police protect whiteness, their own violence cannot be read as violence; because the black male body, prior to any video, is the site and source of danger, a threat, the police effort to subdue this body, even if in advance, is justified regardless of the circumstances. Or rather, the conviction of that justification rearranges and orders the circumstances to fit that conclusion.

The video is not only violently decontextualized, but violently recontextualized ... [Rodney King] becomes, within that schema, nothing other than the site at which that racist violence fears and beats the specter of its own rage.

(Judith Butler)[17]]

16 Frantz Fanon, *Black Skins/White Masks*, tr. C. L. Markmann, New York: Grove Weidenfeld, 1967: 111–12. An abbreviated version of this quote also appears in Hooper to introduce *The Trial*, 1994: 40.

17 Judith Butler, "Endangered/Endangering: Schematic Racism and *White* Paranoia," in Robert Gooding-Williams ed., *Reading Rodney King/Reading Urban Uprising*, 1993: 17–18, 20. Note the highlighting here of another pair of *de-re* terms revolving around the crucial concept of contextualization.

[And what was the crime of Rodney King? He was a young black man, not yet dead, and not yet ready, and not yet willing, to die: He was black. He should have been dead. He should not have been born.

(June Jordan)[18]]

They put my picture up with silence
'Cause my identity by itself causes violence

(NWA)[19]

Prosecuting Attorney: You can't look at that video and say that every one of those blows is reasonable, can you? Officer Stacey Koon: Oh I can if I put my perceptions in . . . I saw him looking through me . . . *It is what I thought that matters.*

(Court TV)[20]

[For those of us who dare to desire differently, who seek to look away from the conventional ways of seeing blackness and ourselves, the issue of race and representation is not just a question of critiquing the *status quo*. It is also about transforming the image, creating alternatives, asking ourselves questions about what types of images subvert, pose critical alternatives, and transform our worldviews and move away from dualistic thinking about good and bad.

(bell hooks)[21]]

Somatography: the order in place

Henri Lefebvre suggests that power survives by producing space; Michel Foucault suggests that power survives by disciplining space; Gilles Deleuze and Felix Guattari suggest that to reproduce social control the state must reproduce spatial control. What I hope to suggest is that the space of the human body is perhaps the most critical site to watch the production and reproduction of power . . .

I now describe *the order in place*, the "conceptual matrix" by which and through which the "fate" of Rodney King was fixed. I have named this order *somatography*, body writing, a hierarchical differentiating of flesh that began

18   June Jordan, "Burning All Illusions Tonight," in *Inside the L.A. Riots: What Really Happened – And Why It will Happen Again*, New York: Institute for Alternative Journalism, 1992: 77. This richly illustrated collection of essays is the best of the publications that immediately followed the events in Spring 1992.
19   From the rap music of NWA/Niggers with Attitude, "Fuck tha Police." Lead quote in Hooper, *The Trial*.
20   Court TV, "The Rodney King Case: What the Jury Saw in *California v. Powell*," Courtroom Television Network, 1992; in Hooper, 1994: 43, 47, 48.
21   bell hooks, *Black Looks: Race and Representation*, Boston: South End Press, 1992: 4. Hooks again takes us back to the power of images, simulations, simulacra, and to the need to develop new ways to subvert these images, to find critical and transformative alternatives that transcend the simplistic binaries such as good–bad, white–black, that confine critical interpretation to the status quo.

millennia ago with the division of body and mind and that, like geography, earth writing, orders ambiguous substances of matter as political meanings and territories.

Note: I use the term somatography with reservation. The idea of body writing can imply a cultural construction that is applied to, mapped on, etched into the flesh of a passive material body (clothes hung on a paper doll) – an idea I do not wish to perpetuate. By human body I do not mean either a product of culture nor a creation of biology: it is both of these and more. It is a concrete physical space of flesh and bone, of chemistries and electricities; it is a highly mediated space, a space transformed by cultural interpretations and representations; it is a lived space, a volatile space of conscious and unconscious desires and motivations – a body/self, a subject, an identity: it is, in sum, a social space, a complexity involving the workings of power and knowledge *and* the workings of the body's lived unpredictabilities . . .

The pieces of this order . . . accumulate the story of Citizen Rodney King. My central concern is what this story suggests about the production of political subjects in the contemporary context and about current debates on the political meanings of *reason* – particularly the viability of reason as a tool for producing democracy. Weaving in and out of the text, worrying it, are the linked ideas of order, reason, and mastery: ideas that exist as relations of ruling embedded in the hierarchical opposition of body and mind. Also present throughout the text, playing in and out of its lines, is my fantasy of *disorder*: a material/symbolic/lived disorder that would make it impossible to situate Rodney King with such dangerous precision; a fantasy that makes me ask, with Maria Lugones,

> If something or someone is neither/nor,
> but kind of both, not quite either,
> if something is in the middle of
> either/or,
> if it is ambiguous, given the available
> classification of things,
> if it is *mestiza*,
> if it threatens by its very ambiguity
> the orderliness of the system . . .
>
>   (Maria Lugones)[22]

what might the verdict have been then?
I will begin.

ONE: Ordering is the practice of "keeping at a distance the forces of chaos knocking at the door" (Deleuze and Guattari). It is the production of social space as Order; it is an ordering of social space that functions individually and collectively as a method of *orientatio*: as mastery; as protection from ambigu-

---

22 Maria Lugones, "Purity, Impurity, and Separation," *Signs* 19, Winter 1994: 459. See also the references to Lugones in *Thirdspace* 1996: 129–31.

ity and multiplicity, from the terror of "vertigo brought on by disorientation," from the experience of being thrown into the "limitless, unknown and threatening extension" (Eliade) that is the space beyond the skin, the spacing between self and other, us and them . . . It is the practice of purity, of ritual cleanliness . . . of binarism and dualism. Its opposite is disorder: i.e., danger and threat; what occurs when the "forces of chaos" storm the doors, when lines don't hold, borders are crossed, definitions burst seams. It is impurity, ambiguity, multiplicity, chaos, dangerous communications, thrill, miscegenation, resistance, anarchy, revolution. It is pollution, which, for the ancient Greeks, meant *out of place.*[23]

TWO: The world receives its order, and the objects in the world their *identities*, from schemes of classification rooted in contingent and transitory modes of social life – an *orientatio* of social control which positions the individual and the collective along the coordinates of *time, space, and being* [emphasis added]. Subject-citizens, as members of a particular society, acquire knowledge of their space and accede to their status as subjects by acting within that space and comprehending it (Lefebvre, 1991).[24]

THREE: Every society produces its own order; its own geographies and spaces, its own natures, its own knowledges and truths, its own bodies and cities and texts . . . they are *socially produced spaces* which are always in formation, always in flux, existing simultaneously and indivisibly in their material, symbolic, and lived dimensions. As social spaces they are produced by *spatial praxis* . . . the operation of power through which material, symbolic, and lived spaces are hierarchically ordered and produced.

FOUR: Order is not neutral, transcendent, universal, it is always partisan and conflictual . . . *Ordering is politics* . . . The production of political subjects is the spatial praxis of ordering and disordering of social space . . . of ordering, dividing, classifying, categorizing, disciplining, enclosing, partitioning, and ranking . . . a "system of differentiations" which permits one to act upon the actions of others:

> differentiations determined by the law or by traditions of status and privilege; economic differences in the appropriation of riches and goods, shifts in the process of production, linguistic or cultural differences, differences in know-how and competence, and so forth. Every relationship of power puts

23   The references are to Gilles Deleuze and Felix Guattari, *A Thousand Plateaus*, Minneapolis: University of Minnesota Press, 1987: 320; and Mircea Eliade, *A History of Religious Ideas*, vol. I, Chicago: University of Chicago Press, 1978: 3. Hooper here is taking the critique of binary thinking in new directions by radically disrupting and disordering its underpinnings in the power of rationalism.

24   Hooper begins to "ontologize" the key concept of *citizenship* here, with a particular emphasis on its spatiality and with obvious, and not so obvious, connections to contemporary debates on democracy and justice.

into operation differentiations which are at the same time conditions and results.

(Michel Foucault)[25]

FIVE: While these orderings vary across time and place and subject position, in all their variations and discontinuities there is a commonality, a shared vocabulary and intent that it is possible to generalize as the *transformation of a named chaos into a named order* . . . In the west, chaos has been named body, sin, flesh, the profane, immorality, revolution, nature, animal, the unconscious, dark, matter, female, savage, the masses, the particular, the Other. Similarly, order has been named mind, spirit, the human, the divine, the sacred, truth, the universal, the natural order of things, the invisible hand, the common good, the heavenly city, the city of reason, democracy, socialism, capitalism, light, white, male . . . [I]n all these names and guises . . . the production of the binary chaos/order is mobilized by *the desire to master* . . .

SIX: The desire for mastery . . . is not transhistorical, transgeographical, but varies in its manifestations across time and space. In the modern west, these desires have been authored primarily in the name of reason: God does not order, Nature does not order, Fate does not order: Man orders with his science and reason. While these authorings have not gone uncontested, unopposed, unresisted, they have been hegemonic.

SEVEN: Intimate with reason, with order and domination, is the idea of *difference*: reasoning, in its origins, is described by Plato as judgments of *sameness* (affirmation) and *difference* (negation), the faculty through which one apprehends *the pattern of the world*. Difference, as a spatial praxis and politics, is located with reason in the foundations of western thought – specifically, in the western philosophical and scientific tradition as it is based in a system of hierarchical binarism . . . This binarism, which is still potent today, is a mode of conceptualizing that disciplines the world into rigidly bordered, oppositional spaces – A and not-A, Form and Matter, Subject and Object, Male and Female, Mind and Body . . . Hierarchical binarism, then, is a spatial praxis that is the production of difference: a *spacing* which is a differentiating between the Same and the Other; a *spatialized strategy of domination* through which the produced differences are materialized as the hierarchized orderings, the margins and centers, the politicized geographies of bodies, cities, and texts. It is, in essence, a re-location policy, a "spatial fix," an "uneven development" through which the hegemonic order maintains its advantageous position via the production and location of an inferiorized other in subordinate, devalued spaces . . .

25   Michel Foucault, "Afterword: The Subject and Power," in *Michel Foucault: Beyond Structuralism and Hermeneutics*, Hubert L. Dreyfus and Paul Rabinow eds., Chicago: University of Chicago Press, 1983: 223.

EIGHT: *Somatography* is a practice of power/knowledge organized according to hierarchical binarism . . . Like geography, it is related to what Gayatri Chakravorty Spivak has called "the notion of the worlding of a world on a supposedly uninscribed territory . . . a texting, textualization, of making into art, a making into an object to be understood" (Spivak, 1990: 1). In this making of ambiguity into objects to be understood, ambiguous, polymorphous bodies . . . are ordered and stabilized as a series of hierarchical binaries: i.e., classified, subjugated, made productive, disciplined for use and exchange . . .

Border work is the ongoing negotiation of the produced definitions of bodies and subjectivities through which the political subjects of a culture are either maintained as defined – the sustained move of the hegemon – or disrupted and disordered – the counter-hegemonic, subaltern operation. Because the "phenomenon of bordering" is what provides the stability of the definition (Deleuze and Guattari, 1987: 245), the zone of the border is always a site of conflict and contestation . . . All of power exists in the "narrow zone of the line" that separates the binary categories.

> [The boundaries of ethnicity do yield brilliant work. In some cases these boundaries provide safer places that allow us to work in atmospheres where we are supported and can support the work of others. In some cases it's very exciting to work with like-minded people in similar fields of interest. In other cases these boundaries have been crucial to the development of identity and the only conceivable response to a popular culture and a mainstream that denied the possibility of the development of an identity. On the other hand the price we pay is that few of us can really look at the story of race in its complexity and its scope. If we were able to move more frequently beyond these boundaries, we would develop multifaceted identities and we would develop a more complex language . . . Our race dialogue desperately needs this more complex language.
>
> (Anna Deveare Smith)[26]]

NINE: Racism; sexism; orientalism; homophobia; xenophobia; imperialism; colonialism; the productions of science and knowledge – all are a body politics through which the hegemon . . . reads and represents the Other as a projection of impulses and desires the culture fears in itself, yet still finds compelling, fascinating . . .

> A rich web of signs and references for the idea of difference arises out of a society's communal sense of control over its world. No matter how this control is articulated, whether it is political power, social status, religious mission, or

---

26 Anna Deveare Smith, *Twilight*, 1994: xxv. Smith's urging that we move beyond boundaries to develop multifaceted identities resonates well with Hooper's *border work* as well as that of bell hooks. See my discussion of bell hooks in chapter 3 of *Thirdspace*.

geographical and economic domination, it provides an appropriate vocabulary for the sense of difference. Difference is what threatens order and control; it is the polar opposite to "our" group.

(Sander Gilman)[27]

TEN: The difference produced between *body and mind*, between raw matter and thinking substance, is among the most potent of the west's binary orderings: it is *the ur-form of order* itself; it is the template of the desire for mastery, a desire which becomes, in the west, a virulent politics of somatophobia . . . The mastered body, the planned city, the carefully reasoned text, the proof, the elegantly excised truth: all are viewed as sites where knowledge and power become organized and institutionalized according to the dictates of reason . . . The most important work of reason, of reason's order, is to serve as fortification against the ever-present danger of body/chaos . . .

ELEVEN: While all bodies are dangerous, some are more dangerous than others . . . laboring bodies – animal, female, dark, poor, barbarian, slave – who do the body-work of the polis . . . Thus, as produced in the west, reason functions less as a named mode of thought than as an unnamed relation of ruling, a form of domination over all produced as reason's Others . . . As Elaine Scary suggests [see note 15, above], "Power entails an inequality of disembodiment: to be a voice and possess a symbolic relation to the world is to be powerful, while vulnerability and powerlessness grow with embodiment."

[King is still *silent* and manifestly invisible, in proper person. It is as though he is sickeningly caught forever in the graceless heaviness of his attempts – crudely videotaped – to escape the next crushing blow from the bold officers of the LAPD. He has not been *heard* from as the trial begins. And – stunningly – to the amazement of so very many – he is not called . . . to testify in his own behalf . . . nor are the two black men who were in the car with him. King is *silent*, and barely seen outside the repetitive scene of video-ed violence.

(Now . . . this *silence* lends . . . in an age where reality is only sound and images marking what Lyotard calls the "postmodern condition" . . . this *silence* lends the possibility of a heroic interpretation of the unheard victim of the video-tape . . . But the age of information overwhelms this solacing interpretation . . .)

But we have not heard from Rodney King himself, nor have we been historically or semiotically astute enough to conduct our own hearing of the American scene of violence as it has immemorially sounded itself in the New World. We thus wait in vain for something which a hearing of Rodney King – in all the reverberant energies and echolalic resonances of times and scenes of violence gone by – will never produce. That "something" is, of course, *a scene truly heard*.

(Houston A. Baker)[28]]

---

27   Sander L. Gilman, *Difference and Pathology: Stereotypes of Sexuality, Race, and Madness*, Ithaca: Cornell University Press, 1985: 21.
28   Houston A. Baker, "Scene . . . Not Heard," in Gooding-Williams, *Reading Rodney King*, 1993: 43–4.

TWELVE: The story I have narrated thus far is largely a fiction. Differences do not exist: they are artifactual – imagined, produced, desired. There is no order, no chaos, no body, no mind, only the lines drawn and forced between them; lines which are not real but are simply the fantasy of separation – the fantasy of body/mastery that is the desire for order and control . . . Nonetheless, what has been imagined has been hegemonic. So forceful has this imagined thing been, so potent in its effects, that the produced division between body and mind may be, in fact, the entire difference out of which western politics has been made.

THIRTEEN: Body and the body politic, body and social body, body and city, body and citizen-body, are intimately linked productions . . . The practice of using the individual body as a metaphor for the social body, of deploying it as a sign of the health or disease of the social body, both as metaphor and source, develops in the Athenian polis with ideas of democracy and reason and continues into the present. Body and city are the persistent subjects of a social/civic discourse, of an imaginary obsessed with the fear of unruly and dangerous elements and the equally obsessive desire to bring them under control: fears of pollution, contagions, disease, things out of place; desires for . . . controlling and mastering that is the spatial practice of enclosing unruly elements within carefully guarded spaces. These acts of differentiation, separation, and enclosure involve material, symbolic, and lived spaces (the spaces of knowledge, of art and science, of economics and politics, of conscious and unconscious, of bodies and cities and texts) and are practiced as a politics of difference, as segregation and separation:

> In the first instance, discipline proceeds from the distribution of individuals in space.
>
> (Michel Foucault)[29]

In times of social crisis – when centers and peripheries will not hold – collective and individual anxiety rise and the politics of difference become especially significant. The instability of the borders heightens, and concern with either their transgression or maintenance is magnified. When borders are crossed, disturbed, contested, and so become a threat to order, hegemonic power acts to reinforce them: the boundaries around territory, nation, ethnicity, race, gender, sex, class, erotic practice, are trotted out and vigorously disciplined. At the same time, counter-hegemons are working to harness the disorder . . . for political use . . . In these periods, bodies, cities, and texts become key sites of hegemonic and counter-hegemonic contestations . . . In the late twentieth century, it is *the global megacity* [emphasis added] with its restless (teeming, breeding) populations, and (in the USA) the sensationalized,

---

29   Michel Foucault, *Discipline and Punish: The Birth of the Prison*, New York: Vintage Books, 1979: 141. Here is another example of what we can learn by putting space first.

demonized bodies of black males and urban gangs who have taken on the role of representing social disorder and pathology.

FOURTEEN: Disorder is the global condition that produces the case of Rodney King. It is a condition that is marked in Los Angeles, as in other global cities, by major economic, cultural, and demographic restructurings, by territorial struggles for voice and space . . . These restructurings have produced a heightened concern over borders; a situation of struggle over spaces and meanings; a milieu of fear that manifests as a ferocious racism and xenophobia, as a concern for the pathology of bodies and cities which are produced as dangerous carriers of the disorder, incubators and contagions in the global epidemic of shrinking western power.

Greg: The hotel is full. Time to put out the no vacancy sign. Too many here. Too many of the wrong people . . .
Doug: . . . The values we learned have turned to shit or are turning to shit because of the alien problem.
Greg: It's really us against them . . .
Hack: . . . the problem down there [South Central] is no family structure. You see children having children with no fucking idea who the father is . . . All the mothers have six, eight kids and no fucking idea where they are. And they couldn't give a damn because they are too busy pumping out another kid. Picking up the government check. Every Cadillac and Mercedes you stop in the south end of town has food stamps in the glove box. They're on welfare and we're out here driving Volkswagens while they're driving Bentleys . . .
Greg: You want to fix this city? I say you start out with carpet-bombing, level some buildings, plow all this shit under and start all over again.
Doug: [Y]eah, there'd be some innocent people, but not that many. There's just some areas of Los Angeles that can't be saved.
                                (Conversation between LAPD officers)[30]

The trial, *California v. Powell*, occurs as a dramatization of these fears and concerns; as a discourse on the politics of order, and disorder, of us versus them. The courtroom in Simi Valley becomes a scopic device, a spectacle . . . for producing perception according to inherited logics linking reason, order, and control with mind (as sited in white male) and those linking disorder, danger, violence, threat, with body (with not-white, with Other) . . .

The Trial: Us v. Them

[ES: In the "compensatory drama" presented below, I have extracted from Hooper's text her reports on the trial, *California v. Powell*, as derived from

30 Conversation between LAPD officers in April 1992, cited in Marc Cooper, "LA's State of Siege: City of Angels, Cops from Hell," in *Inside the L.A. Riots*, Institute for Alternative Journalism, 1992: 16–19.

Court TV and other sources. The key actors are Terence White, the lead prosecuting attorney; the defendants Laurence Powell, Stacey Koon, Theodore Briseno, and Timothy Wind (who does not testify); Koon's attorney Daryll Mounger; expert witness for the defense Charles S. Duke, Jr.; Powell's attorney Michael Stone; and Wind's attorney Paul DePasquale (who makes a statement on Wind's behalf). The script presented does not follow any sequence relating to the trial but, rather, the flow captured by Hooper in her text.]

White (addressing the jury):   You can't need to be an expert to look at that video and say that is wrong, that is bad, that is criminal . . . What more could you ask for? You have the videotape that shows objectively, without bias, impartially, what happened that night. The videotape shows conclusively what happened that night. It can't be rebutted . . . Who are you going to believe? The defendants or your own eyes?

White (addressing Koon):   You can't look at that video and say that every one of those blows is reasonable, can you?

Koon: Oh I can if I put my perceptions in . . . Sometimes police work is brutal. That's just a fact of life.

Mounger (opening the trial):   The state says that Stacey Koon is responsible for all his actions as supervisor. The evidence is going to show you that he's not in charge of this situation. There's only one person in charge and that is Rodney Glenn King . . . Rodney King displayed the objective symptoms of being under the influence of something. Sergeant Koon will tell you he knew this.

Koon (describing King):   . . . bucked out . . . an individual who is very pumped up as far as muscles . . . was probably an ex-con . . . blank stare . . . watery eyes . . . perspiration . . . I saw him looking through me . . . he wasn't complying . . . on the rise . . . torso was off the ground . . . legs were cocked . . . bear-like yell [*in response to taser shock*] . . . would not go down . . . repeated his groan similar to, like a wounded animal . . . I could see the vibrations on him . . . a policeman's nightmare . . . individual is super-strong . . . one-track mind . . . equate with a monster . . . It is what I thought that matters.

Powell (describing King):   . . . scared to death that if this guy got back up he was going to take my gun away from me . . . blank stare . . . slow, stiff movements . . . sweat glistening on his face . . . wasn't complying with verbal commands . . . I was scared that this guy was under PCP . . . great strength and resistance in his arms . . . He had very powerful arms. This was a big man . . . acting like an animal.

Depasquale: Wind acted in accordance with his training . . . direct responses to King's movements . . . stood and watched. When Mr. King tried to rise, Tim Wind moved in and used the strokes as per his training, then he backed up . . . The force used was proper according to the policy of the LAPD.

Briseno (explaining that he was "helping King" by putting his foot on King's neck):   . . . Officer Powell was out of control . . . didn't understand it . . . couldn't see what they were looking at . . . I'm thinking evidently they saw something I didn't see.

Stone: . . . as the suspect's movements and activities create an increase in the threat to the officers, or an increase in the resistance to arrest, or an increase in the attempt to escape, the officers are taught to escalate force. As the suspect becomes more compliant or ceases the threat, or ceases the resistance, the officers are taught to de-escalate force.

Duke (expertly detailing the "distinct uses of force"):   . . . there was an escalation and a de-escalation, an assessment period, and then an escalation and de-escalation again. And another assessment period.

White: We see a blow being delivered. Is that correct?

Duke: That's correct. The force has been again escalated to the level it had been previously, and the de-escalation has ceased.

White: And at, and at this point which is, for the record, four thirteen twenty nine, we see a blow being struck and thus the end of the period of de-escalation. Is that correct . . . ?

Duke: That's correct. Force has now been elevated to the previous level, after this period of de-escalation.

White (observing King moving his right hand behind his back, seemingly for hand-cuffing):   That would be the position you'd want him in. Is that correct?

Duke: Not, not with the way he is. His, his leg is bent in this area . . . That causes me concern.

White: Does it also cause you concern that someone's stepped on the back of his neck?

Duke: No it does not.

White (as the video shows King moving further into a "compliance mode"):   So would you again consider this to be a nonaggressive movement by Mr. King?

Duke: At this time no I wouldn't.

White: It is aggressive?

Duke: Yes. It's starting to be. His foot is laying flat, there's starting to be a bend in his leg, in his butt. The buttocks area has started to rise. Which would put us at the beginning of our spectrum again . . . They're taught to evaluate. And that's what they were doing in the last two frames. Or three frames.

White: Can you read their mind, Sgt. Duke?

Duke: I can form an opinion based on my training and having trained people, what I can perceive their perceptions are.

White: Well, what's Mr. King's perceptions at this time?

Duke: I've never been a suspect. I don't know.

White (to Powell):   Mr. King is a human being, right?

Powell: Yes, sir.

White: He should be treated like a human being?

Powell: Yes, sir.

White: Even though he is a suspect suspected of committing a crime this man is still a human being isn't he?

Powell: Yes, sir.

White: He deserved to be treated like a human being, didn't he?

Powell: Yes, sir.
White: He wasn't an animal was he?
Powell: No sir, just acting like one.

In interpreting evidence in the case of Rodney King, the juror-analysts, the judge, the expert witnesses, the millions of "lay" witnesses around the globe, are presumed to possess reason: the faculty allowing humans to make judgments of sameness and difference; to act as objective minds making conscious decisions; to analyze the evidence and make sense of it – i.e., to make order of the chaotic perceptual field and with this order to make judgments. This is in accord with the western scientific and philosophic tradition of thinking of the truth as hidden, something that is buried, masked, but that with the use of reason, the right methods of observation and analysis, can be discovered, discerned. Together, these are the presumptions upon which the entire legal system rests.

But there are problems with these assumptions . . . In his essay "Nietzsche, Genealogy, History," Foucault (1984) writes that the idea of deep hidden meanings is a cultural belief and nothing more; there is, to the contrary, a profound visibility to everything: all is visible, all is interpretation: "If interpretation is a never-ending task, it is simply because there is nothing to interpret. There is nothing absolutely primary to interpret because, when all is said and done, underneath it all everything is already interpretation."[31] . . . There is also the order in place: that vast convoluted strategy of knowledge and power ordering our thoughts into binaries, urging us into either/or, saturating our everyday analyses and perceptions.

This is how the jury saw, how they judged: according to the assumptions, without attending to the problems. By involving themselves in the drama of disembodying truth; by seeing through a "racially saturated field of vision"; by having available a logic of difference, a somatography of order and disorder, they were able to transcend, to escape, to become minds, experts privy to special knowledge, masters of the terror, the danger that was the body of Rodney King.

We are all witnesses . . .

---

31   Foucault's essay is in Paul Rabinow ed., *The Foucault Reader*, New York: Vintage, 1990: 76–100; the quote is from Dreyfus and Rabinow eds., *Michel Foucault*, 1983: 107.

Chapter 13
LA 1992: The Spaces of Representation

Event-Geography-Remembering

. . . I try to follow the perverse journey that the George Holliday video of the Rodney King beating has taken. The shock value obscures entire stages in the political history of collective memory. And the traces from one reception to the next are too faint in themselves to build much of a case. The mystery therefore is not how to find clues to an "abject" crime. It is about perception itself-as a political context. Why do people fail to see "the obvious"? Why is imaginary identification so difficult for things so clearly in one's best interest? Like Poe's famous "purloined letter," the clues sit openly on the mantelpiece, but are utterly unfindable. Something in the obviousness of them makes them instantly forgettable.

(Norman Klein)[1]

[Spaces of representation] need obey no rules of consistency or cohesiveness. Redolent with imaginary and symbolic elements, they have their source in history-in the history of a people as well as in the history of each individual belonging to that people. Ethnologists, anthropologists and psychoanalysts are students of such representational spaces, whether they are aware of it or not, but they nearly always forget to set them alongside those representations of space which coexist, concord or interfere with them; they even more frequently ignore social [sic-the original French was spatial] practice . . . Representational space is alive; it speaks. It has an affective kernel or centre: Ego, bed, bedroom, dwelling, house; or: square, church, graveyard. It embraces the loci of passion, of action, of lived situations, and thus immediately implies time. Consequently it may be

---

1 Norman M. Klein, *The History of Forgetting: Los Angeles and the Erasure of Memory*, London: Verso, 1997: 4. Klein uses Poe's "hyper-obtrusive" purloined letter, in full view yet invisible, to open up a discussion of an "evacuated presence," the loss of memory and remembering that often accompanies historical knowledge and seems particularly intense in the geohistory of Los Angeles. He refers specifically to John Muller and William Richardson eds., *The Purloined Letter: Lacan, Derrida and Psychoanalytic Reading*, Baltimore: Johns Hopkins University Press, 1988. His observations, and indeed the whole of this excellent book, provide an apt introduction to a geographical remembering of the events of 1992. Klein is a critic and historian of mass culture who teaches at the California Institute of the Arts, an important center of critical cultural studies in the Los Angeles region.

qualified in various ways: it may be directional, situational or relational, because it is essentially qualitative, fluid and dynamic.

(Henri Lefebvre)[2]

The perceived-conceived-lived triad (in spatial terms: spatial practice, representations of space, representational spaces) loses all force if it is treated as an abstract "model". If it cannot grasp the concrete (as distinct from the "immediate"), then its import is severely limited, amounting to no more than that of one ideological mediation among others.

(Lefebvre continued)[3]

Visible antipodes: Inner versus Outer City

After years of neglecting the pent-up misery of the inner cities, the country shuddered at the bloody wake-up call. Out of a city endlessly burning, out of the heart of Simi Valley and the soul of South-Central Los Angeles, a verdict seen as a miscarriage of justice induced a convulsion of violence that left 44 dead, 2,000 bleeding and $1 billion in charred ruins. The 56 videotaped blows administered by Los Angeles police to Rodney King last year had landed hard on everyone's mind. But they fell like feathers on a suburban jury that acquitted the cops of using excessive force. "That verdict was a message from America," said Fermin Moore, owner of an African artifacts shop near Inglewood. The reply from the inner city was a reciprocal "F – you." First South-Central blew. The fires licked up to Hollywood, south to Long Beach, west to Culver City and north to the San Fernando Valley. The nation's second largest city began to disappear under billows of smoke.

(Newsweek)[4]

2   Henri Lefebvre, *The Production of Space*, tr. Donald Nicholson-Smith, Oxford, UK and Cambridge, MA: Blackwell, 1991: 41–2. Lefebvre's notion of *les espaces de représentation* was translated as "representational spaces" rather than the more direct, and I think less confusing, phrase "spaces of representation," which I use for the title of this chapter. Lefebvre always tried to make sure that these spaces of representation were associated with fully *lived* space, rather than only with the perceived world of *spatial practices* and the conceived world described through *representations of space*, the two other components of Lefebvre's well-known triad. Unfortunately, the translator frequently eliminates Lefebvre's persistent injections of the lived in his discussions of "representational spaces." The excerpt cited here, for example, excludes the phrase *vécus plus que conçus* (lived more than conceived) that in the original (1974: 52) follows what I bracket as [Spaces of representation], substituting instead the innocuous phrase "on the other hand." Adding further to the confusion is another mistranslation that diminishes Lefebvre's explicitly spatial emphasis. In noting what is frequently forgotten in the work of enthnologists, anthropologists, and psychoanalysts, the translation reads as "social practice." The original is *la pratique spatiale*, or *spatial* practice. I bring up these details here not only to suggest that the ongoing revisioning of the events of 1992 is an attempt to understand lived space/thirdspace in all its incohesive and inconsistent, material and symbolic, passionate and fluid, real-and-imagined fullness, but also to make sure we remember that it is a critical spatial perspective that is leading the way.

3   Lefebvre, 1991: 40. Here is another *reminder* that whatever approach we take to understanding the postmetropolitan transition, the aim is to grasp the concrete rather than just respond to the "immediate."

4   *Newsweek*, May 11, 1992. The events of spring 1992 were set up for the world to see as a battle between Inner and Outer Cities, South-Central Los Angeles and Simi Valley, and by association black versus white and urban poor versus suburban rich. For many, this is all that is remembered, as the events in Los Angeles immediately began to disappear under billows of smoke.

The image of insurrection, in short, is part of a narrative that sees the relations of police and Blacks in L.A., not as the disaggregated dyad of state official and private citizen, mediated by neutral legal norms of reasonableness and nondiscrimination, but instead in terms of the power-laden relationship of communities defined by race, within which whites, through the police, exercise a kind of occupying power, and within which Black neighborhoods appear as something like colonies. In these terms, an "insurrection" is not the blindly irrational acts of "rioters" (who, in the dominant narrative, should be expected to protest peacefully), but the concerted action of a community determined to raise the cost of peace to the colonizers, and thereby to increase its leverage on the continuing power relations.

(Kimberley Crenshaw and Gary Peller)[5]

I'm not saying I told you so but rappers have been reporting from the front for years.

(Ice T)[6]

The overwhelming majority of LAPD officers are white. Most are first- or second-generation immigrants from the South or Midwest. They look at the city they police today and they see it as a formidable, threatening, unpredictable, *foreign* land . . . [T]o the older LA police officers who grew up in the near-rural, all-white suburbs of the city, and to the recruits from Kansas lured to the force by $40,000 salaries, South Central is an exotic, harrowing, terrifying land inhabited by unruly natives . . .

(Marc Cooper)[7]

Los Angeles has been, as Langston Hughes once wrote, "no crystal stair," full of "tacks" and "splinters," but the journey upward hasn't been hopeless or for naught. This body of work is an attempt to offer an alternative vision, radically different from the mainstream media's careless commentaries full of "theys" and "thems" peopled by "thugs" and "packs," a race made that much more one-dimensional by the outside's sheer ignorance of the city grid, an unschooled view that renders the deep dark thicket south of Pico, south of the I-10 Freeway, the heart of "the community," the interzone known as South Central L.A.

Black Los Angeles isn't just the chaos one tunes in to every evening at six and again at eleven. It is as well a 9-to-5, a bungalow, front lawns. It is family, per-

5 Kimberley Crenshaw and Gary Peller, "Reel Time/Real Justice," in Robert Gooding-Williams ed., *Reading Rodney King/Reading Urban Uprising*, New York and London: Routledge 1993: 68. Echoed here is the rousing call that was heard, if not listened to, during and after the events: No Justice, No Peace! Cutting through the still ongoing debates about what to call what happened in 1992, my preference is the Justice Riots, keeping in mind the simultaneously social and spatial definitions of justice.
6 Ice T, *Los Angeles Sentinel*, May 7, 1992. I thank Clyde Woods for finding this quote from the major African American newspaper in Los Angeles.
7 Marc Cooper, "LA's State of Siege," in *Inside the L.A. Riots*, New York: Institute for Alternative Journalism, 1992: 13–14. Klein (1997) notes that by the spring of 1993, at least twelve books had been published on the "Rebellion." By 1996, the number had passed fifty, with nearly a thousand articles and government documents. One of the first to appear, *Inside the L.A. Riots*, organized largely around the work of journalists associated with the region's leading progressive newspaper, the *LA Weekly*, remains one of the best.

severance and resilience. These teachers, musicians, community organizers, visionaries, preachers, filmmakers, civic leaders, students, *griots*, authors and photographers have shared their stories, have over the years become an extended family of sorts, an inspiration. They are just a few of many out there making their roots into rich soil, not sand. They make it easier for me to realize why people still come to wrestle with the ugly beauty that Los Angeles has become, but more important, they help me slowly to understand just why it is so imperative to stay.

(Lynell George)[8]

Fifty miles northwest of the LAPD's Parker Center slumbers the glorified desert truck stop known as Castaic – home to Sergeant Stacey Koon . . . Numerous other LAPD officers live out here, as well as in even more remote hamlets up the road toward Bakersfield. The mailing list of LAPD personnel is kept secret, for security reasons, but as many as 90 percent or more of the force is thought to live outside the city it is paid to police.

But in LA, there are no equivalents of Queens or Yonkers. Rather, a one- or two-hour drive away, in the desert or the mountains – not in suburbs, nor even in what we have come to call "bedroom communities," but in that peculiarly Southern California-type cantonment known as "housing developments" – live most of the members of the LAPD. Spiritless, soulless, pre-fabricated neighborhoods with no history, not even an immediate identity beyond the huge signs that announce "3 Bedrooms – 2 Baths – Security Gate – $119,000!"

Along a dusty half-mile stretch of access road along Interstate 5, the entirety of the Castaic business community sits as if at one big National Franchise Expo: a McDonalds, a 7-Eleven, a Del Taco, a Fosters Freeze and two chain motels. A single strip mall is the only reminder of urban life, and it's an hour away down the highway. At its center is a CB [Citizen's Band] Supply store with a faded Confederate Stars and Bars hanging over the doorway . . . On the hill above the mall are three residential developments, all filled with Spielbergian tract homes on loan from the *E.T.* set, all identical, all the same sandstone color, most with garages that serve as Saturday workshops. There's an extraordinary number with small boats in the driveways . . . This is cop utopia. No minorities, no gangs, no crime (except for an occasional trucker's dust-up at the Country Girl Saloon) – "a great place to raise kids," as they say. A perfectly ordered uniformity and predictability. A whole town of compliance, if you will. Safely distant from the dystopia of the daily beat and its deviants, perverts, criminals and aliens, desert towns like Castaic are a perfect incubator for the LAPD's closed political culture.

(Marc Cooper continued)

If ever there was a community where the four cops who beat Rodney King could be judged by a jury of their peers, Simi Valley [ES: pronounce it "Sim-mee'," the inhabitants tell us, not "See'-mee" or "Seamy"] is the place. Just over the Santa Susana Pass, on LA County's northwest border, Simi Valley (population 100,000) is home to no less than 2,000 LAPD, Sheriff's Department and other law enforce-

8 Lynell George, *No Crystal Stair: African-Americans in the City of Angels*, New York: Doubleday Anchor Books, 1992: 5–6.

ment personnel who make the daily commute over the rolling hills along Freeway 118 to Parker Center and dozens of other police stations around Los Angeles County . . . [Los Angeles Deputy DA Terry] White has acknowledged he faced an uphill battle when the case was moved to Ventura County. Of some 300 prospective jurors, all had ties to the Southern California law-enforcement community. The 27 who did not were excluded by the defense.

(Kevin Uhrich)[9]

Normalized enclosures: the development of common interests

In Simi Valley, the expression of normative values is closely associated with the practices of normalization. The mayor, for instance, is quick to note: "There is no question, in this community, that somebody out of the ordinary sticks out quickly. And people are very quick to report anything suspicious, very quick to call the police, and expect them to be there." In the minds of the residents of Simi Valley, it is a lifestyle that separates those who live in the suburbs from urban others. Those that are different are perceived as dangerous.

Residents insist that what binds them is not their common race or ethnicity, but a shared middle-class lifestyle. "We're living in a place with educated people, people who believe as we do," said [the mayor] . . . "But I don't believe skin color is a criteria . . . There's a black person up our street and we say 'Hi' like he's a normal person . . . This isn't about race, It's about whether you let your property run down." "Or whether you sell drugs out of your house," his wife . . . interjected. In the normalized community, the best that a minority can be is "like a normal person . . .

The normalized community is itself an enclosed space . . . with sharply delineated points of entry and exit. Simi Valley is described as a very safe place, in part because of its plan. "The geographic configuration of the 12-mile long valley, and its carefully planned street grid, makes a safe place safer. Just as each subdivision in Simi Valley is a self-contained web of cul-de-sacs so the whole city can, in effect, be cordoned off simply by blocking four highway exits." Such a system of streets encloses Simi Valley from the dangerous people of the outside world. People feel safe because they are surrounded with a familiar sameness. Those who are different are far away, spatially. Those who invade will be contained and removed . . .

In the American version of normalized society, the least normal (and most despised) group of people are young black men . . . A Sentencing Project Report, using U.S. Department of Justice and Census Bureau data, has shown that as of 1990 23% of black men between the ages of 18 and 30 in the United States were

9 Kevin Uhrich, "Policeville: Why People Who Know West [sic] Ventura County Weren't Surprised by the Verdict," in *Inside the L.A. Riots*, Institute for Alternative Journalism, 1992: 57–8. Uhrich, a staff writer for the Pasadena *Star News*, discusses the persistent racism rampant in this subregion of *East Ventura County*, home also to the Ronald Reagan Presidential Library located on 40 Presidential Drive in, where else, Simi Valley. It might be added that the Library was the recipient of a bomb threat in the week after the verdict.

in prison, in jail, or on probation or parole, versus 6% of white men in the same age category. The report noted, "The number of *young* black men under the control of the criminal justice system – 609,690 – is greater than the *total* number of Black men of *all ages* enrolled in college – 436,000 as of 1986. For white males, the comparable figures are 4,600,000 total in higher education and 1,054,508 age 20–29 in the criminal justice system."

(Thomas L. Dumm)[10]

First of all, I . . . I don't think it was a fund-raiser.
I don't think it was a fund-raiser at all
It was a group of
people
who were in opposition
to Proposition F.[11]
We were talking about long-term support.

. . .

And they begged me to be there
and I said I would and this is before we knew the . . . the,
uh, verdicts were coming in
and I didn't wanna go.
I didn't like those things, I don't like them at all,
but
strong supporters and I said I'll drop by for a little while.

. . .

I was in constant contact with my office.
I have radio beepers, telephones,
uh,
a portable telephone . . .
telephone in my car
just about everything you'd need
to communicate anywhere within our power.

. . .

When I . . . when I thought things were getting
to the point that I had . . . we were having some serious problems,
I was almost there.

10   All the above passages are taken from Thomas L. Dumm, "The New Enclosures: Racism in the Normalized Community," in Gooding-Williams, *Reading Rodney King*, 1993: 189–90. The quoted material on Simi Valley is from Jane Gross, "In Simi Valley, Defense of a Shared Way of Life," *New York Times*, May 4, 1992, A15. This normalization process plays a major role in the "history of forgetting" and the "erasure of memory" in Los Angeles, as well as in the material discussed earlier in chapters 10 and 11.
11   Proposition F was an attempt to impose tighter controls over the LAPD and reduce its powerful autonomy within city government. It passed in 1992.

My intent was to drop in say, "Hey,
I think we got a . . . a, uh,
riot blossoming.
I can't stay. I gotta get out of here."
And that's basically what I did.
The problem was
I was further away.
I thought it was in Bel Air. It turned out to be Pacific Palisades.
And my driver kept saying,
"We're almost there, we're almost there."
You know, he was kinda . . .
he wasn't sure of the distance either.
"we're almost there, Chief, we're almost there."

(Daryl Gates)[12]

Go ahead and kill us, we're already dead.

(Anonymous)[13]

we saw them
beat him.
they beat him, and they beat him,
and they beat him,
they beat him;
81 seconds and
56 blows.

they were tried
by a jury of their peers.
Lady Justice is not
blind.
she has been
blindfolded.
no justice.
no peace
America's black
whitemare raging
once again in the streets:

you say
you just don't understand.
you say
we look dangerous
to you.
you pretend

---

12 Daryl Gates, "It's Awful Hard to Break Away," in Anna Deveare Smith, *Twilight – Los Angeles, 1992*, New York: Doubledag Anchor, 1994: 180–3. Gates was the "lost" police chief during the Justice Riots.
13 Anonymous participant, reported in *USA Today*, May 1, 1992.

you don't know why
we are so angry.
you try so hard not to remember,
you depend on us
to live and
forget . . .

(Mwatabou S. Okantah)[14]

The Invisible Riots Remembered[15]

Downtowns: this is not the 1960s

We are in front of Police Chief Daryl F. Gates's house – a.k.a. Parker Center – which is surrounded on three sides by the LAPD. But it doesn't matter: We can do anything we want. The later it gets, the angrier we get. We throw rocks. We snap a No Parking sign. We torch a parking-lot guard booth. Get that LAPD patrol car! With 25 pairs of arm and leg muscles, turn it over! Torch it! Now the Rolls Royce! Listen to the hollow thud of crowbar against windshield glass. The riot police follow us at a distance, never confronting. Trees in large round concrete planters roll down the street. Bus benches become barricades. We hold burning copies of the *LA Times* to the leaves of the palm trees that peek out above the 101 overpass. We stare in awe at the flaming palms and at the drivers down below, who slam on their brakes and attempt desperate U-turns. One car screeches to a halt in the slow lane before two burning American flags that frame a Robbie Conal "Daryl Gates" poster. We yell, "No Justice, No Peace!" and we spray-paint the walls of City Hall East and City Hall West and City Hall South and the *LA Times* building. We are Revolutionary Communist Party types (manning the megaphone and spray-painting detail), we are barrio kids from East LA and South Central, we are bohemians from Echo Park, we are ACT-UP activists and we are journalists, a unified organism of about 300 cells on foot, on skateboards, on bikes, wearing "X" caps and Soundgarden T-shirts, moving like a big jellyfish, nudged by the waves of the LAPD.

(Ruben Martinez)[16]

---

14   Mwatabou S. Okantah, "America's Poem, or, 81 Seconds and 56 Blows," in Haki R. Madhubuti ed., *Why L.A. Happened: Implications of the '92 Los Angeles Rebellion*, Chicago: Third World Press, 1993: 136–40.
15   Here I try to draw out some of the less visible dimensions of the Justice Riots, especially with respect to what was screened to the rest of the world in 1992.
16   Ruben Martinez, "Riot Scenes," in *Inside the L.A. Riots*, Institute for Alternative Journalism, 1992: 31. It is often forgotten that the first night of the uprising was centered on a direct confrontation within the citadel of Los Angeles, the core of urban power. The most obvious point of attack was Parker Center, the bastion of the LAPD, but after being repelled by the police the remarkably heterogeneous crowd of protesters moved next door into the Civic Center to demonstrate and disturb the peace around the County Courthouse and other public buildings. Nothing like this multicultural confrontation took place in the 1965 uprising in Watts or in the other urban riots of the 1960s. For at least a few fleeting moments, the urban memory most stirred was that of the Paris Commune in 1871.

What happened in Los Angeles . . . was neither a race riot nor a class rebellion. Rather, this monumental upheaval was a multiracial, trans-class and largely male display of justified social rage. For all its ugly, xenophobic resentment, its air of adolescent carnival and its downright barbaric behavior, it signified the sense of powerlessness in American society. Glib attempts to reduce its meaning to the pathologies of the black underclass, the criminal actions of hoodlums or the political revolt of the oppressed urban masses miss the mark. Of those arrested, only 36 percent were black, more than a third had full-time jobs and most claimed to shun political affiliation. What we witnessed in Los Angeles was the consequence of a lethal linkage of economic decline, cultural decay and political lethargy in American life. Race was the visible catalyst, not the underlying cause.

(Cornel West)[17]

it
began
sometime during the fifteenth
century.
first the Portuguese,
and then the Spanish, and then
the Dutch, and then
the French,
and then the English,
and then the
Americans
raided in Africa.

no African holocaust memorials
in Europe
or America today,
only the slave relics house in Badagri,
only cells on Goree Island,
only dungeons
at Christianborg, Elmina
and Cape Coast Castles
to remind us
the price
paid
for the second class
citizenship of an
exslave.

you say
you just don't understand.
living in ghettoes
reminds us everyday of those things
you so easily forget.

17   Cornel West, "Learning to Talk of Race," *New York Times Magazine*, August 2, 1992. West's words place the events of 1992 directly into the wider framework of the postmetropolitan transition, without reducing the significance of race and racism.

when descendants of rape
victims live
in the house of their
fathers,
they
sleep with the enemy
in themselves . . .

(Okantah's American Poem, continued)

I want to say, "It started long before all this . . ." Long before this afternoon's
bewildering decision left me less astonished than strangely numb. Long before
George Holliday ran tape capturing Rodney G. King's struggle and submission.
Long before Latasha Harlins, Eulia Love and Marquette Frye became cautionary
symbols. Long before Watts shouted its existence into the sky in 1965, sending
up searchlights in the form of flames.

(Lynell George)[18]

In a sense, 1992 is the year of the rehabilitation of white, male heterosexuality,
its return to sites of centeredness, beauty, prosperity, power. Such a rehabilitation is central both to the European community and to the Columbian
quincentenary.

(Ruth Wilson Gilmore)[19]

My fear is that multiculturalism is going to trivialize further the distinct predica-
ment of black Americans – most especially the plight of the young black male.
There are two stories in American history that are singular and of such extraordinary magnitude that they should never be casually compared to the experience of other Americans. One is the story of the American Indian; the other is
the story of the black slave.

(Richard Rodriguez)[20]

There was an insurrection in this city before
and if I remember correctly
it was sparked by police brutality.
We had a Kerner Commission report.
It talked about what was wrong with our society.
It talked about institutionalized racism.
It talked about a lack of services,
lack of a government responsive to the people.
Today, as we stand here in 1992,

18 Lynell George, *No Crystal Stair*, 1992: 9. The names mentioned refer to memorable instances of
police brutality and/or legal miscarriages of justice within the African American community, ranging
back from the more immediate Latasha Harlins case in the early 1990s to the arrest of Marquette Frye
that was one of the triggers of the Watts uprising in 1965.
19 Ruth Wilson Gilmore, "Terror Austerity Race Gender Excess Theater," in Gooding-Williams,
Reading Rodney King, 1993: 30. The symbolism of the 500-year anniversary of Columbus's landfall on
Santo Domingo in 1492 and the beginnings of New World colonialism was appropriately remembered
by many in response to the events in Los Angeles, the so-called "capital" of the Third World.
20 Richard Rodriguez, "Multiculturalism With No Diversity," *Los Angeles Times*, Opinion, May 10,
1992. More forgotten history is being recalled.

if you go back and read the report
it seems as though we are talking about what that report
cited
some twenty years ago still exists today.
Mr. President,
THEY'RE HUNGRY IN THE BRONX TONIGHT
THEY'RE HUNGRY IN ATLANTA TONIGHT
THEY'RE HUNGRY IN ST. LOUIS TONIGHT.
Mr. President,
our children's lives are at stake.
We want to deal with the young men who have been dropped
off of
America's agenda.
Just hangin' out
chillin',
nothin' to do,
nowhere to go.
They don't show up on anybody's statistics.
They're not in school,
they have never been employed,
they don't really live anywhere.
They move from grandmama
to mama to girlfriend.
They're on general relief and
they're sleepin' under bridges.

. . .

The fact of the matter is,
whether we like it or not,
riot
is the voice of the unheard.

(Maxine Waters)[21]

During the Watts riots, [then LAPD Police Chief William] Parker would speak
the unspeakable, and say for all to hear on a local TV show what would never
again – in the post-civil-rights era – be so frankly uttered by a public official. "It
is estimated that by 1970," said Parker, "45 percent of the metropolitan area of
Los Angeles will be Negro; if you want any protection for your home and family
. . . you're going to have to get in and support a strong police department. If you
don't do that, God help you."

(Joe Domanick)[22]

---

21 Maxine Waters, "The Unheard," in Anna Deveare Smith, *Twilight*, 1994: 159–62. Waters is Con-
gresswoman for the 35th District, in South Central Los Angeles. The performed excerpts are from a
speech Waters gave at the First African Methodist Episcopal Church just after Daryl Gates had resigned
and soon after the events of April 29–May 2, 1992.
22 Joe Domanick, "Police Power," in *Inside the L.A. Riots*, Institute for Alternative Journalism, 1992:
21. See also Joe Domanick, *To Protect and Serve: The LAPD's Century of War in the City of Dreams*, New
York: Pocket Books, 1994.

this is not the 1960s,
no Malcolm
to tell us the dream is a nightmare.
even Martin said
your freedom check has been
returned,
stamped
"Insufficient Funds."
another generation
is burning
and the nation
is bankrupt
today:

you say
you just don't understand
we live in your house.
we are strangers.
we see you in the workplace.
we are invisible.
we die in your wars.
we kill for you.
we make you laugh.
we sing, we dance for you.
you do not see us.
you see us
only when we wreak havoc
in your streets,
framed nightly on your tv screens,
you see us only
when we leap
out of your wildest dreams.

we saw them beat him,
you say
you just don't understand.
you have eyes.
you refuse to see.
to see us,
you have to look into our lives,
into that darkening
terror
mirror reflecting
your deeply
deep felt
why:

you don't understand.
you live in fear.
you have not

listened.
you
turned
a deaf ear . . .

(Okantah's American Poem, continued)

GIVE USA THE HAMMER AND THE NAILS,
WE WILL REBUILD THE CITY.

(Bloods/Crips Proposal)[23]

They are calling for a new Los Angeles. They are calling for every abandoned building to be gutted, for new parks and community centers to be built, for the re-pavement of streets and sidewalks. They are demanding increased lighting and more trees, for businesses which have a stake in the community, for the reconstruction of schools and more books. They are calling for jobs which pay decent and livable wages – not the low-paying jobs they are often offered, if any. And the total cost of the Crips/Bloods package is estimated at $3.726 billion – far less that the $500 billion used to bail out the Savings and Loans.

(Luis Rodriguez)[24]

Paul Gilroy: Yesterday when we were looking at the Bloods and Crips plans for the rebuilding of LA I was struck by the richness and complexity of those proposals, by the absence of any Afrocentric tropes from those plans and thirdly, and this makes me very uncomfortable, by the incredible distance between that vision of social and economic reconstruction and the whole domain of African-American intellectual life which seems reluctant to turn its gaze towards those intractable conflicts.

bell hooks: Though the word "de-colonization" isn't used in that plan, one can read it is that way. If we were to show it to certain thinkers in Third World countries they would recognize it in that way. How it talks about transforming the educational system, for example, its sense of a different approach to pedagogy. There have been very few black academics/intellectuals who have been interested in that area and its implications for rethinking public policy on schools. We can see that happening in the Bloods and Crips proposals for reconstructing LA.

Paul Gilroy: When I read that plan I couldn't help thinking about South Africa and the whole project of social reconstruction and re-building of their educational system which is being engaged in there. The tasks that arise in reckoning with the existence of a whole generation of people who have been

23 See "Bloods/Crips Proposal for LA's Face-Lift," published in Madhubuti, *Why L.A. Happened*, 1993: 274–82. In response to the events of April–May 1992, the Bloods and Crips gangs called a truce and produced a sophisticated planning proposal for rebuilding Los Angeles. Although the truce was maintained for many months after the uprising, the proposals were ignored by government authorities. Although few today remember this truce, it probably played some role in the significant decline of crimes of violence that occurred in the second half of the 1990s, especially in South Central Los Angeles.

24 Luis J. Rodriguez, "From These Black and Brown Streets: L.A. Revisited," in Madhubuti, *Why L.A. Happened*, 1993: 225.

systematically excluded from those spaces. I wonder whether the experience of what has been happening there isn't a resource that we could use a lot more in making sense of some of the things around us in the other overdeveloped countries undergoing processes of de-industrialization. Andre Gorz, the French economist and philosopher, talks about the growth of types of service work here in Europe as being a process of South-Africanization. The return of household servants is one aspect of this that is relevant to what is going on here in London, the new politics of spatiality and zone-based control in our urban centres, the militarization of aspects of policing are other patterns . . .

(Paul Gilroy speaking with bell hooks)[25]

Southward, beyond the high-rise towers of downtown Los Angeles, a symmetrical grid pattern of streets is barely discernible through the usual dim haze. These streets, stretching south to the horizon and east to west, are unknown to most white Angelenos. Crenshaw, Western, Normandie, Vermont, Hoover, Figueroa, Broadway, San Pedro, Main, Avalon, Central, Hooper, Compton, Alameda, Washington, Adams, Jefferson, Vernon, Slauson, Florence, Manchester, Century, Imperial, El Segundo, Rosecrans . . . These are the arteries of South Central Los Angeles. Hundreds of thousands of blacks move along these pathways daily. The fortunate go to places of employment in the metropolitan area, but for most the movement is circular, cyclical and to nowhere. These streets have become the skeletal structure of another "bantustan" in an American city – another defoliated community, manipulated and robbed of its vitality by the ever-present growth pressures of the local economy.

(Cynthia Hamilton)[26]

Arrests of Latino males exceeded that of black males throughout the 6 days from April 30 through May 5. Arrests of Latino and black females were practically tied during the first three days of the riot, but May 3rd saw a surge in arrests for black females while arrests for Latino women continued to drop. We have no explanation for this phenomenon.

(Joan Petersilia and Allan Abrahamse)[27]

The focus on the black body was extended and rendered more complex as black female engagement in revolutionary feminist thinking led to an interrogation of sexism both in regard to the ways white racist aesthetics subjugated and colo-

---

25 Paul Gilroy, "A dialogue with bell hooks," *Small Acts: Thoughts on the Politics of Black Cultures,* London and New York: Serpent's Tail, 1993: 219–20. Gilroy is one of Britain's leading cultural critics. See his *The Black Atlantic: Modernity and Double Consciousness,* Cambridge: Harvard University Press, 1993; and *"There Ain't No Black in the Union Jack": The Cultural Politics of Race and Nation,* Chicago: University of Chicago Press, 1987. Note in particular Gilroy's reference to a more repressive version of "the new politics of spatiality" in his dialogue with bell hooks.
26 Cynthia Hamilton, "The Making of an American Bantustan," *LA Weekly,* December 30, 1988; reprinted in *Inside the L.A. Riots,* Institute for Alternative Journalism, 1992.
27 Joan Petersilia and Allan Abrahamse, "A Profile of Those Arrested," in *The Los Angeles Riots: Lessons for the Urban Future,* Mark Baldassare ed., Boulder, CO: Westview Press, 1994: 141. This book represents the best conventional liberal social science interpretation of the riots.

nized the black body and the ways in which the segregated spheres of black life sanctioned black male domination, subjugation, and exploitation of black females. The critical work of individual black women writing feminist theory broke new ground by constructing an intellectual framework for critical discussions of that body from a standpoint which considered race, gender, and class. Much of this work emerged from critical thinkers who were both black and gay (Audre Lord, Pat Parker, Joseph Bleam, Essex Hemphill, Hilton Als, Marlon Riggs, to name just a few). Feminist and/or queer theory established a broader context for discussion of black body politics.

(bell hooks)[28]

At First AME Church – the establishment founded by ex-slave Biddy Mason, the launching ground for Tom Bradley – the Disney Corporation held interviews for two hundred summer jobs. It was June 1992; the effects of the riot were everywhere. A crowd of working-class kids materialized, wearing their Sunday suits and clothes. A *New York Times* photograph showed one of them, a seventeen-year old girl, smiling with the combination of guilelessness and watchfulness that seems the province of the adolescent. The girl appeared slim and well-attired. She seemed unaware that she represented, as James Baldwin put it, "a social and not a personal or a human problem" that brings to mind "statistics, slums, rapes, injustices, remote violence . . . the beast in our jungle of statistics." The newspaper described her background with its impeccable proletarian credentials: she is the daughter of a nurse and a disabled roofer; her brothers and sisters work in a school cafeteria, as a cashier in Dodger Stadium, as a mail carrier, as a bus driver, as a custodian. In the logic of newspaper fairy tales, she inevitably gets one of the summer jobs at Disneyland and is thrilled; this quite transcends her previous employment at McDonald's. When confronted with her and the rest of the crowd, a Disney spokesman admitted being "taken aback." The sight of several hundred presentable black youngsters eager to work seemed to stun him as he confessed, "We didn't know they were there."

(Susan Anderson)[29]

Pico-Union and the desaparacidos

Whether in political discourse or media reportage, Latino poverty is the consistently missing variable in most explanations of [the 1992] uprising. For all the attention given to their problems, most Mexican or Central American immigrants might as well live on the dark side of the moon. Few politicians or television pundits, for example, have bothered to examine the official riot statistics . . . only 38 percent of those arrested by the LAPD were Black . . . Latinos, in addition to being 51 percent of the total arrestees, also constituted a majority of arson

28   bell hooks, "Feminism Inside: Toward a Black Body Politic," in *Black Male: Representations of Masculinity in Contemporary American Art*, Thelma Golden ed., New York: Whitney Museum of American Art and Harry N. Abrams, Inc., 1994: 128.

29   Concluding paragraph in Susan Anderson, "A City Called Heaven: Black Enchantment and Despair in Los Angeles," in Scott and Soja eds., *The City*, 1996: 336–64. The quotes are from James Baldwin, *Notes of a Native Son*, New York: Bantam, 1972: 18 and 22.

defendants. Moreover, the greatest density of riot-related "incidents" occurred *north* of the Santa Monica Freeway within the Wilshire and Rampart LAPD areas, not in Southcentral LA . . .

The arrest and incident data, in other words, imply that there were actually *two*, parallel Los Angeles uprisings . . . The first, which riveted the attention of the world, occurred in South Los Angeles and adjacent parts of LA County, and was driven by Black anger, although it included significant participation of poor Mexican immigrants in the looting of stores and mini-malls. The *second*, largely invisible, riot occurred in the preponderantly Latino Mid-City Area: an emergent super-slum . . . formed by the addition of the Hollywood flatlands, the mid-Wilshire district (including Koreatown) and the Westlake (or Ramparts) community . . .

The Mid-City area is . . . a huge "rent plantation" – the largest tenement district west of the Mississippi. In the Westlake/Rampart area, in particular, population densities (nearly 100,000 people within a mile radius of MacArthur Park) exceed New York City, and 95 percent of the housing stock is owned by absentee landlords. A detailed analysis of the rental economy of a representative neighborhood has shown that slum property, dense-packed with Latino immigrants in tiny, poorly maintained units, is highly profitable. For example, one sixty-unit structure, which so closely resembles a classical Eastern tenement that it is frequently used by Hollywood as an exterior for "South Bronx" scenes, amortizes its assessed value every ten months. Although Korean landlords have been villainized in popular stereotypes, the study reveals that a majority of landlords are wealthy Anglos. The thousands of Latina maids and house-cleaners, in other words, who ride the bus every day from their Mid-City tenements to Beverly Hills or Hancock Park may well be cleaning mansions financed by their own rack rent.

(Mike Davis)[30]

The Salvadoran barrio explodes Thursday afternoon. Nobody seems to know how it started, it just did. Some say it was *los morenitos* (a racial epithet for blacks), a few groups from South Central who ventured north. Others say it was locals. Whatever the spark, by 2 p.m. crowds are looting stores from Washington to Beverly, from Western to Figueroa. Pico-Union and the surrounding neighborhoods of Westlake and Mid-Wilshire look like San Salvador at the height of the rebel offensive.

(Ruben Martinez)[31]

The armored personnel carrier squats on the corner like *un gran sapo feo* – "a big ugly toad" – according to nine-year-old Emerio. His parents talk anxiously about the *desaparacidos*: Raul from Tepic, big Mario, the younger Flores girl and the cousin from Ahuachapan. Like all Salvadorans, they know about those who "disappear"; they remember the headless corpses and the man whose tongue had been pulled through the hole in his throat like a necktie. That is why they came here – to zip code 90057, Los Angeles, California . . . Now they are counting their friends and neighbors, Salvadoran and Mexican, who are suddenly gone. Some

30 Mike Davis, "Who Killed Los Angeles? The Verdict is Given," *New Left Review* 199, 1993: 37–8, 40.
31 Ruben Martinez, "Riot Scenes," 1992: 32.

are still in the County Jail on Bauchet Street, brown grains of sand lost among the 13,000 other alleged *saqueadores* (looters) and *incendarios* (arsonists) detained after the most violent American civil disturbance since the Irish poor burned Manhattan in 1863. Those without papers are probably already back in Tijuana, broke and disconsolate. Violating city policy, the police and the Sheriff's Department fed hundreds of hapless undocumented *saqueadores* to the INS for deportation before the ACLU or immigrant-rights groups even realized they had been arrested.

(Mike Davis)[32]

I teach at a new school which is a block west of Olympic and Hoover. My students and I watched from our classroom window as a video store burned, flames and smoke easily visible... The majority of looting in the Pico-Union and Wilshire areas was done by Central Americans, not Blacks or Mexican-Americans. They really didn't care or even know who Rodney King is. In Central America, whenever there is a major change of regime by force, or a breakdown of power, the people react by getting what they need and "deserve" while they can... There was no coordination or planning by the people north of the Santa Monica Freeway, other than that provided by the roadmap shown on local TV. Most of my students simply shrugged their shoulders and said: "everyone was doing it, why not us as well?" In the area where I work, the LAPD is a sadistic occupying army. I believe that one of the reasons people were so quick to loot, and break the law, was because they had little or no respect for the police... I do not think that Korean stores were attacked for exclusively ethnic reasons. If Korean-owned liquor stores were burned, Korean travel agencies and beauty shops were not touched. The uprising was directed against the police and rip-off merchants in general. It was driven by economic desperation and class resentment, not race.

(Mike Dreebin)[33]

To be forced to cross the Atlantic as a slave in chains, to cross the Mediterranean or the Rio Grande illegally, heading hopefully North, or even to sweat in slow queues before officialdom, clutching passports and work permits, is to acquire a habit of living between worlds, caught on a frontier that runs through your tongue, religion, music, dress, appearance and life. To come from elsewhere, from "there" and not "here," and hence to be simultaneously "inside" and "outside" the situation at hand, is to live at the intersections of histories and memories, experiencing both their preliminary dispersal and their subsequent translation into new, more extensive, arrangements along emerging routes. It is simultaneously to encounter the languages of powerlessness and the potential intimations of heterotopic futures. This drama, rarely freely chosen, is also the drama of the stranger. Cut off from homelands of tradition, experiencing a constantly challenged identity, the stranger is perpetually required to make herself at home in an interminable discussion between a scattered historical inheritance and a heterogeneous present... As such the stranger is an emblem... a figure that draws our attention to the urgencies of our time: a presence that questions

---

32 Mike Davis, "Burning All Illusions in LA," in *Inside the L.A. Riots*, Institute for Alternative Journalism, 1992: 96.
33 Mike Dreebin, fifth-grade teacher, quoted in Mike Davis, "Who Killed Los Angeles?," 1993: 39.

our present. For the stranger threatens the "binary classification deployed in the construction of order," and introduces us to the uncanny displacement of ambiguity.

(Iain Chambers)[34]

Sa-i-ku *and other commemorations*

We waited for about half an hour
and then my father showed up with a neighbor.
He told me what had happened.
There was no police officer to be found anywhere.
We came back here.
We started calling all the police stations and the hospitals
to see if
anybody had checked in
if they fit the description.
Unfortunately we can't get any kind of answer from anybody.
While that was happening a neighbor called and said you
      better
come down here because
there are hundreds of people and your store's being looted
at this time.
So we packed up our van, four people, five people, including
myself, and we headed down there.
I already knew people were carrying guns,
already knew my mother was shot at that corner.
So it was like going to war.

. . .

As I was approaching the store
one person was carrying to the side –
obviously he was wounded –
and our neighbor,
he was a car dealership and he was trying to hold down the
      store,
trying to keep people back,
and I can see one person still at the corner of the door
with a shotgun and I looked across the street.
There are at least three or four people with handguns firing
      back.
There was an exchange of fire going on.
So I pulled our van – I was driving –
I pulled our van in between our store entrance,
in between the person firing at me in front of the store.

. . .

34   Iain Chambers, *Migrancy, Culture, Identity*, 1994: 6.

I yelled for everybody to stop shooting, yelled
"Don't shoot!"
For a split second, they stopped shooting.
And across the street
I looked, could see three people, they looked at me, and
    they pointed the
guns at me.
And they were so close
I could see the barrels of the guns.
And . . . I knew they were going to start firing.
I got a gut feeling.
And I ducked.
And . . . they started firing at the van.
And . . . I came around the van to the back.
And . . . we had a rifle inside the van.
And . . . I pulled it out,
pulled the trigger,
and it just clicked, because there was no bullet in the chamber.
So I went back,
put the bullet in the chamber, and returned fire at the
    people firing
at us.
I wasn't aiming to hurt anybody.
More or less trying to disperse the people.
I was firing at the general direction that the gunfire was
    coming from.
When that happened, people dispersed.
I guess the people firing at me decided it wasn't worth it
    and they all
took off.
Everybody just went "pa-chew."

(Richard Kim)[35]

Manipulations of Korean Americans into a "model" minority contributed to their "triple scapegoating" following the King verdict. The first layer of attack came from those who targeted Korean-owned stores for looting and arson. The second layer consisted of those in positions of power who were responsible for the sacrifice of Koreatown, Pico-Union, and South Central Los Angeles to ensure the safety of wealthier, whiter communities. The final scapegoating came at the hands of the media, eager to sensationalize the events by excluding Korean perspectives from coverage and stereotyping the immigrant community. These three forces combined to blame the Korean-American community for the nation's most daunting economic and sociopolitical problems . . .

Koreans first were scapegoated by rioters of all colors . . . [T]he early activity following the not guilty verdict . . . centered around a crowd that had gathered in front of Tom's Liquor Store at Florence and Normandie in the late afternoon of 29 April 1992. One of the first targets of the group was the "swap meets"

35 Richard Kim, "Don't Shoot," in Anna Deveare Smith, *Twilight*, 1994: 87–9. Interviewed by Smith in August, 1993, Kim is a Korean American appliance store owner.

because they were Korean-owned. The swap meets were essentially indoor flea markets that operated every day during the week and offered discounted prices on consumer items such as electronics and clothing. Whether these stores provided a service to an underserved community by offering low-priced goods where mega-retailers refused to tread or whether they shamelessly promoted consumerism to an economically disadvantaged population was not at issue. The most oft-stated reason for the targeting of these stores and Korean stores in general was a familiar refrain: Korean owners were rude to African American and Latino customers . . .

Much has been made of the rudeness of Korean owners. Some of the major media outlets that covered the tensions between African Americans and Korean Americans attempted to reduce the conflict to "cultural differences" such as not smiling enough, not looking into the other person's eyes, not placing change in a person's hands. Although Koreans wanted very badly to believe in this reductionism, one making an honest assessment must conclude that far too many Korean shopowners had accepted widespread stereotypes about African Americans as lazy, complaining criminals.

The dominant U.S. racial hierarchy and its concomitant stereotypes are transmitted worldwide to every country that the United States has occupied militarily . . . When Koreans immigrate to the U.S., internationalized stereotypes are reinforced . . . in films, television shows, and other popular forms of cultural production. [These stereotypes], combined with the high crime rate inherent in businesses such as liquor or convenience stores (regardless of who owns them), produced the prejudiced, paranoid, bunker mentality of Soon ja Du who shot Latasha Harlins, a 15-year old African American girl, in the back of the neck during a dispute over a bottle of orange juice . . . On the other hand, many African Americans also internalize stereotypes of Korean Americans. Asian Americans walk a fine line between being seen as model minorities and callous unfair competitors . . . [T]he politics of resentment painted Koreans as callous and greedy invaders who got easy bank loans. As this depiction ran unchecked, it became increasingly easy to consider violence against such a contemptible group. The popular rap artist, Ice Cube, warned Korean shopowners in his song entitled "Black Korea" (on his *Death Certificate* album) to "pay respect to the black fist, or we'll burn your store right down to a crisp." The scene was set for disaster and required simply a spark to ignite the highly inflammable situation.

(Sumi K. Cho)[36]

Situated as we are on the border between those who have and those who have not, between predominantly Anglo and mostly African American and Latino communities, from our recent interstitial position in the American discourse of race, many Korean Americans have trouble calling what happened in Los Angeles an "uprising." At the same time, we cannot quite say it was a "riot." So some of us have taken to calling it *sa-i-ku*, April 29, after the manner of naming other events in Korean history – 3.1 (*sam-il*) for March 1, 1919, when massive protests against Japanese colonial rule began in Korea; 6.25 (*yook-i-o*), or June 25, 1950, when the Korean War began; and 4.19 (*sa-il-ku*), or April 19, 1960, when the first student movement in the world to overthrow a government began in

36 Sumi K. Cho, "Korean Americans vs. African Americans: Conflict and Construction," in Gooding-Williams, *Reading Rodney King*, 1993: 197–201.

South Korea. The ironic similarity between 4.19 and 4.29 does not escape most Korean Americans . . .

I could hardly believe my ears when, during the weeks immediately follow-ing *sa-i-ku*, I heard African American community leaders suggesting that Korean American merchants were foreign intruders deliberately trying to stifle African American economic development, when I knew that they had bought those liquor stores at five times gross receipts from African American owners, who had previously bought them at two times gross receipts from Jewish owners after Watts . . . I was disheartened with Latinos who related the pleasure they felt while looting Korean stores that they believed "had it coming" . . . And I was filled with despair when I read about Chinese Americans wanting to disassoci-ate themselves from us . . . "Suddenly," admitted [one] Chinese American, "I am scared to be Asian. More specifically, I am afraid to be mistaken for Korean." I was enraged when I overheard European Americans discussing the conflicts as if they were watching a dogfight or a boxing match. The situation reminded me of the Chinese film *Raise the Red Lantern,* in which we never see the husband's face. We only hear his mellifluous voice as he benignly admonishes his four wives not to fight among themselves. He can afford to be kind and pleasant because the structure that pits wives against each other is so firmly *in place* [my emphasis] that he need never sully his hands or even raise his voice.

(Elaine Kim)[37]

A repetitive ending

The new Enclosures cannot endure because they cannot sustain themselves. While suburban life is not yet an oxymoron, it will become one if those excluded from its peace are given only the miserable and incommodious lives of exclu-sion to live. That alternative future is upon us in the United States. It can and will result in the replication of the Los Angeles riot. But at the same time it is possible for the emergence of a politics of deterritorialization and reconnection, a politics in which arguments over space – its enclosures, exclusions, and intern-ments – become subjects for debate and discussion, and more important, for resistances and transgressions. The initiation of such a politics is a short step in the long journey to beginning the process of ameliorating the current problem. *Can Americans, for so long lacking a need to think about space, begin to think in spatial terms? Can they begin to act upon those thoughts?* [my emphasis] . . .

After the rioting began, Rodney King went on television to plead with his fellow citizens. Most Americans remember that he asked, "Can we all get along?" But he added, "We all can get along. We've just got to, just got to. *We're all stuck here for awhile.*" King recognized the finitude of the space of Los Angeles. He

---

37   Elaine H. Kim, "Home is Where the *Han* Is: A Korean American Perspective on the Los Angeles Upheavals," in Gooding-Williams, *Reading Rodney King,* 1993: 216–17. Kim notes: "*Han* is a Korean word that means, loosely translated, the sorrow and anger that grows from the accumulated experi-ences of oppression" (1993: 215). As she watched "the destruction of Koreatown," Kim states, "I had a terrible thought that there would be no belonging and that we were, just as I had always suspected, a people destined to carry our *han* around with us wherever we went in the world. The destiny (*p'aljja*) that had spelled centuries of extreme suffering from invasion, colonization, war, and national division had smuggled itself in the U.S. with our baggage" (1993: 216).

resisted the temptation to separate, to enclose, to substitute for the messy and open qualities of heterogeneous urban spaces the closed and deadened spaces of the suburbs. In making his plea he implicitly endorsed an ill-defined notion of toleration and plurality. He gave us a moment to reflect upon the possibility of a democratic existentialism. The world is worlding. The forces of normalization operate to constrain, to separate, to exclude, to intern. Our hope is precisely phrased. We're all stuck here for awhile.

(Thomas L. Dumm)[38]

To conclude this chapter and connect to the next, I return to my own words. What follows, written in the verse style of Anne Deveare Smith's *Twilight–Los Angeles, 1992*, was how I ended the original manuscript for *Thirdspace* more than six years ago, before it was split into two volumes.

To attempt a conclusion
using Iain Chambers' words,[39]
LA 1992 was indeed
a "highly charged punctuation of the cosmopolitan script."
Like so many other events that have marked
the geohistory of the world
        since 1989
(the fall of the Berlin Wall and the Cold War's disappearance,
the Gulf War, Tiananmen Square, the Salman Rushdie affair,
the Columbian quincentenary, the rise of the NICs,
the rebalkanization of southeastern Europe,
the fragmented unity of a Europe of the regions,
and, most recently,
the downfall of Orange County
and the terrorism of Oklahoma City),
the Second Los Angeles Uprising
is igniting
a "new mode of thinking"
that is "neither fixed
nor stable,"
a mode of thinking instigated
by "recent apertures in critical thought"
and tensely pressured by
"the return of the repressed,
the subordinate
and the forgotten
in 'Third World' musics,
literatures,
poverties and populations
as they come to occupy
the economies,

---

38   Thomas L. Dumm, "The New Enclosures," 1993: 192. The first paragraph was cited earlier, in chapter 10.
39   The quoted material is from Iain Chambers, *Migrancy, Culture, Identity*, London: Routledge, 1994: 3.

cities,
institutions,
media
and leisure time
of the First World."
To quote Chambers yet again,
this new mode of (re)thinking the postmetropolis
is "open to the prospect of a continual return to events,
to their   re-elaboration
and   revision,"
to a   "re-telling,
                  re-citing
and   re-siting
of what passes for historical and cultural knowledge,"
to a   "re-calling
and   re-membering
of earlier fragments and traces that flare up and flash
in our present moment of danger,"
to "splinters of light that illuminate our journey
   [to real-and-imagined places]
while simultaneously casting questioning shadows along the path."

For bell hooks and so many
        Others
it is an unconventional mode of rethinking race
and representation,
the relations between the colonizer
and the colonized,
and all alternative images that work to subvert
the status quo
and change our worldviews
and lifeworlds
at the same time and in the same
        lived spaces.
It is also about   real-and-imagined

                                        bodies

                                                                cities

                                texts
what Barbara Hooper called   the "order in place,"
about consciously   spatial praxis
that aims at   disordering

                              deconstructing

                                                        reconstituting
but not destroying or eliminating   difference and reason,
                                                  identity and enlightenment
                                                  philosophy and mastery
It is about   border work/la frontera
                                                  a new cultural politics
                        choosing the margin as a space of radical openness
                                                          and hybridity

about finding those meeting places
where new and radical happenings   can occur
about a politics of | deterritorialization – and – reconnection |
a politics in which arguments over   <SPACE>   its enclosures
                                      exclusions   internments
become subjects for debate and discussion,
and more important, for . . . . resistance and transgression
It is about   recombinant postmodern cultures
                                                              postmodern geographies
                                                                    heterotopologies
                                          the differences that postmodernity makes.
It is about   race
                                                                                   class
                                                                                 gender

            and/also . . .
It is about

                                                            material spatial practices
                                                            representations of space
                                                          lived spaces of representation

            and/also . . .
It is about

                                                                             Firstspace
                                                                          Secondspace
                                                                            Thirdspace

            and/also . . .

Only one ending is possible: **TO BE CONTINUED . . .**

Chapter 14
Postscript: Critical Reflections on the Postmetropolis

The real-and-imagined "new enclosures" of Los Angeles were cracked open for a few days just before and after May Day 1992. What was immediately exposed was clearly opaque, informatively deceptive, routinely spin-doctored by the media with images of random violence, intractable poverty, and racial polarization. But there was much more that flowed from what some have called the Second Los Angeles Uprising than these immediate images. Taking advantage of "recent apertures in critical thought," I use this final chapter to recollect, re-envision, and reflect upon what has happened since this "highly charged punctuation of the cosmopolitan script."[1] Los Angeles remains the representative center of attention, as it has in every previous chapter. But my aim continues to be to stimulate critical and comparative generalization from these particularities, to explore what can be learned from the Los Angeles experience by those who live in other places and spaces. What follows, then, is not a summing up of all that has come before, but a further opening up of the contemporary discourses on the postmetropolis.

New Beginnings I: Postmetropolis in Crisis

Looking back to the future, still another "new" Los Angeles seemed to burst on to the scene in 1992 and in its short life it has already begun to instigate significant revisions of the discursive scripts of postmodern urbanism. As the nation's second largest city began to disappear in smoke and fire during that violent spring, many of the most confident interpretations of the new urbanization processes seemed as if they too were being engulfed in flames. It is not that the discourses on the postmetropolis that had been developing over the past thirty years became entirely irrelevant post-1992, but rather that the material, symbolic, and lived spaces charted by each discursive framework, each

---

1 The quoted phrases refer back to the passage from Iain Chambers, *Migrancy, Culture, Identity* (1994), contained in chapter 12.

mode of interpreting the postmetropolitan transition, took an unexpected twist. For nearly three decades, crisis-generated restructuring processes emanating in large part from the worldwide urban irruptions of the 1960s dominated the discourse of those trying to make practical and theoretical sense of Los Angeles and its exemplifications of the contemporary urban condition. After 1992, however, the urban realities and hyperrealities of Los Angeles and other global city-regions no longer seemed so readily interpretable under the prevailing rubric of urban restructuring. The new urbanization processes that had so profoundly transformed the modern metropolis were themselves being tangibly disrupted and disordered, exposing their inherent tensions and resultant injustices for all the world to see.

What was happening in 1992, viewed with hindsight from the edge of a new millennium, may very well have been a profound local turning point, marking with other events before and after a shift from a period of crisis-generated restructuring to the onset of a new era of *restructuring-generated crises*. In other words, the full-grown postmetropolis has reached a stage when it appears to be exploding under the weight of its newnesses. Those same innovative practices and restructured urban spatialities that proved most successful in restoring robust economic growth and in effectively controlling social unrest after the 1960s are now showing signs of disturbing dysfunctionality. The flexibly specialized and unevenly developed industrial landscapes of postfordism; the heterogeneous globalizations of capital, labor, and culture in the polychromatic Cosmopolis; the stretched and rewoven urban fabric of the recentered and edge-citied Exopolis; the gaping metropolarities and mixed-up class boundaries of the dis-ordered Fractal City; the protective fortresses and tightly policed turfs of the increasingly gated-and-guarded Carceral Archipelago; and the anaesthetic urban imaginary of the spin-doctored Simcity's enchanting and duplicitous hyperrealities have, in effect, moved from being solutions to become part of the problem.

Every one of these postmetropolitan subworlds took on a different color and cast in the extended twilight of the Second Los Angeles Uprising, suggesting that what happened in 1992 was not just a localized event but rather one of many global expressions, stretching from the fall of the Berlin Wall and the events in Tienanmen Square in 1989 to the current world financial turmoil, of a more general crisis of postmodernity, postfordism, globalization, neoliberalism, and specifically postmetropolitan urban forms and ways of life. A few brief glimpses of post-1992 Los Angeles help us learn more about these interlocking crises and conflicts and some of the new directions being taken in response to them.

The downturn of postfordism

The *Postfordist Industrial Metropolis* of Los Angeles, one of the great economic success stories of the late twentieth century, had already begun to disintegrate by April, 1992. *Perestroika*, that potent Russian form of restructuring, and the precipitous end of the Cold War simultaneously weakened the most propulsive forces behind the postfordist regional economy and toppled many of the ideological pillars that had supported the tightening of social discipline by local and federal keepers of the peace. Between the fall of the Berlin Wall and the bankruptcy of Orange County, roughly 1989–1995, median household income in Los Angeles County fell by as much as 20 percent in by far the worst regional recession since the Great Depression. As the militarized technopolis careened into steep decline, so too did its supportive FIRE sector, creating a recessionary spiral that seemed to go deeper in Southern California than almost anywhere else in the country.

Massive job losses hit unusually hard at the upper "bubble" of the bimodal labor market: bankers and brokers, highly paid aerospace workers and the new technocracy, lawyers, accountants, and real estate agents, yuppies and beemers (BMW-drivers), the flush legatees of the Reagan-Bush era. As the hopeful prospects of defense industry conversion went unfulfilled, poverty and homelessness, already at high levels, burst out from their enclaves of despair to infiltrate the entire urban landscape. With painful irony, what was once the world's most robust job machine became radically downsized, leaner and meaner. Unemployment rates rose above national levels and were prevented from climbing still further only by the continued growth of the fabulous entertainment industry (now again "the" industry of Los Angeles) and the "temp" or contingent labor market. In both a real and imagined sense, the ascendant model of the postfordist industrial metropolis began rapidly to lose at least some of its luster as the darkside of the new economy became increasingly apparent.

There has been significant regional recovery since 1996, propelled especially by technological innovations in multi-media industries and the expansion of "cultural production" activities, but even here there are signs that many aspects of the crisis of neoliberal postfordism have continued to worsen. Traditionally liberal Hollywood–the symbolic core of the entertainment industry-led the local economic recovery in the early 1960s through the expansion of a dense network of small and middle-sized firms allied to the larger studios and organized around flexibility, innovation, job-generation, and a broad base of skilled craftsmen and other specialized workers. Since the mid-1990s, however, there has been what one observer describes as a significant "upward flow of wealth" at the expense of the craft and blue-collar workforce, leading to reduced wages, much lower job growth, and worsening work conditions and employment security.[2] The simplistic bottom-line addiction of corporate America to get lean and mean by drastically cutting workers' wages and benefits while often ballooning upper executive and, for Hollywood, celebrity salaries has entered the entertainment industry in full force as we have arrived

2 David Friedman, "The Jackpot Economy," *Los Angeles Times*, May 9, 1999. One of the leading business-oriented boosters of the new Los Angeles (see chapter 8), Friedman in this recent Opinion piece calls for a new working-class politics to fight against the negative effects of the reinvigorated jackpot or casino economy. He does not, or chooses not to, notice, however, the robust new working-class politics that has been emerging in recent years.

at the century's end, contributing to, rather than helping to resolve, the widening income gap.

California and New York continue today to rank alongside Mississippi as the states with the highest income disparities, and their largest cities, New York even more so than Los Angeles, remain near the top of the world list in terms of metropolarity, the urban gap between the wealthy and the poor. A recent report of the Select Committee on the California Middle Class shows that between 1994 and 1996, when the recovery was beginning, the labor market of Los Angeles County intensified its bipolarization and middle-class squeeze, dropping still larger numbers of lower middle-class workers into the ranks of the working poor. For example, the proportion of county residents living in households earning less than $20,000 a year increased by 13.5 percent between 1994 and 1996. This meant that 41 percent of the entire county population were living in households close to or below the poverty level. This magnified an already severe housing crisis as the working poor became still further compacted in already overcrowded and aging residential areas. Another recent report, by the Center on Budget and Policy Priorities in Washington DC, identified Los Angeles as leading the country in the ratio of low-income renters to the number of low-cost rental units available (more than 4 to 1).

In stark contrast, households earning $100,000–500,000 increased by 29.7 percent (to 7.3 percent of the county total) and those with incomes over $500,000 jumped more than 40 percent (to a total of 0.5 percent). Meanwhile, households earning $40,000–100,000 dropped from 30 to 26 percent of the county population during these two years of relative economic expansion. What these figures indicate is that the Los Angeles job machine, today again reputed to be among the most robust in the country, has continued to generate huge numbers of bare subsistence jobs for increasing numbers of the working poor as well as an expanding small stream of high-end job opportunities for the fortunate 10 percent of the labor market. Topping it all off, the numbers of households in Los Angeles county earning more than $25 million a year more than doubled between 1994 and 1996, from 65 to 143. It is easy to see why Los Angeles since the Justice Riots has become one of the national centers for coalition-building around securing a "living wage" for its workers.[3]

Too fulsome globalization?

The *Cosmopolis* continued to be unsettled and turbulent after the Justice Riots. For every new cross-cultural achievement in the arts, in business, and in local

---

3   These figures are reported in Harold Meyerson, "No Justice, No Growth," *LA Weekly* July 17–23, 1998. The subtitle for this article, which will be referred to again later in this chapter, is "A New Labor–Left Alliance Scrambles L.A.'s Growth Politics – and Creates Middle-Income Jobs in a City where They're Vanishing." Harold Meyerson, political editor for this important free weekly newspaper, is also a leading commentator on local and national politics.

politics, there appeared new kinds of inter-ethnic conflict as scores of different cultural worlds continued to collide without mixing. More and more poor immigrants were added to the population, saturating even the most absorptive local labor markets and cruelly ballooning welfare dependency in what had now become the neoliberal post-welfare state. Like the affordable housing crisis, an already severe public health crisis intensified and was made still worse by the welfare reforms of the Clinton administration, a series of local hospital closures and reorganizations, and the continuing high cost of health insurance. The streets of Los Angeles became even more densely filled with the homeless, the unhealthy, and the starving. Finding better ways to distribute food to poor communities, such as through urban gardening and the recycling of produce from the growing network of farmers' markets, has become an urgent concern for the region's activists and community-based organizations in the aftermath of what some called the "Food Riot" of 1992. For example, the Los Angeles Regional Foodbank, a network of more than 750 groups, currently provides nourishment for nearly 200,000 people a week.

At the same time as the flow of immigrant labor continued, the influx of foreign capital has slowed down. An eventuality once considered inconceivable by many financial experts, Japanese-owned hotels, office buildings, and businesses were sold or went into bankruptcy, reflecting not just local events but also the severe recession in Japan. Most obviously hard-hit was the new downtown, instigating revivals of older debates about regenerating the "heart of our city" and the need for a downtown "renaissance." What was maintained most stubbornly, however, was a fundamentally unresponsive government system, seemingly incapable of adapting to the changed circumstances of this most intensively globalized city-region. Globalization was reduced in city government to insipid claims of having become "world-class" or to celebrations of "diversity," with little mention of the expanding landscapes of poverty and despair that these accomplishments have helped to generate. In 1999, there was an attempt in the City of Los Angeles to revise the seriously outdated City Charter, but there is little indication that whatever changes scheduled to be are made will make any difference to the ability of city government to respond to the intensified problems arising from economic restructuring and globalization.

It has become increasingly clear that the glocalizations of capital, labor, and culture that had helped to make Los Angeles boom are now beginning to overburden the multicultural regional economy. This has fanned anti-immigrant feelings and led to the passage of new state laws on welfare rights, affirmative action, and bilingual education that constrain still further the abilities of the immigrant working poor to survive and prosper in the postmetropolis. Adding further to these difficulties throughout the country has been the welfare reform legislation of the Clinton administration, especially its popular welfare-to-work policies, which take increasing numbers of the "truly disadvantaged" off direct government benefits to fill subsidized jobs at well below the minimum wage. This has artificially reduced the national unemployment rate and created the image if not the reality of accelerated job-generation and plummeting welfare expenditures. But at the same time it has captured and used the deepest underclass as still another tool to discipline the industrious working poor, who find themselves unable to compete with the proud new burger-slingers or dishwashers being paid $2 an hour.

And as much as ever before, the whole world is watching Los Angeles. While the Watts Rebellion could be seen as a regional event, as localized civil unrest, as strangely far away, the Second Los Angeles Uprising was a truly global urban spectacle, presenting and representing the first World City exploding from its too fulsome globalization. As the crisis of the Cosmopolis continues, what is being seen in Los Angeles and elsewhere today is a further crumbling of the myth of inexorable globalization as the panacea for all the world's ills. In the wake of this dissolution and disillusion, new communities of resistance to globalization are beginning to express their discontent and to search for better ways to resist and/or control globalization's increasingly evident negative social and spatial consequences. The allegedly irresistible force is now starting to become a movable object of contention.

Suddenly everywhere is Pomona

Although the Justice Riots were most intense in the "old downtowns" of Los Angeles and Long Beach, they reached well into the edgy cities and the post-suburban strongholds of the *Exopolis*; and they overflowed into Las Vegas, the Bay Area, Omaha, Minneapolis, Atlanta, Toronto, London, Seoul, leaping scales. Once-steadfast boundaries between citadel and ghetto, Inner and Outer City, urban and suburban, metropolis and region, center and periphery, Los Angeles and the rest of the world, seemed to disappear, at least momentarily, in puffs of smoke. Even more so today, the Nowhere City is now-here and everywhere, integrally disintegrated, being recomposed again as a dystopian symbol of a contemporary world run amok. For its inhabitants, there is no longer any place to hide inside the peculiarly compacted Exopolis. Suddenly, everywhere is Pomona.

With I-told-you-so confidence, Mike Davis in his newly revamped *Ecology of Fear* (1998) continues his tactical projections of downward-spiraling trends to plunge contemporary Los Angeles ever deeper into apocalypse now, a veritable theme park of disaster. And he is not alone, for many who not long ago were forced to recognize the successful exemplariness of Los Angeles now revert to older stereotypes, forgetting what they once had seen to focus on the new urban crises of this still exemplary postmetropolis. When, for example, the film *Independence Day* presented the alien destruction of New York City, the audience was usually quiet and somber. When Los Angeles, once projected as the capital of the twenty-first century, was destroyed, it was reported that many audiences cheered. For much of the world, the Edge City maxim, that every American city is growing in the fashion of Los Angeles, has become much more of a foreboding threat than a hopeful promise.

The splintered social labyrinth that intertwined with the fractured, unevenly developed, spatially disordered Exopolis created the incendiary conditions that, as much as anything else, generated the events of 1992. Academic studies of the panorama of polarization and inequality inscribed in the *Fractal City* had provided some anticipatory warnings. But beneath the surface of these restratified socialities was a hidden tinderbox of extraordinary violence, oppression, and racism, unseen in those dedicated attempts to impose a rational order on what Barbara Hooper called the erratic, fragmented, and disorderly "social body." Perhaps the most serious oversight in these still-continuing academic studies was the depth of despair and frustration building up in African American communities, especially among young black men and women, unconvinced by intellectual explanations of their plight. Amidst still-heated debates about whether race really matters or whether immigrants compete for the same jobs as African Americans or whether corporate hiring practices are a product of rational choice or "statistical discrimination" rather than racial bias, the postfordist economy has continued its protracted "disciplining" of African Americans to the point of stimulating not entirely outrageous Afrocentric claims of genocide and racial cleansing.

There have been other unforeseen developments. The depth of poverty and malnutrition among the immigrant Latino population made 1992 as much a food riot as anything else, and these pressures persist with little amelioration. Made more visible in their swelling and spreading numbers, the homeless population has increasingly turned many once sympathetic Angelenos into frantic not-in-my-back-yard antagonists, fanning still further the ecology of fear. The new ethnic division of labor, once proclaimed by many as the linchpin of a successful multicultural economy, has also increasingly become an uncontrollable battlefield of competing entrepreneurial ethnicities, each jostling for its own indigenous positioning and each competition fought out not just in segregated residential enclaves or major employment nodes but everywhere in cityspace. Here, in this growing ubiquity of city-like heterogeneity, reaching its most unexpected pathologies in such "postsuburban slums" as Palmdale, Lancaster, and Moreno Valley, we can see the process of mass regional urbanization taking its negative toll.

Repadded white bunkers

Arising from the fortressed enclaves of the *Carceral Archipelago*, less visible in 1992 but more rampant today in the anti-immigrant hysteria that fueled the passage of Proposition 187 in 1994 and the growing neoconservative and neoliberal movements against affirmative action, multicultural education, civil rights, and social and spatial justice, has been the consolidation of white right-wing nativism, backed by an increasingly visible paramilitary army of angry-white-male vigilantes and their equally armed children. There are more connections between Los Angeles 1992 and the apple-pie terrorism in

Oklahoma City three years later, as well as the most recent mass murders at Colorado's Columbine High School and Granada Hills Jewish Community Center, than may initially meet the interpretive eye. It is almost as if the rising prominence of radical women of color in the academic, political, and public arenas of the 1990s has induced its polar opposite: the insurgence of reactionary white straight men.

Since 1992, a new kind of paramilitary Outer City has been taking shape in the Los Angeles postmetropolis. It stretches from the bunkered "urban villages" of Ventura County (Simi Valley, Camarillo, Thousand Oaks) through the booming high desert outposts of northern Los Angeles County (Castaic, Lancaster, Palmdale, Santa Clarita) into the low desert fringes of the urbanized region, where the nearby Angeles National Forest is used for tactical maneuvers and elaborate "defense" sites by such groups as the "secret" USA Enforcement Agency. The zone extends still further to the borderlands of San Diego and Orange counties in Camp Pendleton and nearby Fallbrook, home to Tom Metzger, former Grand Dragon of the Ku Klux Klan, once Republican candidate for Congress, and now a consulting agitator for the White Aryan Resistance, or WAR.[4]

In this strange new world, redolent of older Aryan dreams, 1992 served as an almost biblical call for militant white racial re-empowerment against "Degenerate Los Angeles" (title of one of Metzger's WAR videos) and against not only the federal government but also the local "police state," seen by some to have been co-opted and corrupted in the imprisonment of such racial heroes and homeboys as Stacey Koon and Lawrence Powell. There have even been claims that the federal government, in alliance with local police, has been secretly training and equipping the Crips and Bloods for an allied counteroffensive against the Aryan militias. Stimulated to even more intense paranoia by the earthquakes, floods, and fires that followed the events of 1992, privatopia and common interest developments have taken on more sinister meanings.

Deconstructed modes of regulation

In order to understand better the post-1992 consolidation of this underground crescent of anti-minority, anti-government, white supremacist fanaticism, it is important to recognize just how much the events of 1992 represented and initiated a general crisis of social control in both the Carceral Archipelago and the cyberspatial Simcity, the twin peaks of the postmodern/postfordist mode of social and spatial regulation. To illustrate with intentionally subversive imagery this symbolic and strategic disordering, let us return briefly to the

---

4   For a fictional account of this terrorist borderland overlapping Orange and San Diego counties, see the thriller written by T. Jefferson Parker, *The Triggerman's Dance*, New York: Hyperion, 1996. Parker here and in his other detective stories, *Laguna Heat*, *Pacific Beat*, *Summer of Fear*, and *Little Saigon*, offers novel insights into the postsuburban angst of Orange County life.

corner of Florence and Normandie, the real-and-imagined starting point for the Justice Riots and also so much more.

As the violent beating of white truck driver Reginald Denny was beamed around the world, a peculiar revisioning of power could be seen as taking place both in the "real" turfs controlled by the Space Police and in the hyper-real spaces of the urban imaginary. The former is easier to describe: the police failed to protect and serve the Carceral Archipelago, failed to confine the riots and looting to their proper places, failed in their surveillance and control of the purported enemy within. Replacing *polis* with *police* simply did not work and the potential power of the underclasses was forcefully expressed, threat-ening even the most heavily guarded and gated normalized communities. With the breakdown of "official" police and governmental control, increasing numbers of those who felt most threatened by the readily apparent expres-sion of angry black power became convinced that well-armed and indepen-dent white militias might be their only hope for survival in the postmetropolis, and began to act accordingly.

The revisioning of power in the Simcity also took on a more subtle and sub-versive imagery within the media-savvy African American population. This insurgent urban imaginary emerged most provocatively in the documentary theater performance captured in the videotaping of the Reginald Denny beating. Staged on the corner of Florence and Normandie were two happen-ings, one a brutal explosion of frustration by angry black youth enraged at the Rodney King verdict; the second an inquisitive media mini-drama about the hyperrealities of racism in SimAmerica, a performance that pointedly asked a disturbing question: if a videotape of many white men kicking and beating up a lone black man could be dismissed as a misleading picture of reality, would it be possible for the same result to occur with a videotape of many black men kicking and beating up a lone white man?

At the trial of the "LA Four" charged with the attempted murder of Regi-nald Denny, the mini-drama of subversive imagery continued. The mother of one of the defendants was shown some stills from the videotape. They portrayed, full-face on, staring straight at the helicopter camera with fist raised high, what appeared very clearly to be the mother's son Damian. Asked if she could identify the person in the picture the mother was firmly noncom-mittal, saying that, well . . . , hmmm . . . , it could be my son, but then again, you know, pictures can be very deceiving, I really don't know for sure. Through it all, Denny refused to vilify his attackers, instead referring with anti-racist gratitude to the four non-white citizens who came to his rescue. Eventually, nearly all the charges against the LA Four were dismissed except in the case of Damian Williams, the leading performer, who was sentenced to a maximum of ten years in prison for the attacks on the body of Citizen Reginald Denny.

It is possible to see in such multivalent events another side of what occurred in 1992. The electronic cyberspaces, Simcities, and hyperrealities of everyday life were being slowly infiltrated by, as bell hooks described them, those who dare to desire differently, to look away from the conventional ways of seeing and acting upon the oppressions of race, class, and gender to open new spaces for struggle that work to transform prevailing imagery, create strategic alternatives, and project new images that subvert and transform our established worldviews. The Simcity is no longer just an enchanting diversion that helps to maintain an invisible apparatus of social control. It has also become a site for resistance and counter-simulation, for what Celeste Olalquiaga called an "iconic radicalism" and Iain Chambers an "uprooting and rerouting" of established histories and geographies, structures and traditions.[5]

Simgovernment in crisis

Driven by a desire to forget, the immediate response of local, state, and federal governments to the Justice Riots in 1992 concentrated around still another hypersimulation, the creation of a super-committee of civic and business leaders whose stated aim was to "rebuild" Los Angeles. Initially headed by Peter Ueberoth, key organizer of the localized spectacle of the 1984 Olympics and resident of Orange County where many of the athletic events took place, the Rebuild LA committee (later shortened to just RLA) was rife with hidden meaning and intent. Although it was represented as the primary governmental response to the Justice Riots, it actually symbolized the full retreat of government from any significant responsibility in dealing with the deep social and spatial problems that so obviously instigated the uprising. In a hollow triumph of neoliberalism, the rebuilding of Los Angeles–and symbolically the future of all American cities – was handed over by the Mayor, the Governor, and the President of the USA to the corporate sector and its globalized networks of economic power. Two activities dominated the work of this faux governmental committee, located at the real and imagined interface between public and private interests. The first was to encourage corporate investment in what was considered the primary if not only source of the riots and unrest, that now globally iconic fusion zone of all urban problems, South Central LA. The second was much more ambitious and urgent: to rebuild the public and private image of Los Angeles as an ascendant global city-region, a "world-class" economic and cultural capital of late twentieth-century America.

Rebuild LA/RLA would eventually involve important local activists and organizers from Black, Latino, Asian, and other minority communities, and have some minor successes in achieving both their investment and image-spinning goals. But its most lasting effect has had less to do with its specific activities than with what it came to symbolize for the urban future. After the Watts Rebellion in 1965, there was at least the pretense that responsible government could significantly assist in resolving the problems of racism, poverty, and unemployment that were among the root causes of the unrest. After 1992,

---

5   It is worth rereading the passage from Chambers (1990: 47–8) presented in the Introduction to Part II.

even the pretense seemed to disappear behind thickly spun blankets of hyper-reality. Rebuilding LA became very much like other tales of the Simcity, a game of Simgovernment in which models of the real substituted for the real itself, exposing that there was little left behind the simulations except homespun spitting images. Even without such Baudrillardian references, it became clear to many that the new Los Angeles that had emerged from thirty years of intensive restructuring was even more impotent than the old in dealing with major urban crises.

These (hyper)realizations have had relatively little effect on the vast majority of the population. For the most part, urban life and urban governance in Los Angeles have continued with little change in the years following the Justice Riots. But at the same time, there have been some new developments that need to be recognized and understood. Especially for those actively participating in the public arena from all parts of the political spectrum, three very different streams of political reaction seemed to grow directly out of the events of 1992 and their immediate aftermath. The first and probably the most widespread swept up those formerly progressive citizens who abandoned any hope that the globalized regional economy and the established hierarchy of federal, state, local, and municipal governments could have a significant effect on resolving the problems of social and spatial justice that were peaking in places such as Los Angeles and New York. Their response, after years of more confident expectations, was to retreat into political apathy and/or sniping cynicism. Only the dark side of the postmetropolis and the inevitability of additional violence and unrest remained in view, moving many even deeper into bunkered lifestyles and further weakening the power of the remaining progressive forces in the city-region.

A second, much smaller but much more violent, stream of political reaction has arisen from a newly emboldened and angry white nativism. Fueled by the easy availability of guns and other weapons of destruction, this increasingly activated reactionary fringe blames riots and urban unrest, as well as nearly all problems in America, on immigrants and African Americans, and secondarily on what is perceived as their excessively favorable coddling by both the government and the corporate sectors. Every place and space – from the freeway and the shopping mall to the high school and the community center to the television studio and the movie theater – becomes a potential battlefield site for the expression of rage and frustration in the fearful ecology of the postmetropolis. Here a very different kind of cultural and identity politics of place and space is operative.

A third group of activists, also feeling abandoned by the established order, has responded not by withdrawal or reactionary violence but with reinvigorated efforts to assert the power of local and non-governmental community movements and a more progressively insurgent civil society. Out of these developments, slowly but surely, there is emerging a more spatially conscious network of creative resistance and redirection with regard to the new urbanization processes, an active practice of a progressive cultural politics of place, space, and region that consciously crosses and disrupts existing boundaries of class, race, gender, and locality to deal with the specific injustices and inequities embedded in the restructured urban-regional milieu. I conclude *Postmetropolis* with a closer look at some of these innovative new forms of rebuilding a better Los Angeles, for they represent the most hopeful and progressive new beginnings to have emerged from the Justice Riots of 1992.

New Beginnings II: Struggles for Spatial Justice and Regional Democracy

A new critical discourse on cities and regions has developed in the 1990s in the attempt to make practical and theoretical sense of the emerging crises of the postmetropolis. Theoretically informed by poststructuralist epistemologies, postmodern feminism, queer theory, postmarxist analyses, postcolonial and other anti-racist critiques, and increasingly empowered with particular conviction by radical women of color, this still evolving discourse has been triggering new modes of thinking about the generalizable particularities and spatial specificities of Los Angeles and other globalized city-regions. Entwined with this refocusing of critical studies of cities and regions and the concurrent spatial turn so integral to it has been the onset of something even more significant, the emergence of an active and situated practice of a cultural politics that is consciously driven by increasingly spatialized notions of social justice, participatory democracy, and citizenship rights and responsibilities. The impact of these spatially conscious practices has not been very great as yet, but there are sufficient indications to suggest that they are likely to play a major role in shaping the postmetropolitan future.

Brief references to these actual and potential struggles for spatial justice as they have been developing in Los Angeles are contained in all the chapters of Part II. I have argued, for example, that growing out of the more general discourses on industrial urbanism and globalization has been a call for new forms of *regional democracy* that could contend more effectively with the growing challenges and opportunities embedded in postmetropolitan city-regions. Allen Scott translated his vision of this socially and spatially democratic regionalism into "concerted institution-building" to increase regional economic productivity and competitiveness as well as "massive investment in social overhead capital" to improve the quality of the workforce and provide decent living wages for "currently underprivileged groups." In Scott's work and that of other New Regionalists such as Michael Storper, these policy objectives tend to revolve primarily around the creation of regional industrial councils or "directorates" that, with associated development banks, can coordinate information- and technology-sharing, job training, public and private investment allocations, and other activities that increase regional productivity and global competitiveness while at the same time fostering greater equity and expanded worker's rights in the regional labor market. Little has yet been done to implement these suggestions in Los Angeles, but they have helped to place the New Regionalism and the concept of regional democracy on the public policy agenda and to support, implicitly at least, a shift in academic attention to addressing more directly the problems of increasing social and spatial inequalities.

In Los Angeles and elsewhere, the regionality of cityspace and the new opportunities for promoting greater regional democracy in an age of information technology, globalization, and postfordism are being more widely recognized as we have arrived at the century's end. Take, for example, the work of Myron Orfield on the "metropolitics" of global city-regions.[6] Based in the Twin Cities of Minneapolis-St. Paul, Orfield's work has been receiving attention from urban governments throughout the country, including Los Angeles, where one of his regional revitalization projects is currently in progress. Orfield's approach to fostering regional democracy and reducing what I have called metropolarities revolves primarily around regional tax-base or revenue sharing, increasing control over investment policies, and the building of new political coalitions between older suburbs and central cities within a confederation of governmental and planning authorities. While such calls for redistributive justice are certainly not new, what is different today is their explicit attachment to a community-based regional agenda and a growing public consciousness of how geographically uneven development and the spatial specificities of the restructured urban-regional economy work to generate and maintain social and economic injustices and inequalities.[7]

Promoting similar demands for regional democracy is the work of critical legal scholars such as Gerald Frug and Richard T. Ford, who advocate radical revisions in local governance and voting regulations to stimulate regional consciousness and center it on achieving greater spatial and racial justice.[8] One of their more creative ideas has been to give multiple votes to urban residents, allowing anyone to allocate their voting power to any constituency in the metropolitan region, local or otherwise. The main aim here is to heighten public consciousness of regional interdependencies and to assist in struggles against recalcitrant localisms and racisms. In an indirect way, these ideas build on earlier legal precedents such as the Mount Laurel case of 1975, which established the principle of territorial or regional responsibility in which municipal land-use decisions have to take into account possible negative spillover effects into other jurisdictions – a breakthrough in recognizing the larger spatial obligations of local governments in an urban region and in providing a potential framework for more effective and equitable regional land-use plan-

6   Myron Orfield, *Metropolitics: A Regional Agenda for Community and Stability*, Washington, DC: Brookings Institution Press, and Cambridge, MA: Lincoln Institute of Land Policy, 1997.

7   For a further analysis of community-based regionalism with a particular focus on Los Angeles, see Manuel Pastor Jr., Peter Dreier, J. Eugene Grigsby III, and Mart Lopez-Garza, *Growing Together: Linking Regional and Community Development in a Changing Economy*, Minneapolis: University of Minnesota Press, 1999.

8   Gerald Frug, "Decentering Decentralization," *The University of Chicago Law Review* 60, Spring 1993: 253–338; Richard T. Ford, "The Boundaries of Race: Political Geography in Legal Analysis," *Harvard Law Review* 107, June 1994: 1843–1921, and "Geography and Sovereignty: Jurisdictional Formation and Racial Segregation," *Stanford Law Review* 49, July 1997: 1365–1446.

ning based in the legal system. Constitutional arguments and property rights laws severely constrained any ambitious extension of these principles of spatial or territorial responsibility, but there may be some room for their tactical revival in connection with reinvigorated movements for greater regional democracy and spatial justice.[9]

Iris Marion Young, a critical philosopher of public policy, has also been adding her insights to the resurgence of interest in democratic regionalism. Young is currently completing a book with the tentative title *Inclusion and Democracy* that contains a specific discussion and advocacy of the idea of regional democracy, especially with regard to ameliorating the most negative effects of residential segregation and what she describes more broadly as the "spatial structures of privilege" that lie at the source of increasing metropolarities. Young has been a key figure in rethinking the concepts of community, difference, and diversity in cities and in redefining civil society, and by extension regional democracy, around what she has called a "heterogeneous public" assertively open to "unassimilated otherness" and a collective sense of "togetherness-in-difference." Her past work has attracted attention from both geopolitical economists and critical cultural scholars working on cities, and she is likely to continue to play a role in the future in encouraging a productive interaction between these two often highly competitive groups of scholars.

In their interpretations of globalization and the new Cosmopolis in chapter 7, Engin Isin and Leonie Sandercock contribute their views to the current debates on regional democracy and spatial justice. Isin focuses his attention on contemporary struggles over citizenship and the rights to regional city-space, especially in postmetropolitan Toronto, where a more conservative form of the new regionalism has recently taken hold. Sandercock echoes his attention to the related rights to the city-region and to difference. In her imagined but approachable postmodern utopia, a transformative politics of difference is seen as leading the way in creating new spaces for justice, community, and connection. The ancient concept of citizen's rights and responsibilities, the re-empowerment of civil society, and the 1960s demand for greater rights to the city or *le droit à la ville*, Henri Lefebvre's trenchant phrase that played a key part in mobilizing the May 1968 uprising in Paris, are given new life in these writings. Especially significant here and also noted in chapter 7 are Raymond Rocco's concrete studies of associational rights claims and situated spatial practices in the Latino communities of Los Angeles.[10]

The definition of democratic citizenship is being significantly rethought in the 1990s in such new journals as *Citizenship Studies* as well as in practice, especially with regard to the growing immigrant population and extraordinary

---

9 The original Mount Laurel Case, *Southern Burlington County NAACP v. Township of Mount Laurel* (New Jersey) was subsequently watered down and significantly despatialized into a state Council on Affordable Housing. See Charles M. Haar, *Suburbs under Siege: Race, Space, and Audacious Judges*, Princeton: Princeton University Press, 1996.

10 See pp. 231–2 above.

cultural diversity characterizing the postmetropolis. In Los Angeles and other city-regions, for example, proposals have been raised to give voting rights to non-citizen resident "aliens" (another term that needs redefinition) in local elections, at least for issues and offices that directly affect family health, welfare, education, work, and safety. These proposals arise from a more general mobilization of significantly disenfranchised groups and the working poor for greater social and spatial justice, ranging from the now widespread Living Wage movement to more spatially specific struggles for environmental justice and residential rights to public services in transportation, health, education, and welfare. The recent success of the Bus Riders Union, discussed in chapter 8, is indicative of how these local community mobilizations, especially in the form of community-based regionalism, are becoming connected to a greatly expanded notion of civil rights (as residential rights to cityspace) and new visions of specifically regional participatory democracy.

These developments are raising awareness of the degree to which the long-entrenched administrative structures of governance in the fragmented postmetropolis severely constrain the possibilities of attaining greater justice and democracy. This is leading some toward to a rethinking of the exclusive dependence of local government on such units as the municipality and the county, and to new visions for a democratic regional governance system more responsive to the restructured needs of postmetropolitan cityspace. Even sympathetic observers recognize the formidable barriers that exist to prevent the implementation of these new visions, but it is nevertheless useful to imagine how they might be constructed. It will be necessary, for example, to move beyond simply collecting together existing city and county authorities in relatively powerless COGs (councils of governments). Emphasis needs to shift instead to the creation of a more innovative form of urban confederalism which allocates greater fiscal and allocative powers to both regional *and* local community organizations simultaneously. These new city-region confederations or congresses of local communities might also involve ties to significant NGOs or non-governmental organizations, including labor unions, philanthropic institutions, more progressive regional industrial councils and religious organizations, and other active units of civil society to assist in assuring that local government meets regional needs – and vice versa.

One can go into further detail on how such confederations might be organized, and I hope others will be stimulated to do so. But the key objective of such exercises must remain focused on increasing awareness of the interrelated notions of democratic regionalism and spatial justice. This means, above all, an obligation to deal directly with the most troubling and challenging conclusion derived from all the discourses on the postmetropolis: *that the new urbanization processes have built into their impact the magnification of economic and extra-economic (racial, gender, ethnic) inequalities along with destructive consequences for both the built and natural environments.* There can be little doubt that the resurgence of inequality associated with the postmetropolitan transition has been particularly intense in Los Angeles and continues to generate serious problems, even after a limited recovery from the extraordinary explosion of frustrations linked to its consequences. While relatively little has yet been accomplished in reversing this surge in inequality, there are encouraging signs that new movements are arising that have the potential to respond to the restructuring-generated crises in significantly progressive ways. The Bus Riders Union and the growing multiracial and cross-class coalitions for environmental justice are but a few of the limited but crucially important examples of the new cultural and spatial politics being organized around labor, community, locality, and region. An even more promising and comprehensive coalition has recently burst on to the local scene and has quickly become a major force in progressive local and regional politics, the Los Angeles Alliance for a New Economy (LAANE).

At the heart of LAANE's activities is the assertive recognition that the Los Angeles economy has become a free-wheeling inequality-generating machine. Its explicit target in constructing a "new economy" is the postmetropolitan labor market and its polarization of the region into an explosive duality of working poor and super-rich neighborhoods jostling ever closer together. Adapting the resounding calls emanating from the streets in 1992, its motto can be described as No Justice, No Growth or, as it is defined more temperately by the organization itself, Growth with Equity. The current leaders of LAANE spearheaded the local Living Wage Campaign, which achieved its first major success with the passage of a new ordinance in the City of Los Angeles in 1997 that guaranteed increased minimum wages and health benefits for all City contract workers.[11] Since that initial victory, LAANE's organizers have expanded their efforts significantly to take on the private sector as well, collectively bargaining for all low-wage service workers, even those who are not yet union members, at selected strategic sites planned for large-scale development.

LAANE's strategy is very consciously place-based and focused, with militant particularism, at key sites of location-dependent development, such as the tourist and entertainment industries as well as local government authorities. In these locally rooted sites, capital investment and related commitments are much less mobile and free to relocate than, say, in large manufacturing plants, which were the earlier focus of the local labor movement. That these three sectors and their offshoots (hotels, restaurants, shopping malls, etc.) probably employ a majority of service workers in the region and represent, perhaps more than any others, the imagery attached to Los Angeles by the rest of the world, gives added strength to their efforts. It was no surprise, for example, that the richly iconic CityWalk in the popular Universal Studios theme park, both scheduled for major expansion, became a primary target. In

---

11 An excellent and politically impassioned analysis of Living Wage campaigns around the country and especially in Los Angeles can be found in an as yet unpublished paper by Andy Merrifield, "The Urbanization of Labor: Living Wage Activism in the American City." Merrifield's notion of the urbanization of labor relates to the arguments presented here about growing spatial consciousness and the important role of place and the spatial specificities of urbanism in the contemporary American labor movement.

July 1998, LAANE helped to organize a broad-based coalition of more than sixty unions, religious groups, and community organizations (including some local homeowners' associations) that successfully pressured Universal as well as Loew's theaters into agreeing to pay a living wage and to provide adequate health insurance for the 8,000 new service workers that would be added by the expansion.

Earlier in the same year, another protest based on innovative applications of land-use and economic-development law had achieved significant success in Hollywood, where the developer involved in rebuilding Times Square in New York, Trizec-Hahn, was planning to do something similar to the area around Mann's Chinese Theater along symbolic but seedy Hollywood Boulevard. Backed by a close ally, City Council member Jackie Goldberg, author of the City's Living Wage Ordinance and a leading figure in local struggles for lesbian and gay rights, LAANE was able to achieve a remarkable agreement with Trizec-Hahn. It assured that the up-to-800 new employees for the proposed hotel and theater complex would be unionized and that the new shops to be built would lease their space to companies that would hire local Hollywood residents and pay them a living wage. In addition, the $12.5 million developer's fee paid to the City is to be used to set up a local hiring hall and to develop a special health plan in which all companies contracted to pay a living wage can enroll their employees.[12]

A look at the leading figures and organizational alliances that constitute LAANE is revealing. Its executive director and most prominent strategist is Madeline Janis-Aparicio, a UCLA law graduate who was formerly director (1990–3) of CARACEN, one of the most important advocacy groups for Central American and other immigrants' rights, and especially active in the aftermath of the Justice Riots and the expulsion of many Salvadoran and Guatemalan residents. Building on these experiences, Janis-Aparicio founded the Tourist Industry Development Council (TIDC) in 1993, a labor-based organization that aimed at improving wages for hotel, restaurant, and other service workers in the notoriously low-paying tourist industry. The TIDC was particularly active in pressuring developers, the LA City Council, and the Community Redevelopment Agency over the expansion of the Convention Center and, more recently, the LA version of the new downtown sports stadium-shopping complexes that have become so attractive to other central city redevelopment projects throughout the country. Using her experiences in CARACEN and TIDC, which was renamed LAANE in early 1998, Janis-Aparicio has helped significantly in organizing the much larger coalition currently struggling for Growth with Equity.

---

12   This information has been taken from Harold Meyerson, "No Justice, No Growth," footnote 3. Meyerson describes LAANE's take on Los Angeles in this way: "Our number-one problem is no longer overdevelopment and underdevelopment [the progressive program ten years ago]. It's our immense disparity in incomes. It's that we have become the simultaneous capital of shit jobs and insulated affluence."

Two of the leading players in the broad coalition are Local 1877 of the Service Employees International Union (SEIU) and Local 11 of the Hotel Employees and Restaurant Employees union (HERE), both headed by progressive if not radical women of color. In the aftermath of LAANE's earlier failure to extract living wage concessions for the new developments planned at LAX, the huge international airport complex, the two unions joined together with LAANE to successfully organize 2,500 security workers (SEIU) and 1,000 food concession workers (HERE) to obtain higher wages and benefits. Their efforts were supported significantly by the national AFL-CIO, which has turned increasingly to Los Angeles as an important indicative site for new developments in the American labor movement.

The SEIU, with 325,000 members in California, today reputedly hires more organizers than any other organization in the region. Under the leadership of Eliseo Medina, it is currently engaged in a major campaign to organize county home-health-care workers, Catholic hospital-service employees, and other sectors of the huge health care industry. As perhaps the leading force in the renaissance of a community-based labor movement in Los Angeles, the SEIU draws strength from its earlier role in one of the most successful union-organizing campaigns in late twentieth-century America, Justice for Janitors.[13] Justice for Janitors began in 1985 in cities such as Pittsburgh and Denver, and was extended to Los Angeles in 1988. Across the country, this was a time of massive downtown redevelopment fed largely by Urban Development Block Grants aimed at regenerating blighted areas of the city centers feeling the effects of globalization, economic restructuring, and the growth of Outer Cities. With little social control over the process, these grants essentially stimulated and subsidized private corporations to engage in a speculative orgy of building convention centers, office towers, entertainment complexes, luxury apartment blocks, and especially hotels – perhaps the greatest hotel-building spree in American history.[14] What all this redevelopment shared was an increased need for cheap service labor, most basically janitorial help.

Among large American cities, Los Angeles occupied a special niche with respect to janitors. In the 1980s, the janitorial workforce doubled to nearly 30,000, union membership dropped 77 percent, and wages fell even more,

---

13 For more on this remarkable example of what might be called postmodern labor organizing, see Roger Waldinger et al., "Justice for Janitors," *Dissent*, Winter 1997, 44: 37–44; and "Helots No More: A Case Study of the Justice for Janitors Campaign in Los Angeles," in Kate Bronfenbrenner et al. eds., *Organizing to Win: New Research on Union Strategies*, Ithaca: Cornell University Press, 1998; Lydia Savage, "Geographies of Organizing: Justice for Janitors in Los Angeles," in Andrew Herod ed., *Organizing the Landscape: Geographical Perspectives on Labor Unionism*, Minneapolis: University of Minnesota Press, 1998; SEIU Local 399, *A Penny for Justice: Janitors and L.A.'s Commercial Real Estate Market*, Los Angeles: SEIU, 1995; and "Janitors' Union Uses Pressure and Theatrics to Expand its Ranks," *The Wall Street Journal*, March 21, 1994.

14 See Bernard Frieden and Lynne Sagalyn, *Downtown, Inc.*, Cambridge, MA: MIT Press, 1989. See also David Harvey, "From Managerialism to Entrepreneurialism: The Transformation of Urban Governance in Late Capitalism," *Geografiska Annaler* 71B, 1989: 3–17; and Merrifield, "The Urbanization of Labor," footnote 11.

from a high of $12.50 per hour in 1983 to a low of $3.35 five years later, lower than in any major city in the country. Then Local 399 (it would merge into statewide Local 1877 in 1997) moved into this worsening scene, first in the heavily subsidized and skyscrapered developments of the new downtown and, after significant success, into the next largest target agglomeration of offices, hotels, and entertainment, Century City. In May 1990, a strike of janitors was called against International Service Systems (ISS), a Danish multinational cleaning conglomerate active throughout the USA. The strike was almost immediately globalized as SEIU officials flew to Denmark to picket the ISS headquarters and gained significant support from the SEIU local in New York. A month later, the campaign was glocalized again in a richly iconic demonstration that stormed Century City as if it were a postmodern Bastille, with drums beating, people chanting about justice, and red-t-shirted activists occupying security-stationed lobbies and strategic road intersections in what was once the backlots of the Twentieth-Century Fox movie studios. The police soon reacted violently, beating the protesters and clearing them from the visible streets. While there was no immediate victory, the event gained significant public sympathy for the plight of janitors, especially after there was some admission that overzealous police officers were responsible for the violence. In the next five years, union membership increased rapidly to 90 percent in Century City, janitors' wages rose 50 percent, and workers were provided, for the first time, with full family health coverage. The Justice for Janitors campaign would become a model for the SEIU, the Living Wage Campaign, and for the new labor movement in Los Angeles and elsewhere in the USA.

María Elena Durazo, president of Local 11 of HERE, has been another key figure in achieving living wage benefits, in this case for hotel and restaurant workers, and in the wider struggle for immigrants' rights, especially with regard to the activities of the Immigration and Naturalization Service (INS). In late 1997, in a campaign begun in that symbolic bastion of postmodern urbanism, the Bonaventure Hotel, HERE negotiated a contract with six big hotels that increased wages over a six-year period, prohibited subcontracting work to non-unionized firms, and provided significant protection for workers dismissed because of their immigrant status. Durazo was also instrumental in another form of protest by the working poor, a video called *City on the Edge* (a strategic play on Edge City enthusiasm?) produced soon after the Justice Riots in 1992 and creating a major stir in the tourist industry and in the image wars over downtown redevelopment. Predicting the likelihood of more violence without significant efforts to achieve greater justice, the video echoed with iconic radicalism the cry of 1992: No Justice – No Peace. Sometimes, but not always, Durazo is allied in her work with her husband, Miguel Contreras, a disciple of Cesar Chavez and currently head of the nearly 740,000 member County Federation of Labor, AFL-CIO, for many years the most powerful if not always very progressive labor voice in the region.

LAANE's labor–Left alliance has been built primarily around the urgent needs of the Latino immigrant working poor, but it connects to many other groups as well. A particularly active organization has been KIWA (Korean

Immigrant Workers Access), which has been involved in various SEIU and HERE campaigns and played an important role in the Bus Riders Union strike, organized by another prominent local multicultural coalition, the Labor/Community Strategies Center. Also active and effective has been AGENDA (Action for Grassroots Empowerment and Neighborhood Development Alternatives), led by former Black Panther Anthony Thigpenn. AGENDA has been involved in organizing South Los Angeles residents around such issues as community policing and increased social welfare, while also challenging economic concessions given to large-scale developments such as DreamWorks in the still highly contentious space of Playa Vista (see chapter 8). Another key figure is the activist and mystery story writer, Gary Phillips, leader of the MultiCultural Collaborative, a broad-based coalition of community groups formed in 1992 and particularly active in educational reform.[15] Although to a somewhat more limited extent, major arts, religious, environmental, feminist, and gay and lesbian activist organizations have also become associated with these larger movements. Particularly noteworthy has been the interfaith organization CLUE (Clergy and Laity United for Economic Justice), inspired by its own form of iconic radicalism.[16]

Although it would be stretching things too much to claim that all these organizations, leaders, and movements are driven by the explicit goals of regional democracy and spatial justice, there seems little doubt that these goals are today more on the agenda of progressive local and regional politics than they ever have been before. It is this spatial consciousness, along with a greater sensitivity to cross-cultural, transnational, and gender issues, that most distinguishes these movements from their earlier union and civil rights predecessors. I do not want to exaggerate the power and achievements of these emerging – and, I would add, critically postmodern – struggles over the spatial specificities and structures of privilege in the postmetropolis, but neither should they be buried under either the edenic visions of urban boosterism or the apocalyptic predictions of a cynical Left withdrawing from the challenging conditions of postmodernity. Here again, in optimistic conclusion, the synekism of Los Angeles will be worth watching and learning from as we move into the twenty-first century.

---

15 For some new insights on the Justice Riots and their aftermath, see Gary Phillips, *Violent Spring*, Portland, OR: West Coast Crime, 1994; and *Perdition, U.S.A.*, New York: Berkley, 1995.

16 Merrifield, "The Urbanization of Labor," describes CLUE's strategic use of the Old Testament Book of Deuteronomy (24:14): "You shall not withhold the wages of poor and needy laborers, whether other Israelites or aliens who reside in your land in one of your towns." See also Richard W. Gillett, "Living Wage Ordinance: A Victory for the Working Poor," *Tikkun* 12, 1997: 47–8. Gillet, a presbyterian minister, has been active in labor-community issues for many years and played a key role in the Coalition to Stop Plant Closures in the 1980s.

Bibliography

Abu-Lughod, Janet L. 1991: *Changing Cities*. New York: HarperCollins.

Agnew, John 1996: "Spacelessness versus Timeless Space in State-Centered Social Sciences," *Environment and Planning A* 28: 129–32.

Allen, James P., and Eugene Turner 1997: *The Ethnic Quilt: Population Diversity in Southern California*. Northridge: Center for Geographical Studies, California State University, Northridge.

——1996: "Ethnic Diversity and Segregation in the New Los Angeles." In *EthniCity: Geographic Perspectives on Ethnic Change in Los Angeles*, C.C. Roseman, G. Thieme, and H.D. Laux eds., Lanham, MD: Rowman and Littlefield: 1–29.

——1995: "Ethnic Differentiation by Blocks within Census Tracts," *Urban Geography* 16: 344–64.

——1989: "The Most Ethnically Diverse Urban Places in the United States," *Urban Geography* 10: 523–39.

Amin, Ash ed. 1994: *Post-Fordism: A Reader*. Oxford, UK, and Cambridge, MA: Blackwell.

Anderson, Benedict 1983: *Imagined Communities: Reflections on the Origins and Spread of Nationalism*. London: Verso.

Appadurai, Arjun 1996: *Modernity at Large: Cultural Dimensions of Globalization*. Minneapolis and London: University of Minnesota Press.

Baldassare, Mark 1998: *When Government Fails: The Orange County Bankruptcy*. Berkeley and Los Angeles: University of California Press, with the Public Policy Institute of California.

——ed. 1994: *Los Angeles Riots: Lessons for the Urban Future*. Boulder, CO: Westview Press.

——1986: *Trouble in Paradise: The Suburban Transformation in America*. New York: Columbia University Press.

Banham, Reyner 1971: *Los Angeles: The Architecture of the Four Ecologies*. New York: Harper and Row.

Barnett, Jonathan 1995: *The Fractured Metropolis: Improving the New City, Restoring the Old City, Reshaping the Region*. New York: HarperCollins.

Barth, Lawrence 1996: "Immemorial Visibilities: Seeing the City's Difference," *Environment and Planning A* 28, 471–93.

Barton, Stephen, and Carol J. Silverman 1994: *Common Interest Communities: Private Governments and the Public Interest*. Berkeley: Institute of Governmental Studies Press.

Bauböck, Rainer 1994: *Transnational Citizenship: Membership and Rights in International Migration*. Cheltenham: Edward Elgar.

Baudrillard, Jean 1988: *America*. London and New York: Verso.

——1983: *Simulations*. New York: Semiotext(e).

Benedikt, Michael ed. 1992: *Cyberspace: First Steps*. Cambridge, MA: MIT Press.

Berman, Marshall 1982: *All That is Solid Melts into Air*. New York: Simon and Schuster.

Berry, Brian J.L. 1991: *Long-Wave Rhythms in Economic Development and Political Behavior*. Baltimore: Johns Hopkins University Press.

——ed. 1976: *Urbanization and Counter-Urbanization*. Urban Affairs Annual Review 11, Beverly Hills: Sage Publications.

——and John D. Kasarda 1977: *Contemporary Urban Ecology*. New York and London: Macmillan.

Bhabha, Homi 1994: *The Location of Culture*. London and New York: Routledge.

—— 1990: *Nation and Narration*. New York and London: Routledge.

Blakely, Edward J., and Mary Gail Snyder 1997: *Fortress America: Gated Communities in the United States*. Washington, DC: Brookings Institution Press, and Cambridge, MA: Lincoln Institute of Land Policy.

Bloch, Robin 1994: *The Metropolis Inverted: The Rise and Shift to the Periphery and the Remaking of the Contemporary City*. Los Angeles: Unpublished doctoral dissertation in Urban Planning, UCLA.

Blomley, Nicholas 1994: *Law, Space, and the Geographies of Power*. New York and London: Guilford Press.

Bluestone, Barry, and Bennett Harrison 1982: *The Deindustrialization of America*. New York: Basic Books.

Bookchin, Murray 1995: *From Urbanization to Cities: Towards a New Politics of Citizenship*. New York: Cassell.

Borja, Jordi, and Manuel Castells 1996: *Local and Global: Management of Cities in the Information Age*. London: Earthspan Publications.

Borjas, George J. 1990: *Friends or Strangers? The Impact of Immigrants on the U.S. Economy*. New York: Basic Books.

Boyer, M. Christine 1996: *CyberCities: Visual Perception in the Age of Electronic Communication*. New York: Princeton Architectural Press.

——1994: *The City and Collective Memory: Its Historical Imagery and Architectural Entertainments*. Cambridge, MA: MIT Press.

——1988: "The Return of Aesthetics to City Planning," *Society*: 49–56.

——1983: *Dreaming the Rational City: The Myth of American City Planning, 1893–1945*. Cambridge, MA: MIT Press.

Bremer, Michael 1993a: *SimCity Classic – User Manual*. Orinda, CA: Maxis.

——1993b: *SimCity 2000 – User Manual*. Orinda, CA: Maxis.

Brenner, Neil 1998: "Global Cities, Glocal States: Global City Formation and State Territorial Restructuring in Contemporary Europe," *Review of International Political Economy* 5: 1–37.

——1997: "State Territorial Restructuring and the Production of Spatial Scale," *Political Geography* 16: 272–306.

Brown, Jeffrey 1998: "Race, Class, Gender and Public Transportation: Lessons from the Bus Riders Union Lawsuit," *Critical Planning* 5: 3–20.

Burbach, Roger, Orlando Núñez, and Boris Kagarlitsky 1997: *Globalization and its Discontents: The Rise of Postmodern Socialisms*. London: Pluto Press.

Caldeira, Teresa P.R. 1999: *City of Walls: Crime, Segregation, and Citizenship in Sao Paulo*. Berkeley and Los Angeles: University of California Press.

——1996: "Fortified Enclaves: The New Urban Segregation," *Public Culture* 8: 303–28.

Calthorpe, Peter 1993: *The Next American Metropolis: Ecology, Community, and the American Dream.* Princeton: Princeton Architectural Press.

Calvino, Italo 1974: *Invisible Cities,* tr. William Weaver. New York: Harcourt Brace Jovanovich.

Carnoy, Martin, Manuel Castells, Stephen S. Cohen, and Fernando H. Cardoso eds. 1993: *The New Global Economy in the Information Age: Reflections on Our Changing World.* University Park, PA: Penn State University Press.

Castells, Manuel 1996/7/8: *The Information Age: Economy, Society and Culture.* 3 vols: I *The Rise of the Network Society,* II *The Power of Identity,* III *End of Millennium.* Oxford, UK, and Cambridge, MA: Blackwell Publishers.

——1989: *The Informational City: Information, Technology, Economic Restructuring and the Urban-Regional Process.* Oxford, UK, and Cambridge, MA: Blackwell Publishers.

—— 1983: *The City and the Grass Roots.* Berkeley and Los Angeles: University of California Press.

——1977: *The Urban Question.* London: Edward Arnold.

——and Peter Hall 1994: *Technopoles of the World: The Making of Twenty-first Century Industrial Complexes.* London: Routledge.

Cauvin, Jacques and Paul Sanlavalle eds 1981: *Préhistoire du Levant: Chronologie et organisation de l'espace depuis les origines jusqu'au VIe millénaire.* Paris: Editions du Centre National de la Recherche Scientifique.

Cenzatti, Marco 1993: *Los Angeles and the L.A. School: Postmodernism and Urban Studies.* West Hollywood, CA: Los Angeles Forum for Architecture and Urban Design.

Chambers, Iain 1994: *Migrancy, Culture, Identity.* London and New York: Routledge.

——1990: *Border Dialogues: Journeys in Postmodernity.* London and New York: Routledge.

——1986: *Popular Culture: The Metropolitan Experience.* London and New York: Routledge.

Chang, Edward T., and Russell C. Leong eds. 1993: *Los Angeles – Struggles toward Multiethnic Community.* Seattle and London: University of Washington Press.

Childe, V. Gordon 1981: *Man Makes Himself* (illustrated edn.). Bradford-on-Avon: Moonraker Press/Pitman.

Clark, David 1996: *Urban World/Global City.* London and New York: Routledge.

Cohen, Stephen, and John Zysman 1984: *Manufacturing Matters: The Myth of the Post-Industrial Economy.* New York: Basic Books.

Courchene, Thomas J. 1995: "Glocalization: The Regional/International Interface," *Canadian Journal of Regional Science* 18: 1–20.

Cox, Kevin ed. 1997: *Spaces of Globalization: Reasserting the Power of the Local.* New York and London: Guilford Press.

Davis, Mike 1998: *Ecology of Fear: Los Angeles and the Imagination of Disaster.* New York: Metropolitan Books-Henry Holt.

——1994: "Cannibal City: Los Angeles and the Destruction of Nature." In *Urban Revisions,* R. Ferguson ed., Los Angeles: Museum of Contemporary Art, and Cambridge, MA: MIT Press.

——1993a: "Who Killed Los Angeles? A Political Autopsy," *New Left Review* 197: 3–28.

——1993b: "Who Killed Los Angeles? The Verdict is Given," *New Left Review* 199: 29–54.

——1993c: "Dead West: Ecocide in Marlboro Country," *New Left Review* 200: 49–73.

——1992a: *Beyond Blade Runner: Urban Control and the Ecology of Fear.* Westfield, NJ: Open Magazine Pamphlet Series.

——1992b: *L.A. Was Just the Beginning – Urban Revolt in the United States*. Westfield, NJ: Open Magazine Pamphlet Series.

——1990: *City of Quartz: Excavating the Future in Los Angeles*. London and New York: Verso.

Dear, Michael, H. Eric Schockman, and Greg Hise eds. 1996: *Re-Thinking Los Angeles*. Thousand Oaks, CA: Sage Publications.

de la Croix, Horst, Richard G. Tansey, and Diane Kirkpatrick 1991: *Art through the Ages* (9th edn.). New York: Harcourt Brace Jovanovich.

Deleuze, Gilles, and Felix Guattari 1987: *A Thousand Plateaus*. Minneapolis: University of Minnesota Press.

——1983: *Anti-Oedipus*. Minneapolis: University of Minnesota Press.

Deveare Smith, Anna 1994: *Twilight – Los Angeles, 1992*. New York: Doubleday Anchor Books.

Diamond, Jared 1997: *Guns, Germs, and Steel: The Fates of Human Societies*. New York: Norton.

Dicken, Peter 1992: *Global Shift: The Internationalization of Economic Activity*. New York: Guilford Press.

Domanick, Joe 1994: *To Protect and Serve: The LAPD's Century of War in the City of Dreams*. New York: Pocket Books.

Duchacek, Ivo D., Daniel Latouche, and Garth Stevenson eds. 1988: *Perforated Sovereignties and International Relations: Trans-sovereign Contacts of Subnational Governments*. New York: Greenwood Press.

Dumm, Thomas L. 1993: "The New Enclosures: Racism in the Normalized Community." In *Reading Rodney King/Reading Urban Uprising*, R. Gooding-Williams ed.: 178–95.

Eco, Umberto 1986: *Travels in Hyperreality*. San Diego: Harcourt.

Edmonston, Barry, and Jeffrey S. Passel eds. 1994: *Immigration and Ethnicity: The Integration of America's Newest Arrivals*. Washington, DC: Urban Institute Press.

Ellin, Nan 1996: *Postmodern Urbanism*. Oxford, UK, and Cambridge, MA: Blackwell.

Fainstein, Susan 1994: *The City Builders: Property, Politics, and Planning in London and New York*. Oxford, UK, and Cambridge, MA: Blackwell.

——and Scott Campbell eds. 1996: *Readings in Urban Theory*. Oxford, UK, and Cambridge, MA: Blackwell.

——, Ian Gordon, and Michael Harloe eds. 1994: *Divided Cities: New York and London in the Contemporary World*. Oxford, UK, and Cambridge, MA: Blackwell.

Fanon, Frantz 1967: *Black Skins/White Masks*, tr. C.L. Markmann. New York: Grove Weidenfeld.

Feagin, Joe R., and Vera Hernán 1994: *White Racism: The Basics*. New York and London: Routledge.

Featherstone, Mike ed. 1990: *Global Culture: Nationalism, Globalization and Modernity*. Newbury Park, CA: Sage.

Featherstone, Mike, and R. Burrows eds. 1995: *Cyberspace/Cyberbodies/Cyberpunk*. London: Sage.

Featherstone, Mike, Scott Lash, and Roland Robertson eds. 1995: *Global Modernities*. London: Sage.

Fishman, Robert 1987: *Bourgeois Utopias: The Rise and Fall of Suburbia*. New York: Basic Books.

Flusty, Steven 1994: *Building Paranoia: The Proliferation of Interdictory Space and the Erosion of Spatial Justice*. West Hollywood, CA: Los Angeles Forum for Architecture and Urban Design.

Fogelson, Robert M. 1967 and 1993: The *Fragmented Metropolis: Los Angeles 1850–1930*. Cambridge, MA: Harvard University Press; reissued Berkeley and Los Angeles: University of California Press.

Fong, Timothy P. 1994: *The First Suburban Chinatown: The Remaking of Monterey Park, California*. Philadelphia: Temple University Press.

Ford, Richard T. 1999: "Law's Territory: A History of Jurisdiction," *Michigan Law Review* 97–4: 843–930.

—— 1997: "Geography and Sovereignty: Jurisdictional Formation and Racial Segregation," *Stanford Law Review* 49: 1365–1446.

—— 1994: "The Boundaries of Race: Political Geography in Legal Analysis," *Harvard Law Review* 107: 1843–1921.

—— 1992: "Urban Space and the Color Line: The Consequences of Demarcation and Disorientation in the Postmodern Metropolis," *Harvard Blackletter Journal* 9: 117–47.

Foucault, Michel 1988: *Politics, Philosophy, Culture: Interviews and Other Writings*, L. Kritzman ed. New York and London: Routledge.

—— 1986: "Of Other Spaces," *Diacritics* 16: 22–7.

—— 1977: *Discipline and Punish: The Birth of the Prison*. New York: Vintage Books.

Friedmann, John 1995: "Where We Stand: A Decade of World City Research." In P. Knox and P. Taylor, *World Cities in a World System*: 21–47.

—— 1986: "The World City Hypothesis," *Development and Change* 17: 69–84.

—— and Michael Douglas eds. 1998: *Cities for Citizens: Planning and the Rise of Civil Society in a Global Age*. Chichester: John Wiley.

—— and Goetz Wolff 1982: "World City Formation: An Agenda for Research and Action," *International Journal of Urban and Regional Research* 6: 309–44.

Frug, Gerald 1993: "Decentering Decentralization," *The University of Chicago Law Review* 60: 253–338.

Fulton, William 1997: *The Reluctant Metropolis: The Politics of Urban Growth in Los Angeles*. Point Arena, CA: Solano Press.

—— 1996: *The New Urbanism: Hope or Hype for American Communities*. Cambridge, MA: Lincoln Institute of Land Policy.

Garreau, Joel 1991: *Edge City: Life on the New Frontier*. New York: Doubleday.

George, Lynell 1992: *No Crystal Stair: African-Americans in the City of Angels*. New York: Doubleday Anchor Books.

Gibson, William 1994: *Virtual Light*. New York: Bantam Books.

—— 1984: *Neuromancer*. New York: Ace Books.

Giddens, Anthony 1998: *The Third Way: The Renewal of Social Democracy*. Cambridge: Polity Press.

—— 1994: *Beyond Left and Right: The Future of Radical Politics*. Stanford: Stanford University Press.

—— 1990: *The Consequences of Modernity*. Cambridge: Polity Press.

Gilroy, Paul 1993: *Small Acts: Thoughts on the Politics of Black Cultures*. London and New York: Serpent's Tail.

Gimbutas, Marija 1989: *The Language of the Goddesses: Unearthing the Hidden Symbols of Western Civilization*. San Francisco: Harper and Row.

—— 1974: *The Goddesses and Gods of Old Europe, 6500–3500 BC.: Myths and Cult Images*. Berkeley: University of California Press.

Goldsmith, William W., and Edward J. Blakely 1992: *Separate Societies: Poverty and Inequality in U.S. Cities*. Philadelphia: Temple University Press.

Gooding-Williams, Robert ed. 1993: *Reading Rodney King/Reading Urban Uprising*. New York and London: Routledge.

Gordon, David 1978: "Capitalist Development and the History of American Cities." In *Marxism and the Metropolis*, W. Tabb and L. Sawers eds., New York: Oxford University Press.

——1977: "Class Struggle and the Stages of Urban Development." In D. Perry and A. Watkins eds. *The Rise of the Sunbelt Cities*, Beverly Hills: Sage: 55–82.

Gottdeiner, Mark 1997: *The Theming of America*. Boulder, CO: Westview Press.

Gottlieb, Robert 1993: *Forcing the Spring: The Transformation of the American Environmental Movement*. Washington DC: Island Press.

Gottmann, Jean, and Robert A. Harper eds. 1990: *Since Megalopolis: The Urban Writings of Jean Gottmann*. Baltimore: Johns Hopkins University Press.

Graham, Stephen, and Simon Marvin eds. 1996: *Telecommunications and the City: Electronic Spaces, Urban Places*. London and New York: Routledge.

Hall, Peter 1998: *Cities and Civilization*. New York: Pantheon.

——and Paschal Preston 1988: *The Carrier Wave: New Information Technology and the Geography of Innovation, 1846–2003*. London and Boston: Unwin Hyman.

Hannerz, Ulf 1996: *Transnational Connections: Culture, People, Places*. London and New York: Routledge.

——1992: *Culture, Cities and the World*. Amsterdam: Centrum voor Grootstedelijk Onderzoek.

Haraway, Donna 1991: *Simians, Cyborgs, and Women: The Reinvention of Nature*. New York and London: Routledge.

Harris, Chauncey, and Edward Ullman 1945: "The Nature of Cities," *Annals of the American Academy of Political and Social Sciences* 242: 7–17.

Harrison, Bennett 1994: *Lean and Mean: The Changing Landscape of Corporate Power in the Age of Flexibility*. New York: Basic Books.

——1988: *The Great U-Turn: Corporate Restructuring and the Polarizing of America*. New York: Basic Books.

Harvey, David 1996: *Justice, Nature and the Geography of Difference*. Oxford, UK, and Cambridge, MA: Blackwell.

——1995: "Globalization in Question," *Rethinking Marxism* 8: 1–17.

——1989: *The Condition of Postmodernity*. Oxford, UK, and Cambridge, MA: Blackwell.

——1988: "Urban Places in the 'Global Village': Reflections on the Urban Condition in Late Twentieth Century Capitalism." In *World Cities and the Future of the Metropolis*, Luigi Mazza ed., Milano: Electa: 21–33.

——1985a: *The Urbanization of Capital*. Baltimore: Johns Hopkins University Press and Oxford: Basil Blackwell.

——1985b: *Consciousness and the Urban Experience*. Baltimore: Johns Hopkins University Press and Oxford: Basil Blackwell.

——1982: *Limits to Capital*. Oxford: Basil Blackwell and Chicago: University of Chicago Press.

——1978: "The Urban Process under Capitalism," *International Journal of urban and Regional Research* 2: 101–31.

——1973: *Social Justice and the City*. Baltimore: Johns Hopkins University Press.

——1969: *Explanation in Geography*. New York: St. Martin's and London: Edward Arnold.

——and Allen J. Scott 1989: "The Practice of Human Geography: Theory and Empirical Specificity in the Transition from Fordism to Flexible Accumulation." In B. Macmillan ed., *Remodeling Geography*, Oxford: Blackwell: 217–29.

Hawley, Amos 1950: *Human Ecology: A Theory of Urban Structure*. New York: Ronald Press.

Held, David 1996: *Democracy and the Global Order: From the Modern State to Cosmopolitan Globalism*. Stanford, CA: Stanford University Press.

Herbert, Steve 1997: *Policing Space: Territoriality and the Los Angeles Police Department*. Minneapolis and London: University of Minnesota Press.

Herington, John 1984: *The Outer City*. London: Harper and Row.

Heskin, Allan David 1991: *The Struggle for Community*. Boulder, CO: Westview Press.

Hirst, Paul, and Grahame Thompson 1996: *Globalization in Question*. Cambridge: Polity Press.

Hise, Greg 1997: *Magnetic Los Angeles: Planning the Twentieth-Century Metropolis*. Baltimore and London: Johns Hopkins University Press.

Hobsbawm, Eric 1994: *The Age of Extremes: 1914–1991*. New York: Pantheon.

——1987: *The Age of Empire, 1875–1914*. New York: Pantheon.

——1975: *The Age of Capital, 1848–1878*. New York: Charles Scribner's.

——1962: *The Age of Revolution, 1789–1848*. New York: New American Library.

Hodder, Ian ed. 1996: *On the Surface: Çatalhöyük 1993–1995*. Cambridge: McDonald Institute for Archeological Research and Ankara: British Archeological Institute.

——1992: *Theory and Practice in Archeology*. London and New York: Routledge.

——1991: *Reading the Past: Current Approaches to Interpretation in Archeology*. Cambridge: Cambridge University Press.

——1990: *The Domestication of Europe: Structure and Contingency in Neolithic Societies*. Oxford, UK, and Cambridge, MA: Blackwell.

——ed. 1987: *The Archeology of Contextual Meanings*. Cambridge: Cambridge University Press.

——et al. eds. 1995: *Interpreting Archeology: Finding Meaning in the Past*. London and New York: Routledge.

Holston, James, and Arjun Appadurai 1996: "Cities and Citizenship," *Public Culture* 19: 187–204.

hooks, bell 1994: "Feminism Inside: Toward a Black Body Politic." In *Black Male: Representations of Masculinity in Contemporary American Art*, T. Golden ed., New York: Whitney Museum of American Art and Harry N. Abrams, Inc.

——1992: *Black Looks: Race and Representation*. Boston: South End Press.

——1990: *Yearning: Race, Gender, and Cultural Politics*. Boston: South End Press.

Hooper, Barbara 1998: "The Poem of Male Desires: Female Bodies, Modernity, and 'Paris, Capital of the Nineteenth Century'." In L. Sandercock ed., *Making the Invisible Visible: A Multicultural Planning History*: 227–54.

——1994: "Bodies, Cities, Texts: The Case of Citizen Rodney King," unpublished manuscript.

Horton, John 1995: *The Politics of Diversity: Immigration, Resistance, and Change in Monterey Park, California*. Philadelphia: Temple University Press.

——1992: "The Politics of Diversity in Monterey Park, California." In *Structuring Diversity: Ethnographic Perspectives on the New Immigration*, L.Lamphere ed., Chicago: University of Chicago Press: 215–45.

——1989: "The Politics of Ethnic Change: Grass-Roots Responses to Economic and Demographic Restructuring in Monterey Park," *Urban Geography* 10: 578–92.

Institute for Alternative Journalism 1992: *Inside the L. A. Riots: What Really Happened – And Why It Will Happen Again*. New York: Institute for Alternative Journalism.

Isin, Engin 1997: "Who is the New Citizen? Towards a Genealogy," *Citizenship Studies* 1: 115–32.

—— 1996a: "Metropolis Unbound: Legislators and Interpreters of Urban Form." In J. Caulfield and L. Peake eds., *City Lives and City Forms: Critical Urban Research and Canadian Urbanism*, Toronto: University of Toronto Press: 98–127.

—— 1996b: "Global City-Regions and Citizenship." In D. Bell, R. Keil, and G. Wekerle eds., *Global Processes, Local Places*, Montreal: Black Rose Books: 21–34.

Jackson, Kenneth 1985: *Crabgrass Frontier: The Suburbanization of the United States*. New York: Oxford University Press.

Jacobs, Jane 1984: *Cities and the Wealth of Nations: Principles of Economic Life*. New York: Random House.

—— 1969: *The Economy of Cities*. New York: Random House.

Janik, Allan, and Stephen Toulmin 1973: *Wittgenstein's Vienna*. New York: Simon and Schuster.

Jencks, Charles 1993: *Heteropolis: Los Angeles, the Riots, and the Strange Beauty of Hetero-Architecture*. London: Academy Editions.

Jencks, Christopher 1994: *The Homeless*. Cambridge, MA: Harvard University Press.

—— and Paul E. Peterson eds. 1991: *The Urban Underclass*. Washington, DC: Brookings Institution.

Judd, Dennis R. 1995: "The Rise of the New Walled Cities." In *Spatial Practices*, H. Liggett and D. C. Perry eds.: 144–66.

Katz, Peter 1994: *The New Urbanism: Toward an Architecture of Community*. New York: McGraw-Hill.

Kelley, Ron, Jonathan Friedlander, and Anita Colby eds. 1993: *Irangeles: Iranians in Los Angeles*. Berkeley and Los Angeles: University of California Press.

Kelly, Barbara M. ed. 1989: *Suburbia Re-examined*. New York: Greenwood Publishers.

Kenyon, Kathleen 1960: *Archeology in the Holy Land*. London: Ernest Benn.

—— 1957: *Digging Up Jericho*. London: Ernest Benn.

Kern, Stephen 1983: *The Culture of Time and Space, 1880–1918*. Cambridge, MA: Harvard University Press.

King, Anthony ed. 1996: *Re-Presenting the City: Ethnicity, Capital and Culture in the twenty-first Century Metropolis*. Basingstoke and London: Macmillan.

—— ed. 1991: *Culture, Globalization and the World-System*. London and Binghamton, NY: Macmillan.

—— 1990: *Global Cities: Post-Imperialism and the Internationalization of London*. London and New York: Routledge.

Klein, Norman M. 1997: *The History of Forgetting: Los Angeles and the Erasure of Memory*. London and New York: Verso.

Kling, Rob, Spencer Olin, and Mark Poster eds. 1991: *Postsuburban California: The Transformation of Orange County since World War II*. Berkeley and Los Angeles: University of California Press.

Knox, Paul ed. 1993: *The Restless Urban Landscape*. Englewood Cliffs, NJ: Prentice Hall.

Knox, Paul, and Peter Taylor eds. 1995: *World Cities in a World-System*. Cambridge and New York: Cambridge University Press.

Kotkin, Joel 1993: *Tribes: How Race, Religion, and Identity Determine Success in the New Global Economy*. New York: Random House.

Kowinski, William S. 1985: *The Malling of America: An Inside Look at the Great Consumer Paradise*. New York: W. Morrow.

Kunstler, James H. 1996: *Home from Nowhere: Remaking Our Everyday World for the Twenty-First Century*. New York: Simon and Schuster.

—— 1993: *The Geography of Nowhere: The Rise and Decline of America's Man-Made Landscape*. New York: Simon and Schuster.

Lamphere, Louise ed. 1992: *Structuring Diversity: Ethnographic Perspectives on the New Immigration.* Chicago: University of Chicago Press.

Lefebvre, Henri 1996: *Writings on Cities/Henri Lefebvre.* Selected, tr., and intro. by Eleonore Kofman and Elizabeth Lebas. Oxford, UK, and Cambridge, MA: Blackwell.

——1991: *The Production of Space,* tr. D. Nicholson-Smith, Oxford, UK and Cambridge, MA: Blackwell.

——1976: *The Survival of Capitalism,* tr. F. Bryant, London: Allison and Busby.

——1974: *La Production de l'espace.* Paris: Anthropos.

LeGates, Richard T., and Frederic Stout 1996: *The City Reader.* London and New York: Routledge.

Liggett, Helen, and David C. Perry 1995: *Spatial Practices: Critical Explorations in Social/Spatial Theory.* Thousand Oaks, CA: Sage.

Light, Ivan, and Edna Bonacich 1988: *Immigrant Entrepreneurs.* Berkeley and Los Angeles: University of California Press.

——and Carolyn Rosenstein eds. 1995: *Race, Ethnicity, and Entrepreneurship in Urban America.* Hawthorne, NY: Aldine de Gruyter.

Lipietz, Alain 1993: "The Local and the Global: Regional Individuality or Interregionalism," *Transactions of the Institute of British Geographers* 18: 8–18.

——1992: *Towards a New Economic Order: Post Fordism, Ecology and Democracy.* Cambridge: Polity Press.

——1977: *Le Capital et son espace.* Paris: Maspero.

Lippard, Lucy 1997: *The Lure of the Local: Senses of Place in a Multi-Centered Society.* New York: New Press.

Lo, Clarence Y. H. 1990: *Small Property versus Big Government: Social Origins of the Property Tax Revolt.* Berkeley and Los Angeles: University of California Press.

Lo, Fu-Chen, and Yue-Man Yeung 1998: *Globalization and the World of Large Cities.* Tokyo, New York, Paris: United Nations University Press.

Longstreth, Richard 1997: *From City Center to Regional Mall.* Cambridge, MA: MIT Press.

MacKenzie, Evan 1994: *Privatopia: Homeowner Associations and the Rise of Residential Private Government.* New Haven and London: Yale University Press.

Madhubuti, Haki R. ed. 1993: *Why L. A. Happened: Implications of the '92 Los Angeles Rebellion.* Chicago: Third World Press.

Maisels, Charles Keith 1993: *The Near East: Archeology in the "Cradle of Civilization."* London and New York: Routledge.

——1990: *The Emergence of Civilization: From Hunting and Gathering to Agriculture, Cities, and the State in the Near East.* London and New York: Routledge.

Mandel, Ernest 1980: *Long Waves and Capitalist Development: The Marxist Interpretation.* Cambridge, UK: Cambridge University Press.

——1975: *Late Capitalism.* London: Verso.

Mann, Eric, et al. 1996: *A New Vision for Urban Transportation: The Bus Riders Union Makes History at the Intersection of Mass Transit, Civil Rights, and the Environment.* Los Angeles: Labor/Community Strategy Center.

——et al. 1991: *LA's Lethal Air: New Strategies for Policy, Organizing, and Action.* Los Angeles: Labor/Community Strategy Center.

Marcus, Steven 1974: *Engels, Manchester and the Working Class.* New York: Vintage.

Markley, Robert ed. 1996: *Virtual Realities and Their Discontents.* Baltimore: Johns Hopkins University Press.

Markusen, Ann, P. Hall, S. Campbell, and S. Dietrick eds. 1991: *The Rise of the Gunbelt.* New York: Oxford University Press.

Massey, Doreen 1994: *Space, Place and Gender*. Oxford: Blackwell, and Cambridge: Polity Press.

——1984: *Spatial Divisions of Labour*. New York and London: Routledge.

——and John Allen eds. 1984: *Geography Matters! A Reader*. Cambridge: Cambridge University Press.

Massey, Douglas, and Nancy Denton 1994: *American Apartheid: Segregation and the Making of the Underclass*. Cambridge, MA: Harvard University Press.

Mellaart, James 1967: *Çatal Hüyük*. London: Thames and Hudson.

——1964: "A Neolithic City in Turkey," *Scientific American* 210–4: 94–104.

Meltzer, Jack 1984: *Metropolis to Metroplex: The Social and Spatial Planning of Cities*. Baltimore: Johns Hopkins University Press.

Merrifield, Andy, and Erik Swyngedouw eds. 1996: *The Urbanization of Injustice*. London: Lawrence and Wishart.

Miller, Gary 1981: *Cities by Contract: The Politics of Municipal Incorporation*. Cambridge, MA: MIT Press.

Min, Pyong Gap 1996: *Caught in the Middle: Korean Merchants in Multiethnic America*. Berkeley and Los Angeles: University of California Press.

Mitchell, William 1995: *City of Bits: Space, Place, and the Infobahn*. Cambridge, MA: MIT Press.

Mittelman, J. H. 1996: "Rethinking the New Regionalism in the Context of Globalization," *Global Governance* 2: 189–213.

Mlinar, Zdravko 1992: *Globalization and Territorial Identities*. Aldershot, UK, and Brookfield, VT: Avebury.

Mollenkopf, John, and Manuel Castells eds. 1991: *Dual City: Restructuring New York*. New York: Russell Sage Foundation.

Morley, David, and Kevin Robins 1995: *Spaces of Identity: Global Media, Electronic Landscapes and Cultural Boundaries*. London and New York: Routledge.

Morris, A. E. J. 1972 (new edn. 1994): *History of Urban Form: Before the Industrial Revolutions*. Harlow: Addison Wesley Longman.

Muller, Peter O. 1976: *The Outer City: Geographical Consequences of the Urbanization of the Suburbs*. Washington, DC: Association of American Geographers Resource Paper, no. 5: 75-2.

Mumford, Lewis 1961: *The City in History*. New York: Harcourt Brace Jovanovich.

Newman, Oscar 1972: *Defensible Space: Crime Prevention through Urban Design*. New York: Macmillan.

O'Brien, Richard 1992: *Global Financial Integration: The End of Geography*. New York: Council on Foreign Relations Press, and London: Pinter.

Ohmae, Kenichi 1995: *The End of the Nation State*. New York: Free Press.

——1993: "The Rise of the Region-State," *Foreign Affairs* 71: 78–87.

——1990: *The Borderless World*. New York: Harper Business.

Olalquiaga, Celeste 1992: *Megalopolis*. Minneapolis: University of Minnesota Press.

Oliver, Melvin L., and Thomas M. Shapiro 1995: *Black Wealth/White Wealth: A New Perspective on Racial Inequality*. New York and London: Routledge.

Omi, Michael, and Howard Winant 1994: *Racial Formation in the United States: From the 1960s to the 1990s*. New York and London: Routledge.

Ong, Paul, Edna Bonacich, and Lucie Cheng eds. 1994: *The New Asian Immigration in Los Angeles and Global Restructuring*. Philadelphia: Temple University Press.

Orfield, Myron 1997: *Metropolitics: A Regional Agenda for Community and Stability*. Washington, DC: Brookings Institution Press, and Cambridge, MA: Lincoln Institute of Land Policy.

Painter, Jo, and Chris Philo 1995: "Spaces of Citizenship: An Introduction," *Political Geography* 14: 107–20.

Park, Robert E., Ernest W. Burgess, and Roderick D. Mackenzie eds. 1925: *The City*. Chicago: University of Chicago Press (New edn., intro. Morris Janowitz, 1967).

Pastor, Manuel 1993: *Latinos and the Los Angeles Uprising: The Economic Context*. Claremont, CA: Tomas Rivera Center.

——, Peter Dreier, J. Eugene Grigsby, and Mart Lopez-Garza 1999: *Growing Together: Linking Regional and Community Development in a Changing Economy*. Minneapolis: University of Minnesota Press.

Peck, Jamie 1996: *Work-Place: The Social Regulation of Labor Markets*. New York and London: Guilford Press.

Peet, Richard 1991: *Global Capitalism: Theories of Societal Development*. London and New York: Routledge.

Peterson, Paul (ed.) 1985: *The New Urban Reality*. Chicago: University of Chicago Press.

Petrella, Riccardo 1992: "Techno-Apartheid for a Global Underclass," *Los Angeles Times*, August 6.

——1991: "World City-States of the Future," *New Perspectives Quarterly* 8: 59–64.

Pierce, Neil R., Curtis W. Johnson, and John Stuart Hall 1993: *Citistates: How Urban America Can Prosper in a Competitive World*. Washington, DC: Seven Locks Press.

Piore, Michael, and Charles F. Sabel 1984: *The Second Industrial Divide: Possibilities for Prosperity*. New York: Basic Books.

Pollard, Jane S. 1995: *Industry Change and Labor Segmentation: The Banking Industry in Los Angeles, 1970–1990*. Los Angeles: Unpublished doctoral dissertation in Urban Planning, UCLA.

Portes, Alejandro, and Ruben G. Rumbaut 1990: *Immigrant America*. Berkeley and Los Angeles: University of California Press.

Preucel, Robert, and Ian Hodder eds. 1996: *Contemporary Archeology in Theory*. Oxford, UK, and Cambridge, MA: Blackwell.

Price, T. Douglas, and Anne Birgitte Gebauer 1995: *Last Hunters – First Farmers: New Perspectives on the Prehistoric Transition to Agriculture*. Santa Fe, NM: School of American Research Press.

Purcell, Mark 1998: *Power in Los Angeles: Neighborhood Movements, Urban Politics, and the Production of Urban Space*. Los Angeles: Unpublished doctoral dissertation, Geography, UCLA.

Putnam, Robert 1993: *Making Democracy Work: Civic Transactions in Modern Italy*. Princeton NJ: Princeton University Press.

Rabinow, Paul 1984: "Space, Knowledge, and Power." In P. Rabinow ed., *The Foucault Reader*. New York: Pantheon: 239–56.

Rheingold, Howard 1993: *The Virtual Community: Homesteading on the Electronic Frontier*. Reading, MA: Addison-Wesley.

——1991: *Virtual Reality: A Revolutionary Technology of Computer-Generated Artificial Worlds – and How It Promises to Transform Society*. New York: Simon and Schuster.

Rieff, David 1991: *Los Angeles: Capital of the Third World*. New York: Simon and Schuster.

Robertson, Roland 1995: "Glocalization: Time-Space and Homogeneity-Heterogeneity." In Featherstone et al. eds., *Global Modernities*, 25–44.

——1994: "Glocalization: Space, Time, and Social Theory," *Journal of International Communication* 1.

——1992: *Globalization: Social Theory and Global Culture*. London: Sage.

Rose, Gillian 1993: *Feminism and Geography: The Limits of Geographical Knowledge*. Cambridge: Polity Press.

Ruddick, Susan 1996: *Young and Homeless in Hollywood: Mapping Social Identities*. New York and London: Routledge.

Sadler, David 1992: *The Global Region: Production, State Policies, and Uneven Development*. Oxford and New York: Pergamon Press.

Said, Edward 1979: *Orientalism*. New York: Vintage.

Sandercock, Leonie 1998a: *Towards Cosmopolis*. Chichester: John Wiley.

——ed. 1998b: *Making the Invisible Visible: A Multicultural Planning History*. Berkeley and Los Angeles: University of California Press.

Sassen, Saskia 1996: *Losing Control? Sovereignty in an Age of Globalization*. New York: Columbia University Press.

——1994: *Cities in a World Economy*. Thousand Oaks, CA: Pine Forge/Sage.

——1991: *The Global City: New York, London, Tokyo*. Princeton: Princeton University Press.

——1988: *The Mobility of Capital and Labor*. London: Cambridge University Press.

Sayer, Andrew, and Richard Walker 1992: *The New Social Economy: Reworking the Division of Labour*. Oxford: Balckwell.

Schor, Juliet B. 1991: *The Overworked American: The Unexpected Decline of Leisure*. New York: Basic Books.

Scott, Allen J. 1998: *Regions and the World Economy: The Coming Shape of Global Production, Competition, and Political Order*. Oxford: Oxford University Press.

——1997: "The Cultural Economy of Cities," *International Journal of Urban and Regional Research* 21: 323–39.

——1996a: "Regional Motors of the Global Economy," *Futures* 28: 391–411.

——1996b: "The Craft, Fashion, and Cultural-products Industries of Los Angeles: Competitive Dynamics and Policy Dilemmas in a Multisectoral Image-producing Complex," *Annals of the Association of American Geographers* 86: 306–23.

——1995: "Industrial Urbanism in Southern California: Post-Fordist Civic Dilemmas and Opportunities," *Contention* 5–1: 39–65.

——1993: *Technopolis: High Technology Industry and Regional Development in Southern California*. Berkeley and Los Angeles: University of California Press.

——1988a: *Metropolis: From Division of Labor to Urban Form*. Berkeley and Los Angeles: University of California Press.

——1988b: *New Industrial Spaces: Flexible Production. Organization and Regional Development in North America and Western Europe*. London: Pion.

——1986: "Industrialization and Urbanization: A Geographical Agenda," *Annals of the Association of American Geographers* 76: 25–37.

——and Edward W. Soja eds. 1996: *The City: Los Angeles and Urban Theory at the End of the Twentieth Century*. Berkeley and Los Angeles: University of California Press.

——and Michael Storper eds. 1986: *Production, Work, Territory: The Geographical Anatomy of Industrial Capitalism*. Boston: Allen and Unwin.

Sensiper, Sylvia 1994: *The Geographic Imaginary: An Anthropological Investigation of Gentrification*. Los Angeles: Unpublished doctoral dissertation in Urban Planning, UCLA.

Smith, Michael Peter ed. 1992: *After Modernism: Global Restructuring and the Changing Boundaries of City Life*. New Brunswick and London: Transaction.

——and Luis Eduardo Guarnizo eds. 1998: *Transnationalism from Below*. New Brunswick and London: Transaction.

Smith, Neil 1997: "The Satanic Geographies of Globalization: Uneven Development in the 1990s," *Public Culture* 10–11: 169–89.

——1996a: *New Urban Frontier: Gentrification and the Revanchist City*. London and New York: Routledge.

——1996b: "After Tompkins Square Park: Degentrification and the Revanchist City." In A. King ed., *Re-Presenting the City*: 93–107.

Soja, Edward W. 1999: "Thirdspace: Expanding the Scope of the Geographical Imagination." In D. Massey, J. Allen, and P. Sarre eds., *Human Geography Today*. Cambridge: Polity Press: 260–78.

——1997: "Six Discourses on the Postmetropolis." In *Imagining Cities*, S. Westwood and J. Williams, eds.: 19–30.

——1996a: *Thirdspace: Journeys to Los Angeles and Other Real-and-Imagined Places*. Oxford, UK and Cambridge, MA: Blackwell.

——1996b: "Margin/Alia: Social Justice and the New Cultural Politics." In *The Urbanization of Injustice*, A. Merrifield and E. Swingedouw eds.: 180–99.

——1995: "Postmodern Urbanization." In *Postmodern Cities and Spaces*, S. Watson and K. Gibson eds.: 125–37.

——1992: "Inside Exopolis." In *Variations on a Theme Park*, M. Sorkin ed.: 94–122.

——1989: *Postmodern Geographies: The Reassertion of Space in Critical Social Theory*. London: Verso.

——1985: "Regions in Context: Spatiality, Periodicity, and the Historical Geography of the Regional Question," *Society and Space* 3: 175–90.

——1980: "The Socio-Spatial Dialectic," *Annals of the Association of American Geographers* 70: 207–25.

——, Rebecca Morales, and Goetz Wolff 1983: "Urban Restructuring: An Analysis of Social and Spatial Change in Los Angeles," *Economic Geography* 59: 195–230.

Sonenshein, Raphael J. 1993: *Politics in Black and White: Race and Power in Los Angeles*. Princeton, NJ: Princeton University Press.

Sorkin, Michael ed. 1992: *Variations on a Theme Park*. New York: Hill and Wang-Noonday Press.

Spivak, Gayatri Chakravorty 1990: *The Post-Colonial Critic*, S. Harasym, ed. New York and London: Routledge.

Storper, Michael 1997: *The Regional World: Territorial Development in a Global Economy*. New York and London: Guilford Press.

——1995: "Regional Technology Coalitions: An Essential Dimension of National Technology Policy," *Research Policy* 24: 895–911.

——and Susan Christopherson 1987: "Flexible Specialization and Regional Industrial Agglomerations: The Case of the USA Motion Picture Industry," *Annals of the Association of American Geographers* 77: 104–17.

——and Robert Salais 1997: *Worlds of Production: The Action Frameworks of the Economy*. Cambridge, MA: Harvard University Press.

——and Allen, J. Scott eds. 1993: *Pathways to Industrialization and Regional Development*. London: Routledge.

——and Richard Walker eds. 1989: *The Capitalist Imperative: Territory, Technology, and Industrial Growth*. Oxford: Basil Blackwell.

Sudjic, Deyan 1992: *The 100 Mile City*. London: Flamingo/HarperCollins.

Suttles, Gerald 1972: *The Social Construction of Communities*. Chicago: University of Chicago Press.

Suttles, Gerald D. 1968: *The Social Order of the Slum*. Chicago and London: University of Chicago Press.

Swyngedouw, Erik 1997: "Neither Global nor Local: 'Glocalization' and the Politics of Scale." In K. R. Cox ed., *Spaces of Globalization*: 137–66.

——1992: "The Mammon Quest: 'Glocalisation,' Interspatial Competition and the Monetary Order: The Construction of New Scales." In M. Dunford and G. Kafkalas eds., *Cities and Regions in the New Europe: The Global-Local Interplay and Spatial Development Strategies*. London: Belhaven Press: 39–68.

Teaford, Jon C. 1997: *Post-Suburbia: Government and Politics in the Edge Cities*. Baltimore: Johns Hopkins University Press.

Toulmin, Stephen 1990: *Cosmopolis: The Hidden Agenda of Modernity*. New York: Free Press.

Turner, Eugene, and James P. Allen 1991: *An Atlas of Population Patterns in Metropolitan Los Angeles and Orange Counties, 1990*. Northridge: Department of Geography, California State University-Northridge.

UCLA Research Group on the Los Angeles Economy 1989: *The Widening Divide: Income Inequality and Poverty in Los Angeles*. Los Angeles: Urban Planning Department, unpublished report.

Van de Mieroop, Marc 1992: *Society and Enterprise in Old Babylonian Ur*. Berlin: Dietrich Reimer Verlag.

Vergara, Camilo 1995: *The New American Ghetto*. New Brunswick, NJ: Rutgers University Press.

Waldinger, Roger 1996: *Still the Promised City? New Immigrants and African-Americans in Post-Industrial New York*. Cambridge, MA: Harvard University Press.

——and Mehdi Bozorgmehr eds. 1996: *Ethnic Los Angeles*. New York: Russell Sage Foundation.

Waters, Malcolm 1995: *Globalization*. London and New York: Routledge.

West, Cornel 1990: "The New Cultural Politics of Difference." In *Out There*, R. Ferguson et al. eds., Cambridge, MA: MIT Press, and New York: New Museum of Contemporary Art.

Westwood, Sallie, and John Williams eds. 1997: *Imagining Cities: Scripts, Signs, Memory*. London and New York: Routledge.

Wheatley, Paul 1971: *The Pivot of the Four Quarters*. Chicago: University of Chicago Press.

Wilson, Rob, and Wimal Dissanayake eds. 1996: *Global/Local: Cultural Production and the Transnational Imaginary*. Durham and London: Duke University Press.

Wilson, William Julius 1996: *When Work Disappears: The World of the New Urban Poor*. New York: Vintage.

——1987: *The Truly Disadvantaged: The Inner City, the Underclass, and Public Policy*. Chicago: University of Chicago Press.

Wirth, Louis 1938: "Urbanism as a Way of Life," *American Journal of Sociology* 44: 1–24.

Wolch, Jennifer, and Michael Dear 1989: *The Power of Geography: How Territory Shapes Social Life*. Boston: Unwin Hyman.

Woods, Clyde 1998: *Development Arrested: Race, Power, and the Blues in the Mississippi Delta*. London: Verso.

——1995: "The Blues Epistemology and Regional Planning History," *Planning Theory* 13: 53–72.

Woolley, Sir Leonard 1982: *Ur "of the Chaldees," The Final Account: Excavations at Ur*, revised and updated by P. R. S. Moorey. London: Herbert Press.

Wright, Gwendolyn, and Paul Rabinow 1982: "Spatialization of Power: A Discussion of the Work of Michel Foucault." *Skyline* 14–15.

Young, Iris Marion 1990: *Justice and the Politics of Difference*. Princeton, NJ: Princeton University Press.

Yu, Eui-Young, and Edward T. Chang eds. 1995: *Multiethnic Coalition Building in Los Angeles*. Los Angeles: Regina Books for Institute for Asian and Pacific American Studies, California State University-Los Angeles.

Zukin, Sharon 1995: *The Cultures of Cities*. Oxford, UK, and Cambridge, MA: Blackwell.

——1991: *Landscapes of Power: From Detroit to Disney World*. Berkeley and Los Angeles: University of California Press.

Name Index

Subject Index